Street by Str...

C000148930

SOUT
YORKSHIRE
PLUS DRONFIELD, HEMSWORTH, HOLMFIRTH, WORKSOP
Enlarged Areas Barnsley, Doncaster, Rotherham, Sheffield

1st edition May 2001

© Automobile Association Developments Limited 2001

This product includes map data licensed from Ordnance Survey® with the permission of the Controller of Her Majesty's Stationery Office. © Crown copyright 2000. All rights reserved. Licence No: 399221.

Published by AA Publishing (a trading name of Automobile Association Developments Limited, whose registered office is Norfolk House, Priestley Road, Basingstoke, Hampshire, RG24 9NY. Registered number 1878835).

Mapping produced by the Cartographic Department of The Automobile Association.

A CIP Catalogue record for this book is available from the British Library.

Printed in Italy by Printer Trento srl

Ref: MD074

Key to map pages — ii-iii

Key to map symbols — iv-1

Enlarged scale pages — 2-9

Street by Street — 10-211

Index – towns & villages — 212-214

Index – streets — 215-273

Index – featured places — 273-280

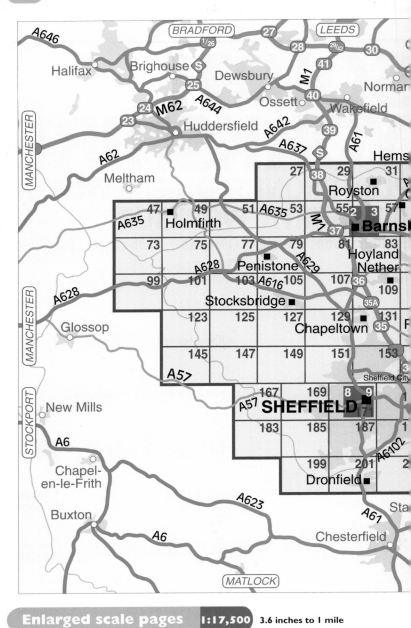

A646
BRADFORD 1/26
27
LEEDS
28
29/42
30
Halifax
Brighouse S
Dewsbury
41
M1
Normar
25
MANCHESTER
24 M62
A644
Ossett
40
Wakefield
23
A62
Huddersfield
A642
A61
39
Hems
A637
S
Meltham
27
38
29
31
Royston
47
49
51 A635 53
55 2
3
57
A635
Holmfirth
M1
37
Barnsl
73
75
77
79
81
83
A628
Penistone
A629
Hoyland
Nether
MANCHESTER
99
101
103 A616 105
107 36
109
A628
Stocksbridge
35A
Glossop
123
125
127
129
131
Chapeltown
35
F
145
147
149
151
153
A57
3
Sheffield City
STOCKPORT
New Mills
167
169
8
9
A57
SHEFFIELD
7
A6
183
185
187
1
Chapel-
en-le-Frith
199
201
2
A6102
Dronfield
A623
Buxton
A61
Sta
A6
Chesterfield
MATLOCK

Enlarged scale pages 1:17,500 3.6 inches to 1 mile

0   1/2   miles   1

0   1/2   1   kilometres   1 1/2

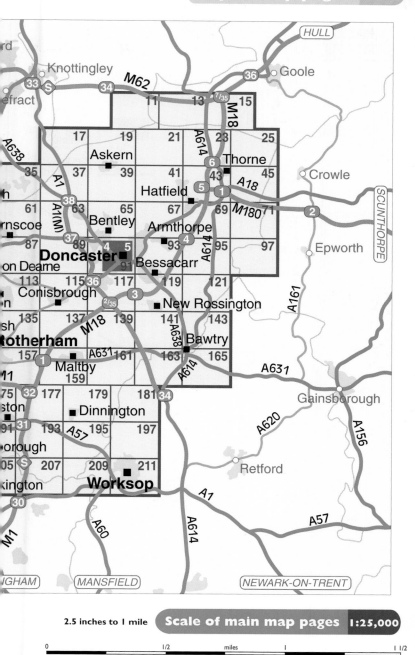

HULL

Knottingley   M62   36   Goole

33 S   34   11   13   7/35   15

efract   M18

A638   17   19   21   A614   23   25

Askern   6   Thorne   Crowle

35   37   39   41   43   A18   45

A1   5   1

Hatfield   A18

61   A1(M)   63   65   67   69   M180   71   2   SCUNTHORPE

rnscoe   Bentley   Armthorpe   4   95   97   Epworth

87   37   69   4   5   93   A614

Doncaster

on Dearne   91   Bessacarr

113   115   36   117   119   121   A161

Conisbrough   3

n   New Rossington

135   137   139   141   143

M18   A638

otherham   Bawtry

157   A631   161   163   165   A631

1   Maltby   A614

M1   159

75   32   177   179   181   34   Gainsborough

ston   Dinnington   A620

91   31   193   A57   195   197   A156

orough

05   S   207   209   211   Retford

kington   Worksop

30

A60   A614   A1   A57

M1

IGHAM   MANSFIELD   NEWARK-ON-TRENT

2.5 inches to 1 mile   **Scale of main map pages**   1:25,000

0   1/2   miles   1   1 1/2

0   1/2   1   kilometres   1 1/2   2

iv

Junction 9	Motorway & junction
Services	Motorway service area
	Primary road single/dual carriageway
Services	Primary road service area
	A road single/dual carriageway
	B road single/dual carriageway
	Other road single/dual carriageway
	Restricted road
	Private road
← ←	One way street
	Pedestrian street
= = = =	Track/ footpath
	Road under construction
⌐ = = = ⌐	Road tunnel
P	Parking

P+	Park & Ride
	Bus/coach station
	Railway & main railway station
	Railway & minor railway station
⊖	Underground station
⊖	Light railway & station
+++++++++	Preserved private railway
LC	Level crossing
•—•—•—	Tramway
---------	Ferry route
....	Airport runway
—·—·—·—	Boundaries- borough/ district
⌄⌄⌄⌄⌄⌄	Mounds
93	Page continuation 1:25,000
7	Page continuation to enlarged scale 1:17,500

River/canal lake, pier

Aqueduct lock, weir

465
▲
Winter Hill
Peak (with height in metres)

Beach

Coniferous woodland

Broadleaved woodland

Mixed woodland

Park

Cemetery

Built-up area

Featured building

City wall

A&E
Accident & Emergency hospital

Toilet

Toilet with disabled facilities

Petrol station

PH Public house

PO Post Office

Public library

Tourist Information Centre

Castle

Historic house/ building

Wakehurst Place NT
National Trust property

M Museum/ art gallery

✝ Church/chapel

Country park

Theatre/ performing arts

Cinema

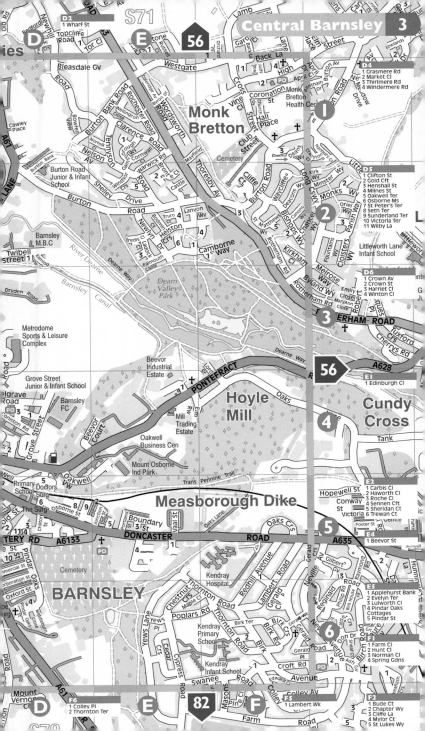

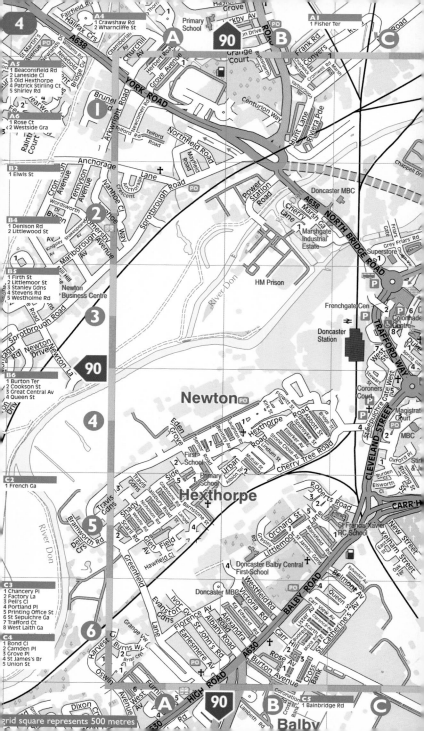

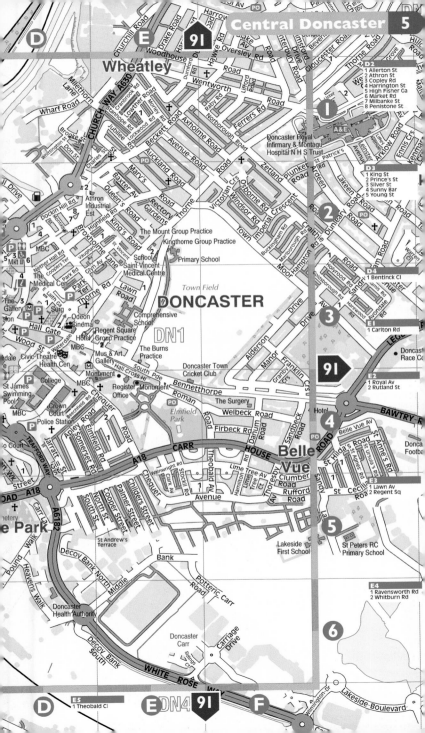

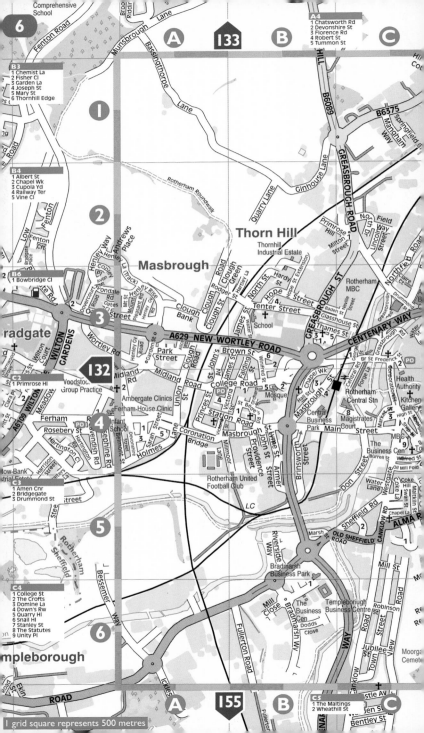

D2
1 Denman St
2 Jennings Cl
3 Owen Cl
4 Selwyn St

Parkgate Business Park

133

D3
1 Carlisle St
2 Eastwood La
3 Ellcott Ct
4 Henry St
5 Kenneth St
6 Nottingham St
7 Rawson Rd

River Don

Chesterton Road
Eastwood Trading Estate

Sycamore Road

Eastwood

D4
1 Catherine St
2 Chatham St
3 Doncaster Ga
4 Douglas St
5 Morpeth St
6 Percy St
7 Summerfield
8 Whybourne Gv

A630

Hardwicke Rd
Eldon Road
Bethel Road
Shakespeare
Shaw Road
Halsbury Road
Haidan Road
Finlay St
St John's Road
Foljambe Road
Doncaster

Child Welfare & Sch Clinic
Comprehensive School

Doctors Surgery

FITZWILLIAM ROAD
A630
Sumner Road
Bowen
Cranworth
Rd
Clarendon Road
Coleridge Road
Cranworth Close

Doncaster Road JMI School

North Far Crs
East Crs

D5
1 Aldred Ct
2 Hollowgate
3 Horace St
4 Moorgate Rd
5 Pinfold La

York Rd
St Stephen's Road
Leonard's St
Ridge Road
The Surg
Old Gdn
Oxford Street
Lord Street
Davis Rd

East Dene

Far Place
Broadway
Middle Place
Alpha Road
Delta Pl

ST ANN'S RD
Erskine St
Russell St
Selborne St
Lindley St
Bramwell St
Ann's Medical Cen
Rotherham MBC
Norfolk
Doncaster Road
Danum Drive
Rotherham St
Cambridge St
Oval Rd
The Lane

A6021
Doctors Surgery
Civic Theatre
Rotherham MBC
Art Gallery & Museum

Clifton

Clifton Comprehensive School

Clifton Park

Rotherham Health Authority

134

E3
1 St Leonard's La
2 St Leonard's Pl

Guild Rd

Badsley Moor Lane JMI School

Osmith Rd
Goldsmith Rd
Shelley Drive

County Court
Clifton Bank
Clifton Mt
Albion Rd
CLIFTON LANE
Parkfield
Lister Street
Gilberthorpe Street
Clifton Gv
Middleton
Clifton
Newton St
Byron Lane
Tennyson
Campbell St

E4
1 Clifton La
2 Ellesmere Ter
3 Gordon Ter
4 Granville Ter
5 Harcourt Ter

WELLGATE
WARWICK
Sherwood
Albany
William Street
Aldred
Carlton Ave
Badsley South
Badsley St South
Clifton Av
Moor
Wordsworth Dr
Burns Road
Longfellow
Chaucer
Marlowe Road
Beaumont

Godstone Rd
Warwick St
Lilian St
Gerard
Rugby Club
Rotherham Town Cricket Club
Boswell
Brunde Road
Spenser Rd
Marlowe Drive

5

E5
1 Carrington St
2 Frances St
3 Garfield Mt
4 Mabel St

Ramsden Road
Richard Road
Hall Road
Welham Drive
Broom Ter
Broom Grove
Treherne Rd
Fraser Rd
Broom Valley Road
Broomfield Grove
BROOM ROAD
Preparatory School
Broom Crs
Dryden Rd
Chatterton Rd
Shenstone

ROTHERHAM

A618
Moorgate La
Heather Close
MOORGATE ROAD
Moorgate Grove
Winston Grove
Oxley Grove
Guest
Wharncliffe
Brunswick Road
Shawsfield Rd
Norrel's Cft
Lisle Road
Broom Road
Oakwood
Carlingford Rd
Fenway Road

Broom
Broom Valley Junior & Infant School
Thomas Rotherham College
Hotel
Brunswick Road

A6021 **WICKERSLEY ROAD**

Herringthorpe Junior & Infant
F2
1 Coleridge Rd

6

Ledsham
Beechwood Rd
Oakwood Rd
Broom Avenue
Vernon Rd

F4
1 Badsley Ct
2 Gilberthorpe Dr

Sitwell Vale
155
Lane Medical Centre
B6410

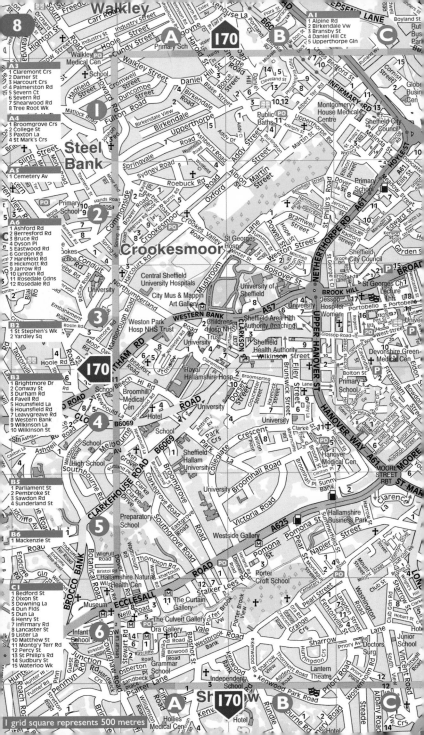

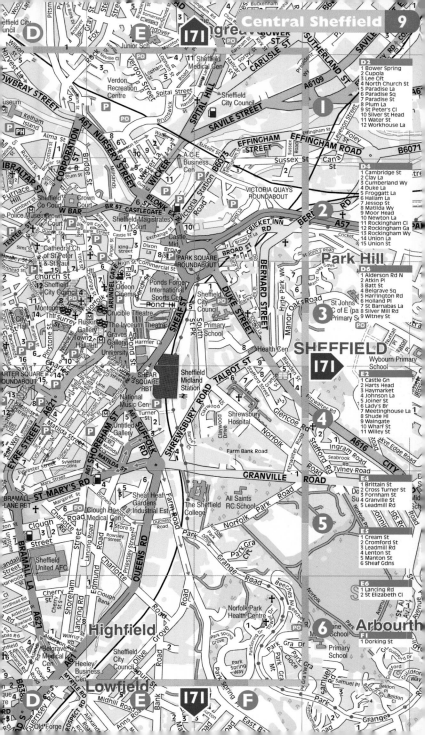

10

Hollins Farm

Intake Lane

Mill Balk

Intake Lane

Main Street

A B C D E

Whitley 1

2

Heck Lane

Balne Moor

3 Balne Moor Road

West End Farm

Westend Lane

Haigh Lane

4 Hazing Lane

The Grange

Yewtree Farm

Thorntree Lane

Balne

Highgate LC

West End

5 Jenny Lane

Park Lane

Ash Tree Farm

Little Common Lane

A19

6 Neville Pits Lane

Gore Lane

Toadham Lane

Chapel Hill

LC

7

South End Lane

South End

SELBY ROAD

A19

8

Badger Lane

River Went

Lockpits Road

North Yorkshire County
Doncaster

A B 19 C D E

1 grid square represents 500 metres

1 Canal Garth
2 Pinfold Vw
3 Water Way Garth

F G H J K

EWDALL   BROACH

M62   A645

Lodge Farm

Snaith Road

snaith

Road

North Yorkshire County
East Riding of Yorkshire

eck Hall
arm

And Pollington Lane

Heck   And   Pollington Lane

I

Frignall
Lane

Cowgill Lane

Balk Lane

Balk Lane

Long Lane

2

Pinfold
Lane

West End
Gardens

West End

Oak Tree Close

PO

Greensdens

Pollingto

Main

Street

Main Street

Willow Close

Willow Lane

3

Aire and Calder Navigation

Bridge Lane

Lock Close

Water Way
Garth

4

I2

Balne Moor Road

Crossfill Lane

Pollington
Balne C of E
School

Knottingley & Goole Canal

Highgate

Cross Hill

East Riding of Yorkshire
North Yorkshire County

Cat Lane

Balne Hill Road

Pollington
Grange

5

Crow Croft Lane

Lowgate

Lowgate

Balne Hall

6

Balne

Lowgate Farm

7

North Yorkshire County
Doncaster

8

Topham

F G H **20** J K

Rawcliffe
Bridge

Dobella
Farm

Dutch River

Decoy

West Way Junior &
Infant
School

Bridge Lane

Place Hill Road

Road

Moor Road

Hookmoor
Farm

Top House

Moor Road

LC

Priory Farm

Rawcliff
Moors

LC

LC

Snaith & Cowick Moors

LC

LC

mons

nland

F **G** **H** **J** **K**

I

2

3

4

5

6

7

8

F **G** **H** **24** **J** **K**

18

A B C D E

1

Common Lane

Walden
Stubbs

LC

LC

River Went

Wentbank House

2

Went
Bridge

rth Yorkshire County
Doncaster

Norton
Priory

3

Norton Mill

Walden Stubbs Road

Stubbs Lane

Norton
Common Farm

ck
Lane

rs C bse

End

1 Tratford Rd
Arundel
Rd
2 Adelaide Rd

Lyndhurst
Close

Denver
Road

Lyndhurst
Rise

Magot Garth

Station
Road

Quarry Road

LC

Norton Common Lane

4

Norton

17

Pinfold
Lane

Common Lane

Cridling
Gardens

New Road

County

School

Balk

5

Stygate Lane

Campsall

Norton Common Road

6

Church

Wellfield
Drive

Glebe Road

Park

Grange
Road

Willow Road

Field Road

Cemetery

Drive

Beech

Campsall Park

Vaughan
Road

Campsall

LC

DN6

Willow

7

Mount

Loversall

Church View

Street

Askern
Swimming
Pool

Campsall

Selby Road

Station
Rd

LC

Askern
Health
Centre

Sunnymede Crs
Sunnymede Av
King's
Road

Infant
Sch

Highfield

Marboroup

8

Sutton

Lane

Alan Crs

Sherwood Av

Davis Rd

Instoneville

Llewelyn
Crescent

Hill

Market Place

High Street

Instone Terrace

ASKERN

Green Lane

The Avenue

A19

Llewelyn
Crs

Alfred
Road

A B

38

C

Manor Way

D E

Askern Spa
Junior School

Littlemoor

Manor Road

A19

Rushy
Moor

grid square represents 500 metres **utton**

Fenwick

Moss

Haywood

Went Farm
Fenwick Lane
Moat Hill Farm
Fenwick Common
Cemetery
Ladythorpe Farm
Fenwick Lane

Fenwick Common Lane

Kells Lane

Haggs

London Lane

Moss Haven

Moss Road

Lane

Trumfleet

Pinfold

Bri... ... Lane

Clough Lane

Lane

Askern Grange Lane
Heyworth Lane
Eden
Coniston
Grange
Orange
Windsor
Richmond Drive
Lowness Dr...
The Drive
...ck Road
Moss Road

Moor Lane

Rushy Moor

Moor Road

Haywood Lane

Wrancarr Lane

Went

Nor... ...hire County
Doncaster

...bbs
...ange

Common Lane

F G H 10 J K I

F G H 39 J K

2 3 4 20 5 6 7 8

20

A B II C D E

I

Fenwick

Riddings Farm

Fenwick Hall

West

2

Lawn Lane

Lane

West End

3

Fenwick Comm

Flashley Carr Lane

Lane

4

Fenwick Grange

19

5

Jett Hall

Farnley Carr Lane

Moss Road

Moseley Grange

Cordon Lane

Moss Lane

Moss Road

6

Moss

Lane

Pinfold

Turnfleet Lane

Kirk Gre

Moss Road

7

Brick Kiln Lane

8

Hawkhouse Green

Hawkhouse Green Lane

Turnfleet Lane

arr Lane

A B 40 C D E

Willow Bridge Lane

Willow Bridge Lane

grid square represents 500 metres

Moor Lane

North Lane

Lane

Sykehouse Road

F **G** Thorseby Hall **H** **12** **J** Marsh Hill Farm **K**

Pringle Lane

Bate Lane

PO

Mawson Green

Sykehouse

Mawson Green

I

Starkbridge Lane

Broad Lane

Tideworth Hague Lane

2

Green Royd Farm

Mill Hill Road

Manor Farm Lane

Salex Lane

Kirk Lane

Kirk Lane

Trans Pennine Trail

3

Bell Gn

Snatchells Lane

New Junction Canal

Smallhedge Farm

4 Lane

22

5 Foste

Westfield House

New House Farm

6

Westfield Lane

Mill Fiel

East La

7 ar Bank

Kirkhouse Green Road

Westfield Road

Trundle Lane

Bank La

Pear Tree Lane

Lodge Lane

Jack Row Lane

Woodhouse Green Road

Nab

8

Nab

F **G** **H** **41** **J** **K**

Trans Pennine Trail

New Junction Canal

Thorne Round Walk

Plumtree Hill

Inge Lane

Plumtree Nab

Thorne N

A4
1 The Hermitage

A3
1 Grange Gv
2 Grange Sq
3 Thrislington Sq

A   LC   B   15   C   D   E

1

Moor
Ends

2

Moorends

3

Grove
East Gate
Darlington
Road
Belvedere
Close
The Surgery

Alexandra Rd
High
Road
Park Road
Richmond
Road
Grange
The Green
Micklethwaite Rd   Chapel
The Fairway
HMB Road

West Road
First School
West Road
Wembley Road
Orchard
Lane
Vermuyden Rd
Silkstone Oval

Windlestone Sq
Eldon
Grove
Shildon
Grove
Locomo...
Road
Barnsley Road
Barnsley Rd
South Road

4

Laurel
Avenue
Road
Fernhill

23

Moorends
Clinic
Moorends
Marshland
First School

Newfields Avenue
Newfields Drive
Newfields

5

Wilkinson
Avenue
Marshland

Broadbent Gate
Road

Dairy Farm

Tween Bridge
Moors

Thorne Waste

Willow
Grove
Willow
Grove

6

Coulman
Road
Albert
Street

Coulman Road

King Edward
First School

7

THORNE

Street
Balk

Moor Edges Road

Causeway Farm

Grammar
Thorne
Swimming
Baths
Church

Longwood
Road
Lockwood Close

Sand Moors
or South Moors

DN8

8

Elmhirst
Glebe Road
Cemetery
Haynes
Gardens
Haynes
Grove

Wike Gate Road
Travis
Ave

Sandmoor Farm

Moor Owner...

Cemetery
Thorne South
Common
First School

Warren Road
Miller
Lane

School

Sandmoor Farm

A   B   44   C   D   E

grid square represents 500 metres

F G H J K

I

2

3

Will
Pitts

4

5

6

7

8

East Riding of Yorkshire
Doncaster

Thorne Moors
or Waste

Doncaster
North Lincolnshire

F G H 45 J K

F4
1 Grasmere Crs

F5
1 Langcliffe Cl
2 Roeburn Cl

F G H J K

Woolley
Hall
College

BARNSLEY ROAD

George Lane

Manor Close

Notton

1

New Road

Woodcote Farm

A61

F6
1 Bloomfield Ri
2 Grove Rd
3 Sunningdale Av

2

G5
1 Moorcrest Ri
2 Stamford Wy
3 Wheatley Ri

Woodhouse Lane

BARNSLEY ROAD

Warren Lane

Notton
Park

Barnsley
Wakefield

3

G6
1 Melford Cl

Lee Lane Farm

4

LEE LANE

30

Staincross

Staincross

Bourne Walk

The Balk

Common

Limes Avenue

Barnsley Municipal
Golf Club

Doctors
Surgery

Bourne
Court

B6428

5

G7
1 Broomhead Ct
2 Longlands Dr
3 Ravens Cl
4 Spark La

Redland
Grove

SHAW LA

A61

Paddock Road

WAKEFIELD ROAD

6

H6
1 Butterton Cl
2 Cherry Tree Cl
3 Church St
4 Greenside
5 Greenside Pl

Athersley
North Primary
School

Mapplewell

GREENSIDE

TOWNGATE

Mapplewell
Health Cen

Cloverlands
Drive

Eastfield Ct

Lindhurst
Rd

7

H7
1 Beaulieu Vw
2 Carr Green La
3 Hamble Ct
4 Maythorne Cl
5 Wentworth Crs
6 Wentworth Dr

BLACKER ROAD

Malincroft

BAR LANE B6131

SPARK LANE

B6428

Blacker

WAKEFIELD ROAD

A61

New Lodge

Wakefield

8

Swallow Hill

Swallow Hill Road

River Dearne

F G H 55 J K

30

B8
1 Dale Cl
2 Peak Rd
3 Peveril Crs

B3
1 Linburn Cl

A8
1 Croft Dr
2 Selby Rd

A7
1 High Croft Dr
2 Watnall Rd

A6
1 Carr Furlong
2 Chilwell Cl
3 Chilwell Gdns
4 Egmanton Rd
5 Greenbank
6 Thrumpton Rd

C2
1 Birkdale Rd
2 Cutts Field Vw

C3
1 Boswell Cl
2 Clevedon Wy
3 Petworth Cft
4 Summer Rd

C4
1 Hallcroft Ri
2 Whitewood Cl

C8
1 Blackheath Cl
2 Carlton Rd
3 Derwent Cl

B3
1 Kent Cl
2 Queensway
3 Well Hill Gv

B5
1 Brownroyd Av

B6
1 Lambecroft

B7
1 Springbank Cl

1 Robin Hood Av
2 Rowland St

E7
1 Wharncliffe St
2 Woodmoor St

E8
1 Baycliff Cl
2 Cartmel Ct
3 Kirkham Pl
4 St Francis Bvd

A B C D E

Notton

Royston Comprehensive School

Barnsley Metropolitan Borough Council

HIGH STREET B6428

ROYSTON

29

Athersley North

Athersley South

Carlton Industrial Estate

St Michaels RC Comprehensive School

56

grid square represents 500 metres

F1
1 Hawthorne Crs
2 Highfield Pl
3 Lime Tree Ct Ct
4 Marton Av

G1
De 1 Beechwood Mt
2 Hawthorne Av

G2
1 Penlington Cl
2 Thornton Cl

K5
1 Aaron Wilk'on Ct
2 George B'ley Ct

H1
Street Names for
these grid squares
are listed at the
back of the index

SOUTH
KIRKBY

Howell Wood

Burntwood
Hall

Brierley
Manor

Burntwood
Sports & Leisure
Centre

Wakefield
College

Hemsworth
R U F C

Stocksgate
First School

South Kirkby
School

West
Haigh
Wood

34

59

WF9

B4
1 Spring Vale Rd

Elmsall Lodge

A6
1 Fenton Cl
2 Flavell Cl
3 Mountfields Wk
4 Newhill

A4
1 Hague Park Cl
2 Hague Park Wk

1

B5
1 Royles Cl

2

C4
1 Waterton Cl

3

D4
1 Blundell St
2 Diamond Av
3 Everdale Mt
4 New St

ROAD A/22

4

33

5

D6
1 Springfield Mt

6

3
Marlborough Cft

SOUTH KIRKBY

7

4
Dearne St
Exchange St
Kirkbridge Wy

8

Cemetery
Standish Crs
Leville Cl
Temple Rd
Wentworth Drive
Brierley
Beacon Vw
Northfield St
Northfield Gv
Northfield Lane
Northfield School
Kings Cft
Beech
WHITE APRON STREET B6422
Church Fld
Grove Drive
Grove
Grove Mount
Stockingate Surgery
Church Mount
Church Vis
Bull Lane
Park Av
Sullivan Rd
The Levs
Stockingate First School
South Kirkby School
Broad Lane
Faith St
Brooksfield
Holt
Crawley Av
Powell St
Clock Rw
Clock Rw Gv
Clock Rw Mt
BARNSLEY
South Kirkby Middle & First School
Cemetery
Moorthorpe Station
ROAD
PO
Moorthorpe
Industrial Estate
Burntwood V & I School
Burntwood Gv
Mayfields
Bradshaw
Carlton Vw
Parkgate
Broadway
Broad Lane
Broad Lane Farm
Langthwaite Beck
Langthwaite Road
Suzanne Crs
Pendle Av
Dennholme Meadow
Hammerton
Hirst Street
Beaumont Av
Hinds Crt
South Ellis Health Ce
South Ellis Surgery
North Av
Pine Street
Vickers Av
Lime Crt
Lime Gans
Porton
Hoods Ct
Bradley Carr Terrace
Oak St
Walnut St
Gordon P

Wakefield Doncaster

E5
1 Carlton Rd
2 Central Av
3 Clifford St
4 Holly Cl

grid square represents 500 metres

36

Wrangbrook

A **B** **16** **C** **D** **E**

I

Ash
Wrangbrook
Sleep Hill Lane

Hollins Farm

Sleep Hill Lane

Lane

Barnsdale

Skelbrooke

A1(1)

2

Lane

Coal Pit

Doncaster Road

Straight Lane

3

ROAD

Doncaster Lane

4

Wakefield

Stubbs Hall

35

Lane

Hazel

Doncaster

5

A638

Stubbs Bridge

Hazel La

Leys La

Moorhouse Lane

6

Hampole Field Lane

Moorhouse Gap

A638

Main Street

Hampole

Old Street

North Ings Rd

7

Denny Balk

8

Old Street

Hampole Wood

Hampole Grange

Junction

A **B** **62** **C** **D** **E**

Hampole Wood

Field Road

G6
1 Cromwell Ct

H5
1 Buttercross Cl
2 Cromwell Gv
3 Crossfield Ho Cl

Woodfield Farm

F G H **17** J K

I

H6
1 Buttercross
2 French St
3 Old Hall Rd
4 Windermere Cl

2

J6
1 Hobcroft Ter

3

J8
1 Woodcock Wy

4

38

5

K7
1 Croasdale Gdns
2 Martindale Wk

6

Burghwallis

Skellow

Carcroft

HAMPOLE BALK B1220

7

8

F G H **63** J K

Adwick Station

F G H **19** J K

I

Moor Lane

Road

2

Wrancarr Lane

Rushy Moor Road

Haywood Lane

Haywood

LC

Clay Bank

Wrancarr House

3

Hatfield Lane

Narrow Lane

Thorpe Grange Lane

Thorpe Lane

Blacker Green Lane

Thorpe Grange

LC

LC

Storrs

4

40

LC

Airey Lane

Thorpe Lane

5

Thorpe in Balne

Middle Lane

Archery Lands Lane

Owston Grange

LC

LC

LC

Bell Lane

Croft Lane

Croft Lane

Applehurst Lane

6

Sickle Croft

LC

Station Road

7

Field

Ash

Plantation Road

Thorpe Road

Lowfield Balne Road

8

Lane

Plantation Road

LC

The Balk

F G H **65** J K

40

Ⓐ Ⓑ **20** Ⓒ Ⓓ Ⓔ

D8
1 Rosewood Dr

D7
1 The Paddock

B7
1 West Service Rd

Hawkhouse Green Lane

Hawkhouse
Green

ancarr Lane

Ⓘ

E7
1 Arren Cl
2 Browning Rd
3 Burns Rd
4 Kipling Rd
5 Sheridan Rd
6 Swinburne Cl

Willow Bridge Lane

Willow Bridge Lane

Braithwaite

2

Trumfleet La

Trumfleet
Grange

Trumfleet

3

Moss Lane

Highfield Lane

Highfield Lane

Marsh

Marsh
Road

4

River Don

Chegl

39

Thorpe Lane

5

Lane

Thorpe

Thorpe Bank

Marsh Lane

Home Field Lane

New Ings Lane

Broad

Ings

Lane

**Thorpe
in Balne**

Lane

6

Ap

Lane

Sickle
Croft

LC

LC

Woodford
Road

7

Station

Ash

Road

Road

West

Farm

Plantation Railway

Lower Boundary Road

Ash Fields Road

North Road

Road

S Spruce Wood

Precipitator
Road

Road

Thorpe Bank

Cemetery

The Cross

Church Lane

Church Lane

Marsh Lane

Sycamore Rd

Windam

St Ann's

Partridge Hill Rd

Maple Gr

4 2

Rosedale

Mrlowe
Road

Primary
School

8

Thorpe

Mere

River

Plantation Road

Marsh

Marsh Lane

Forstead

Lane

Marcus Cons

Ⓐ Ⓑ **66** Ⓒ Ⓓ Ⓔ

Fox
Covert

Marsh Lane

I grid square represents 500 metres

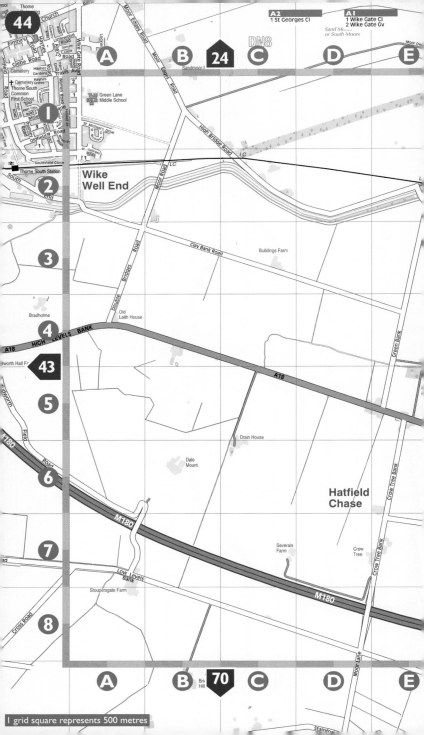

44

Thorne
Church
Elmhirst
Road
Clebe Road
Cemetery
Thorne South
Common
First School
Thorne South Station

A
B
24
DN8
C
D
E

A2
1 St Georges Cl
A1
1 Wike Gate Cl
2 Wike Gate Gv

Sand Mo......
or South Moors

Green Lane
Middle School

St. Michael's Drive

Southfield Close

2

Wike
Well End

Moor Edges Road
Moor Edges Road
Wike Gate Road
High Bridge Road
LC
LC

Moor Dr...

3

Clay Bank Road
Buildings Farm

Double Bridges Road

Bradholme
Old Laith House

4
HIGH LEVELS BANK
A18

...worth Hall F...

43

A18

5

M180

Field Road

Drain House

Dale
Mount

6
M180

**Hatfield
Chase**

Green Bank

Crow Tree Bank

7

Low Levels Bank

Severals
Farm

Crow
Tree

Stoupersgate Farm

M180

8

Cross Road

Crow Tree Bank

Moor Lane

A
B
70
Bri...
Hill...
C
D
E

Stainfor...

I grid square represents 500 metres

F G H **25** J K

I

Medge Hall

2

Stainforth & Keadby Canal

3

4 Dirtness Levels

Sandhill Farm

5

Red House

Boating Dike

Hains Farm

6

Jacque's Farm

Bank House Farm

A18

Smaque Farm

HIGH LEVELS BANK

High Levels Bank

A18

7

Elder House

Plains House Farm

Doncaster

North Lincolnshire

8

M180

M180

F G H **71** J K

w Levels Bank

Plains Lane

Holmfirth 47

MOOR

G2
1 Lower Mdw
2 Lydgetts
3 Netherhouses

H2
1 Five Lane Ends

Holmfirth Swimming Pool

Holmfirth Health Centre

Wolfstones Height

Home Valley Circular Walk

The Oval

HUDDERSFIELD

A635 NEW

Wooldale Cliff Road

Wolfstones Road

Mark Bottoms Lane

Huddersfield Technical College

1

J2
1 Little La

Upperthong

Health Centre

Hill Lane

Holmfirth

Cooper Lane

Highway

STATION ROAD

2

K1
1 Summervale

Town Gate

Hill Lane

Broad Lane

Upperthong Lane

Picture Drome Cinema Museum

Holmfirth Craft Museum

Victoria

Hotel

Last of Summer Wine Exhibition

New Rd

B6106

Swan Bank Court

3

K2
1 Beech St
2 Carr House Rd
3 Crown La
4 Norridge Bottom
5 Town Hall St

A635

Infant School

Briar Ct

Spring Bank Croft

GREENFIELD ROAD

A6024

WOODHEAD ROAD

Cemetery

Cemetery Road

Swan Bank Lane

ngley Green

Booth House Lane

Uphill Bank Road

Burnlee Road

Shaw Lane

Lower Holme

Ward Place Lane

Cartworth Road

Under Bank

4

DUNE

Yew Tree Lane

Hinchcliffe Mill

Woodhead Road

Old Road

Spring Lane

Hinchcliffe Mill County School

Dropp

Acre Lane

White Gate Road

Royd

Mill House Road

Gill Lane

Cartworth

Cartworth Fold

Dunkley Bank Road

Brow

Bank

Dover Lane

Well Road

Cartworth Road

Green Lane

Washpit

Rich Gate

CROSS ROAD

48

5

Lower Longley

Longley Edge Lane

Longley Edge

6

Woodhouse Lane

White Gate

Cote Lane

Hill Top

Cartworth Moor Road

Arrunden Lane

Arrunden

River Ribble

Greave Road

Bent Lane

Primary School

Hill Top View

7

B6106

Copthurst Road

Weather Hill Lane

West Gate

Kirklees Wy

Dunford Road

Abbey Cl

Abbey

Hade Edge

8

Daisy Lee Moor

Ramsden Road

Crossley's Plantation

Close Road

F   G   H   73   J   K

Fulstone

F   G   H   J   K   I

Hall

White Ley Bank

Holme Valley Circular Walk

Edson House Lane

Acre Lane

Wood End Lane

Close

Long

Matlon Lane

Row Gate

Top Row

LANE HEAD ROAD

Carr Lane

Cross Lane

Cumberworth

Lane Head

A635

Piper Well Lane

ROAD

Gate

Foot

Lane

The Gully

Deershaw Lane

Wall Nook Lane

Park Head

Lane

Deershaw sike Lane

Dearne

Dike

Lane

2

Park Head

Holme Valley Circular Walk

Hirst Lane

Dearne Head

Haddingley Lane

Broadstone Rd

Birds Edge Lane

3

4

Hole

Lane

Side

Dick

Edge

Lane

Cheese Gate Nab

Daisy Gate

Windmill Lane

Kirklees Barnsley

Low Common

Birdsnest Lane

50

5

Mill

Shaw

Lane

Lane

Hey Slack Lane

Slack Top Lane

Lane

Birdsnest

Slack Beck

Broadstone Reservoir

6

Snug Lane

Gate Head Lane

Barnside

A616

Old Bar Lane

Wood Royd

Mill Lane

Crime

Cross Lane

Hogg

Lane

Lower

Maythorn

Upper Maythorn Lane

Lane

Potters

Gate

Edge

Brown's

Road

Upper Maythorn

7

Kirklees

Barnsley

Road

Edge

Victoria

Hepshaw

Lower Maythorn

Calf

Hey Lane

Lane

Whitley Common

8

Whitley Road

F   G   H   **75**   J   K

Shidbrook Crs

Crow Edge

A   B   **26**   C   D   E

I

Exley
Gate

2

Nether
End

Denby
Hall

3

BARNSLEY ROAD   A635

4

51

Hazel House

5

North Lane

6

Carr Lane

Gadding
Moor

New Road

7

Cat
Hill

Kidfield
House

Cross Lane

8

A   B   **78**   C   D   E

Hoylandswaine

Bleffer
Wood

Kirklees
Barnsley

Jowett
House   Jowett H

Barnsley Boundary Walk

Rawling House

South
Lane

The
Nook

PO   Road

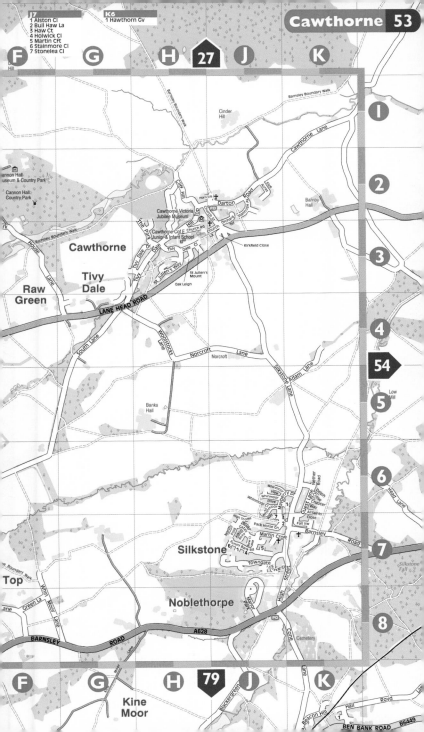

J7
1 Alston Cl
2 Bull Haw La
3 Haw Ct
4 Holwick Cl
5 Martin Cft
6 Stainmore Cl
7 Stonelea Cl

K6
1 Hawthorn Gv

F G H 27 J K

Barnsley Boundary Walk

Cinder Hill

Cawthorne Lane

1

Cannon Hall Museum & Country Park

Cannon Hall Country Park

2

Cliff Hill

Horn Cft

Darton Road

Barnby Hall

Cawthorne Victoria Jubilee Museum

Orchard

Cawthorne C of E Church Rd

Cawthorne C of E Junior & Infant School

Cem Church

Cawthorne

Tivy Dale Dr

Tivy Dale

Kirkfield Close

3

Raw Green

Tivy Dale

St Julien's Way

St Julien's Mount

Oak Leigh

House Lane

Barnsley Boundary Walk

LANE HEAD ROAD

4

South Lane

Woodcocks Lane

Norcroft Lane

Norcroft

Silkstone Lane

Adam Lane

54

Low Hill

5

Banks Hall

Head Lane

6

Whitworth Dr

Nether Road

Whitmore View

Whitmore

Drive

Queen's Drive

Dearn

Chapel

Castle

All Saints Close

7

High Thorns

Pack Horse Gn

Martin Cft

Fall Vw

Barnsley Road

Silkstone

Silkstone Fall

Silkstone

Noblethorpe

Towngate

Barnsley Boundary Walk

Top

Green La

Whin Moor Lane

8

Noblethorpe

High Street

Cone Lane

Cemetery

BARNSLEY ROAD A628

F G H 79 J K

Kine Moor

Blacker Green La

Beacon Hill

Hall Royd Lane

BEN BANK ROAD B6449

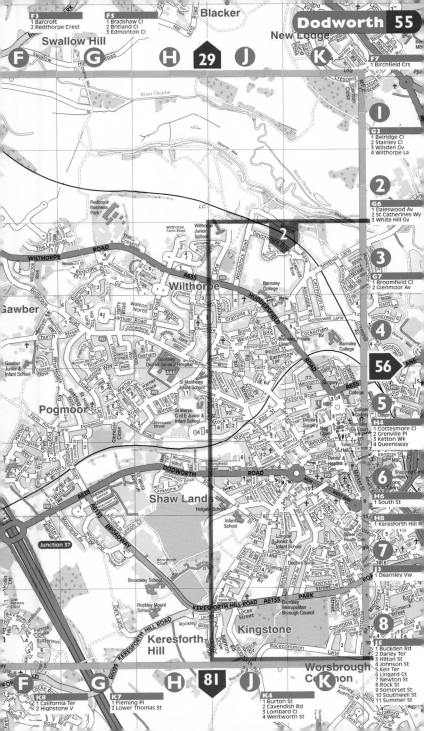

Blacker

New Lodge

Swallow Hill

F3
1 Barcroft
2 Redthorpe Crest

F5
1 Bradshaw Cl
2 Britland Cl
3 Edmonton Cl

F Swallow **G** Road **H** **29** **J** **K**

F7
1 Birchfield Crs

1

G3
1 Belridge Cl
2 Stainley Cl
3 Wilsden Gv
4 Wilthorpe La

2

River Dearne

Redbrook
Business
Park

G6
1 Daleswood Av
2 St Catherines Wy
3 White Hill Gv

3

Wilthorpe
Farm Road

2

G7
1 Broomfield Cl
2 Glenmoor Av

Wilthorpe

Gawber

Barnsley
College

4

Honeywell Lane

Honeywell

Barnsley
College

Barnsley
District General Hospital

Barnsley
Private
Clinic

56

Cockerham

H4
1 Cottesmore Cl
2 Grenville Pl
3 Ketton Wk
4 Queensway

Gawber
Junior &
Infant School

St Matthews
Infant School

St Marys
C of E Junior &
Infant School

5

Odeon

Pogmoor

Barnsley
Metropolitan
Borough Council

H6
1 South St

6

Shaw Lands

Junction 37

Broadway School

DODWORTH ROAD

Infant
School

Longcar
Junior &
Infant School

H8
1 Keresforth Hill Rd

7

Holgate School

Rockley Mount
School

KERESFORTH HILL ROAD

J3
1 Dearnley Vw

8

J5
1 Buckden Rd
2 Darley Ter
3 Hilton St
4 Johnson St
5 Keir Ter
6 Lingard Ct
7 Newton St
8 Rock St
9 Somerset St
10 Southwell St
11 Summer St

Keresforth
Hill

Kingstone

Worsbrough
Common

F **G** **H** **81** **J** **K**

K8
1 California Ter
2 Highstone V

K7
1 Fleming Pl
2 Lower Thomas St

K4
1 Burton St
2 Cavendish Rd
3 Lombard Cl
4 Wentworth St

F3
1 Abbey Sq
2 Hickson Dr

B1, B2, B7, B8
Street Names for
these grid squares
are listed at the
back of the index

F4
1 Darrington Pl

A5,A6,A7, A8
Street Names for
these grid squares
are listed at the
back of the index

F5
1 Harwood Ter
2 Trueman Ter
3 Wycombe St

F8
1 Nursery Gdns
2 Wheatley Rd

G4
1 The Close
2 Vincent Rd

Sudwo
Commo

G7
1 Alexandra Ter
2 Chapel St
3 Crown Well HI
4 Foxroyd CI
5 Scarfield CI

H1
1 Co-operative St
2 Thornwell Gv

H2
1 Newdale Av

H7
1 Ambleside Gv
2 Eskdale Rd
3 Hillside

H8
1 St Christoph's
2 St Clements Ck
3 St Leonards W
4 Winchester W

West
Green

CUDWORTH

Stairfoot

Ardsley

Low
Laithes

Horse
Carr
Wood

K3
1 Belmont

K2
1 Lakeland CI
2 Meadowland RI
3 White Cross Ct
4 White Cross Mt

J2
1 Edgelands RI
2 Newtown Gn

J1
1 Churchfield Av
2 Churchfield Cr
3 Churchfield Te
4 Quarry Bank R
5 Somerset St
6 Stonegarth C

I grid square represents 500 metres

G4
1 Mileswood Cl

H5
1 Woodlands Vw

F G H 33 J K

I
H6
1 Oak Haven Av
2 Old Hall Wk

2
H8
1 Belmont Crs

3
J6
1 Ebenezer St

4

60

5

6

7

8

West Haigh Wood

Burntwood Hall

Howell Lane

Houghton Lodge

Howell House

Howell Lane

Shortwood Lane

Clayton

Hostler Lane

Little Park

Park Lane

MOOR LANE B6273

Crabtree Drive
Park Lane
Cemetery
Pinewood Close

Great Houghton

HIGH STREET B6273
Pear Tree Close
PO

Pinfold Close
Potts Crescent
Pleasant Avenue

Clayton Lane

B6411 THURNSCOE LANE
John Street
Wescoe Avenue
Norfolk Road

Great Houghton Clinic
Primary School
Edward St
New Street
Turner Street

Sandhill

Little Houghton

B6195

Chapel Lane
Buttercross Drive
Middlecliff Lane

Houghton Main Welfare & Sports Club

ROTHERHAM ROAD
Middlecliff Lane
West Kirk Lane

Billingley Lane

HOUGHTON ROAD

Rectory Close
Rectory Lane
Southfield

Common

Burns Close

Taylor Crescent
B6273
Mary Street

Back Lane
High Street

Chapel Lane

Fitzwilliam Road
PO
ROAD

F Middlecliffe G H 85 J Billingley K

Bentley 65

F   G   H   39   J   K

1

2   Almholme

3

4

66

5

6

7   A630

Wheatley Park

8

Shaftholme

The Balk

Almholme Lane

Almholme Lane

Common Lane

Marsh Lane

Rich Farm Close   The Croft
Pine Oaks

Arksey

Chadwick Gdns

Stockbridge

Amy Road

Elm Crescent

New Village

Station

Cemetery

Arksey County Junior & Infant School

Colvin Close

Kenrock Close

Arksey Lane

Marsh Lane

Common Lane

Ings Lane

Dog Croft Lane

River Don

Bentley Common

Bentley   LC

Common Lane

River Don

WHEATLEY

ROAD

Wheatley Hall Business Centre

Hereford Road

Guildford Road

Kingfisher First School

Norwich

Brocker

Worcester Av

HALL

Worcester Av

Parkway

Beckett Road

Exeter

DN2

F   G   H   91   J   K

40

A   B   C   D   E

Map labels and grid references:

B8
1 Endcliffe Wy
2 Parkstone Wy
3 Woodlea Wy

B7
1 Sandalwood Cl

A8
1 Kingfisher Cl
2 Rockley Nook

1

D3
1 Orchard Cl

2 Almholme

D5
1 Marian Rd
2 St Nicholas Cl

3

D6
1 Eleanor Ct

4

65

5

E1
1 Pinfold Ct

6

E2
1 Rainford Sq

7

Wheatley
P

8

3
Cowley Pl
Prince's Sq
St Helen's Sq
St James Cl
Stanley Sq
Windermere Crs
Windle Sq

Fox Covert

River Don

Sandall
Grove

Moor
Lane

Kirk Sandall
Station

Works

Kirk Sandall
Infant School

Guildhall
Industrial Estate

Long
Sandall

Doncaster MBC

Edenthorpe
Surgery

Hungerhill
Comprehensive
School

THORNE

Curlew
Junior School

Plumb
Estates

Hungerhill Lane

WHEATLEY HALL RD

A650

Wheatley Hall
Business Centre

Hereford Road

THORNE ROAD

Shaw Lane
Industrial Estate

Shaw Wood Way

Golf Course

Kingfisher
School

DN2

A   B   C   D   E

92 Wheatley Hills

E4
1 Camellia Dr
2 Magnolia Cl
3 Thirlmere Gdns

E5
1 Milton Gv
2 Sherwood Av

Doncaster Road

grid square represents 500 metres

Kirk Sandall **67**

Parks

Barr F1
1 Heathfield Cl
2 Limedale Vw
Dun 3 Mill Field Ct

F3
1 Longton Rd
2 Tarleton Cl
3 Tynedale Ct

F · G · H · **41** · J · K

I
F4
1 Fernhall Cl

2

F5
1 Holme Wood Ct
2 Worral Ct

Dunsville

St George
Avenue
Kenneth
Avenue

3

F6
1 Beechwood Cl
2 Farm Cl
3 Robin Hood Crs

HIGH STREET

Dunsville Centre

Wyndthorpe Hall

Sandall Grange

4

68

West Moor

5

G1
1 Lowfield Cl

THORNE ROAD A18

Green Lane Farm

6

H8
1 Cedar Rd

West Moor Farm

Park Hill Grange

County Primary School

Edenthorpe

Hatfield Lane

A630

7

K3
1 Cathedral Ct
2 St Catherine's Dr

A630

West Moor Lane

8

DN3

Meadowview Industrial Estate

Armthorpe High School

F · G · H · **93** · J · K

E6
1 Aspen Cl
2 Oakdale Cl

ARMTHORPE

70

A **B** **44** **C** **D** **E**

Stoupersgate Farm

M180

Moor Lane

I

Brier
Hills Farm

Stainforth Moor Road

orth   Moor   Road

2

Moor Farm

3

4

69

olme Bank Road

5

Lindholme Bank   Road

6

Lindholme
Hall

Hatfield Moors

7

8

A **B** **96** **C** **D** **E**

Doncaste
rth Lincoln

I grid square represents 500 metres

F 30

G

H

45

J

K

I

M180

M180

Plains House Farm

Doncaster
North Lincolnshire

Plains Lane

evels Bank

2

Goodcop Farm

Sandtoft

3

Lindholme Grange

Low Levels

4

West Hale Farm

5

Doncaster
North Lincolnshire

North Idle Drain

West Carr

6

West Carr Houses

Idle Bank

7

Roe Carr

8

F

G

H

97

J

K

wah m

72

Holme

Rake Head R

A

B

46

C

D

E

Riding
Wood
Reservoir

WOODHEAD ROAD

Burnt Bank Lane

Holme
Woods

Kiln Bank Road

Yateholme
Reservoir

I

Kaye
Edge

WOODHEAD ROAD

A6024

Holme Woods Lane

2

3

Upper
Heyden

4

A6024

Kirklees
Derbyshire County

Twizle
Head
Moss

5

White
Low

Stable
Clough

6

Heyden
Moor

Binns

A6024

Heyden Brook

West
Withens
Clough

7

Tup
Stones

Dewhill
Naze

Withens
Moor

W
E

8

Butterley
Moss

Great
Intake

Little
Intake

Cat
Clough

A

Bridge

Stone
Low

B

98

C

D

Pikenaze
Moor

E

sike
gh

1 grid square represents 500 metres

Edge

(F) (G) (H) **47** (J) (K)

Road

Crossley's
Plantation

Linshaws Road

Close Road
Dunford

Daisy
Lee
Moor

Green Abbey

Abbey Ct

ttle Road

lees Way

I

Dunford Road

Kirklees
Beaumont Road
ley

2

Snailsden Reservoir

Snailsden

Harden
Clough

Ha

3

rden
h

Kirklees
Barnsley

4

74

5

Great
Grains
Clough

Grains
Moss

6

Barnsley
byshire County

Upper
Dead
Edge

7

Wike Head

Windle Edge

8

(F) (G) (H) **99** (J) (K)

Longside
Moss

74

Hade Edge

A   **B**   **48**   **C**   **D**   **E**

PENISTONE ROAD B6106

I

2

Kirklees
Bear Bones Road
Barnsley

3

Harden Clough

Harden Reservoir

Harden

Flight Hill

Law Slack Road

Law Common Road

Barnsley Boundary Walk

Snittlegate

Dunford Road

Close Road

4

73

5

Winscar Reservoir

Townhead

Dunford Road

Windle Edge

Don View

6

Dunford Bridge

Longdendale Trail

7

Lower Windleden Reservoirs

Thurlstone Moors

8

Upper Windleden Reservoirs

Windle Edge

A   **B**   **100**   **C**   **D**   **E**

grid square represents 500 metres

Victoria

Lower
Maythorn

Kirklees

Barnsley

shaw

Common

Whitley Road

Crow
Edge

Eltock Farm

Middlecliffe
Drive

Studbrook Dike

LANE

B6106

BENTS

ROAD

LEE LANE B610

Carlecotes

Town Brook

Soughley

Lane

Hazlehead

River Don

WHAMS ROAD

Wogden
Clough

Flouch
Inn

Old   Manchester   Road

A616

Brook House Lane

Badger   Lane

Brook House Lane

F   G   H   J   K

I

2

3

4

5

6

7

8

F   G   H   J   K

76

row
dge

A616

Hazlehead

A **B** **50** **C** **D** **E**

Soher House Lane

Annat Royd Lane

High Lane

Barnsley Boundary Walk

Whitley Road

Whitley Road

Penistone Boundary

I

2

3 LEE LANE B6106

Hollin La

LEE LANE

4

75

5

6

7

8

WHAMS ROAD

High Peak

Royd Lane

Royd

Millhouse Green

B6106

West End Avenue

Penistone Boundary Walk

Catshaw Lane

Catshaw

River Don

Ranah Stones Farm

Bullhouse Lane

MANCHESTER ROAD

Lilley Lane

Ee

Field Lane

Long Lane

Flouch Inn

Old Manchester Road

A616

A628

A616(T)

Ecklands Road

Hartcliff Road

Paw Hill Lane

New Ho Lan

Fullshaw

Brook House Lane

Badger Lane

Badger Lane

A **B** **102** **C** **D** **E**

Edge Lane

Brown's Lane

Newbing Lane

Gilbert Hill

Langsett

Kirklees

I grid square represents 500 metres

78

Cat Hill

A5
1 Barnside Cl
2 Harden Cl
3 Wilson Av

A4
1 Hodgkinson Av
2 Sycamore Wk
3 Wentworth Ms

A3
1 Waterhall Vw

D1
1 Green Hill Gv

A B **52** C D E

Hoylandswaine

I

2

Penistone Grammar School

HALIFAX ROAD

Wellhouse Way
Viewlands Close

3

Penistone Sports Centre

ROAD

High Lee

HIGH LEE LANE

A628

BRIDGE STREET

Talbot Rd

Stottercliffe Rd

Wentworth

Town Councillors

Wentworth Road

CHURCH ST

SHREWSBURY ROAD

ST MARY'S

4

Schole Avenue

77

Victoria St

Market

Ward Street

Unwin St

River Don

Penistone Station

Spring Vale

School

SHEFFIELD ROAD

Don Street

Queen Street

High Oxspring

OXSPRING LANE

A629

5

Clarel Street

Chapel Lane

Downing

Green Road

Westgate

Castle Lane

Castle Close

Bower Powell

Castle Green

6

Gledhill Av

The Green

Mortimer Road

Callis Lane

Nook Lane

Long Lane

Old Manor Drive

Foxfields

Oxspring Junior & Infant School

Cubley

7

Mortimer Road

Royd Field

Thicett Lane

Oxspring Road

Long Lane

Back Lane

Roughbirchworth

8

Cliff House

Ossley Road

A B **104** C D E

Cranberry Farm

Cranberry Road

Salter

Snowden Hill

grid square represents 500 metres

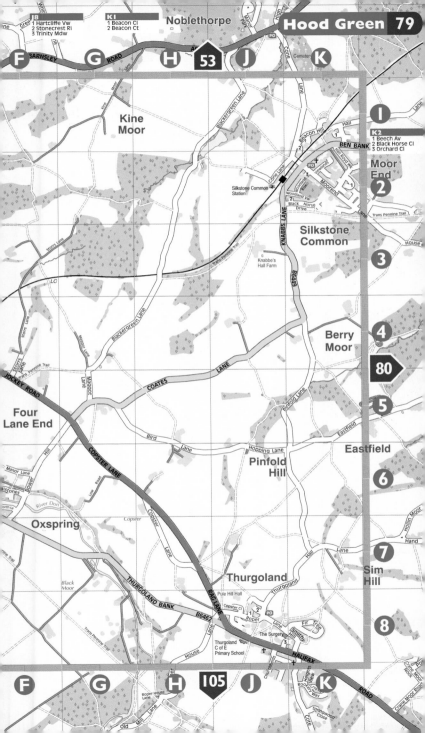

Noblethorpe

J8
1 Hartcliffe Vw
2 Stonecrest Ri
3 Trinity Mdw

K1
1 Beacon Cl
2 Beacon Ct

K2
1 Beech Av
2 Black Horse Cl
3 Orchard Cl

BARNSLEY ROAD

F G H `53` J K

Kine Moor

Silkstone Common Station

BEN BANK

Moor End

`I`

`2`

Knabbe's Hall Farm

Silkstone Common

Trans Pennine Trail

`3`

Berry Moor

`4`

`80`

`5`

COATES LANE

Four Lane End

JOCKEY ROAD

Eastfield

`6`

COPSTER LANE

Bird Lane

Hopping Lane

Pinfold Hill

Manor Lane

River Don

Oxspring

Copster

Black Moor

Tram Pennine Trail

Sim Hill

`7`

Thurgoland

Pule Hill Hall

THURGOLAND BANK

B6462

RAG LANE

Copster Cl

Roper

The Surgery

Thurgoland C of E Primary School

Fir Tree

HALIFAX ROAD

`8`

F G H `105` J K

1 Chatsworth Ri
2 Hardwick Gv
3 Needlewood
4 Nostell Fold
5 Pilley Hl
6 Rob Royd
7 Saville Hall La
8 Woburn Pl

1 St John's Cl

A **B** **54** **C** **D** **E**

Bank Crescent

MITCHELSON A

STATION RD

Dodworth
Health
Centre

Cemetery

Dodworth
C of E
School

Ratten
Row

Cemetery

Saville Hall

I

Royd   Lane

Hall

LC

Dodworth
Green

DODWORTH GREEN ROAD

Dodworth
Bottom

BEN BANK ROAD B6449

2

Moor
End

Lane

Trans Pennine Trail

Trans Pennine Trail

Silkstone
Common

3

House Carr La

Bank

4
Moor

79

Fairthwaite Green Lane

Lovve Lane

Wentworth
College of E

Stainborough
Castle

5

Lane

Eastfield

Wood Hill

Hood Green Road

Greno
View

Castle
Drive

Stainborough

Lane

Hood
Green

Bagger
Wood

Wood   Road

Bagger

6

Eastfield

Stainborough
Fold

7

Hollin Moor Lane

Hand   Lane

Stainborough

Manor
Farm

Sim
Hill

8

Crane Moor

Cliffe La

Dance Lane

Cliffe
Farm

Fir Tree

HALIFAX

ROAD

Crane Moor Road

Pog Lane

Crane Croke Lane

Cliffe

Common

Hermit
Hill

Hermit Hill

A **B** **106** **C** **D** **E**

I grid square represents 500 metres

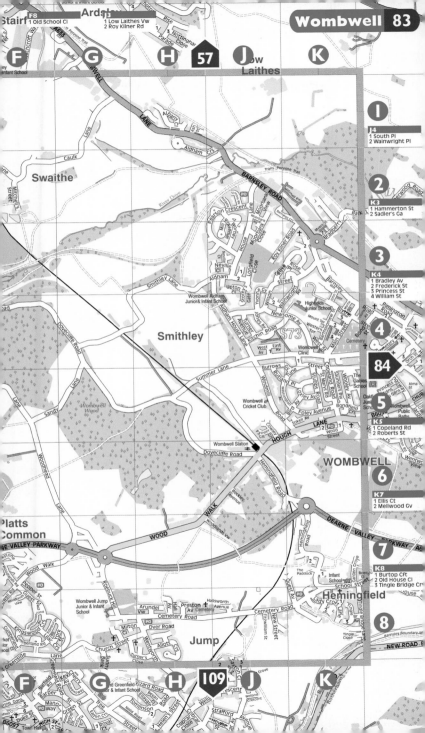

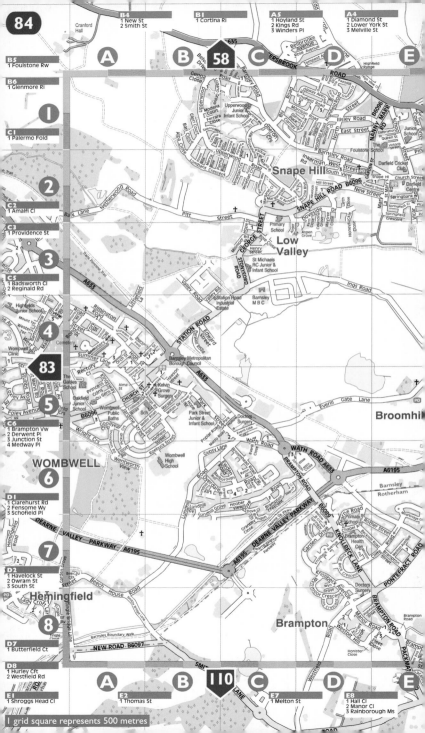

A635

A

B

62

LEY

A635

C

D

Marr

E

Church Lane

PO

Grove Ct

Scarborough Lane

1

2

3

4

87

5

6

7

8

Hangman Stone Road

Mellinder Lane

Melton Wood

Ladyfield Farm

Sheep Lane Farm

St Helen's Lane

Hangman Stone Road

Ludwell Hill

Ox Pasture

Sheep Lane

Melton Mill Lane

Doncaster Road

Barnburgh Grange

Doncaster College

High Melton

Cusby Lane

Garden Lane

Dearne Bridge

A

B

114

C

D

E

Pasture

F G H 69 J K

I

Gate
Wood End

Boston
Park

Poor
Piece

2

3

Torne Bridge

4 Farm

96

Long
Plantation

God's
Cross

5

Common Lane

Acomb Farm

6

A614

THORNE ROAD

Levels Lane

Blaxton
Common

Nesson Bank

Candley Bank

7

Ninescores Lane

8

F G H 121 J K

Maxton

Springbank
Close
Summerfield
Drive

Elephant
Parkland Walk

Finningly
Grange Farm

Wroot Road

A B **70** C D E

1
2
3
4
95
5
6
7
8

A B C D E

Doncaster
North Lincolnshire

Ellerholme
Farm

Moor
Lane

Acres Lane

Sand Lane

High Street

Wroot

Woodsi

PO

Woodside

Candy Farm

God's
Cross

Field House
Farm

Candle Bank

Nan Sampson Bank

Field Lane

Ninescores
Farm

Ninescores Lane

Ninescores
Lane

Peat
Carr

Peat Carr Track

ly
Farm

grid square represents 500 metres

F G H **71** J K

I

2

3

4

5

6

7

8

Ninevah Farm

Tunnel Pits

River Torne

Poles Bank

Aucklands Farm

DN9

South Engine Drain

Greenholme Bank

Harvester Farm

Haxey Turbary

Thorn Bank

Greenholme Bank Farm

Star Carr

Charity Farm

F G H J K

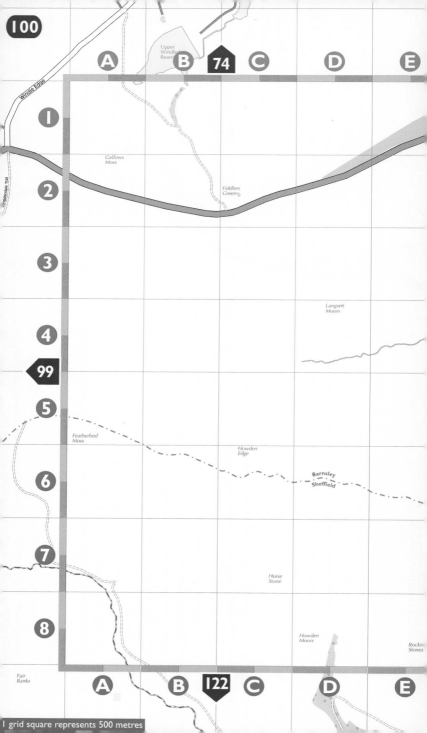

A **B** 74 **C** **D** **E**

Windle Edge

Upper
Windfield
Reservoir

1

Gallows
Moss

Longdendale Trail

2

Fiddlers
Green

3

Langsett
Moors

4

99

5

Featherbed
Moss

Howden
Edge

Barnsley
Sheffield

6

7

Horse
Stone

Fair
Banks

8

Howden
Moors

Rocking
Stones

A **B** 122 **C** **D** **E**

1 grid square represents 500 metres

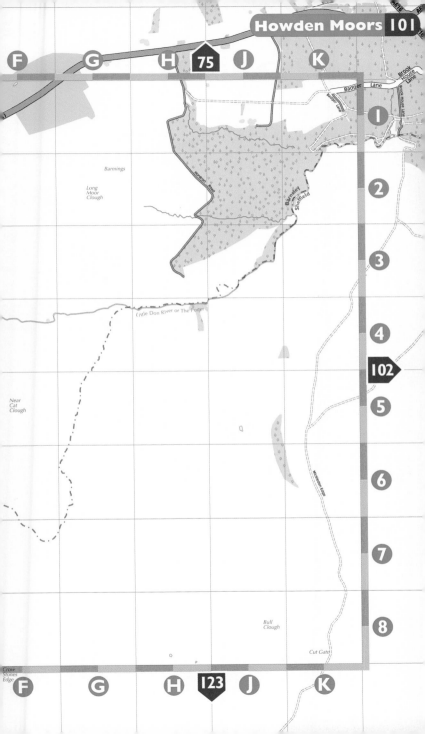

F G H **75** J K

I

2

3

4

102

5

6

7

8

F G H **123** J K

Barmings

Long
Moor
Clough

Morgan Fam

Barnsley
Shefield

Little Don River or The Porter

Near
Cat
Clough

Mickleden Edge

Bull
Clough

Cut Gate

Crow
Stones
Edge

Badger Lane

Brook
House
Lane

Brook House Lane

Badger Lane

102

A   **B**   **76** **C** Fullshaw   **D**   **E**

Paw Hill Lane   Neth Hous Lane

A616   A628   A616(T)

Brook House Lane

Badger Lane   Brow

1

Langsett   Kirklees   Sheffield

A616(T)

Oliphet Hill

2   Langsett Reservoir   Midhope Cliff Lane

S36

Upper Midhope

3   Joseph Lane   Midnor

Ringstone Lane

4   Stocks   Low Moor Lane   Low Moor

Thickwoods Lane

101

5

Mickleden Edge

6

7   Fenny Common

Pike Lowe Stones

8   Pike Lowe

Cut Gate

A   **B** **124** **C**   **D**   **E**

F   G   H **77** J   K

Scuff Hill Road

Brock

Brock Holes

Alderman's Head Farm

Mossley Road

Cranberr

1

Cranberry Farm

Judd Field Lane

Mortimer Road

Sheephouse

2

Lane

Dark Lane

Sheephouse Wood

3

A616(T)

Midhope Hall Lane

Chapel Lane

Chapel Lane

Miller Lane

Midhope Reservoir

Midhopestones

Oaks Lane

Underbank Reservoir

4

Stony Croft Lane

104 103

A616

5

Gill Royd Lane

6

Barnside Moor

Barnside Farm

Long Lane

Ewden Height

Mortimer Road

Wind Hill Lane

7

Ewden

8

F   G   H **125** J   K

Ewden Beck

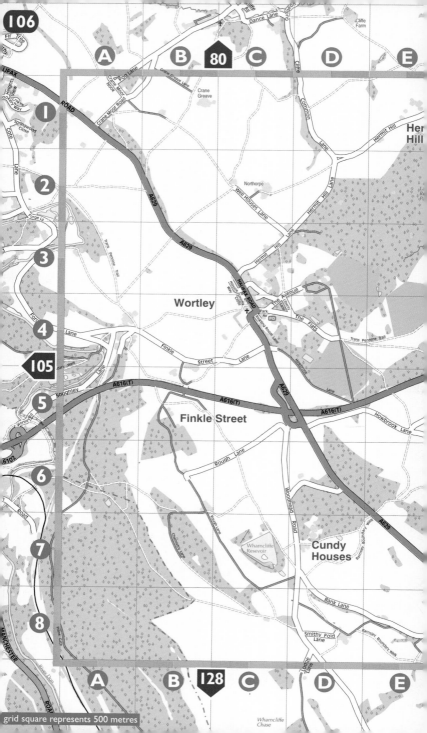

grid square represents 500 metres

F1
1 Booth St
2 Hall St
3 Little Leeds
4 Milton Rd
5 St Andrews Crs
6 Tithe Laithe
7 Vicarage Cl

F2
1 Alder Ms
2 George St

F3
1 Primrose Wy
2 Roseberry Cl

G1
1 Rock Mt

G2
1 Southlea Cl
2 Wentworth Vw

H1
1 Stirling Cl
2 Sunny Bank Ri

H2
1 Beacon Vw
2 The Croft

J1
1 Aberford Gv
2 Hambleton Cl
3 Ledsham Ct
4 Wendel Gv

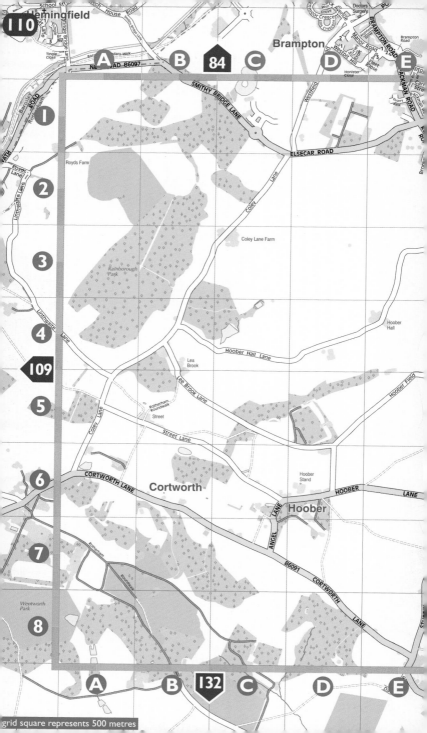

Wath upon Dearne 111

G2 1 Thompson Cl   **G2** 1 Wombwell Av

F   **G**   **H**   **85**   **J**   **K**

West Melton & I School

B6097 MELTON HIGH ST

ton Ellis School

West Melton

Wath JMI School

WEST STREET

WATH U

1

G7
1 Wharncliffe Cl
2 Woodhouse Cl

2

G8
1 Humphries Av
2 The Steadlands

Wath Upon Dearne Comprehensive School

Newhill

3

H1
1 Brook Farm Ms
2 Church La
3 Church St
4 Montgomery Rd
5 Thornhill Pl

Abdy

112

4

Racecourse Road

5

H5
1 The Parade

WATH WOOD ROAD

Wath Wood

WARREN VALE RD

BLACKAMOOR

B6092

6

J1
1 Moor Rd
2 Wharncliffe Av

WENTWORTH

ROAD   B6090

7

J2
1 Cherry Tree Pl
2 Fir Cl
3 Marshall Gv
4 Sycamore Crs

Upper Haugh

Ryecroft

8

J4
1 Beechwood Cl

Rawmarsh Monkwood JMI School

Monkwood Health Centre

F   **G**   **H**   **133**   **J**   **K**

K2 1 Hawthorne Rd   **J8** 1 Pipe House La   **J12** 1 Macmanus Av

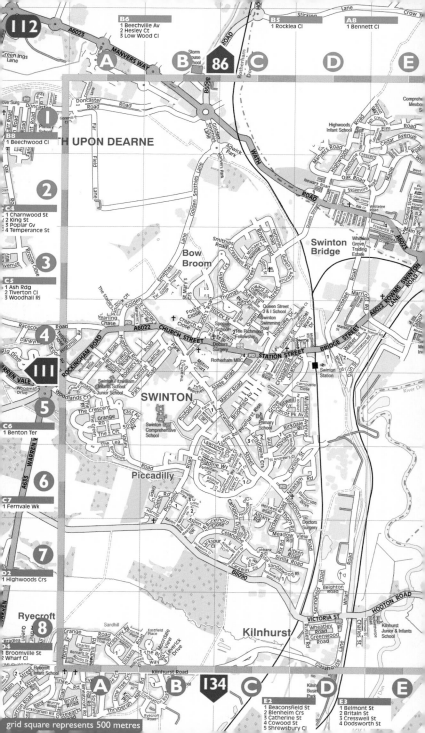

112

B6
1 Beechville Av
2 Hesley Ct
3 Low Wood Cl

B5
1 Rocklea Cl

A8
1 Bennett Cl

A MANVERS WAY **B** **86** **C** **D** **E**

Sticking Lane

Crow ?

Green Ings Lane

A6023

Storm House School

ROTHERHAM

B6090

1

B8
1 Beechwood Cl

H UPON DEARNE

Doncaster Road

Doncaster Road

Adwick Park

WATH

2

C4
1 Charnwood St
2 King St
3 Poplar Gv
4 Temperance St

ROAD

Newark Road

Oak Road

Sycamore Road

Highwoods Infant School

Manvers Road

Highwoods Crescent

Elm Road

Cedar Avenue

West

Main St

A6022

3

C5
1 Ash Rdg
2 Tiverton Cl
3 Woodhall Ri

Bow Broom

Smithies Road

Cresswell Rd

Swinton Bridge

Whitelee Grove Trading Estate

Frederick ?

4

Yearling Chase

A6022 CHURCH STREET

Church Close

Queen Street 3 & I School

Swinton Swimming Pool

The Richmond Fellowship

STATION STREET

BRIDGE STREET

A6022 TOWNS SWINTON LANE

Market ?

Walker St

111
WARREN VALE

ROCKINGHAM ROAD

Woodman Drive

Doctors Surgery

Rotherham MBC

Swinton Station

River Do?

Woodlands Crs

5

C6
1 Benton Ter

SWINTON

The Crescent

Grange Rd

The Cft

The Green

The Lea

Swinton Fitzwilliam Infants School Junior School

Swinton Comprehensive School

Slade Road

Manor Road

Birkdale

Primary School

St Andrew's Cl

Carnoustie Ave

6

A633

Piccadilly

Laurence Dr

Caladine Wy

St Andrew's Cl

7

C7
1 Fernvale Wk

D2
1 Highwoods Crs

Glebe Rd

Harrop

Aspen

Buckthorn Close

Celandine

Albany Rd

Holywell Road

Meadow View

Sivilla Road

Doctors Surgery

B6090

Larkspur

Canalway

Beighton Road

Victoria St

Wharf

HOOTON ROAD

8

Ryecroft

D4
1 Broomville St
2 Wharf Cl

Sandhill

Eastfield Place

Mortake View Drive

The Brig

Kilnhurst Road

Kilnhurst

Wheatley Road Greenwood Road

Russell St

Charles St

Kilnhurst Junior & Infants School

grid square represents 500 metres

A **B** **134** **C** **D** **E**

Glasshouse Lane

Kilnhurst Business Park

E2
1 Beaconsfield St
2 Blenheim Crs
3 Catherine St
4 Cowood St
5 Shrewsbury Cl

E3
1 Belmont St
2 Britain St
3 Cresswell St
4 Dodsworth St

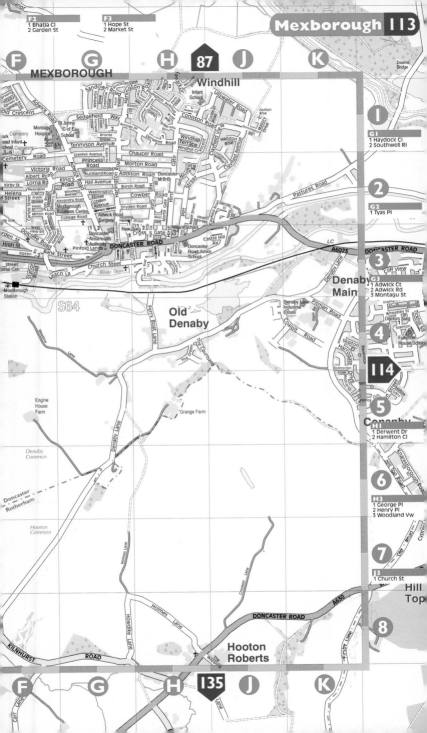

F2
1 Bhatia Cl
2 Garden St

F3
1 Hope St
2 Market St

F **G** **H** **87** **J** **K**

MEXBOROUGH

Windhill

Dearne
Bridge

1
1 Haydock Cl
2 Southwell Rl

2
G2
1 Tyas Pl

Pastures Road

LC
A6023 DONCASTER ROAD
3
Cliff View

G3
1 Adwick Ct
2 Adwick Rd
3 Montagu St

Denaby
Main

S64

Old
Denaby

Denaby Lane
Industrial
Estate

Pitman Road

Craypit Road

4
Stainton
114

5
Denaby
H1
1 Derwent Dr
2 Hamilton Cl

Engine
House
Farm

'Grange Farm'

6
H3
1 George Pl
2 Henry Pl
3 Woodland Vw

Denaby
Common

Doncaster
Rotherham

Hooton
Common

7
J3
1 Church St

Holmes Lane

Howdike Lane

Crooked Lane

Hill
Top

A630

Finkhy Lane

8

KILNHURST
ROAD

DONCASTER ROAD
A630

Hooton
Roberts

F **G** **H** **135** **J** **K**

Carr Lane

F **G** **H** **89** **J** **K** **I**

F5
1 Brook Rd
2 Butt Hole Rd
3 Templestowe Ga

H6
1 Bower V
2 Grainger Cl

Nursery Lane

I6
1 Mount Vw
2 Windermere Gra

Warmsworth Primary School

Mill Lane

Warmsworth

SHEFFIELD ROAD A630

A630

Warmsworth

SHEFFIELD ROAD

K5
1 Church Rein Cl
2 Coronation Gdns

Cemetery

2

3

K4
1 Boundary Cl
2 Century Ct
3 Fielders Wy
4 Johnson Ct
5 Larwood Gv

Edlington Victoria Primary School

Staveley Street

Victoria Road

Middle School

EDLINGTON LANE

B6376

4

116

St Marys Catholic School

Doctors Surgery

Bungalow Road

Market Place

The Health Centre

Markham Road

Grange Road

Springfield Road

5

K5
1 Newbridge Gv

Thompson Avenue

Baines Avenue

Carr Road

Broomhouse

Lilac Crescent

Violet Avenue

Martin Well Road

Roberts Road

St Mary's Road

Hill Top Junior & Infant School

New Edlington

Edlington Wood

Highbury Vale

Hillside

Tait Avenue

Avenue

Eccles Dr

Top View

Edlington School

6

7

Conisbrough Common

Common Road

Snake Lane

EDLINGTON LANE

B6376

CARR LANE

Rectory Gdns

Back Lane

Wood Lane

Old Edlington

8

F **G** **H** **137** **J** **K**

B6376 COCKHILL

116

B2
1 Beechcroft Rd
2 Pinewood Av
3 Whitney Cl

B1
1 Apostle Cl
2 Cambria Dr
3 Hyland Crs
4 Mannering Rd
5 Sandycroft Crs

D1
1 Dirleton Dr
2 Grosvenor Ter

90

A B C D E

Junction 36

WARMSWORTH A630

C1
1 Blackwood Av
2 Finch Rd
3 Springwell Gdns
4 W'bourne Gdns

2

C2
1 Millwood Rd
2 The Spinney

3

D1
1 Byron Av
2 Ruskin Rd

4

115

5

6

New

E8
1 Vicarage Dr

7

E1
Street Names for these grid squares are listed at the back of the index

8

A B 138 C D E

grid square represents 500 metres

118

D
1 Broughton Rd

C7
1 King Georges Cl

CI
1 Winterton Cl

BESSACARR

A   B   92   C   D   E

Potteric Carr
Nature Reserve

I

D2
1 Mattersey Cl
2 Torksey Cl

2

D7
1 Skipwith Gdns

3

EI
1 Dunniw'd Reach

4

117

5

6

St Catherine's

7

8
Carr

A   B   140   C   D   E

Stancil Lane

grid square represents 500 metres

NEW
ROSSINGTON

Rossington
Grange Farm

Holmes Carr
Great Wood

Doncaster
Metropolitan
Borough Council

Rossington
Parish Council

Rossington
Swimming
Pool &
Sports Centre

Pheasant
Bank Junior School

Holmescarr
Junior Mixed
School

Bankwood Lane
Industrial
Estate

Park
Wood

River Torn

Mother Dra

F6
1 Primrose Cir

F7
1 Cherry Gv
2 Kier Hardie Av
3 Sandbeck Ct
4 Wilkinson Av

F **G** **H** 93 **J** **K**

B1396

Riverside Gdns

I

F8
1 Kingsway Cl

Twelve Months Carr

2

G1
1 Gleneagles Dr
2 Sunningdale Cl

Hayfield Comprehensive School

3

G6
1 Canon Cl
2 Cardinal Cl
3 Deacon Cl
4 Littleworth Cl
5 Whitwell Vw

4

120

5

6

Hay Field

River Torne

Warnington

Hotel

BAWTRY ROAD A638

The Warren

Doncaster Golf Course

Rossington Bridge

BRIDGE LANE B6463

SHEEP LANE

Rossington

Littleworth

School

Warren House Farm

Hotel

7

8

Hall View Road

Common Lane LC

F **G** **H** 141 **J** **K**

Rossington Hall School

F4
1 Church La
2 Honeysuckle Ct
3 Pinfold Cl
4 St Oswald's Dr

G1
1 Foxglove Cl

G4
1 Silver Birch Gv

F **G** **H** **95** **J** **K**

I

2

3

4

5

6

7

8

Finningley Grange Farm

Old Bank End Farm

Whin Covert

BANK END ROAD B1396

BANK

END

ROAD

THORNE

Woot Road

Springbank Close
Shepherds Croft
Summerfields
Prickland Walk
Drive
Park
New St
The Crscent
Blue Bell Court
B1396

Bell's Close

Road

LC

Harvey Cl
Wood
Lane
Chapel Lane
Lindley Cl
Tenter Hill Clo
Grange Close
Elm Drive
School
Kinsley Ct
Croft Court
Ashley

Finningley

WROOT ROAD

The Green

BAWTRY ROAD A614

A614

Croft Road

A614

Pickle Wood

Flow Wood

Misson Grange

Spring Hill

Deeps Lane

Springs Farm

Red House

Road

SPRI

Firbeck Road

F **G** **H** **143** **J** **K**

Middle Wood Lane

Middle Wood Farm

Bracken

122

Fair Banks

Upper Small Clough

Ronksley Moor

Lower Small Clough

Sheffield
Derbyshire County
Deer Holes

River Derwent

Howden Moors

Mosley Bank

Slippery Stones

Ox Hey

Linch Clough

Ridge Nether Moor

Cow Hey

Banktop Hey

Sheffield Derbyshire County

Fox's Piece

How... ...er

100

144

grid square represents 500 metres

Bull
Clough

F

G

H

101

J

Cut

K

ow
nes
ge

1

Bull
Stones

2

Bull
Clough

3

546
▲
Margery
Hill

Cranberry
Clough

4

124

5

Cold
Side

Penistone
Stile

6

Featherbed
Moss

7

Howden Clough

8

Howden
Moors

F

G

H

145

J

K

Abbey Brook

Howden
Dean

124

Cut Gate

Pike Lowe

A B **102** C D E

1

2 *Upper Commons*

Ewden Beck

3

Stainery Clough

4

123

5 *Middle Moss*

6

Featherbed Moss

7

8

A B **146** C D E

grid square represents 500 metres

126

Ⓐ   Ⓑ   **104**   Ⓒ   Ⓓ   Ⓔ

Stone
Moor

Heads Lane

Waldershaigh

1

2

Broomhead
Hall

Allas
Lane

Allas Dike Lane

Broomhead
Reservoir

3

Moor   Lane

Wigtwizzle

Rushy Lane

Mill Lane

New Road

Fee   Lane

Dwarriden   Lane

Canyards

White
Farm

4

◄125

Canyards   Hills   Lane

Walker   Edge

5

Mortimer   Road

Penistone Road

Load   Field   Road

White
Lee
Moor

Smallfield

6

Agden
Bridge

Agden   side   Road

Smallfield Lane

West
Nab

7

Penistone   Road

8

Mortimer Road

Ⓐ   Ⓑ   **148**   Ⓒ   Ⓓ   Ⓔ

Windy   Bank

Brown
House

1 grid square represents 500 metres

A8
1 Jackey Hl

A6
1 Damasel Cl

Bank A5
1 Brightholmlee Ct
2 Damasel Rd

A

B

106

C

Smith

D

E

Barnsley Boundary Walk

MANCHESTER

1

ROAD

Mouse Park

Plank Gate

Wharncliffe
Chase

Lodge Lane

2

Plank Gate

Langworthcliffe's Road

Lodge Lane

3

Lane

Wharncliffe
Lodge

Barnsley Boundary Walk

A6102

MAIN

4

Woodhead Drive

Carton st East

The Grove

127

rightholmlee Lane

Wharncliffe Side
Primary School

Dixon Drive

PO

Stedman

Gap

Old View Gate

Mouse Park Gate

S

Wharnc Side

Swinnock Hall

5

ROAD

Port Avenue

Storth

Wharncliffe
Wood

Storth
Lane

6

Damasel Lane

Green

Spring Gv

Storms

Stack Flats
Lane

Cockshutts

Foldrings

Owler

Gate

Hilltop
Dr

Lane

LANGSETT ROAD NORTH

Plank Gate

7

Raynor Sike Lane

Horse Croft Lane

Onesacre

Crag View
Close

Crag View

Bedford Road

Plants Lane

Wortley Drive

Oughtibridge Lane

Lumb Lane

8

Green Lane

Conway Hill

Long Lane

Lane

Station Lane

Bedford Road

Station
Lane

Police
Station

Oughtibridge

Sheffield
Health
Authority

LOW ROAD

Wheel Lane

Church Street

Poplar
Road

Alford Av
Primary
School

Naylor
Road

Birks Wood

Edward Drive

LANGSETT ROAD SOUTH

A6102

Coumes Farm

Burton Lane

Rollin
Road

HILL

Burton
Cemetery

Boggard
Lane

B

150

Rarer's Road

Wheel Lane

Hope
Road

C

Bertram Road

D

E

1 grid square represents 500 metres

G2
1 Chapelfield Crs
2 Chapelfield Mt
3 Chapel Field Pl
4 Flanders Ct
5 Kirkcroft Cl

G3
1 Thorntree Cl

H1
1 Kingfisher Ri
2 Lapwing V

F   G   H   **109**   J   K

1

Strafford Place

Chapelfield Road

Peacock Close

Avocet Way

Raven Close

Bittern View

Nightingale Croft

Morley Pond

2

THORPE STREET

Chestnut Grove

The Paddock

Thorpe Hesley

Wentworth Road

Kirkcroft Avenue

Slough Hall Close

Oaken Wood Close

The Surgery

Thorpe Hesley Clinic

Thorpe Hesley Infant School

3

WORTLEY ROAD

Wortley Mews

Brook Hill

Windsor Road

Thorpe Hesley Junior School

Newton Place

Scholes

Scholes Green

Scholes Lane

Kirkstead Abbey Mews

132

S61

4

Tumble Lane

Louden Close

Louden Rd

Keppel Drive

Scholes Coppice

Keppel Column

Admirals Crest

Hesley Grange

Wentworth Place

5

Sunmoor Road

The Coppice

Monks Close

Oaks Lane

Lady Road

Redscope

6

UPPER WORTLEY ROAD

A629

Dropping Well

Trans Pennine Trail

Hurst Lane

Upper Wortley Road

7

Grange Lane

DEEP LA

Grange Mill Lane

MT

Thundercliffe Grange

Watson Green

Farm Road

Hill View Rd

Farm View Close

8

Abbey School

Green Lane

Droppingwell Road

Little Common Lane

Winterhill Road

The Bawne

Wood Road

Sheffield Council

Ecclesfield

Blackburn

Bolsterstone County Junior Mixed School

Barber Wood Road

West Hill

153

Hill Top

F   G   H   **153**   J   K

F8
1 Amory's Holt Cl
2 Everson Cl
3 Surtees Cl

F G H 115 J K

Rectory Gdns

Bac... Lane
Wood   Lane

...ton
...ton

1

B6376
B6094

COCKHILL LANE

M18

LONG   B6376

2   Cockhill Farm

clifton

Shipman   Balk
Green Balk

Ruddle Lane

B6094

Newland's Farm
Cockhill Lane
Rates Lane

3

New
Road

Field   Lane
Cockhill
LANE

4

DONCASTER B6376 RD

138

Lane
Hole

Cockhill Lane

ng   Micklebring Lane

Birchwood Gdns

Church
Grove

Austwood   Lane

5

Chapel Lane

Ruddle Mill

The Ruddle Mill

Cardwell
Court   B6376 HIGH ST   Low Pas...

Braithwell

Ashton Lane

B6427 HOLYWELL LANE

6

Holme
Hall Farm

HOLME

Croft   Lane

Holy...
Crescent

B6376 LANE

MALTBY

B6427
FISH POND LANE

Lambcote Grange

7

Stainton Lane

8

Amory's Holt Drive

Halds Road
Dale Hill Road
Acre Close

Underfield Road

Greenland Av

LANE

F G H 159 J K

Salisbury
Morwood   Manor   Clarence

BRAITHWELL R

Davy Drive
Highfield Park

Ticket Dr

ORANGE

138

A

B

116

C

D

E

Gospel Well

Lane

Lane

Garth

CHURCH ROAD

I

short Gate

B6094

WILSIC ROAD

Wilsic

Cockhill Farm

2

LONG GATE

B6094

B6094

Both

Woodlands Farm

Wilsic Hall School

Rakes Lane

3

Stainton Lane

Wilsic

Lodge Farm

4

137

Chapel Hole

Cockhill Lane

Tickhill Back Lane

5

Limekiln Lane

Ruddle Mill Lane

The Ruddle Mill

Hirst Lane

Wood Lane

Broad

Riding

Stainton Little Wood

6

Holme Hall Farm

Holme Hall Lane

Stainton

Stainton Woodhouse Farm

7

Rawl Lane

Stainton Lane

Schogt Lane

8

ne

Limekiln Lane

A

B

160

C

Scotch Spring Lane

D

E

grid square represents 500 metres

A   B   118   C   D   E

Carr   Bank
Stancil Lane

Rossington
Grange Farm

A8
Radburn   1 Orange Cft
Whitc
Wildflower
Close
Kepple
Close
Regent
Grove

I

Stancil
Lane

Park
Wood

2   Wellingley

Stancil

3   Stancil
Lane

Coolei Dike or River Torne

Bog
Wood

4

139

5

Limpool Farm

Dumpling
Castle

6   East

Hooyard Lane

Sheepwash Lane

Lane

Tickfield
Eastfield Primary
School

Common

Common
Lane

High

7   Airedale Avenue

Alderson Close

The

8   SUNDERLAND STREET A631

A631

Spital
Hill

Beech Avenue
Wainut Av

Paper Mill Lane

Sunderland

Broom
Close

Lumley Dy

Lindrick

GATE60

A   B   162   C   D   E

Moorhouse Farm

BLYTH ROAD

1 grid square represents 500 metres

F
G
H
119
J
K

I

2

3

4

142

5

6

7

8

F
G
H
163
J
K

Hunster
Grange Farm

New
Lodge

Common Lane LC

Rossington
Hall School

RSPCA
Centre

GREAT NORTH ROAD

A1(M)

Martin
Common Farm

Bawtry
Forest

Martin Lane

Martin
Beck

Martin Grange

Martin Lane

Martin Lane

Tickhill
Grange

Martin Beck Lane

Grange Av
Ingham
Cliff
Martin Lane

Maple
Grove
Yew
Oak Tree Rd
Elm Tree

TICKHILL ROAD

Madison
Dr

Bircotes
Court

Leeming Court

Doncaster
Nottinghamshire

122

Hov
Rese

Fox's
Piece

Fagney
Clough

Beaver's
Croft

He
Da

Green
Clough

Upper Derwent Valley

irchin
t

Birchinlee
Pasture

Birchinlee

Alport
Castles

The
Tower

Der
Rese

Ouzelden
Clough

Gores Fa

ucklow
ees Barn

Rowlee
Pasture

Derwent
Dale

Gores
Heights

Lockerbrook
Heights

Lockerbrook Farm

Gillot
Hey Farm

Nab
Wood

Rowlee Farm

Hagg Fa

Blackley
Hey

Asl

grid square represents 500 metres

I

2

3

4

146

5

6

7

8

Howden
Moors

Abbey Brook

Howden
Dean

Little
Howden
Moor

Abbey
Bank

Lost
Lad

Howshaw
Tor

Green
Sitches

Far
Deep
Clough

Gusset

Cakes
of Bread

John
Field
Howden

Dovestone
Clough

Derwent
Edge

Sheffield
Derbyshire County

Dovestone
Tor

Fairholmes

Mill Brook

Salt
Cellar

Derwent Lane

Whi
Tor

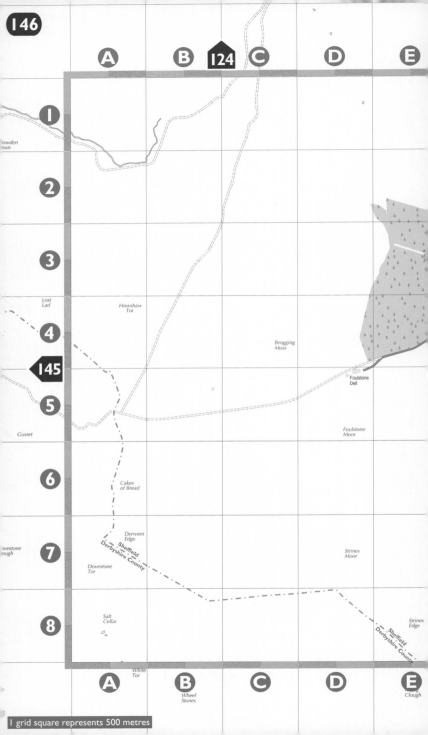

F   G   H   **125**   J   K

1

2

3

4

148

5

6

7

8

F   G   **166**   J   K

Bradfield
Moors

Thornseat
Delf

Thornseat Road

Mortimer Road

Mortimer Road

Dale Road

Thornseat

Thompson House
Green

Lane

Bradfie
Dale

Hall

Lane Head

Road

Blindside Lane

Bole Edge
Plantation

Hallfield

Tor Farm

Dale Dike
Resevoir

We

PH

Strines

Strines
Resevoir

Sugworth

Road

Bradfield
Moors

Sugworth Road

Sugworth
Hall

Bents
House

Moor
Lodge

Stake Hill Road

Ughill Moors

Sugworth Road

Woodsea

Moscar
Cross

oss Road

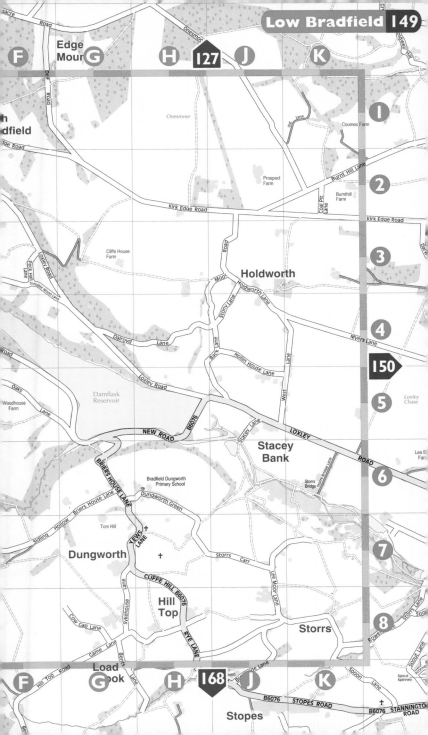

152

C7
1 Passhouses Rd

B4
1 Piper Ct

B5
1 Bishopsholme Rd
2 Busk Knoll

A4
1 Southey Cl
2 Southey Green Cl

CB
1 Brandon St

130

A · B · C · D · E

Monteney Middle & Primary School

1

D2
1 Kinnaird Av

CHAUCER ROAD

B6087

Chaucer School

Parson Cross

Deerlands Avenue

2

D3
1 Crestwood Gdns
2 Swanbourne Pl

Buchanan

BARNSLEY ROAD A6135

HIGHGREAVE

Deerlands Special School

3

D6
1 Fir Vale Pl

Wordsworth

Buchanan Road

Crowder Avenue

Crowland Road

S5

STUBBIN LANE

Pis H

Longley Estate

Fir Pa

4

151

HERRIES

Southey Crescent

Everingham

Herries Drive

Longley Hall Road

Hucklow Primary School

The Oval

5

D7
1 Cawston Rd
2 Gayton Rd
3 Osgathorpe Crs

Doctors Surgery

Shirecliffe

Boynton Road

Buck Park

ABOVE

Norwood Gra

Fir Vale

Calder Way

6

D8
1 Ella Rd
2 Grimesthorpe Rd
3 Lucas St
4 Lyons St

Wardsend Cemetery

Crumpsall Drive

Musgrave

Norwood Close

Goddard Hall Road

Skinnerthorpe Road

Grime

Whiteways Junior School

Osgathorpe Drive

S4

erton ding ate

7

E2
1 Hatfield House Ct
2 Molineaux Cl

Standish Avenue

Firshill Rise

Firs Hill Junior School

BARNSLEY ROAD A6135

Pexton

Scott

Pitsmoor

8

E3
1 Lindley Rd
2 Mortlake Rd

Parkwood Springs

Sheffield Ski Village

S3

Pitsmoor Sug

Sheffield City Council

Pitsmoor Dental Health Centre

Byron Wood Primary School

Melton Street

Sixty Temple Lyons Street

Carwood Street

E6
1 Bolsover Rd East
2 Heathcote St

B6074 NEEPSEND LANE

A · B · 171 · C · D · E

E7
1 Earl Marshal Dr
2 Whiteways Dr

E8
1 Carwood Gv
2 Jamaica St

Burngreave

Masbroug

Abbey School

1 Siemens Cl

B5

Common Lane

Little

Crane Dr

Old Hall Comprehensive School

A

Winter Hill

B

132

Fenton

B1
1 Clement Ms
2 Roman Ct

Kimberworth

Oates Street

Clough Bank

A5
1 Plumper's Rd

Bradgate

D

Street

E

Hill

1

Regent
Upper
Clifton

Woodstock Bower
Group Practice

Ambergate Clinics

Ferham House Clinic

West Hill

C6
1 Ackworth Dr

Meadowhall Junior School

Deepdale Rd

Ferham
Rosebery St

Holmes

Meadow Bank
Industrial Estate

Magno

2

D1
1 Ferham Park Av
2 Meadowbank Cl

MEADOW BANK

A6109

Jordan

Street

Trans Pennine Trail

Rotherham
Sheffield

A6109

MEADOW BANK ROAD

3

D6
1 Ambleside Cl
2 St Georges Dr

River Don

Templeborough

Langman's Hos

Rd

4

153

A6178 SHEFFIELD ROAD

Bessemer Way

DO WHALL WAY

Junction 34

Mesque Lane

Street

Dundas

Tinsley

Bawtry Gate

Newman

Highgate

5

E1
1 Chatsworth Rd
2 Devonshire St
3 Florence Rd
4 Robert St
5 Tummon St

VULCAN ROAD

The Surgery

The Medical
Centre

Junction Thirty Four
Industrial Estate

Greasbro Road

Tinsley
Junior
School

A631 BAWTRY ROAD

Bawtry Rd

Brinsworth
Medical
Centre

BONET LANE

Crownhill Road

Bawtry Road

Pringle Road

Godric Drive

Manor
School

6

SHEFFIELD ROAD

1 Ellen Tree Cl

Meadowhall
Retail Park

LANE

M1

Park House Lane

Sheffield United
Cricket Club

St Andrews
Walk

Kirkstall

Winchester Way

Brinsworth

Pringle Road

7

G1, G7, H1
Street Names for
these grid squares
are listed at the
back of the index

Trans Pennine Trail

Trans Pennine Trail

Brinsworth
Comprehensive
School

Brinsworth
Road

Brinsworth Road

8

Tinsley Pk Rd

S9

Trans Pennine Trail

BRINSWORTH

Green Lane

GREENLAND

A631

A

Europa

B

173

Link

C

City Airport

D

Tinsley

E

grid square represents 500 metres

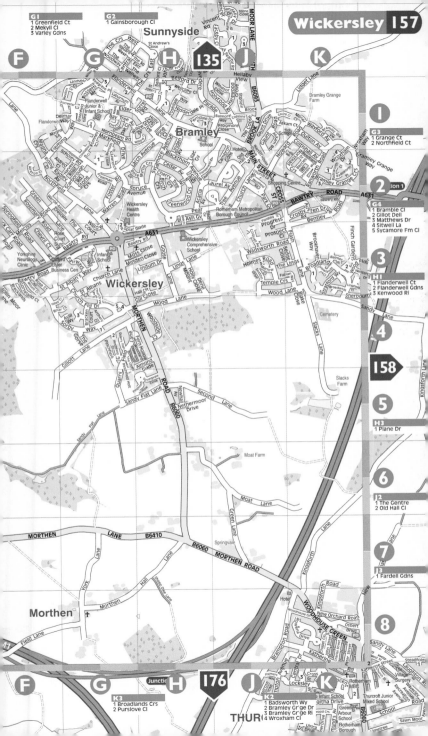

F1
1 Aldrin Wy
2 Fretwell Cl
3 Gladstone Rd

F3
1 St Barbara's Cl
2 St Barth'mew's Cl
3 St Phillip's Cl

Stainton Lane

137

Greenland Av

MALTBY

Hooton Levitt

Hooton

G1
1 Dale Hill Cl
2 Norwood Cl
3 Springvale Cl

H1
1 Cavendish Pl

H2
1 Southey Rd

160

H3
1 Ascension Cl
2 Deacon Crs
3 Queen Av
4 Scarbrough Crs

H4
1 Millicent Sq
2 Queen Mary St

7 Roche Abbey

J1
1 Haslam Pl
2 Lambcote Wy
3 Nookery Cl

178

J4
1 Adelaide St

J3
1 Bedford St
2 Scholfield Crs
3 Somerset St

J2
1 Heatherdale Rd
2 Howard Rd
3 Seymour Rd
4 Staffordshire Cl
5 Stone Park Cl

F **G** **H** **139** **J** **K**

SUNDERLAND STREET A63

St Mary's
Saffron
Kesfield
St Mary's Rd
ST GATE
Davy Gallery

Tickhill Dr
St Mary's
C of E
School
Kg Edwards
Castle
Sarahs Gallery

I

Paper Mill Dike

Crown Road
Pinfold
NEW RD
Pinfold
Lane

WEST GATE A60

Lindrick
Lane

Castle Cl
Castle
Davy
Road

Lindrick

Limestone
Hill

A631

ROTHERHAM ROAD

A60 WORKSOP ROAD

Lindrick
Lane

2

Water Lane

Wittery Hough Lane

A631

Crooked Head Lane

3

Bagley Farm

Blyth Gate Lane

A60

4

Folds   Lane

162

South
Wongs Farm

Dam
Nottinghamshire County

5

Folds

Folds Farm

Lane

A60   MALPAS HILL   A60

Styrrup
Carr

6

Styrrup Lane

7

Thornbury Hill Lane

Park
House

Rotherham
Nottinghamshire County

A60

8

B6463

F **G** **H** **180** **J** Oldcote **K**

A63 MALTBY ROAD

Wynlea
Drive

BLYTH ROAD

Elmsmere
Drive

Weirside

F2
1 Welbeck Rd

F3
1 Holderness Cl
2 Sandymount E
3 Sandymount W

F G H **141** J K

Drive
Chestnut
Drive

TICKHILL ROAD

Madison
Dr

1

Leeming
Court

Doncaster

Nottinghamshire County

Swinnow
Wood

2

Plumtree Farm
Estate

North Border County
Secondary School

Bircotes
Sports
Centre

Galway
Road

3

Gibbet Hill La

Harworth
Medical
Centre

WEST STREET

White House Road

Essex Road

Suffolk Road

Cumberland
Close

Westmorland Ct

St Patricks
Primary
School

Beverley Road

Norfolk
Road

Milne
Drive

4

Infant
School

Crewe
Rd

Junior
School

The
Crescent

164

Khan Medical
Centre

Scrooby Road

Bircotes

Scroo

5

Saracens

Droversdale
Wood

6

Harworth Park
Industrial Estate

Ruins
Plantation

The
Holt

Neale's
Covert

7

Blyth Road

A614

Round
Holt

Green Lane

Noble Flatt
Wood

Serlby

8

BAWTRY ROAD

A614

Serlby Park
Golf Club

F G H J K

Harworth
Avenue

The
Woodlands

A614

Bishopfield
Farm

River Ryton

K4
1 Old Post Office St
River Idle

F G H **143** J K

Pasture Farm

Claybank Farm

I

Everton
Carr

2

Pasture Lane

Hazel
Barn Lane

Carr
Hill

3

Foe Lane

Barrow
Hills

A631

Harwell

Harwell   Lane

Everton

Everton
Sluice
Lane

Windmill Ridge

Church St
Ferry
La
1
Brewery
La
High
Piln

Croft
Farm Cl

4

Carr

St

Crow

Long Mdw

PO

GAINSBOROUGH ROAD

A631

5

Tethering
Lane

Pusto
Hill
Lane

Cemetery

**Mattersey
Thorpe**

Newall
Dr
Wilson
Cl

Wilson
Crescent

6

Plantation
Drive

Ton Green

Pusto
Hill Farm

Mattersey
Road

B6045

Cunningham
Close

Bader View

7

Broomfield Lane

Wilson Close

EEL POOL ROAD

B6045

Mattersey
Grange

Brecks Lane

Thorpe Road

Cemetery

MATTERSEY ROAD

Abbey Road

8

Mattersey
Primary
School

Dene
Close

Wood
View

Mattersey

MAIN STREET

Job Lane

F G H J K

Mattersey
Hill

166
Strines
Edge

Sheffield
Derbyshire County

A **B** 147 **C** **D** **E**

Moor
Lodge

Sugworth Road

Stake Hill Road

Ughill Moors

Rising
Clough

1

Moscar
Cross

Moscar Cross Road

2

Moscar
House

Heathy Lane

Moscar
Lodge

Hollow
Mead

3

A57

Moscar
Fields

4

5

Stanage
End

Jarvis
Clough

6

Moscar
Moor

High Lad
Ridge

7

Crow
Chin

8

457
High Neb

A **B** 182 **C** Stanage Edge **D** **E**

Sheffield
Derbyshire County

Buck Stone

1 grid square represents 500 metres

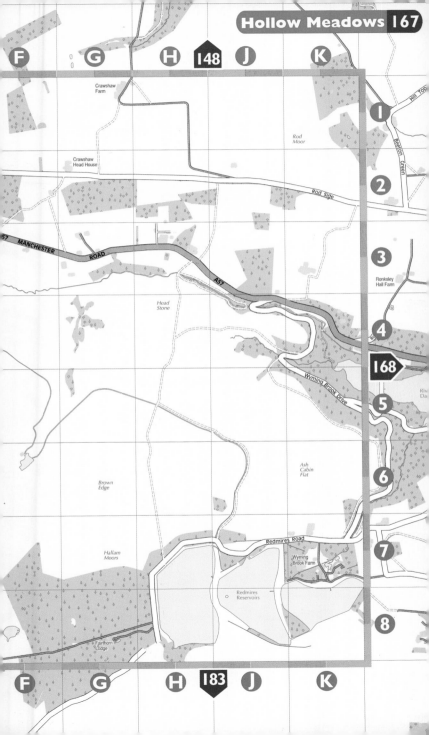

F G H 148 J K

Crawshaw
Farm

I

Rod
Moor

Beeton Green

Hill Top

Crawshaw
Head House

Rod Side

2

57 MANCHESTER ROAD

A57

3

Ronksley
Hall Farm

Head
Stone

4

168

Wyming Brook Drive

River
Da

5

Brown
Edge

Ash
Cabin
Flat

6

Redmires Road

7

Wyming
Brook Farm

Hallam
Moors

Redmires
Reservoirs

8

Fairthorn
Lodge

F G H 183 J K

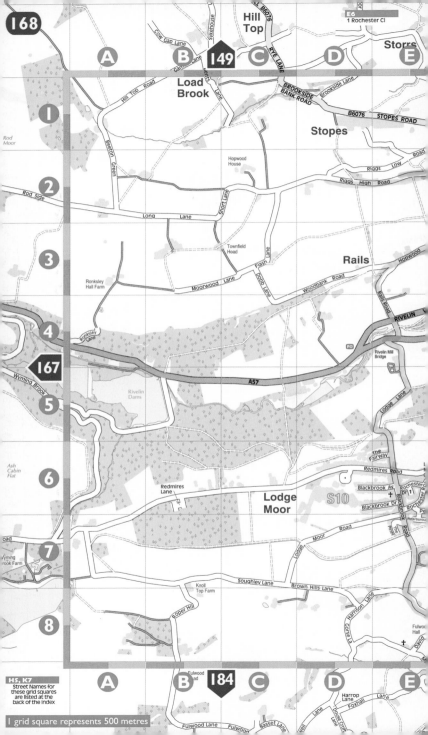

168

A **B** **149** **C** **D** **E**

Hill Top

Storrs

E6
1 Rochester Cl

Cow Gap Lane

Sikehouse Lane

Rye Lane

Load
Brook

Garth House Lane

Hill Top Road

BROOKSIDE
BANK ROAD

Brookside Lane

B6076 STOPES ROAD

I

Rod
Moor

Beeton Green

Stopes

Hopwood
House

Riggs Low Road

2

Rod Side

Short Lane

Riggs High Road

Long Lane

3

Townfield
Head

Flash Lane

Rails

Hopwood

Ronksley
Hall Farm

Moorwood Lane

Dobb Lane

Woodbank Road

Rails Road

RIVELIN

4

Ronksley Lane

167

Wyming Brook

Rivelin Mill
Bridge

A57

5

Rivelin
Dams

Lodge Lane

Ash
Cabin
Flat

The
Fairway

6

Redmires
Lane

Redmires Road

Blackbrook Av

Rochester Dr

**Lodge
Moor**

S10

Blackbrook Dr

Blackbrook Rd

Rochester Rd

Peterborou

Road

Lodge Moor Road

7

Wyming
Brook Farm

Piper Lane

8

Knoll
Top Farm

Roper Hill

Soughley Lane

Brown Hills Lane

Harrison Lane

Gosse La

Fulwood
Hall

David

H5, K7
Street Names for
these grid squares
are listed at the
back of the index

A **B** **184** **C** **D** **E**

Fulwood
Road

Harrop
Lane

Foxhall

Lane

Well Lane

House Croft

Lane

Fulwood Lane

Fulwood

Basset Lane

1 grid square represents 500 metres

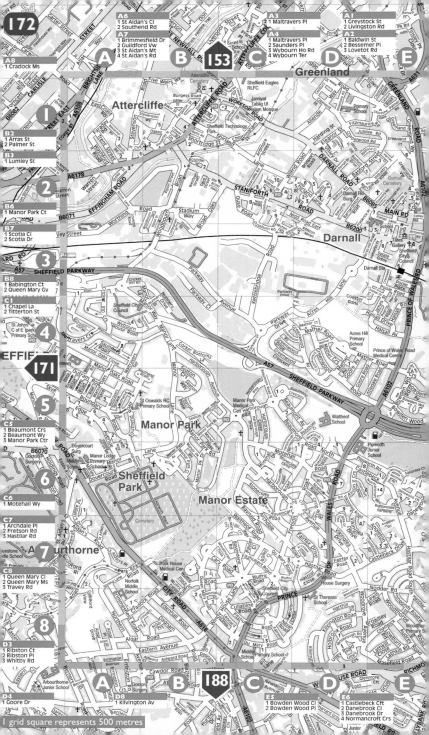

A6
1 St Aidan's Cl
2 Southend Rd

A7
1 Brimmesfield Dr
2 Guildford Vw
3 St Aidan's Mt
4 St Aidan's Rd

A3
2 Maltravers Pl

A4
1 Maltravers Pl
2 Saunders Pl
3 Wybourn Ho Rd
4 Wybourn Ter

A1
2 Greystock St
3 Livingston Rd

A2
1 Baldwin St
2 Bessemer Pl
3 Lovetot Rd

A8
1 Cradock Ms

B2
1 Arras St
2 Palmer St

B3
1 Lumley St

B6
1 Manor Park Ct

B7
1 Scotia Cl
2 Scotia Dr

B8
1 Babington Ct
2 Queen Mary Gv

C1
1 Chapel La
2 Titterton St

C5
1 Beaumont Crs
2 Beaumont Wy
3 Manor Park Ctr

D
Surgery

C6
1 Motehall Wy

C7
1 Archdale Pl
2 Fretson Rd
3 Hastilar Rd

C8
1 Queen Mary Cl
2 Queen Mary Ms
3 Travey Rd

D3
1 Ribston Ct
2 Ribston Pl
3 Whitby Rd

D4
1 Goore Dr

D8
1 Kilvington Av

E5
1 Bowden Wood Cl
2 Bowden Wood Pl

E6
1 Castlebeck Cft
2 Danebrook Cl
3 Danebrook Dr
4 Normancroft Crs

I grid square represents 500 metres

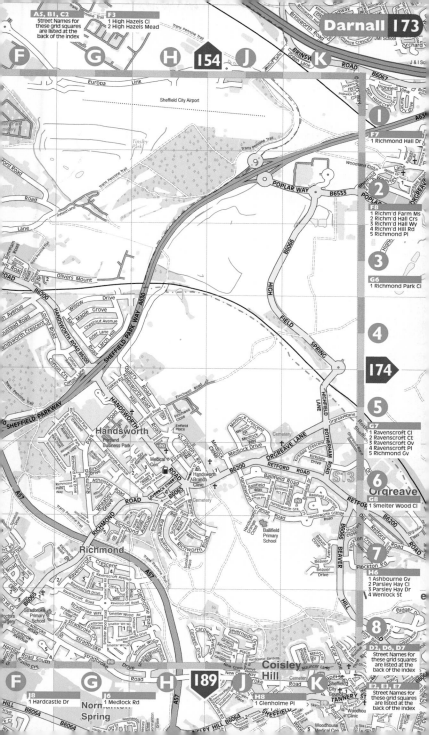

F **G** **H** 154 **J** **K**

Europa Link

Sheffield City Airport

Trans Pennine Trail

Tinsley Park

POPLAR WAY   B6533

1

2

3

Olivers Mount

SHEFFIELD PARK WAY A630

HIGH   FIELD   SPRING

4

174

5

Willow Drive
Maple Grove
Chestnut Avenue
Alder Lane
Larch Hill

HANDSWORTH ROAD B6200

Finchwell Road

Enfield Place

Medlock Crescent
Medlock Drive

ORGREAVE LANE

HIGHFIELD LANE

ROTHERHAM ROAD

S13

Cemetery

Handsworth

Portland
Business Park

Medical Cen

Handsworth
Branch
Clinic

RETFORD   ROAD

Ballifield Road
Ballifield Way

6
Orgreave

Richmond

Ravenscroft Crescent
Ravenscroft Avenue
Ravenscroft Drive
Ravenscroft Road

RICHMOND   ROAD

A57

Handsworth Grange Road

Ballifield
Primary
School

BEAVER HILL

Beaver
Drive

7

Stradbroke
Primary
School

SMELTER WOOD

Severnside Drive
Severnside Place

Flockton Rd

RETFORD ROAD B6200

8

Coisley Hill

Cemetery Road

F **G** **H** 189 **J** **K**

Normanton
Spring

SHEFFIELD

Woodhouse
Medical Cen

G8
1 Knaresboro' Cl

H5
1 Manor Farm

M1

F   A618   G   Upper   Whiston   Lane   H   156   J   Field Lane   K   M1

Guilthwaite

Upper Whiston

Morthen Lane

Stow Bridge Lane

I
H6
1 Woodlands Cl

Guilthwaite

Common Lane

Ulley Country Park

Stoket Lane

2
H7
1 Aunby Dr
2 Darcy Cl

PLEASLEY ROAD   A618

Reservoir Road

Ulley Reservoir

Penny Hill Lane

Main Street

Ulley

3
H8
1 Alison Cl
2 Manvers Cl
3 Orchard Lea Dr

Green Lane

Poynton Avenue

Ulley Lane

Turnshaw Road

Carr Lane

4

B6067

TREETON LANE B6067

176

5
J7
1 Wharncliffe Av

AUGHTON

Coral Drive

Well Lane

Hall Farm Lane

ASTON LANE B6067

Infant School

West Lane

Hall Road

Mason Drive

Aston Comprehensive School

Cemetery

Avenue

Aston Springwood Junior School

Ulley Lane

6
J8
1 Aylsham Dr
2 Burford Crs
3 Legion Dr
4 Regents Wy

Alexandra Road

Nursery Road

AUGHTON ROAD A618

Eden Grove

Millstone Drive

Worksop Road

AUGHTON LANE

Stanley Grove

Cemetery

7
K7
1 Stanley Gv
2 Willow Gv

Aston Swallownest Junior & Infant School

Manvers Road

HIGH STREET A618

Rotherham

Swallownest Health Centre

Swallownest Drive

Newington Drive

All Saints Way

WORKSOP ROAD

B6067

Park Hill

Main Street

Swallownest

CHESTERFIELD RD

MANSFIELD ROAD

H   191   J   Elizabeth Way   Fair View   Church Lane   K

Moorland View

ASTON

Aston Cricket Club

8

F   G   Field Road   H   191   J   Vickerwood Drive   Wedgewood View   K

K8
1 Hardwick Cl

F1
1 Riddings Cl
2 South St

G1
1 Autumn Cl

Brook House

F

G

H

158

J

Brookhouse

K

Slade View

I

J4
1 Station Wy

2

K6
1 Roddis Cl

3

K8
1 Bedford Cl
2 Marlborough Cl

4

178

ROAD B64

5

Dinnington
Business Ce

B6060

6

Athorpe Road

7

8

NURSERY

Steadfolds Lane

Steadfolds Lane

Laughton Road

Village

Avenue

Avenue

Surgery

Junior School

The Crescent

West

Clarke

South

Laughton

Sawn Moor

Arbour Drive

Sawn Moor

Road

ARBOUR ROAD

Cemetery

B6060

LAUGHTON COMMON ROAD

Common Lane

Lane

Rose Lane

Brookhouse Lane

Rotherham Lane

All Saints C of E School

Church Corner

High Street

Pub

Rose

Old Hall Close

Castle Green

Laughton Junior & Infant Sch

School Road

Lane

Hangman

School View

STATION ROAD

Laughton Common

OUTGANG LANE

St Leger Avenue

BECWITH

Lumley

HATFIELD

CRESCENT

MEADOW St

Meadow

Kieran Close

Princes Street

Part Lane

Monksbridge Trading Estate

MONKSBRIDGE ROAD

Rotherham

Church Lane

Booker's Lane

Common Farm

Booker's Lane

Bookers Way

Bookers Way

Abbey Way

Houghton Road

Jerobeand's

Donstone View

Canfitt Crescent

Market

Athorpe Road

Church Lane

Limehand Road

Crescent

Lilac Crescent

Elm

Close

Midhope

Close

Common Road

Common Road

TODWICK ROAD

B6463

Anston Brook

North Anston Business Centre

Rutland

Wellington

Devonshire Terrace

Romans

Drive Way

Nursery

Crescent

Orchard Avenue

Ennerdale Way

The Oval

Sunnyside Close

Burne Farm

North Anston

Canfitt Road

Sanctuary Fields

Quarry Road

Penny Piece Place

Lane

Hall Close

Lodge Farm

F

G

H

193

J

K

odwick

A57(T)

178 **Slade Hooton**

A6
1 Broadoaks Cl
2 Broadoaks Rd

A3
1 Longthwaite Cl
2 St John's Ct

A2
1 Eastfield Crs
2 Hooton Cl
3 Orchard Cl

A **B** **159** **C** **D** **E**

1

A7
1 Burgley Cl
2 Meadowpark Cft
3 Washington Cl

2

A8
1 Manvers Cl
2 Newcastle Cl
3 Scarborough Cl

3

B4
1 Hunters Ct
2 Hunters Gdns
3 Hunters Gn

Laughton en le Morthen

St John's

Throapham

4

177 COMMON ROAD B6463   OLDCOATES ROAD

5

B5
1 Clarke Ct
2 Oldcoates Cl
3 Poynton Dr
4 Revill Ct
5 St Leger Wy

6

B6
West Garth Cl

7

B7
1 Laughton Rd
Leopold Av

8

B8
Hawkshead Crs
Langdale Wy

Dinnington

Lodge Farm

A **B** **194** **C** **D** **E**

C6
1 Clarence Sq
2 Quarry Pl

C7
1 Masefield Ct
2 Tennyson Cl
3 Wordsworth Av

grid square represents 500 metres

F G H **160** J K

I

2

3

4

Flat Lane

St Martin's C

Lime Avenue

Salt Hill

Firbeck ✚

New Road

Kid Lane

Lingodell Farm

Hill

Penny

Park Hill Farm

Park Hill Drive

Thwaite House Farm

B6463

NE

Ranmer Road

Ivy Lodge Lane

Letwell ✚

Barker

Hades

180 ▶

PO

Church Lane

5

Langold Farm

6

Gildingwells Road

Burrs Lane

Burrs Farm

7

Red Quarry Lane

Rotherham Baulk

8

Gildingwells

Home Farm

Road

F G H **195** ▼ J K

Brand's Lane

Woodsetts

wells Lane

D7
1 Sutherland Cl

D4
1 Wembley Rd

C8
1 Cedar Cl
2 Chiltern Wy
3 Hambleton Ct
4 Lowther Sq
5 Pentland Dr

Park House

A
B
161
C
D
E

Oldcotes

A634 MALTBY ROAD

Wynlea Drive

Elmsmere Drive

Weirside

BLYTH ROAD

Main Street

D8
1 Harvest Cl
2 North Wy
3 Plough Dr
4 Ramsden Crs

I

LAMB LANE B6463

Hermeston Hall

2

Goldthorpe F

3

Dyscarr Wood

Chestnut Rd

Langold

Harrison Drive Business Centre

Laburnum Road

Langold Dyscarr Junior School

Harrison Drive

Firbeck Crescent

Goldthorpe Av

School Avenue

White Avenue

Markham Road

4

179

Knott End

Riddell Avenue

PO

Cemetery

Salt Hill Road

Ramsden Street

Langold Health Centre

5

Lodge Lane

Road

Cross Street

DONCASTER ROAD

A60

Mellish

Hodsock Grange

Church Street

The Lakeside Surgery

Langold Farm

Langold Lake

Langold Country Park

Hodsock Woodhou

6

7

Costhorpe Industrial Estate

Costhorpe

Road

8

Lawn Road Industrial Estate

Lawn Road

Northumberland Avenue

Westmoor

Cumberland Road

Rotherham Balk

Lilac Close

Willow Av

Beech

Harrison Way

Oak Tree Rise

Lime Road

Dadley

Avon Drive

Pasture Close

Mulberry Crs

Knaton Road

Le Brun Square

Becket Avenue

A

B

196

Stewart Road

Kingston Road

C

Oxford Road

D

ham Health

E

Nor

ng Lane

Windsor Gardens

Carnaroon

Curthie

Craigston Road

Glamis Close

Pembroke Drive

Conway Drive

Balmoral Drive

Strathmore Road

Strathaven Drive

Kenilworth Drive

Warwick Avenue

Windsor Road

Grange Close

Greenway

F **G** **H** 162 **J** **K**

I

2

3

4

5

6

7

8

Holme Farm

Whitewater Lane

DONCASTER BY-PASS

Harworth Avenue

Whitewater Common

Whitewater Lane

A634

A634

Junction 34

Nornay Close

Meadow Lane

A634

River Ryton

Hotel

Market Club

Park Drive

Priory Close

Blyth

SHEFFIELD ROAD

The Mews

WORKSOP

Briber

BRIBER HILL

Hodsock Plantation

Hodsock Park

Hodsock Lodge Farm

Lane

Willow Holt

B6045

Hodsock Red Bridge

Elm Wood

Hodsock

Hodsock Lane

F **G** **H** 197 **J** **K**

rlton

Black Screed

Carlton

Lane

457
▲
High Neb

166

Stanage Edge

Stanedge
Lodge

Sheffield
Derbyshire County

Buck Stone

Long Causeway

The Cough

Sheepwash
Bank

Dennis
Knoll

Greens House

Gatehouse

North
Lees

Rob
Hoo

Hoo
Car

Upper
Hurst Farm

Hurstclough Lane

Nether
Hurst

Birley Lane

Brookfield
Manor

Kimber
Court
Farm

Thorpe Farm

Cunliffe House

Birley Farm

Cookers Lane

Towers Lane

Hill Lane

Car Head

Church Bank

Ranmoor Hill

Banmoor
Lane

Derwent
Lane

Higher
Bank Lane

Church
Bank

Hungry Lane

The D

Jagger's

Castleton
Road

HATHERSAGE ROAD

CASTLETON ROAD

A6187

Lane

Cliffe
Lane

Park
Edge

Hathersage

Hotel

PH

School Ln

St Michaels
C of E
School

Dale Bottom

1

Hotel

2

Crossland
Road

Hathersage
Swimming Pool

Moorland Rd

SHEFFIELD ROAD

Nether Hall

Dore Lane

BACK Nanholme La

A6187

fferton
all

Stoop

Broadhay
Farm

STATION ROAD

Hathersage Station

A6187

th
Boot

PH

Callow Farm

Went

Redmires
Reservoirs

F G H 167 J K

1

2

3

4

184

5

6

7

8

Stanedge
Pole

White
Path
Moss

Friar's Ridge

Cowper
Stone

Overstones
Farm

Toothill
Farm

Callow
Bank

Callow

Mitchell
Field

Hathersage
Moor

Burbage
Moor

Derbyshire County
Sheffield

Winyards
Nick

Parson's
House Farm

F G H J K

A625

A B **168** C D E

1

2

3

183

4

5

6

7

8

A B **198** C D E

Fulwood
Head

Harrop
Lane Foxhall
Lane

Fulwood Lane Fulwood Head Road Basset Lane Greenhouse Lane Dobbie Croft Lane Clough

Bassett

Brown
Edge
Farm

Porter
Clough

Ringinglo

Cam   Height

Lady's
Cinning's
Plantation

Ox Stones

Jumble   Road Sheephill Road

Burbage
Moor

Houndkirk Road

Dore
Moor

Houndkirk
Moor

Whitel

Parson's
House

Round
Farm

HATH....AGE ROAD

A625

I grid square represents 500 metres

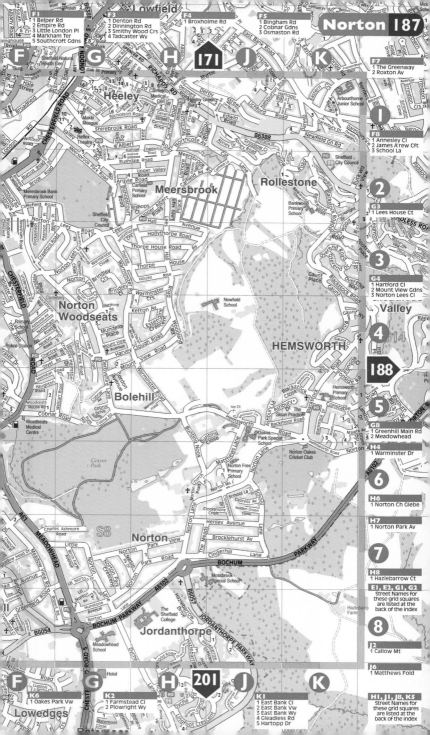

F1
1 Belper Rd
2 Empire Rd
3 Little London Pl
4 Markham Ter
5 Southcroft Gdns

F3
1 Denton Rd
2 Dinnington Rd
3 Smithy Wood Crs
4 Tadcaster Wy

F4
1 Broxholme Rd

F5
1 Bingham Rd
2 Cobnar Gdns
3 Osmaston Rd

F7
1 The Greenway
2 Roxton Av

F8
1 Annesley Cl
2 James A'rew Cft
3 School La

G3
1 Lees House Ct

G4
1 Hartford Cl
2 Mount View Gdns
3 Norton Lees Cl

G8
1 Greenhill Main Rd
2 Meadowhead

H4
1 Warminster Dr

H6
1 Norton Ch Glebe

H7
1 Norton Park Av

H8
1 Hazlebarrow Ct

E1, E2, G1, G2
Street Names for these grid squares are listed at the back of the index

J2
1 Callow Mt

J6
1 Matthews Fold

K6
1 Oakes Park Vw

K2
1 Farmstead Cl
2 Plowright Wy

K1
1 East Bank Cl
2 East Bank Vw
3 East Bank Wy
4 Gleadless Rd
5 Hartopp Dr

H1, J1, J8, K5
Street Names for these grid squares are listed at the back of the index

171

188

201

172

187

202

A5
1 Constable Cl
2 Gibbons Wy
3 Landseer Pl
4 Orpen Wy
5 Sandby Ct
6 Sandby Cft

A3
1 Spotswood Cl

N3
1 Newfield Farm Cl
2 Spotswood Dr
3 Spotswood Mt
4 Toll Bar Av

B1
1 Dagnam Pl

B3
1 Ashleigh Pl
2 Grassmoor Cl

B3
1 Gleadless Bank

C1
1 Ridgeway Rd

C2
1 Chatsw'th Pk Av
2 Chatsw'th Pk Dr
3 Chatsw'th Pk Gv
4 Durlstone Cl
5 Leadbeater Dr

C4
1 Gleadless Mt
2 Herdings Ct
3 Little Wood Rd

C5
1 Welwyn Cl

D4
1 Basegreen Pl
2 Lister Cl
3 Lister Pl

D5
1 Woodland Dr

E1
1 Carpenter Gdns

E2
1 Alnwick Dr
2 Hollinsend Pl
3 Wadsworth Rd

C3, D1, K4
Street Names for these grid squares are listed at the back of the index

E3
1 Fox Lane Ct

E4
1 Basegreen Wy

E5
1 Basegreen Rd

Intake

Hollins End

Gleadless

Gleadless Valley

HEMSWORTH

Charnock Hall

Lightwood

1 grid square represents 500 metres

Woodhouse

F2
1 Rowdale Crs
2 Wadsworth Cl

F3
1 Stanton Crs

F4
1 Hayfield Crs
2 Thornbridge Gv
3 Thornbridge Pl

173

F **G** **H** **J** **K**

Coisley
Hill

G1
1 Linley La

Normanton
Spring

G2
1 Birley Moor Cl

I

Woodhouse
Clinic

G4
1 Birley Moor Cl
2 East Glade Sq
3 Hazelbadge Crs
4 Newstead Cl
5 Newstead Gv
6 Thornbridge La

Hackenthorpe

2

H4
1 Spa View Ter
2 Weakland Wy

H5
1 Ardsley Gv
2 Darfield Cl

3

I1
1 Hollis Cft
2 Sheffield Rd

I4
1 Cotleigh Cl
2 Cotleigh Pl
3 Fairmount Gdns
4 Redbrook Cft
5 Redbrook Gv
6 Spring Water Cl
7 Wilthorpe Gdns

190

Owlthorpe

5

J5
1 Brampton Ct
2 Cranford Ct
3 Deanhead Ct
4 Kingswood Cl
5 Kingswood Cft
6 Royston Cft
7 Royston Gv

Moorhole

6

J6
1 Bishopdale Ct

Highlane

7

I7
1 Bishopdale Dr
2 Parkgate Cl
3 Parkgate Cft

Ridgeway

8

Mosborough
Medical Centre

K1
1 Birks Av
2 Cross Dr
3 Water Slacks Cl

Plumbley

F Ford **G** **H** **203** **J** **K**

K8
1 Meadow Crs

K7
1 Owlthorpe Cl

K5
1 Broadlands Cft
2 Broadlands Rl
3 Rylstone Ct

192

WORKSOP ROAD

B6067

Worksop Road

Worksop Road · A57

A

B

176

C

D

E

Aston Hall
Cricket Club

ASTON

A57

M1

1

Goose Carr Lane

Upper
Common Farm

E2
1 De Houton Cl
2 Furnival Cl
3 Horbiry End

2

Nickerwood Farm

St Paul

The Pastu

Storth Lane

Barber Balk

E5
1 Victoria Cl
2 Victoria Ct

Low
Laithes Farm

Mil

3

Manor Road

Orchard
Cft

E8
1 Hudson Cl

M1

Wales

S26

Forge
Rd

Meadows
Junior
School

Wales
High
School

Kiv
P

4

Wales Bar

Storth
Lane

Grove

Chestnut Avenue

Highfield Av

191

Manor Road

Old Quarry
Av

Maple
Grove

Highfield Av

Lane

SCHOOL ROAD

Fir Tree Drive

B6059

Myrtle
Grove

Station
Road

STATION RD

Kiveton P
Infant Sch

Green Oak Drive

Wales
Junior &
Infant School

WALES

ROAD

Thomas St

Kiveton Bridge Station

Stone

5

Cherry Tree

Church Street

Sycamore Avenue

Kiveton
Park Group
Practice

Chapel Way

Mackenzie
Way

Church
Close

Walesmoor
Longlands
Avenue

Greenside

High House Farm
Court

Stockwell
Lane

Stockwell Av

Norwood Cr

6

Cemetery

Cuckoo Way

Cuckoo Way

Rotherham Road

7

Norwood

Rotherham
Derbyshire County

Waleseber Lane

North Farm
Close

Woodside
Avenue

8

Cinder Lane

Dawber Lane

MANSFIELD

A

B

206

C

D

E

Killamarsh
Lane

Woodall Lane

Woodall Lane

Jacksy
Lane

Doctors
Surgery

orchard

Woodall

Greystones
Court

Woodall Lane

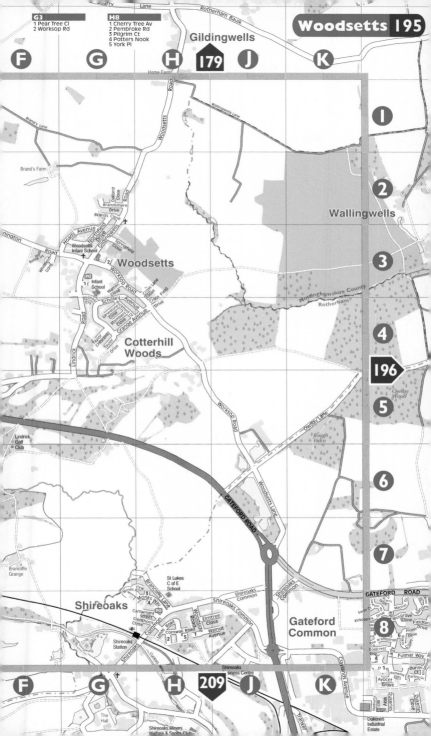

C1
1 Stewart Cl

B8
1 Farndon Gv
2 Gateford Gv
3 Swallow Gv

A8
1 Chaffinch Ms
2 Cuckoo Holt
3 Greenfinch Dl
4 Heron Gld
5 Magpie Cl
6 The Mallards

180

A **B** **C** **D** **E**

1

C7
1 Anson Cl
2 Blenheim Ri
3 Stirling Cl
4 Windermere Cl

2

D7
1 Campbell Cl
2 Doncaster Rd
3 Hemmingfield Cl
4 Hemmingfield Ri

ingwells

3

D8
1 Thievesdale Av

4

195

5

E2
1 Chapel Ga
2 Church Field Cl

6

E7
1 Hemmingfl'ld Wy
2 Mossdale
3 Ribblesdale

7

E8
1 Bishopdale
2 Close Barn
3 Forest Hill Rd
4 Littondale
5 Mercia Cl
6 Stable Cl
7 Worcester Cl

ateford
ommon

8

A **B** **210** **C** **D** **E**

Carlton in
Lindrick

South
Carlton

Gateford

I grid square represents 500 metres

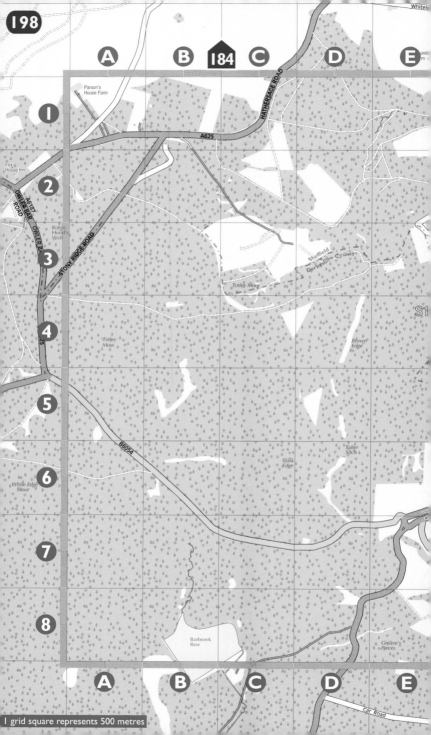

A **B** 184 **C** **D** **E**

1
2
3
4
5
6
7
8

A **B** **C** **D** **E**

HATHERSAGE ROAD

A625

Parson's House Farm

Fox House Inn

A6187 OWLER BAR ROAD

OWLER BAR

STONY RIDGE ROAD

Robin Hood's Well

Totley Moor

Totley Moss

Blown Edge

Sheffield Derbyshire County

S1

B6054

Salter Sitch

Flask Edge

White Edge Moor

Barbrook Resr

Greave's Pieces

Car Road

Whitel...

...und...
...m

1 grid square represents 500 metres

G1
1 Overdale Ri

H2
1 Totley Brook Cl
2 Totley Brook Cft
3 Totley Brook Gln
4 Totley Brook Wy

Dore

185

Doctors Surg

Dore Junior & Infant School

Abbeydale Park

Abbeydale Park Sports Club

I

H3
1 Stocks Green Dr
2 Totley Grange Cl

Totley Rise

2

I2
1 Devonshire Gv

King Egbert Secondary School

Totley Brook

King Egbert Road

Totley Brook Grove

Totley Bents

The Surgery

3

I3
1 Grove House Ct
2 Mountford Cft
3 Oakbank Ct

Marstone

Stonecroft Road

Baslow Road Surgery

BASLOW ROAD

Mickley Lane

Greenway Natural Health Centre

Totley All Saints C of E Primary School

New Totley

St George's Farm

4

A621

BASLOW ROAD

Lane Head Road

Overcroft Rise

Oldwell Cl

Totley

Stocks Green Court

200

5

J3
1 Aldam Cl
2 Aldam Wy
3 Green Oak Crs
4 Green Oak Dr
5 Laverdene Cl

A621

BASLOW ROAD

Moorwood's Hall Farm

Moorwood Lane

Owler Lea

6

K1
1 Brinkburn Cl
2 Devonshire Cl
3 Devonshire Gln
4 West View Cl
5 West View La

Fanshaw Gate

Storth House Farm

Old Hall

B6054

7

MAIN

K2
1 Glover Rd

B6054

Lidgate

Holmesfield Common

Horsleygate

8

HORSLEYGATE RD

F

G

HORSLEYGATE

H

Horsleygate

Horsleygate Lane

J

K3
1 Laverdene Wy

K

ROAD

B6051

Fox Lane

Cordwell

Millthorpe

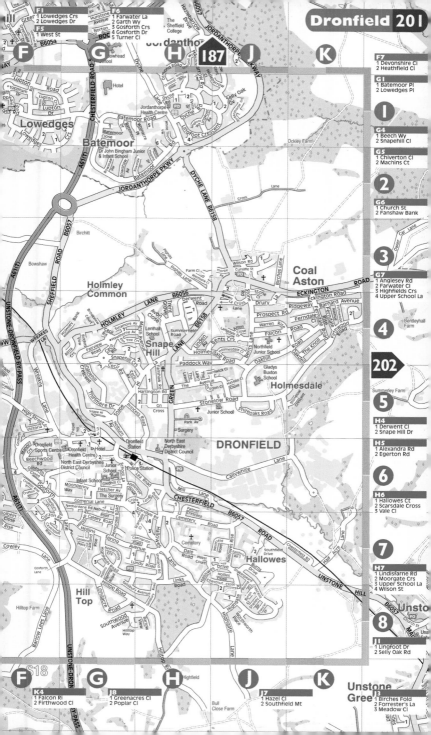

F1
1 Lowedges Crs
2 Lowedges Dr

F6
1 Farwater La
2 Garth Wy
3 Gosforth Crs
4 Gosforth Dr
5 Turner Cl

F3
1 West St

F7
1 Devonshire Cl
2 Heathfield Cl

G1
1 Batemoor Pl
2 Lowedges Pl

G4
1 Beech Wy
2 Snapehill Cl

G5
1 Chiverton Cl
2 Machins Ct

G6
1 Church St
2 Fanshaw Bank

G7
1 Anglesey Rd
2 Farwater Cl
3 Highfields Crs
4 Upper School La

H4
1 Derwent Cl
2 Snape Hill Dr

H5
1 Alexandra Rd
2 Egerton Rd

H6
1 Hallowes Ct
2 Scarsdale Cross
3 Vale Cl

H7
1 Lindisfarne Rd
2 Moorgate Crs
3 Upper School La
4 Wilson St

J1
1 Lingfoot Dr
2 Selly Oak Rd

G18

K4
1 Falcon Ri
2 Firthwood Cl

J8
1 Greenacres Cl
2 Poplar Cl

J7
1 Hazel Cl
2 Southfield Mt

J3
1 Birches Fold
2 Forrester's La
3 Meadow Cl

K4 1 Sandown Cl
K5 1 Randall St

F G H **189** J K

Plumbley

Litfield Farm

Ford

Ridgeway Moor

Birleyhay

Bramley

Bramley Moor

Marsh Lane

Middle Handley

Nether Handley

204

F G H J K

204

Plumbley

B
1 Ladybank Rd
2 Oakworth Dr
3 Oats Orch
4 Parsonage Cl
5 Ralston Ct
6 Streetfield Crs
7 William Cl

190

STATION ROAD

A4
1 Fanshaw Dr
2 Hazel Rd
3 Valley View Cl

A4
1 Greenfields

Halfway

Oxclose

1

B3
1 Camms Cl

2

D1
1 Arms Park Dr
2 Middle Ox Cl

3

D2
1 Hall Meadow Gv
2 Twickenham Gln

4

ECKINGTON

203

WEST STREET

5

6

C1
Street Names for
these grid squares
are listed at the
back of the index

7

Red Lodge
Farm

8

A White Lodge

B

C

D

E

grid square represents 500 metres

GATEFORD ROAD

Gateford
Common

F **G** **H** **195** **J** **K**

1 Tylden Wy   1 Tylden Rd

Shireoaks Common

Shireoaks
Station

Shireoaks
Business Centre

The
Hall

Shireoaks Miners'
Welfare & Sports Club

Shireoaks Road

I

Dukeries
Industrial
Estate

2

A57(T)

Shireoaks Road

Rhodesia

Spring Lane

Spring Lane

Steetley Lane

Primary
School

Cecil
Close

Holme
Carr

Lady
Lee
Farm

3

High Grounds Way

High Grounds Rd

River Ryton

4

Lodge Farm

210

5

Ladylea
Close

Meadow

Mansfield Rd

Featherbed Lane

Darfoulds

Harness
Grove

A619

6

West
Wood

MANSFIELD ROAD

A60

7

Ratcliffe
Grange

MANSFIELD ROAD

A60

8

F **G** **H** **J** **K**

rpe

New Farm

196

209

C3
1 Humber St

C4
1 Colbeck St
2 Cresswell St
3 Manvers St
4 Portland St
5 Shaw St

C5
1 Bull Yd
2 Forrest's Yd
3 Hardy St
4 Westgate Vw
5 White Hart Yd

C6
1 Chestnut Cl

D1
1 Derwent Cl

D3
1 Portland Pl

E1
1 Beechcroft
2 Coventry Dr
3 Northumbria Cl
4 Northwood
5 Primrose Wy
6 Prospect Prec
7 Ravenscourt
8 Ridgeway
9 Ringwood
10 Sunnymede
11 Wessex Cl

C2
1 Holmhurst Cl

B1
1 Clarendon Dr

A1
1 Lark Spinney

E2
1 Holmefield Cl
2 Inglemere Cl

E4
1 High Hoe Ct

E5
1 Lowtown Cl

E7
1 Martlet Wy

A   B   C   D   E

F1
1 Fingleton
2 Larwood

F2
1 Farnes Ct
2 Lindwall Ct
3 Statham Ct
4 Trueman Ct

F | G | H | 197 | J | K

F3
1 Stevenson Rd

F6
1 Woodland Av

Kilton Forest
Golf Club

Larwood Health
Centre

Kilton
Junior
School

Black
Hill
Clump

Rayton
Angle

Gravel Pit
Wood

Chesterfield Canal

Rayton Lane

Rayton
Farm

RETFORD ROAD

B6079

Coleridge Road

Rossetti
Gardens

Scott
Close
Nash
Close
Macaulay
Close
Brooke
Close

B6040

Cemetery

Forest Lane

Manton Villas

Gorselands
Avenue

South Av

South Av

Manton
Junior
School

Manton
Infant
School

Kingston Road

Kingston Close

Rufford Street

A57(T)

B6040

A57(T)

A57(T)

Workshop College

Windmill Lane

Old Coach Road

Manton
For

F | G | H | J | K

Abbeydale ... 186 B6
Abbeydale Park ... 199 J1
Abdy ... 111 G5
Adwick Le Street ... 63 J2
Adwick upon Dearne ... 87 F7
Aldwarke ... 133 K5
Almholme ... 65 K2
Apperknowle ... 202 D6
Arbourthorne ... 171 K7
Ardsley ... 57 G8
Arksey ... 65 H5
Armthorpe ... 93 G1
Arrunden ... 47 J6
Askern ... 18 D8
Aston ... 175 K8
Athersley North ... 30 A7
Athersley South ... 30 B8
Attercliffe ... 172 A1
Auckley ... 94 B8
Aughton ... 175 F5
Austerfield ... 142 D5
Balby ... 90 E8
Balne ... 10 D4
Barlborough ... 206 B7
Barnburgh ... 87 J4
Barnby Dun ... 41 F8
Barnes Hall ... 129 J3
Barnside ... 49 F7
Barnsley ... 3 D6
Barrow ... 109 G6
Barugh ... 54 D1
Barugh Green ... 54 D3
Bassett ... 184 B2
Batemoor ... 201 G2
Bawtry ... 142 C8
Beauchief ... 186 B7
Beighton ... 190 D3
Belle Green ... 31 K8
Belle Vue ... 5 F4
Bentley ... 64 E8
Bentley Rise ... 90 D1
Berry Moor ... 79 K4
Bessacarr ... 92 D8
Billingley ... 85 J1
Bircotes ... 163 J3
Birds Edge ... 50 B3
Birdwell ... 81 K7
Birley Carr ... 151 G2
Birley Edge ... 151 H1
Birleyhay ... 202 E2
Blackburn ... 131 J8
Blacker ... 29 H8
Blacker Hill ... 82 D6
Blaxton ... 121 F1
Bolehill ... 187 G5
Bolsterstone ... 127 F1
Bolton Upton Dearne ... 86 C5
Bow Broom ... 112 B3
Bradgate ... 132 C8
Bradway ... 200 C2
Braithwaite ... 40 D2
Braithwell ... 137 H5
Bramley ... 157 H1
Bramley ... 203 H4
Brampton ... 84 C8
Brampton en le Morthen ... 176 D2
Branton ... 93 J6
Brecks ... 156 E3
Brick Houses ... 185 G7
Brierholme Carr ... 43 H6
Brierley ... 32 C4
Brightholmlee ... 127 J4
Brightside ... 153 G7
Brincliffe ... 186 C1
Brodsworth ... 62 B3
Bromley ... 107 F5
Brookhouse ... 158 D8
Broom ... 7 E6
Broomhill ... 84 E5
Burghwallis ... 37 J3
Burncross ... 129 K2
Burngreave ... 114 E1
Cadeby ... 18 A7
Campsall ... 23 H8
Canal Side ... 23 H8
Canklow ... 155 G4
Cantley ... 93 G6
Carbrook ... 153 H7
Carcroft ... 37 K5
Carlecotes ... 75 F4
Carlton ... 30 E6
Carlton in Lindrick ... 196 D2
Carr ... 158 D6
Carter Knowle ... 186 D2
Cartledge ... 200 A8
Cartworth Fold ... 47 J4
Castle Green ... 78 C5
Catcliffe ... 174 B1
Cat Hill ... 52 A8
Catshaw ... 76 C4
Cawthorne ... 53 C3
Chapeltown ... 130 C1
Charltonbrook ... 129 H2
Charnock Hall ... 188 C5
Clayton ... 60 B3

Clayton West ... 26 D5
Clifton ... 7 E4
Clifton ... 137 F2
Coal Aston ... 201 K3
Coisley Hill ... 189 J1
Conanby ... 114 A5
Conisbrough ... 114 B4
Cortworth ... 110 B6
Costhorpe ... 180 C7
Cotterhill Woods ... 195 G4
Cowley ... 200 D8
Crane Moor ... 80 B7
Crookes ... 170 B3
Crookesmoor ... 8 A2
Crow Edge ... 75 K1
Cubley ... 77 K7
Cudworth ... 57 J1
Cudworth Common ... 58 A3
Cundy Cross ... 56 E6
Cundy Hos ... 106 D7
Cusworth ... 89 K2
Dalton ... 134 C6
Dalton Magna ... 134 E8
Dalton Parva ... 134 D7
Darfield ... 84 E2
Darfoulds ... 209 G6
Darnall ... 172 D3
Darton ... 28 D7
Dean Head ... 104 E2
Dearne ... 86 E2
Deepcar ... 105 J8
Denaby Main ... 113 K3
Denby Dale ... 51 J1
Dinnington ... 178 D7
Dodworth ... 54 E8
Dodworth Bottom ... 80 D1
Dodworth Green ... 80 C1
Doncaster ... 5 E3
Dore ... 185 J8
Drakehouse ... 190 B4
Dronfield ... 201 J6
Dronfield Woodhouse ... 200 B5
Dropping Well ... 131 J6
Dunford Bridge ... 74 C6
Dungworth ... 149 G7
Dunscroft ... 68 B1
Dunsville ... 67 K2
East Dene ... 7 F3
Eastfield ... 79 K6
East Herringthorpe ... 134 C8
Eastwood ... 7 D2
Ecclesall ... 186 A2
Ecclesfield ... 130 C6
Eckington ... 204 A4
Ecklands ... 76 E5
Edenthorpe ... 67 F6
Edge Mount ... 127 G8
Elscar ... 109 H2
Emmett Carr ... 205 G7
Eskholme ... 12 C7
Everton ... 165 J3
Ewden Village ... 127 F2
Far Bank ... 22 A7
Felkirk ... 31 H1
Fenwick ... 20 A2
Finkle Street ... 106 B5
Firbeck ... 179 J2
Firth Park ... 152 E4
Fir Vale ... 152 D6
Fishlake ... 22 C8
Flush House ... 46 E4
Foldrings ... 127 K6
Ford ... 203 F1
Fosterhouses ... 22 A5
Four Lane End ... 79 F5
Frecheville ... 188 E5
Fullshaw ... 76 C8
Fulwood ... 169 G7
Garden Village ... 104 C6
Gateford ... 196 B7
Gateford Common ... 195 K8
Gawber ... 55 F4
Gildingwells ... 179 H8
Gilroyd ... 81 F2
Gleadless ... 188 C3
Gleadless Valley ... 188 A4
Goldthorpe ... 86 D2
Gosforth Valley ... 200 D5
Greasbrough ... 133 F3
Great Houghton ... 59 H5
Greenhill ... 186 E8
Greenland ... 153 J8
Green Moor ... 105 H4
Greenside ... 202 D4
The Green ... 78 A6
Grenoside ... 129 J7
Greystones ... 169 K8
Grimesthorpe ... 152 E6
Grimethorpe ... 32 D8
Guilthwaite ... 175 F1
Hackenthorpe ... 189 C3
Hade Edge ... 48 A8
Haigh ... 27 K3
Halfway ... 190 C8
Hall Broom ... 148 E7

Hallowes ... 201 C
Hampole ... 36 C
Handsworth ... 173 C
Hangsman Hill ... 23 C
Harden ... 74 E
Hardwick ... 176 C
Harley ... 108 E
Harlington ... 87 C
Harthill ... 207 H
Harwell ... 165 H
Harworth ... 162 C
Hatfield ... 42 F
Hatfield Chase ... 44 E
Hatfield Woodhouse ... 69 F
Hathersage ... 182 E
Hay Field ... 119 K
Haywood ... 39 F
Hazlehead ... 75 F
Heeley ... 187 C
Hellaby ... 158 C
Hemingfield ... 83 K
Hemsworth ... 187
Hepworth ... 48
Hermit Hill ... 106 E
Herringthorpe ... 156 E
Hexthorpe ... 4 A
Hickleton ... 61 H
Higham ... 54 E
Higham Common ... 54 E
High Bradfield ... 149 F
Highfield ... 9 E
Highfields ... 63 H
High Flatts ... 50 E
Highgate ... 86 A
High Green ... 107
High Hoyland ... 27 C
Highlane ... 189 C
High Melton ... 88 C
High Moor ... 205
Hillsborough ... 150 E
Hill Side ... 77 C
Hill Top ... 52 E
Hill Top ... 114 A
Hill Top ... 149 H
Hill Top ... 153 K
Hill Top ... 201 C
Hinchcliffe Mill ... 47 C
Hodsock ... 181
Hogley Green ... 47 H
Holbrook ... 190 E
Holdworth ... 149
Hollins End ... 188 D
Hollow Meadows ... 166 E
Holmbridge ... 46 D
Holme ... 46 E
Holmesdale ... 201
Holmesfield ... 200 A
Holmfirth ... 47 H
Holmley Common ... 201 C
Hoober ... 110 C
Hood Green ... 80 C
Hood Hill ... 108 E
Hooton Levitt ... 159 F
Hooton Pagnell ... 61 H
Hooton Roberts ... 113
Howbrook ... 107 C
Hoyland ... 108 E
Hoyland Common ... 108 E
Hoylandswaine ... 78 B
Hoyle Mill ... 3 F
Hundall ... 202 C
Hyde Park ... 4
Ingbirchworth ... 51 F
Instoneville ... 18 C
Intake ... 91 K
Intake ... 188 C
Jackson Bridge ... 48 C
Jordanthorpe ... 187 H
Jordon ... 154 C
Jump ... 83 H
Kendray ... 82 C
Keresforth Hill ... 55 H
Kexbrough ... 28 E
Killamarsh ... 204 E
Kilnhurst ... 112 C
Kilton ... 211 E
Kimberworth ... 132 E
Kimberworth Park ... 132 C
Kine Moor ... 79 C
Kingstone ... 2 E
Kirk Bramwith ... 40 E
Kirk Sandall ... 66 E
Kirk Smeaton ... 16 D
Kiverton Park ... 193
Kiveton Park ... 192 E
Lane End ... 130 B
Lane Head ... 49 J
Langold ... 180 C
Langsett ... 102 C
Laughton Common ... 177
Laughton en le Morthen ... 178
Letwell ... 179 H
Lidgate ... 199 C
Lidget ... 120 E
Lightwood ... 188 E

...sterdale ... 156 E2
...ttle Houghton ... 59 G7
...ttle Smeaton ... 17 G1
...ttleworth ... 119 H6
...oad Brook ... 168 B1
...odge Moor ... 168 C6
...ongley Estate ... 152 C4
...ong Sandall ... 66 C4
...oversall ... 117 G5
...ow Barugh ... 54 E1
...ow Bradfield ... 148 D5
...owedges ... 201 F1
...ower Denby ... 51 J3
...ower Longley ... 47 K6
...ower Maythorn ... 49 J8
...owfield ... 171 G8
...ow Laithes ... 57 J8
...ow Valley ... 84 C3
...oxley ... 150 B7
...undwood ... 57 F4
...alinbridge ... 151 F8
...altby ... 159 H2
...anor Estate ... 172 B6
...anor Park ... 172 A5
...anton ... 210 E6
...applewell ... 29 H6
...arr ... 62 D8
...arsh Lane ... 203 H4
...asbrough ... 6 A3
...attersley ... 165 K8
...attersley Thorpe ... 165 F6
...awson Green ... 13 F8
...eadow Hall ... 153 J4
...eadow Head ... 186 E6
...eal Hill ... 48 E4
...easborough Dike ... 3 E5
...eersbrook ... 187 H2
...exborough ... 87 F8
...icklebring ... 136 E5
...ickley ... 200 B4
...iddlecliffe ... 85 F1
...iddle Handley ... 203 H7
...iddlewood ... 150 E3
...idhopestones ... 103 G4
...illhouse Green ... 76 D4
...illhouses ... 85 G2
...illhouses ... 186 B4
...ilton ... 109 F2
...insthorpe ... 34 E2
...isson ... 143 J5
...onk Bretton ... 3 E1
...oor End ... 80 A2
...oorends ... 24 A2
...oorgate ... 155 J5
...oorhole ... 189 J6
...oorhouse ... 35 J6
...oorthorpe ... 34 E4
...orthen ... 157 F8
...ortomley ... 107 K8
...osborough ... 190 A7
...oss ... 19 K6
...ether Edge ... 186 E1
...ether End ... 52 A2
...ether Haugh ... 110 E8
...ew Edlington ... 115 K6
...ewhill ... 111 H3
...ewington ... 142 E6
...ew Lodge ... 29 J8
...ew Rossington ... 118 C7
...ewton ... 4 A4
...ew Totley ... 199 J3
...ew Village ... 65 F5
...oblethorpe ... 53 H8
...ormanton Spring ... 189 G1
...orth Anston ... 177 J8
...orth Carlton ... 196 E1
...orth Elmsall ... 35 G1
...orton ... 17 K4
...orton ... 187 H7
...orton Woodseats ... 187 G4
...orwood ... 191 K7
...otton ... 30 A1
...utwell ... 93 J2
...dcotes ... 180 D1
...d Denaby ... 113 H4
...d Edlington ... 115 H8
...nesacre ... 128 A7
...ngreave ... 174 A6
...ughtibridge ... 128 D8
...wler Bar ... 198 E7
...wlerton ... 151 J7
...wlthorpe ... 189 K5
...wston ... 38 B4
...xclose ... 204 E1
...xspring ... 79 F7
...arkgate ... 133 J5
...ark Head ... 50 A2
...arkhead ... 185 K4
...ark Hill ... 171 K4
...ark Mill ... 26 D3
...ie Parks ... 42 A3
...arkwood Springs ... 152 A8
...arson Cross ... 152 A2
...enistone ... 77 J4
...ccadilly ... 112 A6

Pickburn ... 62 E4
Pilley ... 107 H2
Pincheon Green ... 13 H8
Pinfold Hill ... 79 J6
Pismire Hill ... 152 E3
Pitsmoor ... 152 C8
Platts Common ... 83 F7
Plumbley ... 189 K8
Pogmoor ... 55 F5
Pollington ... 11 K3
Potter Hill ... 107 G8
Rails ... 189 F1
Ranmoor ... 169 J6
Ravenfield ... 135 J4
Raw Green ... 53 F3
Rawmarsh ... 133 K3
Renishaw ... 204 E8
Rhodesia ... 209 H2
Richmond ... 173 G7
Ridgeway ... 189 G7
Ridgeway Moor ... 203 G1
Ringinglow ... 184 E3
Rollestone ... 187 J2
Rossington ... 119 F6
Rostholme ... 64 C5
Rotherham ... 7 E5
Roughbirchworth ... 78 D8
Royd ... 76 E3
Royd Moor ... 77 F2
Royston ... 30 B5
Ryecroft ... 111 K8
St Helen's ... 56 D2
Sandhill ... 59 G6
Sandtoft ... 71 J3
Sandygate ... 169 J5
Scaftworth ... 164 D3
Scawsby ... 90 A1
Scawthorpe ... 64 A7
Scholes ... 48 C4
Scholes ... 131 K3
Scout Dike ... 77 J1
Scrooby ... 164 A5
Serlby ... 163 J7
Shafton ... 31 H4
Shafton Two Gates ... 31 H5
Sharrow ... 170 D8
Shaw Lands ... 55 H6
Sheffield ... 9 F3
Sheffield Park ... 172 A6
Shirecliffe ... 152 B6
Shiregreen ... 153 G2
Shireoaks ... 195 G8
Silkstone ... 53 H7
Silkstone Common ... 79 K3
Sim Hill ... 79 K7
Skelbrooke ... 36 D2
Skellow ... 37 H5
Slade Hooton ... 158 E8
Slay Pits ... 43 F8
Smithies ... 56 A2
Smithley ... 83 H4
Snape Hill ... 84 C2
Snape Hill ... 201 H4
Snowden Hill ... 104 D1
Sothall ... 190 D6
Soughley ... 75 J5
South Anston ... 193 J3
South Bramwith ... 41 H4
South Carlton ... 196 E3
South Elmsall ... 35 G4
South Hiendley ... 31 K1
South Kirkby ... 33 K6
South Lane ... 52 E6
Spinkhill ... 205 H5
Spital Hill ... 140 D8
Spring Vale ... 78 B4
Sprotbrough ... 89 K6
Stacey Bank ... 149 J6
Staincross ... 29 G5
Stainforth ... 42 A3
Stainton ... 138 B7
Stairfoot ... 57 F8
Stannington ... 169 H1
Steel Bank ... 170 C2
Stockbridge ... 65 F5
Stocksbridge ... 105 F7
Stone ... 160 C7
Stone Hill ... 43 H8
Stopes ... 168 D1
Storrs ... 149 K8
Stubbley ... 200 D4
Styrrup ... 162 C6
Sunnyfields ... 90 B1
Sunnyside ... 135 H8
Sutton ... 38 A1
Swaithe ... 83 F2
Swallow Hill ... 29 F8
Swallownest ... 175 G8
Swinton ... 112 A5
Swinton Bridge ... 112 D3
Sykehouse ... 21 J1
Tankersley ... 107 K5
Tapton Hill ... 170 A5
Templeborough ... 154 C3
Thorne ... 23 K7

Thorn Hill ... 6 B2
Thornseat ... 147 K2
Thorpe Hesley ... 131 H2
Thorpe in Balne ... 39 K5
Thorpe Salvin ... 208 A1
Throapham ... 178 B4
Thrybergh ... 134 D4
Thurcroft ... 176 D1
Thurgoland ... 79 J7
Thuristone ... 77 G3
Thurnscoe ... 86 B1
Thurnscoe East ... 60 E7
Tickhill ... 193 J7
Tilts ... 38 E8
Tinsley ... 154 B5
Tivy Dale ... 53 G3
Todwick ... 193 F1
Toll Bar ... 64 D3
Topham ... 11 K8
Totley ... 199 G3
Totley Brook ... 199 H2
Totley Rise ... 199 K2
Totties ... 48 C3
Townhead ... 74 D5
Townhead ... 185 G8
Treeton ... 174 C3
Troway ... 202 C3
Trumfleet ... 40 B2
Turnerwood ... 194 E8
Ughill ... 148 C6
Ulley ... 175 K4
Under Bank ... 47 K4
Under Tofts ... 169 G3
Unstone ... 202 A8
Upper Cudworth ... 31 K7
Upper Cumberworth ... 50 B1
Upper Denby ... 51 F4
Upper Haugh ... 111 G8
Upper Hoyland ... 82 D8
Upper Maythorn ... 49 J7
Upper Midhope ... 102 D3
Upper Tankersley ... 107 H3
Upperthong ... 47 G1
Upperthorpe ... 205 H2
Upper Whiston ... 175 H1
Victoria ... 49 G8
Wadsley ... 150 D5
Wadsley Bridge ... 151 G3
Wadworth ... 139 F1
Walden Stubbs ... 18 B1
Waldershaigh ... 126 D1
Wales ... 192 B4
Wales Bar ... 192 A4
Walkley ... 170 C1
Wallingwells ... 195 K2
Ward Green ... 81 K2
Warmsworth ... 115 J2
Warren ... 108 C7
Washipt ... 47 K5
Waterside ... 22 E7
Waterthorpe ... 190 B5
Wath upon Dearne ... 111 K1
Wentworth ... 109 J6
West End ... 68 E2
Westfield ... 190 C8
West Green ... 57 G1
West Handley ... 202 E7
West Melton ... 111 F1
Westthorpe ... 205 H3
Wharncliffe Side ... 127 K5
Wheatley ... 5 E1
Wheatley Hills ... 92 B1
Wheatley Park ... 65 K8
Whinney Hill ... 134 C5
Whirlow ... 185 K5
Whirlow Brook ... 185 G4
Whiston ... 156 B6
Whitley ... 130 A5
Wickersley ... 157 G3
Wigthorpe ... 196 E4
Wigtwizzle ... 126 A3
Wike Well End ... 44 A2
Wilsic ... 138 E3
Wilthorpe ... 55 H3
Wincobank ... 153 H4
Windhill ... 113 H1
Wingfield ... 132 B4
Wombwell ... 83 K6
Woodall ... 206 C1
Woodhouse ... 174 A8
Woodhouse Mill ... 174 C2
Woodlands ... 23 J3
Wood Seats ... 129 J4
Woodsetts ... 195 G3
Woodside ... 96 E4
Woolley ... 29 F1
Worksop ... 210 D3
Worrall ... 150 C3
Worsbrough Bridge ... 82 B4
Worsbrough Common ... 81 K1
Worsbrough Dale ... 82 B3
Wortley ... 106 B4
Wrangbrook ... 16 A8
Wroot ... 96 D4

USING THE STREET INDEX

Street names are listed alphabetically. Each street name is followed by its postal town or area locality, the Postcode District, the page number, and the reference to the square in which the name is found.

Aaron Wilkinson Ct *HEM/SK/SE* WF9.........................**33** K5 🔟

Some entries are followed by a number in a blue box. This number indicates the location of the street within the referenced grid square. The full street name is listed at the side of the map page.

GENERAL ABBREVIATIONS

ACC.....................ACCESS	GAL.....................GALLERY	PLNS.....................PLAIN
ALY.....................ALLEY	GDN.....................GARDEN	PLZ.....................PLA
AP.....................APPROACH	GDNS.....................GARDENS	POL.....................POLICE STATIC
AR.....................ARCADE	GLD.....................GLADE	PR.....................PRINC
ASS.....................ASSOCIATION	GLN.....................GLEN	PREC.....................PRECINC
AV.....................AVENUE	GN.....................GREEN	PREP.....................PREPARATOR
BCH.....................BEACH	GND.....................GROUND	PRIM.....................PRIMAR
BLDS.....................BUILDINGS	GRA.....................GRANGE	PROM.....................PROMENAD
BND.....................BEND	GRG.....................GARAGE	PRS.....................PRINCE
BNK.....................BANK	GT.....................GREAT	PRT.....................POR
BR.....................BRIDGE	GTWY.....................GATEWAY	PT.....................POIN
BRK.....................BROOK	GV.....................GROVE	PTH.....................PAT
BTM.....................BOTTOM	HGR.....................HIGHER	PZ.....................PIAZZ
BUS.....................BUSINESS	HL.....................HILL	QD.....................QUADRAN
BVD.....................BOULEVARD	HLS.....................HILLS	QU.....................QUEE
BY.....................BYPASS	HO.....................HOUSE	QY.....................QUA
CATH.....................CATHEDRAL	HOL.....................HOLLOW	R.....................RIVE
CEM.....................CEMETERY	HOSP.....................HOSPITAL	RBT.....................ROUNDABO
CEN.....................CENTRE	HRB.....................HARBOUR	RD.....................ROA
CFT.....................CROFT	HTH.....................HEATH	RDG.....................RIDG
CH.....................CHURCH	HTS.....................HEIGHTS	REP.....................REPUBL
CHA.....................CHASE	HVN.....................HAVEN	RES.....................RESERVO
CHYD.....................CHURCHYARD	HWY.....................HIGHWAY	RFC.....................RUGBY FOOTBALL CLU
CIR.....................CIRCLE	IMP.....................IMPERIAL	RI.....................RIS
CIRC.....................CIRCUS	IN.....................INLET	RP.....................RAM
CL.....................CLOSE	IND EST.....................INDUSTRIAL ESTATE	RW.....................RO
CLFS.....................CLIFFS	INF.....................INFIRMARY	S.....................SOU
CMP.....................CAMP	INFO.....................INFORMATION	SCH.....................SCHOO
CNR.....................CORNER	INT.....................INTERCHANGE	SE.....................SOUTH EAS
CO.....................COUNTY	IS.....................ISLAND	SER.....................SERVICE ARE
COLL.....................COLLEGE	JCT.....................JUNCTION	SH.....................SHO
COM.....................COMMON	JTY.....................JETTY	SHOP.....................SHOPPIN
COMM.....................COMMISSION	KG.....................KING	SKWY.....................SKYWA
CON.....................CONVENT	KNL.....................KNOLL	SMT.....................SUMM
COT.....................COTTAGE	L.....................LAKE	SOC.....................SOCIE
COTS.....................COTTAGES	LA.....................LANE	SP.....................SPU
CP.....................CAPE	LDG.....................LODGE	SPR.....................SPRIN
CPS.....................COPSE	LGT.....................LIGHT	SQ.....................SQUAR
CR.....................CREEK	LK.....................LOCK	ST.....................STREE
CREM.....................CREMATORIUM	LKS.....................LAKES	STN.....................STATIO
CRS.....................CRESCENT	LNDG.....................LANDING	STR.....................STREA
CSWY.....................CAUSEWAY	LTL.....................LITTLE	STRD.....................STRAN
CT.....................COURT	LWR.....................LOWER	SW.....................SOUTH WES
CTRL.....................CENTRAL	MAG.....................MAGISTRATE	TDG.....................TRADIN
CTS.....................COURTS	MAN.....................MANSIONS	TER.....................TERRA
CTYD.....................COURTYARD	MD.....................MEAD	THWY.....................THROUGHW
CUTT.....................CUTTINGS	MDW.....................MEADOWS	TNL.....................TUNN
CV.....................COVE	MEM.....................MEMORIAL	TOLL.....................TOLLW
CYN.....................CANYON	MKT.....................MARKET	TPK.....................TURNPI
DEPT.....................DEPARTMENT	MKTS.....................MARKETS	TR.....................TRA
DL.....................DALE	ML.....................MALL	TRL.....................TRA
DM.....................DAM	ML.....................MILL	TWR.....................TOWE
DR.....................DRIVE	MNR.....................MANOR	U/P.....................UNDERPA
DRO.....................DROVE	MS.....................MEWS	UNI.....................UNIVERSI
DRY.....................DRIVEWAY	MSN.....................MISSION	UPR.....................UPP
DWGS.....................DWELLINGS	MT.....................MOUNT	V.....................VA
E.....................EAST	MTN.....................MOUNTAIN	VA.....................VALL
EMB.....................EMBANKMENT	MTS.....................MOUNTAINS	VIAD.....................VIADU
EMBY.....................EMBASSY	MUS.....................MUSEUM	VIL.....................VIL
ESP.....................ESPLANADE	MWY.....................MOTORWAY	VIS.....................VIS
EST.....................ESTATE	N.....................NORTH	VLG.....................VILLAG
EX.....................EXCHANGE	NE.....................NORTH EAST	VLS.....................VILL
EXPY.....................EXPRESSWAY	NW.....................NORTH WEST	VW.....................VIE
EXT.....................EXTENSION	O/P.....................OVERPASS	W.....................WE
F/O.....................FLYOVER	OFF.....................OFFICE	WD.....................WOO
FC.....................FOOTBALL CLUB	ORCH.....................ORCHARD	WHF.....................WHA
FK.....................FORK	OV.....................OVAL	WK.....................WA
FLD.....................FIELD	PAL.....................PALACE	WKS.....................WAL
FLDS.....................FIELDS	PAS.....................PASSAGE	WLS.....................WEL
FLS.....................FALLS	PAV.....................PAVILION	WY.....................WA
FLS.....................FLATS	PDE.....................PARADE	YD.....................YAR
FM.....................FARM	PH.....................PUBLIC HOUSE	YHA.....................YOUTH HOST
FT.....................FORT	PK.....................PARK	
FWY.....................FREEWAY	PKWY.....................PARKWAY	
FY.....................FERRY	PL.....................PLACE	
GA.....................GATE	PLN.....................PLAIN	

POSTCODE TOWNS AND AREA ABBREVIATIONS

BRD	Abbeydale Road
RMTH	Armthorpe
TT	Attercliffe
U/AST/KP	Aughton/Aston/Kiveton Park
WLS/ASK	Adwick le Street/Askern
SLY	Barnsley
SLYN/ROY	Barnsley north/Royston
SVR	Bolsover
TLY	Bentley
WTY	Bawtry
HPT/GREN	Chapeltown/Grenoside
ONI	Conisbrough
UD/GR	Cudworth/Grimethorpe
ARN/MH	Darnall/Meadowhall
EARNE	Wath upon Dearne/ Bolton upon Dearne
OD/DAR	Dodworth/Darton
ON	Doncaster
ONS/BSCR	Doncaster south/Bessacarr
RON	Dronfield
CC	Ecclesall
CK/KIL	Eckington/Killamarsh

EDL/UDV	Edale/Upper Derwent Valley
EPW	Epworth
FUL	Fulwood
GLE	Goole
GLSP	Glossop
GLV	Gleadless Valley
HACK//IN	Hackenthorpe/Intake
HAN/WDH	Handsworth/Woodhouse
HATH/EYAM	Hathersage/Eyam
HEM/SK/SE	Hemsworth/ SouthKirby/South Elmsall
HOLM/MEL	Holmfirth/Meltham
HOR/CROF	Horbury/Crofton
HOY	Hoyland
HTFD	Hatfield
KBTN	Kirkburton
KIMB	Kimberworth
MALT	Maltby
MEX/SWTN	Mexborough/Swinton
MOS	Mosborough
NROS/TKH	New Rossington/Tickhill
OWL	Owlerton

PONT	Pontefract
RAW	Rawmarsh
RHAM	Rotherham
RHAM/THRY	Rotherham/Thrybergh
SCSW/CWLE	Scunthorpe southwest/ Crowle
SHEF	Sheffield
SHEFN	Sheffield north
SHEFP/MNR	Sheffield Park/Manor
SHEFS	Sheffield south
ST/HB/BR	Stannington/ Hillsborough/Bradfield
STKB/PEN	Stocksbridge/Penistone
STV/CWN	Staveley/Clowne
THNE	Thorne
TOT/DORE	Totley/Dore
WHHL	Wheatley Hills
WMB/DAR	Wombwell/Darfield
WRKN	Worksop north
WRKS	Worksop south

Aar - Ald

A

aron Wilkinson Ct		
HEM/SK/SE WF9	33	K5 🔢
he Abbe's Cl AWLS/ASK DN6	37	J2
he Abbe's Wk AWLS/ASK DN6	38	A3
bbey Brook Cl SHEFS S8	186	E6 🔢
bbey Brook Dr SHEFS S8	186	E6
bbey Cl DIN S25	177	K2
bbey Ct HOLM/MEL HD7	47	K8
bbey Crs ABRD S7	186	B6
bbey Ct ABRD S7	186	B6
bbeydale Park Crs		
TOT/DORE S17	199	K1
bbeydale Park Ri		
TOT/DORE S17	185	J8
bbeydale Rd SHEFS S8	186	D4
bbeydale Rd South SHEFS S8	186	B6
TOT/DORE S17	200	A1
bbey Dr HTFD DN7	42	B7 🔢
bbeyfield Rd ATT S4	152	C8
HTFD DN7	42	A7
bbey Flds EPW DN9	121	F4
bbey Gra ABRD S7	186	B6
bbey Gv BSLYN/ROY S71	57	F3
bbey La BSLYN/ROY S71	57	F5
ECC S11	186	A4
MALT S66	159	H7
SHEFS S8	186	E6
bbey Lane Dell SHEFS S8	186	B6
bbey Pl ECK/KIL S21	205	D5
bbey Rd BWTY DN10	165	K8
HTFD DN7	42	B6
bbey Sq BSLYN/ROY S71	57	F3 🔢
bbey St WRKS S80	210	D5
bbey View Rd SHEFS S8	187	G4
bbey Wy DIN S25	177	H6
HTFD DN7	42	B6
bbot La HOR/CROF WF4	29	C1
botsford Dr MALT S66	176	E1 🔢
bots Meadow MOS S20	190	E6 🔢
bots Rd BSLYN/ROY S71	57	C4
bbott St DONS/BSCR DN4	4	B4
bdy Rd KIMB S61	132	A5
RAW S62	111	C5
berconway Crs NROS/TKH DN11	118	E7
bercorn Rd WHHL DN2	92	B3
berford Gv HOY S74	109	J1 🔢
bingdon Gdns KIMB S61	132	E4
bingdon Rd WHHL DN2	92	A2
bney Cl SHEFS S8	187	J1 🔢
bney Dr SHEFS S8	187	J1
bney Rd SHEFS S8	187	J1
bney St SHEF S1	8	C3 🔢
cacia Av CHPT/GREN S35	130	A3
MALT S66	157	H2
MALT S66	158	E2
cacia Crs BTLY DN5	64	D5 🔢
cacia Crs ECK/KIL S21	205	F2
cacia Gv CONI S4 (2)	114	E7
CUD/GR S72	31	K5
cacia Rd AWLS/ASK DN6	37	H5
DONS/BSCR DN4	92	F3
SHEFN S5	153	F3
cer Cl DIN S25	193	K4
ECK/KIL S21	205	G2
cer Cft ARMTH DN3	93	G2

Ackford Dr WRKS S80	210	B4
Ackworth Dr DARN/MH S9	154	C6 🔢
Acomb Common Rd HTFD DN7	43	G7
Acorn Cft KIMB S61	132	E5
Acorn Dr ST/HB/BR S6	169	F1
Acorn Gv HOLM/MEL HD7	48	C4
Acorn Hl ST/HB/BR S6	150	C8
Acorn St OWL S3	8	C1
MALT S66	137	F8
Acre Cl ST/HB/BR S6	169	F1
Acre Ga CHPT/GREN S35	107	J8
Acre La CHPT/GREN S35	127	K7
HOLM/MEL HD7	47	G5
HOLM/MEL HD7	49	G1
STKB/PEN S36	78	A1
Acre Rd CUD/GR S72	57	K3
Acres Hill La DARN/MH S9	172	D4
Acres Hill Rd DARN/MH S9	172	D3
Acres La EPW DN9	96	D2
HOLM/MEL HD7	46	C3
Acton Cl AU/AST/KP S26	175	H6
Adam La DOD/DAR S75	53	K5
Adastral Av HACK//IN S12	188	C5
Addison Rd MALT S66	158	E2
MEX/SWTN S64	113	G2
Addison Sq DIN S25	178	B6
Addy Cl ST/HB/BR S6	8	B1
Addy Crs HEM/SK/SE WF9	34	E4
Addy St ST/HB/BR S6	8	A1
Adelaide Dr AWLS/ASK DN6	18	A4
ECC S11	186	D1
Adelaide St MALT S66	159	J4 🔢
Adelphi St ST/HB/BR S6	8	B1
Adkin Royd DOD/DAR S75	53	J7
Adkins Dr SHEFN S5	151	K4
Adkins Rd SHEFN S5	151	K4
Adlard Rd WHHL DN2	92	A1 🔢
Adlington Crs SHEFN S5	152	A3
Adlington Rd SHEFN S5	152	A3
Admirals Crest KIMB S61	131	J5
Adrian Crs SHEFN S5	152	A3
Adsetts St ATT S4	153	F6
Adwick Av MEX/SWTN S64	113	G3 🔢
Adwick La AWLS/ASK DN6	64	B1
Adwick Pk DEARNE S63	112	C1
Adwick Rd MEX/SWTN S64	86	E8
MEX/SWTN S64	113	G3 🔢
Agden Br ST/HB/BR S6	125	K7
Agden Rd SHEFN S5	152	A3
Agden Side Rd ST/HB/BR S6	126	A6
Agnes Rd BSLY S70	2	B5
DOD/DAR S75	28	C7
Ainsdale Av DEARNE S63	86	D6
Ainsdale Cl BSLYN/ROY S71	56	C2
Ainsdale Rd BSLYN/ROY S71	30	C2
Ainsley Cl EPW DN9	94	A8
Ainsley Rd FUL S10	170	C3 🔢
Ainsty Rd ABRD S7	171	F8 🔢
Aintree Av DONS/BSCR DN4	92	C5
ECK/KIL S21	203	K4
Aintree Cl BTLY DN5	90	A2
Aintree Dr MEX/SWTN S64	113	G1
Aire Cl CHPT/GREN S35	130	A1
Airedale WRKN S80	196	E8
Airedale Av NROS/TKH DN11	139	K7
Airedale Rd DOD/DAR S75	28	B7
ST/HB/BR S6	151	F5
Aireton Cl MALT S66	157	F2
Aireton Rd BSLY S70	2	B3 🔢
Airey La AWLS/ASK DN6	39	J5

Air Mount Cl MALT S66	157	F3
Airstone Rd AWLS/ASK DN6	18	C8
Aisby Dr NROS/TKH DN11	119	F5
Aisthorpe Rd SHEFS S8	187	F4
Aitken Rd MEX/SWTN S64	112	C7
Aizlewood Rd SHEFS S8	171	F8 🔢
Akley Bank Cl TOT/DORE S17	199	K2
Alan Rd DOD/DAR S75	28	C7
Alba Cl WMB/DAR S73	84	B1
Albanus Rdg ST/HB/BR S6	169	F1
Albany Av CHPT/GREN S35	130	C3
Albany Cl WMB/DAR S73	83	H1
Albany Crs HEM/SK/SE WF9	34	E5
Albany La NROS/TKH DN11	118	D6
Albany Rd ABRD S7	171	F8
DONS/BSCR DN4	4	A6
MEX/SWTN S64	112	C6
STKB/PEN S36	104	E6
Albany St HEM/SK/SE WF9	34	E5
RHAM/THRY S65	7	D4
Albert Rd DEARNE S63	85	G8
DEARNE S63	86	D2 🔢
HACK//IN S12	189	K4
KBTN HD8	26	B4
MEX/SWTN S64	113	F2
RAW S62	133	J3
SHEFS S8	187	G1
Albert St BSLY S70	2	C4
CUD/GR S72	31	K7 🔢
DEARNE S63	60	B7
ECK/KIL S21	204	B5
MALT S66	159	J3
MEX/SWTN S64	112	C3
RHAM S60	6	B4 🔢
RHAM S60	6	B4 🔢
THNE DN8	23	K7
WRKS S80	210	D4
Albert Terrace Rd ST/HB/BR S6	8	B1
Albion Cl WRKS S80	210	D4
Albion Dr DEARNE S63	60	D2 🔢
Albion Pl HEM/SK/SE WF9	35	F4
Albion Rd BSLYN/ROY S71	30	D8
RHAM/THRY S65	7	D4
Albion St ST/HB/BR S6	8	B2
Albion Ter DONS/BSCR DN4	4	B5
Alcester Rd ABRD S7	171	F8 🔢
Aldam Cl RHAM/THRY S65	134	C8
TOT/DORE S17	199	J3 🔢
Aldam Cft TOT/DORE S17	199	J3
Aldam Rd DONS/BSCR DN4	116	B1
TOT/DORE S17	199	J3
Aldam Wy TOT/DORE S17	199	J3 🔢
Aldbury Cl BSLYN/ROY S71	56	C1
Aldcliffe Crs DONS/BSCR DN4	116	C3
Aldene Av ST/HB/BR S6	150	E6
Aldene Gld ST/HB/BR S6	150	E6
Aldene Rd ST/HB/BR S6	150	E5
Alder Cl DOD/DAR S75	29	F6
WRKS S80	210	C6
Alder Gv DONS/BSCR DN4	90	D8
THNE DN8	23	K4
WMB/DAR S73	84	C3
Alder Holt Cl ARMTH DN3	93	H2
Alder La DARN/MH S9	173	G4
Alder Ms HOY S74	109	F2 🔢
Alderney Rd SHEFP/MNR S2	171	G8 🔢
Aldervale Ct NROS/TKH DN11	119	F7
Alderson Av RAW S62	133	J1
Alderson Cl NROS/TKH DN11	140	A7
Alderson Dr BSLYN/ROY S71	56	B1
NROS/TKH DN11	140	A7
WHHL DN2	5	F3
Alderson Pl SHEFP/MNR S2	9	D6
Alderson Rd SHEFP/MNR S2	8	C6

WRKS S80 .... 210 C6
Alderson Rd North
SHEFF/MNR S2 .... 9 D6
Aldervale Cl MEX/SWTN S64 .... 112 C7
Aldesworth Rd DONS/BSCR DN4 .... 92 D6
Aldfield Wy SHEFN S5 .... 152 C6
Aldham Crs WMB/DAR S73 .... 83 H1
Aldham House La WMB/DAR S73 .... 83 J4
Aldred Cl ECK/KIL S21 .... 191 J7
MALT S66 .... 157 F2
Aldred Ct RHAM/THRY S65 .... 7 D5
Aldred Rd FUL S10 .... 170 C2
Aldred St RHAM/THRY S65 .... 7 D5
Aldred St East WRKS S80 .... 210 E5
Aldrens Cl CONI DN12 .... 136 E5
Aldrin Wy MALT S66 .... 159 F1
Aldwarke La RHAM/THRY S65.. .... 133 K5
Aldwarke Rd RAW S62 .... 133 J4
Alexander Dr WRKN S81 .... 196 B7
Alexander St BTLY DN5 .... 64 E6
Alexandra Cl KIMB S61 .... 132 B7
Alexandra Rd AU/AST/KP S26 .... 175 G7
AWLS/ASK DN6 .... 64 A1
BTLY DN5 .... 64 E6
DONS/BSCR DN4 ....
DRON S18 .... 201 H5
MEX/SWTN S64 .... 113 G2
NROS/TKH DN11 .... 163 G3
SHEFP/MNR S2 .... 171 G8
THNE DN8 .... 24 A3
Alexandra St MALT S66 .... 159 H3
THNE DN8 .... 23 J6
Alexandra Ter BSLYN/ROY S71 .... 57 G7
Alford Av CHPT/GREN S35 .... 128 C3
Alfred Rd AWLS/ASK DN6 .... 18 B8
DARN/MH S9 .... 153 G8
Alfred St BSLYN/ROY S71 .... 51 F5
Algar Cl SHEFP/MNR S2 .... 172 A8
Algar Crs SHEFP/MNR S2 .... 172 A8
Algar Dr SHEFP/MNR S2 .... 172 A8
Algar Pl SHEFP/MNR S2 .... 172 A8
Algar Rd SHEFP/MNR S2 .... 172 A8
Alice Rd KIMB S61 .... 6 A3
Alison Cl AU/AST/KP S26 .... 175 H8
Alison Crs SHEFP/MNR S2 .... 172 D6
Alison Dr AU/AST/KP S26 .... 175 H8
Allan St RHAM/THRY S65 .... 7 D1
Allas Dike La STKB/PEN S36 .... 126 B3
Allas La STKB/PEN S36 .... 126 B3
Allatt Cl BSLY S70 .... 2 C5
Alldred Crs MEX/SWTN S64 .... 112 B6
Allenby Cl SHEFS S8 .... 186 E8
Allenby Crs NROS/TKH DN11 .... 118 D7
Allenby Dr SHEFS S8 .... 186 E8
Allendale BSLY S70 .... 82 D2
Allendale Gdns BTLY DN5 .... 90 C4
Allendale Rd BTLY DN5 .... 90 C4
DOD/DAR S75 .... 2 B1
DOD/DAR S75 .... 28 C7
HOY S74 .... 108 E2
RHAM/THRY S65 .... 156 B3
Allende Wy DARN/MH S9 .... 172 D1
Allen Rd MOS S20 .... 190 D5
Allen St OWL S3 .... 8 C2
WRKS S80 .... 210 C4
Allergill Pk HOLM/MEL HD7 .... 47 G2
Allerton St DON DN1 .... 5 D2
Allestree Dr DRON S18 .... 200 C6
All Hallowes Dr NROS/TKH DN11 .... 139 J8
All Hallows Dr MALT S66 .... 159 F3
Alliance St ATT S4 .... 171 K1
Allott Cl HEM/SK/SE WF9 .... 34 E4
RHAM/THRY S65 .... 135 J7
Allott Crs HOY S74 .... 83 H8
Allott St HOY S74 .... 108 C2
All Saints Cl DOD/DAR S75 .... 53 K7
All Saints Wy AU/AST/KP S26 .... 175 J3
Allsopp Dr WRKN S81 .... 210 D1
Allt St RAW S62 .... 133 J3
Alma Cl DRON S18 .... 201 G4
Alma Rd CHPT/GREN S35 .... 107 J8
RHAM S60 .... 6 C5
Alma Rw RHAM S60 .... 156 B6
Alma St BSLY S70 .... 2 A4
OWL S3 .... 9 D1
WMB/DAR S73 .... 84 A5
Almholme La BTLY DN5 .... 65 J2
Almond Av ARMTH DN3 .... 67 G8
CUD/GR S72 .... 31 J8
Almond Cl EPW DN9 .... 120 D3
HEM/SK/SE WF9 .... 35 F2
MALT S66 .... 158 E2
Almond Dr ECK/KIL S21 .... 205 G2
Almond Gld MALT S66 .... 157 H4
Almond Gv WRKS S80 .... 210 C7
Almond Rd DONS/BSCR DN4 .... 92 E7
Almond Tree Rd AU/AST/KP S26 .... 191 K5
Almshils Crs ECC S11 .... 185 K4
Almshill Dr ECC S11 .... 185 K4
Almshill Gld ECC S11 .... 185 K4
Alms Hill Rd ECC S11 .... 185 K4
Alney Pl ST/HB/BR S6 .... 151 J3
Alnwick Dr HACK/IN S12 .... 188 E2
Alnwick Rd HACK/IN S12 .... 188 D2
Alperton Cl BSLYN/ROY S71 .... 57 G2
Alpha Rd RHAM/THRY S65 .... 134 A8
Alpine Cl STKB/PEN S36 .... 104 D6
Alpine Ct WRKS S80 .... 209 K5

Alpine Rd ST/HB/BR S6 .... 8 A1
SHEFP/PEN S36 .... 104 D6
Alport Av HACK/IN S12 .... 189 G3
Alport Dr HACK/IN S12 .... 189 G2
Alport Gv HACK/IN S12 .... 189 G3
Alport Pl HACK/IN S12 .... 189 G3
Alport Ri DRON S18 .... 200 D5
Alport Rd HACK/IN S12 .... 189 G2
Alric Dr BSLYN/ROY S71 .... 57 F6
RHAM S60 .... 154 E6
Alsing Rd DARN/MH S9 .... 153 K4
Alston Cl DOD/DAR S75 .... 53 J7
DONS/BSCR DN4 .... 92 C8
Alston Rd DONS/BSCR DN4 .... 118 C1
Alton Cl DRON S18 .... 200 D7
ECC S11 .... 186 A5
Alton Wy DOD/DAR S75 .... 29 F6
Alverley La DONS/BSCR DN4 .... 116 D3
Alwyn Av BTLY DN5 .... 64 B8
Alwyn Rd THNE DN8 .... 23 K8
Amalfi Ct WMB/DAR S73 .... 84 C2
Amanda Av WRKN S81 .... 196 D1
Amanda Dr HTFD DN7 .... 42 C8
Amanda Rd NROS/TKH DN11 .... 162 E5
Ambassador Gdns ARMTH DN3 .... 93 H2
Amberley Ri AWLS/ASK DN6 .... 37 G5
Amberley St DARN/MH S9 .... 153 H7
Ambler Ri AU/AST/KP S26 .... 175 G6
Ambleside Cl MOS S20 .... 204 C1
RHAM S60 .... 154 D6
Ambleside Crs BTLY DN5 .... 89 H6
Ambleside Gra WRKN S81 .... 196 D7
Ambleside Gv BSLYN/ROY S71 .... 57 H7
Ambleside Wk DIN S25 .... 194 A1
Ambrose Av HTFD DN7 .... 42 D7
Amen Cnr RHAM S60 .... 6 C3
America La DEARNE S63 .... 111 F4
Amersall Cr BTLY DN5 .... 64 B7
Amersall Rd BTLY DN5 .... 64 B7
Amory's Holt Cl MALT S66 .... 137 F8
Amory's Holt Dr MALT S66 .... 137 F8
Amory's Holt Rd MALT S66 .... 137 F8
Amory's Holt Wy MALT S66 .... 158 E1
Amos Rd DARN/MH S9 .... 153 J5
Amwell Gn HTFD DN7 .... 68 B1
Amy Rd BTLY DN5 .... 65 F4
Anchorage Crs BTLY DN5 .... 4 A2
Anchorage La BTLY DN5 .... 90 C3
Ancient La HTFD DN7 .... 69 F2
Ancona Ri WMB/DAR S73 .... 84 C2
Ancote Cl DOD/DAR S75 .... 55 F6
Andover Dr OWL S3 .... 171 G1
Andover St OWL S3 .... 171 G1
Andrew La OWL S3 .... 9 E1
Andrews Rd KIMB S61 .... 132 D7
Andrew St OWL S3 .... 9 E1
Andwell La FUL S10 .... 184 C2
Anelay Rd DONS/BSCR DN4 .... 90 C8
Anfield Rd DONS/BSCR DN4 .... 92 D8
Angel La RAW S62 .... 110 C6
Angel St DEARNE S63 .... 86 C6
SHEF S1 .... 9 E2
Angerford Av SHEFS S8 .... 187 G3
Anglesey Rd DRON S18 .... 201 G7
Angleton Av SHEFP/MNR S2 .... 172 C7
Angleton Cl SHEFP/MNR S2 .... 172 E7
Angleton Gdns SHEFP/MNR S2 .... 172 E7
Angleton Gn SHEFP/MNR S2 .... 172 E7
Angleton Ms SHEFP/MNR S2 .... 172 C7
Angram Rd CHPT/GREN S35 .... 107 J3
Annan Rd DOD/DAR S75 .... 54 D2
Anna Rd AWLS/ASK DN6 .... 18 C8
Annat Pl CHPT/GREN S35 .... 107 H8
Annat Royd La STKB/PEN S36 .... 50 D8
Anne Crs CUD/GR S72 .... 32 A2
Annesley Cl SHEFS S8 .... 187 F8
Annesley Rd SHEFS S8 .... 187 F7
Anne St DIN S25 .... 178 B4
Annet La ST/HB/BR S6 .... 148 C3
Anns Rd SHEFP/MNR S2 .... 171 G8
Anns Rd North SHEFP/MNR S2 .... 171 H8
Ansell Rd ECC S11 .... 186 A1
Anson Gv RHAM S60 .... 155 G7
Anson St SHEFP/MNR S2 .... 9 F3
Anston Av AU/AST/KP S26 .... 192 E4
WRKN S81 .... 210 C2
Anston Crs DONS/BSCR DN4 .... 92 D6
Anston Cl DIN S25 .... 193 K1
Anston Dr HEM/SK/SE WF9 .... 35 K2
Antrim Av FUL S10 .... 8 A4
Anvil Cl ST/HB/BR S6 .... 169 J1
Anvil Crs CHPT/GREN S35 .... 130 C7
Apley Rd DON DN1 .... 5 D4
Apollo St RAW S62 .... 112 A8
Apostle Cl DONS/BSCR DN4 .... 116 B1
Appgirdle Cl DOD/DAR S75 .... 28 E6
Appleby Cl WRKN S81 .... 196 D7
Appleby Pl AWLS/ASK DN6 .... 37 G5
Appleby Rd WHHL DN2 .... 92 B3
Appleby Wk DIN S25 .... 178 B8
Applegarth Cl HAN/WDH S13 .... 188 D1
Applegarth Dr HACK/IN S12 .... 188 C1
Apple Gv EPW DN9 .... 120 B3
Applehaigh Gv BSLYN/ROY S71 .... 30 A3
Applehaigh La HOR/CROF WF4 .... 30 B1
Applehaigh Vw BSLYN/ROY S71 .... 30 B3

Applehurst Bank BSLY S70 .... 3 E5
Applehurst La BTLY DN5 .... 39 K6
Appleton Wy BSLY S70 .... 82 B2
BTLY DN5 .... 64 C1
Appletree Dr DRON S18 .... 201 C6
Applewood Cl WRKN S81 .... 196 B2
April Cl BSLYN/ROY S71 .... 3 F7
April Dr BSLYN/ROY S71 .... 56 E3
Apy Hill La NROS/TKH DN11 .... 139 F7
Aqueduct St BSLYN/ROY S71 .... 2 C2
Arbour Crs MALT S66 .... 177 F7
Arbour Dr MALT S66 .... 177 F7
Arbour La CONI DN12 .... 135 K3
RHAM/THRY S65 .... 135 K3
Arbourthorne Rd SHEFP/MNR S2 .... 188 A1
Archdale Cl SHEFP/MNR S2 .... 172 D7
Archdale Pl SHEFP/MNR S2 .... 172 C7
Archdale Rd SHEFP/MNR S2 .... 172 C6
Archer Ga ST/HB/BR S6 .... 150 C6
Archer La ABRD S7 .... 186 D2
Archer Rd SHEFS S8 .... 186 D4
Archery Cl MALT S66 .... 157 G4
Archibald Rd ABRD S7 .... 186 E1
Arcon Pl RAW S62 .... 133 K3
Arcubus Av AU/AST/KP S26 .... 175 H7
Ardeen Rd WHHL DN2 .... 91 K3
Arden Ga DONS/BSCR DN4 .... 116 C3
Ardmore St DARN/MH S9 .... 172 C2
Ardsley Av AU/AST/KP S26 .... 191 J8
Ardsley Cl MOS S20 .... 189 H5
Ardsley Dr MOS S20 .... 189 H5
Ardsley Gv MOS S20 .... 189 H5
Ardsley Rd BSLY S70 .... 82 D2
Argosy Cl BWTY DN10 .... 142 A7
Argyle La NROS/TKH DN11 .... 118 D6
Argyle Rd SHEFS S8 .... 187 G2
Argyle St MEX/SWTN S64 .... 113 F2
Argyll Av WHHL DN2 .... 92 A3
Arklow Rd WHHL DN2 .... 91 K3
Arksey Common La BTLY DN5 .... 65 H5
Arksey La BTLY DN5 .... 64 E6
Arkwright Rd BTLY DN5 .... 90 C2
Arley St SHEFP/MNR S2 .... 9 D5
Arlington Av AU/AST/KP S26 .... 175 K7
Arlott Wy CONI DN12 .... 115 K6
Armer St RHAM S60 .... 6 B4
Armitage Rd DONS/BSCR DN4 .... 90 C8
STKB/PEN S36 .... 105 G7
Armley Rd DARN/MH S9 .... 153 H7
Armroyd La HOY S74 .... 109 G3
Arms Park Dr MOS S20 .... 204 D1
Armstead Rd MOS S20 .... 190 D4
Armstrong Wk MALT S66 .... 159 F1
Armthorpe La ARMTH DN3 .... 67 F2
WHHL DN2 .... 91 K2
Armthorpe Rd ECC S11 .... 169 K7
WHHL DN2 .... 91 K2
Armyne Gv BSLYN/ROY S71 .... 57 F6
Arncliffe Dr BSLY S70 .... 55 G6
CHPT/GREN S35 .... 130 A2
Arndale Gv HOLM/MEL HD7 .... 48 A3
Arnold Av BSLYN/ROY S71 .... 30 A7
HACK/IN S12 .... 188 D6
Arnold Crs MEX/SWTN S64 .... 113 F1
Arnold Rd RHAM/THRY S65 .... 156 A1
Arnold St ST/HB/BR S6 .... 170 C1
Arnside Rd MALT S66 .... 159 H1
SHEFS S8 .... 186 E2
Arran Hl RHAM/THRY S65 .... 134 E4
Arran Rd FUL S10 .... 170 B4
Arras St DARN/MH S9 .... 172 B2
Arren Cl ARMTH DN3 .... 40 E7
Arrunden La HOLM/MEL HD7 .... 47 J6
Arthington La SHEFS S8 .... 187 G1
Arthur Av BTLY DN5 .... 64 E5
Arthur Pl BTLY DN5 .... 64 E5
Arthur Rd STKB/PEN S36 .... 104 D6
Arthur St BSLY S70 .... 82 B2
BTLY DN5 .... 64 E4
RAW S62 .... 111 K8
Artisan Vw SHEFS S8 .... 187 G1
Arundel Av RHAM S60 .... 174 C3
RHAM/THRY S65 .... 134 C6
Arundel Cl DRON S18 .... 200 D6
Arundel Cottages RHAM S60 .... 174 C3
Arundel Crs RHAM S60 .... 174 B3
Arundel Dr WRKN S81 .... 196 D1
Arundel Gdns BTLY DN5 .... 64 C7
Arundel Ga SHEF S1 .... 9 D3
Arundel La SHEF S1 .... 9 E4
Arundel Rd BSLYN/ROY S71 .... 57 C3
AWLS/ASK DN6 .... 18 A4
CHPT/GREN S35 .... 107 J8
RHAM S60 .... 174 C3
RHAM/THRY S65 .... 7 E5
Arundel St RHAM S60 .... 174 B3
SHEF S1 .... 9 D4
Arundel Vw HOY S74 .... 83 H8
Ascension Cl MALT S66 .... 159 H3
Ascot Av DONS/BSCR DN4 .... 92 C6
Ascot Cl MEX/SWTN S64 .... 113 C1
Ascot Dr BTLY DN5 .... 90 A1
Ascot St SHEFP/MNR S2 .... 9 D5
Ashberry Cl DEARNE S63 .... 60 C7
Ashberry Rd ST/HB/BR S6 .... 8 A1
Ashbourne Gv CHPT/GREN S35 .... 150 D1
HAN/WDH S13 .... 173 H6
Ashbourne Rd BSLYN/ROY S71 .... 30 B8
HAN/WDH S13 .... 173 H6

Ashburnham Cl AWLS/ASK DN6 ...... 18 B4
Ashburnham Gdns BTLY DN5 .... 90 B4
Ashburnham Rd THNE DN8 .... 23 H8
Ashburton Cl AWLS/ASK DN6 .... 63 H1
Ashbury Dr SHEFS S8 .... 187 J5
Ashbury La SHEFS S8 .... 187 J5
Ashby Cl BSLY S70 .... 2 A5
Ash Cl ECK/KIL S21 .... 205 G2
RHAM/THRY S65 .... 156 C3
WRKS S80 .... 210 C6
Ash Ct DIN DN5 .... 90 A6
MALT S66 .... 158 E1
Ash Crs ECK/KIL S21 .... 203 K6
MEX/SWTN S64 .... 112 D1
Ashdale Cl ARMTH DN3 .... 66 E6
Ash Dale Rd CONI DN12 .... 115 J5
Ashdell ECC S11 .... 170 C5 🔲
Ashdell La ECC S11 .... 170 C5 🔲
Ashdell Rd ECC S11 .... 170 C5
Ashdene Ct MEX/SWTN S64 .... 112 C7
Ashdown Pl BTLY DN5 .... 64 B7
Ash Dyke Cl DOD/DAR S75 .... 28 C8
Asher Rd ABRD S7 .... 8 C6 🔲
Ashes La RAW S62 .... 109 G7
Ashes Park Av WRKN S81 .... 196 E6
Ashfield Av THNE DN8 .... 43 H1
Ashfield Cl DOD/DAR S75 .... 55 H4
HACK/IN S12 .... 188 B3
Ashfield Dr HACK/IN S12 .... 188 B3
Ashfield Gv HTFD DN7 .... 42 A3
Ashfield Rd DONS/BSCR DN4 .... 33 G2
HEM/SK/SE WF9 .... 33 G2
HTFD DN7 .... 42 A8
STKB/PEN S36 .... 105 G6 🔲
THNE DN8 .... 43 F2
Ash Fields Rd ARMTH DN3 .... 40 B7
BTLY DN5 .... 39 K7
Ashford Rd DRON S18 .... 200 D7
ECC S11 .... 8 A6 🔲
Ashfurlong Cl TOT/DORE S17 .... 185 K8
Ashfurlong Dr TOT/DORE S17 .... 185 K8
Ashfurlong Pk TOT/DORE S17 .... 185 K8
Ashfurlong Rd TOT/DORE S17 .... 185 J8
Ashgate Cl ECC S11 .... 170 C5
Ashgate La FUL S10 .... 170 C5 🔲
Ashgate Rd ECC S11 .... 170 C5
Ash Gv ARMTH DN3 .... 69 H8
AU/AST/KP S26 .... 192 C4
BSLY S70 .... 56 E8
CONI DN12 .... 114 B6
EPW DN9 .... 120 B4
FUL S10 .... 8 A4
HEM/SK/SE WF9 .... 35 F3
MALT S66 .... 157 H2
MALT S66 .... 159 J1
RAW S62 .... 133 K2
Ash Grove Rd HOLM/MEL HD7 .... 47 H2
Ash Hill Cl HTFD DN7 .... 42 C8
Ash Hill Rd GLE DN14 .... 21 F2
HTFD DN7 .... 42 C8
Ash Holt Dr WRKN S81 .... 196 D7
Ash House La TOT/DORE S17 .... 185 H6
Ashland Rd ABRD S7 .... 186 E2
ECK/KIL S21 .... 204 C4
Ash La DRON S18 .... 202 B4
ECK/KIL S21 .... 202 E1
KBTN HD8 .... 26 E1
STKB/PEN S36 .... 105 H6
Ashleigh CUD/GR S72 .... 32 D4
Ashleigh Av HACK/IN S12 .... 188 B2
Ashleigh Ct ECK/KIL S21 .... 204 A6
Ashleigh Cft HACK/IN S12 .... 188 B2
Ashleigh Dr HACK/IN S12 .... 188 B2
Ashleigh Pl HACK/IN S12 .... 188 B2 🔲
Ashleigh Rd STV/CWN S43 .... 206 A3
Ashley Cl ECK/KIL S21 .... 205 H1 🔲
Ashley Ct EPW DN9 .... 121 F4
HEM/SK/SE WF9 .... 33 J6
WRKN S81 .... 210 C1
Ashley Gdns BSLYN/ROY S71 .... 30 C3
Ashley Gv AU/AST/KP S26 .... 175 H8
Ashley La ECK/KIL S21 .... 205 H1
Ashley Rd WRKN S81 .... 210 C1
Ashmore Av ECK/KIL S21 .... 203 K5
Ashover Cl BSLY S70 .... 82 E3 🔲
Ashpool Cl HAN/WDH S13 .... 189 J1
Ash Rdg MEX/SWTN S64 .... 112 C5 🔲
Ash Rd AWLS/ASK DN6 .... 37 J5
CUD/GR S72 .... 32 A5
DEARNE S63 .... 111 J2
Ash St MOS S20 .... 190 A8
Ash Ter ECK/KIL S21 .... 170 E1
WMB/DAR S73 .... 83 H1
Ashton Av BTLY DN5 .... 64 A6
Ashton Cl ECK/KIL S21 .... 205 G1
Ashton Dr ARMTH DN3 .... 66 D3
Ashton La MALT S66 .... 137 G6
Ash Tree Av BWTY DN10 .... 142 A8
Ash Tree Rd THNE DN8 .... 43 J1
Ashurst Cl ST/HB/BR S6 .... 150 D8
Ashurst Dr ST/HB/BR S6 .... 150 D8
Ashurst Pl ST/HB/BR S6 .... 150 D8
Ashurst Rd ST/HB/BR S6 .... 150 D8
Ash Vw CHPT/GREN S35 .... 130 A3
KIMB S61 .... 132 E4
Ashville NROS/TKH DN11 .... 119 F7
Ashwell Cl CUD/GR S72 .... 31 K4

Ashwell Rd HAN/WDH S13 .... 189 J1
Ashwood Cl ARMTH DN3 .... 93 H8
BSLY S70 .... 82 C3 🔲
CHPT/GREN S35 .... 107 H7
Ashwood Gv CUD/GR S72 .... 59 G4
Ashwood Rd CHPT/GREN S35 .... 107 H7
RAW S62 .... 133 J5
WRKS S80 .... 210 C6
Ashworth Dr KIMB S61 .... 132 A5
Askam Ct MALT S66 .... 157 J1
Askam Rd MALT S66 .... 157 J1
Askern Grange La AWLS/ASK DN6 ... 19 F7
Askern Rd AWLS/ASK DN6 .... 38 B6
BTLY DN5 .... 64 D3
Askew Ct STKB/PEN S36 .... 105 F7
Askrigg Cl DONS/BSCR DN4 .... 92 E8 🔲
Asline Rd SHEFP/MNR S2 .... 9 D6
Aspen Cl ARMTH DN3 .... 66 E6 🔲
ECK/KIL S21 .... 205 G1
Aspen Gv WMB/DAR S73 .... 84 D3
Aspen Rd ECK/KIL S21 .... 203 K6
Aspen Wy MEX/SWTN S64 .... 112 B7
Asquith Rd DARN/MH S9 .... 64 E6
DARN/MH S9 .... 153 J3 🔲
Aster Cl DIN S25 .... 193 K3
MOS S20 .... 190 D4
Aston Cl DRON S18 .... 201 J4
Aston Dr BSLYN/ROY S71 .... 56 B1
Aston Gn HTFD DN7 .... 68 B1
Aston La AU/AST/KP S26 .... 175 H5
Aston St SHEFP/MNR S2 .... 171 K3
Astwell Gdns CHPT/GREN S35 ... 129 K1 🔲
Athelstan Cl HAN/WDH S13 .... 173 G6
Athelstan Crs ARMTH DN3 .... 66 E4
Athelstane Dr MALT S66 .... 176 E2
Athelstane Rd CONI DN12 .... 114 C5
Athelstan Rd HAN/WDH S13 .... 173 G6
WRKS S80 .... 210 B6
Athersley Crs BSLYN/ROY S71 .... 56 B1
Athersley Gdns MOS S20 .... 189 J5
Athersley Rd BSLYN/ROY S71 .... 56 B1
Atherton Cl SHEFP/MNR S2 .... 188 B1
Atherton Rd SHEFP/MNR S2 .... 188 B1
Atholl Crs WHHL DN2 .... 92 B2
Athol Rd SHEFS S8 .... 186 E3
Athorpe Gv DIN S25 .... 178 A6
Athorpe Rd DIN S25 .... 178 A6
Athron Dr RHAM/THRY S65 .... 156 B3
Athron St DON DN1 .... 5 D2 🔲
Atkin Pl SHEFP/MNR S2 .... 9 D6 🔲
Atlantic Dr SHEFS S8 .... 200 D1
Atlantic Rd SHEFS S8 .... 200 D1
Atlantic Wy SHEFS S8 .... 200 C1
Atlas St ATT S4 .... 171 K1
RHAM S60 .... 155 F6
Atlas Wy ATT S4 .... 153 F8
Atterby Dr NROS/TKH DN11 .... 119 F5
Attercliffe Common
  DARN/MH S9 .... 153 H8
Attercliffe Rd DARN/MH S9 .... 172 B1
Attlee Av NROS/TKH DN11 .... 118 C2
Attlee Crs MALT S66 .... 159 J3
Attlee Rd MALT S66 .... 159 J3
Attlee Wy WMB/DAR S73 .... 85 F2
Auburn Rd CONI DN12 .... 115 J5
Auckland Av ST/HB/BR S6 .... 150 D7
Auckland Dr MOS S20 .... 204 B1
Auckland Ri MOS S20 .... 204 C1
Auckland Rd DON DN1 .... 5 E1
  MEX/SWTN S64 .... 113 G2
Auckland Wy MOS S20 .... 204 C1
Audrey Rd HAN/WDH S13 .... 172 E8
Aughton Av AU/AST/KP S26 .... 175 G6
Aughton Cl HAN/WDH S13 .... 173 F8
Aughton Crs HAN/WDH S13 .... 172 E7
Aughton Dr HAN/WDH S13 .... 172 E7 🔲
Aughton La AU/AST/KP S26 .... 175 J7
Aughton Rd AU/AST/KP S26 .... 175 H7 🔲
Augustus Rd RHAM S60 .... 155 F5 🔲
Aukley Rd SHEFS S8 .... 187 F2
Aunby Dr AU/AST/KP S26 .... 175 H7 🔲
Austen Av DONS/BSCR DN4 .... 116 B1
Austen Dr MALT S66 .... 157 K2
Austin Cl ST/HB/BR S6 .... 150 D7
Austin Ct ST/HB/BR S6 .... 150 D6
Austwick Cl DOD/DAR S75 .... 29 F5
  DONS/BSCR DN4 .... 116 C3
Austwood La MALT S66 .... 137 H5
Autumn Cl MALT S66 .... 177 G1 🔲
Autumn Dr MALT S66 .... 159 H1
Avenue Rd AWLS/ASK DN6 .... 18 C8
  DEARNE S63 .... 111 K1
  WHHL DN2 .... 5 E1
The Avenue AWLS/ASK DN6 .... 17 K6
  AWLS/ASK DN6 .... 18 C8
  BSLYN/ROY S71 .... 31 F3
  BTLY DN5 .... 65 F6
  BTLY DN5 .... 87 G6
  CHPT/GREN S35 .... 106 C4
  DARN/MH S9 .... 172 E3 🔲
  DOD/DAR S75 .... 107 J1
  DONS/BSCR DN4 .... 92 B6
  DRON S18 .... 201 H5
  ECK/KIL S21 .... 138 B7
  MALT S66 .... 158 D6
  MOS S20 .... 190 D3
  THNE DN8 .... 23 K3
Aviemore Rd DONS/BSCR DN4 ..... 116 B1

Avill Wy MALT S66 .... 157 G4
Avisford Dr SHEFN S5 .... 151 J4
Avisford Rd SHEFN S5 .... 151 J3
Avoca Av WHHL DN2 .... 91 K3
Avocet Gv WRKN S81 .... 210 A1
Avocet Wy KIMB S61 .... 131 G1
Avon Cl DOD/DAR S75 .... 54 D4
  DRON S18 .... 201 H4
  MALT S66 .... 159 G1
  WMB/DAR S73 .... 84 C6
Avon Ct EPW DN9 .... 94 B8
Avondale Dr BSLYN/ROY S71 .... 30 D6
Avondale Rd KIMB S61 .... 132 D8
  ST/HB/BR S6 .... 151 G7 🔲
  WHHL DN2 .... 91 K4
Avon Gv CHPT/GREN S35 .... 129 K1
Avon Mt KIMB S61 .... 132 D8
Avon St BSLYN/ROY S71 .... 3 D4
Avon Wy WRKN S81 .... 196 C8
Axholme Gn THNE DN8 .... 43 K1 🔲
Axholme Rd WHHL DN2 .... 5 E1
Axle La DIN S25 .... 193 J3
Aylesbury Crs DARN/MH S9 .... 153 J4
Aylesbury Rd WHHL DN2 .... 92 A5
Aylesford Cl BSLYN/ROY S71 .... 2 C2 🔲
Aylsham Dr AU/AST/KP S26 .... 175 J8 🔲
Aylward Cl SHEFP/MNR S2 .... 172 B8
Aylward Rd SHEFP/MNR S2 .... 172 B8
Aymer Dr MALT S66 .... 176 E2
Ayots Gn HTFD DN7 .... 68 B1
Aysgarth Av BSLYN/ROY S71 .... 57 J7
Aysgarth Ri AU/AST/KP S26 .... 175 G7
Aysgarth Rd ST/HB/BR S6 .... 151 H3
Ayton Wk BTLY DN5 .... 64 D5 🔲
Azalea Cl DIN S25 .... 193 K4

B

Babbage Wy WRKS S80 .... 210 B3
Babington Cl SHEFP/MNR S2 .... 172 B8
Babington Ct SHEFP/MNR S2 .... 172 B8
Babur Rd ATT S4 .... 171 K1 🔲
Back Field La HTFD DN7 .... 42 E8
Backfield Ri CHPT/GREN S35 .... 130 B1
Backfields SHEF S1 .... 9 D3
Back La AWLS/ASK DN6 .... 17 K7
  AWLS/ASK DN6 .... 17 K3
  BSLYN/ROY S71 .... 56 D2
  BTLY DN5 .... 60 B3
  BTLY DN5 .... 61 J2
  BTLY DN5 .... 89 K2
  BWTY DN10 .... 143 J5
  CONI DN12 .... 115 H8
  CUD/GR S72 .... 59 J8
  DIN S25 .... 194 A1
  DRON S18 .... 202 B6
  ECK/KIL S21 .... 204 A4
  EPW DN9 .... 120 E2
  FUL S10 .... 169 F1
  HATH/EY S32 .... 182 C8
  HEM/SK/SE WF9 .... 35 F1
  HOLM/MEL HD7 .... 47 K2
  HOR/CROF WF4 .... 29 F1
  HTFD DN7 .... 41 K3
  KBTN HD8 .... 26 D4
  MALT S66 .... 136 E2
  MALT S66 .... 136 E5
  MALT S66 .... 158 B4
  RAW S62 .... 133 F1
  RHAM/THRY S65 .... 134 E3
  RHAM/THRY S65 .... 135 J1
  ST/HB/BR S6 .... 149 J1
  STKB/PEN S36 .... 78 A4
  STKB/PEN S36 .... 78 D7
  STKB/PEN S36 .... 102 D3
  STKB/PEN S36 .... 104 C1
  STKB/PEN S36 .... 104 A4
  WRKS S80 .... 208 D1
Back La West BSLYN/ROY S71 .... 30 E3
Backmoor Crs SHEFS S8 .... 187 J5
Backmoor Rd SHEFS S8 .... 187 J5
Back Rd DRON S18 .... 202 B6
Bacon La DARN/MH S9 .... 172 A2
Baden La KBTN HD8 .... 26 D3
Bader Rd BWTY DN10 .... 165 H7
Bader Vw BWTY DN10 .... 165 H7 🔲
Badger Cl HAN/WDH S13 .... 174 A8
Badger Dr HAN/WDH S13 .... 174 A8
Badger La AWLS/ASK DN6 .... 18 D1
  STKB/PEN S36 .... 101 K1
Badger Pl HAN/WDH S13 .... 174 A8
Badger Ri HAN/WDH S13 .... 174 A8
Badger Rd HAN/WDH S13 .... 174 A8
Badsley Ct RHAM/THRY S65 .... 7 F4 🔲
Badsley Moor La RHAM/THRY S65 ... 7 E5
Badsley St RHAM/THRY S65 .... 7 E4
Badsley St South RHAM/THRY S65 ... 7 F5
Badsworth Cl MALT S66 .... 157 K2
  WMB/DAR S73 .... 84 C5 🔲
Badsworth Pl MALT S66 .... 157 K2
Badsworth Rd DONS/BSCR DN4 ... 115 K2
Badsworth Wy MALT S66 .... 157 K2 🔲
Bagden La KBTN HD8 .... 52 E1
Bagger Wood Hl DOD/DAR S75 ...... 80 C4
Bagger Wood Rd DOD/DAR S75 ..... 80 B6

Bagley Rd ATT S4 ... 152 E6
Bagshaw's Rd HACK/IN S12 ... 188 D1
Bagshot St ECC S11 ... 8 A6
Bahram Rd DONS/BSCR DN4 ... 92 B7
Bailey Crs SHEF/SK/SE WF9 ... 35 F2
Bailey Dr ECK/KIL S21 ... 191 J7
Bailey La HTFD DN7 ... 42 E3
  SHEF S1 ... 8 C3
Bailey St SHEF S1 ... 9 D5
Bainbridge Rd DONS/BSCR DN4 ... 4 C5
Baines Av CONI DN12 ... 115 H6
Bainton Dr BSLY S70 ... 2 A6
Bakehouse La DOD/DAR S75 ... 55 F4
Baker Dr ECK/KIL S21 ... 205 G1
Bakers Hl SHEF S1 ... 9 E3
Bakers La SHEF S1 ... 8 C2
Baker St DARN/MH S9 ... 172 B1
Bakewell Rd BSLYN/ROY S71 ... 56 B1
Bala St BSLYN/ROY S71 ... 2 C4
Balby Carr Bank DONS/BSCR DN4 ... 91 G8
Balby Rd DONS/BSCR DN4 ... 4 B6
Balcarres St NROS/TKH DN11 ... 118 E6
Baldwin St DARN/MH S9 ... 172 A2
Balfour Dr DARN/MH S9 ... 172 D2
Balfour Rd BTLY DN5 ... 65 F6
  DARN/MH S9 ... 172 D2
Balk La BSLY S70 ... 81 K6
  CLE DN14 ... 11 K6
  HEM/SK/SE WF9 ... 35 J3
  KBTN HD8 ... 50 D1
  RHAM S60 ... 154 D5
Balkley La WMB/DAR S73 ... 85 F2
The Balk BTLY DN5 ... 65 H1
  DOD/DAR S75 ... 29 H5
Ballam Av BTLY DN5 ... 65 H1
Ballfield La DOD/DAR S75 ... 28 B7
Ballfield Av HAN/WDH S13 ... 173 J6
Ballfield Cl HAN/WDH S13 ... 173 K6
Ballfield Crs HAN/WDH S13 ... 173 K6
Ballfield Dr HAN/WDH S13 ... 173 K6
Ballfield Pl HAN/WDH S13 ... 173 J6
Ballfield Ri HAN/WDH S13 ... 173 K6
Ballfield Rd HAN/WDH S13 ... 173 J6
Ballfield Wy HAN/WDH S13 ... 173 J6
Ball Rd ST/HB/BR S6 ... 151 G8
Ball St OWL S3 ... 8 C1
Balmain Dr ST/HB/BR S6 ... 151 G6
Balmain Rd ST/HB/BR S6 ... 151 G6
Balmer Ri MALT S66 ... 157 K3
Balm Gn SHEF S1 ... 9 D3
Balmoral Cl BTLY DN5 ... 87 H4
  STKB/PEN S36 ... 77 H5
  WRKN S81 ... 196 D1
Balmoral Crs DRON S18 ... 200 D5
Balmoral Rd HAN/WDH S13 ... 190 A1
Balmoral Wy MALT S66 ... 157 J1
Balne Croft La GLE DN14 ... 12 B5
Balne Hall Rd GLE DN14 ... 11 J3
Balne Moor Rd GLE DN14 ... 10 C3
  GLE DN14 ... 11 G4
Baltic Rd DARN/MH S9 ... 172 B1
Bamford Av BSLYN/ROY S71 ... 56 B1
Bamford Cl DOD/DAR S75 ... 54 D8
Bamforth St ST/HB/BR S6 ... 151 J8
Bank Cl ABRD S7 ... 186 E1
  KIMB S61 ... 132 C6
Bank End Av BSLY S70 ... 82 D2
Bank End Cl KBTN HD8 ... 26 D6
Bank End Rd BSLY S70 ... 26 E6
  BWTY DN10 ... 121 K3
  EPW DN9 ... 121 G2
Bankfield Dr HOLM/MEL HD7 ... 47 F5
Bankfield La ST/HB/BR S6 ... 169 G1
Bankfield Rd ST/HB/BR S6 ... 151 F8
Bank House Rd FUL S10 ... 170 C2
Bank La CHPT/GREN S35 ... 106 D8
  HOLM/MEL HD7 ... 46 E5
  HOLM/MEL HD7 ... 47 G3
  KBTN HD8 ... 51 G3
  STKB/PEN S36 ... 127 H2
Bank Side CHPT/GREN S35 ... 127 F4
Bank St BSLY S70 ... 2 C6
  BSLYN/ROY S71 ... 57 F7
  CUD/GR S72 ... 31 J8
  DIN S25 ... 193 K3
  HOLM/MEL HD7 ... 48 D3
  HOY S74 ... 109 G3
  MEX/SWTN S64 ... 113 F3
  SHEF S1 ... 9 D2
Bank Top La HOLM/MEL HD7 ... 46 D4
Bank Top Rd RHAM/THRY S65 ... 156 C3
Bankwood Cl SHEFS S8 ... 187 K2
Bankwood La NROS/TKH DN11 ... 118 C4
Bankwood Rd SHEFP/MNR S2 ... 187 K2
Banmoor La HATH/EY S32 ... 182 A7
Banner Ct ECC S11 ... 185 J1
Banner Cross Dr ECC S11 ... 186 B1
Bannerdale Cl ECC S11 ... 186 C1
Bannerdale Rd ECC S11 ... 186 C1
Bannerdale Vw ECC S11 ... 186 C1
Bannham Rd DARN/MH S9 ... 173 G3
Bannister La AWLS/ASK DN6 ... 36 D2
Bar Av DOD/DAR S75 ... 29 J7
Barbados Wy MALT S66 ... 158 B2
Barber Balk Cl KIMB S61 ... 132 C6
Barber Balk Rd KIMB S61 ... 132 C2
Barber Cl AU/AST/KP S26 ... 192 E2

Barber Crs ST/HB/BR S6 ... 8 A2
Barber Pl FUL S10 ... 8 A2
Barber Rd FUL S10 ... 8 A2
Barberry Wy RHAM/THRY S65 ... 135 K7
Barber's Av RAW S62 ... 133 J3
Barber's Crs RAW S62 ... 133 J2
Barber's La ECK/KIL S21 ... 191 H7
Barbers Pth MEX/SWTN S64 ... 112 E1
Barber St HOY S74 ... 109 F1
Barber Wood Rd KIMB S61 ... 133 J1
Barbot Hill Rd KIMB S61 ... 133 F5
Barcroft DOD/DAR S75 ... 55 F5
Barden Crs RHAM S60 ... 155 F7
Barden Dr DOD/DAR S75 ... 55 G4
Bardolf Rd DONS/BSCR DN4 ... 92 D6
Bardon Rd ARMTH DN3 ... 66 E5
Bard St SHEFP/MNR S2 ... 9 F2
Bardwell Rd OWL S3 ... 8 A2
Barfield Av RHAM S60 ... 155 K6
Barfield Rd HOY S74 ... 109 F1
Barholm Rd FUL S10 ... 169 K5
Baring Rd KIMB S61 ... 153 J1
Barkby Rd DARN/MH S9 ... 153 H3
Barker Hades Rd WRKN S81 ... 179 J4
Barker's Pl ST/HB/BR S6 ... 151 H6
Barker's Pool SHEF S1 ... 9 D5
Barker's Rd ECC S11 ... 186 D1
Barker St MEX/SWTN S64 ... 112 D1
Bark House La DOD/DAR S75 ... 53 F3
Bark Mdw DOD/DAR S75 ... 55 F8
Barkston Rd BSLYN/ROY S71 ... 30 D8
Barleycroft La DIN S25 ... 208 D2
Barley Ms DRON S18 ... 200 C6
Barley Vw DEARNE S63 ... 60 C8
Barleywood Rd DARN/MH S9 ... 172 E1
Barlow Dr ST/HB/BR S6 ... 170 A1
Barlow Lees La DRON S18 ... 201 F8
Barlow Rd ST/HB/BR S6 ... 151 F8
Barlow Vw DRON S18 ... 201 H8
Barmouth Rd ABRD S7 ... 186 C2
Barnard Av DRON S18 ... 201 K4
Barnardiston Rd DARN/MH S9 ... 172 D2
Barnburgh La DEARNE S63 ... 86 D3
Barnby Dun Rd WHHL DN2 ... 66 B7
Barncliffe Cl FUL S10 ... 169 G7
Barncliffe Crs FUL S10 ... 169 F6
Barncliffe Dr FUL S10 ... 169 F6
Barncliffe Gln FUL S10 ... 169 F7
Barncliffe Rd FUL S10 ... 169 G7
Barnes Av DRON S18 ... 200 D5
Barnes Ct SHEFP/MNR S2 ... 9 E4
Barnes Hall Rd CHPT/GREN S35 ... 129 J3
Barnes La DRON S18 ... 200 B3
Barnet Av ECC S11 ... 185 J2
Barnet Gn HTFD DN7 ... 68 B1
Barnet Rd ECC S11 ... 185 J2
Barnfield Av FUL S10 ... 169 J4
Barnfield Cl FUL S10 ... 169 J5
Barnfield Dr FUL S10 ... 169 J5
  HATH/EY S32 ... 182 B8
Barnfield Rd FUL S10 ... 169 J4
Barnfields HATH/EY S32 ... 182 B8
Barnsdale Av MOS S20 ... 189 J5
Barnsdale Ms AWLS/ASK DN6 ... 17 K7
Barnsdale Wy AWLS/ASK DN6 ... 17 J3
Barnside Cl STKB/PEN S36 ... 78 A5
Barnside La HOLM/MEL HD7 ... 48 E6
Barnsley Av CONI DN12 ... 114 B5
Barnsley Boundary Wk
  CHPT/GREN S35 ... 105 K5
  CHPT/GREN S35 ... 128 E6
  DOD/DAR S75 ... 53 F5
  HOLM/MEL HD7 ... 74 D1
  HOY S74 ... 109 G3
  KBTN HD8 ... 51 J4
  STKB/PEN S36 ... 50 D8
  WMB/DAR S73 ... 84 A8
Barnsley Rd ATT S4 ... 152 E6
  BTLY DN5 ... 61 J8
  CUD/GR S72 ... 32 C4
  CUD/GR S72 ... 57 H1
  DEARNE S63 ... 85 G8
  DOD/DAR S75 ... 28 D7
  DOD/DAR S75 ... 53 K7
  DOD/DAR S75 ... 54 D1
  HEM/SK/SE WF9 ... 34 C4
  HOY S74 ... 82 E7
  KBTN HD8 ... 26 B6
  KBTN HD8 ... 50 D1
  KIMB S61 ... 109 F8
  OWL S3 ... 152 C8
  SHEFN S5 ... 152 D2
  STKB/PEN S36 ... 78 A3
  THNE DN8 ... 24 A4
  WMB/DAR S73 ... 58 C8
  WMB/DAR S73 ... 83 K3
Barnstone St DONS/BSCR DN4 ... 4 A5
Barnwell Crs WMB/DAR S73 ... 83 J2
Barossa St SHEF S1 ... 9 D5
Barrack Rd DRON S18 ... 202 C6
Barracks Fold HOLM/MEL HD7 ... 48 D5
Barratt Rd ECK/KIL S21 ... 204 B5
Barrel La DONS/BSCR DN4 ... 116 A1
Barret Rd DONS/BSCR DN4 ... 92 E6

Barretta St ATT S4 ... 152 E2
Barrie Crs SHEFN S5 ... 152 A
Barrie Dr SHEFN S5 ... 152 A
Barrie Gv MALT S66 ... 158 C
Barrier Bank GLE DN14 ... 13 K
Barrie Rd DONS/BSCR DN4 ... 116 E1
  SHEFN S5 ... 152 A
Barrowby Rd RHAM S60 ... 155 K
Barrow Field La RAW S62 ... 109 H
Barrowfield Rd DEARNE S63 ... 60 D
  HOY S74 ... 82 E
Barrow Hl RAW S62 ... 109 C
Barrow Rd DARN/MH S9 ... 153 J
Bartholomew Cl RHAM S60 ... 156 C5
Bartholomew St WMB/DAR S73 ... 83 K
Bartle Av HACK/IN S12 ... 188 E
Bartle Dr HACK/IN S12 ... 188 E
Bartle Rd HACK/IN S12 ... 188 E
Bartle Wy HACK/IN S12 ... 188 E
Bartlett Cl ST/HB/BR S6 ... 169 G2
Bartlett Rd SHEFN S5 ... 152 A
Bartle Wy HACK/IN S12 ... 188 E
Barton La ARMTH DN3 ... 93 F
Barton Pl CONI DN12 ... 114 C
Barton Rd SHEFS S8 ... 187 C
Barton Wy HEM/SK/SE WF9 ... 35 F
Barugh Green Rd DOD/DAR S75 ... 54 D
Barugh La DOD/DAR S75 ... 54 E
Basegreen Av HACK/IN S12 ... 188 D
Basegreen Cl HACK/IN S12 ... 188 E
Basegreen Crs HACK/IN S12 ... 188 E
Basegreen Dr HACK/IN S12 ... 188 D
Basegreen Pl HACK/IN S12 ... 188 D4
Basegreen Rd HACK/IN S12 ... 188 E5
Basegreen Wy HACK/IN S12 ... 188 E4
Basford Cl DARN/MH S9 ... 172 D
Basford Dr DARN/MH S9 ... 172 D
Basford Ms DARN/MH S9 ... 172 E2
Basford Pl DARN/MH S9 ... 172 D2
Basford St DARN/MH S9 ... 172 C
Basil Av ARMTH DN3 ... 66 E
Basildon Rd DEARNE S63 ... 60 D
Baslow Crs DOD/DAR S75 ... 54 C
Baslow Rd BSLYN/ROY S71 ... 30 C
  TOT/DORE S17 ... 199 F
Bassett La FUL S10 ... 184 C
Bassett Pl SHEFP/MNR S2 ... 171 F
Bassett Rd SHEFP/MNR S2 ... 172 A
Bassingthorpe La KIMB S61 ... 132 E
Bassledene Rd SHEFP/MNR S2 ... 172 C
Bastock Rd ST/HB/BR S6 ... 151
Bate La GLE DN14 ... 12 A
Bateman Cl CUD/GR S72 ... 31 F
Bateman Rd MALT S66 ... 158 C
Batemoor Cl SHEFS S8 ... 201 C
Batemoor Dr SHEFS S8 ... 201 C
Batemoor Pl SHEFS S8 ... 201 G1
Batemoor Rd SHEFS S8 ... 201 C
Bates Gdn MOS S20 ... 190 C
Bath St OWL S3 ... 8 C4
Battison La DEARNE S63 ... 111 C
Battle Cl HTFD DN7 ... 69 C
Batt St SHEFP/MNR S2 ... 9 D6
Batty Av CUD/GR S72 ... 57 H
Batworth Dr ATT S4 ... 152 E
Batworth Rd SHEFN S5 ... 152 E
Baulk Farm Cl RAW S62 ... 132 E
Baulk La HATH/EY S32 ... 182 C
  NROS/TKH DN11 ... 162 E
  WRKN S81 ... 210 C
The Baulk WRKN S81 ... 210 D
Bawtry Cl NROS/TKH DN11 ... 162 E
Bawtry Ga DARN/MH S9 ... 154 E
Bawtry Rd BWTY DN10 ... 142 C
  BWTY DN10 ... 143 H
  BWTY DN10 ... 165 C
  BWTY DN10 ... 165 C
  DARN/MH S9 ... 154 C
  DONS/BSCR DN4 ... 91 K
  DONS/BSCR DN4 ... 118 E
  HTFD DN7 ... 69 C
  MALT S66 ... 157 K
  NROS/TKH DN11 ... 162 E
  NROS/TKH DN11 ... 163 F
  RHAM S60 ... 154 J
  RHAM/THRY S65 ... 156 D3
  WRKN S81 ... 163 C
Baxter Av DON DN1 ... 5 E
Baxter Cl ST/HB/BR S6 ... 151 H
Baxter Dr ST/HB/BR S6 ... 151 H
Baxter Ga DON DN1 ... 4 C
Baxter Rd ST/HB/BR S6 ... 151 H
Baycliff Cl BSLYN/ROY S71 ... 30 E8
Bay Ct ECK/KIL S21 ... 205 C
Bayfield Cl HOLM/MEL HD7 ... 48 A
Baylee St HEM/SK/SE WF9 ... 33 H1
Baysdale Cft MOS S20 ... 190 E
Bay Tree Av MALT S66 ... 157 C
Baytree Gv EPW DN9 ... 120 A
Beacon Cl DARN/MH S9 ... 153 C
  DOD/DAR S75 ... 79 K1
Beacon Ct DOD/DAR S75 ... 79 K1
Beacon Cft DARN/MH S9 ... 153 C
Beacon Hl DOD/DAR S75 ... 79 K
Beacon La MALT S66 ... 136 E
Beacon Rd DARN/MH S9 ... 153 C
Beaconsfield Rd DONS/BSCR DN4 ... 4 A5
  RHAM S60 ... 155 H
Beaconsfield St BSLY S70 ... 2 B4
  MEX/SWTN S64 ... 112 E2

Beacon Sq *MALT* S66 .... 137 F2
Beacon Vw *HEM/SK/SE* WF9 .... 34 B4
HOY S74 .... 109 H2 🔲
Beacon Wy *DARN/MH* S9 .... 153 C5
Beale Wy *RAW* S62 .... 133 C5
Beamshaw *HEM/SK/SE* WF9 .... 34 A6
Bean Av *WRKS* S80 .... 211 F4
Beancroft Cl *NROS/TKH* DN11 .... 117 F8
Bear Bones Rd *HOL/MEL* HD7 .... 74 A2
Bear Tree Cl *RAW* S62 .... 133 J3 🔲
Bear Tree Rd *RAW* S62 .... 133 J3
Bear Tree St *RAW* S62 .... 133 J4 🔲
Beauchamp Rd *KIMB* S61 .... 132 C6
Beauchief Abbey La *SHEFS* S8 .... 186 C7
Beauchief Cl *STKB/PEN* S36 .... 105 J7 🔲
Beauchief Dr *SHEFS* S8 .... 186 C8
Beauchief Ri *SHEFS* S8 .... 186 C6
Beaufort Cdns *BWTY* DN10 .... 142 A8
Beaufort Rd *FUL* S10 .... 8 A3
WHHL DN2 .... 92 A3
Beaufort Wy *WRKS* S81 .... 196 C7
Beaulieu Cl *DOD/DAR* S75 .... 29 H7
BSLY S70 .... 55 C6
HEM/SK/SE WF9 .... 34 E4
SHEFP/MNR S2 .... 172 C5
Beaumont Av *SHEFP/MNR* S2 .... 172 D5
Beaumont Crs *SHEFP/MNR* S2 .... 172 C5 🔲
Beaumont Dr *HOR/CROF* WF4 .... 27 J1
RHAM/THRY S65 .... 156 A2
Beaumont Ms *SHEFP/MNR* S2 .... 172 D6 🔲
Beaumont Ri *WRKS* S80 .... 210 B4
Beaumont Rd *DOD/DAR* S75 .... 28 B8
Beaumont North
SHEFP/MNR S2 .... 172 C5
Beaumont St *HOY* S74 .... 108 C2
Beaumont Wy *SHEFP/MNR* S2 .... 172 C5 🔲
Beaver Av *HAN/WDH* S13 .... 173 K7
Beaver Cl *HAN/WDH* S13 .... 173 K7
Beaver Dr *HAN/WDH* S13 .... 173 K7
Beaver Hill Rd *HAN/WDH* S13 .... 173 K7
Beaver Pl *WRKS* S80 .... 210 D4
Beccles St *BSLYN/ROY* S71 .... 2 C5
Beck Cl *MEX/SWTN* S64 .... 112 C6
SHEFN S5 .... 131 F8
Becket Crs *KIMB* S61 .... 132 A5
Becket Rd *SHEFS* S8 .... 200 E1
Beckett Av *WRKN* S81 .... 180 D8
Beckett Rd *DON* DN1 .... 5 E1
WHHL DN2 .... 65 K8
Beck Ri *BSLYN/ROY* S71 .... 2 C3
Beckfield Gv *DEARNE* S63 .... 86 A4
Becknoll Rd *WMB/DAR* S73 .... 84 D7
Beck Rd *SHEFN* S5 .... 130 E8
Beckton Av *MOS* S20 .... 190 C5
Beckton Cl *MOS* S20 .... 190 D5
Beckton Gv *MOS* S20 .... 190 C5
Beck Vw *HOR/CROF* WF4 .... 30 B1
Beckwith Rd *DIN* S25 .... 177 J5
RHAM/THRY S65 .... 134 B8
Bedale *WRKN* S81 .... 196 E7
Bedale Rd *BTLY* DN5 .... 64 A8
SHEFS S8 .... 187 F1
Bedding Edge Rd *HOLM/MEL* HD7 .... 75 F1
Bedford Cl *DIN* S25 .... 177 K8 🔲
Bedford Rd *CHPT/GREN* S35 .... 128 C7
Bedford St *BSLY* S70 .... 2 C6
CUD/GR S72 .... 58 D2
MALT S66 .... 159 J3 🔲
ST/HB/BR S6 .... 8 C1 🔲
Bedford Ter *BSLYN/ROY* S71 .... 56 B2
Bedgebury Cl *MOS* S20 .... 191 F6 🔲
Bedgrave Cl *ECK/KIL* S21 .... 191 K7
Beecham Ct *MEX/SWTN* S64 .... 112 B6
Beech Av *CUD/GR* S72 .... 31 J7
DOD/DAR S75 .... 79 K2 🔲
EPW DN9 .... 120 B3
NROS/TKH DN11 .... 140 A8
RAW S62 .... 134 A2
RHAM/THRY S65 .... 156 D5
WRKN S81 .... 210 D1
Beech Cl *CUD/GR* S72 .... 32 D4
HEM/SK/SE WF9 .... 34 A5
MALT S66 .... 158 D2
WMB/DAR S73 .... 83 K7
Beech Crs *ECK/KIL* S21 .... 203 K6
MEX/SWTN S64 .... 205 G2
HTFD DN7 .... 42 A3
MEX/SWTN S64 .... 112 D2
Beechcroft *WRKN* S81 .... 210 E1 🔲
Beechcroft Cl *CHPT/GREN* S35 .... 107 J7 🔲
Beechcroft Cl *DEARNE* S63 .... 86 B5
Beechfield Rd *DON* DN1 .... 5 D4
HTFD DN7 .... 42 A8
Beech Gv *BSLY* S70 .... 2 A6
BTLY DN5 .... 64 E7 🔲
CONI DN12 .... 114 C6
DIN S25 .... 178 B8
DONS/BSCR DN4 .... 115 K1

Beech Hi *CONI* DN12 .... 114 D6
Beech Hill Rd *FUL* S10 .... 170 C5
Beech House Rd *WMB/DAR* S73 .... 84 A7
Beech Wy *AU/AST/KP* S26 .... 175 F7
Beech Rd *ARMTH* DN3 .... 67 G8
AWLS/ASK DN6 .... 18 A6
AWLS/ASK DN6 .... 37 H6
CUD/GR S72 .... 32 A5
DEARNE S63 .... 111 K1
MALT S66 .... 158 E2
NROS/TKH DN11 .... 119 F7
NROS/TKH DN11 .... 165 F2
Beech St *BSLY* S70 .... 2 C5
HEM/SK/SE WF9 .... 34 D6
HOLM/MEL HD7 .... 47 K2 🔲
Beech Tree Av *THNE* DN8 .... 43 K1
Beech Tree Cl *ARMTH* DN3 .... 93 G6
Beechville Av *MEX/SWTN* S64 .... 112 B6 🔲
Beech Wy *AU/AST/KP* S26 .... 175 F7
DRON S18 .... 201 G4 🔲
Beechwood Cl *ARMTH* DN3 .... 67 F6 🔲
DEARNE S63 .... 111 J4 🔲
RAW S62 .... 112 B8 🔲
Beechwood Crs *HEM/SK/SE* WF9 .... 33 F1
Beechwood Mt *HEM/SK/SE* WF9 .... 33 G1 🔲
Beechwood Rd
CHPT/GREN S35 .... 129 K3 🔲
DRON S18 .... 201 F6
RHAM/THRY S65 .... 7 F5
ST/HB/BR S6 .... 151 G7
STKB/PEN S36 .... 104 E7
Beehive Rd *FUL* S10 .... 8 A2
Beeley St *SHEFP/MNR* S2 .... 8 C5 🔲
Beeley Wood La *ST/HB/BR* S6 .... 151 F3
Beeley Wood Rd *ST/HB/BR* S6 .... 151 H4
Beely Rd *CHPT/GREN* S35 .... 150 D1
Beeston Dr *DRON* S18 .... 200 C5 🔲
Beeston Sq *BSLYN/ROY* S71 .... 30 A7 🔲
Beeton Gn *ST/HB/BR* S6 .... 168 A1
Beeton Rd *SHEFS* S8 .... 187 F2
Beet St *DEARNE* S63 .... 86 E2
Beever Cl *BSLYN/ROY* S71 .... 3 D4
Beever La *DOD/DAR* S75 .... 55 F4
Beevers Rd *KIMB* S61 .... 132 A5
Beevor St *DEARNE* S63 .... 86 E2
Beevor Cl *BSLYN/ROY* S71 .... 3 E4 🔲
Begonia Cl *DIN* S25 .... 193 J3
Beighton Dr *HACK/IN* S12 .... 189 K4
HAN/WDH S13 .... 190 B1
MEX/SWTN S64 .... 112 D7
Beighton Rd East *MOS* S20 .... 190 A4
Belcourt Rd *RHAM/THRY* S65 .... 156 C3
Beldon Cl *SHEFP/MNR* S2 .... 171 K8
Beldon Pl *SHEFP/MNR* S2 .... 171 K8
Beldon Rd *SHEFP/MNR* S2 .... 171 K8
Belford Cl *MALT* S66 .... 157 H1
Belford Dr *MALT* S66 .... 157 H1
Belfry Gdns *DONS/BSCR* DN4 .... 93 F8 🔲
Belfry Wy *DIN* S25 .... 178 D2
Belgrave Ct *BWTY* DN10 .... 142 A8 🔲
Belgrave Dr *FUL* S10 .... 169 H6
Belgrave Pl *AU/AST/KP* S26 .... 175 G8
Belgrave Rd *BSLYN/ROY* S71 .... 3 D4
FUL S10 .... 169 H6
Belgrave Sq *SHEFP/MNR* S2 .... 9 D6 🔲
Belklane Rd *ECK/KIL* S21 .... 191 J8
Bell Bank Vw *BTLY* DN5 .... 82 A2
Bellbrooke Av *WMB/DAR* S73 .... 58 C8
Bell Butts La *EPW* DN9 .... 120 A1
Bell Croft La *BTLY* DN5 .... 39 J6
Belifield St *OWL* S3 .... 8 B2
Belle Green Cl *CUD/GR* S72 .... 31 K8 🔲
Belle Green Gdns *CUD/GR* S72 .... 31 K8
Belle Green La *CUD/GR* S72 .... 31 K8
Bellerby Pl *AWLS/ASK* DN6 .... 37 G5
Bellerby Rd *AWLS/ASK* DN6 .... 37 G5
Belle Vue Av *MEX/SWTN* S64 .... 113 F3
Belle Vue Ter *THNE* DN8 .... 23 J8
The Bellfields *KIMB* S61 .... 131 F2
Bellgreave Av *HOLM/MEL* HD7 .... 48 A8
Bell Gn *GLE* DN14 .... 21 J3
Bellhagg Rd *ST/HB/BR* S6 .... 170 D1
Bellhouse Rd *SHEFN* S5 .... 153 F3
Bellmont Crs *HEM/SK/SE* WF9 .... 33 H1
Bellows Rd *RAW* S62 .... 133 J2
Bellrope Acre *ARMTH* DN3 .... 93 G2
Bells Sq *SHEF* S1 .... 9 D3 🔲
Bellwood Crs *HOY* S74 .... 108 D2
Belmont *CUD/GR* S72 .... 57 K3 🔲
Belmont Av *BSLYN/ROY* S71 .... 56 C1
CHPT/GREN S35 .... 130 B2
DONS/BSCR DN4 .... 4 C5
Belmont Cl *ARMTH* DN3 .... 93 K7
Belmont Crs *DOD/DAR* S75 .... 59 H8 🔲
Belmont Dr *STKB/PEN* S36 .... 105 F6 🔲
Belmont St *KIMB* S61 .... 114 D1
MEX/SWTN S64 .... 112 E3 🔲
Belmont Wy *HEM/SK/SE* WF9 .... 35 G4
Belper Rd *SHEFS* S8 .... 187 F1 🔲
Belridge Cl *DOD/DAR* S75 .... 55 G3 🔲
Belsize Rd *ECC* S11 .... 169 H7
Belton Cl *DRON* S18 .... 200 C5 🔲
Belvedere *DONS/BSCR* DN4 .... 116 C1

Belvedere Cl *AWLS/ASK* DN6 .... 18 E7
CUD/GR S72 .... 31 K5 🔲
DIN S25 .... 194 B2
Belvedere Dr *THNE* DN8 .... 23 K4
WMB/DAR S73 .... 58 B8
Belvedere Pde *MALT* S66 .... 135 H8
Belvoir Av *BTLY* DN5 .... 77 H4
Bembridge *WRKN* S81 .... 211 F1
Ben Bank Rd *DOD/DAR* S75 .... 79 K1
Bence Cl *DOD/DAR* S75 .... 28 D8
Bence La *DOD/DAR* S75 .... 28 B8
Ben Cl *ST/HB/BR* S6 .... 150 E6
Benita Av *MEX/SWTN* S64 .... 113 H3
Ben La *ST/HB/BR* S6 .... 150 E6
Benmore Dr *MOS* S20 .... 191 F6 🔲
Bennett Cl *RAW* S62 .... 112 A8 🔲
Bennetthorpe *WHHL* DN2 .... 5 E4
Bennett St *KIMB* S61 .... 154 B1
SHEFP/MNR S2 .... 8 C6 🔲
Benson Rd *SHEFP/MNR* S2 .... 172 A5
Bentfield Av *RHAM/THRY* S65 .... 156 B4
Bentham Dr *BSLYN/ROY* S71 .... 56 B3
Bentham Wy *DOD/DAR* S75 .... 29 F5
Bent Hills La *CHPT/GREN* S35 .... 127 H6
Bentinck Cl *DON* DN1 .... 5 D4 🔲
Bentinick St *CONI* DN12 .... 114 E5 🔲
Bent La *HOLM/MEL* HD7 .... 47 K7
Bent Lathes Av *RHAM* S60 .... 156 B4
Bentley Av *DONS/BSCR* DN4 .... 4 A4
Bentley Cl *BSLYN/ROY* S71 .... 57 F2
Bentley Common La *BTLY* DN5 .... 65 F7
Bentley Moor La *AWLS/ASK* DN6 .... 38 A8
Bentley Rd *BTLY* DN5 .... 64 E8
CHPT/GREN S35 .... 130 C3
FUL S10 .... 170 A2
MALT S66 .... 157 K3
Bentley St *RHAM* S60 .... 155 G4
Benton Ter *MEX/SWTN* S64 .... 112 C6 🔲
Benton Wy *KIMB* S61 .... 132 C8
Bent Rd *HOLM/MEL* HD7 .... 48 C8
Bents Cl *CHPT/GREN* S35 .... 130 B2 🔲
ECC S11 .... 185 J2
Bents Crs *DRON* S18 .... 201 J4
ECC S11 .... 185 K3
Bents Dr *ECC* S11 .... 185 J1
Bents Green Av *ECC* S11 .... 185 J2
Bents Green Rd *ECC* S11 .... 185 J2 🔲
Bents Green Rd *ECC* S11 .... 185 K2
Bents La *DRON* S18 .... 201 J4
ST/HB/BR S6 .... 149 G8
Bents Rd *ECC* S11 .... 185 K2
KIMB S61 .... 132 C6
STKB/PEN S36 .... 75 H3
Bent St *STKB/PEN* S36 .... 77 K3
Benty La *FUL* S10 .... 169 K4
Beresford Rd *MALT* S66 .... 159 J3
Beresford St *BTLY* DN5 .... 64 E6
Berkeley Cft *BSLYN/ROY* S71 .... 30 C3
Berkley Cl *BSLY* S70 .... 82 A2
Bernard Rd *ATT* S4 .... 171 K3
CONI DN12 .... 115 J6
SHEFP/MNR S2 .... 9 F2
Bernard St *RAW* S62 .... 112 A8
RHAM/THRY S65 .... 7 D5
SHEFP/MNR S2 .... 9 F2
Berners Cl *SHEFP/MNR* S2 .... 188 A2
Berners Dr *SHEFP/MNR* S2 .... 188 A1
Berners Pl *SHEFP/MNR* S2 .... 188 A1
Berners Rd *SHEFP/MNR* S2 .... 187 K1
Berneslai Cl *BSLY* S70 .... 2 B3
Berne Sq *DIN* S25 .... 195 F3
Bernshall Crs *SHEFS* S8 .... 130 C8
Berresford Rd *ECC* S11 .... 8 A6 🔲
Berridge La *GLE* DN14 .... 12 A3
Berrington Cl *DONS/BSCR* DN4 .... 116 D3
Berry Av *ECK/KIL* S21 .... 204 A4
Berrydale *BSLY* S70 .... 82 B2
Berry Dr *AU/AST/KP* S26 .... 193 F4 🔲
Berry Holme Cl *CHPT/GREN* S35 .... 130 B2 🔲
Berry Holme Ct
CHPT/GREN S35 .... 130 B2 🔲
Berry Holme Dr *CHPT/GREN* S35 .... 130 B2 🔲
Berry La *CHPT/GREN* S35 .... 107 F7
Berrywell Av *STKB/PEN* S36 .... 78 B5
Bertram Rd *CHPT/GREN* S35 .... 150 D1
Bessacarr La *DONS/BSCR* DN4 .... 118 D1
Bessemer Pl *DARN/MH* S9 .... 172 A2 🔲
Bessemer Rd *DARN/MH* S9 .... 172 A1
Bessemer Ter *STKB/PEN* S36 .... 104 E5 🔲
Bessemer Wy *RHAM* S60 .... 154 D2
Bessingby Rd *ST/HB/BR* S6 .... 151 H8
Bethel Rd *RHAM/THRY* S65 .... 7 E2
Bethel St *HOY* S74 .... 109 G1
Betjeman Gdns *ECC* S11 .... 170 C6 🔲
Betony Cl *ECK/KIL* S21 .... 205 F2
Between Rivers La *GLE* DN14 .... 13 J3
Beulah Rd *ST/HB/BR* S6 .... 151 J6
Bevan Av *NROS/TKH* DN11 .... 118 E6
Bevan Cl *HOY* S74 .... 109 H1
Bevan Crs *MALT* S66 .... 159 G1
Bevan Wy *CHPT/GREN* S35 .... 130 A3
Bevercotes Rd *SHEFN* S5 .... 152 E4
Beverley Av *BSLY* S70 .... 82 A1
Beverley Cl *AU/AST/KP* S26 .... 175 H8
BSLYN/ROY S71 .... 29 K8
Beverley Gdns *BTLY* DN5 .... 90 A2
Beverley Rd *NROS/TKH* DN11 .... 163 F3
WHHL DN2 .... 91 K1
Beverleys Rd *SHEFS* S8 .... 187 G3

Beverley St *DARN/MH* S9 ...... 172 C1
Bevin Pl *RAW* S62 ...... 134 A1
Bevre Rd *ARMTH* DN3 ...... 67 F7
Bewicke Av *BTLY* DN5 ...... 90 A1
Bhatia Cl *MEX/SWTN* S64 ...... 113 F2
Bib La *DIN* S25 ...... 158 D8
Bierlow Rd *ST/HB/BR* S6 ...... 151 H5
Bierlow Vl *WMB/DAR* S73 ...... 84 D6
Bigby Wy *RHAM/THRY* S65 ...... 135 H8
Bignor Pl *ST/HB/BR* S6 ...... 151 J3
Bignor Rd *ST/HB/BR* S6 ...... 151 J2
Bilham La *BTLY* DN5 ...... 61 H4
Bilham Rd *KBTN* HD8 ...... 26 D5
Billam Pl *KIMB* S61 ...... 203 K4
Billingley Dr *DEARNE* S63 ...... 60 B8
Billingley Green La *CUD/GR* S72 ...... 85 J1
Billingley La *CUD/GR* S72 ...... 59 J7
Billingley Vw *DEARNE* S63 ...... 86 A5
Billy Wright's La *NROS/TKH* DN11 ...... 139 J2
Bilston St *ST/HB/BR* S6 ...... 151 J8
Binbrook Ct *BWTY* DN10 ...... 164 A1
Binders Rd *KIMB* S61 ...... 132 B6
Binfield Rd *SHEFS* S8 ...... 187 F2
Bingham Park Crs *ECC* S11 ...... 170 A7
Bingham Park Rd *ECC* S11 ...... 170 A8
Bingham Rd *SHEFS* S8 ...... 187 F5
Bingley La *ST/HB/BR* S6 ...... 169 F3
Bingley St *DOD/DAR* S75 ...... 2 A5
Binns Rd *HOLM/MEL* HD7 ...... 47 J2
Binsted Av *SHEFN* S5 ...... 151 J3
Binsted Cl *SHEFN* S5 ...... 151 J4
Binsted Crs *SHEFN* S5 ...... 151 J4
Binsted Cft *SHEFN* S5 ...... 151 J4
Binsted Dr *SHEFN* S5 ...... 151 J4
Binsted Gdns *SHEFN* S5 ...... 151 J4
Binsted Gld *SHEFN* S5 ...... 151 J4
Binsted Gv *SHEFN* S5 ...... 151 J4
Binsted Rd *SHEFN* S5 ...... 151 J4
Binsted Wy *SHEFN* S5 ...... 151 J4
Birchall Av *RHAM* S60 ...... 156 A6
Birch Av *AWLS/ASK* DN6 ...... 37 H6
  CHPT/GREN S35 ...... 130 A3
  EPW DN9 ...... 120 B4
Birch Cl *BTLY* DN5 ...... 90 A6
  ECK/KIL S21 ...... 205 G2
Birch Crs *MALT* S66 ...... 157 H2
Birchdale Cl *ARMTH* DN3 ...... 66 E6
Birchen Cl *DONS/BSCR* DN4 ...... 118 D2
  DRON S18 ...... 200 D6
Birches Fold *DRON* S18 ...... 201 J3
Birches La *DRON* S18 ...... 201 J3
Birch Farm Av *SHEFS* S8 ...... 187 G7
Birchfield Crs *DOD/DAR* S75 ...... 55 F7
Birchfield Dr *WRKS* S80 ...... 209 K5
Birchfield Wk *DOD/DAR* S75 ...... 55 G5
Birch Gv *CHPT/GREN* S35 ...... 150 C5
  CONI DN12 ...... 114 E5
Birch House Av *CHPT/GREN* S35 ...... 150 C5
Birchitt Cl *TOT/DORE* S17 ...... 200 C3
Birchitt Pl *TOT/DORE* S17 ...... 200 C2
Birchitt Rd *TOT/DORE* S17 ...... 200 C2
Birchitt Vw *DRON* S18 ...... 201 C4
Birchlands Dr *ECK/KIL* S21 ...... 205 H2
Birch Rd *BSLY* S70 ...... 56 E8
  DARN/MH S9 ...... 172 A1
  DONS/BSCR DN4 ...... 92 E7
Birch Tree Cl *ARMTH* DN3 ...... 40 E8
Birchtree Rd *KIMB* S61 ...... 131 G4
Birch Tree Rd *STKB/PEN* S36 ...... 104 E1
Birchvale Rd *HACK/IN* S12 ...... 189 F4
Birchwood Av *MALT* S66 ...... 158 E1
  MOS S20 ...... 190 C7
  THNE DN8 ...... 23 J6
Birchwood Cft *MOS* S20 ...... 190 C7
Birchwood Dell *DONS/BSCR* DN4 ...... 119 C7
Birchwood Dr *RHAM/THRY* S65 ...... 135 H7
Birchwood Gdns *MALT* S66 ...... 137 H5
  MOS S20 ...... 190 C7
Birchwood Gv *MOS* S20 ...... 190 C7
Birchwood Pk *HOLM/MEL* HD7 ...... 48 D1
Birchwood Ri *MOS* S20 ...... 190 C7
Birchwood Rd *ECK/KIL* S21 ...... 203 F4
Birchwood Vw *MOS* S20 ...... 190 C7
Bircotes Wk *NROS/TKH* DN11 ...... 119 G6
Bird Av *WMB/DAR* S73 ...... 83 K3
Bird La *STKB/PEN* S36 ...... 79 H5
Birds Edge La *KBTN* HD8 ...... 50 A4
Birdsnest La *HOLM/MEL* HD7 ...... 49 H6
  KBTN HD8 ...... 49 K5
Birdwell Rd *ATT* S4 ...... 153 G6
  DOD/DAR S75 ...... 81 F1
  MEX/SWTN S64 ...... 112 C2
Birk Av *BSLY* S70 ...... 3 F6
Birkbeck Ct *CHPT/GREN* S35 ...... 107 J7
Birk Crs *BSLY* S70 ...... 3 F6
Birkdale *WRKS* S81 ...... 211 F1
Birkdale Av *DIN* S25 ...... 178 B7
Birkdale Cl *CUD/GR* S72 ...... 31 K7
  DONS/BSCR DN4 ...... 119 C3
Birkdale Ri *MEX/SWTN* S64 ...... 112 C5
Birkdale Rd *BSLYN/ROY* S71 ...... 30 C2
Birkendale *ST/HB/BR* S6 ...... 8 A1
Birkendale Rd *ST/HB/BR* S6 ...... 8 A1
Birkendale Vw *ST/HB/BR* S6 ...... 8 A1
Birk Gn *BSLY* S70 ...... 56 E8

Birk House La *BSLY* S70 ...... 56 E8
Birklands Av *HAN/WDH* S13 ...... 173 G6
Birklands Cl *HAN/WDH* S13 ...... 173 C6
Birklands Dr *HAN/WDH* S13 ...... 173 C6
Birk Rd *BSLY* S70 ...... 3 F6
Birks Av *HAN/WDH* S13 ...... 189 K1
  STKB/PEN S36 ...... 77 F4
Birks Holt Dr *MALT* S66 ...... 159 J4
Birks La *STKB/PEN* S36 ...... 77 F5
Birks Rd *KIMB* S61 ...... 132 B6
Birks Wood Dr *CHPT/GREN* S35 ...... 150 C1
Birk Ter *BSLY* S70 ...... 3 F6
Birkwood Av *CUD/GR* S72 ...... 57 K2
Birley La *HACK/IN* S12 ...... 189 F5
  HATH/Y S32 ...... 182 B5
Birley Moor Av *HACK/IN* S12 ...... 189 G4
Birley Moor Cl *HACK/IN* S12 ...... 189 G4
Birley Moor Crs *HACK/IN* S12 ...... 189 G5
Birley Moor Pl *HACK/IN* S12 ...... 189 G5
Birley Moor Rd *HACK/IN* S12 ...... 189 F5
Birley Moor Wy *HACK/IN* S12 ...... 189 G4
Birley Ri Cl *HACK/IN* S12 ...... 189 G4
Birley Rise Crs *ST/HB/BR* S6 ...... 151 H3
Birley Rise Rd *ST/HB/BR* S6 ...... 151 H3
Birley Spa Dr *HACK/IN* S12 ...... 189 K3
Birley Spa La *HACK/IN* S12 ...... 189 J3
Birley Vale Av *HACK/IN* S12 ...... 188 E3
Birley Vale Cl *HACK/IN* S12 ...... 188 E3
Birley Vw *CHPT/GREN* S35 ...... 150 C2
Birthwaite Rd *DOD/DAR* S75 ...... 28 A7
Bisby Rd *RAW* S62 ...... 133 K1
Biscay Wy *DEARNE* S63 ...... 111 J2
Bishopdale *WRKS* S81 ...... 196 E8
Bishopdale Ct *MOS* S20 ...... 189 J6
Bishopdale Dr *HACK/IN* S12 ...... 189 J7
Bishopdale Ri *HACK/IN* S12 ...... 189 J7
Bishop Gdns *HAN/WDH* S13 ...... 189 J1
Bishopgarth Cl *BTLY* DN5 ...... 90 E1
Bishop Hl *HAN/WDH* S13 ...... 189 J1
Bishops Ct *SHEFS* S8 ...... 187 G2
Bishopscourt Rd *SHEFS* S8 ...... 187 G2
Bishopsholme Rd *SHEFN* S5 ...... 152 B5
Bishopston Wk *MALT* S66 ...... 159 F1
Bishops Wy *BSLYN/ROY* S71 ...... 8 C4
Bisley Cl *BSLYN/ROY* S71 ...... 31 F4
Bismarck St *BSLY* S70 ...... 2 C6
Bittern Vw *WRKS* S81 ...... 131 H1
Blacka Moor Crs *TOT/DORE* S17 ...... 199 H1
Blackamoor Rd *RAW* S62 ...... 111 J6
Blacka Moor Rd *TOT/DORE* S17 ...... 199 G5
Blacka Moor Vw *TOT/DORE* S17 ...... 199 G5
Black Bank *BWTY* DN10 ...... 143 K7
Blackbird Av *RHAM* S60 ...... 155 G7
Blackbrook Av *FUL* S10 ...... 168 D6
Blackbrook Dr *FUL* S10 ...... 168 D6
Blackbrook Rd *FUL* S10 ...... 168 E6
Blackburn Crs *CHPT/GREN* S35 ...... 129 K5
Blackburn Cft *CHPT/GREN* S35 ...... 130 A1
Blackburn Dr *CHPT/GREN* S35 ...... 129 K2
Blackburne St *ST/HB/BR* S6 ...... 151 J8
Blackburn La *BSLY* S70 ...... 82 B2
  DOD/DAR S75 ...... 2 A3
  KIMB S61 ...... 153 J1
Blackburn Rd *KIMB* S61 ...... 153 J1
Blackburn St *BSLY* S70 ...... 82 B2
Blackdown Av *MOS* S20 ...... 190 B5
Blacker Green La *BTLY* DN5 ...... 39 G3
Blackergreen La *STKB/PEN* S36 ...... 79 G4
Blacker La *BSLY* S70 ...... 82 B5
  CUD/GR S72 ...... 31 K4
Blacker Rd *DOD/DAR* S75 ...... 29 H7
Blackheath Cl *BSLYN/ROY* S71 ...... 30 C8
Blackheath Rd *BSLYN/ROY* S71 ...... 30 C8
Blackheath Wk *BSLYN/ROY* S71 ...... 30 C8
Black Hill Rd *RHAM/THRY* S65 ...... 156 C3
Black Horse Cl *STKB/PEN* S36 ...... 79 K2
Black Horse Dr *STKB/PEN* S36 ...... 79 K2
Black La *HOY* S74 ...... 108 A5
  ST/HB/BR S6 ...... 150 C8
Blackmoor Crs *RHAM* S60 ...... 154 E6
Blackmore St *ATT* S4 ...... 171 K2
Black Sike La *HOLM/MEL* HD7 ...... 47 F2
Blacksmith La *CHPT/GREN* S35 ...... 129 H7
Blacksmith's La *BTLY* DN5 ...... 88 D1
Blackstock Cl *SHEFS* S8 ...... 187 K5
Blackstock Crs *SHEFS* S8 ...... 187 K5
Blackstock Dr *SHEFS* S8 ...... 187 K5
Blackstock Rd *SHEFP/MNR* S2 ...... 187 K5
  SHEFS S8 ...... 187 K5
Black Syke La *GLE* DN14 ...... 22 D4
Blackthorn Av *MALT* S66 ...... 157 H2
Blackthorn Cl *CHPT/GREN* S35 ...... 107 J7
Blackthorne Cl *CONI* DN12 ...... 115 H6
Blackthorn Ri *RHAM/THRY* S65 ...... 135 K7
Blackwell Cl *SHEFP/MNR* S2 ...... 9 F5
Blackwell Pl *SHEFP/MNR* S2 ...... 9 F5
Blackwood Av *DONS/BSCR* DN4 ...... 116 C1
Blagden St *SHEFP/MNR* S2 ...... 9 F5
Blair Athol Rd *ECC* S11 ...... 186 B1
Blake Av *DEARNE* S63 ...... 85 F8
  WHHL DN2 ...... 91 J1
Blake Cl *MALT* S66 ...... 157 K3
Blake Grove Rd *ST/HB/BR* S6 ...... 8 B1
Blakeley Cl *BSLYN/ROY* S71 ...... 30 C8
Blakeney Rd *FUL* S10 ...... 170 C4
Blake St *ST/HB/BR* S6 ...... 8 A1

Bland La *ST/HB/BR* S6 ...... 150 E
Bland St *ATT* S4 ...... 153 F
Blast La *ATT* S4 ...... 9 F
  SHEFP/MNR S2 ...... 9 F2
Blaxton Cl *MOS* S20 ...... 189 J
Blayton Rd *ATT* S4 ...... 152 D
Blazley Rd *SHEFP/MNR* S2 ...... 188 B
Bleachcroft Wy *BSLY* S70 ...... 57 F
Bleak Av *CUD/GR* S72 ...... 31 K
Bleakley Av *HOR/CROF* WF4 ...... 30 C
Bleakley Cl *CUD/GR* S72 ...... 31 K
Bleakley La *BSLYN/ROY* S71 ...... 30 C
Bleakley Ter *HOR/CROF* WF4 ...... 30 C
Bleasdale Gv *BSLYN/ROY* S71 ...... 3 D
Blenheim Av *BSLY* S70 ...... 2 B
Blenheim Cl *DIN* S25 ...... 178 A
  HTFD DN7 ...... 68 B1
  MALT S66 ...... 135 H
Blenheim Crs *MEX/SWTN* S64 ...... 112 C2
Blenheim Dr *EPW* DN9 ...... 120 E
Blenheim Gdns *ECC* S11 ...... 186 A2
Blenheim Ri *BWTY* DN10 ...... 164 A1
  WRKN S81 ...... 196 C
Blenheim Rd *BSLY* S70 ...... 2 A
  EPW DN9 ...... 120 E
  HTFD DN7 ...... 69 H
Blindside La *ST/HB/BR* S6 ...... 148 A
Bloemfontein St *CUD/GR* S72 ...... 57 H
Blonk St *OWL* S3 ...... 9 E
Bloomfield Ri *DOD/DAR* S75 ...... 29 F6
Bloomfield St *DOD/DAR* S75 ...... 28 E
Bloomhill Cl *THNE* DN8 ...... 23 K
Bloom Hill Gv *THNE* DN8 ...... 23 K
Bloomhill Rd *THNE* DN8 ...... 23 K
Bloomhouse La *DOD/DAR* S75 ...... 28 C
Blossom Av *AWLS/ASK* DN6 ...... 18 E
Blow Hall Crs *CONI* DN12 ...... 115 H
Blucher St *BSLY* S70 ...... 2 E
Bluebell Av *STKB/PEN* S36 ...... 77 K
Bluebell Cl *HOY* S74 ...... 108 D
  SHEFN S5 ...... 153 F
Blue Bell Ct *EPW* DN9 ...... 121 F
Bluebell Rd *DOD/DAR* S75 ...... 28 C
  SHEFN S5 ...... 153 C
Bluebird Ml *AU/AST/KP* S26 191
Blue Boy St *OWL* S3 ...... 8 C2
Blundell Cl *BSLYN/ROY* S71 ...... 56 E2
Blundell St *HEM/SK/SE* WF9 ...... 34 C4
Blyde Rd *SHEFN* S5 ...... 152 C
Bly Rd *WMB/DAR* S73 ...... 84 C
Blyth Av *RAW* S62 133
Blyth Cl *RHAM* S60 ...... 156 C
Blythe St *WMB/DAR* S73 ...... 83 H
Blyth Gate La *NROS/TKH* DN11 161
Blyth Gv *WRKN* S81 ...... 210 B
Blyth Rd *MALT* S66 159
  NROS/TKH DN11 ...... 162 E
  WRKN S81 187
  WRKN S81 190
  WRKN S81 ...... 210 D
Boardman Av *RAW* S62 ...... 111 F
Boating Dyke Wy *THNE* DN8 23
Boat La *BTLY* DN5 89
Bochum Pkwy *SHEFS* S8 187
Bocking Cl *SHEFS* S8 ...... 186 D
Bocking Hl *STKB/PEN* S36 ...... 105 C
Bocking La *SHEFS* S8 186
Bocking Ri *SHEFS* S8 ...... 186 E
Boden La *SHEF* S1 ...... 8 C5
Boden Pl *DARN/MH* S9 ...... 172 E2
Bodmin St *BSLYN/ROY* S71 ...... 3 B
Bodmin St *DARN/MH* S9 ...... 172 B1
Boggard La *CHPT/GREN* S35 150
  STKB/PEN S36 77
Boiley La *ECK/KIL* S21 205
Boland Rd *TOT/DORE* S17 200
Bold St *DARN/MH* S9 153
Bole Cl *WMB/DAR* S73 84
Bole Hl *RHAM* S60 174
Bolehill La *ECK/KIL* S21 203
  FUL S10 170
Bole Hill Rd *FUL* S10 169
Bolsover Rd *SHEFN* S5 152
Bolsover Rd East *ATT* S4 ...... 152 E6
Bolsover St *OWL* S3 8
Bolsterstone Rd *ST/HB/BR* S6 126
Bolton Hill Rd *DONS/BSCR* DN4 119
Bolton Rd *DEARNE* S63 86
Bolton St *CONI* DN12 114
  OWL S3 9
Bond Cl *DON* DN1 ...... 4 C4
Bondfield Av *NROS/TKH* DN11 119
Bondfield Crs *WMB/DAR* S73 83
Bondhay La *WRKS* S80 207
Bond Rd *DOD/DAR* S75 2
Bond St *NROS/TKH* DN11 119
  WMB/DAR S73 83
Bone La *AWLS/ASK* DN6 17
Bonemill La *WRKN* S81 210
Bonet La *RHAM* S60 154
Bonington Ri *MALT* S66 159
Booker Rd *SHEFS* S8 ...... 186 E5
Booker's La *DIN* S25 177
Bookers Wy *DIN* S25 177
Bootham Cl *HTFD* DN7 42
Bootham Crs *HTFD* DN7 42
Bootham La *HTFD* DN7 42
Bootham Rd *HTFD* DN7 42

ooth Cl MALT S66 .... 177 G1
   MOS S20 .... 190 B5
ooth Cft MOS S20 .... 190 B5
ooth House La HOLM/MEL HD7 ... 47 F3
ooth Pl RAW S62 .... 111 H7
ooth Rd CHPT/GREN S35 .... 107 H8
ooth St HOY S74 .... 109 F1 🔢
   KIMB S61 .... 132 E3
orough Rd ST/HB/BR S6 .... 151 J7
orrowdale La AWLS/ASK DN6 .... 57 H7
   BSLYN/ROY S71 .... 57 H7
   MOS S20 .... 204 C3 🔢
orrowdale Crs DIN S20 .... 178 B3
orrowdale Dr MOS S20 .... 190 B8
orrowdale Rd MOS S20 .... 204 C1
oston Castle Gv RHAM S60 .... 7 D6
oston St SHEFP/MNR S2 .... 8 C5
osville Cl RHAM/THRY S65 .... 135 J4 🔢
osville Rd FUL S10 .... 170 B4 🔢
osville St RHAM/THRY S65 .... 134 C7 🔢
   STKB/PEN S36 .... 78 B5
oswell Cl BSLYN/ROY S71 .... 30 C3 🔢
   CHPT/GREN S35 .... 107 H7
   NROS/TKH DN11 .... 118 D7
oswell Rd DEARNE S63 .... 111 J3
   DONS/BSCR DN4 .... 92 B8
oswell St RHAM/THRY S65 .... 7 E5
osworth Cl HTFD DN7 .... 68 B2 🔢
osworth St AWLS/ASK DN6 .... 63 H1
osworth St FUL S10 .... 170 C6
otanical Rd FUL S10 .... 170 C6
otany Bay La ARMTH DN3 .... 41 H8
otham St ATT S4 .... 153 F7
oughton Rd WRKS S80 .... 209 J2
oulder Bridge La CUD/GR S72 .... 31 C5
e Boulevard ARMTH DN3 .... 66 D5
oulton Dr ARMTH DN3 .... 93 G6
oundary Av WHHL DN2 .... 66 B8
oundary Cl CONI S63 .... 115 K4 🔢
oundary Cl CUD/GR S72 .... 32 D4 🔢
oundary Gn RAW S62 .... 133 J3
oundary Rd SHEFP/MNR S2 .... 172 A5
oundary Rw WRKS S80 .... 210 D5
oundary St BSLY S70 .... 3 E5
oundary Wk RHAM S60 .... 134 D7
ourne Cl DOD/DAR S75 .... 29 C5
ourne Mill Cl STV/CWN S43 .... 206 B8
ourne Rd BSLY S70 .... 82 A3
   SHEFN S5 .... 152 D3
ourne Wk DOD/DAR S75 .... 29 C5
owbridge Cl DRON S18 .... 6 B6 🔢
owden Gv DOD/DAR S75 .... 54 E8
owden Wood Av DARN/MH S9 ..... 172 E5
owden Wood Cl DARN/MH S9 ..... 172 E5 🔢
owden Wood Crs DARN/MH S9 .... 172 E5
owden Wood Dr DARN/MH S9 ..... 172 E5
owden Wood Pl DARN/MH S9 ..... 172 E5 🔢
owden Wood Rd DARN/MH S9 .... 172 E5
owdon St SHEF S1 .... 8 C4
owen Dr RHAM/THRY S65 .... 134 C5
owen Rd RHAM/THRY S65 .... 7 E2
ower Cl KIMB S61 .... 132 B6
ower Hl STKB/PEN S36 .... 79 F6
ower La CHPT/GREN S35 .... 129 C6
ower Rd FUL S10 .... 8 A2
   MEX/SWTN S64 .... 112 C3
ower Spring OWL S3 .... 9 D2 🔢
ower St OWL S3 .... 9 D2
ower V CONI S63 .... 115 H6 🔢
owfell Vw BSLYN/ROY S71 .... 3 D1
owfield Rd SHEFN S5 .... 152 D3
owland Cl BTLY DN5 .... 64 C7
owland Crs BSLY S70 .... 82 A3
owland Dr CHPT/GREN S35 .... 129 K2
owlease Gdns DONS/BSCR DN4 ..... 92 D7
owling Green St OWL S3 .... 9 D2
owman Cl HACK/IN S12 .... 188 B5
owman Dr HACK/IN S12 .... 188 B5
owness Cl DRON S18 .... 159 F1
owness Rd AWLS/ASK DN6 .... 19 F7
owness Rd ST/HB/BR S6 .... 151 H8
owood Rd ECC S11 .... 8 A6
owshaw Cl SHEFS S8 .... 201 G2
owshaw Cl SHEFS S8 .... 201 G2
owshaw Vw SHEFS S8 .... 201 G2
w St CUD/GR S72 .... 31 J8
oyce St ST/HB/BR S6 .... 8 A1
oyd Rd DEARNE S63 .... 111 J4
yland St OWL S3 .... 171 F1
ynton Crs SHEFN S5 .... 152 B5
ynton Rd SHEFN S5 .... 152 A5
abbs Rd HTFD DN7 .... 42 D7
acebridge WRKS S80 .... 210 E5
acebridge Av WRKS S80 .... 211 F4
acebridge Gv WRKS S80 .... 210 E5
ackenbury Cl BTLY DN5 .... 114 E1 🔢
acken Cl ARMTH DN3 .... 93 K6
acken Cl MALT S66 .... 157 G4
ackenfield Gv HACK/IN S12 .... 189 F3
acken Heen La HTFD DN7 .... 42 D7 🔢
acken Hl CHPT/GREN S35 .... 129 J3
   HEM/SK/SE WF9 .... 34 C5
acken Hill La BWTY DN10 .... 143 H1
acken Moor La STKB/PEN S36 ..... 105 F7
acken Rd SHEFN S5 .... 153 F3
acken Wy NROS/TKH DN11 .... 162 C5

Brackley St OWL S3 .... 171 H1
Bradberry Balk La WMB/DAR S73 ... 83 K3
Bradbury's Cl RAW S62 .... 133 J4 🔢
Bradbury St BSLY S70 .... 2 A4
   SHEFS S8 .... 187 G1 🔢
Bradfield Rd ST/HB/BR S6 .... 151 H7
Bradgate Cl KIMB S61 .... 132 D8
Bradgate La KIMB S61 .... 132 C8
Bradgate La KIMB S61 .... 132 C8
Bradgate Pl KIMB S61 .... 132 D7
Bradgate Rd KIMB S61 .... 132 D8
Bradley Av WMB/DAR S73 .... 83 K4 🔢
Bradley Carr Ter HEM/SK/SE WF9 ... 34 D7
Bradley St FUL S10 .... 170 B2
Bradmarsh Wy RHAM S60 .... 6 B6
Bradshaw Av RHAM S60 .... 174 B1
Bradshaw Rd DOD/DAR S75 .... 55 F5 🔢
Bradshaw Rd HOLM/MEL HD7 .... 46 E1
Bradshaw Wy RHAM S60 .... 174 D4 🔢
Bradstone Rd RHAM/THRY S65 .... 134 B8
Bradway Cl TOT/DORE S17 .... 200 B2 🔢
Bradway Dr TOT/DORE S17 .... 200 B2
Bradway Grange Rd
   TOT/DORE S17 .... 200 C2 🔢
Bradway Grange Rd TOT/DORE S17 .. 200 B2
Bradwell Av DOD/DAR S75 .... 81 F2
Bradwell Cl DRON S18 .... 200 C6
Bradwell St SHEFP/MNR S2 .... 171 H8
Braemar Rd WHHL DN2 .... 91 K4 🔢
Braemore Rd ST/HB/BR S6 .... 151 F6
Brailsford Av SHEFN S5 .... 130 B7
Brailsford Rd SHEFN S5 .... 130 B7
Braithwaite La HTFD DN7 .... 20 E8
   HTFD DN7 .... 40 E2
Braithwell Rd BTLY DN5 .... 64 D5
   RHAM/THRY S65 .... 159 G1
Braithwell Wy MALT S66 .... 158 B1
Bramah St BSLYN/ROY S71 .... 30 D6
Bramall La SHEFP/MNR S2 .... 9 D5
   STKB/PEN S36 .... 104 C5
Bramble Cl MALT S66 .... 157 G4 🔢
The Brambles CHPT/GREN S35 ..... 130 B7
Bramble Wy DEARNE S63 .... 110 E1
   EPW DN9 .... 120 B3
   NROS/TKH DN11 .... 162 D5
The Bramblings DONS/BSCR DN4 .. 119 F2
   WRKN S81 .... 196 A8
Bramcote Av BSLYN/ROY S71 .... 29 K7 🔢
Brameld Rd MEX/SWTN S64 .... 112 C4 🔢
   RAW S62 .... 133 J2
Bramham Ct DARN/MH S9 .... 172 D7 🔢
Bramham Rd DARN/MH S9 .... 172 D2 🔢
   DONS/BSCR DN4 .... 92 E5
Bramley Av AU/AST/KP S26 .... 75 C7
   HAN/WDH S13 .... 173 H7
Bramley Cl MOS S20 .... 204 A1
Bramley Dr HAN/WDH S13 .... 173 H6
Bramley Grange Crs MALT S66 .... 157 K2 🔢
Bramley Grange Dr MALT S66 ..... 157 K2 🔢
Bramley Grange Ri MALT S66 ...... 157 K2 🔢
Bramley Grange Vw MALT S66 .... 157 K1
Bramley Grange Wy MALT S66 .... 157 J2
Bramley Hall Rd HAN/WDH S13 .... 173 H7
Bramley La HAN/WDH S13 .... 173 H6
   MALT S66 .... 136 B7
Bramleymoor La ECK/KIL S21 ...... 203 G6
Bramley Park Cl HAN/WDH S13 .... 173 H7
Bramley Park Rd HAN/WDH S13 ... 173 H6
Bramley Wy ECK/KIL S21 .... 203 G6
Brampton Av MALT S66 .... 158 B1
Brampton Cl ARMTH DN3 .... 93 F2
Brampton La HEM/SK/SE WF9 .... 35 F2 🔢
   MOS S20 .... 189 J5 🔢
Brampton Crs WMB/DAR S73 .... 84 C6
Brampton La ARMTH DN3 .... 93 F2
Brampton Mdw MALT S66 .... 176 D1
Brampton Rd DEARNE S63 .... 84 E8
   MALT S66 .... 176 D1
   WMB/DAR S73 .... 84 C6
Brampton St WMB/DAR S73 .... 84 C6
Brampton Vw WMB/DAR S73 .... 84 C6 🔢
Bramshill Cl MOS S20 .... 190 E6 🔢
Bramshill La MOS S20 .... 190 E6 🔢
Bramwell Cl OWL S3 .... 8 B2
Bramwell St OWL S3 .... 7 D3
   RHAM/THRY S65 .... 7 D3
Bramwith La ARMTH DN3 .... 40 D7
   HTFD DN7 .... 40 E5
Bramwith Rd ECC S11 .... 169 K7 🔢
Bramworth Rd DONS/BSCR DN4 .... 90 C6
Brancliffe La WRKN S81 .... 195 H7
Brandeth Rd ST/HB/BR S6 .... 8 B1
Brand La BTLY DN5 .... 89 J3
Brandon St OWL S3 .... 152 C8 🔢
Brandreth Cl ST/HB/BR S6 .... 8 B1
Brands Cl WRKN S81 .... 195 G2
Brand's La DIN S25 .... 178 D8
Brandsmere Dr WRKN S81 .... 195 G2
Branksome Av BSLY S70 .... 55 H6
Bransby St ST/HB/BR S6 .... 8 A1 🔢
Bransdale WRKN S81 .... 196 E7
Branstone Rd BTLY DN5 .... 89 J5
Branton Gate Rd or
   Whiphill Top La ARMTH DN3 .... 93 K5
Brantwood Crs DONS/BSCR DN4 .... 92 E6
Brathay Cl ATT S4 .... 153 C6

Brathay Rd ATT S4 .... 153 G6 🔢
Bray St DARN/MH S9 .... 172 C2 🔢
Brayton Gdns AWLS/ASK DN6 .... 17 K6
Brearley Av STKB/PEN S36 .... 105 G7
Brechin WRKN S81 .... 211 F2
Brecklands MALT S66 .... 157 F3
   RHAM/THRY S65 .... 156 B3
Breck La BWTY DN10 .... 165 H8
   DIN S25 .... 178 B5
   ECK/KIL S21 .... 204 A3
Brecks Crs RHAM/THRY S65 .... 156 D2
Brecks La ARMTH DN3 .... 67 F3
   RHAM/THRY S65 .... 134 C8
Brecon Cl MOS S20 .... 190 E5
Breezemount Ct HTFD DN7 .... 42 A3 🔢
Brendon Cl WMB/DAR S73 .... 84 C6
Brentwood Av ECC S11 .... 186 D1 🔢
Brentwood Cl HOY S74 .... 108 D2 🔢
Brentwood Rd ECC S11 .... 186 D1
Bressingham Cl ATT S4 .... 171 J1 🔢
Bressingham Rd ATT S4 .... 171 H1
Bretby Cl DONS/BSCR DN4 .... 92 E8
Brett Cl RAW S62 .... 111 F7
Bretton Cl DOD/DAR S75 .... 28 B7
   HTFD DN7 .... 68 B1
Bretton Gv HACK/IN S12 .... 189 F4
Bretton Rd DOD/DAR S75 .... 28 C7
Bretton Vw CUD/GR S72 .... 57 H2
Brewery La BWTY DN10 .... 165 K4
Brewery Rd DEARNE S63 .... 85 H8
Breydon Av BTLY DN5 .... 90 B2
Briar Cl EPW DN9 .... 120 B3
   WRKS S80 .... 210 A5
Briar Ct HOLM/MEL HD7 .... 47 G3
   MALT S66 .... 157 F4
   NROS/TKH DN11 .... 162 D3
Briar Cft DONS/BSCR DN4 .... 4 A6
Briarfield Av HACK/IN S12 .... 188 C4
Briarfield Crs HACK/IN S12 .... 188 C5
Briarfields La CHPT/GREN S35 ..... 150 B2
Briar Gv CUD/GR S72 .... 32 D4
   STKB/PEN S36 .... 78 A5
Briar Lea WRKS S80 .... 210 A5
Briar Ri BSLY S70 .... 82 B3
Briar Rd ABRD S7 .... 186 E1
   ARMTH DN3 .... 67 F8
   AWLS/ASK DN6 .... 37 H6
Briars Cl ECK/KIL S21 .... 205 H2
Briars La HTFD DN7 .... 42 A2
Briary Av CHPT/GREN S35 .... 107 J3
Briary Cl RHAM S60 .... 155 F8
Brickhouse La TOT/DORE S17 ...... 185 G7
Brick Kiln La AWLS/ASK DN6 .... 20 A7
Brick St FUL S10 .... 170 B3
Bridby St HAN/WDH S13 .... 190 A1
Bride Church La NROS/TKH DN11 . 139 K8
Bridge Cl KBTN HD8 .... 26 B5 🔢
Bridgedate RHAM S60 .... 6 C3
Bridge Gv BTLY DN5 .... 90 C2
Bridge Hl HTFD DN7 .... 41 K3 🔢
Bridge Inn Rd CHPT/GREN S35 .... 130 B1
Bridgelake Dr DONS/BSCR DN4 ... 116 E3
Bridge La GLE DN14 .... 11 J4
   HOLM/MEL HD7 .... 47 K1
Bridge Pl WRKS S80 .... 210 D4
Bridge Rd DONS/BSCR DN4 .... 92 B7
Bridge St BSLY S70 .... 57 F7 🔢
   BSLYN/ROY S71 .... 2 C3
   DOD/DAR S75 .... 28 D6
   DONS/BSCR DN4 .... 4 B4
   ECK/KIL S21 .... 191 H8
   MEX/SWTN S64 .... 112 D2
   OWL S3 .... 9 E2
   RHAM S60 .... 7 F5
   STKB/PEN S36 .... 77 K3
   THNE DN8 .... 23 J8
   WRKS S80 .... 210 C5
Bridgewater Park Dr
   AWLS/ASK DN6 .... 37 G5
Bridle Cl CHPT/GREN S35 .... 130 B1
Bridle Crs CHPT/GREN S35 .... 130 B1
Bridle Stile MOS S20 .... 190 A8
Bridle Stile Cl MOS S20 .... 190 A8 🔢
Bridle Stile Gdns MOS S20 .... 189 K8
The Bridleway RAW S62 .... 112 B8
Bridport Rd DARN/MH S9 .... 172 D2
Brier Cl MOS S20 .... 190 B6
Brierey Cl DOD/DAR S75 .... 29 F7
Brierfield Rd DOD/DAR S75 .... 55 H5
Brierfield Rd HACK/IN S12 .... 188 C4
Brierholme Carr Rd HTFD DN7 ...... 43 G7
Brierholme Cl HTFD DN7 .... 43 F6
Brierholme Ings Rd HTFD DN7 ...... 43 G7
Brierley Crs HEM/SK/SE WF9 .... 34 B4
Brierley Rd CUD/GR S72 .... 32 A5
   DONS/BSCR DN4 .... 92 C8
Brierly Rd RHAM/THRY S65 .... 134 D6
Briers House La ST/HB/BR S6 .... 149 G6
Brier St ST/HB/BR S6 .... 151 H7 🔢
Briggs Rd BSLYN/ROY S71 .... 30 D6
Brightholmlee Ct
   CHPT/GREN S35 .... 128 A5 🔢
Brightholmlee La CHPT/GREN S35.. 127 K4
Brightholmlee Rd
   CHPT/GREN S35 .... 127 J5
Bright Meadow MOS S20 .... 204 E2
Brightmore Dr OWL S3 .... 8 B3 🔢
Brighton St CUD/GR S72 .... 32 D8
Brighton Terrace Rd FUL S10 .... 170 C3

Brightside La DARN/MH S9 .... **172** A1
Brightside Wy ATT S4 .... **153** G7
Brimmesfield Dr
  SHEFP/MNR S2 .... **172** A7 🔟
Brimmesfield Rd SHEFP/MNR S2 ... **172** B8
Brimmsfield Cl SHEFP/MNR S2 .... **172** B8
Brinckman St BSLY S70 .... **2** C5
Brincliffe Crs ECC S11 .... **170** C8
Brincliffe Edge Cl ECC S11 .... **186** C1
Brincliffe Edge Rd ECC S11 .... **186** B1
Brincliffe Gdns ECC S11 .... **170** C8
Brincliffe Hl ECC S11 .... **170** B8
Brindley Cl SHEFS S8 .... **187** G3
Brindley Ct SHEFS S8 .... **187** G3 🔟
Brindley Crs SHEFS S8 .... **187** G3
Brinkburn Cl TOT/DORE S17 ...... **199** K1 🔟
Brinkburn Dr TOT/DORE S17 ...... **199** K1
Brinkburn Vale Rd TOT/DORE S17 .. **199** K1
Brinsford Rd RHAM S60 .... **155** F6
Brinsworth Hall Av RHAM S60 ..... **154** E7
Brinsworth Hall Crs RHAM S60 .... **154** E7
Brinsworth Hall Dr RHAM S60 ..... **154** E7
Brinsworth Hall Gv RHAM S60 ..... **154** E7
Brinsworth La RHAM S60 .... **154** E7
Brinsworth Rd DARN/MH S9 .... **154** D7
  RHAM S60 .... **174** A1
Brinsworth St DARN/MH S9 .... **172** B1
  RHAM S60 .... **6** B5
Bristol Gv WHHL DN2 .... **91** K1
Bristol Rd ECC S11 .... **170** C6
Britain St MEX/SWTN S64 .... **112** E3 🔟
Britannia Cl BSLY S70 .... **2** C5 🔟
Britannia Rd DARN/MH S9 .... **172** E5
Britland Cl DOD/DAR S75 .... **55** F5 🔟
Britnall St DARN/MH S9 .... **172** C1
Briton Sq DEARNE S63 .... **60** D6
Briton St DEARNE S63 .... **60** D6
Brittain St SHEF S1 .... **9** E4 🔟
Broachgate BTLY DN5 .... **64** B7
Broadbent Gate Rd THNE DN8 ..... **25** K6
Broad Bridge Cl AU/AST/KP S26 ... **192** E5
Broadcarr Rd HOY S74 .... **108** C2
Broadcroft Cl MOS S20 .... **190** E4
Broad Dyke Cl AU/AST/KP S26 .... **193** H1
Broad Elms Cl ECC S11 .... **185** K3 🔟
Broad Elms La ECC S11 .... **185** J4
Broadfield Pk HOLM/MEL HD7 ..... **47** F5
Broadfield Rd SHEFS S8 .... **187** F1
Broadgate House Cl KIMB S61 .... **132** C8 🔟
Broad Gates DOD/DAR S75 .... **53** J7
Broadhead Dr STKB/PEN S36 ...... **105** G6
Broad Inge Crs CHPT/GREN S35 .. **129** K2
Broad Ings La ARMTH DN3 .... **40** C5
Broadlands MALT S66 .... **157** K3
Broadlands Av FUL S10 .... **169** F8
Broadlands Crs FUL S10 .... **169** G8
Broadlands Dr FUL S10 .... **169** F8 🔟
Broadlands Rd AWLS/ASK DN6 .... **37** K8
Broadlands Wy DIN S25 .... **177** K6
Broad La GLE DN14 .... **21** G2
  HEM/SK/SE WF9 .... **33** K6
  HOLM/MEL HD7 .... **47** G2
  SHEF S1 .... **8** C3
Broad Lane Ct SHEF S1 .... **8** C3 🔟
Broadley Rd HAN/WDH S13 ...... **172** D8
Broad Oak La NROS/TKH DN11 ... **139** G7
  STKB/PEN S36 .... **52** A6
Broad Oaks DARN/MH S9 .... **172** A3
Broadoaks Cl DIN S25 .... **178** A6 🔟
Broadoaks La DIN S25 .... **178** A6 🔟
Broad Riding MALT S66 .... **138** B6
Broadstone Rd KBTN HD8 .... **50** A3
Broad St HOY S74 .... **108** E1
  RAW S62 .... **133** J4
  SHEF S1 .... **9** E2
  SHEFP/MNR S2 .... **9** F2
Broad Street La SHEFP/MNR S2 ... **9** F2
Broadwater DEARNE S63 .... **86** A6 🔟
Broadwater Dr HTFD DN7 .... **42** B8 🔟
  HTFD DN7 .... **68** B1 🔟
Broadway BSLY S70 .... **22** C6
  DOD/DAR S75 .... **29** G7
  HEM/SK/SE WF9 .... **34** D6
  HTFD DN7 .... **42** B7
  HTFD DN7 .... **68** A1
  MEX/SWTN S64 .... **112** A5
  RHAM S60 .... **154** E8
  RHAM/THRY S65 .... **134** A8
Broadway Av CHPT/GREN S35 .... **130** C3
Broadway Cl MEX/SWTN S64 ..... **112** A5
Broadway East RHAM/THRY S65 .. **134** A8
The Broadway DONS/BSCR DN4 ... **116** C2
Brocco Bank ECC S11 .... **170** C7
Brocco Cl OWL S3 .... **8** C2
Brocco St OWL S3 .... **8** C2 🔟
Brockenhurst Rd HTFD DN7 ...... **42** E3 🔟
Brockfield Cl DIN S25 .... **82** B2 🔟
Brockholes La ARMTH DN3 .... **93** J8
  STKB/PEN S36 .... **77** H8
Brockhurst Wy RHAM/THRY S65 .. **134** E5
Brockhurst Rd BSLY S70 .... **82** E1
  SHEFS S8 .... **187** J7
Brockwood Cl HAN/WDH S13 ... **174** A8 🔟
Broc-o-bank AWLS/ASK DN6 ..... **17** K4
Brodsworth Wy NROS/TKH DN11 .. **119** G7
Bromcliffe Pk BSLYN/ROY S71 .... **57** F2
Bromley Carr Rd CHPT/GREN S35 .. **107** G6

Brompton Rd BTLY DN5 .... **89** K6
  DARN/MH S9 .... **153** H8
Bromwich Rd SHEFS S8 .... **186** E5
Bronte Av DONS/BSCR DN4 ...... **116** C1
Bronte Cl BSLY S70 .... **3** E2
Bronte Gv HEM/SK/SE WF9 ...... **33** F1
  MEX/SWTN S64 .... **113** G1
Bronte Pl RAW S62 .... **112** A8
Brook Cl DIN S25 .... **193** K2
Brook Cft DIN S25 .... **8** B2
Brooke Cl WRKN S81 .... **211** G3
Brooke Dr DEARNE S63 .... **111** G1
Brooke St DON DN1 .... **5** D1
  HOY S74 .... **108** E1
  THNE DN8 .... **23** H7
Brook Farm Ms DEARNE S63 ..... **111** H1 🔟
Brookfield Av MEX/SWTN S64 .... **112** C5
Brookfield Cl ARMTH DN3 .... **93** G2 🔟
  RHAM/THRY S65 .... **134** C6
  THNE DN8 .... **23** H7
Brookfield Rd SHEFS S8 .... **171** F8 🔟
Brookhaven Wy MALT S66 .... **157** K3
Brook Hl KIMB S61 .... **131** C3
  OWL S3 .... **8** B3
Brook Hill La STKB/PEN S36 ..... **74** E4
Brookhill Rd DOD/DAR S75 ...... **28** A7
Brookhouse Cl HACK/IN S12 ..... **189** K4
Brookhouse Dr HACK/IN S12 ..... **189** K4
Brookhouse Hl ECC S11 .... **169** G8
Brookhouse La DIN S25 .... **177** J1
Brook House La STKB/PEN S36 ... **76** A8
  STKB/PEN S36 .... **102** A1
Brookhouse Rd AU/AST/KP S26 .. **191** H1
Brooklands MALT S66 .... **158** D5
Brooklands Av FUL S10 .... **169** F8
Brooklands Crs FUL S10 .... **169** G8
Brooklands Dr FUL S10 .... **169** F8 🔟
Brooklands Wy DIN S25 .... **177** K6
Brook La CHPT/GREN S35 .... **128** B8
  CHPT/GREN S35 .... **129** H7
  HACK/IN S12 .... **189** K4
  MALT S66 .... **157** J1
  OWL S3 .... **8** B3
Brooklyn Pl SHEFS S8 .... **187** G2 🔟
Brooklyn Rd SHEFS S8 .... **187** G2 🔟
Brook Rd CHPT/GREN S35 .... **129** K1
  CONI DN12 .... **115** F5 🔟
  RHAM/THRY S65 .... **134** C3
  SHEFS S8 .... **187** F2
Brook Rw STKB/PEN S36 .... **105** F7
Brooksfield HEM/SK/SE WF9 ..... **34** C3
Brookside CONI DN12 .... **114** D6 🔟
  MEX/SWTN S64 .... **112** A6
  RHAM/THRY S65 .... **156** B2
Brookside Bank Rd ST/HB/BR S6 . **168** B2
Brookside Cl HACK/IN S12 ...... **189** K4
Brookside Crs DEARNE S63 ...... **110** B3
Brookside Dr BSLY S70 .... **82** E1
Brookside La ST/HB/BR S6 ...... **168** D1
Brookside Ms HEM/SK/SE WF9 .. **34** E4
Brook St ECK/KIL S21 .... **205** G8
  RHAM S60 .... **156** A6 🔟
Brook Ter WRKS S80 .... **210** C5
Brookvale BSLYN/ROY S71 .... **56** E4 🔟
Brookview Ct DRON S18 .... **201** G4
Brook Wy BTLY DN5 .... **65** G6
Broom Av RHAM/THRY S65 ...... **156** A3
Broombank KBTN HD8 .... **51** G2
Broom Cl BSLY S70 .... **82** E1
  DEARNE S63 .... **89** F6
  DOD/DAR S75 .... **8** C5
  ECC S11 .... **140** A8
  NROS/TKH DN11 .... **140** A8
Broom Ct HTFD DN7 .... **42** B8
Broom Crs RHAM/THRY S65 ..... **7** E6
Broomcroft Pk ECC S11 .... **185** K4 🔟
Broom Dr RHAM S60 .... **156** A4
Broome Av MEX/SWTN S64 ...... **112** C4
Broomfield Cl BSLY S70 .... **55** G7 🔟
Broomfield Ct STKB/PEN S36 .... **105** G7 🔟
Broomfield Gv RHAM/THRY S65 .. **7** F6
  STKB/PEN S36 .... **105** F6
Broomfield La FUL S10 .... **8** A4
  STKB/PEN S36 .... **105** G6
Broom Gn OWL S3 .... **8** C4
Broom Gv DIN S25 .... **193** K4
  RHAM/THRY S65 .... **7** E5
Broomgrove Crs FUL S10 .... **8** A4 🔟
Broomgrove La FUL S10 .... **8** A4
Broomgrove Rd FUL S10 .... **8** A4
Broomhall Pl FUL S10 .... **8** B4
Broomhall Rd FUL S10 .... **8** B4
Broomhall St OWL S3 .... **8** C4 🔟
Broomhead Cl DOD/DAR S75 .... **29** G7 🔟
Broomhead Rd WMB/DAR S73 ... **84** C6
Broomhill Av WRKN S81 .... **196** C4
Broomhill Av WRKN S81 .... **26** A1 🔟
Broomhill Cl ECK/KIL S21 .... **203** K4
  HOLM/MEL HD7 .... **48** C4
Broom Hill Dr DONS/BSCR DN4 .. **92** E8
Broomhill La DEARNE S63 .... **85** F4
Broomhill Vw DEARNE S63 ...... **86** A6
Broomhouse Cl KBTN HD8 ...... **51** H2
Broomhouse La CONI DN12 ..... **115** J6

DONS/BSCR DN4 .... **116** C2
Broom La RHAM/THRY S65 ...... **7** F6
Broom Riddings KIMB S61 ...... **132** E8 🔟
Broom Rd RHAM/THRY S65 ...... **7** E6
Broomroyd BSLY S70 .... **82** C3
Broom Royd CHPT/GREN S35 ... **128** A4
Broomspring Cl OWL S3 .... **8** B4 🔟
Broomspring La FUL S10 .... **8** B4 🔟
  OWL S3 .... **8** C4 🔟
Broom St FUL S10 .... **8** B4
Broom Ter RHAM/THRY S65 ..... **7** D6
Broomvale Wk CONI DN12 ...... **115** H6
Broom Valley Rd RHAM S60 ..... **7** E6
  RHAM/THRY S65 .... **7** D5
Broomville St MEX/SWTN S64 ... **112** D4 🔟
Broomwood Cl MOS S20 .... **190** E4 🔟
Broomwood Gdns MOS S20 ..... **190** E4
Brosley Av ARMTH DN3 .... **40** E8
Brotherton St OWL S3 .... **171** H7
Broughton Av BTLY DN5 .... **64** D8
Broughton La DARN/MH S9 ..... **153** J3
Broughton Rd DONS/BSCR DN4 . **118** D1 🔟
  ST/HB/BR S6 .... **151** H1
Brow Cl BSLY S70 .... **82** A7
Brow Crs MOS S20 .... **190** C8
Brow Hill Rd MALT S66 .... **159** F7
Brow La HOLM/MEL HD7 .... **47** H6
  KBTN HD8 .... **52** A7
Browell St OWL S3 .... **8** C2
Brownhill La HOLM/MEL HD7 ... **46** E6
Brown Hills La FUL S10 .... **168** C5
Brown House La ST/HB/BR S6 ... **148** E5
Browning Av DONS/BSCR DN4 .. **116** E1
Browning Cl BSLYN/ROY S71 .... **56** C2 🔟
  ST/HB/BR S6 .... **151** J2
  WRKN S81 .... **211** E5
Browning Dr RHAM/THRY S65 .. **156** A1 🔟
  ST/HB/BR S6 .... **151** J2
Browning Rd ARMTH DN3 .... **40** E7
  DEARNE S63 .... **85** F7
  MEX/SWTN S64 .... **113** F1
  RHAM/THRY S65 .... **156** A5
  ST/HB/BR S6 .... **151** H1
Brown La DRON S18 .... **201** J1
  SHEF S1 .... **9** D
The Brow RHAM/THRY S65 ...... **156** D6
Brow Vw DEARNE S63 .... **86** A1
Broxholme La DON DN1 .... **5** D6
Broxholme Rd SHEFS S8 .... **187** F4 🔟
Bruce Av BSLY S70 .... **82** A7
Bruce Crs WHHL DN2 .... **92** A8
Bruce Rd ECC S11 .... **8** A6
Brunel Cl NROS/TKH DN11 ...... **162** E5
Brunel Ga NROS/TKH DN11 ..... **162** E5
Brunel Rd BTLY DN5 .... **90** C2
Brunswick Cl BSLYN/ROY S71 ... **56** A4
Brunswick Rd OWL S3 .... **9** F4
  RHAM S60 .... **7** E4
Brunswick St DEARNE S63 ...... **60** D8
  FUL S10 .... **8** B4
Brunt Rd RAW S62 .... **134** A4
Brushfield Gv HACK/IN S12 ..... **189** F4
Bryans Close La BWTY DN10 .... **143** G5
Bryony Cl ECK/KIL S21 .... **205** F5
Bubup Hl NROS/TKH DN11 ...... **117** F7
Bubwith Rd DARN/MH S9 .... **153** J5
Buchanan Crs SHEFN S5 .... **151** K1
Buchanan Dr SHEFN S5 .... **151** K1
Buchanan Rd SHEFN S5 .... **152** A3
Buckden Rd BSLY S70 .... **2** A3
Buckenham St ATT S4 .... **171** J2
Buckingham Cl DRON S18 ...... **200** D5 🔟
Buckingham Ri WRKN S81 ...... **196** B3
Buckingham Rd CONI DN12 ..... **114** C3
  WHHL DN2 .... **5** F4
Buckingham Wy BSLYN/ROY S71 .. **30** C
  MALT S66 .... **159** H
  RHAM S60 .... **155** G7
Buckleigh Dr DEARNE S63 ...... **111** H
Buckley Ct BSLY S70 .... **2** C5
Buckthorn Cl MEX/SWTN S64 ... **112** B
Buck Wood Vw SHEFP/MNR S2 .. **187** K6
Bude Ct BSLYN/ROY S71 .... **56** B3
Bude Rd DONS/BSCR DN4 .... **4** B
Bud La CHPT/GREN S35 .... **127** H
Bullcroft Cl AWLS/ASK DN6 ..... **37** K
Bullen Rd ST/HB/BR S6 .... **151** H
Bullenshaw Rd HEM/SK/SE WF9 .. **33** C
Bullfinch Cl RHAM S60 .... **155** C
Bull Haw La DOD/DAR S75 ...... **53** J7
Bullhouse La STKB/PEN S36 .... **76** D
Bull La HTFD DN7 .... **43** H7
Bull La HEM/SK/SE WF9 .... **34** E
Bull Moor Rd HTFD DN7 .... **43**
Bull Yd WRKS S80 .... **210** C5
Bungalow Rd CONI DN12 .... **115**
The Bungalows KBTN HD8 ...... **26** E
  RHAM S60 .... **174** C
Bunker S Hl ECK/KIL S21 .... **205**
Bunkers Hl HOLM/MEL HD7 ..... **47** H
Bunting Cl SHEFS S8 .... **187**
Bunting Nook SHEFS S8 .... **187** F
Burbage Cl DRON S18 .... **200** D5

Burbage Gv HACK/IN S12 .... 189 F2
Burcot Rd SHEFS S8 .... 187 F2
Burcroft Cl HOY S71 .... 57 J4
Burcroft Hl CONI DN12 .... 114 E4
Burford Av DONS/BSCR DN4 .... 116 B2
Burford Crs AU/AST/KP S26 ... 175 J8 🆘
Burgar Rd THNE DN8 .... 43 J2
Burgen Rd KIMB S61 .... 132 B6 🆘
Burgess Rd DARN/MH S9 .... 172 B1
Burgess St SHEF S1 .... 9 D3
Burghwallis La AWLS/ASK DN6 ..... 37 K2
Burghwallis Rd AWLS/ASK DN6 ..... 17 K8
Burgley Cl DIN S25 .... 178 A7 🆘
Burgoyne Cl ST/HB/BR S6 .... 170 D1
Burgoyne Rd ST/HB/BR S6 .... 170 D1
Burkinshaw Av RAW S62 .... 111 J7
Burleigh Ct BSLY S70 .... 2 C4 🆘
Burleigh Rd ST/HB/BR S6 .... 8 B1 🆘
Burleigh St THNE DN8 .... 2 C4
Burn Gv CHPT/GREN S35 .... 179 J6
Burlington Ar BSLY S70 .... 2 C4 🆘
Burlington Cl ST/HB/BR S6 .... 8 B1 🆘
Burlington Gln TOT/DORE S17 ..... 185 J8 🆘
Burlington Gv TOT/DORE S17 ...... 185 J8
Burlington Rd TOT/DORE S17 ...... 185 J8
Burlington St ST/HB/BR S6 .... 8 B1
Burman Rd DEARNE S63 .... 111 J1
Burnaby Ct ST/HB/BR S6 .... 151 J8
Burnaby Crs ST/HB/BR S6 .... 151 J8
Burnaby Grn ST/HB/BR S6 .... 151 J8
Burnaby St ST/HB/BR S6 .... 151 J8
Burnaston Cl DRON S18 .... 200 C6 🆘
Burncross Dr CHPT/GREN S35 ...... 130 A2
Burncross Rd CHPT/GREN S35 ...... 129 K2
Burnell Rd ST/HB/BR S6 .... 151 H7
Burngreave Bank ATT S4 .... 171 H1
Burngreave Rd ATT S4 .... 152 C8
Burngreave St ATT S4 .... 171 H1
Burn Gv CHPT/GREN S35 .... 130 D3
Burnham Av DOD/DAR S75 .... 29 G8
Burnham Cl DONS/BSCR DN4 .... 92 A8
Burnham Wy WMB/DAR S73 .... 84 C2
Burnlee Rd HOLM/MEL HD7 .... 47 H3
Burn Pl BSLY/ROY S71 .... 29 K8 🆘
Burnsall Crs RHAM S60 .... 155 F7
Burnsall Gv BSLY S70 .... 2 B6
Burns Av HEM/SK/SE WF9 .... 33 J6
Burns Cl CHPT/GREN S35 .... 130 A2
DRON S18 .... 201 J7
RHAM/THRY S65 .... 156 A1
Burnside DEARNE S63 .... 60 B6
Burnside Av SHEFS S8 .... 187 G2
Burnside Dr HOLM/MEL HD7 .... 47 H3
Burns Rd ARMTH DN3 .... 40 E7 🆘
DIN S25 .... 178 C7
DONS/BSCR DN4 .... 116 E1 🆘
MALT S66 .... 159 H4
RHAM/THRY S65 .... 7 F4
ST/HB/BR S6 .... 8 A2
WRKN S81 .... 211 F3
Burns St BTLY DN5 .... 64 E6
Burns Wy DEARNE S63 .... 85 F8
DONS/BSCR DN4 .... 4 A6
Burnt Hill La CHPT/GREN S35 ...... 149 K2
Burnt Stones Cl FUL S10 .... 169 H5
Burnt Stones Dr FUL S10 .... 169 H5
Burnt Stones Gv FUL S10 ..... 169 H5 🆘
Burnt Tree La OWL S3 .... 8 C2 🆘
Burntwood Av HEM/SK/SE WF9 ..... 34 B5
Burntwood Bank HEM/SK/SE WF9 .. 33 G2
Burntwood Cl DEARNE S63 .... 60 A8
Burntwood Crs RHAM S60 ..... 174 C2 🆘
Burntwood Dr HEM/SK/SE WF9 ..... 34 A5
Burntwood Gv HEM/SK/SE WF9 ..... 34 B5
Burnt Wood La CUD/GR S72 .... 33 H6
Burntwood Rd CUD/GR S72 .... 58 E1
Burrell St RHAM S60 .... 6 C4
Burrowlee Rd ST/HB/BR S6 .... 151 H6
Burrows Dr SHEFN S5 .... 152 B5
Burrows Gv WRKN S81 .... 83 J5
Burrs La WRKN S81 .... 179 H7
Burton Av BSLY/ROY S71 .... 56 E3
DONS/BSCR DN4 .... 4 B6
Burton Bank Rd BSLY/ROY S71 ..... 3 D2 🆘
Burton Crs BSLY/ROY S71 .... 57 F2
Burton La CHPT/GREN S35 .... 150 B1
Burtonlees Ct DONS/BSCR DN4 ..... 92 D8 🆘
Burton St BSLY/ROY S71 .... 3 F2
BTLY DN5 .... 2 B2 🆘
HEM/SK/SE WF9 .... 33 J1
ST/HB/BR S6 .... 151 J8
Burton Ter DONS/BSCR DN4 .... 4 B6 🆘
Burtop Cft WMB/DAR S73 .... 83 K8 🆘
Burying La RAW S62 .... 109 F4
Bushey Wood Rd TOT/DORE S17 ... 199 J1
Bushfield Rd DEARNE S63 .... 111 G2
Bush St HEM/SK/SE WF9 .... 33 H1 🆘
Buskler La KBTN HD8 .... 26 A6
Busk Knoll SHEFN S5 .... 152 B5 🆘
Busk Meadow SHEFN S5 .... 152 B5
Busk Pk SHEFN S5 .... 152 B5
Busley Gdns BTLY DN5 .... 64 D7 🆘
Butcher St DEARNE S63 .... 60 B7
Butchill Av SHEFN S5 .... 130 B7
Bute St FUL S10 .... 170 B4
Butler Rd ST/HB/BR S6 .... 151 F8
Butler Rd ECK/KIL S21 .... 191 G8
Butten Meadow BWTY DN10 .... 142 D5

Butterbusk CONI DN12 .... 115 F5
Buttercross DN HACK/IN S12 .... 37 H6 🆘
Buttercross Cl AWLS/ASK DN6 ...... 37 H5 🆘
Buttercross Dr CUD/GR S72 .... 59 F7
Butterfield Cl GLE DN14 .... 13 J1
Butterfield La WMB/DAR S73 ..... 84 D7 🆘
Butterill Dr ARMTH DN3 .... 93 J2
Butterley Dr BSLY S70 .... 82 E1 🆘
Butterley La HEM/SK/SE WF9 .... 48 E2
Butterleys DOD/DAR S75 .... 55 F8
Buttermere Cl DRON S18 .... 86 B6 🆘
DEARNE S63 .... 86 B6 🆘
DIN S25 .... 178 A8
Buttermere Rd SHEFS S8 .... 186 E3
Buttermere Wy BSLY/ROY S71 ..... 57 J7 🆘
Butterthwaite Crs SHEFN S5 .... 131 F8
Butterthwaite La CHPT/GREN S35 .. 130 D7
Butterthwaite Rd SHEFN S5 .... 130 D7
Butterton Cl DOD/DAR S75 .... 29 H6 🆘
Butt Hole Rd CONI DN12 .... 115 F5 🆘
Butt La BTLY DN5 .... 61 J3
HOLM/MEL HD7 .... 48 D5
Button Hl ECC S11 .... 186 B5
Button Row STKB/PEN S36 .... 105 F6 🆘
Butts Hl TOT/DORE S17 .... 199 H3
Buxton Rd BSLY/ROY S71 .... 30 B8
Byland Wy BSLY/ROY S71 .... 3 F3
Byrley Rd KIMB S61 .... 132 B6
Byrne Cl DOD/DAR S75 .... 54 D3
Byron Av AWLS/ASK DN6 .... 17 K6 🆘
BTLY DN5 .... 90 C3
CHPT/GREN S35 .... 130 A3
DONS/BSCR DN4 .... 116 D1 🆘
Byron Cl DRON S18 .... 201 J8
Byron Crs DEARNE S63 .... 85 F8
RHAM/THRY S65 .... 7 F4
Byron Rd ABRD S7 .... 186 D1
DIN S25 .... 178 C7
MALT S66 .... 159 H3
MEX/SWTN S64 .... 113 G2
MOS S20 .... 190 E5 🆘
Byron St CUD/GR S72 .... 59 H6
Byron Wy WRKN S81 .... 211 F3

C

Cadeby Av CONI DN12 .... 114 B5
Cadeby La BTLY DN5 .... 88 D7
Cadman Cl MOS S20 .... 204 B5
Cadman La SHEF S1 .... 9 E5 🆘
Cadman Rd HACK/IN S12 .... 188 D1
Cadman St ATT S4 .... 9 F2 🆘
DEARNE S63 .... 111 K1
MOS S20 .... 204 A1
Cadwell Cl CUD/GR S72 .... 31 K7
Caernarvon Crs DEARNE S63 .... 86 A5
Caernarvon Dr BTLY DN5 .... 87 H4
Caernarvon Rd DRON S18 .... 201 G7
Caine Gdns KIMB S61 .... 154 B1
Cairns Rd FUL S10 .... 169 K5
MOS S20 .... 190 D3
Caister Av CHPT/GREN S35 .... 130 A1
Caistor Av BSLY S70 .... 55 H8
Calcot Park Av MEX/SWTN S64 .... 112 C5
Caldbeck Gv CHPT/GREN S35 ..... 107 J7 🆘
Caldbeck Pl DIN S25 .... 178 B8
Calder Av BSLY/ROY S71 .... 56 E8
Calder Crs BSLY S70 .... 11 J4
GLE DN14 .... 11 J4
Calder Rd DEARNE S63 .... 86 C6
KIMB S61 .... 132 C5
Caldervale BSLY/ROY S71 .... 31 F3
Calder Wy SHEFN S5 .... 152 D5
Caldey Rd DRON S18 .... 201 G7
Calf Hey La STKB/PEN S36 .... 49 J8
California Crs BSLY S70 .... 2 C6 🆘
California Dr CHPT/GREN S35 .... 130 B3
RHAM S60 .... 174 A2 🆘
California La STV/CWN S43 .... 206 A8
California St BSLY S70 .... 2 B6
California Ter BSLY S70 .... 2 B6 🆘
Calladine Wy MEX/SWTN S64 ...... 112 B6
Callis La STKB/PEN S36 .... 78 B6
Callis Wy STKB/PEN S36 .... 78 A5
Callow Dr SHEFP/MNR S2 .... 187 K2
Callow Mt SHEFS S8 .... 187 J2 🆘
Callow Rd SHEFP/MNR S2 .... 187 J2
Callywhite La DRON S18 .... 201 J6
Calner Cft MOS S20 .... 191 F5
Calver Cl DOD/DAR S75 .... 81 F2
Calvert Rd DARN/MH S9 .... 172 E1
Camborne Cl ST/HB/BR S6 ... 151 H2 🆘
Camborne Rd ST/HB/BR S6 .... 151 H2
Camborne Wy BSLY/ROY S71 .... 3 F2
Cambourne Cl AWLS/ASK DN6 .... 63 J1
Cambria Dr DONS/BSCR DN4 ...... 116 B1 🆘
Cambrian Cl BTLY DN5 .... 89 H6 🆘
Cambria Ter WRKS S80 .... 210 A5
Cambridge Cl BTLY DN5 .... 87 G5
Cambridge Crs RHAM/THRY S65 ... 7 F3
Cambridge Pl RHAM/THRY S65 .... 7 F3
Cambridge Rd NROS/TKH DN11 .. 162 E5 🆘
SHEFS S8 .... 187 H1
STKB/PEN S36 .... 105 J7
Cambridge St HEM/SK/SE WF9 ..... 34 D4

Cambron Gdns MALT S66 .... 157 J2
Camdale Ri HACK/IN S12 .... 189 H6
Camdale Vw HACK/IN S12 .... 189 H6
Camden Pl DON DN1 .... 4 C4 🆘
Camellia Cl CONI DN12 .... 114 E6 🆘
Camellia Dr ARMTH DN3 .... 66 E4 🆘
Cam Height ECC S11 .... 184 B4
Cammell Rd SHEFN S5 .... 152 E5
Camms Cl ECK/KIL S21 .... 204 B5 🆘
Camm St ST/HB/BR S6 .... 170 C1
Campbell Cl WRKN S81 .... 196 D7 🆘
Campbell Dr RHAM/THRY S65 ...... 156 A2
Campbell St RAW S62 .... 133 F3
Camping La SHEFS S8 .... 186 E4
Campion Cl DEARNE S63 .... 86 A4 🆘
Campion Dr ECK/KIL S21 .... 205 G1 🆘
MEX/SWTN S64 .... 112 C6
Campo La SHEF S1 .... 9 D3
Camp Rd HEM/SK/SE WF9 .... 33 J6
Campsall Balk AWLS/ASK DN6 ...... 18 A5
Campsall Dr FUL S10 .... 170 A4
Campsall Field Cl DEARNE S63 .... 111 H3
Campsall Field Rd DEARNE S63 ... 111 H2
Campsall Hall Rd AWLS/ASK DN6 .. 17 K6
Campsall Park Rd AWLS/ASK DN6 . 17 K6
Campsall Rd AWLS/ASK DN6 .... 18 C7
Campsmount AWLS/ASK DN6 ...... 17 K7 🆘
Canada St ATT S4 .... 152 E8
BSLY S70 .... 2 B6
Canal Br ECK/KIL S21 .... 205 H1
Canal Garth GLE DN14 .... 11 J3 🆘
Canal Rd WRKS S80 .... 210 D4
Canal St ATT S4 .... 171 K3
BSLY/ROY S71 .... 2 C2
Canal Ter WRKS S80 .... 210 E4
Canberra Av HTFD DN7 .... 69 H8
Canberra Ri DEARNE S63 .... 86 A5
Candy Bank EPW DN9 .... 96 A5
Canklow Hill Rd RHAM S60 .... 155 G4
Canklow Rd RHAM S60 .... 6 C5
Canning St SHEF S1 .... 8 C5 🆘
Cannock St ST/HB/BR S6 .... 151 H7 🆘
Cannon Flds HATH/KY SS2 .... 182 B7 🆘
Cannon Hall Rd SHEFN S5 .... 152 D7
Cannon Wy DOD/DAR S75 .... 54 E2
Canon Cl NROS/TKH DN11 .... 119 G6 🆘
Canons Wy BSLY/ROY S71 .... 3 F2
Canterbury Av FUL S10 .... 169 G7
Canterbury Cl BTLY DN5 .... 90 B1 🆘
WRKN S81 .... 196 E8
Canterbury Crs FUL S10 .... 169 G7
Canterbury Dr FUL S10 .... 169 G7
Canterbury Rd HTFD DN7 .... 42 B7
SHEFS S8 .... 187 H2
WHHL DN2 .... 91 J1
Cantilupe Crs AU/AST/KP S26 ..... 175 H7
Cantley La DONS/BSCR DN4 .... 92 C6
DONS/BSCR DN4 .... 93 F7 🆘
Cantley Manor Av
DONS/BSCR DN4 .... 93 F8
Cantley Riding WHHL DN2 .... 92 D2
Canyards Hills La ST/HB/BR S6 .... 126 B4
Capel St ST/HB/BR S6 .... 151 J8
Caperns Rd DIN S25 .... 194 B2
Capri Ct WMB/DAR S73 .... 84 B1
Caraway Gv MEX/SWTN S64 .... 112 C7
Carbis Cl BSLY/ROY S71 .... 3 E2 🆘
Carbrook Hall Rd DARN/MH S9 ... 153 J6
Carbrook St DARN/MH S9 .... 153 J6
Cardew Cl RAW S62 .... 133 K2
Cardiff St DARN/MH S9 .... 153 H7
Cardigan Rd WHHL DN2 .... 92 B2
Cardinal Cl NROS/TKH DN11 .... 119 G6 🆘
Cardoness Dr FUL S10 .... 169 J5
Cardoness Rd FUL S10 .... 169 K5
Cardwell Av HAN/WDH S13 .... 173 H8
Cardwell Cl MALT S66 .... 137 G5
Cardwell Dr HAN/WDH S13 .... 173 H8
Carey Av BSLY/ROY S71 .... 3 D4
Carfield Av SHEFS S8 .... 187 H2
Carfield La SHEFS S8 .... 187 J2
Car Hl KIMB S61 .... 133 F5
Carisbrooke Rd WHHL DN2 .... 91 K3 🆘
Carisbrook Rd WRKN S81 .... 196 C1
Carlby Rd ST/HB/BR S6 .... 150 D6
Carley Dr MOS S20 .... 190 D6
Carling Av WRKS S80 .... 210 B5
Carlingford Rd RHAM S60 .... 174 C3
Carlin St HAN/WDH S13 .... 189 G2
Carlisle Rd ATT S4 .... 153 F7
WHHL DN2 .... 66 A8
Carlisle St MEX/SWTN S64 .... 112 C6
RHAM/THRY S65 .... 7 D3 🆘
RHAM/THRY S65 .... 7 D3 🆘
Carlisle St East ATT S4 .... 171 K1
Carlthorpe Gv CHPT/GREN S35 .... 107 H8
Carlton Av RHAM/THRY S65 .... 7 F5
WRKN S81 .... 210 C1
Carlton Cl ARMTH DN3 .... 93 K7
HEM/SK/SE WF9 .... 33 F1
MOS S20 .... 204 A1
WRKN S81 .... 196 C8
Carlton Dr BWTY DN10 .... 164 A1
Carlton Gdns HEM/SK/SE WF9 ...... 34 E4

Carlton Hall La *WRKN* S81 .... **196** D2
Carlton Ri *CHPT/GREN* S35 .... **128** A4
Carlton Rd *BSLYN/ROY* S71 .... 30 C8 ▣
  BSLYN/ROY S71 .... **56** C1
  HEM/SK/SE WF9 .... **34** E5 ▣
  RAW S62 .... **133** J5
  ST/HB/BR S6 .... **151** C5
  WHHL DN2 .... **5** E1 ▣
  WRKN S81 .... **196** D6
  WRKN S81 .... **210** D3
  WRKS S80 .... **210** D4
Carlton St *BSLYN/ROY* S71 .... **2** B1
  CUD/GR S72 .... **31** J8
  CUD/GR S72 .... **32** A8
Carlyle Rd *MALT* S66 .... **159** H3
Carlyle St *MEX/SWTN* S64 .... **113** F2
Carnaby Rd *ST/HB/BR* S6 .... **151** H8
Carnarvon St *ST/HB/BR* S6 .... **8** B1 ▣
Carnforth Rd *BSLYN/ROY* S71 .... **56** C2
Carnley St *DEARNE* S63 .... **110** E1
Carnoustie *WRKN* S81 .... **211** F2
Carnoustie Cl *MEX/SWTN* S64 .... **112** D5
Carolina Wy *DONS/BSCR* DN4 .... **91** K8
Carpenter Cft *HACK/IN* S12 .... **188** E1
Carpenter Gdns *HACK/IN* S12 .... **188** E1 ▣
Carr Bank Cl *ECC* S11 .... **169** K7
Carr Bank Dr *ECC* S11 .... **169** K7 ▣
Carr Bank La *ECC* S11 .... **169** J7
Carr La *CI RHAM* S60 .... **154** D7
Carrcroft Ct *STKB/PEN* S36 .... **105** J7 ▣
Carrfield Cl *DOD/DAR* S75 .... **28** C7 ▣
Carr Field La *DEARNE* S63 .... **86** A4
Carrfield Dr *SHEFS* S8 .... **187** H1
Carrfield La *SHEFP/MNR* S2 .... **187** H1
Carrfield Rd *SHEFS* S8 .... **187** H1
Carrfield St *SHEFP/MNR* S2 .... **187** H1
Carr Forge Cl *HACK/IN* S12 .... **189** J3
Carr Forge La *HACK/IN* S12 .... **189** J3
Carr Forge Mt *HACK/IN* S12 .... **189** J3
Carr Forge Pl *HACK/IN* S12 .... **189** K3
Carr Forge Rd *HACK/IN* S12 .... **189** J3
Carr Forge Ter *HACK/IN* S12 .... **189** J3
Carr Forge Vw *HACK/IN* S12 .... **189** K3
Carr Furlong *BSLYN/ROY* S71 .... **30** A6 ▣
Carr Gn *DEARNE* S63 .... **86** B4
Carr Green La *DOD/DAR* S75 .... **29** H7 ▣
Carr Cv *STKB/PEN* S36 .... **105** H7
Carr Head La *CHPT/GREN* S35 .... **107** G6
Carr Head Rd *CHPT/GREN* S35 .... **107** G6
Carr Hl *KBTN* HD8 .... **50** B1
Carr House La *CHPT/GREN* S35 .... **127** C4
Carr House Rd *DON* DN1 .... **4** C5
  DONS/BSCR DN4 .... **4** B6
  HOLM/MEL HD7 .... **47** K2 ▣
Carriage Dr *DONS/BSCR* DN4 .... **5** F6
The Carriage Wy *NROS/TKH* DN11 .... **119** G6
Carrill Dr *ST/HB/BR* S6 .... **151** H1
Carrill Rd *ST/HB/BR* S6 .... **151** H1
Carrington Av *DOD/DAR* S75 .... **2** B1
Carrington Rd *ECC* S11 .... **170** B7
Carrington St *DOD/DAR* S75 .... **2** A2 ▣
  RHAM/THRY S65 .... **7** E5 ▣
Carr La *AU/AST/KP* S26 .... **175** K4
  CHPT/GREN S35 .... **107** H3
  CONI DN12 .... **115** F7
  DOD/DAR S75 .... **107** H2
  DON DN1 .... **5** D5
  DONS/BSCR DN4 .... **118** D2
  DRON S18 .... **200** C5
  GLE DN14 .... **12** E2
  HEM/SK/SE WF9 .... **34** E3
  HOLM/MEL HD7 .... **46** E3
  KBTN HD8 .... **50** A1
  MALT S66 .... **158** D7
  NROS/TKH DN11 .... **139** F1
  RHAM/THRY S65 .... **135** F1
  STKB/PEN S36 .... **51** J8
Carr Mt *KBTN* HD8 .... **50** B1
Carroll Ct *HEM/SK/SE* WF9 .... **34** D4
Carron Dr *DOD/DAR* S75 .... **29** H7
Carr Rd *CONI* DN12 .... **115** H6
  DEARNE S63 .... **111** K1
  ST/HB/BR S6 .... **170** C1
  STKB/PEN S36 .... **105** G8
Carr Side La *HTFD* DN7 .... **68** D3
Carrs La *CUD/GR* S72 .... **57** J2
Carr St *BSLYN/ROY* S71 .... **56** E2
Carr Vw *BWTY* DN10 .... **165** K4
Carr View Av *DONS/BSCR* DN4 .... **4** B6
Carr View Rd *HOLM/MEL* HD7 .... **48** D5
Carrville Dr *ST/HB/BR* S6 .... **151** J3
Carrville Rd *ST/HB/BR* S6 .... **151** J3
Carrville Rd West *ST/HB/BR* S6 .. **151** H3 ▣
Carrwell La *HTFD* DN7 .... **151** H4
Carrwood Rd *BSLY* S70 .... **57** F6
  ECK/KIL S21 .... **205** F7
Carsick Cv *FUL* S10 .... **169** H6
Carsick Hill Crs *FUL* S10 .... **169** H6
Carsick Hill Dr *FUL* S10 .... **169** J6
Carsick Hill Rd *FUL* S10 .... **169** H6
Carsick Hill Wy *FUL* S10 .... **169** H6 ▣
Carsick View Rd *FUL* S10 .... **169** H6
Carson Mt *HACK/IN* S12 .... **188** D4
Carson Rd *FUL* S10 .... **170** B4
Carter Hall La *HACK/IN* S12 .... **188** D5

Carterhall Rd *HACK/IN* S12 .... **188** D5
Carter Knowle Av *ECC* S11 .... **186** B2
Carter Knowle Rd *ECC* S11 .... **186** B2
Carter Lodge Av *HACK/IN* S12 .... **189** J3
Carter Lodge Dr *HACK/IN* S12 .... **189** K3
Carter Lodge Pl *HACK/IN* S12 .... **189** K3
Carter Lodge Ri *HACK/IN* S12 .... **189** K3
Carter Pl *SHEFS* S8 .... **187** H1
Carter St *SHEFS* S8 .... **187** G1
Cartledge La *DRON* S18 .... **200** A7
Cartmel Cl *DRON* S18 .... **200** E6 ▣
  MALT S66 .... **159** H1
Cartmel Ct *BSLYN/ROY* S71 .... **30** E8 ▣
Cartmell Crs *SHEFS* S8 .... **186** E3
Cartmell Rd *SHEFS* S8 .... **186** E3
Cartmel Wk *DIN* S25 .... **178** B8
Cartworth Moor Rd
  HOLM/MEL HD7 .... **47** H7
Cartworth Bank Rd
  HOLM/MEL HD7 .... **47** J5
Cartworth La *HOLM/MEL* HD7 .... **47** J4
Cartworth Rd *HOLM/MEL* HD7 .... **47** K4
Cartwright St *WRKN* S81 .... **195** C8
Car Vale Dr *SHEFP/MNR* S2 .... **172** E7
Car Vale Vw *SHEFP/MNR* S2 .... **172** E7
Carver Cl *AU/AST/KP* S26 .... **206** E1
Carver Dr *DIN* S25 .... **178** A7
Carver La *SHEF* S1 .... **9** D3
Carver St *SHEF* S1 .... **9** D3
Carver Wy *AU/AST/KP* S26 .... **206** E1
Carwood Cl *ATT* S4 .... **152** E8
Carwood Gv *ATT* S4 .... **152** E8 ▣
Carwood Rd *ATT* S4 .... **152** E8
Cary Rd *ECK/KIL* S21 .... **203** K4
  SHEFP/MNR S2 .... **172** B7
Casson Dr *AU/AST/KP* S26 .... **192** E8
Casson's Rd *THNE* DN8 .... **23** H7
Castell Cfs *DONS/BSCR* DN4 .... **92** D6
  RHAM S60 .... **155** G4
Castlebeck Av *SHEFP/MNR* S2 .... **172** D6
Castlebeck Cft *SHEFP/MNR* S2 .. **172** E6 ▣
Castlebeck Dr *SHEFP/MNR* S2 .... **172** E7
Castle Cl *BSLYN/ROY* S71 .... **9** F3
  BTLY DN5 .... **90** B5
  NROS/TKH DN11 .... **139** K8
  STKB/PEN S36 .... **78** B5
Castle Ct *CONI* DN12 .... **114** D4
Castle Crs *CONI* DN12 .... **114** D4
Castledale Cft *SHEFP/MNR* S2 .. **172** D7 ▣
Castledale Gv *SHEFP/MNR* S2 .... **172** D7
Castledale Pl *SHEFP/MNR* S2 .. **172** D7 ▣
Castledine Cl *DONS/BSCR* DN4 .... **116** E3
Castledine Cft *DARN/MH* S9 .... **153** H5
Castledine Gdns *DARN/MH* S9 .... **153** H5
Castle Dr *DOD/DAR* S75 .... **80** D3
Castle Farm La *WRKS* S80 .... **210** C8
Castle Ga *NROS/TKH* DN11 .... **161** K1
Castlegate *OWL* S3 .... **9** E2
Castle Gn *DIN* S25 .... **177** K3
  SHEF S1 .... **9** E2 ▣
Castle Gv *BTLY* DN5 .... **89** J6 ▣
Castle Hl *CONI* DN12 .... **114** D5
  ECK/KIL S21 .... **204** B3
Castle Hill Av *MEX/SWTN* S64 .... **113** H3
Castle Hill Cl *ECK/KIL* S21 .... **204** B3
Castle Hill Fold *BTLY* DN5 .... **61** H8
Castle Hills Rd *BTLY* DN5 .... **64** B6
Castle La *STKB/PEN* S36 .... **78** B5
Castle Ms *BTLY* DN5 .... **64** C6
Castlereagh St *BSLY* S70 .... **2** B4
Castlerigg Wy *DRON* S18 .... **200** E6 ▣
Castlerow Cl *TOT/DORE* S17 .... **200** A1
Castlerow Dr *TOT/DORE* S17 .... **200** B1
Castle St *BSLY* S70 .... **2** B5
  CONI DN12 .... **114** D5
  SHEF S1 .... **9** E2
  WRKS S80 .... **210** D5
Castle Ter *CONI* DN12 .... **114** D5
Castleton Rd *HATH/EY* S32 .... **191** J2
Castle Vw *BSLY* S70 .... **81** K7
  CONI DN12 .... **115** J6
  ECK/KIL S21 .... **204** B4
Castlewood Crs *FUL* S10 .... **169** F7 ▣
Castlewood Dr *FUL* S10 .... **169** F7
Castor Rd *DARN/MH* S9 .... **153** C8 ▣
Catania Ri *WMB/DAR* S73 .... **84** B1
Catcliffe Rd *DARN/MH* S9 .... **172** E3 ▣
Cathedral Ct *HTFD* DN7 .... **67** K3 ▣
Catherine Av *AU/AST/KP* S26 .... **175** H8
Catherine Rd *ATT* S4 .... **171** H1
Catherine St *MEX/SWTN* S64 .... **112** E2 ▣
  OWL S3 .... **171** H1
  RHAM/THRY S65 .... **7** D4 ▣
Cat Hill La *STKB/PEN* S36 .... **52** A7
Cathill Rd *WMB/DAR* S73 .... **85** F3
Cat La *GLE* DN14 .... **11** G5
  SHEFS S8 .... **187** J2
Cattey Rd *DARN/MH* S9 .... **172** E2
Catling La *ARMTH* DN3 .... **40** E8
Catshaw La *STKB/PEN* S36 .... **76** C4
Cattal St *DARN/MH* S9 .... **172** C2 ▣
Catterick Cl *CONI* DN12 .... **113** K5
Caulk La *BSLY* S70 .... **83** C2
Causeway Gdns *TOT/DORE* S17 .. **185** G7 ▣
Causeway Gld *TOT/DORE* S17 ...... **185** G7
Causeway Head Rd
  TOT/DORE S17 .... **185** G7
The Causeway *TOT/DORE* S17 ...... **185** H8

Cavendish Av *ST/HB/BR* S6 .... **150** D
  TOT/DORE S17 .... **185**
Cavendish Cl *BWTY* DN10 .... **164** A
  RHAM/THRY S65 .... **156** C
Cavendish Ct *OWL* S3 .... **8** C4
Cavendish Pl *MALT* S66 .... **159** H1
Cavendish Ri *DRON* S18 .... **201** F
Cavendish Rd *BTLY* DN5 .... **64** D
  DOD/DAR S75 .... **2** B2
  ECC S11 .... **170** C
  KIMB S61 .... **154** D
  WRKS S80 .... **210** E
Cavendish St *OWL* S3 .... **8** C
Cave St *DARN/MH* S9 .... **172** B
Cavill Rd *SHEFS* S8 .... **187** C
Cawdor Rd *SHEFP/MNR* S2 .... **188** E
Cawdor St *BTLY* DN5 .... **64** E6
Cawdron Ri *RHAM* S60 .... **155** F
Cawley Pl *BSLYN/ROY* S71 .... **5** D
Cawston Rd *ATT* S4 .... **152** D7
Cawthorne Cl *RHAM/THRY* S65 ...... **134** E
  SHEFS S8 .... **186** E
Cawthorne Gv *SHEFS* S8 .... **186** E
Cawthorne La *DOD/DAR* S75 .... **53** H
Cawthorne Rd *DOD/DAR* S75 .... **54** C
  RHAM/THRY S65 .... **134** C
Cawthorne Vw *STKB/PEN* S36 .... **78** C
Caxton La *ECC* S11 .... **170** E
Caxton Rd *AWLS/ASK* DN6 .... **63**
  ECC S11 .... **170** C5
Caxton St *BSLY* S70 .... **2** E
Caythorpe Cl *BSLYN/ROY* S71 .... **57** H
Cayton Cl *BSLYN/ROY* S71 .... **29** K8
Cecil Av *DONS/BSCR* DN4 .... **115** H
  DRON S18 .... **201** C
Cecil Cl *WRKS* S80 .... **209**
Cecil Rd *DRON* S18 .... **201** C
Cecil Sq *SHEFP/MNR* S2 .... **8** C
Cedar Av *HTFD* DN7 .... **42** B3
  MALT S66 .... **157** H
  MEX/SWTN S64 .... **112** E
Cedar Cl *BSLYN/ROY* S71 .... **30** E
  DONS/BSCR DN4 .... **116** A
  ECK/KIL S21 .... **203** H
  ECK/KIL S21 .... **205** H
  EPW DN9 .... **120** B3
  STKB/PEN S36 .... **104** H
  WRKN S81 .... **180** C8
Cedar Crs *BSLY* S70 .... **3**
Cedar Dr *MALT* S66 .... **158** E
  RHAM/THRY S65 .... **136** C
Cedar Gv *CONI* DN12 .... **114** H
Cedar Rd *ARMTH* DN3 .... **67** H8
  DONS/BSCR DN4 .... **116** A
  STKB/PEN S36 .... **104** H
  THNE DN8 .... **23**
Cedar Wk *AWLS/ASK* DN6 .... **17**
Cedar Wy *CHPT/GREN* S35 .... **130** A3
Cedric Av *CONI* DN12 .... **114**
Cedric Crs *MALT* S66 .... **157**
Cedric Rd *ARMTH* DN3 .... **66**
Celandine Ct *TOT/DORE* S17 ...... **200** A2
Celandine Gdns *TOT/DORE* S17 ...... **200**
Celandine Gv *WMB/DAR* S73 .... **84** E
Celandine Ri *MEX/SWTN* S64 .... **112**
Cemetery Av *ECC* S11 .... **8** A5
Cemetery Rd *AWLS/ASK* DN6 .... **63**
  BSLY S70 .... **J6**
  CUD/GR S72 .... **32**
  DEARNE S63 .... **86**
  DEARNE S63 .... **111**
  DRON S18 .... **201**
  ECC S11 .... **8**
  HOLM/MEL HD7 .... **47**
  HOY S74 .... **83**
  HTFD DN7 .... **43**
  MEX/SWTN S64 .... **113**
  WMB/DAR S73 .... **84**
  WRKS S80 .... **210**
Centenary Wy *RHAM* S60 .... **6**
  RHAM S60 .... **155** F4
Central Av *AWLS/ASK* DN6 .... **63**
  BTLY DN5 .... **64**
  CUD/GR S72 .... **32**
  DIN S25 .... **178**
  HEM/SK/SE WF9 .... **34** E8
  MALT S66 .... **135**
  MEX/SWTN S64 .... **112**
  RHAM/THRY S65 .... **134**
  WRKS S80 .... **210**
Central Bvd *WHHL* DN2 .... **92**
Central Dr *BSLYN/ROY* S71 .... **30**
  BWTY DN10 .... **142**
  MALT S66 .... **76**
  NROS/TKH DN11 .... **118**
  RAW S62 .... **111**
Central Rd *RHAM* S60 .... **6**
Central St *DEARNE* S63 .... **86**
  HOY S74 .... **108** C2
Centre St *HEM/SK/SE* WF9 .... **35** F4
Centurion Wy *BTLY* DN5 .... **4**
Century Ct *CONI* DN12 .... **115** K0
Century Gdns *BTLY* DN5 .... **65**
Century St *DARN/MH* S9 .... **172**
Century Vw *RHAM* S60 .... **154**
Chadbourne Cl *ARMTH* DN3 .... **93**
Chaddesden Cl *DRON* S18 .... **200** C8
Chadwick Dr *MALT* S66 .... **159**
Chadwick Gdns *BTLY* DN5 .... **65**

Chadwick Rd *AWLS/ASK* DN6 .... 63 H3
BTLY DN5 .... 4 B1
HAN/WDH S13 .... 172 E8
THNE DN8 .... 24 A3
Chaff Cl *RHAM* S60 .... 156 A6
Chaffinch Av *RHAM* S60 .... 155 G7 ⬛
Chaffinch Ms *WRKN* S81 .... 196 A8 ⬛
Chaff La *RHAM* S60 .... 156 A6
Challenger Crs *DEARNE* S63 .... 60 B6
Challenger Dr *BTLY* DN5 .... 90 B4
Challoner Gn *MOS* S20 .... 190 C7 ⬛
Challoner Wy *MOS* S20 .... 190 C7 ⬛
Chalmers Dr *WHHL* DN2 .... 66 C6
Chamberlain Av *CONI* DN12 .... 90 C1
Chamberlain Ct
   CHPT/GREN S35 .... 130 A1 ⬛
Chambers Av *CONI* DN12 .... 114 B5
Chambers La *ATT* S4 .... 153 F6
Chambers Rd *HOY* S74 .... 82 E8 ⬛
   KIMB S61 .... 132 C6
Champion Cl *SHEFN* S5 .... 152 E1
Champion Rd *SHEFN* S5 .... 152 D1
Chancel Wy *BSLYN/ROY* S71 .... 3 F7
Chancery Pl *DON* DN1 .... 4 C3 ⬛
Chancet Wood Cl *SHEFS* S8 .... 187 F7
Chancet Wood Dr *SHEFS* S8 .... 187 F7
Chancet Wood Ri *SHEFS* S8 .... 187 F7
Chandos Crs *ECK/KIL* S21 .... 205 G1
Chandos St *FUL* S10 .... 170 C5 ⬛
Channing Gdns *ST/HB/BR* S6 .... 151 J8
Channing St *ST/HB/BR* S6 .... 151 J8
Chantrey Rd *SHEFS* S8 .... 187 F4
Chantry Cl *DONS/BSCR* DN4 .... 93 F8
Chantry Gv *BSLYN/ROY* S71 .... 30 D4
Chantry Pl *AU/AST/KP* S26 .... 193 F4
Chapel Av *BSLYN/ROY* S71 .... 30 D6
   WMB/DAR S73 .... 84 D7
Chapel Bank *HOLM/MEL* HD7 .... 48 D4
Chapel Cl *BSLY* S70 .... 81 K8 ⬛
   CHPT/GREN S35 .... 129 K2
   CUD/GR S72 .... 31 K4
   EPW DN9 .... 121 F4
   FUL S10 .... 169 K6 ⬛
   MALT S66 .... 157 K8
Chapel Ct *BSLY* S70 .... 81 K8
Chapelfield Crs *KIMB* S61 .... 131 G2 ⬛
Chapelfield Dr *KIMB* S61 .... 131 G2
Chapelfield La *KIMB* S61 .... 131 G2
Chapel Field La *STKB/PEN* S36 .... 77 K5
Chapelfield Mt *KIMB* S61 .... 131 G2 ⬛
Chapel Field Pl *KIMB* S61 .... 131 G2 ⬛
Chapelfields *HEM/SK/SE* WF9 .... 34 A5
Chapelfields *KIMB* S61 .... 131 F1 ⬛
Chapelgate *HOLM/MEL* HD7 .... 48 C4
Chapel Ga *WRKN* S81 .... 196 E2 ⬛
Chapel Hl *AWLS/ASK* DN6 .... 18 D7
   BTLY DN5 .... 60 B3
   HOY S74 .... 82 E6
   KBTN HD8 .... 26 C5
   MEX/SWTN S64 .... 112 B4
   RHAM S60 .... 156 A6
Chapel Hole La *MALT* S66 .... 137 K5
Chapel La *ARMTH* DN3 .... 93 K7
   BSLYN/ROY S71 .... 30 C1
   BWTY DN10 .... 164 B5
   BWTY DN10 .... 165 J4
   CHPT/GREN S35 .... 105 H4
   CONI DN12 .... 114 D6
   CUD/GR S72 .... 59 G6
   CUD/GR S72 .... 85 J1
   DARN/MH S9 .... 172 C1 ⬛
   DEARNE S63 .... 60 D6
   DRON S18 .... 202 C6
   EPW DN9 .... 121 F3
   GLE DN14 .... 12 B8
   HEM/SK/SE WF9 .... 35 C4
   PONT WF8 .... 16 E1
   RHAM S60 .... 6 C5
   STKB/PEN S36 .... 77 K5
   STKB/PEN S36 .... 103 J3
   THNE DN8 .... 23 J8 ⬛
Chapel Pl *BSLYN/ROY* S71 .... 57 G7
Chapel Ri *DIN* S25 .... 193 K2
Chapel Rd *CHPT/GREN* S35 .... 107 K7 ⬛
   CHPT/GREN S35 .... 129 K5
   DOD/DAR S75 .... 107 H1
Chapel St *AWLS/ASK* DN6 .... 37 J7
   BSLY S70 .... 81 K8
   BSLYN/ROY S71 .... 57 G7 ⬛
   BTLY DN5 .... 64 E7
   CUD/GR S72 .... 31 K4
   CUD/GR S72 .... 58 D1
   DEARNE S63 .... 60 B7
   DEARNE S63 .... 86 B5
   DEARNE S63 .... 111 H2
   HAN/WDH S13 .... 189 K1
   KIMB S61 .... 108 C2
   KIMB S61 .... 132 E3
   MEX/SWTN S64 .... 112 D2
   MOS S20 .... 204 A1
   RAW S62 .... 133 J2
Chapel Ter *FUL* S10 .... 169 K6
Chapeltown Rd *CHPT/GREN* S35 .... 130 C5
Chapel Wk *RAW* S62 .... 111 G8
   RHAM S60 .... 6 B4 ⬛
   SHEF S1 .... 9 D5 ⬛
   WRKS S80 .... 210 C5
Chapel Wy *AU/AST/KP* S26 .... 192 D5

RAW S62 .... 111 G8
Chapelwood Rd *DARN/MH* S9 .... 172 D1
Chapel Yd *DRON* S18 .... 201 G5
Chapman St *DARN/MH* S9 .... 153 J3 ⬛
   DEARNE S63 .... 60 D7 ⬛
Chappell Cl *STKB/PEN* S36 .... 78 C1
Chappell Dr *BTLY* DN5 .... 4 C2
Chappell Rd *STKB/PEN* S36 .... 78 C1
Chapter Wy *BSLYN/ROY* S71 .... 3 F2 ⬛
   DOD/DAR S75 .... 53 K6
Charity St *BSLYN/ROY* S71 .... 57 G1
Charles Ashmore Rd *SHEFS* S8 .... 187 F7
Charles La *SHEF* S1 .... 9 D5 ⬛
Charles Rd *DEARNE* S63 .... 111 J2
Charles St *ARMTH* DN3 .... 93 H3
   AWLS/ASK DN6 .... 37 J5
   BSLY S70 .... 82 B3 ⬛
   BSLY S70 .... 82 B3 ⬛
   CUD/GR S72 .... 31 K7
   CUD/GR S72 .... 32 B2
   CUD/GR S72 .... 58 D1 ⬛
   CUD/GR S72 .... 59 G8
   DEARNE S63 .... 86 C2 ⬛
   DIN S25 .... 178 B5
   DON DN1 .... 5 D2
   MALT S66 .... 176 E1
   MEX/SWTN S64 .... 112 C5
   RAW S62 .... 112 A8
   SHEF S1 .... 9 D3
Charlotte La *SHEF* S1 .... 8 C3 ⬛
Charlotte Rd *SHEF* S1 .... 9 D5
   SHEFP/MNR S2 .... 9 E5
Chariton Brook Crs
   CHPT/GREN S35 .... 129 K1
Chariton Clough *CHPT/GREN* S35 .... 129 J2
Chariton Dr *CHPT/GREN* S35 .... 129 K1
Chariton Hill Ri *CHPT/GREN* S35 .... 129 J1
Charnell Rd *MALT* S66 .... 159 H2
Charnley Av *ECC* S11 .... 186 C2
Charnley Cl *ECC* S11 .... 186 B1
Charnley Dr *ECC* S11 .... 186 C2
Charnley Ri *ECC* S11 .... 186 C2
Charnock Av *HACK/IN* S12 .... 188 D5
Charnock Crs *HACK/IN* S12 .... 188 C4
Charnock Dale Rd *HACK/IN* S12 .... 188 C5
Charnock Dr *BTLY* DN5 .... 90 C2 ⬛
   HACK/IN S12 .... 188 C4
Charnock Gv *HACK/IN* S12 .... 188 D5
Charnock Hall Rd *HACK/IN* S12 .... 188 C5
Charnock View Rd *HACK/IN* S12 .... 188 C5
Charnock Wood Rd *HACK/IN* S12 .... 188 D5
Charnwood Ct *MOS* S20 .... 190 C5 ⬛
Charnwood Dr *DONS/BSCR* DN4 .... 116 B2
Charnwood Gv *KIMB* S61 .... 154 C1
Charnwood St *MEX/SWTN* S64 .... 112 C4
Charter Dr *BTLY* DN5 .... 63 K7
Charter Rw *SHEF* S1 .... 8 C4
Charter Square Rbt *SHEF* S1 .... 8 C4
Chase Rd *ST/HB/BR* S6 .... 150 C7
The Chase *AU/AST/KP* S26 .... 191 J1
Chatfield Rd *SHEFS* S8 .... 186 E5
Chatham St *OWL* S3 .... 9 D1
   RHAM/THRY S65 .... 7 D4 ⬛
Chatsworth Av *MEX/SWTN* S64 .... 113 J2
Chatsworth Cl *AU/AST/KP* S26 .... 175 K8
Chatsworth Crs *BTLY* DN5 .... 64 C7
Chatsworth Dr *NROS/TKH* DN11 .... 119 G7
Chatsworth Park Av
   HACK/IN S12 .... 188 C2 ⬛
Chatsworth Park Dr
   HACK/IN S12 .... 188 C2 ⬛
Chatsworth Park Gv
   HACK/IN S12 .... 188 C2 ⬛
Chatsworth Park Rd
   HACK/IN S12 .... 188 C2
Chatsworth Ri *DRON* S18 .... 200 D5 ⬛
Chatsworth Ri *DOD/DAR* S75 .... 80 E1 ⬛
   RHAM S60 .... 155 G7 ⬛
Chatsworth Rd *BSLYN/ROY* S71 .... 56 B1
   KIMB S61 .... 6 A4 ⬛
   TOT/DORE S17 .... 199 J1
   WRKN S81 .... 196 D8
Chatterton Dr *RHAM/THRY* S65 .... 156 A3
Chaucer Cl *SHEFN* S5 .... 151 J1 ⬛
Chaucer Dr *DRON* S18 .... 201 J8
Chaucer Rd *MEX/SWTN* S64 .... 156 A5
   RHAM/THRY S65 .... 156 A5
   SHEFN S5 .... 151 K1
Cheadle St *ST/HB/BR* S6 .... 151 H7 ⬛
Cheapside *BSLY* S70 .... 2 C4 ⬛
   WRKS S80 .... 210 E5
Checkstone Av *DONS/BSCR* DN4 .... 118 D2
Chedworth Cl *DOD/DAR* S75 .... 28 D8
Cheese Gate Nab Side
   HOLM/MEL HD7 .... 49 F5
Cheetham Dr *MALT* S66 .... 159 H1
Chelmsford Av *AU/AST/KP* S26 .... 175 J7
Chelmsford Dr *WHHL* DN2 .... 91 J1
Chelsea Ct *ECC* S11 .... 170 C8
Chelsea Ri *ECC* S11 .... 170 C8
Chelsea Rd *ECC* S11 .... 186 C1
Cheltenham Ri *BTLY* DN5 .... 90 A2 ⬛
Cheltenham Rd *WHHL* DN2 .... 92 B2
Chemist La *RHAM* S60 .... 6 E3 ⬛
Chemistry La *CHPT/GREN* S35 .... 106 B7
Chepstow Dr *MEX/SWTN* S64 .... 113 G1
Chepstow Gdns *BTLY* DN5 .... 90 A2
Chequer Av *DONS/BSCR* DN4 .... 5 E4

Chequer La *HTFD* DN7 .... 40 E4
Chequer Rd *DON* DN1 .... 5 D4
Cheriton Av *AWLS/ASK* DN6 .... 63 H1
Cherry Bank Rd *SHEFS* S8 .... 187 G4
Cherry Cl *BSLYN/ROY* S71 .... 30 B3
   CUD/GR S72 .... 31 J7
Cherry Garth *AWLS/ASK* DN6 .... 17 K7
   BTLY DN5 .... 64 E1
   HEM/SK/SE WF9 .... 33 F1
Cherry Gv *CONI* DN12 .... 114 A7
   NROS/TKH DN11 .... 119 F7 ⬛
Cherry Hills *DOD/DAR* S75 .... 29 F6
Cherry La *BTLY* DN5 .... 4 B2
   KBTN HD8 .... 26 C5 ⬛
Cherrys Rd *BSLYN/ROY* S71 .... 56 E5
Cherry St *SHEFP/MNR* S2 .... 9 D6
Cherry St South *SHEFP/MNR* S2 .... 9 D6
Cherry Tree Av *WRKN* S81 .... 195 H8 ⬛
Cherry Tree Cl *DOD/DAR* S75 .... 29 H6 ⬛
   ECC S11 .... 170 D8 ⬛
   RHAM S60 .... 155 G7 ⬛
Cherry Tree Crs *MALT* S66 .... 157 H2
Cherry Tree Dell *ECC* S11 .... 170 D8 ⬛
Cherry Tree Dr *ABRD* S7 .... 170 D8 ⬛
   ECK/KIL S21 .... 205 G2
   HTFD DN7 .... 42 B7 ⬛
   THNE DN8 .... 23 J6 ⬛
Cherry Tree Gv *HTFD* DN7 .... 42 B6
Cherry Tree Pl *DEARNE* S63 .... 111 J2 ⬛
Cherry Tree Rd *ABRD* S7 .... 170 D8 ⬛
   ARMTH DN3 .... 93 G1
   AU/AST/KP S26 .... 192 A5
   DONS/BSCR DN4 .... 4 B4
   MALT S66 .... 158 C2
Cherry Tree St *HOY* S74 .... 109 G1
Cherry Wk *CHPT/GREN* S35 .... 130 B3 ⬛
Chesham Rd *BSLY* S70 .... 2 A4
Chessel Cl *SHEFS* S8 .... 187 G3
Chesterfield Rd *AU/AST/KP* S26 .... 191 F1
   DRON S18 .... 201 H6
   ECK/KIL S21 .... 203 K5
   ECK/KIL S21 .... 205 F2
   SHEFS S8 .... 187 F1
Chesterfield Rd South *SHEFS* S8 .... 201 G1
Chesterhill Av *RHAM/THRY* S65 .... 134 D6
Chester La *SHEF* S1 .... 8 C4 ⬛
Chester Rd *WHHL* DN2 .... 65 J8
Chester St *SHEF* S1 .... 8 C3 ⬛
Chesterton Dr *WRKN* S81 .... 211 F2
Chesterton Rd *DONS/BSCR* DN4 .... 117 F1 ⬛
Chesterton Wy *RHAM/THRY* S65 .... 134 A6
Chesterwood Dr *FUL* S10 .... 170 B5 ⬛
Chestnut Av *ARMTH* DN3 .... 93 G1
   AU/AST/KP S26 .... 192 C5
   AWLS/ASK DN6 .... 37 J6
   CUD/GR S72 .... 32 C4
   DARN/MH S9 .... 173 G4
   DEARNE S63 .... 111 J3
   ECK/KIL S21 .... 203 K5
   ECK/KIL S21 .... 205 F2
   HTFD DN7 .... 42 B3
   MOS S20 .... 190 D2
   NROS/TKH DN11 .... 119 F7
   RHAM/THRY S65 .... 134 A8
   STKB/PEN S36 .... 104 E7
   THNE DN8 .... 43 K1 ⬛
   WHHL DN2 .... 66 A8
Chestnut Cl *DRON* S18 .... 201 H7
   MALT S66 .... 157 C1
   WRKS S80 .... 210 C6 ⬛
Chestnut Ct *BSLY* S70 .... 2 C2 ⬛
   BTLY DN5 .... 64 D5 ⬛
Chestnut Crs *BSLY* S70 .... 3 E6
Chestnut Dr *BWTY* DN10 .... 142 A8
   CHPT/GREN S35 .... 129 K3
   CUD/GR S72 .... 32 A2
   EPW DN9 .... 120 B3
Chestnut Gv *BTLY* DN5 .... 89 J7 ⬛
   CONI DN12 .... 114 B6
   DEARNE S63 .... 60 C8
   DIN S25 .... 178 B5
   HEM/SK/SE WF9 .... 33 J2
   MALT S66 .... 158 E1
Chestnut Rd *AU/AST/KP* S26 .... 175 F7
   WRKN S81 .... 180 D3
Chestnut St *CUD/GR* S72 .... 58 C2
   HEM/SK/SE WF9 .... 34 E6
Chevet Ri *BSLYN/ROY* S71 .... 30 B3
Chevet Vw *BSLYN/ROY* S71 .... 30 B3
Cheviot Cl *THNE* DN8 .... 43 H1
Cheviot Dr *BTLY* DN5 .... 64 C8
Chevril Ct *MALT* S66 .... 157 F3
Cheyne Wk *BWTY* DN10 .... 142 A8
Chichester Rd *FUL* S10 .... 170 B3 ⬛
Childers Dr *FUL* S10 .... 94 B8
Childers St *DONS/BSCR* DN4 .... 5 E5
Chiltern Crs *BTLY* DN5 .... 89 H6
Chiltern Ri *RHAM* S60 .... 155 G8
Chiltern Rd *BTLY* DN5 .... 64 C8
   ST/HB/BR S6 .... 151 G7
Chiltern Wy *WRKN* S81 .... 180 C8 ⬛
Chilton St *BSLY* S70 .... 3 D5
Chilwell Cl *BSLYN/ROY* S71 .... 30 A6 ⬛
Chilwell Gdns *BSLYN/ROY* S71 .... 30 A6 ⬛
Chinley St *DARN/MH* S9 .... 172 C2 ⬛
Chippingham Pl *DARN/MH* S9 .... 172 B1 ⬛
Chippingham St *DARN/MH* S9 .... 172 C1 ⬛
Chippinghouse Rd *ABRD* S7 .... 171 F1 ⬛
   SHEFS S8 .... 171 F8 ⬛

Chiverton Cl *DRON* S18 .... 201 G5 🔟
Choppards Bank Rd
　HOLM/MEL HD7 .... 47 K6
Choppards La *HOLM/MEL* HD7 ... 47 K5
Chorley Av *FUL* S10 .... 169 G7 🔟
Chorley Dr *FUL* S10 .... 169 G7 🔟
Chorley Pl *FUL* S10 .... 169 G8
Chorley Rd *FUL* S10 .... 169 H7
Christchurch Av *AU/AST/KP* S26 ... 175 J7
Christchurch Rd *DEARNE* S63 .... 85 F8
Christ Church Rd *OWL* S3 .... 152 C8
Chu Rw *HEM/SK/SE* WF9 .... 34 B5
　THNE DN8 .... 133 H5
Church Balk *ARMTH* DN3 .... 66 E4
　THNE DN8 .... 23 K8
Church Balk Gdns *ARMTH* DN3 ..... 66 E4
Church Bank *HATH/EY* S32 .... 182 C7
Church Cl *AU/AST/KP* S26 .... 192 B5
　CHPT/GREN S35 .... 128 C8
　DOD/DAR S75 .... 28 D7
　ECK/KIL S21 .... 205 F7
　MALT S66 .... 159 G3
　MEX/SWTN S64 .... 112 B4
　RHAM/THRY S65 .... 135 H4
　THNE DN8 .... 23 K8
Church Cnr *DIN* S25 .... 177 K2
Church Cottage Ms
　DONS/BSCR DN4 .... 90 B8
Church Ct *DIN* S25 .... 194 A3 🔟
　DONS/BSCR DN4 .... 92 E8 🔟
Church Cft *RAW* S62 .... 133 H3
Churchdale Rd *HACK/IN* S12 .... 189 F3
Church Dr *CUD/GR* S72 .... 32 C5
　HEM/SK/SE WF9 .... 34 B5
Churchfield *BSLY* S70 .... 2 B3 🔟
Churchfield Av *CUD/GR* S72 .... 57 J1 🔟
　DOD/DAR S75 .... 28 E7 🔟
Churchfield Cl *BTLY* DN5 .... 64 D8
　DOD/DAR S75 .... 28 A7
Church Field Cl *WRKN* S81 .... 196 E2 🔟
Churchfield Crs *CUD/GR* S72 .... 57 J1 🔟
Church Field Dr *MALT* S66 .... 157 G3
Churchfield La *DOD/DAR* S75 .... 28 A7
Church Field La *RAW* S62 .... 133 H3
Church Field Rd *NROS/TKH* DN11... 119 G5
　BTLY DN5 .... 60 B5
Churchfields *CHPT/GREN* S35 .... 105 J1
Church Flds *KIMB* S61 .... 132 B8
Church Fields Rd *NROS/TKH* DN11.. 119 C5
Churchfield Ter *CUD/GR* S72 .... 57 J1 🔟
Church Field Vw
　DONS/BSCR DN4 .... 90 B8 🔟
Church Gn *DEARNE* S63 .... 111 H4
Church Gv *BSLYN/ROY* S71 .... 3 F1
　HEM/SK/SE WF9 .... 34 B5
　MALT S66 .... 137 H5
Church Hl *BSLYN/ROY* S71 .... 30 E4
Churchill Rd *FUL* S10 .... 170 C4 🔟
　STKB/PEN S36 .... 104 C5
　WHHL DN2 .... 91 H1
Church Hts *STKB/PEN* S36 .... 52 C8
Church La *ARMTH* DN3 .... 40 D1
　AU/AST/KP S26 .... 175 K8
　AWLS/ASK DN6 .... 63 K1 🔟
　BSLY S70 .... 2 B3 🔟
　BSLY S70 .... 82 A5
　BTLY DN5 .... 62 D8
　BTLY DN5 .... 87 H5
　BWTY DN10 .... 164 B5
　CUD/GR S72 .... 31 H1
　DEARNE S63 .... 111 H2 🔟
　DIN S25 .... 177 K6
　DIN S25 .... 178 A7
　DIN S25 .... 179 G5
　DOD/DAR S75 .... 27 G4
　DOD/DAR S75 .... 53 J3
　DONS/BSCR DN4 .... 92 E8
　DONS/BSCR DN4 .... 116 A1
　DONS/BSCR DN4 .... 118 D1
　ECK/KIL S21 .... 205 J1
　EPW DN9 .... 121 F4 🔟
　HACK/IN S12 .... 190 A4
　HAN/WDH S13 .... 189 K1
　HOY S74 .... 107 K4
　HTFD DN7 .... 22 C8 🔟
　KBTN HD8 .... 26 C5
　MALT S66 .... 136 E2
　MALT S66 .... 157 J2
　MALT S66 .... 157 G3
　MALT S66 .... 159 G3
　MOS S20 .... 190 E4
　NROS/TKH DN11 .... 138 E1
　NROS/TKH DN11 .... 139 K8
　NROS/TKH DN11 .... 162 D3
　RHAM S60 .... 174 A1 🔟
　RHAM S60 .... 94 B3
　RHAM/THRY S65 .... 135 J4
　STKB/PEN S36 .... 52 C8
　TOT/DORE S17 .... 199 H1
　WRKN S81 .... 196 D3
Church Lane Ms *MALT* S66 .... 157 J2
Church Lea *HOY* S74 .... 109 F3
Church Meadow Rd
　NROS/TKH DN11 .... 119 G7

　MEX/SWTN S64 .... 113 H3
　MOS S20 .... 190 B8 🔟
Church Mt *HEM/SK/SE* WF9 .... 34 B5
Church Rein Cl
　DONS/BSCR DN4 .... 115 K1 🔟
Church Rd *ARMTH* DN3 .... 40 D7
　ARMTH DN3 .... 66 E3
　CONI DN12 .... 114 B3
　CONI DN12 .... 115 J4
　DOD/DAR S75 .... 53 H3
　HTFD DN7 .... 41 K3
　NROS/TKH DN11 .... 138 E1
　NROS/TKH DN11 .... 163 H3
Church St *ARMTH* DN3 .... 40 D7
　AU/AST/KP S26 .... 192 B5
　BSLY S70 .... 2 B3 🔟
　BSLYN/ROY S71 .... 30 A4
　BSLYN/ROY S71 .... 3 H1
　BTLY DN5 .... 64 D7 🔟
　BWTY DN10 .... 164 B1
　BWTY DN10 .... 165 K4
　CHPT/GREN S35 .... 128 B8
　CHPT/GREN S35 .... 130 B6
　CONI DN12 .... 114 D5
　CUD/GR S72 .... 32 C4
　CUD/GR S72 .... 57 J1
　CUD/GR S72 .... 59 H5
　DEARNE S63 .... 60 B7
　DEARNE S63 .... 86 B5
　DEARNE S63 .... 111 H4 🔟
　DOD/DAR S75 .... 28 D7
　DOD/DAR S75 .... 29 H6 🔟
　DOD/DAR S75 .... 53 H2
　DOD/DAR S75 .... 55 F4
　DRON S18 .... 201 G6 🔟
　DRON S18 .... 202 A8
　ECK/KIL S21 .... 204 C3
　HEM/SK/SE WF9 .... 35 F5
　HOLM/MEL HD7 .... 48 E1 🔟
　HOY S74 .... 83 G8
　HOY S74 .... 109 H2
　HTFD DN7 .... 22 C8 🔟
　KIMB S61 .... 132 B8
　KIMB S61 .... 132 D3
　MALT S66 .... 177 F1
　MEX/SWTN S64 .... 112 B4
　MEX/SWTN S64 .... 113 J3 🔟
　MEX/SWTN S64 .... 113 G3
　RAW S62 .... 133 H3
　SHEF S1 .... 9 D3
　ST/HB/BR S6 .... 169 G2
　STKB/PEN S36 .... 78 A4
　STV/CWN S43 .... 206 B8
　THNE DN8 .... 23 J8
　WMB/DAR S73 .... 55 J6
　WRKN S81 .... 180 C5
Church Ter *HOLM/MEL* HD7 .... 47 K2
　KBTN HD8 .... 26 A6
Church Top *HEM/SK/SE* WF9 .... 34 B5
Church Vw *AU/AST/KP* S26 .... 175 J8
　AU/AST/KP S26 .... 192 A5
　AWLS/ASK DN6 .... 63 K1 🔟
　BWTY DN10 .... 164 B5 🔟
　CONI DN12 .... 115 H6
　CUD/GR S72 .... 57 J1
　DOD/DAR S75 .... 55 H4
　DON DN1 .... 4 C2
　ECK/KIL S21 .... 191 J8
　HAN/WDH S13 .... 190 A1
　HEM/SK/SE WF9 .... 34 B4
　HOLM/MEL HD7 .... 46 E3
　HOY S74 .... 108 C2
　MALT S66 .... 157 G3
　NROS/TKH DN11 .... 138 E1
　RHAM/THRY S65 .... 134 E4
　STV/CWN S43 .... 206 B8
Church View Crs *STKB/PEN* S36 ... 78 A4
Church View Rd *STKB/PEN* S36 .... 78 A4
Church Vls *HEM/SK/SE* WF9 .... 34 B5
Church Wk *CONI* DN12 .... 114 B3
　NROS/TKH DN11 .... 162 D3
　WRKS S80 .... 210 D4
Church Wy *DON* DN1 .... 5 E1
Cinder Bridge Rd *RAW* S62 .... 133 F3
Cinder Hill La *CHPT/GREN* S35 .... 129 J7
Cinderhill La *CHPT/GREN* S35 ...... 187 J7
Cinderhill Rd *KIMB* S61 .... 132 B5
Cinder Hills Rd *HOLM/MEL* HD7 ... 48 A3
Cinder Hills Wy *DOD/DAR* S75 ...... 55 F8 🔟
Cinder La *ECK/KIL* S21 .... 191 K8
Circle Cl *SHEFP/MNR* S2 .... 172 D7
The Circle *NROS/TKH* DN11 .... 118 D6
　SHEFP/MNR S2 .... 172 D6
The Circuit *AWLS/ASK* DN6 .... 63 G1
Circular Dr *ECK/KIL* S21 .... 205 F7
City Rd *SHEFP/MNR* S2 .... 171 K5
Claire Ct *RHAM* S60 .... 6 C3
Clanricarde St *BSLYN/ROY* S71 ..... 2 B2
Clara Pl *KIMB* S61 .... 154 C1
Clarehurst Rd *WMB/DAR* S73 .... 84 D1 🔟
Clarel Cl *STKB/PEN* S36 .... 77 K5
Clarell Gdns *DONS/BSCR* DN4 ...... 92 D6
Clarel St *STKB/PEN* S36 .... 77 K5
Claremont Crs *FUL* S10 .... 8 A3 🔟
Claremont Pl *FUL* S10 .... 8 A3
Claremont St *KIMB* S61 .... 154 C1
Clarence Av *DONS/BSCR* DN4 .... 4 B6
Clarence La *SHEFP/MNR* S2 .... 8 C5
Clarence Pl *MALT* S66 .... 159 H1

Clarence Rd *BSLYN/ROY* S71 .... 3 E1
　ST/HB/BR S6 .... 151 G2
　WRKS S80 .... 210 C3
Clarence Sq *DIN* S25 .... 178 C6 🔟
Clarence St *DEARNE* S63 .... 85 J3 🔟
　DIN S25 .... 178 C6
Clarendon Dr *WRKN* S81 .... 210 B1 🔟
Clarendon Rd *ECC* S11 .... 169 J8
　RHAM/THRY S65 .... 7 E3
Clarendon St *BSLY* S70 .... 2 A4
Clark Av *CONI* DN12 .... 115 J7
　DONS/BSCR DN4 .... 5 E4
Clarke Av *MALT* S66 .... 177 G1 🔟
Clarke Ct *DIN* S25 .... 178 B5 🔟
Clarke Dell *FUL* S10 .... 8 A5
Clarke Dr *FUL* S10 .... 8 A5
Clarkegrove Rd *FUL* S10 .... 8 A4
Clarkehouse Rd *FUL* S10 .... 170 C6
Clarke Sq *SHEFP/MNR* S2 .... 8 C6
Clarke St *DEARNE* S63 .... 60 D7 🔟
　DOD/DAR S75 .... 2 A2
　FUL S10 .... 8 B4
Clark Gv *ST/HB/BR* S6 .... 169 H1
Clarks Ct *AWLS/ASK* DN6 .... 63 J1
Clarkson St *BSLY* S70 .... 82 D2
　FUL S10 .... 8 B3
Clark St *HOY* S74 .... 82 E8
Clarney Av *WMB/DAR* S73 .... 84 C1
Clarney Pl *WMB/DAR* S73 .... 84 C1
Clay Bank *AWLS/ASK* DN6 .... 39 K2
Clay Bank La *BWTY* DN10 .... 143 K8
Clay Bank Rd *THNE* DN8 .... 44 B3
Claycliffe Av *DOD/DAR* S75 .... 54 E3
Claycliffe Rd *DOD/DAR* S75 .... 54 E2
Clayfield Av *MEX/SWTN* S64 .... 113 J2
Clayfield La *RAW* S62 .... 109 J6
Clayfield Rd *MEX/SWTN* S64 .... 113 J2
Clayfields *DONS/BSCR* DN4 .... 116 D2
Clayfield Vw *MEX/SWTN* S64 .... 113 J2
Clay Flat La *NROS/TKH* DN11 .... 118 E7
Claylands Av *WRKN* S81 .... 195 K8
Claylands Cl *WRKN* S81 .... 210 B1
Claylands La *WRKN* S81 .... 210 B2
Clay La *SHEF* S1 .... 9 D4 🔟
　WHHL DN2 .... 66 C7
Clay La West *WHHL* DN2 .... 66 B6
Clay Pit La *RAW* S62 .... 133 K2
Clay Pits La *STKB/PEN* S36 .... 104 A5
Clayroyd *BSLY* S70 .... 82 B3
Clay St *DARN/MH* S9 .... 153 G8
Clayton Av *DEARNE* S63 .... 60 A6
Clayton Crs *MOS* S20 .... 190 C5
Clayton Dr *DEARNE* S63 .... 60 A7
Clayton Hollow *MOS* S20 .... 190 C5
Clayton Holt *HEM/SK/SE* WF9 .... 34 A6
Clayton La *BTLY* DN5 .... 61 H2
　DEARNE S63 .... 60 A6
Clayton Vw *HEM/SK/SE* WF9 .... 34 A6
Clay Wheels La *ST/HB/BR* S6 .... 151 G3
Claywood Dr *SHEFP/MNR* S2 .... 9 F4
Claywood Rd *SHEFP/MNR* S2 .... 9 F5 🔟
Clayworth Dr *DONS/BSCR* DN4 ...... 92 A8 🔟
Clear Vw *CUD/GR* S72 .... 32 C7
Clearwell Cft *BTLY* DN5 .... 90 C2
Cleeve Hill Gdns *MOS* S20 .... 190 B5
Clematis Rd *SHEFN* S5 .... 153 G4
Clement Ms *KIMB* S61 .... 154 B1 🔟
Clementson Rd *FUL* S10 .... 170 C3 🔟
Clement St *DARN/MH* S9 .... 172 D1
　KIMB S61 .... 154 B1
Clevedon Crs *BTLY* DN5 .... 64 C6
Clevedon Wy *BSLYN/ROY* S71 .... 30 C3 🔟
Cleveland Rd *ARMTH* DN3 .... 93 H1
Cleveland St *DON* DN1 .... 4 C3
　ST/HB/BR S6 .... 8 B1
Cleveland Wy *HTFD* DN7 .... 42 C7
Clevland Cl *WRKN* S81 .... 180 C8
Cliff Crs *DONS/BSCR* DN4 .... 115 J5
Cliff Dr *WMB/DAR* S73 .... 85 F2
　CHPT/GREN S35 .... 80 C7
Cliffe Bank *MEX/SWTN* S64 .... 112 C5
Cliffe Cl *CUD/GR* S72 .... 32 C5
Cliffe Common La *CHPT/GREN* S35 .. 80 D8
Cliffe Ct *BSLYN/ROY* S71 .... 3 F2
Cliffe Crs *DOD/DAR* S75 .... 54 D8 🔟
Cliffedale Crs *BSLY* S70 .... 82 C1
Cliffe Farm Dr *ECC* S11 .... 170 A8 🔟
Cliffefield Rd *MEX/SWTN* S64 .... 112 C5
　SHEFS S8 .... 187 F2
Cliffe Hl *ST/HB/BR* S6 .... 170 A2
　WMB/DAR S73 .... 84 E7
Cliffe House Ms *SHEFN* S5 .... 152 C3
Cliffe La *BSLYN/ROY* S71 .... 3 F2 🔟
　HATH/EY S32 .... 182 B7
Cliffe Rd *ST/HB/BR* S6 .... 170 A2
　WMB/DAR S73 .... 84 E7
Cliffe St *KBTN* HD8 .... 26 C5
Cliffe Vw *KBTN* HD8 .... 26 C5
Cliffewood Ri *KBTN* HD8 .... 26 B5 🔟
Cliff Hl *DOD/DAR* S75 .... 53 H2
　MALT S66 .... 158 E2
Cliff Hill Rd *AWLS/ASK* DN6 .... 17 J4
Cliff Hills Cl *MALT* S66 .... 159 F2
Cliff House La *HOLM/MEL* HD7 ..... 48 A1
Cliff La *CUD/GR* S72 .... 32 B5
　HOLM/MEL HD7 .... 48 A1 🔟
Clifford Av *RHAM/THRY* S65 .... 135 F5 🔟
Clifford Rd *ECC* S11 .... 170 D8
　HEM/SK/SE WF9 .... 34 A5

KIMB S61 .... **132** B6
MALT S66 .... **158** B3
lifford St *CUD/GR* S72 .... **31** K6
HEM/SK/SE WF9 .... **34** E5 🔟
liff Rd *HOLM/MEL* HD7 .... **46** D3
HOLM/MEL HD7 .... **48** A2
ST/HB/BR S6 .... **169** H1
WMB/DAR S73 .... **85** F3
liff St *ECC* S11 .... **8** C5
MEX/SWTN S64 .... **113** F3
liff Vw *CONI* DN12 .... **114** A3
lifton Av *BSLYN/ROY* S71 .... **29** K7
DARN/MH S9 .... **173** C4
HOLM/MEL HD7 .... **48** A1
RHAM/THRY S65 .... **7** F4
STV/CWN S43 .... **206** A8
lifton Bank *RHAM/THRY* S65 .... **7** D4
lifton Cl *BSLYN/ROY* S71 .... **29** K7
lifton Ct *THNE* DN8 .... **23** H7
lifton Crs *BSLYN/ROY* S71 .... **30** A6
DARN/MH S9 .... **173** F4
WHHL DN2 .... **92** A1
lifton Crs North *RHAM/THRY* S65 .... **7** E4
lifton Crs South *RHAM/THRY* S65 .... **7** E4
lifton Dr *BTLY* DN5 .... **90** A5
lifton Gdns *CUD/GR* S72 .... **32** B4
lifton Gv *RHAM/THRY* S65 .... **7** E4
lifton In *CONI* DN12 .... **114** E6
lifton La *DARN/MH* S9 .... **173** C5
RHAM/THRY S65 .... **7** E4 🔟
lifton Mt *RHAM/THRY* S65 .... **7** D4
lifton Ri *MALT* S66 .... **159** F1
lifton Rd *CUD/GR* S72 .... **32** D8
lifton St *BSLY* S70 .... **3** D5 🔟
DARN/MH S9 .... **153** J7
HEM/SK/SE WF9 .... **33** F1
lifton Ter *RHAM/THRY* S65 .... **7** D4
linthill La *WRKS* S80 .... **208** A8
linton Pl *FUL* S10 .... **8** B5
linton St *WRKS* S80 .... **210** E6
lipstone Av *BSLYN/ROY* S71 .... **30** A7
lipstone Gdns *DARN/MH* S9 .... **172** E1
lipstone Rd *DARN/MH* S9 .... **172** E1
lock Row Av *HEM/SK/SE* WF9 .... **34** C4
lock Row La *HEM/SK/SE* WF9 .... **34** C4
lock Row Mt *HEM/SK/SE* WF9 .... **34** C4
he Cloisters *DONS/BSCR* DN4 .... **93** F8
loisters Wy *BSLYN/ROY* S71 .... **56** E5
loonmore Cft *SHEFS* S8 .... **187** H6
loonmore Dr *SHEFS* S8 .... **187** J6
lose Barn *WRKN* S81 .... **196** E8 🔟
he Close *ARMTH* DN3 .... **93** J7
AWLS/ASK DN6 .... **18** A4
BSLYN/ROY S71 .... **30** D6
BSLYN/ROY S71 .... **57** G4 🔟
BTLY DN5 .... **60** B3
KBTN HD8 .... **26** E5 🔟
loudberry Wy *DOD/DAR* S75 .... **29** J7
SHEFP/MNR S2 ....
lough Bank *KIMB* S61 .... **6** A3
lough La *FUL* S10 .... **9** E6
lough Fields Rd *HOY* S74 .... **108** D2
lough Foot La *HOLM/MEL* HD7 .... **47** K8
lough Gn *KIMB* S61 .... **6** A3
lough House La *KBTN* HD8 .... **51** K1
lough La *AWLS/ASK* DN6 .... **19** F4
ECC S11 .... **184** E2
lough Rd *HOY* S74 .... **108** C2 🔟
KIMB S61 .... **6** A3
SHEF S1 .... **9** D5
lough St *KIMB* S61 .... **6** A3
lough Wood Vw *CHPT/GREN* S35 ..... **150** C5
lovelly Rd *ARMTH* DN3 .... **66** E5
lover Cl *WRKN* S81 .... **197** F8
lover Gdns *SHEFS* S8 .... **153** F4
lover Rd *DONS/BSCR* DN4 .... **5** F5
FUL S10 .... **169** A6
lumber St *DOD/DAR* S75 .... **2** A3
lun Rd *ATT* S4 .... **171** J1
lun St *ATT* S4 .... **171** J1
lyde Rd *SHEFS* S8 .... **187** F1
lyde St *BSLYN/ROY* S71 .... **2** C4
oach Gate La *STKB/PEN* S36 .... **52** A5
oach House La *BSLY* S70 .... **82** A1 🔟
he Coach Houses *FUL* S10 .... **8** A2 🔟
oach Rd *KIMB* S61 .... **132** E5
oalbush Av *HAN/WDH* S13 .... **174** B7
oalbrook Gv *HAN/WDH* S13 .... **174** B7
oalbrook La *HAN/WDH* S13 .... **174** B7
oalbrook Rd *HAN/WDH* S13 .... **174** B7
oalpit La *KBTN* HD8 .... **51** G4
oal Pit La *CHPT/GREN* S35 .... **149** K2
CONI DN12 .... **136** D5
CUD/GR S72 .... **57** K2
HEM/SK/SE WF9 .... **35** K3
HOLM/MEL HD7 .... **48** B1
PONT WF8 .... **16** A4

STKB/PEN S36 .... **104** E8
Coalpit Rd *CONI* DN12 .... **113** K4
Coates La *STKB/PEN* S36 .... **79** H5
Coates St *SHEFP/MNR* S2 .... **9** F4 🔟
Cobb Ct *MEX/SWTN* S64 .... **112** C6
Cobb Dr *MEX/SWTN* S64 .... **112** B6
Cobcar Av *HOY* S74 .... **109** J2
Cobcar Cl *HOY* S74 .... **109** H1
Cobcar La *HOY* S74 .... **109** H1
Cobcar St *HOY* S74 .... **109** H2
Cobden Av *MEX/SWTN* S64 .... **113** G2
Cobden Pl *FUL* S10 .... **170** C3 🔟
Cobden View Rd *FUL* S10 .... **170** B3
Cobnar Av *SHEFS* S8 .... **187** G5
Cobnar Dr *SHEFS* S8 .... **187** G5
Cobnar Gdns *SHEFS* S8 .... **187** F5 🔟
Cobnar Rd *SHEFS* S8 .... **187** F5
Cockayne Pl *SHEFS* S8 .... **187** F3
Cockerham Av *DOD/DAR* S75 .... **2** B2
Cockerham La *DOD/DAR* S75 .... **2** B2
Cockhill Cl *BWTY* DN10 .... **164** B1
Cockhill Field La *MALT* S66 .... **137** H5
Cock Hill La *BWTY* DN10 .... **164** A1
Cockhill La *CONI* DN12 .... **137** J3
Cockshot La *STKB/PEN* S36 .... **105** F8
Cockshutt Dr *SHEFS* S8 .... **186** D7
Cockshutt Dr *SHEFS* S8 .... **186** D7
Cockshutt Rd *SHEFS* S8 .... **186** D7
Cockshutts La *CHPT/GREN* S35 .... **128** A6
Coggers La *HATH/EY* S32 .... **182** B6
Coisley Hl *HAN/WDH* S13 .... **189** H2
Coisley Rd *HAN/WDH* S13 .... **189** J1
Coit La *ECC* S11 .... **185** H4
Coke Hl *RHAM* S60 .... **6** C5
Coke La *RHAM* S60 .... **6** C5
Colbeck St *WRKS* S80 .... **210** C4 🔟
Colby Pl *ST/HB/BR* S6 .... **169** K2
Colchester Ct *BTLY* DN5 .... **90** B1
Colchester Rd *FUL* S10 .... **170** B3 🔟
Cold Side *EDL/UDV* S33 .... **125** F5
Coldstream Av *DONS/BSCR* DN4 ..... **116** A1
Coldwell Hl *CHPT/GREN* S35 .... **128** A8
Coldwell La *FUL* S10 .... **169** J4
Cold Well La *HOLM/MEL* HD7 .... **46** E3
Coleford Rd *DARN/MH* S9 .... **173** F2
Coleman St *RAW* S62 .... **133** J4 🔟
Coleridge Av *BSLYN/ROY* S71 .... **3** E1
Coleridge Rd *ARMTH* DN3 .... **40** E7
DARN/MH S9 .... **153** J8
DEARNE S63 .... **85** F8
MALT S66 .... **159** H3
RHAM/THRY S65 .... **7** E3
RHAM/THRY S65 .... **7** F2 🔟
WRKN S81 .... **211** F2
Coley La *RAW* S62 .... **110** A5
Colister Dr *DARN/MH* S9 .... **172** D3
Colister Gdns *DARN/MH* S9 .... **172** D4
College La *WRKS* S80 .... **211** F6
College Park Cl *RHAM* S60 .... **115** H4
ECK/KIL S21 .... **205** G6
MEX/SWTN S64 .... **113** G2
College St *FUL* S10 .... **8** A4 🔟
RHAM/THRY S65 .... **6** C4 🔟
Collegiate Crs *FUL* S10 .... **8** A5
Colley Av *BSLY* S70 .... **82** D1
SHEFN S5 .... **152** B1
Colley Cl *SHEFN* S5 .... **152** B1
Colley Crs *BSLY* S70 .... **82** D1
SHEFN S5 .... **152** C1
Colley Dr *SHEFN* S5 .... **152** C1
Colley Pl *BSLY* S70 .... **3** F6 🔟
Colley Rd *SHEFN* S5 .... **152** B1
Colliers Cl *HAN/WDH* S13 .... **189** K1
Colliers Wy *KBTN* HD8 .... **26** C3
Colliery Cl *DIN* S25 .... **178** A5
Colliery La *DEARNE* S63 .... **86** C1
Colliery Rd *ATT* S4 .... **153** H6
AU/AST/KP S26 .... **192** D5
NROS/TKH DN11 .... **165** G4
Colliery Yd *DOD/DAR* S75 .... **107** J3
Collin Av *ST/HB/BR* S6 .... **151** F6
Collindridge Rd *WMB/DAR* S73 ...... **84** A5
Collingbourne Av *MOS* S20 .... **190** E6
Collingbourne Dr *MOS* S20 .... **190** E6 🔟
Collingham Rd *AU/AST/KP* S26 .... **191** J2
Collins Cl *DOD/DAR* S75 .... **54** D8
Collins Rd *SHEFN* S5 .... **152** D1
Colonel Ward Dr *MEX/SWTN* S64 ... **112** D4
Colster Cl *DONS/BSCR* DN4 .... **55** F5
Colsterdale *WRKN* S81 .... **197** F8
Coltfield *BSLY* S70 .... **82** A6
Coltishall Av *MALT* S66 .... **157** K1
Coltsworth La *STV/CWN* S43 .... **206** D7
Columbia St *BSLY* S70 .... **2** B6
Columbus Wy *MALT* S66 .... **158** E1
Colver Rd *SHEFP/MNR* S2 .... **9** D6
Colvin Cl *BTLY* DN5 .... **65** H6
Colwall St *DARN/MH* S9 .... **172** B1
Commerce St *CHPT/GREN* S35 .... **130** B2
Commercial Rd *DEARNE* S63 .... **86** B3
Commercial St *BSLY* S70 .... **3** G3 🔟
SHEF S1 .... **9** E3
Common Farm Cl
RHAM/THRY S65 .... **135** J7
Common La *ARMTH* DN3 .... **41** H8
AWLS/ASK DN6 .... **18** D1
AWLS/ASK DN6 .... **18** A4
BSLYN/ROY S71 .... **30** D3

BTLY DN5 .... **60** B2
BTLY DN5 .... **65** K3
CONI DN12 .... **114** E8
DEARNE S63 .... **86** C7
DEARNE S63 .... **112** A4
DIN S25 .... **177** H3
DONS/BSCR DN4 .... **116** A2
ECC S11 .... **185** H2
EPW DN9 .... **94** B8
GLE DN14 .... **19** F2
KBTN HD8 .... **51** J1
MALT S66 .... **176** D2
NROS/TKH DN11 .... **139** K7
NROS/TKH DN11 .... **140** B7
NROS/TKH DN11 .... **141** G1
NROS/TKH DN11 .... **162** D3 🔟
RHAM/THRY S65 .... **136** B6
STKB/PEN S36 .... **105** H8
Common Rd *AU/AST/KP* S26 .... **177** F6
AU/AST/KP S26 .... **207** G2
CONI DN12 .... **115** F7
CUD/GR S72 .... **32** D4
DEARNE S63 .... **60** A7
DIN S25 .... **178** A5
WRKS S80 .... **208** B2
Common Road Av
HEM/SK/SE WF9 .... **33** K6
Commonside *FUL* S10 .... **170** C3
The Common *CHPT/GREN* S35 .... **130** C5
Commonwealth Vw *DEARNE* S63 .... **86** A5
Compton St *ST/HB/BR* S6 .... **170** B1
Conalan Av *TOT/DORE* S17 .... **200** B2
Conan Rd *CONI* DN12 .... **114** C5
Concord Rd *SHEFN* S5 .... **153** F1
Concord View Rd *KIMB* S61 .... **153** K2
Conduit La *FUL* S10 .... **170** C5 🔟
Conduit Rd *FUL* S10 .... **170** C5
Cone La *DOD/DAR* S75 .... **53** K8
STKB/PEN S36 .... **79** J2
Conery Cl *RHAM/THRY* S65 .... **135** F5
Coney Rd *BTLY* DN5 .... **64** D3 🔟
Congress St *SHEF* S1 .... **8** C5 🔟
Coningsburgh Rd *ARMTH* DN3 .... **66** E5
Coningsby Rd *SHEFN* S5 .... **152** D6
Coniston Av *DOD/DAR* S75 .... **29** F5
Coniston Cl *DIN* S25 .... **194** D1 🔟
STKB/PEN S36 .... **78** A3
Coniston Dr *DEARNE* S63 .... **86** B6
Coniston Pl *BTLY* DN5 .... **64** C7 🔟
Coniston Rd *ARMTH* DN3 .... **66** E3
AWLS/ASK DN6 .... **19** F7
BSLYN/ROY S71 .... **3** D4
DRON S18 .... **200** E6
MEX/SWTN S64 .... **113** H1
SHEFS S8 .... **186** E2
WHHL DN2 .... **92** B3
WRKN S81 .... **196** C7
Coniston Ter *SHEFS* S8 .... **186** E2 🔟
Connaught Dr *ARMTH* DN3 .... **66** E3
Conrad Cl *WRKS* S80 .... **211** F4
Conrad Dr *MALT* S66 .... **159** F1
Constable Cl *DRON* S18 .... **200** E7
GLV S14 .... **188** A5 🔟
MALT S66 .... **157** G2
Constable Dr *SHEFS* S8 .... **187** K5
Constable La *DIN* S25 .... **178** A6
Constable Pl *DEARNE* S63 .... **111** H1
GLV S14 .... **188** A5
Constable Rd *SHEFS* S8 .... **187** K5
Constable Wy *SHEFS* S8 .... **187** K5 🔟
Convent Gv *DONS/BSCR* DN4 .... **92** C7
Convent Pl *OWL* S3 .... **8** C3 🔟
Convent Wk *OWL* S3 .... **8** C3
Conway Crs *RHAM/THRY* S65 .... **134** B7
Conway Dr *ARMTH* DN3 .... **93** J7
BTLY DN5 .... **87** H4
WRKN S81 .... **196** D1
Conway Pl *WMB/DAR* S73 .... **84** C6
Conway St *BSLY* S70 .... **56** E7
OWL S3 .... **8** B5 🔟
Conway Ter *MEX/SWTN* S64 .... **113** F1
Conyers Dr *AU/AST/KP* S26 .... **175** H7
Conyers Rd *BTLY* DN5 .... **4** B1
Coo Hi *HAN/WDH* S13 .... **190** A1
Cook Av *MALT* S66 .... **159** F1
Cooke St *BTLY* DN5 .... **64** D7
Cookson Cl *SHEFN* S5 .... **151** J3
Cookson Rd *SHEFN* S5 .... **151** J4
Cookson St *DONS/BSCR* DN4 .... **4** B6
Cooks Rd *MOS* S20 .... **190** E5
Cooks Wood Rd *OWL* S3 .... **152** B8
Coombe Pl *FUL* S10 .... **170** C4 🔟
Coombe Rd *FUL* S10 .... **170** B4
Co-operative St *CUD/GR* S72 .... **57** H1 🔟
DEARNE S63 .... **85** G8 🔟
Cooper La *HOLM/MEL* HD7 .... **47** K2
STKB/PEN S36 .... **52** E8
Cooper Rd *DOD/DAR* S75 .... **28** B7
Coopers Ter *DON* DN1 .... **5** D3
Cooper St *DONS/BSCR* DN4 .... **5** E5
Co-op La *HOLM/MEL* HD7 .... **47** G4
Copeland Rd *WMB/DAR* S73 .... **83** K5 🔟
Cope St *BSLY* S70 .... **2** C6
Copley Av *CONI* DN12 .... **114** B5
Copley Crs *BTLY* DN5 .... **89** K1
Copley Pl *KIMB* S61 .... **132** D8
Copley Rd *DON* DN1 .... **5** D2 🔟
Copperas Ct *STKB/PEN* S36 .... **77** F4
Copper Cl *BSLY* S70 .... **2** C5 🔟

Copper St *OWL* S3 .... 9 D2
Coppice Av *DOD/DAR* S75 .... 55 G3
   HTFD DN7 .... 68 B1
Coppice Cl *STKB/PEN* S36 .... 104 C5
Coppice Gdns *KIMB* S61 .... 132 E5
Coppice Gv *HTFD* DN7 .... 42 C8
Coppice La *ST/HB/BR* S6 .... 169 F3
Coppice Rd *AWLS/ASK* DN6 .... 63 J5
   WRKN S81 .... 196 D8
The Coppice *KIMB* S61 .... 131 K5
Coppice Vw *FUL* S10 .... 169 K4 ⬛
Coppice Wy *WRKN* S81 .... 180 D8
Coppicewood Ct
   DONS/BSCR DN4 .... 117 F3
Coppins Cl *MALT* S66 .... 157 J1
Coppin Sq *SHEFN* S5 .... 130 A8 ⬛
The Copse *MALT* S66 .... 157 J1
Copster Cl *CHPT/GREN* S35 .... 79 J8
Copster La *STKB/PEN* S36 .... 79 H6
Copthurst Rd *HOLM/MEL* HD7 .... 47 C7
Coquet Av *MALT* S66 .... 157 J3
Coral Cl *AU/AST/KP* S26 .... 175 G5
Coral Dr *AU/AST/KP* S26 .... 175 G5
Coral La *AU/AST/KP* S26 .... 175 G5
Coral Wy *AU/AST/KP* S26 .... 175 G5
Corby St *ATT* S4 .... 171 K1
Corker Bottoms La
   SHEFP/MNR S2 .... 172 B4
Corker Cl *ST/HB/BR* S6 .... 148 D7
Corker Rd *HACK/IN* S12 .... 188 C1
Corn Hl *CONI* DN12 .... 114 E6
Cornish St *OWL* S3 .... 8 C1
Cornish Wy *RAW* S62 .... 133 H5
Cornwall Cl *BSLYN/ROY* S71 .... 3 E1
Cornwall Rd *WHHL* DN2 .... 92 A2
   WRKN S81 .... 195 H8
Cornwell Cl *RAW* S62 .... 111 F7
Corona Dr *THNE* DN8 .... 23 J7
Coronation *AU/AST/KP* S26 .... 192 C5
Coronation Av *BSLYN/ROY* S71 .... 3 F1
   DEARNE S63 .... 60 D8
   WMB/DAR S73 .... 84 E1
Coronation Br *RHAM* S60 .... 6 A4
Coronation Dr *DEARNE* S63 .... 86 A5
Coronation Gdns
   DONS/BSCR DN4 .... 115 K1 ⬛
Coronation Rd *DEARNE* S63 .... 111 K1
   DOD/DAR S75 .... 54 C3
   DONS/BSCR DN4 .... 90 E8
   HOY S74 .... 108 E1
   HTFD DN7 .... 42 A3
   MEX/SWTN S64 .... 112 D4
   RAW S62 .... 134 B1
   STKB/PEN S36 .... 104 A1
Coronation Ter *BSLYN/ROY* S71 .... 57 G7
Corporation St *BSLY* S70 .... 3 D6
   OWL S3 .... 9 D2
   RHAM S60 .... 6 C3
Cortina Ri *WMB/DAR* S73 .... 84 B1 ⬛
Cortworth La *RAW* S62 .... 110 A6
Cortworth Rd *ECC* S11 .... 186 A3
Corwen Pl *HAN/WDH* S13 .... 189 J1
Cossey Rd *ATT* S4 .... 171 J1
Cote La *CHPT/GREN* S35 .... 105 K1
   HOLM/MEL HD7 .... 47 K7
Coterel Crs *DONS/BSCR* DN4 .... 92 E6
Cotleigh Av *HACK/IN* S12 .... 189 J4
Cotleigh Cl *HACK/IN* S12 .... 189 J4 ⬛
Cotleigh Crs *HACK/IN* S12 .... 189 J4
Cotleigh Dr *HACK/IN* S12 .... 189 J4
Cotleigh Gdns *HACK/IN* S12 .... 189 J4 ⬛
Cotleigh Pl *HACK/IN* S12 .... 189 J4 ⬛
Cotleigh Rd *HACK/IN* S12 .... 189 J4
Cotleigh Wy *HACK/IN* S12 .... 189 J4
Cotswold Av *CHPT/GREN* S35 .... 129 K2
Cotswold Cl *DOD/DAR* S75 .... 55 G5 ⬛
Cotswold Crs *RHAM* S60 .... 156 B5
Cotswold Dr *AU/AST/KP* S26 .... 175 J8
   BTLY DN5 .... 89 H6
Cotswold Gdns *BTLY* DN5 .... 64 C8 ⬛
Cotswold Rd *ST/HB/BR* S6 .... 151 G6
   THNE DN8 .... 43 H1
Cottage La *ECC* S11 .... 185 G2
Cottam Cl *RHAM* S60 .... 156 B6
Cottam Rd *CHPT/GREN* S35 .... 107 H8
Cottenham Rd *RHAM/THRY* S65 .... 7 E3
Cottesmore Cl *DOD/DAR* S75 .... 55 H4 ⬛
Cottingham St *DARN/MH* S9 .... 172 D5
Cotton Mill Rw *OWL* S3 .... 9 D1 ⬛
Cotton St *OWL* S3 .... 9 D2
Coulman Rd *THNE* DN8 .... 24 A7
Coulman St *THNE* DN8 .... 23 K6
Coultas Av *STKB/PEN* S36 .... 105 G7
Countess Dr *SHEF* S1 .... 9 D5 ⬛
County Wy *BSLY* S70 .... 2 C3
Coupland Ct *BTLY* DN5 .... 90 A1
Coupland Rd *RHAM/THRY* S65 .... 134 B7
Court Cl *BTLY* DN5 .... 90 A1
The Courtyard *CONI* DN12 .... 113 H4
Coventry Dr *WRKN* S81 .... 210 E1 ⬛
Coventry Gv *WHHL* DN2 .... 66 A8
Coventry Rd *DARN/MH* S9 .... 172 C2
   THNE DN8 .... 23 K8
Cover Cl *RAW* S62 .... 108 E6
Coverdale *WRKN* S81 .... 197 F8

Coverdale Rd *ABRD* S7 .... 186 E2
Cover Dr *WMB/DAR* S73 .... 84 E1
Coverleigh Rd *DEARNE* S63 .... 111 J3
Coward Dr *CHPT/GREN* S35 .... 128 C8
Cowcliff Hill Rd *HOLM/MEL* HD7 .... 48 C7
Cow Gap La *ST/HB/BR* S6 .... 149 G8
Cow House La *ARMTH* DN3 .... 46 A7
Cowick Rd *GLE* DN14 .... 23 F1
Cow La *ECC* S11 .... 186 A4
Cowley Bottom *DRON* S18 .... 200 E7
Cowley Dr *CHPT/GREN* S35 .... 130 D3
Cowley Gdns *MOS* S20 .... 190 C7
Cowley Gv *WMB/DAR* S73 .... 83 J5
Cowley Hl *CHPT/GREN* S35 .... 130 D3
Cowley La *DRON* S18 .... 200 D7
Cowley Pl *ARMTH* DN3 .... 66 E3 ⬛
Cowley Vw *CHPT/GREN* S35 .... 150 C1
Cowley View Rd *CHPT/GREN* S35 .... 130 C4
Cowlishaw Rd *ECC* S11 .... 170 C4
Cowood St *MEX/SWTN* S64 .... 112 E2 ⬛
Cowper Av *ST/HB/BR* S6 .... 151 J1
Cowper Cl *WRKN* S81 .... 211 F2
Cowper Crs *ST/HB/BR* S6 .... 151 J1
Cowper Dr *RHAM/THRY* S65 .... 156 A3
   ST/HB/BR S6 .... 151 J1
Cowper Rd *MEX/SWTN* S64 .... 113 H2
Cowrakes Cl *RHAM* S60 .... 156 B6
Cow Rakes La *RHAM* S60 .... 156 B6
Cox Pl *ST/HB/BR* S6 .... 150 E6
Cox Rd *ST/HB/BR* S6 .... 150 E6
Crabgate Dr *AWLS/ASK* DN6 .... 37 F5
Crabgate La *AWLS/ASK* DN6 .... 37 F5
Crabtree Cl *SHEFN* S5 .... 152 D6
Crabtree Dr *SHEFN* S5 .... 152 D6
Crabtree Dr *CUD/GR* S72 .... 59 G4
   SHEFN S5 .... 152 D6
Crab Tree La *PONT* WF8 .... 16 C5
Crabtree La *SHEFN* S5 .... 152 C7
Crabtree Pl *SHEFN* S5 .... 152 C6
Crabtree Rd *HTFD* DN7 .... 42 A6
   SHEFN S5 .... 152 C6
Cradley Dr *AU/AST/KP* S26 .... 175 J8
Cradock Ms *SHEFP/MNR* S2 .... 172 A8 ⬛
Cradock Rd *SHEFP/MNR* S2 .... 172 A8
Cragdale Gv *MOS* S20 .... 190 B8
Crags Rd *CONI* DN12 .... 114 C3
Crag Vw *CHPT/GREN* S35 .... 105 K1
Crag View Cl *CHPT/GREN* S35 .... 128 C7
Crag View La *CHPT/GREN* S35 .... 128 B7
Craigston Rd *WRKN* S81 .... 196 C1
Craig Wk *MALT* S66 .... 157 K2
Craithie Rd *WHHL* DN2 .... 5 F2
   WRKN S81 .... 196 C1
Crakehall Rd *CHPT/GREN* S35 .... 130 B4
Cramfit Cl *DIN* S25 .... 193 K1
Cramfit Crs *DIN* S25 .... 177 K7
Cramfit Rd *DIN* S25 .... 177 J8
Cramlands *DOD/DAR* S75 .... 55 F8 ⬛
Cranberry Rd *STKB/PEN* S36 .... 104 A1
Cranborne Dr *DOD/DAR* S75 .... 28 E6 ⬛
Cranbrook Rd *DON* DN1 .... 5 E1
Cranbrook St *BSLY* S70 .... 2 A5 ⬛
Crane Dr *KIMB* S61 .... 132 B8
Crane Greave La *CHPT/GREN* S35 .... 80 B3
Crane Moor Cl *BTLY* DN5 .... 87 H5
Crane Moor Nook
   CHPT/GREN S35 .... 106 A1
Crane Moor Rd *CHPT/GREN* S35 .... 106 A1
Crane Rd *KIMB* S61 .... 132 B5
Crane Well La *DEARNE* S63 .... 86 D5
Cranfield Cl *ARMTH* DN3 .... 93 G2
Cranfield Dr *AWLS/ASK* DN6 .... 37 G5
Cranford Ct *MOS* S20 .... 189 J5 ⬛
Cranford Dr *HACK/IN* S12 .... 189 J4
Cranford Gdns *BSLYN/ROY* S71 .... 30 C3
Cranleigh Gdns *AWLS/ASK* DN6 .... 63 J7
Cranston Cl *BSLYN/ROY* S71 .... 56 E3
Cranwell Rd *DONS/BSCR* DN4 .... 4 A4 ⬛
Cranworth Pl *OWL* S3 .... 171 K1 ⬛
Cranworth Rd *OWL* S3 .... 171 K1 ⬛
   RHAM/THRY S65 .... 7 E2
Craven Cl *BSLYN/ROY* S71 .... 30 C3
   DARN/MH S9 .... 172 E2 ⬛
   DONS/BSCR DN4 .... 92 D7 ⬛
Craven Rd *HEM/SK/SE* WF9 .... 33 G1
   HTFD DN7 .... 42 A7
Craven St *OWL* S3 .... 8 C2 ⬛
   RAW S62 .... 133 J4
Craven Wood Cl *DOD/DAR* S75 .... 55 F4
Crawford Rd *SHEFS* S8 .... 187 F3
Crawley Av *HEM/SK/SE* WF9 .... 34 C4
Crawshaw Av *SHEFS* S8 .... 186 D7
Crawshaw Gv *SHEFS* S8 .... 186 D7
Crawshaw Rd *DONS/BSCR* DN4 .... 4 A4 ⬛
Cream St *SHEFP/MNR* S2 .... 9 E5 ⬛
Crecy Av *WHHL* DN2 .... 92 B3
Creighton Av *RAW* S62 .... 134 A2 ⬛
Cresacre Av *BTLY* DN5 .... 87 H4
Crescent *AU/AST/KP* S26 .... 206 E2
The Crescent East *MALT* S66 .... 157 H1
The Crescent End *MALT* S66 .... 177 F1
Crescent Rd *ABRD* S7 .... 170 E8
The Crescent *ARMTH* DN3 .... 66 E5
   ARMTH DN3 .... 93 H2
   AWLS/ASK DN6 .... 63 G3
   CONI DN12 .... 114 B5
   CONI DN12 .... 115 J5
   DEARNE S63 .... 86 B4
   DIN S25 .... 178 C6

   DOD/DAR S75 .... 55 C3
   DRON S18 .... 200 A7
   EPW DN9 .... 121 G2
   HOLM/MEL HD7 .... 48 D1 ⬛
   HTFD DN7 .... 42 A6
   MALT S66 .... 177 G2
   MEX/SWTN S64 .... 112 A5
   NROS/TKH DN11 .... 163 H3
   TOT/DORE S17 .... 199 J2
The Crescent West *MALT* S66 .... 135 G8
Cresswell Rd *DARN/MH* S9 .... 172 E3
   MEX/SWTN S64 .... 112 C3
   WRKN S80 .... 210 C3
Cresswell St *DOD/DAR* S75 .... 55 H1
   MEX/SWTN S64 .... 112 C3 ⬛
   WRKN S80 .... 210 C4 ⬛
Crest Rd *SHEFN* S5 .... 152 C3
Crestwood Ct *SHEFN* S5 .... 152 D3
Crestwood Gdns *SHEFN* S5 .... 152 D3 ⬛
Creswick Av *SHEFN* S5 .... 130 A8
Creswick Cl *RHAM/THRY* S65 .... 134 C7
Creswick Greave *SHEFN* S5 .... 129 K8
Creswick La *CHPT/GREN* S35 .... 129 K7
Creswick Rd *RHAM/THRY* S65 .... 134 C7
Creswick St *ST/HB/BR* S6 .... 170 D1
Creswick Wy *ST/HB/BR* S6 .... 170 D1
Crewe Rd *NROS/TKH* DN11 .... 163 G3
Crich Av *BSLYN/ROY* S71 .... 30 B8
Cricket Inn Crs *SHEFP/MNR* S2 .... 172 A3
Cricket Inn Rd *SHEFP/MNR* S2 .... 9 F2
Cricket View Rd *RAW* S62 .... 108 E6
Cridling Gdns *AWLS/ASK* DN6 .... 18 B4
Crimicar Av *FUL* S10 .... 169 F7
Crimicar Cl *FUL* S10 .... 169 G8
Crimicar Dr *FUL* S10 .... 169 F7
Crimicar La *FUL* S10 .... 169 F6
Cripps Av *NROS/TKH* DN11 .... 119 F6
Cripps Cl *MALT* S66 .... 159 J3
Crispin Cl *HACK/IN* S12 .... 188 C3 ⬛
Crispin Gdns *HACK/IN* S12 .... 188 C2
Crispin Rd *HACK/IN* S12 .... 188 C3 ⬛
Croasdale Gdns *AWLS/ASK* DN6 .... 37 K7
Crochley Cl *DONS/BSCR* DN4 .... 92 E6 ⬛
Croft Abbey *ECK/KIL* S21 .... 205 G2
Croft Av *BSLYN/ROY* S71 .... 30 C4
Croft Cl *DOD/DAR* S75 .... 29 F6
   ECC S11 .... 185 K4 ⬛
Croft Ct *ARMTH* DN3 .... 90 D6
   EPW DN9 .... 121 F4
Croft Dr *BSLYN/ROY* S71 .... 30 A8 ⬛
   DOD/DAR S75 .... 29 G8
   NROS/TKH DN11 .... 139 K2
   STKB/PEN S36 .... 77 F2
Crofters Cl *ECK/KIL* S21 .... 205 G2
Croft Farm Cl *BWTY* DN10 .... 165 K2
Croft La *ECC* S11 .... 185 K4
Croft Lea *DRON* S18 .... 200 C5
Crofton St *ST/HB/BR* S6 .... 151 G5
Crofton Cl *DRON* S18 .... 201 F6
Crofton Dr *DEARNE* S63 .... 86 B4
Crofton Ri *CHPT/GREN* S35 .... 129 J1
   DRON S18 .... 201 F6
Croft Rd *BSLY* S70 .... 3 F6
   BWTY DN10 .... 121 G5
   DONS/BSCR DN4 .... 116 B2
   HACK/IN S12 .... 188 D2
   HOY S74 .... 82 E8
   RHAM S60 .... 154 E6
Crofts Dr *RHAM/THRY* S65 .... 134 D5 ⬛
Crofts La *HTFD* DN7 .... 41 H7
The Crofts *HATH/EY* S32 .... 182 C7 ⬛
   MALT S66 .... 157 G4
   RHAM S60 .... 6 C4
Croft St *BSLY* S70 .... 82 E2 ⬛
   KIMB S61 .... 65 H4
The Croft *BTLY* DN5 .... 65 H4
   CONI DN12 .... 114 D6
   DOD/DAR S75 .... 54 D2
   HOY S74 .... 109 H2 ⬛
   MEX/SWTN S64 .... 112 A5
   RHAM S60 .... 174 A2
   STKB/PEN S36 .... 78 C1
   THNE DN8 .... 43 K7
   WRKN S80 .... 210 D5
Croft Wy *BWTY* DN10 .... 165 K2
Cromarty Ri *DRON* S18 .... 200 D5
Cromer Cl *RAW* S62 .... 133 J1 ⬛
Cromer Rd *WHHL* DN2 .... 92 B3
Cromer St *CUD/GR* S72 .... 32 D8
Cromford Av *BSLYN/ROY* S71 .... 56 C1 ⬛
Cromford St *SHEFP/MNR* S2 .... 9 E5 ⬛
Crompton Av *BSLY* S70 .... 2 A5
   BTLY DN5 .... 90 C2
Crompton Rd *WHHL* DN2 .... 66 A7
Cromwell Cl *WRKN* S81 .... 196 B3
Cromwell Ct *AWLS/ASK* DN6 .... 37 G6 ⬛
Cromwell Dr *BTLY* DN5 .... 90 B3
Cromwell Gv *AWLS/ASK* DN6 .... 37 H5 ⬛
Cromwell Mt *BSLY* S70 .... 81 K1 ⬛
Cromwell Rd *BTLY* DN5 .... 4 B1 ⬛
   MEX/SWTN S64 .... 113 F7 ⬛
Cromwell St *DEARNE* S63 .... 60 D1
   ST/HB/BR S6 .... 170 C1
Cronkhill La *BSLYN/ROY* S71 .... 30 E1
Crooked La *CONI* DN12 .... 113 J1
Crooked Lane Head
   NROS/TKH DN11 .... 161 H1
Crooke House La *BSLYN/ROY* S71 .... 58 C2
Crookes *FUL* S10 .... 170 B3

rookes Broom Av *HTFD* DN7 ...... 42 C8
rookes Broom La *HTFD* DN7 ...... 42 B8
rookes La *BSLYN/ROY* S71 ...... 30 D6
rookesmoor Dr *ST/HB/BR* S6 ...... 8 A2 🔲
rookesmoor Rd *FUL* S10 ...... 8 A2
rookes Rd *DONS/BSCR* DN4 ...... 116 E1 🔲
...... *FUL* S10 ...... 170 C4
rookes St *BSLY* S70 ...... 2 A4
rookes Valley Rd *FUL* S10 ...... 8 A2
rookhill Rd *CONI* DN12 ...... 114 E5
rook Tree La *HTFD* DN7 ...... 43 F5
ropton Rd *BSLYN/ROY* S71 ...... 30 C4
rosby Av *MALT* S66 ...... 157 K2
rosby Ct *BSLYN/ROY* S71 ...... 56 E2
rosby Rd *SHEFS* S8 ...... 186 E5
rosby St *CUD/GR* S72 ...... 31 J7 🔲
ross Allen Rd *MOS* S20 ...... 190 D5
ross Bank *DONS/BSCR* DN4 ...... 4 B6
ross Burgess St *DEARNE* S63 ...... 9 D5 🔲
ross Butcher St *DEARNE* S63 ...... 60 B7 🔲
ross Chantrey Rd *SHEFS* S8 ...... 187 G4
rosscourt Vw *DONS/BSCR* DN4 ...... 92 B7
ross Dr *HAN/WDH* S13 ...... 189 K1 🔲
rossfield Dr *AWLS/ASK* DN6 ...... 37 H5
...... *DEARNE* S63 ...... 111 H2
rossfield House Cl
...... *AWLS/ASK* DN6 ...... 37 H5 🔲
rossfield La *AWLS/ASK* DN6 ...... 37 H6
ross Ga *BTLY* DN5 ...... 90 D1
...... *MEX/SWTN* S64 ...... 113 H3
rossgate *DEARNE* S63 ...... 60 C8
...... *DOD/DAR* S75 ...... 29 G6
ross Gate Rd *HOLM/MEL* HD7 ...... 48 A5
rossgates *NROS/TKH* DN11 ...... 139 F1
ross Hl *CHPT/GREN* S35 ...... 130 D8
...... *CUD/GR* S72 ...... 32 C4
ross Hill Cl *CHPT/GREN* S35 ...... 130 D8
rosshill La *GLE* DN14 ...... 11 G5
rosshouse Cl *CHPT/GREN* S35 ...... 129 G7
ross House Rd *CHPT/GREN* S35 ...... 129 H7
ross Keys La *HOY* S74 ...... 108 D1
rossland Dr *HACK/IN* S12 ...... 188 C4
rossland Pl *HACK/IN* S12 ...... 188 C3
rossland Rd *HATH/EY* S32 ...... 182 C8
rossland St *MEX/SWTN* S64 ...... 112 C5
ross La *BSLYN/ROY* S71 ...... 31 F4
...... *BWTY* DN10 ...... 142 D2
...... *CHPT/GREN* S35 ...... 107 C6
...... *DRON* S18 ...... 201 J6
...... *DRON* S18 ...... 201 J3
...... *FUL* S10 ...... 170 B4
...... *HOLM/MEL* HD7 ...... 48 B5
...... *KBTN* HD8 ...... 49 K1
...... *SHEFS* S8 ...... 201 J2
ross Lane Cl *WRKN* S81 ...... 195 J3
rossley Cl *MALT* S66 ...... 159 F1
rossley Hill La *WRKN* S81 ...... 197 G3
ross Myrtle Rd *SHEFS* S8 ...... 187 G2 🔲
ross Park Rd *SHEFS* S8 ...... 187 G2 🔲
ross Riding *DONS/BSCR* DN4 ...... 92 D3
ross Rd *HTFD* DN7 ...... 43 K8
ross Road Banner *ECC* S11 ...... 186 B2
ross Smithfield *DEARNE* S63 ...... 8 C2
ross South St *KIMB* S61 ...... 133 F4 🔲
ross St *BSLY* S70 ...... 82 C2
...... *BSLYN/ROY* S71 ...... 3 F1
...... *BTLY* DN5 ...... 64 E6
...... *CONI* DN12 ...... 115 J3
...... *CUD/GR* S72 ...... 58 E1
...... *CUD/GR* S72 ...... 59 H6
...... *DEARNE* S63 ...... 86 D2
...... *DEARNE* S63 ...... 111 H1
...... *DOD/DAR* S75 ...... 2 A2
...... *DOD/DAR* S75 ...... 54 C3
...... *DONS/BSCR* DN4 ...... 90 D8 🔲
...... *ECK/KIL* S21 ...... 191 K8
...... *HAN/WDH* S13 ...... 189 K1
...... *HOY* S74 ...... 108 C2 🔲
...... *KIMB* S61 ...... 133 F4 🔲
...... *KIMB* S61 ...... 154 D1
...... *MALT* S66 ...... 157 J2
...... *MALT* S66 ...... 159 H2
...... *MALT* S66 ...... 176 E1
...... *NROS/TKH* DN11 ...... 118 E7
...... *RAW* S62 ...... 133 J4
...... *RHAM/THRY* S65 ...... 134 D5
...... *WRKN* S81 ...... 180 C5
he Cross *WRKN* S81 ...... 196 E1 🔲
ross Turner St *SHEFP/MNR* S2 ...... 9 E4 🔲
rossway *MEX/SWTN* S64 ...... 112 A5
rossways *DEARNE* S63 ...... 86 B5
...... *HTFD* DN7 ...... 42 A3 🔲
...... *WHHL* DN2 ...... 66 A8
rossways North *WHHL* DN2 ...... 66 A8
rossways South *WHHL* DN2 ...... 92 A1
he Crossways
...... *SHEFP/MNR* S2 ...... 172 D6 🔲
row Croft La *GLE* DN14 ...... 12 K6
rowden Wk *DOD/DAR* S75 ...... 55 F6 🔲
rowder Av *SHEFS* S5 ...... 152 B3
rowder Cl *SHEFS* S5 ...... 152 B4
rowder Crs *SHEFS* S5 ...... 152 B4
rowder Rd *SHEFS* S5 ...... 152 B3

Crowgate *DIN* S25 ...... 193 J4
Crowland Rd *SHEFN* S5 ...... 152 C3
Crow La *DRON* S18 ...... 202 B8
Crowley Dr *DEARNE* S63 ...... 111 H3
Crown Av *BSLY* S70 ...... 3 D6 🔲
...... *CUD/GR* S72 ...... 57 K3
Crown Cl *BSLY* S70 ...... 2 C6
...... *KIMB* S61 ...... 132 B7
Crown Hill Rd *DOD/DAR* S75 ...... 55 F6
Crownhill Rd *RHAM* S60 ...... 154 D6
Crown La *HOLM/MEL* HD7 ...... 47 K2 🔲
Crown Pl *SHEFP/MNR* S2 ...... 9 F3 🔲
Crown Rd *NROS/TKH* DN11 ...... 139 J8
Crown St *BSLY* S70 ...... 3 D6 🔲
...... *HOY* S74 ...... 108 E1
...... *KBTN* HD8 ...... 26 A6
...... *MEX/SWTN* S64 ...... 112 C4
...... *WRKS* S80 ...... 210 C3
Crown Well Hl *BSLYN/ROY* S71 ...... 57 G7 🔲
Crowther St *SHEFP/MNR* S2 ...... 8 C6 🔲
Crow Tree Bank *THNE* DN8 ...... 44 E7
Crow Tree La *MEX/SWTN* S64 ...... 86 E8
Croydon St *ECC* S11 ...... 8 C6 🔲
Cruck Cl *DRON* S18 ...... 200 C5
Cruise Rd *ECC* S11 ...... 169 K7
Crummock Rd *SHEFS* S8 ...... 186 E2 🔲
Crummock Wy *BSLYN/ROY* S71 ...... 57 J7 🔲
Crumpsall Dr *ST/HB/BR* S6 ...... 152 A5
Crumpsall Rd *SHEFN* S5 ...... 152 A6
Crumwell Rd *KIMB* S61 ...... 132 A5
Crusader Dr *BTLY* DN5 ...... 90 B4
Cubley Rise Rd *STKB/PEN* S36 ...... 77 K6
Cuckoo Holt *WRKN* S81 ...... 196 A8 🔲
Cuckoo La *MALT* S66 ...... 42 D7
Cuckoo Wy *AU/AST/KP* S26 ...... 193 K6
...... *ECK/KIL* S21 ...... 205 F2
Cuckstool Rd *KBTN* HD8 ...... 51 H1
Cudworth Vw *CUD/GR* S72 ...... 58 D1
Cullabine Rd *SHEFP/MNR* S2 ...... 172 C8
Cumberland Av *WHHL* DN2 ...... 92 A5
Cumberland Cl *BSLY* S70 ...... 82 A2
...... *HOY* S74 ...... 83 F8
...... *NROS/TKH* DN11 ...... 163 J3
...... *WRKN* S81 ...... 180 D8
Cumberland Crs
...... *CHPT/GREN* S35 ...... 130 C3 🔲
Cumberland Dr *BSLYN/ROY* S71 ...... 57 G7
Cumberland Wy *HOY* S74 ...... 83 F8
...... *SHEF* S1 ...... 9 D4 🔲
Cumberworth La *KBTN* HD8 ...... 49 K2
Cumbria Rd *WRKN* S81 ...... 210 E1
Cumwell La *MALT* S66 ...... 158 A4
Cundy St *ST/HB/BR* S6 ...... 170 C2
Cunliffe St *DRON* S18 ...... 201 J3
Cunningham Cl *BWTY* DN10 ...... 165 G7
Cunningham Rd *HTFD* DN7 ...... 69 G7
Cupola *OWL* S3 ...... 9 D2 🔲
Cupola La *CHPT/GREN* S35 ...... 129 H6
Cupola Yd *RHAM* S60 ...... 6 B4 🔲
Curlew Av *ECK/KIL* S21 ...... 203 K4
Curlew Rdg *SHEFP/MNR* S2 ...... 171 K5
Curlew Ri *KIMB* S61 ...... 131 H1
Curzen Crs *ARMTH* DN3 ...... 67 F3
Curzon Av *DRON* S18 ...... 201 F7
Curzon Cl *ECK/KIL* S21 ...... 205 H1
Curzon Dr *WRKN* S81 ...... 210 D1
Cusworth La *BTLY* DN5 ...... 90 B2
Cusworth Rd *WRKS* S80 ...... 210 B4
Cuthbert Bank Rd *ST/HB/BR* S6 ...... 151 J8
Cuthbert Rd *ST/HB/BR* S6 ...... 151 J8 🔲
Cutler Cl *ECK/KIL* S21 ...... 191 F8 🔲
Cutlers Av *BSLY* S70 ...... 2 A5
Cuttlehurst *KBTN* HD8 ...... 26 A6
Cutts Av *DEARNE* S63 ...... 111 G2
Cutts Field Vw *BSLYN/ROY* S71 ...... 30 C2 🔲
Cutts Ter *SHEFS* S8 ...... 171 F8 🔲
Cutty La *DOD/DAR* S75 ...... 2 A2
Cyclops St *ATT* S4 ...... 153 F7
Cypress Av *EPW* DN9 ...... 120 A4
...... *SHEFS* S8 ...... 187 J6
Cypress Cl *ECK/KIL* S21 ...... 205 G2 🔲
Cypress Ga *CHPT/GREN* S35 ...... 130 A3
Cypress Gv *CONI* DN12 ...... 114 A7
Cypress Rd *BSLY* S70 ...... 3 E6
Cyprus St *SHEFS* S8 ...... 187 G2 🔲

D

Dadley Rd *WRKN* S81 ...... 180 D8
Dadsley Ct *NROS/TKH* DN11 ...... 139 J7 🔲
Dadsley Rd *NROS/TKH* DN11 ...... 139 J6
Daffodil Rd *SHEFN* S5 ...... 153 G4
Dagnam Cl *SHEFP/MNR* S2 ...... 188 B1
Dagnam Crs *SHEFP/MNR* S2 ...... 172 B8
Dagnam Dr *SHEFP/MNR* S2 ...... 172 B8
Dagnam Pl *SHEFP/MNR* S2 ...... 188 B1 🔲
Dagnam Rd *SHEFP/MNR* S2 ...... 172 B8
Daisy Bank *OWL* S3 ...... 8 B2
Daisy Lee La *HOLM/MEL* HD7 ...... 48 B8
Daisy Wk *MOS* S20 ...... 190 E6
...... *OWL* S3 ...... 8 C2
Dalbury Rd *DRON* S18 ...... 200 B6
Dalby Gdns *MOS* S20 ...... 190 E6
Dalby Gv *MOS* S20 ...... 190 E5
Dale Av *RHAM/THRY* S65 ...... 156 B2

Dale Cl *BSLYN/ROY* S71 ...... 30 B8 🔲
...... *KBTN* HD8 ...... 51 G2
Dale Crt *RAW* S62 ...... 133 J2
Dale Crs *HATH/EY* S32 ...... 182 D7
Dale Cft *ST/HB/BR* S6 ...... 148 D3
Dalecroft Rd *AWLS/ASK* DN6 ...... 37 J7
Dale Green Rd *BSLY* S70 ...... 82 A2
Dale Gv *DEARNE* S63 ...... 86 A6
Dale Hill Cl *MALT* S66 ...... 159 C1 🔲
Dale Hill Rd *MALT* S66 ...... 137 F8
Dale La *HEM/SK/SE* WF9 ...... 35 G2
Dale Pit Rd *HTFD* DN7 ...... 69 G2 🔲
Dale Rd *CONI* DN12 ...... 114 D5
...... *DRON* S18 ...... 201 H7
...... *ECK/KIL* S21 ...... 205 J1
...... *MALT* S66 ...... 157 F3
...... *RAW* S62 ...... 133 J1
...... *RHAM/THRY* S65 ...... 156 B2
...... *ST/HB/BR* S6 ...... 148 A2
Dale St *RAW* S62 ...... 133 J1
Daleswood Av *BSLY* S70 ...... 55 G6 🔲
Daleswood Dr *BSLY* S70 ...... 82 E3 🔲
The Dale *HATH/EY* S32 ...... 182 E7
...... *SHEFS* S8 ...... 187 F4
Dale Vw *HEM/SK/SE* WF9 ...... 33 J1
...... *WRKN* S81 ...... 197 F8
Daleview Rd *SHEFS* S8 ...... 186 D5
Dalewood Av *SHEFS* S8 ...... 186 C6
Dalewood Dr *SHEFS* S8 ...... 186 B6
Dalewood Rd *SHEFS* S8 ...... 186 C6
Dalmore Rd *ECC* S11 ...... 186 C2
Dalroyd La *ST/HB/BR* S6 ...... 149 G4
Dalton Ct *SHEFS* S8 ...... 171 F8 🔲
Dalton La *RHAM/THRY* S65 ...... 134 C7
Damasel Cl *CHPT/GREN* S35 ...... 128 A6 🔲
Damasel La *CHPT/GREN* S35 ...... 128 A5
Damasel Rd *CHPT/GREN* S35 ...... 128 A5 🔲
Dame La *BWTY* DN10 ...... 143 J4
Damer St *FUL* S10 ...... 8 A3 🔲
Dam Rd *NROS/TKH* DN11 ...... 161 K1
Damsteads *DOD/DAR* S75 ...... 55 F8
Danby Rd *AU/AST/KP* S26 ...... 193 F4
Dance La *CHPT/GREN* S35 ...... 80 C8
Danebrook Cl *SHEFP/MNR* S2 ...... 172 E6 🔲
Danebrook Dr *SHEFP/MNR* S2 ...... 172 E6 🔲
Danesfield Rd *WRKS* S80 ...... 210 D6
Danesthorpe Cl *WHHL* DN2 ...... 92 B1
Dane St *DEARNE* S63 ...... 60 D7
Dane St North *DEARNE* S63 ...... 60 D7
Dane St South *DEARNE* S63 ...... 60 D7
Daneswary *BTLY* DN5 ...... 64 C6
Danethorpe Wy *CONI* DN12 ...... 114 B7 🔲
Danewood Av *SHEFP/MNR* S2 ...... 172 E7
Danewood Cft *SHEFP/MNR* S2 ...... 172 E6
Danewood Gdns *SHEFP/MNR* S2 ...... 172 E6
Daniel Hl *ST/HB/BR* S6 ...... 8 B1
Daniel Hill Ct *ST/HB/BR* S6 ...... 8 A1 🔲
Daniel Hill St *ST/HB/BR* S6 ...... 8 A1
Daniel Hill Ter *ST/HB/BR* S6 ...... 8 B1 🔲
Daniel La *RAW* S62 ...... 132 E1
Daniels Dr *AU/AST/KP* S26 ...... 175 G6
Dannemora Dr *DARN/MH* S9 ...... 153 K8
Danum Cl *THNE* DN8 ...... 23 K8
Danum Dr *RHAM/THRY* S65 ...... 7 E3
Danum Rd *DONS/BSCR* DN4 ...... 5 F4
...... *HTFD* DN7 ...... 68 C1 🔲
Dara St *DARN/MH* S9 ...... 153 J2
Darcy Cl *AU/AST/KP* S26 ...... 175 H7 🔲
Darcy Rd *ECK/KIL* S21 ...... 204 A4
Daresbury Dr *SHEFP/MNR* S2 ...... 187 K1
Daresbury Pl *SHEFP/MNR* S2 ...... 187 K1
Daresbury Rd *SHEFP/MNR* S2 ...... 187 K1
Daresbury Vw *SHEFP/MNR* S2 ...... 187 K1
Darfield Av *MOS* S20 ...... 189 H5
Darfield Cl *MOS* S20 ...... 189 H5 🔲
...... *NROS/TKH* DN11 ...... 119 G6
Darfield Rd *CUD/GR* S72 ...... 58 A3
Dargle Av *WHHL* DN2 ...... 91 K2
Dark La *BSLY* S70 ...... 55 G8
...... *BSLY* S70 ...... 82 C4
...... *STKB/PEN* S36 ...... 102 E2
Darley *BSLY* S70 ...... 82 D2
Darley Av *BSLY* S70 ...... 81 K1
...... *BSLYN/ROY* S71 ...... 56 B1
Darley Cl *AU/AST/KP* S26 ...... 206 C1 🔲
...... *BSLYN/ROY* S71 ...... 56 B1
Darley Gv *ST/HB/BR* S6 ...... 150 C8
Darley Ter *DOD/DAR* S75 ...... 2 A3 🔲
Darley Yd *BSLY* S70 ...... 82 C3
Darlington Gv *THNE* DN8 ...... 23 K4
Darnall Dr *DARN/MH* S9 ...... 172 D2
Darnall Rd *DARN/MH* S9 ...... 172 D2
Darrington Dr *DONS/BSCR* DN4 ...... 116 A2
Darrington Pl *BSLYN/ROY* S71 ...... 57 H2 🔲
Dart Gv *EPW* DN9 ...... 94 B8
Darton Hall Cl *DOD/DAR* S75 ...... 28 E6
Darton La *DOD/DAR* S75 ...... 29 F7
Darton Rd *DOD/DAR* S75 ...... 53 J2
Darton St *BSLY* S70 ...... 56 E7
Dartree Cl *WMB/DAR* S73 ...... 84 C1
Dartree Wk *WMB/DAR* S73 ...... 84 C1
Dart Sq *OWL* S3 ...... 8 B2
Darwall Cl *CHPT/GREN* S35 ...... 107 J7 🔲
Darwent La *CHPT/GREN* S35 ...... 130 A3
Darwin Cl *FUL* S10 ...... 169 K5
Darwin La *FUL* S10 ...... 169 K5
Darwin Rd *ST/HB/BR* S6 ...... 151 G5
Darwynn Av *MEX/SWTN* S64 ...... 111 K4
David Cl *HAN/WDH* S13 ...... 174 B8 🔲

David La FUL S10 ... 168 E8
Davies Dr MEX/SWTN S64 ... 112 C6
Davis Rd AWLS/ASK DN6 ... 18 B8
Davis St RHAM/THRY S65 ... 7 F3
Davy Dr MALT S66 ... 159 G1
Davy Rd CONI DN12 ... 113 K4
Dawber La ECK/KIL S21 ... 191 K8
Dawber St WRKN S81 ... 196 B8
Daw Croft Av BSLY S70 ... 82 B2
Dawlands Cl SHEFP/MNR S2 ... 172 D6
Dawlands Dr SHEFP/MNR S2 ... 172 D6
Daw La BTLY DN5 ... 64 E5
  NROS/TKH DN11 ... 117 G7
Dawson Av RAW S62 ... 111 F7
Daw Wd BTLY DN5 ... 64 E4
Daykin Cl DOD/DAR S75 ... 28 C7
Daylands Av CONI DN12 ... 114 B6
Day St BSLY S70 ... 2 A4
Deacon Cl NROS/TKH DN11 ... 119 G6
Deacon Crs MALT S66 ... 159 H3
  NROS/TKH DN11 ... 118 D6
Deacons Wy BSLYN/ROY S71 ... 3 F2
Deadman's Hole La DARN/MH S9 ... 154 B3
Deakins Wk FUL S10 ... 169 K6
Dean Bridge La HOLM/MEL HD7 ... 48 C4
Dean Cl BTLY DN5 ... 90 A5
  NROS/TKH DN11 ... 119 G6
Dean Field Vw MOS S20 ... 190 B5
Deanhead Ct MOS S20 ... 189 J5
Deanhead Dr MOS S20 ... 189 H5
Dean Head La STKB/PEN S36 ... 104 C3
Dean La HOLM/MEL HD7 ... 48 C5
  RHAM/THRY S65 ... 156 D1
Dean Rd HOLM/MEL HD7 ... 47 F1
Deansfield Cl ARMTH DN3 ... 93 G2
Dean St BSLY S70 ... 2 A4
Deans Wy BSLYN/ROY S71 ... 3 F1
Dearden Ct CHPT/GREN S35 ... 130 C7
Dearne Br BTLY DN5 ... 88 A8
Dearne Cl WMB/DAR S73 ... 84 C6
Dearne Dike La WHHL S13 ... 49 K2
Dearne Pk KBTN HD8 ... 26 B5
Dearne Rd DEARNE S63 ... 86 A7
  WMB/DAR S73 ... 84 C5
Dearne Royd KBTN HD8 ... 26 B5
Dearneside Rd KBTN HD8 ... 51 G2
Dearne St CONI DN12 ... 114 D4
  CUD/GR S72 ... 59 H6
  DARN/MH S9 ... 153 H5
  DOD/DAR S75 ... 28 D6
  HEM/SK/SE WF9 ... 34 E4
Dearne Valley Pkwy
  WMB/DAR S73 ... 83 K7
Dearne Vw DEARNE S63 ... 86 C2
Dearneway DEARNE S63 ... 111 J1
Dearne Wy DOD/DAR S75 ... 28 B4
  KBTN HD8 ... 26 B4
  KBTN HD8 ... 50 B3
Dearnfield KBTN HD8 ... 50 D1
Dearnley Vw DOD/DAR S75 ... 2 A1
Decoy Bank North
  DONS/BSCR DN4 ... 5 D5
Decoy Bank South
  DONS/BSCR DN4 ... 5 D6
Deepcar La CUD/GR S72 ... 58 B4
Deepdale Rd KIMB S61 ... 154 B1
Deep La SHEFN S5 ... 131 G7
Deeps La BWTY DN10 ... 121 K8
Deepwell Av MOS S20 ... 204 D1
Deepwell Bank MOS S20 ... 204 D1
Deepwell Ct MOS S20 ... 204 D1
Deepwell Vw MOS S20 ... 204 D1
Deerlands Av SHEFN S5 ... 151 J1
Deerlands Cl SHEFN S5 ... 151 K1
Deerlands Mt SHEFN S5 ... 151 K1
Deer Leap Dr RHAM/THRY S65 ... 135 F5
Deer Park Cl ST/HB/BR S6 ... 169 J1
Deer Park Pl ST/HB/BR S6 ... 169 J1
Deer Park Rd RHAM/THRY S65 ... 135 F4
  ST/HB/BR S6 ... 169 J1
Deer Park Vw ST/HB/BR S6 ... 169 J1
Deer Park Wy ST/HB/BR S6 ... 169 K1
Deershaw La KBTN HD8 ... 49 H2
Deershaw Sike La KBTN HD8 ... 49 H2
De Houton La AU/AST/KP S26 ... 192 E2
Deightonby St DEARNE S63 ... 60 D7
De Lacy Dr BSLY S70 ... 22 B6
Delamere Cl MOS S20 ... 190 E5
De La Salle Dr ATT S4 ... 152 D8
Delf Rd ST/HB/BR S6 ... 127 F8
Delf St SHEFP/MNR S2 ... 171 H8
Della Av BSLY S70 ... 2 A5
Dell Av CUD/GR S72 ... 32 D7
Dell Crs DONS/BSCR DN4 ... 4 B4
Delmar Wy MALT S66 ... 157 F1
Delph Cl DOD/DAR S75 ... 53 K6
Delph Edge CHPT/GREN S35 ... 105 H4
Delph House Rd FUL S10 ... 169 K4
Delta Pl RHAM/THRY S65 ... 134 A8
Delta Wy MALT S66 ... 159 J1
Delves Av HACK/IN S12 ... 190 A4
Delves Cl HACK/IN S12 ... 190 A3
Delves Dr HACK/IN S12 ... 190 A4
Delves La AU/AST/KP S26 ... 191 H4
Delves Pl HACK/IN S12 ... 189 K4
Delves Rd ECK/KIL S21 ... 205 G1
  HACK/IN S12 ... 190 A4

Delves Ter HACK/IN S12 ... 190 A4
Denaby Av CONI DN12 ... 118 B5
Denaby La CONI DN12 ... 113 G6
Den Bank Av FUL S10 ... 169 J4
Den Bank Cl FUL S10 ... 169 K4
Den Bank Crs FUL S10 ... 169 J4
Den Bank Dr FUL S10 ... 169 J4
Denby Hall La KBTN HD8 ... 52 A2
Denby La KBTN HD8 ... 50 E4
Denby Rd BSLYN/ROY S71 ... 30 A8
Denby St BTLY DN5 ... 64 D5
  SHEFP/MNR S2 ... 8 C5
Denby Wy MALT S66 ... 158 B1
Dene Cl BWTY DN10 ... 165 J8
  MALT S66 ... 157 H3
Dene Crs RHAM/THRY S65 ... 134 A7
Denehall Rd ARMTH DN3 ... 67 F4
Dene La OWL S3 ... 8 C4
Dene Rd RHAM/THRY S65 ... 134 A7
Denham Rd FUL S10 ... 8 B5
Denholme Cl OWL S3 ... 9 E1
Denholme Meadow
  HEM/SK/SE WF9 ... 34 E3
Denison Cl BSLY S70 ... 2 C5
Denison Rd DONS/BSCR DN4 ... 4 B4
Denman Rd DEARNE S63 ... 111 G1
Denman St RHAM/THRY S65 ... 7 D2
Denmark St SHEFP/MNR S2 ... 187 H1
Dennis St WRKS S80 ... 210 D5
Dent La MOS S20 ... 189 H5
Denton Rd SHEFS S8 ... 187 F3
Dentons Green La ARMTH DN3 ... 66 E3
Denton St BSLYN/ROY S71 ... 2 C5
Denver Rd AWLS/ASK DN6 ... 18 B4
Derby Pl SHEFP/MNR S2 ... 187 H1
Derby Rd WHHL DN2 ... 66 B7
Derbyshire La SHEFS S8 ... 187 G6
Derby St BSLY S70 ... 2 A4
  SHEFP/MNR S2 ... 187 H1
Derby Ter SHEFP/MNR S2 ... 187 J1
Derriman Av ECC S11 ... 186 B3
Derriman Cl ECC S11 ... 186 B3
Derriman Dr ECC S11 ... 186 B3
Derriman Gln ECC S11 ... 186 A3
Derriman Gv ECC S11 ... 186 B3
Derry Gv DEARNE S63 ... 60 B8
Derwent Cl BSLYN/ROY S71 ... 30 C8
  DIN S25 ... 178 D3
  DRON S18 ... 201 H4
  WRKN S81 ... 210 D1
Derwent Crs BSLYN/ROY S71 ... 30 C8
  RHAM S60 ... 154 E8
Derwent Dr ARMTH DN3 ... 66 F4
  CHPT/GREN S35 ... 129 K2
  MEX/SWTN S64 ... 113 H1
  RAW S62 ... 133 J3
Derwent Gdns DEARNE S63 ... 86 D3
Derwent La EDL/UDV S33 ... 145 G8
  HATH/EY S32 ... 182 A7
Derwent Pl BTLY DN5 ... 89 J6
  WMB/DAR S73 ... 84 C6
Derwent Rd BSLYN/ROY S71 ... 30 B8
  DRON S18 ... 201 H4
  KIMB S61 ... 132 D4
  MEX/SWTN S64 ... 113 H1
Derwent St SHEFP/MNR S2 ... 171 K3
Derwent Ter MEX/SWTN S64 ... 113 F1
Derwent Wy DEARNE S63 ... 84 C7
De Sutton Pl AU/AST/KP S26 ... 206 E2
Deveron Rd MOS S20 ... 190 D8
Devonshire Cl DRON S18 ... 201 F7
  TOT/DORE S17 ... 199 K1
Devonshire Dr DIN S25 ... 178 A8
  DOD/DAR S75 ... 2 A1
  TOT/DORE S17 ... 185 J8
Devonshire Gln TOT/DORE S17 ... 199 K1
Devonshire Gv TOT/DORE S17 ... 199 J1
Devonshire La SHEFS S1 ... 8 C5
Devonshire Rd MALT S66 ... 159 H1
  NROS/TKH DN11 ... 162 E3
  TOT/DORE S17 ... 185 J8
  WHHL DN2 ... 92 A2
Devonshire St KIMB S61 ... 6 A4
  SHEF S1 ... 8 C3
  WRKS S80 ... 210 B5
Dewar Dr ABRD S7 ... 186 C3
De Warren Pl AU/AST/KP S26 ... 207 F2
Dewhill Av RHAM S60 ... 156 A6
Dial Cl SHEFN S5 ... 152 D5
Dial House Rd ST/HB/BR S6 ... 151 F7
Dial Wy SHEFN S5 ... 152 D3
Diamond Av HEM/SK/SE WF9 ... 34 D4
Diamond St WMB/DAR S73 ... 84 A4
Dick Edge La HOLM/MEL HD7 ... 49 G5
Dickens Cl RHAM S60 ... 173 K1
Dickinson Ct CHPT/GREN S35 ... 130 A2
Dickens Rd RAW S62 ... 111 F5
  WRKN S81 ... 211 F3
Dickinson Pl BSLY S70 ... 2 C6
Dickinson Rd BSLY S70 ... 2 C6
  SHEFN S5 ... 130 E8
Digby Cl KIMB S61 ... 132 B7
Digley Rd HOLM/MEL HD7 ... 46 B5
Digley Royd La HOLM/MEL HD7 ... 46 D4
Dike Hl RAW S62 ... 109 F6
Dikelands Mt CHPT/GREN S35 ... 129 J1
Dillington Rd BSLY S70 ... 2 C6
Dillington Sq BSLY S70 ... 2 C6

Dinmore Cl DONS/BSCR DN4 ... 116 D
Dinnington Rd DIN S25 ... 195 D
  SHEFS S8 ... 187 F3
Dirleton Dr DONS/BSCR DN4 ... 116 A1
Dirty La HTFD DN7 ... 22 B
Discovery Wy MALT S66 ... 158 E
Dishwell La AU/AST/KP S26 ... 206 E
Disraeli Gv MALT S66 ... 159 F
Ditchingham St ATT S4 ... 171 J1
Division La SHEF S1 ... 9 D
Division St SHEF S1 ... 9 D
Dixon Crs DONS/BSCR DN4 ... 90 C
Dixon Dr CHPT/GREN S35 ... 128 A
Dixon La SHEF S1 ... 9 E
Dixon Rd CONI DN12 ... 115 H
  ST/HB/BR S6 ... 151 G
Dixon St OWL S3 ... 8 C1
  RHAM/THRY S65 ... 7 D
Dobbin Hl ECC S11 ... 186 A
Dobb La HOLM/MEL HD7 ... 47 F
  ST/HB/BR S6 ... 168 C
Dobb Top Rd HOLM/MEL HD7 ... 46 E
Dobcroft Av ABRD S7 ... 186 B
Dobcroft Cl ECC S11 ... 186 A
Dobcroft Rd ECC S11 ... 186 A
Dobie St BSLY S70 ... 2 C
Dobsyke Cl BSLY S70 ... 82 D
Dockin Hill Rd DON DN1 ... 5 D
Dock Rd WRKS S80 ... 210 C
Doctor La AU/AST/KP S26 ... 206 E
Dodds Cl RHAM S60 ... 6 B
Dodd St ST/HB/BR S6 ... 151 H
Dodson Dr HAN/WDH S13 ... 173 H
Dodsworth St MEX/SWTN S64 ... 112 E3
Dodworth Green Rd
  DOD/DAR S75 ... 80 C
Dodworth Rd BSLY S70 ... 55 H
Doe La ECK/KIL S21 ... 202 D
  SHEFS S8 ... 202 E
Doe Quarry La DIN S25 ... 178 B
Doe Royd Crs SHEFN S5 ... 151 H
Doe Royd Dr SHEFN S5 ... 151 K
Doe Royd La SHEFN S5 ... 151 K
Dog Croft La BTLY DN5 ... 65 K
Dog Hl CUD/GR S72 ... 31 J
Dog Hill Dr CUD/GR S72 ... 31 K
Dog Kennels La AU/AST/KP S26 ... 193 H
Dog La BWTY DN10 ... 164 B
Dolcliffe Rd MEX/SWTN S64 ... 113 F
Doles Av BSLYN/ROY S71 ... 30 C
Doles Crs BSLYN/ROY S71 ... 30 C
Doles La RHAM S60 ... 156 D
  RHAM S60 ... 174 C
  WRKS S80 ... 208 D
Doleswood Dr DIN S25 ... 178 A
Domine La RHAM S60 ... 6 C
Dominoe Gv HACK/IN S12 ... 189 F
Don Av CHPT/GREN S35 ... 128 A
  ST/HB/BR S6 ... 151 F
Doncaster Ga RHAM/THRY S65 ... 7 D4
Doncaster La AWLS/ASK DN6 ... 36 D
  AWLS/ASK DN6 ... 63 K
  AWLS/ASK DN6 ... 63 K4
Doncaster Pl RHAM/THRY S65 ... 7 F
Doncaster Rd ARMTH DN3 ... 66 D
  ARMTH DN3 ... 92 D
  AWLS/ASK DN6 ... 18 D
  AWLS/ASK DN6 ... 38 C
  BSLY S70 ... 3 E
  BSLY S70 ... 56 E7
  BSLYN/ROY S71 ... 57 F
  BTLY DN5 ... 62 E
  BTLY DN5 ... 64 C
  BTLY DN5 ... 87 J
  BWTY DN10 ... 142 B
  CONI DN12 ... 114 A
  CONI DN12 ... 114 E5
  DEARNE S63 ... 86 E
  DEARNE S63 ... 111 K
  EPW DN9 ... 121 F
  HEM/SK/SE WF9 ... 35 F
  HTFD DN7 ... 41 J
  HTFD DN7 ... 68 B2
  MALT S66 ... 137 H
  MEX/SWTN S64 ... 113 G
  NROS/TKH DN11 ... 139 J
  RHAM/THRY S65 ... 7 D
  RHAM/THRY S65 ... 134 C
  WMB/DAR S73 ... 84 E
  WRKN S81 ... 180 D
  WRKN S81 ... 196 D7
Doncaster Rd (Harlington)
  BTLY DN5 ... 87 H
Doncaster St OWL S3 ... 8 C
Don Dr BSLY S70 ... 56 E
Donetsk Wy HACK/IN S12 ... 189 J
Don Hill Height STKB/PEN S36 ... 105 F
Donnington Rd MEX/SWTN S64 ... 113 J
  SHEFP/MNR S2 ... 171 K
Donovan Cl SHEFN S5 ... 151 K
Donovan Rd SHEFN S5 ... 151 K
Don Rd DARN/MH S9 ... 153 G
Donstone Vw DIN S25 ... 177 K
Don St CONI DN12 ... 114 E
  DON DN1 ... 5 D
  RHAM S60 ... 5 D
  STKB/PEN S36 ... 78 C
Don Vw STKB/PEN S36 ... 74 C
Dorchester Pl BSLY S70 ... 82 A

orchester Rd *NROS/TKH* DN11 .... 163 G2
ore Cl *TOT/DORE* S17 .... 186 A8
ore Hall Cft *TOT/DORE* S17 .... 185 H8 🔢
ore La *HATH/EY* S32 .... 182 B8
ore Rd *TOT/DORE* S17 .... 185 J7
orking St *ATT* S4 .... 9 F1 🔢
orothy Av *THNE* DN8 .... 23 G7 🔢
orothy Rd *ST/HB/BR* S6 .... 151 G6
orset Cl *WHHL* DN2 .... 92 B2
orset Dr *NROS/TKH* DN11 .... 162 E3 🔢
orset Rd *FUL* S10 .... 8 B4
ouble Bridges Rd *THNE* DN8 .... 44 A4
oubting La *STKB/PEN* S36 .... 77 J8
ouglas Rd *DONS/BSCR* DN4 .... 90 B8
.... *OWL* S3 .... 152 A8
.... *OWL* S3 .... 171 F1
ouglas St *RHAM* S60 .... 7 D4 🔢
ouse Croft La *FUL* S10 .... 184 D1
ovecliffe Rd *WMB/DAR* S73 .... 83 F4
ovecote La *MOS* S20 .... 84 C6
ovedale *BSLY* S70 .... 22 C5
ovedale Rd *ABRD* S7 .... 186 D2
.... *RHAM/THRY* S65 .... 156 B3
ove La *AU/AST/KP* S26 .... 191 J2
overcourt Rd *KIMB* S61 .... 132 D8
.... *SHEFP/MNR* S2 .... 172 A6
over La *ATT* S4 .... 153 F7
ove Rd *WMB/DAR* S73 .... 84 C6
over Rd *FUL* S10 .... 170 C6
.... *HOLM/MEL* HD7 .... 47 K4
over St *OWL* S3 .... 8 C2
oveside Dr *WMB/DAR* S73 .... 84 D2
owcarr La *AU/AST/KP* S26 .... 206 C3
owland Av *CHPT/GREN* S35 .... 107 J7
owland Cl *CHPT/GREN* S35 .... 107 K7
owland Dr *CHPT/GREN* S35 .... 107 J6
owland Gdns *CHPT/GREN* S35 .... 107 J7
ownes Crs *RHAM/THRY* S65 .... 155 J2
owngate Dr *ATT* S4 .... 153 F7
ownham Rd *SHEFN* S5 .... 152 E4
owning La *OWL* S3 .... 8 C1 🔢
owning Rd *SHEFS* S8 .... 186 E7
owning Sq *STKB/PEN* S36 .... 78 A5
he Downings *AU/AST/KP* S26 .... 207 F2
ownland Cl *DONS/BSCR* DN4 .... 116 C3
ownshutts La *HOLM/MEL* HD7 .... 48 C2 🔢
own's Rw *RHAM* S60 .... 6 C4 🔢
rake Cl *CHPT/GREN* S35 .... 129 K2
rake Head La *CONI* DN12 .... 115 F5
rake House La *MOS* S20 .... 190 B4
rake House La *MOS* S20 .... 190 D4 🔢
rake House La West *MOS* S20 .... 190 D4 🔢
rake House Wy *MOS* S20 .... 190 C4
rake Rd *WHHL* DN2 .... 91 H1
r Anderson Av *HTFD* DN7 .... 42 A3
ransfield Cl *STKB/PEN* S36 .... 78 A5
ransfield Cl *FUL* S10 .... 169 K5 🔢
ransfield Rd *FUL* S10 .... 169 J5
raycott Pl *DRON* S18 .... 200 D7 🔢
riIver St *RHAM* S60 .... 6 C3
ronfield Rd *ECK/KIL* S21 .... 203 J5
roppingwell Farm Cl
.... *KIMB* S61 .... 132 A6 🔢
roppingwell Rd
.... *KIMB* S61 .... 132 A6 🔢
ro.over Cl *CHPT/GREN* S35 .... 129 K1
roversdale Rd *NROS/TKH* DN11 .... 163 H3
rummond Av *BTLY* DN5 .... 63 K8
rummond St *SHEFN* S5 .... 152 C2
rummond St *RHAM* S60 .... 6 C3 🔢
.... *RHAM/THRY* S65 .... 6 C3
rury Farm Ct *DOD/DAR* S75 .... 55 F6 🔢
rury La *DRON* S18 .... 201 J4
.... *TOT/DORE* S17 .... 185 H8
ryden Av *SHEFN* S5 .... 151 K3
ryden Cl *WRKN* S81 .... 211 G4
ryden Dr *SHEFN* S5 .... 151 K3
ryden Rd *BSLYN/ROY* S71 .... 3 D3
.... *DEARNE* S63 .... 85 F8
.... *DONS/BSCR* DN4 .... 77 F1
.... *MEX/SWTN* S64 .... 113 G2
.... *RHAM/THRY* S65 .... 156 A3
.... *SHEFN* S5 .... 151 K3
ryden Wy *SHEFN* S5 .... 151 K3
ry Hill La *KBTN* HD8 .... 51 J2
ublin Rd *WHHL* DN2 .... 91 K3
uchess Rd *SHEFP/MNR* S2 .... 9 K5
uckham Dr *AU/AST/KP* S26 .... 191 J1
ucksett La *ECK/KIL* S21 .... 204 B4
udley Rd *ST/HB/BR* S6 .... 151 G5
.... *WHHL* DN2 .... 92 A4
udley St *RAW* S62 .... 133 J4 🔢
uftons Cl *CONI* DN12 .... 114 E4 🔢
ugdale Dr *SHEFN* S5 .... 130 A8
ugdale Rd *SHEFN* S5 .... 130 A8
uke Av *MALT* S66 .... 159 J3
.... *NROS/TKH* DN11 .... 118 D6
uke Crs *BSLY* S70 .... 2 C5 🔢
.... *KIMB* S61 .... 132 B6
uke La *SHEF* S1 .... 9 D4 🔢
uke of Norfolk La *MALT* S66 .... 156 D3
uke Pl *WRKS* S80 .... 210 C4

Dukeries Cl *WRKN* S81 .... 210 A1
Dukeries Crs *WRKS* S80 .... 211 F6
Dukeries Dr *DIN* S25 .... 178 A8
Dukeries Wy *WRKN* S81 .... 210 A1
Duke's Cft *RHAM/THRY* S65 .... 156 A3
Dukes Pl *RHAM/THRY* S65 .... 156 A3
Dukes Ter *BWTY* DN10 .... 142 B8
Duke St *BSLY* S70 .... 2 C5 🔢
.... *CUD/CR* S72 .... 58 D1
.... *DIN* S25 .... 178 B5
.... *DON* DN1 .... 4 C3
.... *HOY* S74 .... 109 F1
.... *HTFD* DN7 .... 41 K4 🔢
.... *MEX/SWTN* S64 .... 112 C3
.... *MOS* S20 .... 204 B1
.... *SHEFP/MNR* S2 .... 9 F3
Duke Wood Rd *KBTN* HD8 .... 26 B5
Dumb Hall La *AU/AST/KP* S26 .... 208 C3
.... *WRKS* S80 .... 208 C2
Dumbleton Rd *ECK/KIL* S21 .... 205 J2
Duncan Rd *FUL* S10 .... 170 B3
Duncan St *RHAM* S60 .... 155 F6
Duncombe St *ST/HB/BR* S6 .... 8 A1
Dundas Rd *DARN/MH* S9 .... 154 B4
.... *WHHL* DN2 .... 92 C5
Dunedin Gln *MOS* S20 .... 204 C1
Dunedin Gv *MOS* S20 .... 204 C1
Dunella Dr *ST/HB/BR* S6 .... 151 G6
Dunella Pl *ST/HB/BR* S6 .... 151 F6
Dunella Rd *ST/HB/BR* S6 .... 151 F6
Dunelm Crs *THNE* DN8 .... 24 A4
Dun Flds *OWL* S3 .... 8 C1 🔢
Dunford Rd *HOLM/MEL* HD7 .... 48 A8
.... *HOLM/MEL* HD7 .... 74 A1
Dungworth Gn *ST/HB/BR* S6 .... 149 H6
Dunkeld Rd *ECC* S11 .... 186 B2
Dunkerley Rd *ST/HB/BR* S6 .... 150 C6
Dun La *OWL* S3 .... 8 C1 🔢
Dunleary Rd *WHHL* DN2 .... 91 K3
Dunlin Cl *KIMB* S61 .... 131 K5
Dunlin Ct *WRKN* S81 .... 210 A1
Dunlop St *DARN/MH* S9 .... 153 J6
Dunmere Cl *BSLYN/ROY* S71 .... 56 B2 🔢
Dunmow Rd *ATT* S4 .... 153 F7
Dunninc Rd *SHEFN* S5 .... 130 E8
Dunninc Ter *SHEFN* S5 .... 130 E8
Dunniwood Av *DONS/BSCR* DN4 .... 118 E2
Dunniwood Reach
.... *DONS/BSCR* DN4 .... 118 E1 🔢
Dunscroft Gv *NROS/TKH* DN11 .... 119 G6
Dunsley Bank Rd *HOLM/MEL* HD7 .... 47 J5
Dunsley Ter *HEM/SK/SE* WF9 .... 18 D4
Dunstan Crs *WRKS* S80 .... 210 D6
Dunstan Rd *MALT* S66 .... 159 F3
Dunstan St *MEX/SWTN* S64 .... 112 D3
.... *OWL* S3 .... 8 C1
Durham Av *THNE* DN8 .... 23 H7
Durham Cl *WRKN* S81 .... 196 E8
Durham La *FUL* S10 .... 8 B3
Durham Rd *RHAM/THRY* S65 .... 156 A3
Durham Rd *FUL* S10 .... 8 B3 🔢
.... *HTFD* DN7 .... 42 B7
.... *WHHL* DN2 .... 65 J8
Durham St *MALT* S66 .... 159 J3
Durlstone Cl *HACK/IN* S12 .... 188 C2 🔢
Durlstone Crs *HACK/IN* S12 .... 188 C2
Durlstone Dr *HACK/IN* S12 .... 188 C2
Durlstone Gv *HACK/IN* S12 .... 188 C2 🔢
Durmast Gv *ST/HB/BR* S6 .... 169 G1
Durnan Gv *RAW* S62 .... 111 F7
Durnford Rd *WHHL* DN2 .... 5 E1
Dursley Ct *EPW* DN9 .... 94 A8
Durvale Ct *TOT/DORE* S17 .... 199 J1
Dutton Rd *ST/HB/BR* S6 .... 151 J6
Dwarriden La *STKB/PEN* S36 .... 126 D3
Dyche Cl *SHEFS* S8 .... 201 H1 🔢
Dyche Ct *SHEFS* S8 .... 201 H1
Dyche La *SHEFS* S8 .... 187 G8
Dyche Pl *SHEFS* S8 .... 201 H1 🔢
Dycott Rd *KIMB* S61 .... 132 C8 🔢
Dyer Rd *HOY* S74 .... 83 H8
Dykes Hall Gdns *ST/HB/BR* S6 .... 151 G7
Dykes Hall Pl *ST/HB/BR* S6 .... 151 G6
Dykes Hall Rd *ST/HB/BR* S6 .... 151 F6
Dykes La *ST/HB/BR* S6 .... 151 F7
Dyke Vale Av *HACK/IN* S12 .... 189 J3
Dyke Vale Cl *HACK/IN* S12 .... 189 J3
Dyke Vale Pl *HACK/IN* S12 .... 189 J3
Dyke Vale Rd *HACK/IN* S12 .... 189 H2
Dyke Vale Wy *HACK/IN* S12 .... 189 J3
Dykewood Dr *ST/HB/BR* S6 .... 150 E4
Dyscart Cl *WRKN* S81 .... 180 D4
Dyson Cote La *STKB/PEN* S36 .... 104 C2
Dyson La *HOLM/MEL* HD7 .... 70 E6
Dyson Pl *ECC* S11 .... 8 A6 🔢
Dyson St *BSLY* S70 .... 2 A6 🔢

E

Eaden Crs *HOY* S74 .... 109 G1
Eagleton Dr *CHPT/GREN* S35 .... 107 K7
Eagleton Ri *CHPT/GREN* S35 .... 107 K7
Eagle Vw *AU/AST/KP* S26 .... 191 J1
Eaming Vw *BSLYN/ROY* S71 .... 3 D2
Earl Av *MALT* S66 .... 159 H3

NROS/TKH DN11 .... 118 C6
Earldom Cl *ATT* S4 .... 171 J1
Earldom Dr *ATT* S4 .... 171 J1
Earldom Rd *ATT* S4 .... 152 D8
Earldom St *ATT* S4 .... 171 J1
Earlesmere Av *DONS/BSCR* DN4 .... 4 A6
Earl Marshal Cl *ATT* S4 .... 152 E6
Earl Marshal Dr *ATT* S4 .... 152 E7 🔢
Earl Marshal Rd *ATT* S4 .... 152 E6
Earl Marshal wa *ATT* S4 .... 152 D7
Earlsmere Dr *BSLYN/ROY* S71 .... 57 H7
Earlston Dr *BTLY* DN5 .... 90 E1
Earl St *SHEF* S1 .... 9 D4
Earl Wy *SHEF* S1 .... 9 D4
Earnshaw Ter *DOD/DAR* S75 .... 2 A2
Earsham St *ATT* S4 .... 9 F1
.... *ATT* S4 .... 171 J1
East Av *HEM/SK/SE* WF9 .... 35 C3
.... *HTFD* DN7 .... 42 A5
.... *MEX/SWTN* S64 .... 112 A5
.... *RAW* S62 .... 133 J1
.... *WMB/DAR* S73 .... 83 J4
East Bank Rd *HTFD* DN7 .... 41 K2
.... *SHEFP/MNR* S2 .... 187 K1 🔢
East Bank Pl *SHEFP/MNR* S2 .... 187 K1
East Bank Rd *SHEFP/MNR* S2 .... 171 J8
East Bank Vw *SHEFP/MNR* S2 .... 187 K1 🔢
East Bank Wy *SHEFP/MNR* S2 .... 187 K1 🔢
East Bawtry Rd *RHAM* S60 .... 156 A6
.... *RHAM* S60 .... 156 A5 🔢
.... *RHAM* S60 .... 156 B5 🔢
East Cl *STKB/PEN* S36 .... 78 D6
East Coast Rd *DARN/MH* S9 .... 172 A1
East Crs *RHAM/THRY* S65 .... 134 A8
.... *STKB/PEN* S36 .... 104 D6
East Cft *DEARNE* S63 .... 86 B5
Eastcroft Cl *MOS* S20 .... 190 D7
Eastcroft Dr *MOS* S20 .... 190 C8
Eastcroft Gln *MOS* S20 .... 190 D7 🔢
Eastcroft Vw *MOS* S20 .... 190 D8 🔢
Eastcroft Wy *MOS* S20 .... 190 D7 🔢
East End Crs *BSLYN/ROY* S71 .... 31 F4
Eastern Av *DIN* S25 .... 178 C6
.... *SHEFP/MNR* S2 .... 172 A8
Eastern Cl *DIN* S25 .... 178 C6
Eastern Crs *SHEFP/MNR* S2 .... 187 K1
Eastern Dr *SHEFP/MNR* S2 .... 171 K8
Eastfield Av *STKB/PEN* S36 .... 78 A4
Eastfield Cl *DOD/DAR* S75 .... 29 J7
Eastfield Crs *DIN* S25 .... 178 A2 🔢
.... *DOD/DAR* S75 .... 29 J7
Eastfield Dr *AWLS/ASK* DN6 .... 18 D7
Eastfield La *CHPT/GREN* S35 .... 79 K5
East Field La *DIN* S25 .... 178 B2
Eastfield La *EPW* DN9 .... 120 B1
Eastfield Pl *RAW* S62 .... 112 B8
Eastfield Rd *ARMTH* DN3 .... 93 G2
.... *DRON* S18 .... 201 J7
.... *FUL* S10 .... 170 C2 🔢
East Field Rd *HTFD* DN7 .... 22 A7
Eastfields *BSLY* S70 .... 82 C3
Eastgate *BSLY* S70 .... 2 B3 🔢
.... *HEM/SK/SE* WF9 .... 33 H1
East Ga *THNE* DN8 .... 23 K3
Eastgate *WRKS* S80 .... 210 D4
East Glade Av *HACK/IN* S12 .... 189 G4
East Glade Cl *HACK/IN* S12 .... 189 G4
East Glade Crs *HACK/IN* S12 .... 189 G3
East Glade Pl *HACK/IN* S12 .... 189 G4
East Glade Rd *HACK/IN* S12 .... 189 G3
East Glade Sq *HACK/IN* S12 .... 189 G4 🔢
East Glade Wy *HACK/IN* S12 .... 189 G3
Eastgrove Rd *FUL* S10 .... 8 A5
East Laith Ga *DON* DN1 .... 5 D3
East La *HTFD* DN7 .... 41 K3
East Pde *SHEF* S1 .... 9 D3 🔢
East Pinfold *BSLYN/ROY* S71 .... 30 D4
East Rd *RHAM/THRY* S65 .... 134 A8
.... *SHEFP/MNR* S2 .... 171 H8
.... *STKB/PEN* S36 .... 78 D6
East Service Rd *ARMTH* DN3 .... 40 C7
East St *BSLY* S70 .... 82 D3
.... *CUD/CR* S72 .... 32 B2
.... *DEARNE* S63 .... 86 E1
.... *DIN* S25 .... 178 B6
.... *DON* DN1 .... 4 C5
.... *ECK/KIL* S21 .... 205 F7
.... *HEM/SK/SE* WF9 .... 35 C3
.... *HOLM/MEL* HD7 .... 48 D4
.... *NROS/TKH* DN11 .... 163 F2
.... *WMB/DAR* S73 .... 84 D1
East Vale Dr *RHAM/THRY* S65 .... 134 E5
East Vw *AWLS/ASK* DN6 .... 18 A6
.... *BWTY* DN10 .... 142 B7 🔢
.... *CUD/CR* S72 .... 31 J8
.... *MALT* S66 .... 158 C2
East View Av *ECK/KIL* S21 .... 204 A5
Eastwood Av *DIN* S25 .... 194 A2
Eastwood Ct *WRKN* S81 .... 196 D6
Eastwood La *RHAM/THRY* S65 .... 7 D3 🔢
Eastwood Mt *RHAM/THRY* S65 .... 7 F4
Eastwood Rd *ECC* S11 .... 8 A6 🔢
Eastwood V *RHAM/THRY* S65 .... 7 F2
Eaton Pl *SHEFP/MNR* S2 .... 171 K4
Eaton Sq *DIN* S25 .... 87 J4
Eaton Wk *HEM/SK/SE* WF9 .... 35 F2 🔢
Ebenezer Pl *OWL* S3 .... 9 D1 🔢
Ebenezer St *CUD/CR* S72 .... 59 J6 🔢
.... *OWL* S3 .... 9 D1 🔢

Eben St *DARN/MH* S9 .... 153 H5
Ebson House La *HOLM/MEL* HD7 .... 49 G1
Ecclesall Rd *ECC* S11 .... 170 D8
Ecclesall Rd South *ECC* S11 ... 186 A2
Eccles Dr *CONI* DN12 .... 115 J7
Ecclesfield Rd *CHPT/GREN* S35 ... 130 C3
  DARN/MH S9 .... 131 G8
  SHEFN S5 .... 130 E7
Eccles St *DARN/MH* S9 .... 153 J3
Eccleston Rd *ARMTH* DN3 .... 67 F2
Eckington Rd *DRON* S18 .... 201 K4
  DIN S3 .... 30 D7
Eckington Wy *MOS* S20 .... 190 B3
Ecklands Long La *STKB/PEN* S36 ... 76 E7
Edale Ri *DOD/DAR* S75 .... 54 D8
Edale Rd *ECC* S11 .... 186 A1
  KIMB S61 .... 154 B1
Edderthorpe La *WMB/DAR* S73 ... 58 D7
Eddison Cl *WRKN* S81 .... 196 E8
Eddison Park Av *WRKN* S81 ..... 196 C6
Eddyfield Rd *STKB/PEN* S36 .... 78 D6
Eden Cl *DOD/DAR* S75 .... 54 D2
  MALT S66 .... 158 C2
Edencroft Dr *ARMTH* DN3 .... 66 E4
Eden Dr *AWLS/ASK* DN6 .... 19 F7
  ST/HB/BR S6 .... 150 D7
Edenfield Cl *BSLYN/ROY* S71 .... 56 E1
Eden Field Rd *ARMTH* DN3 ...... 67 F5
Eden Gld *AU/AST/KP* S26 .... 175 H8
Eden Gv *AU/AST/KP* S26 .... 175 H7
  DONS/BSCR DN4 .... 4 A4
Eden Grove Rd *ARMTH* DN3 ...... 67 F5
Edenhall Rd *SHEFP/MNR* S2 ..... 172 B8
Edensor Rd *SHEFN* S5 .... 152 C5
Eden Ter *MEX/SWTN* S64 .... 113 F1
Edenthorpe Dell *HACK/IN* S12 .. 189 K5
Edenthorpe Gv *MOS* S20 .... 190 A5
Edgar La *NROS/TKH* DN11 .... 118 C0
Edgbaston Wy *CONI* DN12 .... 115 K4
Edgebrook Rd *ECC* S11 .... 186 C1
Edgecliffe Pl *BSLYN/ROY* S71 ... 56 B2
Edgedale Rd *ECC* S11 .... 186 E2
Edge End La *HOLM/MEL* HD7 ..... 46 D2
Edgefield Rd *ABRD* S7 .... 186 E2
Edge Hill Rd *ABRD* S7 .... 186 D1
Edgehill Rd *DOD/DAR* S75 ...... 29 F5
  WHHL DN2 .... 66 B8
Edgelands Ri *CUD/GR* S72 ...... 57 J2
Edge La *ST/HB/BR* S6 .... 151 H1
Edgemount Rd *ABRD* S7 .... 186 E2
Edge Well Cl *ST/HB/BR* S6 ..... 151 H1
Edge Well Crs *ST/HB/BR* S6 .... 151 H1
Edge Well Dr *ST/HB/BR* S6 ..... 151 H2
Edge Well Pl *ST/HB/BR* S6 ..... 151 H1
Edge Well Ri *ST/HB/BR* S6 ..... 151 H1
Edinburgh Av *DEARNE* S63 ...... 86 A5
Edinburgh Cl *BSLYN/ROY* S71 ... 3 E1
Edinburgh Dr *DIN* S25 .... 178 A8
Edinburgh Rd *HOY* S74 .... 83 F8
  WRKS S80 .... 211 F7
Edinburgh Wk *WRKS* S80 .... 210 E7
Edith Ter *BTLY* DN5 .... 64 A8
Edlington La *CONI* DN12 .... 115 H7
  DONS/BSCR DN4 .... 115 K2
Edmonton Cl *DOD/DAR* S75 ...... 55 F5
Edmund Av *RHAM* S60 .... 155 G8
  TOT/DORE S17 .... 200 C1
Edmund Cl *TOT/DORE* S17 .... 200 D1
Edmund Dr *TOT/DORE* S17 .... 200 C1
Edmund Rd *SHEFP/MNR* S2 .... 9 E6
Edmunds Rd *BSLY* S70 .... 82 D3
Edna St *DEARNE* S63 .... 86 B5
Edward Cl *THNE* DN8 .... 23 K6
Edward Ct *THNE* DN8 .... 23 K6
Edward Rd *AWLS/ASK* DN6 .... 37 J6
  AWLS/ASK DN6 .... 64 A1
  DEARNE S63 .... 85 F7
  DEARNE S63 .... 86 B3
Edwards Ct *WRKS* S80 .... 210 B4
Edward St *ARMTH* DN3 .... 66 E8
  BTLY DN5 .... 64 E6
  CUD/GR S72 .... 59 H6
  DEARNE S63 .... 60 B7
  DIN S25 .... 178 B6
  DOD/DAR S75 .... 29 H7
  ECK/KIL S21 .... 204 B6
  HOY S74 .... 108 E1
  MEX/SWTN S64 .... 113 F1
  NROS/TKH DN11 .... 118 C6
  OWL S3 .... 8 C2
  STKB/PEN S36 .... 105 H6
  WMB/DAR S73 .... 84 B4
  WMB/DAR S73 .... 84 D2
  WRKS S80 .... 210 D4
Edwin Rd *AWLS/ASK* DN6 .... 37 J1
  SHEFP/MNR S2 .... 187 J1
Eel Pool Rd *BWTY* DN10 .... 165 K7
Effingham La *ATT* S4 .... 9 F2
Effingham Rd *ATT* S4 .... 9 F1
  DARN/MH S9 .... 172 A2
Effingham Sq *RHAM* S60 .... 6 C3
Effingham St *ATT* S4 .... 9 F3
  RHAM/THRY S65 .... 7 D3
Egerton Cl *SHEF* S1 .... 8 C4
Egerton La *OWL* S3 .... 8 C4
Egerton Rd *AU/AST/KP* S26 ..... 175 H8
  DRON S18 .... 201 H5
Egerton St *OWL* S3 .... 8 C4

Eggington Cl *ARMTH* DN3 .... 93 G8
Egg La *NROS/TKH* DN11 .... 117 J8
Egmanton Rd *BSLYN/ROY* S71 .... 30 A6
Egremont Ri *MALT* S66 .... 136 E8
Eilam Cl *KIMB* S61 .... 132 B7
Eilam Rd *KIMB* S61 .... 132 B7
Ekin St *RHAM* S60 .... 154 D3
Elcroft Gdns *MOS* S20 .... 190 D4
Elder Av *DIN* S25 .... 198 B2
Elder Ct *ECK/KIL* S21 .... 205 G2
Elder Dr *MALT* S66 .... 157 C1
Elder Gv *CONI* DN12 .... 114 B6
  EPW DN9 .... 120 B2
Eldertree Rd *KIMB* S61 .... 131 G4
Eldon Gv *THNE* DN8 .... 24 B4
Eldon Rd *RHAM/THRY* S65 .... 7 E2
Eldon St *BSLY* S70 .... 2 B4
  SHEF S1 .... 8 C3
Eldon St North *BSLYN/ROY* S71 . 2 C3
Eleanor Ct *ARMTH* DN3 .... 66 D6
Eleanor St *DARN/MH* S9 .... 172 B7
Elgar Dr *MALT* S66 .... 159 K3
Elgin St *FUL* S10 .... 170 D2
Elgitha Dr *MALT* S66 .... 176 E1
Elizabeth Av *ARMTH* DN3 .... 67 F5
  CUD/GR S72 .... 32 B2
Elizabeth Rd *AU/AST/KP* S26 ... 175 H8
Elizabeth St *CUD/GR* S72 ...... 58 D1
  DEARNE S63 .... 86 D2
Elland Cl *BSLYN/ROY* S71 ...... 29 K8
Ella Rd *ATT* S4 .... 152 D8
Ellavale *HOY* S74 .... 109 H1
Ellenbro Rd *ST/HB/BR* S6 ...... 151 G7
Elm Tree Cl *RHAM* S60 .... 154 E7
Ellerker Av *DONS/BSCR* DN4 .... 4 B4
Ellers Av *DONS/BSCR* DN4 ...... 92 B7
Ellers Crs *DONS/BSCR* DN4 ..... 92 B7
Ellers Dr *DONS/BSCR* DN4 ...... 92 B7
Ellershaw La *CONI* DN12 .... 114 B6
Ellershaw Rd *CONI* DN12 .... 114 C6
Ellers La *EPW* DN9 .... 94 B8
Ellers Rd *DONS/BSCR* DN4 ...... 92 B7
Ellerton Gdns *DONS/BSCR* DN4 .. 92 D6
Ellerton Rd *SHEFN* S5 .... 152 E5
Ellesmere Gv *HTFD* DN7 .... 42 C3
  ATT S4 .... 152 D8
Ellesmere Rd *ATT* S4 .... 171 J1
Ellesmere Rd North *ATT* S4 .... 152 D8
Ellesmere Ter *RHAM/THRY* S65 .. 7 E4
Ellington Ct *BSLY* S70 .... 2 A6
Ellin St *SHEF* S1 .... 9 D5
Elliot La *CHPT/GREN* S35 ...... 129 K4
Elliot Rd *ST/HB/BR* S6 .... 8 A2
Elliott Av *MALT* S66 .... 84 A6
Elliott Cl *DEARNE* S63 .... 85 F8
Elliott Ct *RHAM/THRY* S65 ..... 7 D3
Elliott Dr *KIMB* S61 .... 132 C5
Elliottville St *ST/HB/BR* S6 .. 170 C1
Ellis Av *DEARNE* S63 .... 111 G3
Ellis Ct *WMB/DAR* S73 .... 83 K7
Ellis Crs *NROS/TKH* DN11 ...... 118 D6
  WMB/DAR S73 .... 84 D8
Ellisons Rd *ECK/KIL* S21 ...... 191 J7
Ellison St *OWL* S3 .... 8 C2
  THNE DN8 .... 43 J1
Ellis St *OWL* S3 .... 8 C2
  RHAM S60 .... 155 F6
Elliston Av *DOD/DAR* S75 ...... 29 H6
Ellorslie Dr *STKB/PEN* S36 .... 105 F6
Elmbridge Cl *BSLYN/ROY* S71 ... 31 F4
Elm Cl *ARMTH* DN3 .... 40 E8
  ECK/KIL S21 .... 205 G2
Elm Crs *BTLY* DN5 .... 65 F5
  MOS S20 .... 190 A7
Elmdale Cl *MEX/SWTN* S64 ...... 112 C3
Elmdale Dr *ARMTH* DN3 .... 66 E6
Elm Dr *ECK/KIL* S21 .... 205 G2
  EPW DN9 .... 121 G4
Elmfield Av *SHEFN* S5 .... 152 C5
Elm Gld *DON* S1 .... 5 D4
  NROS/TKH DN11 .... 118 E7
Elm Green La *CONI* DN12 .... 114 D5
Elm Gv *HEM/SK/SE* WF9 .... 34 E4
  KIMB S61 .... 132 E4
Elmham Rd *DARN/MH* S9 .... 173 F3
  DONS/BSCR DN4 .... 92 D6
Elmhirst Dr *RHAM/THRY* S65 .... 156 B3
Elmhirst La *DOD/DAR* S75 ...... 54 C7
Elmhirst Rd *THNE* DN8 .... 23 K8
Elm La *SHEFN* S5 .... 152 C3
Elmore Rd *FUL* S10 .... 170 C4
Elm Pl *ARMTH* DN3 .... 67 F8
  BSLYN/ROY S71 .... 56 E3
  RAW S62 .... 133 K2
Elm Rd *CHPT/GREN* S35 .... 130 A3
Elm Rd *ARMTH* DN3 .... 67 F8
  AWLS/ASK DN6 .... 37 H5
  ECK/KIL S21 .... 204 A5
  EPW DN9 .... 120 A4
  MEX/SWTN S64 .... 112 E1
  MOS S20 .... 190 E3
Elm Rw *BSLYN/ROY* S71 .... 3 E4
Elmsall Dr *HEM/SK/SE* WF9 ..... 35 H2
Elmsall La *AWLS/ASK* DN6 ...... 35 G7
Elmsall Wy *HEM/SK/SE* WF9 ..... 35 H2
Elmsdale *BSLY* S70 .... 82 C3
Elmsdale Cl *HEM/SK/SE* WF9 .... 35 G5
Elmsmere Dr *WRKN* S81 .... 180 E1

Elms Rd *WRKS* S80 .... 210 C2
Elm St *HOY* S74 .... 108 C2
Elm Tree Cl *DIN* S25 .... 194 E8
Elmtree Cl *WRKN* S81 .... 195 H6
Elm Tree Crs *DRON* S18 .... 201 C2
Elm Tree Dr *BWTY* DN10 .... 142 A1
Elm Tree Gv *THNE* DN8 .... 43 J1
Elm Tree Rd *KIMB* S61 .... 131 C5
  MALT S66 .... 158 E6
Elmview Rd *DARN/MH* S9 .... 153 J3
Elmville Av *MEX/SWTN* S64 ..... 112 E1
Elm Wy *DEARNE* S63 .... 111 K5
Elmwood Av *AWLS/ASK* DN6 ...... 63 C8
Elmwood Crs *ARMTH* DN3 .... 93 F1
Elmwood Dr *MOS* S20 .... 204 E8
Elsecar Rd *RAW* S62 .... 110 C2
Elsham Cl *RHAM/THRY* S65 ...... 135 G8
Elstead Cl *DOD/DAR* S75 .... 54 C1
Elstree Dr *HACK/IN* S12 .... 188 D2
Elstree Rd *HACK/IN* S12 .... 188 D2
Elsworth Cl *DON* DN1 .... 4 C2
Elvaston Cl *DRON* S18 .... 200 E6
Elwin Ct *DONS/BSCR* DN4 .... 116 B3
Elwis St *BTLY* DN5 .... 4 B2
Elwood Rd *TOT/DORE* S17 .... 200 C1
Ely Cl *WRKS* S80 .... 210 E8
Ely Rd *WHHL* DN2 .... 65 J5
Ely St *NROS/TKH* DN11 .... 118 C3
Embankment Rd *FUL* S10 .... 170 C2
Emerson Av *HTFD* DN7 .... 42 A7
Emerson Cl *SHEFN* S5 .... 152 C2
Emerson Crs *SHEFN* S5 .... 152 C2
Emerson Dr *SHEFN* S5 .... 152 C2
Emily Cl *BSLYN/ROY* S71 .... 56 F1
Emley Dr *BTLY* DN5 .... 63 K6
Emmett Carr Cl *ECK/KIL* S21 ... 205 G2
Emmett Carr Dr *ECK/KIL* S21 ... 205 G2
Emmett Carr La *ECK/KIL* S21 ... 205 G2
Empire Rd *ABRD* S7 .... 171 K2
  SHEFS S8 .... 187 F1
Emsley Av *CUD/GR* S72 .... 57 J1
Endcliffe Av *ECC* S11 .... 170 E5
Endcliffe Crs *ECC* S11 .... 170 E5
Endcliffe Edge *FUL* S10 .... 170 B6
Endcliffe Glen Rd *ECC* S11 .... 170 E5
Endcliffe Grove Av *FUL* S10 ... 170 A5
Endcliffe Hall Av *FUL* S10 .... 170 C5
Endcliffe Rise Rd *ECC* S11 .... 170 E5
Endcliffe Terrace Rd *ECC* S11 . 170 E5
Endcliffe Vale Av *FUL* S10 .... 170 C5
Endcliffe Vale Rd *FUL* S10 .... 170 E5
Endcliffe Wy *WHHL* DN2 .... 66 B8
Endfield Rd *SHEFN* S5 .... 130 A1
Endowood Rd *ABRD* S7 .... 186 A6
Enfield Pl *HAN/WDH* S13 .... 173 C6
Engine La *CUD/GR* S72 .... 32 C5
  DEARNE S63 .... 86 B2
Ennerdale Av *MOS* S20 .... 204 C1
Ennerdale Cl *DIN* S25 .... 178 A5
  DRON S18 .... 200 B5
  MEX/SWTN S64 .... 113 C7
Ennerdale Dr *MOS* S20 .... 204 C1
Ennerdale Rd *BSLYN/ROY* S71 ... 57 H6
  WHHL DN2 .... 92 F4
Ennis Crs *WHHL* DN2 .... 91 K4
Entwhistle Rd *CHPT/GREN* S35 .. 107 K4
Epping Gdns *MOS* S20 .... 190 E5
Epping Gv *MOS* S20 .... 190 E5
Epsom Cl *MEX/SWTN* S64 .... 113 F1
Epsom Rd *DONS/BSCR* DN4 .... 92 F4
Epworth Rd *HTFD* DN7 .... 43 F1
Epworth Rd (West) *HTFD* DN7 ... 42 D1
Eric St *HEM/SK/SE* WF9 .... 35 F1
Errington Av *SHEFP/MNR* S2 .... 172 C4
Errington Cl *SHEFP/MNR* S2 .... 188 A4
Errington Crs *SHEFP/MNR* S2 ... 188 A4
Errington Rd *SHEFP/MNR* S2 .... 172 C4
Errington Wy *SHEFP/MNR* S2 .... 172 C4
Erskine La *SHEFP/MNR* S2 ...... 171 K4
Erskine Rd *RHAM/THRY* S65 ..... 7 E1
  SHEFP/MNR S2 .... 171 K4
Erskine Vw *SHEFP/MNR* S2 ...... 187 K1
Eshton Ct *DOD/DAR* S75 .... 29 G4
Eskdale Cl *DRON* S18 .... 200 C5
  ST/HB/BR S6 .... 151 J4
Eskdale Dr *BTLY* DN5 .... 64 A8
  WRKN S81 .... 196 A5
Eskdale Rd *BSLYN/ROY* S71 ..... 57 H7
  KIMB S61 .... 132 A6
  ST/HB/BR S6 .... 151 J4
Eskholme La *GLE* DN14 .... 12 B6
Esperanto Pl *SHEF* S1 .... 9 E5
Essendine Crs *SHEFS* S8 .... 187 F5
Essex Av *WHHL* DN2 .... 92 A4
Essex Cl *AU/AST/KP* S26 .... 163 K8
Essex Dr *NROS/TKH* DN11 .... 163 H6
Essex Rd *BSLY* S70 .... 2 C6
  NROS/TKH DN11 .... 163 H6
  SHEFP/MNR S2 .... 172 E4
Estate Rd *RAW* S62 .... 111 F6
Estfeld Cl *NROS/TKH* DN11 ..... 139 K4
Estone Dr *AU/AST/KP* S26 ...... 175 H1
Etwall Wy *SHEFN* S5 .... 152 D1
Eunice La *KBTN* HD8 .... 50 C8
Europa Link *DARN/MH* S9 .... 173 G4
Evans St *OWL* S3 .... 8 B5
Evanston Gdns *DONS/BSCR* DN4 .. 4 A5
Eveline St *CUD/GR* S72 .... 57 J1
Evelyn Av *WHHL* DN2 .... 92 A4

elyn Rd *FUL* S10 .... 170 A4
elyn St *RAW* S62 .... 134 A1
elyn Ter *BSLY* S70 .... 3 E5 ⊞
erard Av *TOT/DORE* S17 .... 200 A1
erard Dr *TOT/DORE* S17 .... 200 A2
erard Gld *TOT/DORE* S17 .... 200 A2 ⊞
erdale Mt *HEM/SK/SE* WF9 .... 32 E1
HEM/SK/SE WF9 .... 34 D4 ⊞
eretts Cl *NROS/TKH* DN11 .... 139 J8
erill Cl *WMB/DAR* S73 .... 84 C6
erill Gate La *WMB/DAR* S73 .... 84 C5
eringham Cl *SHEFN* S5 .... 152 B4
eringham Crs *SHEFN* S5 .... 152 A4
eringham Rd *DONS/BSCR* DN4 .... 92 D6
SHEFN S5 .... 152 B4
erson Cl *MALT* S66 .... 137 F8 ⊞
erton Rd *ECC* S11 .... 170 C7
erton Sluice La *BWTY* DN10 .... 165 K3
esham St *DARN/MH* S9 .... 153 J3
eston Rd *WMB/DAR* S73 .... 84 C6
ven Wy *DOD/DAR* S75 .... 55 F6
vers Rd *KIMB* S61 .... 154 C1
wood Dr *DONS/BSCR* DN4 .... 92 D7
xchange Pl *ATT* S4 .... 9 E2
xchange St *HEM/SK/SE* WF9 .... 34 E4 ⊞
SHEF S1 .... 9 E2
xeter Dr *OWL* S3 .... 8 C5 ⊞
xeter Pl *OWL* S3 .... 8 C4 ⊞
xeter Rd *WHHL* DN2 .... 91 K1
xeter Wy *OWL* S3 .... 8 B4 ⊞
yam Cl *DOD/DAR* S75 .... 54 D8 ⊞
yam Rd *FUL* S10 .... 170 B4 ⊞
yncourt Rd *SHEFN* S5 .... 152 E4
yre La *SHEF* S1 .... 9 D5
yre St *SHEF* S1 .... 9 D5

F

bian Wy *MALT* S66 .... 157 J3
ctory La *DON* DN1 .... 4 C3 ⊞
airbank Rd *SHEFN* S5 .... 152 C6
airbank Vw *RHAM* S60 .... 156 B6
airbarn Cl *ST/HB/BR* S6 .... 169 J2 ⊞
airbarn Dr *ST/HB/BR* S6 .... 169 J2
airbarn Pl *ST/HB/BR* S6 .... 169 J2
airbarn Rd *ST/HB/BR* S6 .... 169 J2
airbarn Wy *ST/HB/BR* S6 .... 169 J2
airburn Gdns *RHAM* S60 .... 155 G3 ⊞
airburn Gv *HOY* S74 .... 109 J1
airfax Dr *SHEFP/MNR* S2 .... 172 D7
airfax Rd *SHEFP/MNR* S2 .... 172 D7
WHHL DN2 .... 92 A3
air Fld *BTLY* DN5 .... 82 A6
airfield *DEARNE* S63 .... 86 A5
airfield Ct *DONS/BSCR* DN4 .... 118 C1
MALT S66 .... 135 H8
airfield Rd *BTLY* DN5 .... 90 C1
OWL S3 .... 170 E1
airfields *KBTN* HD8 .... 51 G4
airfields Rd *HOLM/MEL* HD7 .... 47 G4
airford Cl *DONS/BSCR* DN4 .... 119 F1
air Holme Vw *ARMTH* DN3 .... 93 H3
air House La *ST/HB/BR* S6 .... 148 E1
airhurst La *CHPT/GREN* S35 .... 127 G3
airleigh *SHEFP/MNR* S2 .... 172 C8
airleigh Dr *RHAM* S60 .... 7 D6
airmount Gdns *HACK/IN* S12 .... 189 J4 ⊞
airthorn Rd *SHEFN* S5 .... 152 E3
airtree Wk *THNE* DN8 .... 23 J8
air View Av *AWLS/ASK* DN6 .... 63 G2
airview Cl *HOY* S74 .... 108 D2
airview Ct *ARMTH* DN3 .... 66 E1
air View Dr *AU/AST/KP* S26 .... 175 H8
airview Rd *DRON* S18 .... 201 G4
airway *DOD/DAR* S75 .... 81 F1
airway *DOD/DAR* S75 .... 29 H5
airways *MALT* S66 .... 157 G3
e Fairway *FUL* S10 .... 168 E6
ith St *BSLYN/ROY* S71 .... 57 C1
HEM/SK/SE WF9 .... 34 C3
alcon Cl *AWLS/ASK* DN6 .... 63 J1
alcon Ct *NROS/TKH* DN11 .... 119 F6
alcon Dr *BSLY* S70 .... 82 A7
RHAM S60 .... 174 D4
alconer La *HAN/WDH* S13 .... 174 D6
alcon Ri *DRON* S18 .... 201 K4 ⊞
alcon St *BSLY* S70 .... 2 B3
alcon Wy *DIN* S25 .... 178 A8
alding St *CHPT/GREN* S35 .... 130 C2
RHAM S60 .... 6 E8
alkland Dr *DRON* S18 .... 201 G7
alkland Rd *ECC* S11 .... 186 A1
all Bank Crs *DOD/DAR* S75 .... 54 C7
alledge La *STKB/PEN* S36 .... 51 F5
all Head La *DOD/DAR* S75 .... 54 A6
allon Rd *ST/HB/BR* S6 .... 169 H1
allow Ct *WRKN* S81 .... 197 F8
all Vw *DOD/DAR* S75 .... 53 K7
almouth Cl *BSLYN/ROY* S71 .... 3 E3
almouth Rd *ABRD* S7 .... 186 E2
alstaff Crs *SHEFN* S5 .... 152 A3
alstaff Rd *SHEFN* S5 .... 152 A2
althwaite Green La *DOD/DAR* S75 .... 80 C4
ane Crs *AU/AST/KP* S26 .... 175 H7

Fanny Av *ECK/KIL* S21 .... 205 J2
Fanshaw Av *ECK/KIL* S21 .... 204 A5
Fanshaw Bank *DRON* S18 .... 201 G6 ⊞
Fanshaw Dr *ECK/KIL* S21 .... 204 A5 ⊞
Fanshaw Gate La *DRON* S18 .... 199 H7
Fanshaw Rd *DRON* S18 .... 201 H5
ECK/KIL S21 .... 204 A5
Fanshaw Wy *ECK/KIL* S21 .... 204 A5
Faraday Rd *DARN/MH* S9 .... 172 A1
Faranden Rd *DARN/MH* S9 .... 172 C2 ⊞
Far Bank La *HTFD* DN7 .... 22 A8
Farcliff *BTLY* DN5 .... 89 J6
Far Common Rd *HTFD* DN7 .... 43 J8
Far Crs *RHAM/THRY* S65 .... 134 A8
Farcroft Gv *ATT* S4 .... 153 G6 ⊞
Far Dalton La *RHAM/THRY* S65 .... 134 C2
Fardell Gdns *MALT* S66 .... 157 J3 ⊞
Far Field Av *HOLM/MEL* HD7 .... 48 D6
Far Field Dr *HOLM/MEL* HD7 .... 48 D5
Far Field La *BSLYN/ROY* S71 .... 57 F1
DEARNE S63 .... 112 A1
HOLM/MEL HD7 .... 48 D6
Farfield Pk *DEARNE* S63 .... 86 A8
Far Field Rd *ARMTH* DN3 .... 67 F4
RHAM/THRY S65 .... 156 B3
Fargate *SHEF* S1 .... 9 D3 ⊞
Far Golden Smithies
MEX/SWTN S64 .... 112 B3
Farish Pl *SHEFP/MNR* S2 .... 187 H1 ⊞
Far La *HOLM/MEL* HD7 .... 48 D7
RHAM/THRY S65 .... 134 A8
ST/HB/BR S6 .... 151 G6
Farlow Cft *CHPT/GREN* S35 .... 107 H7
Farm Bank Rd *SHEFP/MNR* S2 .... 9 F4
Farm Cl *ARMTH* DN3 .... 67 F6 ⊞
BSLYN/ROY S71 .... 3 F1 ⊞
DRON S18 .... 201 H3
HACK/IN S12 .... 188 C5
RHAM S60 .... 154 E8
Farm Ct *AWLS/ASK* DN6 .... 63 K1
Farm Crs *MOS* S20 .... 204 A1
Farm Fields Cl *MOS* S20 .... 190 B6
Farmhill Cl *BTLY* DN5 .... 90 D2 ⊞
Far Moor Cl *BTLY* DN5 .... 87 H5
Farmoor Gdns *MOS* S20 .... 191 F6 ⊞
Farm Rd *BSLY* S70 .... 82 D1
SHEFP/MNR S2 .... 9 E5
Farmstead Cl *SHEFP/MNR* S2 .... 187 K2 ⊞
KIMB S61 .... 189 K4 ⊞
Farm Vw *HACK/IN* S12 .... 132 A7
Farm View Dr *HACK/IN* S12 .... 189 K4
Farm View Gdns *HACK/IN* S12 .... 189 K4
Farm View Rd *KIMB* S61 .... 131 K7
Farnaby Gdns *CHPT/GREN* S35 .... 107 J7
Farnborough Dr *DONS/BSCR* DN4 .... 119 F1
Farndale *WRKN* S81 .... 197 F8
Farndale Rd *BTLY* DN5 .... 64 A8 ⊞
ST/HB/BR S6 .... 151 H5
Farndon Gv *WRKN* S81 .... 196 E8 ⊞
Farndon St *WRKN* S81 .... 211 F2 ⊞
Farnley Av *ST/HB/BR* S6 .... 151 J3 ⊞
Farnsworth Rd *RHAM/THRY* S65 .... 134 B8
Far Pl *RHAM/THRY* S65 .... 134 A8
Farquhar La *MALT* S66 .... 159 J2
Farrar Rd *SHEFS* S8 .... 171 F8 ⊞
Farrier Ga *CHPT/GREN* S35 .... 129 K1
Farringdon Dr *NROS/TKH* DN11 .... 118 E8
Farrow Cl *DOD/DAR* S75 .... 55 F8
Farthing Gale Ms *BTLY* DN5 .... 90 C2 ⊞
Far Townend *DOD/DAR* S75 .... 55 F8 ⊞
Far View Rd *SHEFN* S5 .... 152 C3
Farwater Cl *DRON* S18 .... 201 C7 ⊞
Farwater La *DRON* S18 .... 201 F6 ⊞
Fathers Gdns *AU/AST/KP* S26 .... 192 D5 ⊞
Favell Rd *OWL* S3 .... 8 B5 ⊞
RHAM/THRY S65 .... 134 C8 ⊞
Fearnehough St *DARN/MH* S9 .... 172 C2 ⊞
Fearn House Crs *HOY* S74 .... 108 D2
Fearnley Cl *HOLM/MEL* HD7 .... 48 C2
Fearnley La *HOLM/MEL* HD7 .... 48 B2
Fearnley Rd *HOY* S74 .... 108 D2
Fearnville Gv *BSLYN/ROY* S71 .... 30 D4
Featherbed La *WRKS* S80 .... 209 G5
Featherston Av *WRKS* S80 .... 211 F5
Felkirk Vw *CUD/GR* S72 .... 31 J4
Fellbrigg Rd *SHEFP/MNR* S2 .... 171 K8
Fellowsfield Wy *KIMB* S61 .... 132 B8
Fell Rd *DARN/MH* S9 .... 153 H8
Fell St *DARN/MH* S9 .... 153 C7
Fellview Cl *HATH/EY* S32 .... 182 C8
Fenland Rd *THNE* DN8 .... 43 H1
Fenney La *ECC* S11 .... 185 J5
Fenn Rd *DOD/DAR* S75 .... 108 A2
Fensome Wy *WMB/DAR* S73 .... 84 D1 ⊞
Fenton Cl *HEM/SK/SE* WF9 .... 34 A6 ⊞
Fenton Cft *KIMB* S61 .... 132 D7
Fenton Flds *KIMB* S61 .... 132 D7
Fenton Rd *KIMB* S61 .... 132 D5
Fenton St *BSLY* S70 .... 2 B4 ⊞
ECK/KIL S21 .... 203 K5
KIMB S61 .... 132 C8
Fentonville St *ECC* S11 .... 8 B6
Fenton Wy *KIMB* S61 .... 132 E5
Fenwick Common La
AWLS/ASK DN6 .... 19 K4
Fenwick La *AWLS/ASK* DN6 .... 19 G5

Feoffees Rd *CHPT/GREN* S35 .... 130 C7 ⊞
Ferguson St *DARN/MH* S9 .... 172 B1
Ferham Cl *KIMB* S61 .... 154 D1
Ferham Park Av *KIMB* S61 .... 154 D1 ⊞
Ferham Rd *KIMB* S61 .... 154 D1
Fern Av *BTLY* DN5 .... 64 D8
MOS S20 .... 190 D3
Fern Bank *AWLS/ASK* DN6 .... 63 J1
Fernbank Dr *ARMTH* DN3 .... 67 G7
ECK/KIL S21 .... 203 K4
Fern Cl *ECK/KIL* S21 .... 203 K4
WHHL DN2 .... 92 A1
WMB/DAR S73 .... 84 C6
Ferncroft Av *MOS* S20 .... 190 A8
Ferndale Cl *DRON* S18 .... 201 K4
Ferndale Dr *MALT* S66 .... 157 H1
THNE DN8 .... 23 K5
Ferndale Pl *HEM/SK/SE* WF9 .... 33 F1
Ferndale Ri *DRON* S18 .... 201 K4
Ferndale Rd *CONI* DN12 .... 114 C5
DRON S18 .... 201 K4
Ferndale Vw *BTLY* DN5 .... 90 B2
Fernhall Cl *ARMTH* DN3 .... 67 F4 ⊞
Fern Hollow *MALT* S66 .... 157 H4
Fernhurst Rd *WHHL* DN2 .... 92 B1
Fernlea Cl *BTLY* DN5 .... 90 C2 ⊞
Fernlea Cv *CHPT/GREN* S35 .... 130 C7 ⊞
Fern Lea Gv *DEARNE* S63 .... 86 A5 ⊞
Fernleigh Dr *RHAM* S60 .... 154 E5
Fern Rd *ST/HB/BR* S6 .... 170 B1
Fernvale Wk *MEX/SWTN* S64 .... 112 C7 ⊞
Fern Wy *ECK/KIL* S21 .... 203 K4
Ferrand Cl *BSLY* S70 .... 81 K8
Ferrara Cl *WMB/DAR* S73 .... 84 B1
Ferrars Cl *DARN/MH* S9 .... 154 C5
Ferrars Dr *DARN/MH* S9 .... 154 C6
Ferrars Rd *DARN/MH* S9 .... 154 B4
Ferrars Wy *DARN/MH* S9 .... 154 C6
Ferrers Rd *WHHL* DN2 .... 5 F1
Ferriby Rd *ST/HB/BR* S6 .... 151 G5
Ferry Boat La *MEX/SWTN* S64 .... 113 H3
CONI DN12 .... 114 D4
Ferry Moor La *CUD/GR* S72 .... 58 A1
Ferry Rd *THNE* DN8 .... 23 F5
Festival Av *NROS/TKH* DN11 .... 163 F3
Festival Cl *AU/AST/KP* S26 .... 192 C5
Festival Rd *DEARNE* S63 .... 111 J2
Fewton Wy *DONS/BSCR* DN4 .... 92 A7
Fiddlers Dr *ARMTH* DN3 .... 93 H3
Field Av *ECK/KIL* S21 .... 205 F7
Field Cl *DRON* S18 .... 200 C5 ⊞
WMB/DAR S73 .... 84 D1
WRKN S81 .... 196 E8
Field Dr *CUD/GR* S72 .... 57 J2
Field End La *HOLM/MEL* HD7 .... 46 E5
Fielders Wy *CONI* DN12 .... 115 K4 ⊞
Fieldfare Dr *WRKN* S81 .... 196 A8
Field Ga *NROS/TKH* DN11 .... 119 F5
Fieldhead La *HOLM/MEL* HD7 .... 46 C6
Field Head Rd *HOY* S74 .... 109 F2
Fieldhead Rd *SHEFP/MNR* S2 .... 171 J8 ⊞
Field House Rd *BTLY* DN5 .... 89 J7 ⊞
Fieldhouse Wy *ATT* S4 .... 152 E8
Fielding Dr *MALT* S66 .... 157 J3
Fielding Gv *RAW* S62 .... 111 J8
Fielding Rd *ST/HB/BR* S6 .... 151 H5
Field La *BSLY* S70 .... 57 F8
ECK/KIL S21 .... 205 F2
EPW DN9 .... 96 E6
HEM/SK/SE WF9 .... 35 J3
RHAM S60 .... 156 B6
STKB/PEN S36 .... 76 E6
Field Rd *HOLM/MEL* HD7 .... 48 A3
HTFD DN7 .... 41 K3
THNE DN8 .... 23 J8
Fields End *STKB/PEN* S36 .... 78 E7
Fieldside *ARMTH* DN3 .... 66 E6
Field Side *THNE* DN8 .... 23 H7
Field Station Rd *BTLY* DN5 .... 39 J7
Field Vw *RHAM* S60 .... 155 F6
Field Wv *RHAM* S60 .... 6 C2
Fife Cl *DARN/MH* S9 .... 153 H3
Fife St *BSLY* S70 .... 2 A5 ⊞
DARN/MH S9 .... 153 H3
Fife Wy *DARN/MH* S9 .... 153 H3
Fifth Av *AWLS/ASK* DN6 .... 63 J4
Filby Rd *BTLY* DN5 .... 90 B2
Filey Av *BSLYN/ROY* S71 .... 30 E5
Filey La *OWL* S3 .... 8 B4
Filey St *FUL* S10 .... 8 B3
Finch Cl *RHAM/THRY* S65 .... 134 E5
Finch Gdns *MALT* S66 .... 157 K3
Finch Ri *AU/AST/KP* S26 .... 191 J7
Finch Rd *DONS/BSCR* DN4 .... 116 C1 ⊞
Finchwell Cl *HAN/WDH* S13 .... 175 H5
Finchwell Crs *HAN/WDH* S13 .... 175 H5
Finchwell Rd *HAN/WDH* S13 .... 175 H5
Findon Crs *ST/HB/BR* S6 .... 151 F7
Findon Pl *ST/HB/BR* S6 .... 151 F7 ⊞
Findon Rd *ST/HB/BR* S6 .... 151 F7
Findon St *ST/HB/BR* S6 .... 151 F7
Finghall Rd *AWLS/ASK* DN6 .... 37 G5
Fingleton *WRKN* S81 .... 211 F1 ⊞
Finkle St *BTLY* DN5 .... 64 E7
HTFD DN7 .... 41 K2
Finkle Street La *CHPT/GREN* S35 .... 106 B4
Finlay Rd *RHAM/THRY* S65 .... 7 F2
Finlay St *OWL* S3 .... 8 B2

Finnley's La *GLE* DN14 .... 13 F1
Firbeck Av *DIN* S25 .... 178 A3
Firbeck Crs *WRKN* S81 .... 180 C4
Firbeck La *DIN* S25 .... 178 A2
Firbeck Rd *DONS/BSCR* DN4 .... 5 F4
SHEFS S8 .... 186 E4 🔢
Firbeck Wy *NROS/TKH* DN11 .... 119 G5
Fir Cl *DEARNE* S63 .... 111 J2 🔢
Fircroft Av *SHEF* S5 .... 152 E2
Fircroft Rd *SHEFN* S5 .... 153 F2
Firethorn Ri *RHAM/THRY* S65 .... 135 K7
Firham Cl *BSLYN/ROY* S71 .... 30 B3
Fir Pl *ECK/KIL* S21 .... 205 G2
Fir Rd *ECK/KIL* S21 .... 203 K5
Firsby La *CONI* DN12 .... 113 K8
Firshill Av *ATT* S4 .... 152 C7
Firshill Cl *ATT* S4 .... 152 C7
Firshill Crs *ATT* S4 .... 152 B7
Firshill Gld *ATT* S4 .... 152 B7
Firshill Ri *ATT* S4 .... 152 C7
Firshill Rd *ATT* S4 .... 152 C7
Firs La *STKB/PEN* S36 .... 52 A8
First Av *AU/AST/KP* S26 .... 63 K3
HEM/SK/SE WF9 .... 33 J6
RHAM/THRY S65 .... 7 F2
The Firs *BSLY* S70 .... 82 D1
BSLYN/ROY S71 .... 30 B3
First La *DIN* S25 .... 194 A4
Fir St *FUL* S10 .... 170 C2
Firth Crs *MALT* S66 .... 159 H3
NROS/TKH DN11 .... 118 D6
Firth Dr *ATT* S4 .... 171 K1
Firth Field Rd *HTFD* DN7 .... 43 F7 🔢
Firth Park Av *SHEFN* S5 .... 152 E4
Firth Park Crs *SHEFN* S5 .... 152 E4
Firth Park Rd *SHEFN* S5 .... 152 E4
Firth Rd *DEARNE* S63 .... 110 E1
Firth St *DONS/BSCR* DN4 .... 4 B5 🔢
KIMB S61 .... 133 F4
Firthwood Av *DRON* S18 .... 201 K4 🔢
Firthwood Cl *DRON* S18 .... 201 K4
Firthwood Rd *DRON* S18 .... 201 K4
Fir Tree *CHPT/GREN* S35 .... 79 K3
Fir Tree Av *EPW* DN9 .... 120 B3
Fir Tree Cl *BTLY* DN5 .... 61 C8
Fir Tree Dr *AU/AST/KP* S26 .... 192 A5
AWLS/ASK DN6 .... 17 K4
Firtree Ri *CHPT/GREN* S35 .... 130 B3 🔢
Firvale *AU/AST/KP* S26 .... 206 E2
Fir Vale Pl *SHEFN* S5 .... 152 D6 🔢
Fir Vale Rd *SHEFN* S5 .... 152 D6
Fish Dam La *BSLYN/ROY* S71 .... 30 E7
Fisher Cl *RHAM* S60 .... 6 B3 🔢
Fisher La *DARN/MH* S9 .... 172 E2
Fisher Rd *MALT* S66 .... 159 J2
Fisher St *BTLY* DN5 .... 64 E5
Fisher Ter *BTLY* DN5 .... 4 A1 🔢
Fishlake Nab *HTFD* DN7 .... 41 K1
Fish Pond La *MALT* S66 .... 137 H7
Fishponds Rd *HAN/WDH* S13 .... 172 E7
Fishponds Rd West
HAN/WDH S13 .... 172 E8
Fitzalan Rd *HAN/WDH* S13 .... 173 H6
Fitzalan Sq *SHEF* S1 .... 9 E5 🔢
Fitzgerald Rd *FUL* S10 .... 170 B3
Fitzhubert Rd *SHEFP/MNR* S2 .... 172 D1
Fitzmaurice Rd *DARN/MH* S9 .... 172 D1
Fitzroy Rd *SHEFP/MNR* S2 .... 187 H1
Fitzwalter Rd *SHEFP/MNR* S2 .... 9 F5
Fitzwilliam Ct *RAW* S62 .... 133 J3
DEARNE S63 .... 111 H2
Fitzwilliam Dr *BTLY* DN5 .... 87 G6
Fitzwilliam Ga *SHEF* S1 .... 8 C4
Fitzwilliam Rd *RHAM/THRY* S65 .... 7 E3
WMB/DAR S73 .... 85 F1
Fitzwilliam Sq *RAW* S62 .... 132 E3
Fitzwilliam St *BSLY* S70 .... 2 A4
HOY S74 .... 108 C2
HOY S74 .... 109 H2
MEX/SWTN S64 .... 112 B5
RAW S62 .... 133 J4
SHEF S1 .... 8 C4
WMB/DAR S73 .... 83 J8
Five Acres *DOD/DAR* S75 .... 53 J2
Five Lane Ends *HOLM/MEL* HD7 .... 47 H2 🔢
Five Oaks *BSLY* S70 .... 65 H4
Five Trees Cl *TOT/DORE* S17 .... 200 A1
Five Trees Dr *TOT/DORE* S17 .... 200 A1
Five Weirs Wk *DARN/MH* S9 .... 172 B1
Flanders Ct *KIMB* S61 .... 131 G2 🔢
Flanderwell Av *MALT* S66 .... 157 H2
Flanderwell La *MALT* S66 .... 157 H1 🔢
Flanderwell Gdns *MALT* S66 .... 157 H1 🔢
Flanderwell La *MALT* S66 .... 135 G8
Flash La *MALT* S66 .... 157 K3
ST/HB/BR S6 .... 168 C3
Flashley Carr La *AWLS/ASK* DN6 .... 20 D6
Flask Vw *ST/HB/BR* S6 .... 150 B8
Flat La *CUD/GR* S72 .... 85 H2
DIN S25 .... 179 J1
MALT S66 .... 160 B7
RHAM S60 .... 156 A6
The Flats *CHPT/GREN* S35 .... 106 C4
Flat St *SHEF* S1 .... 9 E3
Flatts Cl *RHAM* S60 .... 174 C2
Flatts La *DEARNE* S63 .... 111 C1
RHAM S60 .... 174 C2

Flavell Cl *HEM/SK/SE* WF9 .... 34 A6 🔢
Flaxby Rd *DARN/MH* S9 .... 172 D2 🔢
Flax Lea *BSLY* S70 .... 82 B2
Fleet Cl *DEARNE* S63 .... 88 D8
Fleet Hill Crs *BSLYN/ROY* S71 .... 56 B2
Fleet La *HTFD* DN7 .... 41 K2 🔢
Fleets Cl *HTFD* DN7 .... 41 K2
Fleet St *KBTN* HD8 .... 26 A6
Fleetway *WRKN* S81 .... 196 C8
Fleetwood Av *BSLYN/ROY* S71 .... 56 D2
Fleming Pl *BSLY* S70 .... 2 B5 🔢
Fleming Wy *MALT* S66 .... 157 F2
Fletcher Av *DRON* S18 .... 201 G6
Fleury Cl *GLV* S14 .... 188 A3
Fleury Crs *GLV* S14 .... 188 A3
Fleury Pl *GLV* S14 .... 188 A3
Fleury Ri *GLV* S14 .... 188 A3
Fleury Rd *GLV* S14 .... 188 A3
Flight Hl *HOLM/MEL* HD7 .... 74 B2
Flint La *HOLM/MEL* HD7 .... 75 F2
Flint Rd *WHHL* DN2 .... 92 B2
Flintway *DEARNE* S63 .... 111 J4
Flockton Av *HAN/WDH* S13 .... 173 K7
Flockton Crs *HAN/WDH* S13 .... 173 K7
Flockton Dr *HAN/WDH* S13 .... 174 A7
Flockton Rd *HAN/WDH* S13 .... 174 A7
Flodden St *FUL* S10 .... 170 D3 🔢
Floodgate Dr *CHPT/GREN* S35 .... 130 C2
Flora St *ST/HB/BR* S6 .... 170 E1
Florence Av *AU/AST/KP* S26 .... 175 H8
DONS/BSCR DN4 .... 4 A6
Florence Ri *KIMB* S61 .... 6 A4 🔢
Florence Rd *SHEFS* S8 .... 186 E5
Flower St *DEARNE* S63 .... 86 E2
Flowitt St *DONS/BSCR* DN4 .... 4 B4
MEX/SWTN S64 .... 112 E2
Flowright Cl *SHEFP/MNR* S2 .... 187 K2
Flush House La *HOLM/MEL* HD7 .... 46 D4
Folderings La *STKB/PEN* S36 .... 127 F1
Folder La *BTLY* DN5 .... 89 H6
Folds Crs *SHEFS* S8 .... 186 C6
Folds Dr *SHEFS* S8 .... 186 C6 🔢
Folds La *NROS/TKH* DN11 .... 161 G4
SHEFS S8 .... 186 C6
Foley Av *WMB/DAR* S73 .... 83 K5
Foley St *ATT* S4 .... 171 K2
Foljambe Crs *NROS/TKH* DN11 .... 118 C6
Foljambe Dr *RHAM/THRY* S65 .... 134 D6
Foljambe Rd *RHAM/THRY* S65 .... 134 A7
Foljambe St *RAW* S62 .... 133 J5 🔢
Follett Rd *SHEFN* S5 .... 152 D2
Folly La *STKB/PEN* S36 .... 77 G1
Fontwell Dr *MEX/SWTN* S64 .... 113 G1
Footgate Cl *CHPT/GREN* S35 .... 128 C8
Forbes Rd *ST/HB/BR* S6 .... 151 H8
Ford La *HACK/IN* S12 .... 203 G2
STKB/PEN S36 .... 105 F5
Fordoles Head La *MALT* S66 .... 136 D7
Ford Rd *ECC* S11 .... 186 B1
ECK/KIL S21 .... 203 G3
Fordstead La *ARMTH* DN3 .... 40 C8
Fore Hill Av *DONS/BSCR* DN4 .... 118 C1
Foremark Rd *SHEFN* S5 .... 152 E3
Forest Hill Rd *WRKN* S81 .... 196 E8 🔢
Forest La *WRKS* S80 .... 211 G5
Forest Ri *DONS/BSCR* DN4 .... 116 B2
Forest Rd *BSLYN/ROY* S71 .... 30 A7
Forge La *CHPT/GREN* S35 .... 105 K2
ECK/KIL S21 .... 191 F8
HOY S74 .... 109 H3
RHAM S60 .... 6 C4
SHEF S1 .... 9 D5 🔢
Forge Rd *AU/AST/KP* S26 .... 192 B4
Formby Ct *BSLYN/ROY* S71 .... 56 E1 🔢
Forncett St *ATT* S4 .... 171 K1
Fornham St *SHEFP/MNR* S2 .... 9 E4 🔢
Forres Av *FUL* S10 .... 170 A4
Forres Rd *FUL* S10 .... 170 B4
Forrester Cl *MALT* S66 .... 157 G1
Forrester's Cl *AWLS/ASK* DN6 .... 17 K4
Forrester's La *DRON* S18 .... 201 J3 🔢
Forrest's Yd *WRKS* S80 .... 210 C5 🔢
Forster Rd *DONS/BSCR* DN4 .... 116 E1
Forth Av *DRON* S18 .... 200 D5
Fort Hill Rd *DARN/MH* S9 .... 153 G5
Fortway Rd *RHAM* S60 .... 155 F5
Fossard Cl *WHHL* DN2 .... 91 K1
Fossard Wy *BTLY* DN5 .... 64 C6
Fossdale Rd *ABRD* S7 .... 186 D2
Foster Place La *HOLM/MEL* HD7 .... 48 E5
Foster Rd *MALT* S66 .... 157 G2
THNE DN8 .... 23 H7
Foster's Cl *MEX/SWTN* S64 .... 112 B5
Foster St *BSLY* S70 .... 56 E7
Foster Wy *CHPT/GREN* S35 .... 107 J8
Foulstone Rw *WMB/DAR* S73 .... 84 B5 🔢
Foundry La *THNE* DN8 .... 23 H8 🔢
Foundry St *BSLY* S70 .... 2 B5
HOY S74 .... 109 H2
RAW S62 .... 133 J4
Fountain Cl *DOD/DAR* S75 .... 28 D6
Fountain Ct *BSLYN/ROY* S71 .... 29 K6
Fountains Wy *BSLYN/ROY* S71 .... 56 E4
Four Lanes Cl *DOD/DAR* S75 .... 54 D2 🔢
Fourth Av *AWLS/ASK* DN6 .... 63 J4
Four Wells Dr *HACK/IN* S12 .... 189 J4
Fowler Bridge Rd *BTLY* DN5 .... 65 F7
Fowler Crs *NROS/TKH* DN11 .... 118 D6

Fox Cl *KBTN* HD8 .... 26 A1
KIMB S61 .... 132 A1
Foxcote Lea *RHAM/THRY* S65 .... 135 F1
Fox Ct *MEX/SWTN* S64 .... 112 C4
Fox Covert Cl *DEARNE* S63 .... 86 B3
Fox Covert Rd Or
Whin Covert La
PONT WF8 .... 17 F6
Foxcroft Cha *ECK/KIL* S21 .... 205 G5
Foxcroft Dr *ECK/KIL* S21 .... 205 G2
Foxcroft Gv *ECK/KIL* S21 .... 205 G2
Foxcroft Mdw *MALT* S66 .... 159 H8
Foxfields *STKB/PEN* S36 .... 78 C1
Foxfield Wk *BSLY* S70 .... 82 E1
Fox Glen Rd *STKB/PEN* S36 .... 105 G2
Foxglove Cl *EPW* DN9 .... 121 G1
WRKS S80 .... 211 F8
Foxglove Rd *SHEFN* S5 .... 153 F1
Fox Gv *DONS/BSCR* DN4 .... 115 K4
Foxhall La *FUL* S10 .... 184 D1
Fox Hill Av *ST/HB/BR* S6 .... 151 H1
Fox Hill Cl *ST/HB/BR* S6 .... 151 H1
Fox Hill Crs *ST/HB/BR* S6 .... 151 H1
Fox Hill Dr *ST/HB/BR* S6 .... 151 H1
Fox Hill Pl *ST/HB/BR* S6 .... 151 H1
Fox Hill Rd *ST/HB/BR* S6 .... 129 H1
Foxhill Rd *THNE* DN8 .... 43 H6
Fox Hill Wy *ST/HB/BR* S6 .... 151 H1
Fox Hole La *NROS/TKH* DN11 .... 139 G7
Fox Holes Gv *STKB/PEN* S36 .... 75 J4
Foxland Av *MEX/SWTN* S64 .... 111 K5
Fox La *BTLY* DN5 .... 87 H4
HACK/IN S12 .... 188 E2
TOT/DORE S17 .... 200 C2
Fox Lane Ct *HACK/IN* S12 .... 188 E3
Fox Lane Vw *HACK/IN* S12 .... 188 E3 🔢
Fox Rd *ST/HB/BR* S6 .... 170 E1
Foxroyd Cl *BSLYN/ROY* S71 .... 57 G7
Fox St *KIMB* S61 .... 154 E3
OWL S3 .... 171 H5
Foxwood Av *HACK/IN* S12 .... 188 D3
Foxwood Dr *HACK/IN* S12 .... 188 D3
Foxwood Gv *HACK/IN* S12 .... 188 D3
Foxwood Rd *HACK/IN* S12 .... 188 D3
Framlingham Pl *SHEFP/MNR* S2 .... 171 H5
France Rd *ST/HB/BR* S6 .... 150 C2
Frances St *RHAM/THRY* S65 .... 7 E5
France St *RAW* S62 .... 133 J4
Francis Crs North
RHAM/THRY S65 .... 156 C6
Francis Crs South
RHAM/THRY S65 .... 156 C6
Francis Dr *RHAM/THRY* S65 .... 156 C6
Francis Gv *CHPT/GREN* S35 .... 107 G8
Francus Rd *BSLYN/ROY* S71 .... 30 D1
Franklin Crs *WHHL* DN2 .... 5 F2
Frank Pl *DARN/MH* S9 .... 153 H2
Frank Rd *BTLY* DN5 .... 90 B2
Fraser Cl *SHEFS* S8 .... 186 E4
Fraser Crs *SHEFS* S8 .... 186 E4
Fraser Dr *SHEFS* S8 .... 187 F4
Fraser Rd *RHAM/THRY* S65 .... 7 J1
SHEFS S8 .... 186 E4
Frederick Av *BSLY* S70 .... 2 A7
Frederick Dr *CHPT/GREN* S35 .... 129 G2
Frederick St *DARN/MH* S9 .... 172 D2
DEARNE S63 .... 85 G8
DEARNE S63 .... 86 E2
MEX/SWTN S64 .... 112 A4
RHAM S60 .... 6 E5
RHAM S60 .... 174 A1
WMB/DAR S73 .... 83 K4
WRKS S80 .... 210 C2
Frederic Pl *BSLY* S70 .... 2 C6
Fred Mulley Rd *ATT* S4 .... 171 J7
Freedom Ct *ST/HB/BR* S6 .... 151 H8
Freedom Rd *ST/HB/BR* S6 .... 170 C1
Freeman Rd *MALT* S66 .... 157 J3
Freeman St *BSLY* S70 .... 2 C5
Freemans Yd *BSLY* S70 .... 2 C4
Freesia Cl *DIN* S25 .... 193 K7
Freeston Pl *DARN/MH* S9 .... 153 H4
French Ga *DON* DN1 .... 4 C2
French St *AWLS/ASK* DN6 .... 37 H6
BTLY DN5 .... 64 E3
Fretson Rd *SHEFP/MNR* S2 .... 172 C7
Fretwell Cl *MALT* S66 .... 159 F1
Fretwell Rd *MALT* S66 .... 158 E1
RHAM/THRY S65 .... 134 A1
Friar Cl *ST/HB/BR* S6 .... 169 H1
Friars Ga *DON* DN1 .... 4 C5
Friar's Rd *BSLYN/ROY* S71 .... 57 F7
Frickley Bridge La *CUD/GR* S72 .... 32 E3
Frickley La *BTLY* DN5 .... 60 B1
Frickley Rd *ECC* S11 .... 169 K4
Frith Cl *HACK/IN* S12 .... 188 D3
Frith Rd *HACK/IN* S12 .... 188 C3
Frobisher Gv *MALT* S66 .... 159 H4
Froggatt La *SHEF* S1 .... 9 D4
Frogmore Cl *MALT* S66 .... 157 G1
Front St *RHAM* S60 .... 156 A3
Frostings Cl *CHPT/GREN* S35 .... 129 H1
The Frostings *CHPT/GREN* S35 .... 129 H1
Fulford Cl *DARN/MH* S9 .... 172 E2
Fulford Pl *DARN/MH* S9 .... 172 E2
Fullerton Av *CONI* DN12 .... 114 A2
Fullerton Cl *AWLS/ASK* DN6 .... 37 H6
Fullerton Crs *RHAM/THRY* S65 .... 134 A1
Fullerton Dr *RHAM* S60 .... 154 A4

ullerton Rd *RHAM* S60 .... 6 B6
  RHAM S60 .... 155 F4
ullshaw La *STKB/PEN* S36 .... 76 C8
ulmar Wy *KIMB* S61 .... 131 H1
  WRKN S81 .... 196 A8
ulmer CI *BSLYN/ROY* S71 .... 56 C1
ulmere Crs *SHEFN* S5 .... 151 K1
ulmere Rd *SHEFN* S5 .... 151 K1
ulmer Rd *ECC* S11 .... 170 C1
ulney Rd *ECC* S11 .... 169 K7
ulton Rd *FUL* S10 .... 170 C2
ulwood Cha *FUL* S10 .... 169 J7 🔲
ulwood Dr *DONS/BSCR* DN4 .... 116 E3
ulwood Head Rd *FUL* S10 .... 184 C1
ulwood La *FUL* S10 .... 184 B1
ulwood Rd *ECC* S11 .... 169 H8
  FUL S10 .... 170 A6
urlong Ct *DEARNE* S63 .... 86 C4
urlong Rd *BTLY* DN5 .... 87 G6
  DEARNE S63 .... 86 C4
urlong Wy *BTLY* DN5 .... 87 G5
urnace HI *OWL* S3 .... 9 D2
urnace La *HAN/WDH* S13 .... 174 B8
urness CI *DIN* S25 .... 178 B8
  ST/HB/BR S6 .... 150 C8
urness Dene *BSLYN/ROY* S71 .... 56 E2
urness Rd *CHPT/GREN* S35 .... 107 H8
urniss Av *TOT/DORE* S17 .... 199 H1
urniss Ms *TOT/DORE* S17 .... 199 J1
urnival Rd *ATT* S4 .... 9 F2
urnival Rd *AU/AST/KP* S26 .... 192 E2 🔲
urnivall Rd *DONS/BSCR* DN4 .... 4 A6
urnival Rd *ATT* S4 .... 9 F2
  AU/AST/KP S26 .... 192 E2
urnival St *SHEF* S1 .... 9 D4
  WRKS S80 .... 210 E6
urnival St North *WRKS* S80 .... 210 E5
urnival Wy *RHAM* S60 .... 156 C6
ylde CI *BSLYN/ROY* S71 .... 56 E1

G

adding Moor Rd *STKB/PEN* S36 .... 52 C7
ainford St *THNE* DN8 .... 24 A3
ainford Sq *THNE* DN8 .... 24 A4
ainsborough CI *MALT* S66 .... 157 G2 🔲
  BWTY DN10 .... 164 B1
  DRON S18 .... 200 E7
ainsborough Rd *ABRD* S7 .... 170 D8
ainsborough Wy *BSLYN/ROY* S71 .... 3 E2
aitskell CI *DEARNE* S63 .... 86 C4
  MALT S66 .... 159 J3
ala Crs *MALT* S66 .... 158 E1
alley Dr *MOS* S20 .... 190 B6
allon Cft *HEM/SK/SE* WF9 .... 34 D4
allow Tree Rd *RHAM/THRY* S65 .... 156 C3
alpharm Wy *DOD/DAR* S75 .... 54 D7
alsworthy Av *SHEFN* S5 .... 152 A4
alsworthy CI *DONS/BSCR* DN4 .... 116 C2
alsworthy Rd *SHEFN* S5 .... 152 A4
alway Av *NROS/TKH* DN11 .... 163 J2
alway CI *RAW* S62 .... 133 K1
alway Dr *NROS/TKH* DN11 .... 163 J2
alway Rd *NROS/TKH* DN11 .... 163 J2
ame La *ST/HB/BR* S6 .... 149 G8
amston Rd *SHEFS* S8 .... 171 F8
annow Cl *ECK/KIL* S21 .... 191 K8
anton Pl *BSLYN/ROY* S71 .... 29 K8
anton Rd *ST/HB/BR* S6 .... 151 G5 🔲
arbroads Crs *RHAM/THRY* S65 .... 134 D5
arbutt St *DEARNE* S63 .... 86 C6 🔲
arden Av *ECK/KIL* S21 .... 205 F8
arden Crs *RHAM* S60 .... 155 K5
arden Dr *WMB/DAR* S73 .... 84 D7
arden Gv *WMB/DAR* S73 .... 83 K7
arden House CI *BSLYN/ROY* S71 .... 56 D2
arden House Dr *AU/AST/KP* S26 .... 193 H4
ardenia Rd *ARMTH* DN3 .... 66 D4
arden La *BTLY* DN5 .... 88 E8
  RHAM S60 .... 6 B3 🔲
  RHAM/THRY S65 .... 135 J4
ardens La *CONI* DN12 .... 114 C5
he Gardens *DONS/BSCR* DN4 .... 92 C8
arden St *DEARNE* S63 .... 60 C7
  DEARNE S63 .... 85 G8 🔲
  DEARNE S63 .... 86 E2
  KIMB S61 .... 6 A3
  MEX/SWTN S64 .... 113 F2 🔲
  SHEF S1 .... 9 E4
  WMB/DAR S73 .... 84 D2
arden Wk *RHAM* S60 .... 155 K4
ardom CI *DRON* S18 .... 200 D6 🔲
arfield Mt *RHAM/THRY* S65 .... 7 E5 🔲
argrave Crs *HEM/SK/SE* WF9 .... 33 F1
argrave Pl *HEM/SK/SE* WF9 .... 33 F1
arland CI *DON* DN1 .... 5 G7
arland Cft *MOS* S20 .... 190 C8
arland Dr *ST/HB/BR* S6 .... 150 C6
arland Mt *MOS* S20 .... 190 C7 🔲
arland Wy *MOS* S20 .... 190 C8
arraby CI *CUD/GR* S72 .... 59 H5
arry Rd *ST/HB/BR* S6 .... 151 G6
arside St *WRKS* S80 .... 210 E4
arter St *ATT* S4 .... 152 E8
arth CI *DARN/MH* S9 .... 172 C2 🔲
arth Wy *DRON* S18 .... 201 F6 🔲
artrice Gdns *MOS* S20 .... 204 E2
artrice Gv *MOS* S20 .... 204 D2

Gashouse La *MOS* S20 .... 204 B2
Gate Crs *DOD/DAR* S75 .... 54 E7
Gatefield Rd *ABRD* S7 .... 186 E1 🔲
Gate Foot La *KBTN* HD8 .... 49 H1
Gateford CI *WRKN* S81 .... 210 B1
Gateford Dr *WRKN* S81 .... 196 B8 🔲
Gateford Gdns *WRKN* S81 .... 210 B1
Gateford Gld *WRKN* S81 .... 210 C1
Gateford Ri *WRKN* S81 .... 196 B8
Gateford Rd *WRKN* S81 .... 195 J6
  WRKN S81 .... 210 C2
  WRKS S80 .... 210 C3
Gate Head La *HOLM/MEL* HD7 .... 49 F7
Gate House La *EPW* DN9 .... 120 C2
Gatesbridge Pk *EPW* DN9 .... 121 G3
Gateway CI *RAW* S62 .... 133 H5
The Gateway *RAW* S62 .... 133 H5 🔲
Gate Wood La *ARMTH* DN3 .... 94 E3
Gatewood La *HTFD* DN7 .... 68 C5
Gatty Rd *SHEFN* S5 .... 130 E8
Gatton CI *ECK/KIL* S21 .... 205 G1
  GLV S14 .... 187 K4
  MALT S66 .... 157 J1
Gaunt Dr *GLV* S14 .... 187 K4
  MALT S66 .... 157 J1
Gaunt Pl *GLV* S14 .... 187 K3
Gaunt Rd *GLV* S14 .... 187 K3
  MALT S66 .... 157 J1
Gaunt Wy *GLV* S14 .... 187 K4
Gawber Rd *DOD/DAR* S75 .... 55 H4
Gayton CI *DONS/BSCR* DN4 .... 116 D2
Gayton Rd *ATT* S4 .... 152 D7 🔲
Geer La *HACK/IN* S12 .... 202 E2
Geeseness La *GLE* DN14 .... 22 C4
Gelderd Pl *DRON* S18 .... 201 G3
Gell St *OWL* S3 .... 8 C4
Geneva Sq *THNE* DN8 .... 24 A4
Genn La *BSLY* S70 .... 81 J1
Genoa CI *WMB/DAR* S73 .... 58 B8
Genoa St *MEX/SWTN* S64 .... 113 C2
The Gentre *MALT* S66 .... 157 J2 🔲
George Buckley Ct
  HEM/SK/SE WF9 .... 33 K5 🔲
George La *HOR/CROF* WF4 .... 29 K1
George PI *MEX/SWTN* S64 .... 113 H3 🔲
  RAW S62 .... 133 K2
George Sq *BSLY* S70 .... 2 B4 🔲
George St *AWLS/ASK* DN6 .... 37 J5
  BSLY S70 .... 2 B4
  BSLY S70 .... 82 D3
  BSLY S70 .... 82 B3 🔲
  BTLY DN5 .... 64 E5 🔲
  CUD/GR S72 .... 31 K7
  CUD/GR S72 .... 59 G8
  DEARNE S63 .... 60 E8
  DEARNE S63 .... 86 B2
  DOD/DAR S75 .... 29 G6
  HEM/SK/SE WF9 .... 33 H1 🔲
  HOY S74 .... 109 F2 🔲
  RHAM S60 .... 6 C3
  SHEF S1 .... 9 D3
  WMB/DAR S73 .... 84 A5
  WMB/DAR S73 .... 84 C3
  WRKS S80 .... 210 D4
George Yd *BSLY* S70 .... 2 B4
Gerald CI *BSLY* S70 .... 3 F6
Gerald Crs *BSLY* S70 .... 56 E7
Gerald PI *BSLY* S70 .... 3 F6
Gerald Rd *BSLY* S70 .... 3 F6
Gerald St *DARN/MH* S9 .... 153 H8
  BSLY S70 .... 3 F6
Gerard Av *RHAM/THRY* S65 .... 135 F5
Gerard CI *SHEFP/MNR* S2 .... 187 H1 🔲
Gerard Rd *RHAM* S60 .... 7 D5
Gerard St *SHEFS* S8 .... 187 H1
Gervase Av *SHEFS* S8 .... 200 E1
Gervase Dr *SHEFS* S8 .... 200 E1 🔲
Gervase PI *SHEFS* S8 .... 200 E1
Gervase Rd *SHEFS* S8 .... 200 E1 🔲
Gibbet Hill La *BWTY* DN10 .... 164 A3
Gibbing Greaves Rd
  RHAM/THRY S65 .... 156 D3
Gibbons Dr *SHEFS* S8 .... 188 A5
Gibbons Wy *SHEFS* S8 .... 188 A5 🔲
Gibdyke *BWTY* DN10 .... 143 K4
Gibraltar St *OWL* S3 .... 9 D2
Gibriding La *HOLM/MEL* HD7 .... 46 E1
Gibson Rd *HTFD* DN7 .... 69 H7
Gifford Dr *DONS/BSCR* DN4 .... 116 A3
Gifford Rd *SHEFP/MNR* S2 .... 171 G8 🔲
Gig La *HOY* S74 .... 82 C7
Gilbert Cv *BSLY* S70 .... 56 E7
Gilbert Hl *STKB/PEN* S36 .... 102 D1
Gilberthorpe Dr *RHAM/THRY* S65 .... 7 F4 🔲
Gilberthorpe Rd
  DONS/BSCR DN4 .... 90 C8 🔲
Gilberthorpe St *RHAM/THRY* S65 .... 7 F4
Gilbert Rd *NROS/TKH* DN11 .... 163 G3
Gilbert St *SHEFP/MNR* S2 .... 9 E3 🔲
Gildingwells Rd *WRKN* S81 .... 179 H6
  WRKN S81 .... 195 G3
Giles Av *DEARNE* S63 .... 111 F1
Gill CI *MALT* S66 .... 157 H1
Gill Cft *ST/HB/BR* S6 .... 169 C1 🔲
Gilleyfield Av *TOT/DORE* S17 .... 185 J8
Gill La *HOLM/MEL* HD7 .... 47 H5

Gill Mdw *ST/HB/BR* S6 .... 169 C1
Gillot Dell *MALT* S66 .... 157 G4 🔲
Gillott La *MALT* S66 .... 157 G4
Gillott Rd *ST/HB/BR* S6 .... 151 H3
Gill Royd La *STKB/PEN* S36 .... 103 F4
Gill St *DON* DN1 .... 5 D4
  HOY S74 .... 109 G2
Gilpin La *ST/HB/BR* S6 .... 8 B1 🔲
Gilpin St *ST/HB/BR* S6 .... 170 E1 🔲
Gilroyd La *DOD/DAR* S75 .... 81 G2
Gilthwaites Gv *KBTN* HD8 .... 51 H1
Ginhouse La *KIMB* S61 .... 6 B2
Gipsy Green La *DEARNE* S63 .... 111 J3
Gipsyhill La *WRKS* S80 .... 207 J6
Gipsy La *DOD/DAR* S75 .... 28 E2
  DRON S18 .... 202 C6
  MALT S66 .... 159 K6
Gisborne Rd *ECC* S11 .... 186 B1
Glade Cft *HACK/IN* S12 .... 188 C2
Glade Lea *HACK/IN* S12 .... 188 C3
Glade Vw *ARMTH* DN3 .... 66 E3
Gladstone Ms *FUL* S10 .... 169 J6 🔲
Gladstone PI *WRKS* S80 .... 210 C4
Gladstone Rd *DONS/BSCR* DN4 .... 4 A5
  FUL S10 .... 169 J6
  MALT S66 .... 159 F4 🔲
Gladstone St *WRKS* S80 .... 210 C4
Gladys St *RHAM/THRY* S65 .... 7 F4
Glaisdale *WRKN* S81 .... 197 F8
Glaisdale CI *DIN* S25 .... 177 J4
Glamis Rd *WHHL* DN2 .... 91 K4
  WRKN S81 .... 196 C1
Glasshouse La *MEX/SWTN* S64 .... 112 D8
Glasshouse St *RHAM* S60 .... 6 B3
Glastonbury Ga *BTLY* DN5 .... 90 A2
Gleadless Av *HACK/IN* S12 .... 188 B3
Gleadless Bank *HACK/IN* S12 .... 188 B3 🔲
Gleadless Common *HACK/IN* S12 .... 188 B2
Gleadless Ct *SHEFP/MNR* S2 .... 187 H1 🔲
Gleadless Crs *HACK/IN* S12 .... 188 B2
Gleadless Dr *HACK/IN* S12 .... 188 B3
Gleadless Mt *HACK/IN* S12 .... 188 C4 🔲
Gleadless Rd *HACK/IN* S12 .... 188 A2
  SHEFP/MNR S2 .... 187 K1 🔲
  SHEFS S8 .... 171 G8
  SHEFS S8 .... 187 G3 🔲
Glebe Av *AU/AST/KP* S26 .... 192 E8
Glebe CI *MEX/SWTN* S64 .... 112 B6
  WRKS S80 .... 210 A4
Glebe Crs *RHAM/THRY* S65 .... 134 D6
Glebe Farm CI *ARMTH* DN3 .... 93 F1
  AU/AST/KP S26 .... 192 E8
Glebeland CI *RAW* S62 .... 111 H7
Glebelands Rd *STKB/PEN* S36 .... 105 F7
Glebe Rd *AWLS/ASK* DN6 .... 18 A6
  FUL S10 .... 170 C3
  MEX/SWTN S64 .... 112 B6
  THNE DN8 .... 23 K8
Glebe St *DONS/BSCR* DN4 .... 116 A1
Gledhill Av *STKB/PEN* S36 .... 77 K6
Gledhill CI *DRON* S18 .... 201 C6
Glenalmond Rd *ECC* S11 .... 170 B8
Glencoe CI *HTFD* DN7 .... 42 B7 🔲
Glencoe Dr *SHEFP/MNR* S2 .... 9 F4 🔲
Glencoe PI *SHEFP/MNR* S2 .... 9 F4 🔲
Glencoe Rd *SHEFP/MNR* S2 .... 9 F4
Glendale CI *DOD/DAR* S75 .... 55 G6
Glendale Rd *BTLY* DN5 .... 89 J6 🔲
Gleneagles Dr *ARMTH* DN3 .... 119 C1 🔲
  DONS/BSCR DN4 .... 119 C1
Gleneagles Ri *MEX/SWTN* S64 .... 112 C5
Gleneagles Rd *DIN* S25 .... 178 B7
Glen Field Av *DONS/BSCR* DN4 .... 4 A5
Glenholme CI *HAN/WDH* S13 .... 173 G8
Glenholme PI *HAN/WDH* S13 .... 173 H8 🔲
Glenholme Rd *HAN/WDH* S13 .... 173 H8
Glenholme Wy *HAN/WDH* S13 .... 173 G7
Glenmoor Av *BSLY* S70 .... 55 C7 🔲
Glenmore CI *HACK/IN* S12 .... 188 D1
Glenmore Ri *WMB/DAR* S73 .... 84 B6 🔲
Glenorchy Rd *ABRD* S7 .... 186 D2
Glen Rd *ABRD* S7 .... 186 E1
  ARMTH DN3 .... 93 K7
The Glen *ECC* S11 .... 170 B6 🔲
Glenthorn CI *WRKN* S81 .... 195 G8
Glentilt Rd *ABRD* S7 .... 186 D2
Glen View Rd *SHEFS* S8 .... 186 E7
Glenville CI *HOY* S74 .... 108 E2
Glenwood Crs *CHPT/GREN* S35 .... 130 C2
Gliwice Wy *DONS/BSCR* DN4 .... 92 A6
Glossop Rd *FUL* S10 .... 170 C5
  OWL S3 .... 8 B5
Glossop Rw *CHPT/GREN* S35 .... 128 C8
Gloucester Crs *FUL* S10 .... 8 B4 🔲
Gloucester Rd *KIMB* S61 .... 132 C6
  WHHL DN2 .... 91 K2
  WRKN S81 .... 196 E8
Gloucester St *FUL* S10 .... 8 B4
Glover Rd *SHEFP/MNR* S2 .... 171 G8 🔲
  TOT/DORE S17 .... 199 K2 🔲
Glyn Av *DON* DN1 .... 5 D3
Goathland Dr *HAN/WDH* S13 .... 174 A8
Goathland PI *HAN/WDH* S13 .... 174 B8
Goathland Rd *HAN/WDH* S13 .... 174 B8
Goddard Av *STKB/PEN* S36 .... 104 C5 🔲
Goddard Hall Rd *SHEFN* S5 .... 152 D6
Godfrey Rd *THNE* DN8 .... 23 H8 🔲
Godley St *BSLYN/ROY* S71 .... 30 C3
Godric Dr *RHAM* S60 .... 154 E6

Godric Gn *RHAM* S60 .... 154 E6
Godric Rd *SHEFN* S5 .... 130 D8
Godstone Rd *RHAM* S60 .... 7 D5
Goldcrest Ri *WRKN* S81 .... 196 A8
Goldcrest Wk *KIMB* S61 .... 131 H2
Gold Cft *BSLY* S70 .... 3 D5 🔲
Golden Smithies La
  MEX/SWTN S64 .... 112 A4
Goldsborough Rd *WHHL* DN2 .... 91 K4
Goldsmith Dr *RHAM/THRY* S65 .. 156 A1
Goldsmith Rd *DONS/BSCR* DN4 .. 117 F1
  RHAM/THRY S65 .... 156 A1
  WRKN S81 .... 211 F2 🔲
Gold St *BSLY* S70 .... 3 D5
Goldthorpe Av *WRKN* S81 .... 180 C4
Goldthorpe Rd *DEARNE* S63 ...... 86 C3
Gomersal La *DRON* S18 .... 201 G6
Gomersal Av *CONI* DN12 .... 114 A5
Gooder Av *BSLYN/ROY* S71 .... 30 D4
Goodison Bvd *DONS/BSCR* DN4 .. 92 D8
Goodison Ct *ST/HB/BR* S6 .... 169 K1
Goodison Ri *ST/HB/BR* S6 .... 169 K1
Goodwin Av *RAW* S62 .... 133 J1
Goodwin Crs *MEX/SWTN* S64 .... 112 C3
Goodwin Rd *KIMB* S61 .... 132 D3
  SHEFS S8 .... 187 G1 🔲
Goodyear Crs *WMB/DAR* S73 .... 84 A5
Goore Av *DARN/MH* S9 .... 172 D5
Goore Dr *DARN/MH* S9 .... 172 D5
Goore Rd *DARN/MH* S9 .... 172 D5
Gooseacre Av *DEARNE* S63 ...... 60 B6
Goosebutt St *RAW* S62 .... 133 J3
Goose Carr La *AU/AST/KP* S26 .. 176 D8
Goosecroft Av *RHAM/THRY* S65 .. 134 D5 🔲
Gorse Gn *HOLM/MEL* HD7 .... 47 K2
Goosehole La *HEM/SK/SE* WF9 .. 35 G6
Goose La *MALT* S66 .... 157 H3
Gordon Av *SHEFS* S8 .... 187 G5
Gordon Cl *WRKS* S80 .... 211 F4
Gordon Pl *HEM/SK/SE* WF9 ...... 34 C5
Gordon Rd *CONI* DN12 .... 115 J5
  ECC S11 .... 8 A6 🔲
Gordon St *BSLY* S70 .... 57 F7
Gordon Ter *RHAM/THRY* S65 .... 7 E4 🔲
Gorehill Cl *DEARNE* S63 .... 111 K1
Gore La *GLE* DN14 .... 10 B6
Gorse Cl *HTFD* DN7 .... 68 A2
Gorse Dr *ECK/KIL* S21 .... 205 H2 🔲
Gorseland Ct *MALT* S66 .... 157 F3
Gorselands Av *WRKS* S80 .... 211 G6
Gorse La *FUL* S10 .... 157 G4
The Gorse *MALT* S66 .... 157 F4
  RHAM/THRY S65 .... 156 B2
Gorsey Brigg *DRON* S18 .... 200 D6
Gosber Rd *ECK/KIL* S21 .... 204 B4
Gosber St *ECK/KIL* S21 .... 204 B4
Gosforth Cl *DRON* S18 .... 201 F6
Gosforth Crs *DRON* S18 .... 201 F6 🔲
Gosforth Dr *DRON* S18 .... 201 F6 🔲
Gosforth Gn *DRON* S18 .... 201 F6
Gosforth La *DRON* S18 .... 201 F6
Gosling Gate Rd *DEARNE* S63 .... 86 D2
Gotham Rd *RHAM* S60 .... 155 F6
Gough Cl *RHAM/THRY* S65 .... 156 B3
Goulding St *MEX/SWTN* S64 .... 112 C3
Gowdall Gn *BTLY* DN5 .... 64 D4
Gowdall La *GLE* DN14 .... 11 K2
Gower St *ATT* S4 .... 171 J1
  WMB/DAR S73 .... 84 B5
Grace Rd *CONI* DN12 .... 115 K4
Grace St *BSLYN/ROY* S71 .... 57 G1
Graftdyke Cl *NROS/TKH* DN11 .. 119 G3
Grafton St *BSLY* S70 .... 2 A4
  SHEFP/MNR S2 .... 9 F4
  WRKS S80 .... 210 C3
Grafton Wy *RHAM/THRY* S65 ... 7 D2
Graham Av *RHAM* S60 .... 155 G8 🔲
Graham Rd *ARMTH* DN3 .... 66 E4
  ECC S11 .... 169 K7
  FUL S10 .... 169 J7
Graham's Orch *BSLY* S70 .... 2 B4 🔲
Grainger Cl *CONI* DN12 .... 115 H6 🔲
Grampian Cl *BTLY* DN5 .... 90 B2 🔲
  DOD/DAR S75 .... 55 G5 🔲
Grampian Wy *THNE* DN8 .... 43 H2
Granary Ct *WRKN* S81 .... 196 E1
Granby Ct *RHAM* DN3 .... 93 H2
  HEM/SK/SE WF9 .... 35 F2 🔲
Granby Crs *WHHL* DN2 .... 5 F4
Granby La *NROS/TKH* DN11 ..... 118 C3
Granby Rd *CONI* DN12 .... 115 K5
  SHEFN S5 .... 152 E3
Grange Av *AU/AST/KP* S26 .... 175 G6
  BWTY DN10 .... 142 A7
  DONS/BSCR DN4 .... 90 D8 🔲
  DRON S18 .... 200 E6
  HEM/SK/SE WF9 .... 35 F4
  HTFD DN7 .... 42 C7
  WRKN S81 .... 195 G4
Grange Cliffe Cl *ECC* S11 .... 186 B3
Grange Cl *AWLS/ASK* DN6 .... 19 F7
  CUD/GR S72 .... 32 C4 🔲
  DONS/BSCR DN4 .... 118 E1
  HTFD DN7 .... 42 C7 🔲
  MALT S66 .... 176 C2
  WRKN S81 .... 196 E1
Grange Ct *BTLY* DN5 .... 90 D1
  MALT S66 .... 157 G3 🔲
Grange Crs *BSLYN/ROY* S71 ..... 57 F5

DEARNE S63 .... 60 D7
ECC S11 .... 8 B6
Grange Crescent Rd *ECC* S11 .... 8 B6
Grange Dr *KIMB* S61 .... 132 A6
  MALT S66 .... 158 C3
  NROS/TKH DN11 .... 163 F2
Grange Farm *DONS/BSCR* DN4 .. 116 D3
Grange Farm Dr *CHPT/GREN* S35 .. 150 C3
Grangefield Av *NROS/TKH* DN11 .. 118 E6
Grangefield Ter *NROS/TKH* DN11 .. 118 E6
Grange Gv *THNE* DN8 .... 24 A5 🔲
Grange La *AWLS/ASK* DN6 .... 57 H3
  BSLYN/ROY S71 .... 57 F6
  DONS/BSCR DN4 .... 116 B3
  KIMB S61 .... 131 G7
  MALT S66 .... 159 J1
  NROS/TKH DN11 .... 118 C7
  RHAM S60 .... 154 D4
Grange Mill La *SHEFN* S5 .... 131 G7
Grange Pk *ARMTH* DN3 .... 67 F2
Grange Rd *AWLS/ASK* DN6 ...... 18 A6
  AWLS/ASK DN6 .... 63 K4
  BSLYN/ROY S71 .... 30 B4
  BTLY DN5 .... 64 D3 🔲
  CUD/GR S72 .... 32 C5
  DEARNE S63 .... 60 D7
  DONS/BSCR DN4 .... 118 E1
  ECC S11 .... 8 B6
  MEX/SWTN S64 .... 112 A3
  MOS S20 .... 190 E4
  RAW S62 .... 111 K8
  RHAM S60 .... 156 A5
  THNE DN8 .... 24 A3
Grange Sq *THNE* DN8 .... 24 A3 🔲
Grange St *DEARNE* S63 .... 60 D7
Grange Vw *DONS/BSCR* DN4 .... 4 A6
  HEM/SK/SE WF9 .... 33 G1
  HOY S74 .... 82 E6
  NROS/TKH DN11 .... 163 F2
Grange View Crs *KIMB* S61 ...... 132 A7
Grange View Rd *KIMB* S61 .... 132 A7
Grangewood Rd *DIN* S25 .... 178 A3
Grantham St *NROS/TKH* DN11 .. 118 D6
Grantley Cl *WMB/DAR* S73 .... 84 C7
Granville Rd *SHEFP/MNR* S2 ..... 9 F5
Granville St *DOD/DAR* S75 .... 2 A2
  SHEFP/MNR S2 .... 9 E4 🔲
Granville Ter *RHAM/THRY* S65 .. 7 E4 🔲
Grasby Ct *RHAM/THRY* S65 ..... 135 J8 🔲
Grasmere Av *WHHL* DN2 .... 92 B5
Grasmere Cl *DIN* S25 .... 194 D3 🔲
  STKB/PEN S36 .... 78 A3
Grasmere Crs *DOD/DAR* S75 .... 29 F4 🔲
Grasmere Rd *AWLS/ASK* DN6 ... 37 K6
  BSLYN/ROY S71 .... 3 D4 🔲
  CONI DN12 .... 114 C5
  DRON S18 .... 200 E6
  SHEFS S8 .... 186 E2 🔲
  WRKN S81 .... 196 D6
Grassdale Vw *HACK/IN* S12 ..... 189 H4
Grassington Cl *HACK/IN* S12 .... 189 K4 🔲
Grassington Dr *HACK/IN* S12 ... 189 J4
Grassington Wy *CHPT/GREN* S35 .. 130 A1
Grassmoor Cl *HACK/IN* S12 ..... 188 D2 🔲
Grassthorpe Rd *HACK/IN* S12 .. 188 C3
Grattan St *KIMB* S61 .... 154 B1
Graven Cl *CHPT/GREN* S35 ...... 129 G7
Gray Av *AU/AST/KP* S26 .... 175 H6
Gray Cl *RHAM/THRY* S65 .... 7 D2
Gray Gdns *DONS/BSCR* DN4 .... 116 E1 🔲
Grays Ct *CONI* DN12 .... 114 B3
Grayson Cl *RHAM/THRY* S65 .... 135 J7
  STKB/PEN S36 .... 105 F7
Grayson Rd *BSLYN/ROY* S71 .... 132 D3
Gray's Rd *BSLYN/ROY* S71 ...... 30 D6
Gray St *HOY* S74 .... 109 H2
  MOS S20 .... 190 A8
  OWL S3 .... 171 H1
Greasbro Rd *DARN/MH* S9 ...... 154 A5
Greasbrough Cl *RAW* S62 .... 133 G2
Greasbrough Rd *RAW* S62 ...... 133 H4
  RHAM S60 .... 6 C3
Greasbrough St *RHAM* S60 ...... 6 B3
Greasebrough Rd *RHAM* S60 .... 6 C3
Great Bank Rd *RHAM/THRY* S65 .. 156 B3
Great Central Av *DONS/BSCR* DN4 .. 4 E6 🔲
Great Cliffe Rd *DOD/DAR* S75 ... 54 D7
Great Common Cl *STV/CWN* S43 .. 206 B8
Great Cft *DRON* S18 .... 200 D5
Great Eastern Wy *RAW* S62 ..... 133 J5
Great North Av *AWLS/ASK* DN6 .. 63 H2
  BWTY DN10 .... 141 K2
  BWTY DN10 .... 164 B8
  NROS/TKH DN11 .... 119 J5
Great Park Rd *KIMB* S61 .... 132 B7
Greave Rd *HOLM/MEL* HD7 ..... 47 K7
Greaves Cl *ST/HB/BR* S6 .... 169 G1 🔲
Greaves Fold *DOD/DAR* S75 ..... 55 G5 🔲
Greaves La *CHPT/GREN* S35 ..... 107 J5
  ST/HB/BR S6 .... 150 B8
  ST/HB/BR S6 .... 169 G1
Greaves Rd *KIMB* S61 .... 132 D8
  SHEFN S5 .... 130 B7
Greaves Sike La *CONI* DN12 ..... 136 D5
Greaves St *ST/HB/BR* S6 .... 169 G1
Greenacre Dr *KBTN* HD8 .... 51 F4
Greenacre Rd *WRKN* S81 .... 210 E1
Green Acres *HOY* S74 .... 109 F2

RAW S62 133
Greenacres Cl *DRON* S18 .... 201 J8
Green Arbour Rd *MALT* S66 ..... 176 E1
Green Balk *CONI* DN12 137
Greenbank *BSLYN/ROY* S71 ..... 30 A6
Green Bank *THNE* DN8 44
Greenbank Wk *CUD/GR* S72 .... 32 C8
Green Boulevarde
  DONS/BSCR DN4 92
Green Cha *ECK/KIL* S21 204
Green Cross *DRON* S18 201
Greenfield *RAW* S62 133
Greenfield Cl *ARMTH* DN3 67
  ARMTH DN3 .... 93 H2
  KBTN HD8 51
  RHAM/THRY S65 .... 134 C7
  SHEFS S8 187
Greenfield Ct *MALT* S66 .... 157 G1
  MEX/SWTN S64 86
Greenfield Dr *SHEFS* S8 187
Greenfield Gdns *DONS/BSCR* DN4 .. 93
  MALT S66 157
Greenfield La *DONS/BSCR* DN4 .. 4
Greenfield Rd *HEM/SK/SE* WF9 .. 33
  HOLM/MEL HD7 46
  HOY S74 83
  RHAM/THRY S65 134
  SHEFS S8 187
Greenfields *ECK/KIL* S21 .... 204 A4
  GLE DN14 11
Green Finch Cl *RHAM* S60 155
Greenfinch Dl *WRKN* S81 .... 196 A8
Greenfoot Cl *DOD/DAR* S75 2
Greenfoot La *DOD/DAR* S75 2
Green Gate Cl *DEARNE* S63 86
Greengate La *CHPT/GREN* S35 .. 129
  HAN/WDH S13 190
Green Gate Rd *HOLM/MEL* HD7 .. 46
Greengate Rd *HAN/WDH* S13 ... 190
  PONT WF8 17
Greenhall Rd *ECK/KIL* S21 204
Greenhead Gdns *CHPT/GREN* S35 .. 130
Greenhead La *CHPT/GREN* S35 .. 130
Greenhill Av *BSLYN/ROY* S71 ... 2
  MALT S66 158
  SHEFS S8 186
Greenhill Bank Rd *HOLM/MEL* HD7 .. 48
Green Hill Gv *STKB/PEN* S36 ... 78 D1
Greenhill Main Rd *SHEFS* S8 .... 187 G8
Greenhill Pkwy *SHEFS* S8 200
  TOT/DORE S17 200
Greenhill Rd *SHEFS* S8 186
Greenhouse La *FUL* S10 184
Green House Hall *WHHL* DN2 ... 92
Greenhow St *FUL* S10 170
Green Ings *DEARNE* S63 85
Greenland Av *MALT* S66 137
  MALT S66 159
Greenland Cl *DARN/MH* S9 ...... 172 E2
  DIN S25 193
Greenland Ct *DARN/MH* S9 172
Greenland Dr *DARN/MH* S9 172
Greenland La *GLE* DN14 14
Greenland Rd *DARN/MH* S9 172
Greenlands Av *NROS/TKH* DN11 .. 119
Greenland Vw *BSLY* S70 .... 82 A3
  DARN/MH S9 172
Greenland Wy *DARN/MH* S9 172
  MALT S66 159
Green La *ARMTH* DN3 93
  AU/AST/KP S26 175
  AU/AST/KP S26 176
  AWLS/ASK DN6 18
  AWLS/ASK DN6 37
  AWLS/ASK DN6 63
  BTLY DN5 65
  BTLY DN5 67
  BWTY DN10 164
  CHPT/GREN S35 127
  CHPT/GREN S35 128
  CHPT/GREN S35 150
  DEARNE S63 111
  DOD/DAR S75 81
  DOD/DAR S75 81
  DRON S18 201
  ECK/KIL S21 205
  HEM/SK/SE WF9 34
  HOLM/MEL HD7 47
  HOR/CROF WF4 30
  HOY S74 108
  HTFD DN7 68
  KBTN HD8 50
  KIMB S61 131
  MALT S66 157
  MALT S66 157
  NROS/TKH DN11 138
  OWL S3 8
  RAW S62 133
  RHAM S60 154
  RHAM S60 155
  STKB/PEN S36 53
  STKB/PEN S36 104
Greenlaws Ct *HOLM/MEL* HD7 .. 47
Green Lea *DRON* S18 200
Greenleafe Av *WHHL* DN2 66
Green Moor Rd *STKB/PEN* S36 .. 105
Green Oak Av *TOT/DORE* S17 ... 199
Green Oak Crs *TOT/DORE* S17 .. 199 J
Green Oak Dr *AU/AST/KP* S26 .. 192

TOT/DORE S17 .... 199 J3
een Oak Rd TOT/DORE S17 ...... 199 J4
eenock St ST/HB/BR S6 .... 151 G7
een Ri RAW S62 .... 111 G8
een Rd STKB/PEN S36 .... 78 A5
eenset Vw BSLYN/ROY S71 ...... 29 K6
eenside CUD/GR S72 .... 31 J3
DOD/DAR S75 .... 29 H6
KBTN HD8 .... 51 H1
KIMB S61 .... 132 E4
STKB/PEN S36 .... 78 D1
eenside Av AU/AST/KP S26 ...... 192 C5
DOD/DAR S75 .... 29 H6
eenside La HOY S74 .... 109 F1
eenside Ms HACK/IN S12 .... 189 K4
eenside Pl DOD/DAR S75 .... 29 H6
een Spring Av BSLY S70 .... 82 A7
een's Rd HTFD DN7 .... 68 A2
RHAM/THRY S65 .... 156 A1
een St DON S1 .... 82 D3
DONS/BSCR DN4 .... 116 C1
HOY S74 .... 109 G1
KIMB S61 .... 132 E3
STKB/PEN S36 .... 78 D1
DONS/BSCR DN4 .... 116 C1
e Green CONI DN12 .... 113 H4
DEARNE S63 .... 86 B4
DIN S25 .... 193 K1
EPW DN9 .... 94 B8
EPW DN9 .... 121 F4
MEX/SWTN S64 .... 112 A5
NROS/TKH DN11 .... 162 D4
RHAM S60 .... 155 J4
STKB/PEN S36 .... 78 A5
THNE DN8 .... 23 J8
THNE DN8 .... 24 A3
TOT/DORE S17 .... 199 H3
WRKN S81 .... 196 E1
e Green Vw CUD/GR S72 .... 31 J3
eenway AU/AST/KP S26 .... 192 D5
WRKN S81 .... 196 F1
e Greenway SHEFS S8 .... 187 F7
DARN/MH S9 .... 172 C4
DONS/BSCR DN4 .... 90 C7
NROS/TKH DN11 .... 162 E2
eenwood Av BSLY S70 .... 82 C2
eenwood Cl DARN/MH S9 .... 172 C4
eenwood Crs DARN/MH S9 ...... 172 C4
MALT S66 .... 157 H2
eenwood Cl HAN/WDH S13 ...... 174 B8
eenwood Rd CHPT/GREN S35 ... 108 A9
DARN/MH S9 .... 172 C4
MEX/SWTN S64 .... 112 D8
eeton Dr CHPT/GREN S35 .... 150 D1
egg House Crs SHEFN S5 .... 152 E2
egg House Rd SHEFN S5 .... 152 D1
egory Crs NROS/TKH DN11 ..... 162 D3
egory Rd SHEFS S8 .... 187 G1
end Wood Ct CHPT/GREN S35 ... 129 H6
enfell Av MEX/SWTN S64 ...... 113 G2
enfolds Rd CHPT/GREN S35 .... 129 J7
enobank Rd CHPT/GREN S35 ... 129 J7
eno Cs CHPT/GREN S35 .... 129 J7
eno Ga CHPT/GREN S35 .... 129 H6
enomoor Ct CHPT/GREN S35 ... 129 H8
eno Rd MEX/SWTN S64 .... 112 C6
eno Vw DOD/DAR S75 .... 80 D5
HOY S74 .... 108 D2
eno View Rd CHPT/GREN S35 ... 107 J8
enville Pl DOD/DAR S75 .... 55 H4
enville Rd DONS/BSCR DN4 .... 116 B1
esham Av RHAM S60 .... 155 F6
esham Rd ST/HB/BR S6 .... 170 C1
esley Av BWTY DN10 .... 142 B7
esley Rd DONS/BSCR DN4 ...... 4 E5
SHEFS S8 .... 186 E7
ey Friars' Rd DON DN1 .... 4 C2
eystock St ATT S4 .... 172 A1
eystone La NROS/TKH DN11 .... 139 H7
eystones Av BSLY S70 .... 82 A3
ECC S11 .... 170 B8
eystones Cl ECC S11 .... 170 A8
eystones Crs AU/AST/KP S26 .. 206 D1
eystones Ct ECC S11 .... 170 A8
eystones Dr ECC S11 .... 170 A8
eystones Grange Crs
ECC S11 .... 170 A8
eystones Grange Rd ECC S11 .. 170 A8
eystones Hall Rd ECC S11 .... 170 A8
eystones Ri ECC S11 .... 170 A8
eystones Rd ECC S11 .... 169 K8
RHAM S60 .... 156 C6
ce Cl DONS/BSCR DN4 .... 92 E5
ffin Rd MEX/SWTN S64 .... 112 A4
ffiths Cl RAW S62 .... 133 J3
ffiths Rd CHPT/GREN S35 ..... 129 K1
me La HOLM/MEL HD7 .... 49 H6
mesthorpe Rd ATT S4 .... 152 D8
TT S4 .... 152 E7
TT S4 .... 171 J1
methorpe St HEM/SK/SE WF9 .. 34 E5
msell Cl ST/HB/BR S6 .... 129 J8
msell Crs ST/HB/BR S6 .... 129 J8
msell Dr ST/HB/BR S6 .... 129 J8
ndlow Cl SHEFS S8 .... 187 J1
ndlow Dr SHEFP/MNR S2 .... 187 J1
zedale Av MOS S20 .... 190 E5

Grizedale Cl MOS S20 .... 190 E5
Grosvenor Ct HTFD DN7 .... 22 C8
Grosvenor Crs BTLY DN5 .... 65 G5
DONS/BSCR DN4 .... 116 A1
Grosvenor Dr AWLS/ASK DN6 ... 63 J2
NROS/TKH DN11 .... 163 G5
RHAM/THRY S65 .... 7 D2
Grosvenor Sq SHEFP/MNR S2 ... 8 C6
Grosvenor Ter DONS/BSCR DN4 . 116 A1
Grouse Ct ST/HB/BR S6 .... 151 K8
Grove Av BTLY DN5 .... 4 A1
HEM/SK/SE WF9 .... 33 H1
ST/HB/BR S6 .... 151 F5
Grove Cl BTLY DN5 .... 78 A6
Grove Dr HEM/SK/SE WF9 ...... 34 A5
Grove Farm WRKN S81 .... 197 F8
Grove Head HEM/SK/SE WF9 ... 34 A5
Grove Hill Rd WHHL DN2 .... 66 A8
Grove House Ct TOT/DORE S17 . 199 J2
Grove La HEM/SK/SE WF9 ...... 33 H1
HEM/SK/SE WF9 .... 34 A5
Grove Lea Ct HEM/SK/SE WF9 . 33 H1
Grove Mt HEM/SK/SE WF9 ...... 34 A5
Grove Pl DON DN1 .... 4 C4
HEM/SK/SE WF9 .... 33 H1
Grove Rd ABRD S7 .... 186 C4
DEARNE S63 .... 84 E7
DOD/DAR S75 .... 29 F6
HTFD DN7 .... 22 C8
RHAM S60 .... 6 C5
STKB/PEN S36 .... 105 J7
TOT/DORE S17 .... 199 J2
Grove Sq ST/HB/BR S6 .... 151 K8
Grove St BSLY S70 .... 82 D2
BSLYN/ROY S71 .... 3 D4
HEM/SK/SE WF9 .... 34 A5
Grove Ter HEM/SK/SE WF9 ..... 33 H1
The Grove ARMTH DN3 .... 40 D7
CHPT/GREN S35 .... 128 A4
CUD/GR S72 .... 31 J6
HEM/SK/SE WF9 .... 34 E3
MALT S66 .... 157 G2
RAW S62 .... 133 G2
RHAM/THRY S65 .... 134 A8
ST/HB/BR S6 .... 150 D7
TOT/DORE S17 .... 199 J2
WHHL DN2 .... 91 K2
WRKN S81 .... 196 D8
Grove V WHHL DN2 .... 66 B8
Grove Wy HEM/SK/SE WF9 ...... 34 A5
Grudgely La STKB/PEN S36 ..... 104 D1
Gudgeon Hole La
CHPT/GREN S35 .... 80 C8
Guernsey Rd CHPT/GREN S35 ... 171 G8
Guest La DOD/DAR S75 .... 53 K7
DONS/BSCR DN4 .... 90 A8
Guest Rd DOD/DAR S75 .... 2 A2
ECC S11 .... 170 C7
RHAM S60 .... 7 E6
Guest St HOY S74 .... 83 H1
Guilbert Av MALT S66 .... 176 D2
Guildford Av SHEFP/MNR S2 .... 171 K7
Guildford Cl SHEFP/MNR S2 .... 171 K7
Guildford Dr SHEFP/MNR S2 .... 171 K7
Guildford Ri SHEFP/MNR S2 .... 171 K7
Guildford Rd BSLYN/ROY S71 ... 30 C3
WHHL DN2 .... 66 A8
Guildford Vw SHEFP/MNR S2 ... 172 A7
Guildford Wy SHEFP/MNR S2 ... 171 K8
Guild Rd RHAM/THRY S65 ...... 156 A1
Guildway AU/AST/KP S26 .... 192 C3
Guilthwaite Common La
AU/AST/KP S26 .... 175 G2
Guilthwaite Crs RHAM S60 ..... 155 K6
Gullane Dr DONS/BSCR DN4 .... 116 A1
Gulling Wood Dr RHAM/THRY S65 135 F5
Gully Ter HOLM/MEL HD7 .... 48 A3
The Gully KBTN HD8 .... 49 H2
Gunhills La ARMTH DN3 .... 67 H8
Gun La OWL S3 .... 9 E2
Gunthwaite La KBTN HD8 .... 49 H2
Gurney Dr DONS/BSCR DN4 ..... 116 E1
Gurth Av ARMTH DN3 .... 67 F5
Gurth Dr MALT S66 .... 176 E2
Gypsy La WMB/DAR S73 .... 84 B6

H

Habershon Dr CHPT/GREN S35 .. 130 A1
Habershon Rd KIMB S61 .... 132 C6
Hacking La HEM/SK/SE WF9 .... 35 G4
Hackings Av STKB/PEN S36 ..... 77 K6
Hackness La RHAM S60 .... 154 E6
Hackthorn Rd SHEFS S8 .... 187 F4
Haddingley La KBTN HD8 .... 49 J4
Haddon Cl DOD/DAR S75 .... 54 D8
DRON S18 .... 201 H5
HEM/SK/SE WF9 .... 35 F2
Haddon Ri MEX/SWTN S64 ...... 113 J1
Haddon Rd BSLYN/ROY S71 ..... 56 C1
Haddon St OWL S3 .... 171 F1
Haddon Wy AU/AST/KP S26 ..... 175 K8
Hadds La THNE DN8 .... 23 F1

Hadds Nook Rd THNE DN8 .... 23 G3
Haden St ST/HB/BR S6 .... 151 H7
Hadfield St FUL S10 .... 170 C2
WMB/DAR S73 .... 84 B6
Hadleigh Cl RAW S62 .... 133 J3
Hadrian Rd RHAM S60 .... 155 F5
Hadrians Cl NROS/TKH DN11 ... 119 F8
Haggard Rd ST/HB/BR S6 .... 151 J7
Hagg Hl FUL S10 .... 169 K2
ST/HB/BR S6 .... 151 G2
Hagg La BWTY DN10 .... 143 H4
FUL S10 .... 169 H4
Haggs La AWLS/ASK DN6 .... 19 K4
Haggstones Dr CHPT/GREN S35 . 150 C3
Haggstones Rd CHPT/GREN S35 . 150 B1
Hag Hill La KBTN HD8 .... 26 A1
Hague Av ECK/KIL S21 .... 205 F7
RAW S62 .... 111 H7
Hague Crs HEM/SK/SE WF9 ..... 33 H2
Hague La CHPT/GREN S35 ...... 107 H8
ECK/KIL S21 .... 204 E7
KIMB S61 .... 109 J8
Hague Park Cl HEM/SK/SE WF9 . 34 A4
Hague Park La HEM/SK/SE WF9 . 34 A4
Hague Park Wk HEM/SK/SE WF9 . 34 A4
Hague Ter HEM/SK/SE WF9 ..... 33 H1
Haids Cl MALT S66 .... 157 G8
Haids Rd MALT S66 .... 157 F8
Haig Crs NROS/TKH DN11 .... 118 D7
Haigh Cl STKB/PEN S36 .... 78 C1
Haigh Cft BSLYN/ROY S71 ...... 30 C3
Haigh La DOD/DAR S75 .... 28 A3
STKB/PEN S36 .... 52 D8
Haigh Moor Cl HAN/WDH S13 .. 173 G7
Haigh Moor Rd HAN/WDH S13 .. 173 H7
Haigh Moor Wy BSLYN/ROY S71 . 30 C3
Haigh Rd DONS/BSCR DN4 ...... 90 D8
Haig Rd THNE DN8 .... 24 A3
Hail Mary Dr HAN/WDH S13 .... 174 B7
Haise Mt DOD/DAR S75 .... 29 F6
Hakehill Cl DONS/BSCR DN4 .... 118 C1
Halcyon Cl HACK/IN S12 .... 189 H4
Haldane Cl CUD/GR S72 .... 32 C4
Haldane Rd RHAM/THRY S65 ... 7 F2
Haldene BSLY S70 .... 82 C3
Haldynley Gdns ARMTH DN3 .... 93 H1
Hale Hill La HTFD DN7 .... 68 E2
Hale St SHEFS S8 .... 187 F1
Halesworth Rd HAN/WDH S13 .. 173 G5
Half Acre La DRON S18 .... 201 K7
Halfway Dr MOS S20 .... 190 C8
Halfway Gdns MOS S20 .... 190 C8
Halifax Av CONI DN12 .... 114 E5
Halifax Crs BTLY DN5 .... 90 C1
Halifax Dr WRKN S81 .... 196 C7
Halifax Rd CHPT/GREN S35 .... 79 K8
CHPT/GREN S35 .... 106 C3
CHPT/GREN S35 .... 129 J8
SHEFN S5 .... 151 J2
ST/HB/BR S6 .... 151 J5
STKB/PEN S36 .... 77 K1
Halifax St BSLYN/ROY S71 ..... 2 B1
Hallam Cha FUL S10 .... 169 H5
Hallam Ct AU/AST/KP S26 ...... 175 G6
DONS/BSCR DN4 .... 92 B8
Hallamgate Rd FUL S10 .... 170 B5
Hallam Grange Cl FUL S10 .... 169 G7
Hallam Grange Crs FUL S10 ... 169 G6
Hallam Grange Ri FUL S10 .... 169 G6
Hallam Grange Rd FUL S10 .... 169 G6
Hallam La SHEF S1 .... 9 D4
Hallam Pl RAW S62 .... 133 K2
Hallam Rd RHAM S60 .... 155 J5
Hallamshire Cl FUL S10 .... 169 F7
Hallamshire Dr FUL S10 .... 169 F7
Hallamshire Rd FUL S10 .... 169 F8
Hallam Wy CHPT/GREN S35 .... 130 C7
Hall Av HOY S74 .... 83 H8
MEX/SWTN S64 .... 113 G2
Hall Balk La DOD/DAR S75 ..... 2 A2
DONS/BSCR DN4 .... 117 G3
NROS/TKH DN11 .... 117 F4
Hall Brig BTLY DN5 .... 60 B3
Hall Broome Gdns DEARNE S63 . 86 B4
Hallcar St ATT S4 .... 9 F1
Hall Cl BSLY S70 .... 82 B5
DEARNE S63 .... 84 E8
DIN S25 .... 193 K1
DRON S18 .... 200 C5
Hall Close Av RHAM S60 .... 156 B6
Hall Crs RHAM S60 .... 156 A5
Hall Cft MALT S66 .... 157 H3
Hallcroft Dr ARMTH DN3 .... 93 H3
Hallcroft Ri BSLYN/ROY S71 ... 30 C4
Hall Cross Hl DON DN1 .... 5 E3
Hall Dr DEARNE S63 .... 111 G2
Hall Farm Cl AU/AST/KP S26 ... 175 H5
Hall Farm Dr DEARNE S63 ...... 60 C8
Hall Farm Ri STKB/PEN S36 .... 78 D1
Hall Farm Ri DEARNE S63 ...... 60 C8
Hall Flat La DONS/BSCR DN4 ... 116 D1
Hallgate DEARNE S63 .... 60 C8
Hall Ga DON DN1 .... 5 D3
MEX/SWTN S64 .... 113 H2
STKB/PEN S36 .... 78 A4
Hall Gv FUL S10 .... 170 A4
RHAM S60 .... 7 D5
Hall Gv DOD/DAR S75 .... 29 H6
Halliday Cl WRKS S80 .... 210 B4

Halliwell Cl SHEFN S5 .... 151 J4 ☑
Halliwell Crs SHEFN S5 .... 151 K4
Hall La HEM/SK/SE WF9 .... 35 G1
  HTFD DN7 .... 41 C4
  ST/HB/BR S6 .... 147 J3
Hall Meadow Cft MOS S20 .... 204 D2
Hall Meadow Dr MOS S20 .... 204 D2
Hall Meadow Gv MOS S20 .... 204 D2 ☑
Hallowes Ct DRON S18 .... 201 H6 ☑
Hallowes Dr DRON S18 .... 201 H7
Hallowes La DRON S18 .... 201 H7
Hallowes Ri DRON S18 .... 201 J7
Hallowmoor Rd ST/HB/BR S6 .... 151 F7
Hall Park Head ST/HB/BR S6 .... 169 K1
Hall Park Hl ST/HB/BR S6 .... 169 J2
Hall Park Mt ST/HB/BR S6 .... 169 J2 ☑
Hall Pl BSLYN/ROY S71 .... 5 F1
Hall Rd AU/AST/KP S26 .... 175 H6
  DARN/MH S9 .... 173 G4
  HAN/WDH S13 .... 173 G5
  RHAM S60 .... 7 D5
Hall Road Old DARN/MH S9 .... 153 H8
Hall Royd DOD/DAR S75 .... 79 K1
Hall Royd Wk DOD/DAR S75 .... 79 K1
Hallside Ct ARMTH DN3 .... 93 G6
Halit St BTLY DN5 .... 87 J4
  DEARNE S63 .... 86 D3
  HOY S74 .... 109 F1 ☑
  RHAM S60 .... 6 B4
  WMB/DAR S73 .... 84 B5
Hallsworth Av HOY S74 .... 83 H8
Hall Vw BWTY DN10 .... 165 J8
Hall View Rd NROS/TKH DN11 .... 119 F8
Hall Villa La BTLY DN5 .... 64 D2
Hall Wood Rd CHPT/GREN S35 .... 129 H2
Hallyburton Cl SHEFP/MNR S2 .... 187 J1 ☑
Hallyburton Dr SHEFP/MNR S2 .... 187 J1 ☑
Hallyburton Rd SHEFP/MNR S2 .... 187 J1
Halmshaw BTLY DN5 .... 64 D7
Halsall Av DARN/MH S9 .... 172 E4
Halsall Dr DARN/MH S9 .... 172 D4
Halsall Rd DARN/MH S9 .... 172 E4
Halsbury Rd RHAM/THRY S65 .... 7 F2
Halstead Gv DOD/DAR S75 .... 29 F5
Halton Ct HACK/IN S12 .... 190 A4
Hamble Cl DOD/DAR S75 .... 29 H7 ☑
Hambleton Cl DOD/DAR S75 .... 55 G5 ☑
  HOY S74 .... 109 J1 ☑
Hambleton Ct WRKN S81 .... 180 C8 ☑
Hameline Rd CONI DN12 .... 114 C5
Hamilton Cl MEX/SWTN S64 .... 113 H1 ☑
Hamilton Park Av BTLY DN5 .... 90 A1 ☑
Hamilton Rd DEARNE S63 .... 86 E1
  DONS/BSCR DN4 .... 5 F5
  MALT S66 .... 159 J3
  SHEFN S5 .... 152 E5
Hamilton St WRKN S81 .... 210 B1
Hammerton Rd ST/HB/BR S6 .... 151 H8
Hammerton St WMB/DAR S73 .... 83 K3 ☑
Hammond St OWL S3 .... 8 B2
Hampden Crs HTFD DN7 .... 69 H7
Hampden Rd MEX/SWTN S64 .... 113 F3
Hamper La STKB/PEN S36 .... 78 C1
Hample Balk AWLS/ASK DN6 .... 37 G6
Hampole Field La AWLS/ASK DN6 .... 36 A6
Hampton Rd HTFD DN7 .... 42 A7
  SHEFN S5 .... 152 D6
  WHHL DN2 .... 5 F3
Hanbury Cl BSLYN/ROY S71 .... 56 E3
  DONS/BSCR DN4 .... 116 E3
  DRON S18 .... 201 F6
Hand La CHPT/GREN S35 .... 80 A7
Handley St OWL S3 .... 9 E1
Hands Rd FUL S10 .... 170 C5
Handsworth Av DARN/MH S9 .... 172 E4
Handsworth Crs DARN/MH S9 .... 173 F4
Handsworth Gdns ARMTH DN3 .... 93 H1 ☑
Handsworth Grange Cl
  HAN/WDH S13 .... 173 J7
Handsworth Grange Crs
  HAN/WDH S13 .... 173 J6
Handsworth Grange Rd
  HAN/WDH S13 .... 173 J6
Handsworth Rd DARN/MH S9 .... 173 F4
Hanging Water Cl FUL S10 .... 169 K7 ☑
Hangingwater Rd ECC S11 .... 169 K8
Hangman Stone Rd BTLY DN5 .... 88 A5
Hangram La ECC S11 .... 185 J1
Hangsman La DIN S25 .... 177 J4
Hangthwaite La AWLS/ASK DN6 .... 64 A4
Hangthwaite Rd AWLS/ASK DN6 .... 38 A4
Hanley Cl HACK/IN S12 .... 189 K4
Hanmoor Rd ST/HB/BR S6 .... 169 G1
Hannas Crs DARN/MH S9 .... 174 B8
Hannas Royd DOD/DAR S75 .... 55 F8 ☑
Hanover Sq DEARNE S63 .... 60 D7
  OWL S3 .... 8 B4
Hanover St DEARNE S63 .... 60 D6
  OWL S3 .... 8 B4 ☑
Hanover Wy OWL S3 .... 8 B4
Hansby Cl NROS/TKH DN11 .... 140 A8
Hanson Rd ST/HB/BR S6 .... 150 C7
Hanson St BSLY S70 .... 2 C3 ☑
Harbord Rd SHEFS S8 .... 186 E5
Harborough Av SHEFP/MNR S2 .... 172 B4
Harborough Cl SHEFP/MNR S2 .... 172 C5
Harborough Dr SHEFP/MNR S2 .... 172 C5

Harborough Hill Rd
  BSLYN/ROY S71 .... 2 C3 ☑
Harborough Ri SHEFP/MNR S2 .... 172 C5
Harborough Rd SHEFP/MNR S2 .... 172 C5
Harborough Wy SHEFP/MNR S2 .... 172 C6
Harbury St HAN/WDH S13 .... 174 C7 ☑
Harcourt Cl DONS/BSCR DN4 .... 92 B8
Harcourt Crs FUL S10 .... 8 A3
Harcourt Ri CHPT/GREN S35 .... 130 C3
Harcourt Rd FUL S10 .... 8 A3
Harcourt Ter RHAM/THRY S65 .... 7 E4
Hardcastle Dr HAN/WDH S13 .... 173 J8 ☑
Hardcastle Gdns HAN/WDH S13 .... 173 J8
Hardcastle Rd HAN/WDH S13 .... 189 J8
Harden Cl DOD/DAR S75 .... 55 F5
  STKB/PEN S36 .... 78 A5 ☑
Hardie Cl MALT S66 .... 159 J4
Hardie Pl RAW S62 .... 133 J1 ☑
Hardie Rd ECK/KIL S21 .... 204 B5
Harding Av RAW S62 .... 111 C7
Harding Cl DARN/MH S9 .... 172 D1
Harding La RAW S62 .... 111 C8
Hardwick Cl AU/AST/KP S26 .... 175 K8 ☑
  DRON S18 .... 201 H5
Hardwick Crs BSLYN/ROY S71 .... 30 B8
  ECC S11 .... 170 C7
  WRKS S80 .... 211 F5
Hardwick Gv BSLYN/ROY S71 .... 80 E1 ☑
Hardwick La AU/AST/KP S26 .... 176 C7
Hardwick Rd East WRKS S80 .... 211 F6
Hardwick Rd West WRKS S80 .... 211 F5
Hardwick St RHAM/THRY S65 .... 134 C7
Hardy Pl ST/HB/BR S6 .... 8 A1
Hardy Rd WHHL DN2 .... 91 H1
Hardy St KIMB S61 .... 6 B3
  WRKS S80 .... 210 C5 ☑
Harefield Rd ECC S11 .... 8 A6 ☑
Harehills Rd RHAM/THRY S65 .... 7 D5
Harewood Av ARMTH DN3 .... 66 E3
  AWLS/ASK DN6 .... 63 C2
  BSLY S70 .... 55 G6
Harewood Ct NROS/TKH DN11 .... 119 J7
Harewood Gv MALT S66 .... 157 J1
Harewood La PONT WF8 .... 16 A5
Harewood Rd WHHL DN2 .... 91 K4
  WRKN S81 .... 196 D8
Harewood Wy ECC S11 .... 186 A5 ☑
Hargrave Rd RHAM/THRY S65 .... 134 E5
Harland Rd FUL S10 .... 8 B5
Harlech Cl CHPT/GREN S35 .... 130 A5
Harleston St ATT S4 .... 171 J1 ☑
Harley Rd ECC S11 .... 185 K2
  RAW S62 .... 108 E6
Harlington Ct CONI DN12 .... 114 B3
Harlington Rd MEX/SWTN S64 .... 86 E7
  MEX/SWTN S64 .... 115 C2
Harmby Cl AWLS/ASK DN6 .... 37 G5
Harmer La SHEF S1 .... 9 E3
Harmony Wy RHAM S60 .... 174 B1 ☑
Harney Cl RHAM S60 .... 172 E2
Harold Av AWLS/ASK DN6 .... 63 H2
  BSLYN/ROY S71 .... 57 F3
Harold Cft RAW S62 .... 133 F3
Harold St ST/HB/BR S6 .... 170 D1
Harpenden Cl HTFD DN7 .... 68 B2
Harpenden Dr HTFD DN7 .... 68 B1 ☑
Harriet Cl BSLY S70 .... 3 D6 ☑
Harrington Ct BSLYN/ROY S71 .... 57 F3
Harrington Rd SHEFP/MNR S2 .... 9 D6 ☑
Harrington St DON DN1 .... 5 D2 ☑
  WRKS S80 .... 210 B5
Harrison Dr WRKN S81 .... 180 C4
Harrison La FUL S10 .... 168 D8
Harrison Rd ST/HB/BR S6 .... 151 E4
Harrison St KIMB S61 .... 154 D2
Harris Rd ST/HB/BR S6 .... 151 C5
Harrogate Dr CONI DN12 .... 113 K4
Harrogate Rd AU/AST/KP S26 .... 191 G1 ☑
Harrop Dr MEX/SWTN S64 .... 112 B6
Harrop La FUL S10 .... 184 D1
Harrowden Rd DARN/MH S9 .... 154 B5
  WHHL DN2 .... 91 J1
Harrow Rd ARMTH DN3 .... 67 H8
Harrow St ECC S11 .... 8 C5
  HEM/SK/SE WF9 .... 34 D4
Harry Firth Cl DARN/MH S9 .... 172 C2 ☑
Harry Rd DOD/DAR S75 .... 20 C3
Harstoft Av WRKN S81 .... 210 D3
Hartcliff Av STKB/PEN S36 .... 77 K4
Hartcliffe La STKB/PEN S36 .... 77 H1
Hartcliffe Rd CHPT/GREN S35 .... 79 J8 ☑
Hartcliffe Hill Rd STKB/PEN S36 .... 77 C7
Hartcliffe Nick STKB/PEN S36 .... 77 F7
Hartcliffe Rd STKB/PEN S36 .... 76 D7
Hartford Cl SHEFS S8 .... 187 G4 ☑
Hartford Rd SHEFS S8 .... 187 G4
Hart Hl RAW S62 .... 111 C7
Harthill Field Rd AU/AST/KP S26 .... 207 C3
Harthill La STV/CWN S43 .... 206 B8
Harthill Rd AU/AST/KP S26 .... 193 J8
  CONI DN12 .... 114 B6
  HAN/WDH S13 .... 172 D8
Hartington Av ABRD S7 .... 186 C4
Hartington Cl KIMB S61 .... 154 D1
Hartington Rd BSLYN/ROY S71 .... 2 C1
Hartington Rd ABRD S7 .... 186 C4

DRON S18 201
KIMB S61 154
Hartland Av MOS S20 .... 190 E5
Hartland Ct MOS S20 .... 190 E5 ☑
Hartland Crs ARMTH DN3 66
Hartland Dr MOS S20 190
Hartland Rd WRKS S80 210
Hartley Brook Av SHEFN S5 152
Hartley Brook Rd SHEFN S5 152
Hartley La KIMB S61 6
Hartley St MEX/SWTN S64 112
  SHEFP/MNR S2 171
Hartopp Av SHEFP/MNR S2 187
Hartopp Cl SHEFP/MNR S2 .... 187 J1
Hartopp Dr SHEFP/MNR S2 .... 187 K1
Hartopp Rd SHEFP/MNR S2 187
Harts Head SHEF S1 .... 9 E2
Harvest Cl BSLY S70 82
  DONS/BSCR DN4 90
  MALT S66 158
  WRKN S81 .... 180 D8
Harvest La OWL S3 171
Harvest Rd MALT S66 157
Harvey Cl EPW DN9 121
Harvey Clough Ms SHEFS S8 187
Harvey Clough Rd SHEFS S8 187
Harvey Rd CHPT/GREN S35 130
Harvey St BSLY S70 .... 105 G6
  STKB/PEN S36 .... 105 G6
Harwell La BWTY DN10 165
Harwell Rd SHEFS S8 171
Harwell Sluice La BWTY DN10 165
Harwich Rd SHEFP/MNR S2 172
Harwood Cl SHEFP/MNR S2 8
Harwood Dr MOS S20 190
Harwood Gdns MOS S20 190
Harwood St BSLY S70 9
Harwood Ter BSLYN/ROY S71 .... 57 F4
Harworth Av WRKN S81 163
Haslam Crs SHEFS S8 .... 200 E5
Haslam Pl MALT S66 .... 159 J7
Haslam Rd NROS/TKH DN11 118
Haslehurst Rd SHEFP/MNR S2 172
Haslemere Gv BTLY DN5 90
Hassop Cl DRON S18 201
Hastilar Cl SHEFP/MNR S2 172
Hastilar Rd SHEFP/MNR S2 .... 172 C1
Hastilar Rd South HAN/WDH S13 172
  SHEFP/MNR S2 172
Hastings Mt ABRD S7 186
Hastings Rd ABRD S7 186
Hastings St CUD/GR S72 32
Hatchell Dr DONS/BSCR DN4 119
Hatchellwood Vw
  DONS/BSCR DN4 119
Hatfield Cl BSLYN/ROY S71 .... 29 K
Hatfield Crs DIN S25 177
Hatfield Gdns BSLYN/ROY S71 30
Hatfield House Cl SHEFN S5 .... 152 E
Hatfield House Cft SHEFN S5 152
Hatfield House La SHEFN S5 152
Hatfield La ARMTH DN3 40
  ARMTH DN3 67
Hatfield Rd HTFD DN7 43
Hatherley Rd DARN/MH S9 154
  MEX/SWTN S64 112
  RHAM/THRY S65 7
Hathersage Rd TOT/DORE S17 185
  TOT/DORE S17 198
Hatter Dr CONI DN12 115
Hatton Cl DRON S18 200
Hatton Rd ST/HB/BR S6 151
Haugh Gn RAW S62 111
Haugh Head Rd STKB/PEN S36 78
Haugh La ECC S11 185
Haugh Rd RAW S62 111
Haughton Rd SHEFS S8 187
Hauxwell Cl AWLS/ASK DN6 37
Havelock St BSLY S70 .... 2 A
  FUL S10 8
  WMB/DAR S73 .... 84 D9
Haven Hl WRKN S81 130
Havercroft Ri CUD/GR S72 32
Havercroft Rd RHAM S60 156
  SHEFS S8 186
Havercroft Ter ECK/KIL S21 .... 191 F
Haverdale Ri DOD/DAR S75 2
Haverlands La BSLY S70 81
Haverlands Rdg BSLY S70 .... 82 A
The Haverlands
  AWLS/ASK DN6 20
Hawke Cl DOD/DAR S75 .... 53 J
Hawkins Av CHPT/GREN S35 .... 129 K
Hawes Cl MEX/SWTN S64 113
Hawfield Cl DONS/BSCR DN4 4
Hawke Cl RAW S62 111
Hawke Rd WHHL DN2 5
Hawke St DARN/MH S9 153
Hawk Hill La MALT S66 176
Hawkhouse Green La
  AWLS/ASK DN6 20
Hawkshead Av DRON S18 200
Hawkshead Crs DIN S25 .... 178 C5
Hawkshead Rd ATT S4 153
Hawksley Av ST/HB/BR S6 151
Hawksley Ms ST/HB/BR S6 151
Hawksley Ri CHPT/GREN S35 150
Hawksley Rd ST/HB/BR S6 151

awksway ECK/KIL S21 ... 203 K4
awsworth Cl RHAM/THRY S65 ... 134 B8
awsworth Rd RHAM/THRY S65 ... 134 B8
ST/HB/BR S6 ... 170 D1
awkwell Bank BSLY/ROY S71 ... 57 H7
awley St DRON S18 ... 202 C5
RAW S62 ... 133 J2
SHEF S1 ... 9 D2
aworth Bank RHAM S60 ... 155 J6 🔲
aworth Cl BSLYN/ROY S71 ... 3 E2 🔲
aworth Crs RHAM S60 ... 155 J6
awshaw La HOY S74 ... 108 D1
awson St WMB/DAR S73 ... 84 B5
awson Wy WRKN S81 ... 196 A8
awthorn Av ARMTH DN3 ... 67 G7
MALT S66 ... 158 E2
MOS S20 ... 190 B6
awthorne Av DIN S25 ... 193 K4
DRON S18 ... 201 G4
HEM/SK/SE WF9 ... 33 G1 🔲
HTFD DN7 ... 67 K3
RAW S62 ... 133 G2
STKB/PEN S36 ... 104 C5
THNE DN8 ... 23 J6 🔲
awthorne Cl ECK/KIL S21 ... 205 H2 🔲
awthorne Crs AWLS/ASK DN6 ... 37 H6
DOD/DAR S75 ... 54 D7
HEM/SK/SE WF9 ... 33 F1 🔲
MEX/SWTN S64 ... 112 D2
THNE DN8 ... 23 J6 🔲
awthorne Gv BTLY DN5 ... 64 E5
THNE DN8 ... 23 J6 🔲
awthorne Rd DEARNE S63 ... 111 K2 🔲
EPW DN9 ... 120 B3
THNE DN8 ... 23 J6
ne Hawthornes MOS S20 ... 190 D3
awthorne St BSLY S70 ... 2 B5
CUD/GR S72 ... 31 K6
ST/HB/BR S6 ... 170 D1 🔲
awthorne Wy CUD/GR S72 ... 31 K4
awtop La DOD/DAR S75 ... 28 E1
awthorn Gv CONI DN12 ... 53 K6 🔲
awthorn Rd CHPT/GREN S35 ... 107 K8
ECK/KIL S21 ... 203 K5
ST/HB/BR S6 ... 151 G7
awthorn Wy WRKN S81 ... 180 C8
axby Cl HAN/WDH S13 ... 189 G1
axby La EPW DN9 ... 120 B3
axby Pl HAN/WDH S13 ... 189 F4
axby St HAN/WDH S13 ... 189 G2
aydon Rd MALT S66 ... 159 J3
aydock Cl DOD/DAR S75 ... 28 E1
aydock Gv MALT S66 ... 157 G1
ayes Cl MOS S20 ... 204 C1
ayes Cft BSLY S70 ... 2 C4 🔲
ayes Dr MOS S20 ... 204 B1
ayes La HTFD DN7 ... 22 C5
ayfield Cl ARMTH DN3 ... 41 F8
DRON S18 ... 200 D6 🔲
HOLM/MEL HD7 ... 48 C3 🔲
ayfield Ct HACK/IN S12 ... 189 F4 🔲
ayfield Dr HACK/IN S12 ... 188 C4
ayfield La EPW DN9 ... 120 B3
ayfield Pl HACK/IN S12 ... 189 F4
ayfield Vw ECK/KIL S21 ... 203 K4
ay Green La BSLY S70 ... 82 A8
aywood Av RHAM/THRY S65 ... 135 K7
aywood Cl RHAM/THRY S65 ... 134 B8
aywood La BTLY DN5 ... 39 H1
aywood La BSLY S70 ... 82 A8
STKB/PEN S36 ... 105 G6
azel Av ECK/KIL S21 ... 205 G2
EPW DN9 ... 120 B3
azelbadge Crs HACK/IN S12 ... 189 G4
azel Cl DRON S18 ... 201 J7 🔲
RHAM/THRY S65 ... 135 K7
azel Gv ARMTH DN3 ... 67 H8
CHPT/GREN S35 ... 107 H8
CONI DN12 ... 114 C6
MALT S66 ... 157 H2
NROS/TKH DN11 ... 118 E7
azel La CONI DN12 ... 115 J5
azel La AWLS/ASK DN6 ... 36 B5
ECK/KIL S21 ... 204 A5 🔲
HTFD DN7 ... 42 A6 🔲
MALT S66 ... 158 E2
azelshaw DOD/DAR S75 ... 81 F1 🔲
azelwood Cl DRON S18 ... 200 C6 🔲
azelwood Dr MEX/SWTN S64 ... 112 C7
azing La GLE DN14 ... 10 A4
azlebarrow Cl SHEFS S8 ... 187 H8
azlebarrow Ct SHEFS S8 ... 187 H8 🔲
azlebarrow Crs SHEFS S8 ... 187 H8
azlebarrow Dr SHEFS S8 ... 187 H8
azlebarrow Gv SHEFS S8 ... 187 J8 🔲
azlebarrow Rd SHEFS S8 ... 201 H1 🔲
azledene Crs CUD/GR S72 ... 31 K6

Hazledene Rd CUD/GR S72 ... 31 K6
Hazlehurst Gdns WRKS S80 ... 210 C5
Hazlehurst La SHEFS S8 ... 188 B8
Headford Gdns SHEF S3 ... 8 C4
Headford Gv OWL S3 ... 8 C4
Headford Ms OWL S3 ... 8 C4 🔲
Headford St OWL S3 ... 8 C4 🔲
Headingley Av AWLS/ASK DN6 ... 18 A4
Headingley Wy CONI DN12 ... 115 K4
Headland Dr FUL S10 ... 170 A4
Headland Rd FUL S10 ... 170 A4
Headlands Rd HOY S74 ... 108 B8
Heads La ST/HB/BR S6 ... 126 D1
Heath Av ECK/KIL S21 ... 205 H2
Heathcote St ATT S4 ... 152 E6 🔲
Heatherbank Rd DONS/BSCR DN4 ... 92 D8
Heather Cl HEM/SK/SE WF9 ... 34 C4
NROS/TKH DN11 ... 140 A7
RHAM S60 ... 7 D6
Hetherdale Rd MALT S66 ... 159 J2 🔲
Heather Knowle DOD/DAR S75 ... 55 F8 🔲
Heather Lea Av TOT/DORE S17 ... 185 G8
Heather Lea Pl TOT/DORE S17 ... 185 G8
Heather Rd SHEFS S5 ... 153 F4
Heathfield Rd HACK/IN S12 ... 189 F7
Heath Gv DEARNE S63 ... 86 A6
Heath Rd ST/HB/BR S6 ... 151 J3
STKB/PEN S36 ... 105 C7
Heathy La ST/HB/BR S6 ... 166 C2
Heaton Cl DRON S18 ... 200 D6
Heaton Gdns CONI DN12 ... 115 K5
Heavens Wk DONS/BSCR DN4 ... 5 D5
Heavygate Av FUL S10 ... 170 C2
ST/HB/BR S6 ... 170 C1
Heavygate Rd ST/HB/BR S6 ... 170 C1
Heck And Pollington La GLE DN14 ... 11 F1
Heck La GLE DN14 ... 10 B3
Hedge Hill Rd STKB/PEN S36 ... 77 H4 🔲
Hedge La DOD/DAR S75 ... 28 C7
Hedley Bank Rd SHEFP/MNR S2 ... 171 H8
Hedley Gv SHEFP/MNR S2 ... 187 H1
Heels St BSLY S70 ... 7 C5
Heighton Vw AU/AST/KP S26 ... 175 H3
The Heights HOLM/MEL HD7 ... 48 B4
Heights Vw CHPT/GREN S35 ... 105 K1
Helena Cl BSLY S70 ... 2 A5 🔲
Helena St MEX/SWTN S64 ... 113 F2
Helensburgh Cl DOD/DAR S75 ... 55 H5 🔲
Hellaby Hall Rd MALT S66 ... 158 C4
Hellaby La MALT S66 ... 136 C7
Hellaby Vw RHAM/THRY S65 ... 135 J8
Helliwell La STKB/PEN S36 ... 105 H8
Helmsley Av MOS S20 ... 190 B8
Helmsley Cl AU/AST/KP S26 ... 191 G1 🔲
Helmton Dr SHEFS S5 ... 187 G5
Helmton Rd SHEFS S5 ... 187 F5
Helston Crs BSLY/ROY S71 ... 3 E2
Helston Ri ABRD S7 ... 186 C3
Hemingfield Rd WMB/DAR S73 ... 83 J6
Hemmingfield Crs WRKN S81 ... 196 D7 🔲
Hemmingfield Ri WRKN S81 ... 196 D7 🔲
Hemmingfield Rd WRKN S81 ... 196 D8
Hemmingfield Wy WRKN S81 ... 196 E7 🔲
Hemper Gv SHEFS S8 ... 186 D8 🔲
Hemper La SHEFS S8 ... 200 D1
Hemp Pits Rd BTLY DN5 ... 65 G6
Hemsworth Rd HEM/SK/SE WF9 ... 33 H2
SHEFS S8 ... 187 J5
Henderson Gln BSLY/ROY S71 ... 30 B4
Hendon St HAN/WDH S13 ... 173 H6
Hengist Rd BTLY DN5 ... 90 C5 🔲
Henley Av SHEFS S8 ... 187 H4
Henley Grove Rd KIMB S61 ... 6 A3
Henley Gv KIMB S61 ... 132 D7
Henley Ri KIMB S61 ... 6 A3
Henley Rd WHHL DN2 ... 92 B2
Henley Wy KIMB S61 ... 132 D8
Hennings Cl DONS/BSCR DN4 ... 92 A8
Henry Cl CUD/GR S72 ... 31 J4
Henry Ct THNE DN8 ... 23 K6 🔲
Henry La NROS/TKH DN11 ... 118 E7
Henry Pl MEX/SWTN S64 ... 113 H3 🔲
Henry Rd DEARNE S63 ... 111 J1
Henry St BSLY S70 ... 82 E2 🔲
CHPT/GREN S35 ... 107 H8
ECK/KIL S21 ... 204 B4
OWL S3 ... 8 C1 🔲
RAW S62 ... 133 J4
RHAM/THRY S65 ... 7 D5 🔲
WMB/DAR S73 ... 84 C3
Henshall St BSLY S70 ... 3 D5 🔲
Heppenstall La DARN/MH S9 ... 172 B1 🔲
Heptinstall St BSLY S70 ... 82 C2 🔲
Hepworth Crs HOLM/MEL HD7 ... 48 D4
Hepworth Dr AU/AST/KP S26 ... 175 H3
Hepworth Rd DONS/BSCR DN4 ... 90 C8 🔲
HOLM/MEL HD7 ... 48 C8
Herald Rd ARMTH DN3 ... 66 D6
Herbert Rd ABRD S7 ... 186 E1 🔲
BTLY DN5 ... 4 A1
Herbert St KIMB S61 ... 132 B8
MEX/SWTN S64 ... 113 G2
Herdings Ct HACK/IN S12 ... 188 C4

Herdings Rd HACK/IN S12 ... 188 C4
Herdings Vw HACK/IN S12 ... 188 C4
Hereford Cl WRKN S81 ... 210 E1
Hereford Rd WHHL DN2 ... 66 A8
Hereford St SHEF S1 ... 9 D5 🔲
Hereward Ct CONI DN12 ... 115 F5
Hereward Rd SHEFN S5 ... 152 C5
Hermes Cl BWTY DN10 ... 142 A7
Hermitage St SHEFP/MNR S2 ... 8 C5 🔲
The Hermitage THNE DN8 ... 24 A4 🔲
Hermit Hl CHPT/GREN S35 ... 106 E1
Hermit Hill La CHPT/GREN S35 ... 106 D2
Hermit La DOD/DAR S75 ... 54 E5
Heron Gld WRKN S81 ... 196 A8 🔲
Heron Hl AU/AST/KP S26 ... 191 J1
Heron Mt SHEFP/MNR S2 ... 172 A5
Herons Wy BSLY S70 ... 82 A7
Herrick Dr WRKN S81 ... 211 G4
Herrick Gdns DONS/BSCR DN4 ... 117 F1
Herrick Rd ARMTH DN3 ... 40 E7
Herries Av SHEFN S5 ... 152 B5
Herries Dr SHEFN S5 ... 152 B5
Herries Pl SHEFN S5 ... 152 B5
Herries Rd SHEFN S5 ... 151 K5
ST/HB/BR S6 ... 151 H5
Herril Ings NROS/TKH DN11 ... 140 A7
Herringthorpe Av RHAM/THRY S65 ... 156 A3
Herringthorpe Cl RHAM/THRY S65 ... 156 A2 🔲
Herringthorpe Gv RHAM/THRY S65 ... 156 B3
Herringthorpe La l RHAM/THRY S65 ... 156 B3
Herringthorpe Valley Rd RHAM/THRY S65 ... 134 B7
RHAM/THRY S65 ... 156 B4
Herriot Gv NROS/TKH DN11 ... 163 F3
Herschell Rd SHEFS S8 ... 171 F8 🔲
Hesketh Dr ARMTH DN3 ... 67 F3
Hesley Bar KIMB S61 ... 131 F3
Hesley Cl MEX/SWTN S64 ... 112 B6 🔲
Hesley Gra KIMB S61 ... 131 J5
Hesley Gv CHPT/GREN S35 ... 130 D3
Hesley La KIMB S61 ... 131 F3
Hesley Rd NROS/TKH DN11 ... 118 E7
SHEFN S5 ... 130 E8
Hesley Ter SHEFN S5 ... 152 E1
Heslop Ct WRKS S80 ... 210 B4
Heslow Gv KIMB S61 ... 131 F1
Hessey St HAN/WDH S13 ... 189 H1
Hessle Rd ST/HB/BR S6 ... 151 G5
Hewitt Pl AU/AST/KP S26 ... 206 E2
Hewitt St MEX/SWTN S64 ... 113 H2
Hexthorpe Rd DONS/BSCR DN4 ... 4 B4
Heyclifffe Rd HOLM/MEL HD7 ... 48 A2
Heyden Br OLSP SK11.5 ... 98 A1
Heyhouse Dr CHPT/GREN S35 ... 108 B8
Heyhouse Wy CHPT/GREN S35 ... 108 A8
Heysham Gn BSLY/ROY S71 ... 56 E2
Heyworth La AWLS/ASK DN6 ... 19 G7
Hibberd Rd ST/HB/BR S6 ... 151 F7
Hickleton Ct DEARNE S63 ... 60 B8
Hickleton Rd BTLY DN5 ... 87 H5
Hickleton St CONI DN12 ... 114 A4
Hickmott Rd ECC S11 ... 8 A6 🔲
Hickson Dr BSLYN/ROY S71 ... 57 F3 🔲
Hicks St OWL S3 ... 171 G1
Hides St DARN/MH S9 ... 153 J7
Higger La HATH/EY S32 ... 182 B7
High Alder Rd DONS/BSCR DN4 ... 92 E7
Higham Common Rd DOD/DAR S75 ... 54 D3
Higham Cl DOD/DAR S75 ... 54 D6
Higham Vw DOD/DAR S75 ... 28 C8
High Ash Av KBTN HD8 ... 26 C5
High Ash Cl HOR/CROF WF4 ... 30 A1
High Ash Dr DIN S25 ... 193 K4
High Bank La STKB/PEN S36 ... 77 C4
High Bridge Rd THNE DN8 ... 44 B1
Highbury Av DONS/BSCR DN4 ... 92 D7
Highbury V CONI DN12 ... 115 H6
Highcliffe Ct MEX/SWTN S64 ... 112 D4
Highcliffe Dr CHPT/GREN S35 ... 150 C1 🔲
ECC S11 ... 169 K8
MEX/SWTN S64 ... 112 C4
Highcliffe Pl ECC S11 ... 185 K1
Highcliffe Rd ECC S11 ... 169 K8
High Cl DOD/DAR S75 ... 28 C6 🔲
High Common La BWTY DN10 ... 142 B1
NROS/TKH DN11 ... 140 E7
Highcroft HOLM/MEL HD7 ... 47 H2
High Cft OWL S74 ... 109 F2
High Croft Dr BSLYN/ROY S71 ... 30 A7 🔲
Highfield GLE DN14 ... 11 K1
Highfield Av AU/AST/KP S26 ... 192 E4
BSLY S70 ... 82 A1 🔲
BSLYN/ROY S71 ... 56 B1
DEARNE S63 ... 86 C8
KBTN HD8 ... 50 B8
Highfield Cl ARMTH DN3 ... 41 F8 🔲
Highfield Ct KBTN HD8 ... 49 K1
Highfield Crs THNE DN8 ... 23 J7 🔲
Highfield Gv DEARNE S63 ... 84 D8
WRKN S81 ... 197 F2
Highfield La AWLS/ASK DN6 ... 40 A3
High Field La BWTY DN10 ... 142 C4
Highfield La HAN/WDH S13 ... 173 K5

RHAM S60 .... 174 A3
WRKS S80 .... 211 G6
Highfield Pk MALT S66 .... 159 J1
Highfield Pl HEM/SK/SE WF9 .... 33 E1
  SHEFF/MNR S2 .... 9 D6
Highfield Range WMB/DAR S73 .... 58 E1
Highfield Ri ST/HB/BR S6 .... 169 F2
Highfield Rd AWLS/ASK DN6 .... 18 E7
  BWTY DN10 .... 142 C7
  CONI DN12 .... 114 E6
  DON DN1 .... 5 D2
  HEM/SK/SE WF9 .... 33 F1
  KIMB S61 .... 135 F5
  MEX/SWTN S64 .... 112 A4
  WMB/DAR S73 .... 84 D1
Highfields STKB/PEN S36 .... 78 C1
Highfields Crs DRON S18 .... 201 G3 E
High Field Spring HAN/WDH S13 .... 173 J3
Highfields Rd DOD/DAR S75 .... 28 A7
  DRON S18 .... 201 G7
Highfield Vw RHAM S60 .... 174 A1
High Fisher Ga DON DN1 .... 5 D2 E
Highgate DARN/MH S9 .... 84 E5
  DEARNE S63 .... 84 E5
  CLE DN14 .... 10 D4
Highgate Cl NROS/TKH DN11 .... 119 F8
Highgate Ct DEARNE S63 .... 86 B2
Highgate Dr DRON S18 .... 201 J8
Highgate La DEARNE S63 .... 86 B3
  DRON S18 .... 201 J8
Highgreave SHEFN S5 .... 152 D1
High Greave Av SHEFN S5 .... 130 D8
High Greave Cl SHEFN S5 .... 130 C8
High Greave Pl RHAM/THRY S65 .... 134 B8
High Greave Rd RHAM/THRY S65 .... 134 B8
High Grounds Rd WRKS S80 .... 210 A3
High Grounds Wy WRKS S80 .... 209 K3
High Hazel Crs RHAM S60 .... 174 A1
High Hazel Rd THNE DN8 .... 24 A3
High Hazels Cl DARN/MH S9 .... 173 F3 E
High Hazels Md DARN/MH S9 .... 173 F3 E
High Hoe Ct WRKS S80 .... 210 E4 E
High Hoe Dr WRKS S80 .... 210 E4
High Hoe Rd WRKS S80 .... 210 E4
High Hooton Rd DIN S25 .... 159 F7
High House Farm Ct
  AU/AST/KP S26 .... 192 B5
High House Ter ST/HB/BR S6 .... 151 J8
High Hoyland La DOD/DAR S75 .... 26 A8
Highland Gv WRKN S81 .... 210 E2
High La HACK/IN S12 .... 189 G6
  HOLM/MEL HD7 .... 48 B4
  MALT S66 .... 176 C4
  STKB/PEN S36 .... 50 E8
High Lee La STKB/PEN S36 .... 78 C2
High Levels Bank THNE DN8 .... 43 K4
  THNE DN8 .... 45 K7
Highlow Vw RHAM S60 .... 155 F6
High Matlock Av ST/HB/BR S6 .... 169 H1
High Matlock Rd ST/HB/BR S6 .... 169 J1 E
High Meadow BWTY DN10 .... 142 A8
Highmill Av MEX/SWTN S64 .... 111 K4
Highmoor Av AU/AST/KP S26 .... 192 C5
Highnam Crescent Ga FUL S10 .... 170 C8 E
High Nook Rd DIN S25 .... 178 C7
High Rdg BSLY S70 .... 82 A2
High Royd CONI DN12 .... 115 J6
  DONS/BSCR DN4 .... 90 D8
  DONS/BSCR DN4 .... 115 K1
  WRKN S81 .... 196 E2
High Royd Av CUD/GR S72 .... 57 J1
High Royd La STKB/PEN S36 .... 78 D2
Highroyds BSLY S70 .... 82 A2
Highstone Av BSLY S70 .... 2 B6
Highstone Crs BSLY S70 .... 2 B6
Highstone La BSLY S70 .... 82 A1
Highstone Rd BSLY S70 .... 2 C6
Highstone V BSLY S70 .... 2 B6 E
High Storrs Cl ECC S11 .... 185 K1
High Storrs Crs ECC S11 .... 170 A8
High Storrs Dr ECC S11 .... 185 K1
High Storrs Ri ECC S11 .... 170 A8
High Storrs Rd ECC S11 .... 185 K1
High St ARMTH DN3 .... 40 E8
  AU/AST/KP S26 .... 175 J7
  AWLS/ASK DN6 .... 17 K7
  AWLS/ASK DN6 .... 18 D8
  AWLS/ASK DN6 .... 18 A4
  AWLS/ASK DN6 .... 37 K7
  BSLY S70 .... 2 B5
  BSLY S70 .... 3 F1
  BSLYN/ROY S71 .... 30 C4
  BTLY DN5 .... 64 B1
  BTLY DN5 .... 65 G5
  BTLY DN5 .... 87 H4
  BWTY DN10 .... 143 J5
  BWTY DN10 .... 164 B1
  BWTY DN10 .... 165 K4
  CHPT/GREN S35 .... 130 C7
  CONI DN12 .... 114 D5
  CUD/GR S72 .... 31 K5
  CUD/GR S72 .... 32 B2
  CUD/GR S72 .... 58 C1
  CUD/GR S72 .... 59 C3
  CUD/GR S72 .... 85 J1
  DEARNE S63 .... 60 B8
  DEARNE S63 .... 86 D2
  DEARNE S63 .... 86 B5

DEARNE S63 .... 111 J1
DIN S25 .... 177 K2
DIN S25 .... 193 K3
DOD/DAR S75 .... 29 F5
DOD/DAR S75 .... 53 J8
DOD/DAR S75 .... 54 A5
DON DN1 .... 4 C3
DRON S18 .... 201 F5
DRON S18 .... 202 C6
ECK/KIL S21 .... 204 B4
ECK/KIL S21 .... 205 H1
EPW DN9 .... 96 C5
HEM/SK/SE WF9 .... 35 G4
HOY S74 .... 109 F1
HTFD DN7 .... 42 E8
HTFD DN7 .... 67 J3
KBTN HD8 .... 26 C5
KIMB S61 .... 132 B8
MALT S66 .... 137 H5
MALT S66 .... 159 H2
MEX/SWTN S64 .... 113 F5
MOS S20 .... 190 A8
MOS S20 .... 190 E5
NROS/TKH DN11 .... 116 E3
RAW S62 .... 133 J3
RHAM S60 .... 6 C4
RHAM S60 .... 156 A6
SHEF S1 .... 9 E5 E
STKB/PEN S36 .... 78 A5
STV/CWN S43 .... 206 A8
TOT/DORE S17 .... 185 H8
WMB/DAR S73 .... 84 A4
High Street La SHEFF/MNR S2 .... 9 F3 E
High Thorne Wy AU/AST/KP S26 .... 193 F4
Highthorn Rd MEX/SWTN S64 .... 112 C6
High Thorns DOD/DAR S75 .... 53 J7
Highton St FUL S10 .... 170 C1
Hightown La HOLM/MEL HD7 .... 47 K2
High Trees TOT/DORE S17 .... 185 H8
High Vw BSLYN/ROY S71 .... 30 C4
High View Cl WMB/DAR S73 .... 84 D1
High Well Hill La CUD/DAR S75 .... 31 K1
Highwood Cl DOD/DAR S75 .... 28 B7 E
Highwood Pl ECK/KIL S21 .... 204 A4
Highwoods Crs MEX/SWTN S64 .... 112 D2 E
Highwoods Rd MEX/SWTN S64 .... 112 D2
High Wray Cl ECC S11 .... 186 B3
Hilary Wy AU/AST/KP S26 .... 175 H8
Hild Av CUD/GR S72 .... 58 A3
Hill Cl RHAM/THRY S65 .... 156 C3
  ST/HB/BR S6 .... 169 G1
Hillcote Cl FUL S10 .... 169 H6
Hillcote Dr FUL S10 .... 169 H6
Hillcote Ms FUL S10 .... 169 H6
Hillcote Ri FUL S10 .... 169 H6
Hillcrest DEARNE S63 .... 60 B8
Hill Crest HOY S74 .... 108 D2
Hillcrest Dr CHPT/GREN S35 .... 150 B1
  DIN S25 .... 193 K3
Hillcrest Ri STKB/PEN S36 .... 105 J7
Hill Crest Rd CHPT/GREN S35 .... 130 A2
  RHAM/THRY S65 .... 134 A8
Hillcrest Rd STKB/PEN S36 .... 105 J7
  WHHL DN2 .... 61 K4
Hill End Rd DOD/DAR S75 .... 29 H8
Hill Farm Cl DEARNE S63 .... 60 B8 E
Hillfold HEM/SK/SE WF9 .... 35 G4 E
Hillfoot Rd TOT/DORE S17 .... 199 G2
Hill House La HOLM/MEL HD7 .... 47 G5
Hill House Rd HOLM/MEL HD7 .... 47 H5
Hill La HATH/EY S32 .... 182 A7
  HOLM/MEL HD7 .... 47 H2
Hill Park Cv DOD/DAR S75 .... 54 E7
Hills and Hamlets Wk
  HOLM/MEL HD7 .... 47 H4
Hillsborough Pl ST/HB/BR S6 .... 151 H7 E
Hillsborough Rd
  DONS/BSCR DN4 .... 92 D7
  ST/HB/BR S6 .... 151 H7 E
Hills Cl BTLY DN5 .... 90 B5
Hillscroft Rd EPW DN9 .... 121 F2
Hillside BSLYN/ROY S71 .... 57 H7 E
  DIN S25 .... 51 C1
  KBTN HD8 .... 51 C1
  MOS S20 .... 190 A8
Hill Side RHAM S60 .... 156 A6
Hill Side Av HOLM/MEL HD7 .... 48 D5
Hillside Av DRON S18 .... 201 G7
  SHEFN S5 .... 152 C1
Hillside Cl STKB/PEN S36 .... 78 C1
Hillside Ce BTLY DN5 .... 90 B5 E
  HEM/SK/SE WF9 .... 35 F3 E
  KIMB S61 .... 132 B8 E
Hillside Crs CUD/GR S72 .... 32 D5
  WRKN S81 .... 210 D2
Hillside Dr CONI DN12 .... 115 H6
  HOY S74 .... 109 G2
Hill Side La CUD/GR S72 .... 32 D5
Hill Side Mt CUD/GR S72 .... 77 F5
Hillside Wy CHPT/GREN S35 .... 106 C3
Hills Rd STKB/PEN S36 .... 105 G6
Hill St BSLYN/ROY S71 .... 57 F7
  HOLM/MEL HD7 .... 48 D4
  HOY S74 .... 109 H2
  SHEFF/MNR S2 .... 8 C5
  WMB/DAR S73 .... 84 D2
  WRKS S80 .... 210 C2
Hilltop CUD/GR S72 .... 32 C4

Hill Top DOD/DAR S75 .... 53 E
Hill Top Av BSLYN/ROY S71 .... 29 K8
Hilltop Cl MALT S66 .... 158 E5
Hill Top Cl HOR/CROF WF4 .... 30 C0
  KIMB S61 .... 154 A1
  RHAM S60 .... 154 C5
Hill Top Ct NROS/TKH DN11 .... 163 F5
Hill Top Crs CONI DN12 .... 115 J6
  MOS S20 .... 190 E5
  WHHL DN2 .... 62 A3
Hilltop Dr CHPT/GREN S35 .... 128 A2
Hilltop Gdns CONI DN12 .... 114 A6
Hill Top La CHPT/GREN S35 .... 129 G6
  DOD/DAR S75 .... 55 G4
  RHAM/THRY S65 .... 134 B8
  STKB/PEN S36 .... 105 G6
Hill Top Ri CHPT/GREN S35 .... 129 G6
Hilltop Rd DRON S18 .... 201 G7
Hill Top Rd BSLY S70 .... 82 A1
  CHPT/GREN S35 .... 129 G6
  CONI DN12 .... 114 A6
  HOLM/MEL HD7 .... 47 H5
  ST/HB/BR S6 .... 168 A4
Hill Top Vw HOLM/MEL HD7 .... 48 D5
Hilltop Wy DRON S18 .... 201 G7
Hill Turrets Cl ECC S11 .... 185 F5
Hill Vw East KIMB S61 .... 132 A7
Hill View Rd KIMB S61 .... 132 A7
Hillwood Cl WRKS S80 .... 209 J3
Himlian Wy HEM/SK/SE WF9 .... 33 F1
Hilton Dr CHPT/GREN S35 .... 130 A2
Hilton St AWLS/ASK DN6 .... 18 A4
  DOD/DAR S75 .... 2 A3
Hindburn Cl DONS/BSCR DN4 .... 92 B7
Hinde House Crs ATT S4 .... 153 G1
Hinde House Cft ATT S4 .... 153 G1
Hinde House La ATT S4 .... 152 E1
Hinde St ATT S4 .... 153 G1
Hindewood Cl ATT S4 .... 153 G1
Hindle St BSLY S70 .... 2 A4
Hind Rd RHAM S60 .... 156 A6
Hinds Crs HEM/SK/SE WF9 .... 34 A1
Hirst Common La ST/HB/BR S6 .... 151 F4
Hirst Dr RHAM/THRY S65 .... 134 A5
Hirst Ga MEX/SWTN S64 .... 113 G4
Hirst La HOLM/MEL HD7 .... 49 H2
  MALT S66 .... 138 A3
Hoads Av WRKN S81 .... 195 J3
Hoar Stones Rd ST/HB/BR S6 .... 148 B3
Hobart St ECC S11 .... 9 A8
Hobcroft Ter AWLS/ASK DN6 .... 37 J6
Hob La CHPT/GREN S35 .... 137 G2
Hobson Av ST/HB/BR S6 .... 151 J4
Hobson Pl ST/HB/BR S6 .... 151 J4
Hodder Ct CHPT/GREN S35 .... 130 A1 E
Hoddesdon Crs HTFD DN7 .... 68 A1
Hodge La PONT WF8 .... 17 G1
Hodgkinson Av STKB/PEN S36 .... 78 A4 E
Hodgson St OWL S3 .... 8 B5
Hodroyd Cl CUD/GR S72 .... 32 B2
Hodroyd Cottages CUD/GR S72 .... 32 A1
Hodsock La WRKN S81 .... 181 H8
  WRKN S81 .... 196 A1
Hodster La CUD/GR S72 .... 59 F3
Hog Close La HOLM/MEL HD7 .... 49 H1
Hoggarth Ri DRON S18 .... 201 G5
Hogley La HOLM/MEL HD7 .... 47 H2
Holbein Cl DRON S18 .... 201 G5
Holberry Cl FUL S10 .... 8 B4
Holberry Gdns FUL S10 .... 8 B4
Holbourne Gv CHPT/GREN S35 .... 107 F4
Holbrook Av MOS S20 .... 190 C3
Holbrook Dr HAN/WDH S13 .... 188 D1
Holbrook Gn MOS S20 .... 190 C3
Holbrook Ri MOS S20 .... 190 C3
Holbrook Rd HAN/WDH S13 .... 172 B8
Holburn Av DRON S18 .... 201 G5
Holden Ct BSLY S70 .... 2 B4
Holderness Cl NROS/TKH DN11 .... 163 F5
Holderness Dr AU/AST/KP S26 .... 175 G6
Holding WRKN S81 .... 211 H1
Holdings Rd SHEFF/MNR S2 .... 171 H1
Holdworth La ST/HB/BR S6 .... 149 H5
Hole House La STKB/PEN S36 .... 104 E5
Holgate WMB/DAR S73 .... 83 K3
Holgate Av SHEFN S5 .... 152 B1
Holgate Crs SHEFN S5 .... 152 B1
Holgate Dr SHEFN S5 .... 152 B1
Holgate Mt BSLY S70 .... 152 B2
Holgate Rd SHEFN S5 .... 152 B1
Holgate Vw CUD/GR S72 .... 32 E4
Holiwell Cl MALT S66 .... 159 J3
Holkham Ri ECC S11 .... 185 K5
Holland Cl RAW S62 .... 111 K1
Holland Pl SHEFF/MNR S2 .... 9 D6
Holland Rd CHPT/GREN S35 .... 107 F4
  SHEFF/MNR S2 9
Holland St SHEF S1 .... 8 C4
Holles St WRKS S80 .... 210 C2
Hollies Cl DRON S18 .... 201 J8
Hollinberry La CHPT/GREN S35 .... 107 K1
Hollin Bridge La HTFD DN7 .... 69 J3
Hollin Brigg La HOLM/MEL HD7 .... 47 H3
Hollin Busk La STKB/PEN S36 .... 105 F4
Hollin Busk Rd STKB/PEN S36 .... 105 F4
Hollin Cl NROS/TKH DN11 .... 119 G8
Hollin Cft DOD/DAR S75 .... 55 G4
Hollindale Dr HACK/IN S12 .... 188 A1
Hollin Edge KBTN HD8 .... 51 J4

Hollin Edge La STKB/PEN S36 .... 127 J2
Holling Cft STKB/PEN S36 .... 105 H6 🈁
Holling's La RHAM/THRY S65 .... 134 E5
Hollin Hill La RHAM/THRY S65 .... 156 B3
Hollin House La HOLM/MEL HD7 ..... 48 E2
KBTN HD8 .... 26 C8
ST/HB/BR S6 .... 149 J4
Hollin La STKB/PEN S36 .... 76 B3
Hollin Moor La CHPT/GREN S35 .... 80 A7
MALT S66 .... 157 F3
Hollin Rd CHPT/GREN S35 .... 150 B1
Hollins Cl ST/HB/BR S6 .... 169 K2
Hollins Dr ST/HB/BR S6 .... 169 K2
Hollinsend Av HACK/IN S12 .... 188 E2
Hollinsend Pl HACK/IN S12 .... 188 E2 🈁
Hollinsend Rd HACK/IN S12 .... 188 C3 🈁
Hollins La ST/HB/BR S6 .... 170 A1
Hollins Spring Av DRON S18 .... 201 G7
Hollins Spring Rd DRON S18 .... 201 G7
Hollis Cl RAW S62 .... 111 F7
Hollis Cft HAN/WDH S13 .... 189 J1 🈁
SHEF S1 .... 8 C2
Hollowdene DOD/DAR S75 .... 55 C4
Hollowgate BTLY DN5 .... 87 H5
Hollow Ga BTLY DN5 .... 114 D2
CHPT/GREN S35 .... 129 J2
Hollowgate HOLM/MEL HD7 .... 47 K2
RHAM S60 .... 7 D5
Hollow Ga RHAM S60 .... 156 A6 🈁
Hollowgate RHAM/THRY S65 .... 7 D5 🈁
Hollowgate Av DEARNE S63 .... 85 F7
Hollow La MOS S20 .... 204 B1
The Hollows DONS/BSCR DN4 .... 118 D1
EPW DN9 .... 120 B1
Holly Av BTLY DN5 .... 64 D8
Hollybank Av HACK/IN S12 .... 188 E1
KBTN HD8 .... 50 D1
Hollybank Cl HACK/IN S12 .... 189 F1
Hollybank Crs HACK/IN S12 .... 188 E1
Hollybank Dr HACK/IN S12 .... 188 E1
Hollybank Rd HACK/IN S12 .... 188 E2
Hollybank Wy HAN/WDH S12 .... 188 E1
Holly Bush Dr DEARNE S63 .... 60 C7
Hollybush St RAW S62 .... 133 J4
Holly Cl CHPT/GREN S35 .... 130 A3
ECK/KIL S21 .... 205 F2
HEM/SK/SE WF9 .... 34 E5 🈁
Holly Ct NROS/TKH DN11 .... 162 D3
Holly Crs MALT S66 .... 157 H1
Holly Croft Gv RHAM/THRY DN11 .... 140 A7
Holly Dene ARMTH DN3 .... 67 F7
Holly Dr BTLY DN5 .... 64 E5
Holly Gdns HACK/IN S12 .... 188 E1
Hollygate BSLY S70 .... 82 C2
Holly Gv CUD/GR S72 .... 32 D4
DEARNE S63 .... 111 J3
HACK/IN S12 .... 188 E1
NROS/TKH DN11 .... 119 F6
Holly Hall La CHPT/GREN S35 .... 105 J4
Holly La SHEF S1 .... 9 D3 🈁
Holly Mt MALT S66 .... 157 H3
Holly Rd EPW DN9 .... 120 B3
THNE DN8 .... 23 K6
Holly's House Rd RHAM/THRY S65. 136 A6 🈁
Holly St SHEF S1 .... 9 D3
Holly Ter AU/AST/KP S26 .... 175 F7
DONS/BSCR DN4 .... 90 C8
Hollythorpe Crs SHEFS S8 .... 187 G3
Hollythorpe Rd SHEFS S8 .... 187 H5
Hollytree Av MALT S66 .... 158 E1
Hollywell Cl RAW S62 .... 134 A1
Holmclose HOLM/MEL HD7 .... 46 E5
Holme Cl ST/HB/BR S6 .... 151 H7 🈁
Holme Ct DEARNE S63 .... 86 B3 🈁
Holmefield Cl ARMTH DN3 .... 93 H2
WRKN S81 .... 210 E2 🈁
Holmefield Cft BWTY DN10 .... 164 B5 🈁
Holme Fleet La HTFD DN7 .... 40 C5
Holme Gdns HTFD DN7 .... 42 A2
Holme Hall La MALT S66 .... 138 B6
Holme La BTLY DN5 .... 38 E5
CHPT/GREN S35 .... 129 J8
ST/HB/BR S6 .... 151 G8
Holme Oak Wy ST/HB/BR S6 .... 150 B8
Holmeroyd Rd AWLS/ASK DN6 .... 38 B8
Holmes Carr Crs NROS/TKH DN11 .... 118 C6
Holmes Carr Rd DONS/BSCR DN4.... 118 C1
NROS/TKH DN11 .... 118 C5
Holmes Crs RHAM S60 .... 174 C3
Holmesdale Cl DRON S18 .... 201 J4
Holmesdale Rd DRON S18 .... 201 H4
Holmesfield CHPT/GREN S35 .... 150 C1 🈁
Holmesfield Rd DRON S18 .... 200 B6
Holmes La CONI DN12 .... 113 G7
KIMB S61 .... 6 A4
Holmes Rd MALT S66 .... 157 J3
Holme Styes La HOLM/MEL HD7 ..... 47 J7
Holme Valley Circular Wk
HOLM/MEL HD7 .... 46 E7
Holme View Dr HOLM/MEL HD7 ..... 47 G2
Holme View Pk HOLM/MEL HD7 ..... 47 H2
Holme View Rd DOD/DAR S75 .... 28 A7
Holme Wood Dr ARMTH DN3 .... 67 F5 🈁
Holme Wood Gdns
DONS/BSCR DN4 .... 92 D8 🈁
Holme Wood La ARMTH DN3 .... 93 J1
Holme Woods La HOLM/MEL HD7 ... 72 C2
Holmfield KBTN HD8 .... 26 C5 🈁
Holmfield Av KBTN HD8 .... 26 C5 🈁

Holmfield Cl KBTN HD8 .... 26 C5
Holmfield Rd KBTN HD8 .... 26 D5
Holm Flatt St RAW S62 .... 133 H4
Holmhirst Cl SHEFS S8 .... 186 E4
Holmhirst Dr SHEFS S8 .... 186 E4
Holmhirst Rd SHEFS S8 .... 186 E4
Holmhirst Wy SHEFS S8 .... 186 E5
Holmhurst Cl WRKN S81 .... 210 C2 🈁
Holmley Bank DRON S18 .... 201 G4
Holmley La DRON S18 .... 201 G4
Holmoak Cl MEX/SWTN S64 .... 112 C6
Holmshaw Dr HAN/WDH S13 .... 173 G7
Holmshaw Gv HAN/WDH S13 .... 173 G7
Holmsley Av HEM/SK/SE WF9 .... 33 K5
Holmsley Gv HEM/SK/SE WF9 .... 33 K5
Holmsley La CUD/GR S72 .... 33 H5
Holmsley Mt HEM/SK/SE WF9 .... 33 K5
Holt La HOLM/MEL HD7 .... 47 J1
Holtwood Rd ATT S4 .... 152 C8
Holwick Cl DOD/DAR S75 .... 53 J7 🈁
Holyoake Av HAN/WDH S13 .... 173 G6
Holyrood Ri MALT S66 .... 157 J1
Holyrood Rd WHHL DN2 .... 91 K4
Holywell Crs MALT S66 .... 137 H6
Holywell La CONI DN12 .... 114 D6
MALT S66 .... 137 H6
Holywell Rd ATT S4 .... 153 G6
MEX/SWTN S64 .... 112 C6
Homecroft Dr DEARNE S63 .... 86 C2
Home Farm Ct BTLY DN5 .... 61 H8
Homefield Crs BTLY DN5 .... 64 B7
Home Mdw NROS/TKH DN11 .... 161 K1
Homestead Cl SHEFN S5 .... 152 E2
Homestead Dr RAW S62 .... 111 J8
RHAM S60 .... 154 E6
Homestead Garth HTFD DN7 .... 42 C7 🈁
Homestead Rd SHEFN S5 .... 152 D5
Honey Lands La BTLY DN5 .... 39 G5
Honeysuckle Cl WMB/DAR S73 .... 84 D3
Honeysuckle Ct EPW DN9 .... 121 F4 🈁
Honeysuckle Rd SHEFN S5 .... 153 G4 🈁
Honister Cl DEARNE S63 .... 84 D8
Hoober Av ECC S11 .... 186 A2
Hoober Ct RAW S62 .... 111 A2
Hoober Fld RAW S62 .... 110 E5
Hoober Hall La RAW S62 .... 110 C4
Hoober La RAW S62 .... 110 D6
Hoober Rd ECC S11 .... 186 A2
Hoober St DEARNE S63 .... 110 E1
Hoober Vw RAW S62 .... 111 G7
WMB/DAR S73 .... 84 C6
Hood Green Rd DOD/DAR S75 .... 80 D5
Hood St HEM/SK/SE WF9 .... 34 D7
Hoole La FUL S10 .... 170 C5 🈁
Hoole Rd FUL S10 .... 170 C4
Hooton Cl ST/HB/BR S6 .... 151 J2
Hooton Cl DIN S25 .... 178 A2 🈁
Hooton La DIN S25 .... 178 A2
MALT S66 .... 159 F3
RHAM/THRY S65 .... 135 H4
Hooton Rd BTLY DN5 .... 62 A4
MEX/SWTN S64 .... 112 E8
Hoowood La HOLM/MEL HD7 .... 46 B4
Hope Av DEARNE S63 .... 86 B5
Hopedale Rd HACK/IN S12 .... 189 F3
Hopefield Av HACK/IN S12 .... 189 F3
Hope Rd CHPT/GREN S35 .... 150 D1
Hope St BSLYN/ROY S71 .... 57 G1
DOD/DAR S75 .... 2 A3
DOD/DAR S75 .... 23 F5 🈁
MEX/SWTN S64 .... 113 F3 🈁
RHAM S60 .... 6 B3
STKB/PEN S36 .... 105 B3
WMB/DAR S73 .... 84 B5
Hope Street Extension RHAM S60... 6 B3
Hopewell St BSLY S70 .... 56 E7
Hop Hills La HTFD DN7 .... 42 B6
The Hop Inge AU/AST/KP S26 .... 206 C3
Hopping La CHPT/GREN S35 .... 79 J6
Hopwood La ST/HB/BR S6 .... 168 C3
Hopwood St BSLY S70 .... 2 B3
Hopyard La NROS/TKH DN11 .... 140 B6
Horace St RHAM/THRY S65 .... 7 D5 🈁
Horbiry End AU/AST/KP S26 .... 192 E2 🈁
Horbury La CHPT/GREN S35 .... 129 K3
Horbury Rd CUD/GR S72 .... 31 J7
Hordron Rd STKB/PEN S36 .... 101 J2
Hornbeam Cl CHPT/GREN S35 .... 130 A3
Hornbeam Rd MALT S66 .... 157 G3
Hornby St BSLY S70 .... 2 C6 🈁
Horn Cote La HOLM/MEL HD7 .... 49 J1
Horn Cft DOD/DAR S75 .... 53 H2
Horndean Rd SHEFN S5 .... 152 E6
Horner Cl STKB/PEN S36 .... 104 E6
Horner Rd SHEFS S8 .... 171 F8
Hornes La DOD/DAR S75 .... 29 F4
Horninglow Cl DONS/BSCR DN4 ..... 119 F1
SHEFN S5 .... 152 D4
Horninglow Rd SHEFN S5 .... 152 D4
Horn La HOLM/MEL HD7 .... 49 H1
STKB/PEN S36 .... 50 B6
Hornsby Rd ARMTH DN3 .... 93 H2
Hornthorpe Rd ECK/KIL S21 .... 203 K5
Hornthwaite Hill Rd STKB/PEN S36.. 77 G5

Horse Carr Vw BSLYN/ROY S71 .... 57 H7
Horse Croft La CHPT/GREN S35 ..... 128 A7
Horse Fair Gn THNE DN8 .... 23 J8 🈁
Horsehills La ARMTH DN3 .... 93 F2
Horsemoor Rd DEARNE S63 .... 60 A7 🈁
Horseshoe Cl AU/AST/KP S26 .... 192 C4 🈁
Horseshoe La MALT S66 .... 160 B7
Horsewood Cl BSLY S70 .... 55 G7
Horsewood Rd HAN/WDH S13 .... 174 B7
Horsleygate Rd TOT/DORE S17 ..... 199 F7
Horton Cl MOS S20 .... 190 C8 🈁
Horton Dr MOS S20 .... 190 C8
Horton Vw ARMTH DN3 .... 66 D2
Hough La WMB/DAR S73 .... 83 J6
Houghton La DEARNE S63 .... 59 K7
DIN S25 .... 177 H7
Hound Hill La DOD/DAR S75 .... 81 J2
MEX/SWTN S64 .... 86 C8
Houndkirk Rd ECC S11 .... 184 C6
Hounsfield Crs RHAM/THRY S65.... 134 C8
Hounsfield La OWL S5 .... 8 B3 🈁
Hounsfield Rd OWL S5 .... 8 B5 🈁
RHAM/THRY S65 .... 134 C8
Houps Rd THNE DN8 .... 23 K8
House Carr La DOD/DAR S75 .... 80 A3
House Grove Dr KBTN HD8 .... 26 B5
Housley La CHPT/GREN S35 .... 130 A1
Housley Pk CHPT/GREN S35 .... 130 B1
Houstead Rd DARN/MH S9 .... 173 F4
Howard La SHEF S1 .... 9 E4
Howard Rd MALT S66 .... 157 J2
MALT S66 .... 159 J2 🈁
NROS/TKH DN11 .... 163 H3
ST/HB/BR S6 .... 170 C2
Howards Cl DIN S25 .... 177 G1
Howard St BSLY S70 .... 2 C6 🈁
DIN S25 .... 178 C6
RHAM S60 .... 6 C3
SHEF S1 .... 9 E4
WMB/DAR S73 .... 85 F2
WRKS S80 .... 210 E5
Howarth Rd RHAM S60 .... 155 G7
Howbeck Cl CONI DN12 .... 115 H6
Howbeck Dr CONI DN12 .... 115 H6
Howbrook Cl CHPT/GREN S35 .... 107 H7 🈁
Howbrook La CHPT/GREN S35 .... 106 E5
Howden Av AWLS/ASK DN6 .... 37 F6
Howden Cl DOD/DAR S75 .... 28 E6
DONS/BSCR DN4 .... 118 B1
Howden Rd DARN/MH S9 .... 153 H8
Howdike La CONI DN12 .... 113 G8
Howe La MALT S66 .... 159 F7
Howell La CUD/GR S72 .... 59 H1
Howlett Cl RHAM S60 .... 156 C6
Howlett Dr RHAM S60 .... 155 F8
Howse St HOY S74 .... 109 H1
Howson Cl RHAM/THRY S65 .... 135 K7
Howson Rd STKB/PEN S36 .... 105 G6
Howville Av HTFD DN7 .... 69 F1
Hoylake Dr MEX/SWTN S64 .... 112 C6
Hoyland Cl STKB/PEN S36 .... 76 E4
Hoyland Rd HOY S74 .... 108 C2
OWL S5 .... 151 K8
Hoyland St MALT S66 .... 159 J2
WMB/DAR S73 .... 84 A5 🈁
Hoyle Croft La MALT S66 .... 137 F6
Hoyle Mill Rd BSLY S70 .... 56 E7
Hoyle St OWL S5 .... 8 C2
Hucklow La SHEFN S5 .... 152 E5
Huddersfield Rd DOD/DAR S75 ..... 28 A2
DOD/DAR S75 .... 55 H3 🈁
STKB/PEN S36 .... 105 K1
Hudson Av HOR/CROF WF4 .... 30 C1
Hudson Cl AU/AST/KP S26 .... 192 E8 🈁
Hudson Rd HAN/WDH S13 .... 174 C7 🈁
KIMB S61 .... 132 B5
Huggin Carr Rd HTFD DN7 .... 69 F6
Hugh Hill La HTFD DN7 .... 42 C3
Humber Cl AWLS/ASK DN6 .... 37 H6
Humber Dr AWLS/ASK DN6 .... 37 H6
Humberside Wy BSLYN/ROY S71 .... 56 E1
Humber St WRKS S80 .... 210 C3 🈁
Humphrey Rd SHEFS S8 .... 186 E1
Humphries Av RAW S62 .... 111 G8 🈁
Humphries Gdns WRKS S80 .... 210 C6
Hundall La DRON S18 .... 202 B8
Hund Oak Dr HTFD DN7 .... 42 C7 🈁
Hundred Acre La WRKN S81 .... 197 G4
Hungerhill Cl KIMB S61 .... 132 A7
Hungerhill La ARMTH DN3 .... 66 C5
Hunger Hill La RHAM S60 .... 156 B6
Hungerhill Rd KIMB S61 .... 132 A6
Hunger Hill Rd RHAM S60 .... 156 A5
Hungry La HATH/EY S32 .... 182 D7
Hunningley La BSLY S70 .... 56 E8 🈁
BSLY S70 .... 82 E1
Hunsdon Rd ECK/KIL S21 .... 204 A4
Hunshelf Hall La STKB/PEN S36 ..... 104 E3
Hunshelf La CHPT/GREN S35 .... 130 C5
Hunshelf Pk STKB/PEN S36 .... 105 F5
Hunshelf Rd CHPT/GREN S35 .... 130 A2
STKB/PEN S36 .... 104 E5
Hunsley St ATT S4 .... 153 F7
Hunster Gv NROS/TKH DN11 .... 118 E7
Hunstone Av SHEFS S8 .... 187 G8
Hunt Cl BSLYN/ROY S71 .... 3 F1 🈁
Hunter Hill Rd ECC S11 .... 170 C8
Hunter House Rd ECC S11 .... 170 B8
Hunter Rd ST/HB/BR S6 .... 151 G7

Hunter's Av BSLY S70 ... 55 F7
Hunters Cha DIN S25 ... 178 B5
Hunters Cl DIN S25 ... 178 B4
Hunters Ct DIN S25 ... 178 B4 3
Hunters Dr DIN S25 ... 178 B5
Hunters Gdns DIN S25 ... 178 B4 2
  ST/HB/BR S6 ... 150 C6
Hunters Gn DIN S25 ... 178 B4 4
Hunter's La HAN/WDH S13 ... 188 E1
Hunters Pk DIN S25 ... 178 B4
Hunters Ri DOD/DAR S75 ... 55 F6
Hunters Wy DIN S25 ... 178 B4
Huntingdon Crs ECC S11 ... 8 B6
Huntington Rd WHHL DN2 ... 63 D4
Huntington St DN5 ... 64 E5 2
Huntington Wy MALT S66 ... 137 F8
Huntingtower Rd ECC S11 ... 170 B8
Hunt La BTLY DN5 ... 4 B1
Hurl Dr HACK/IN S12 ... 188 B2
Hurley Cft DEARNE S63 ... 84 D8 1
Hurley Av HACK/IN S12 ... 188 C2
Hurlfield Ct HACK/IN S12 ... 188 B1
Hurlfield Dr HACK/IN S12 ... 188 B1
  RHAM/THRY S65 ... 135 J8
Hurlfield Rd HACK/IN S12 ... 188 B2
Hurlingham Cl ABRD S7 ... 186 C3
Hursley Cl MOS S20 ... 190 E6 2
Hursley Dr MOS S20 ... 190 E6
Hurst Gn CHPT/GREN S35 ... 107 J8
Hurst La EPW DN9 ... 120 B2
Hushells La GLE DN14 ... 22 A4
Huskar Cl DOD/DAR S75 ... 53 J7
Hutchinson La SHEFS S8 ... 186 D4 3
Hutchinson Rd RAW S62 ... 133 K1 1
  SHEFS S8 ... 186 D4 2
Hutcliffe Dr SHEFS S8 ... 186 D5 1
Hutcliffe Wood Rd SHEFS S8 ... 186 D5
Huthwaite La CHPT/GREN S35 ... 105 J2
Hut La ECK/KIL S21 ... 205 J3
Hutton Cl EPW DN9 ...
Hutton Dr HEM/SK/SE WF9 ... 35 F5
Hutton Rd KIMB S61 ... 132 B6
Hyacinth Cl DARN/MH S9 ... 153 K8
Hyacinth Rd SHEFN S5 ... 153 G4
Hyde Park Wk SHEFP/MNR S2 ... 9 F3
Hyland Crs DONS/BSCR DN4 ... 116 B1 3
Hyman Cl DONS/BSCR DN4 ... 90 A8

I

Ibberson Av DOD/DAR S75 ... 29 F1
Ibbotson Rd ST/HB/BR S6 ... 170 C1
Ibbotsons Cft HATH/EY S32 ... 182 C7 3
Ickles Wy RHAM S60 ... 6 A6
Icknield Wy RHAM S60 ... 155 F7
Ida Gv MALT S66 ... 158 E1
Ida's Rd ECK/KIL S21 ... 204 B3
Idle Bank EPW DN9 ... 71 J7
Idsworth Rd SHEFN S5 ... 152 E5
Ilkley Crs AU/AST/KP S26 ... 191 G1
Ilkley Rd WMB/DAR S73 ... 152 E5
Ilsley Rd WMB/DAR S73 ... 84 D1
Imperial Crs WHHL DN2 ... 5 F2
Industry Rd BSLYN/ROY S71 ... 30 D8
  DARN/MH S9 ... 172 E2
Industry St ST/HB/BR S6 ... 170 C1
Infield La DARN/MH S9 ... 172 E3
Infirmary Rd OWL S3 ... 8 C1 7
  RAW S62 ... 133 K4
  ST/HB/BR S6 ... 8 B1
Ingbirchworth La STKB/PEN S36 ... 51 F8
Ingbirchworth Rd STKB/PEN S36 ... 77 H3
Ingdale Dr HOLM/MEL HD7 ... 48 A1
Ingelow Av SHEFS S8 ... 152 C2
Ingfield Av DARN/MH S9 ... 154 B5
Ingham Rd BWTY DN10 ... 142 A7
Ingleborough Cft CHPT/GREN S35 ... 130 A1 3
Ingleborough Dr BTLY DN5 ... 90 B5
Ingleby Cl DRON S18 ... 200 C6 3
Ingledene Ms ARMTH DN3 ... 40 E8
Ingle Gv BTLY DN5 ...
Inglemere Cl WRKN S81 ... 210 E2 2
Inglenook Dr THNE DN8 ... 23 K7
Inglewood DOD/DAR S75 ... 28 E6
Inglewood Av MOS S20 ... 190 E6 3
Inglewood Ct MOS S20 ... 190 E6 5
Inglewood Dell MOS S20 ... 190 E6 4
Ingram Ct SHEFP/MNR S2 ... 171 K5 3
Ingram Crs HTFD DN7 ... 42 A8
Ingram Gv HTFD DN7 ... 42 A8 1
Ingram Rd HTFD DN7 ... 68 A7
  SHEFP/MNR S2 ... 171 K5
Ings Cl HEM/SK/SE WF9 ... 34 E6
Ingsfield La DEARNE S63 ... 85 K5
Ingshead Av RAW S62 ... 133 K4
Ings Holt HEM/SK/SE WF9 ... 34 C4
Ings La AWLS/ASK DN6 ... 37 H6
  BTLY DN5 ... 65 H5
  BTLY DN5 ... 65 K5
  BTLY DN5 ... 90 B5
  CUD/GR S72 ... 58 E8
  HTFD DN7 ... 41 K1

Ings Mill Av KBTN HD8 ... 26 C4
Ings Mill Dr KBTN HD8 ... 26 C5
Ings Rd BTLY DN5 ... 91 F1
  BTLY DN5 ... 114 E1
  WMB/DAR S73 ... 84 D3
The Ings KBTN HD8 ... 26 C5 8
Ings Wk HEM/SK/SE WF9 ... 34 C4
Ings Wy BTLY DN5 ... 65 G5
  STKB/PEN S36 ... 50 E6
Inkerman Rd WMB/DAR S73 ... 84 D3
Inkerman St WMB/DAR S73 ... 51 C2
Inkersall Dr MOS S20 ... 190 C7
Innovation Wy DOD/DAR S75 ... 55 H3
Insley Gdns DONS/BSCR DN4 ... 92 D8
Instone Ter AWLS/ASK DN6 ... 38 C1
Intake Crs DOD/DAR S75 ... 80 E1
Intake Rd CUD/GR S72 ... 31 K7
  DOD/DAR S75 ... 55 G5
Inverness Rd HTFD DN7 ... 68 E1
Ironside Cl GLV S14 ... 187 K5
Ironside Pl GLV S14 ... 188 A4
Ironside Rd GLV S14 ... 187 K5
Irving St DARN/MH S9 ... 172 E3
Irwell Gdns DONS/BSCR DN4 ... 92 C5 1
Islay St FUL S10 ... 170 B4
Issott St BSLYN/ROY S71 ... 2 C2
Ivan Brook Cl DRON S18 ... 200 C6 2
Ivanhoe Av AU/AST/KP S26 ... 192 E5
Ivanhoe Cl BTLY DN5 ... 90 C3
Ivanhoe Ms AU/AST/KP S26 ... 175 C2
Ivanhoe Rd ARMTH DN3 ... 66 E6
  CONI DN12 ... 114 C5
  CONI DN12 ... 115 J6
  DONS/BSCR DN4 ... 90 B8
  MALT S66 ... 176 E1
Ivanhoe Wy BTLY DN5 ... 90 C3
Ivatt Cl BWTY DN10 ... 142 B7
Ivor Gv DONS/BSCR DN4 ... 4 A6
Ivy Cl HEM/SK/SE WF9 ... 34 E6
  HTFD DN7 ... 42 E7
  NROS/TKH DN11 ... 119 F6
Ivy Cottage La ECC S11 ... 185 G1
Ivy Ct SHEFS S8 ... 187 J5
Ivy Dr FUL S10 ... 8 A2 8
Ivy Farm Cl BSLYN/ROY S71 ... 30 E6
Ivy Farm Cft RHAM/THRY S65 ... 134 C6
Ivy Gv FUL S10 ... 8 A2 7
Ivy Hall Rd SHEFN S5 ... 131 H6
Ivy House Ct EPW DN9 ... 94 A8
Ivy La MOS S20 ... 190 E3
Ivy Lodge La WRKN S81 ... 179 K3
Ivy Park Rd FUL S10 ... 183 C4
Ivy Rd THNE DN8 ... 23 J6
Ivy Side Cl BSLYN/ROY S71 ... 205 H1
Ivyside Gdns ECK/KIL S21 ... 205 H1
Ivy Ter HEM/SK/SE WF9 ... 35 F4 2

J

Jack Close Orch BSLYN/ROY S71 ... 30 D3
Jackey Hl CHPT/GREN S35 ... 128 A8 1
Jack La CHPT/GREN S35 ... 127 F3
Jack Row La HTFD DN7 ... 21 G8
Jackson Crs RAW S62 ... 111 C8
Jackson St CUD/GR S72 ... 57 H1
  DEARNE S63 ... 86 D2 2
Jackys La AU/AST/KP S26 ... 206 E1
Jacobs Cl SHEFN S5 ... 153 F5
Jacobs Dr SHEFN S5 ... 153 F5
Jacobs Hall La DOD/DAR S75 ... 28 B7 3
Jacques Pl BSLYN/ROY S71 ... 56 E5
Jagger's La HATH/EY S32 ... 182 A7
Jamaica St ATT S14 ... 152 E8 2
James Andrew Cl SHEFS S8 ... 187 F8
James Andrew Crs SHEFS S8 ... 186 E8
James Andrew Cft SHEFS S8 ... 187 F8 1
James Ct THNE DN8 ... 23 K6
James Rd AWLS/ASK DN6 ... 38 A4
James St BSLY S70 ... 82 D2
  BSLYN/ROY S71 ... 2 C5
  CUD/GR S72 ... 32 C2
  DARN/MH S9 ... 172 E4
  MEX/SWTN S64 ... 113 J2
  RHAM S60 ... 6 B3
  WRKN S81 ... 210 C2
Janson St DARN/MH S9 ... 153 H7
Jaque's Bank THNE DN8 ... 45 K4
Jardine WRKN S81 ... 211 F1 3
Jardine Cl DARN/MH S9 ... 153 H5
Jardine St DARN/MH S9 ... 153 J3
  WMB/DAR S73 ... 84 A5
Jarratt St DON DN1 ... 5 D4
Jarrow Rd ECC S11 ... 8 A6 8
Jasmine Av MOS S20 ... 190 D4
Jasmine Cl CONI DN12 ... 114 E6
Jaunty Av HACK/IN S12 ... 188 D4
Jaunty Cl HACK/IN S12 ... 188 D4
Jaunty Crs HACK/IN S12 ... 188 D3
Jaunty Dr HACK/IN S12 ... 188 D4
Jaunty La HACK/IN S12 ... 188 D4
Jaunty Mt HACK/IN S12 ... 188 E4
Jaunty Pl HACK/IN S12 ... 188 D4
Jaunty Rd HACK/IN S12 ... 188 E4
Jaunty Vw HACK/IN S12 ... 188 E4
Jaunty Wy HACK/IN S12 ... 188 D3
Jay La AU/AST/KP S26 ... 191 J1

Jebb La DOD/DAR S75 ... 27
Jedburgh Dr DARN/MH S9 ... 153 H
Jedburgh St DARN/MH S9 ... 153 H
Jeffcock Rd CHPT/GREN S35 ... 107 K
  DARN/MH S9 ... 172 E3
Jefferson Av WHHL DN2 ... 66 C
Jeffery Crs STKB/PEN S36 ... 105 C
Jeffery St SHEFF/MNR S2 ... 187 H1
Jenkin Av DARN/MH S9 ... 153 H
Jenkin Cl DARN/MH S9 ... 153 H
Jenkin Dr DARN/MH S9 ... 153 H
Jenkin Rd DARN/MH S9 ... 153 H
Jennings Cl RHAM/THRY S65 ... 7 D2
Jenny La GLE DN14 ... 10 E
Jepson Rd SHEFN S5 ... 153 C
Jericho St OWL S3 ... 8 B
Jermyn Av HACK/IN S12 ... 189 C
Jermyn Cl HACK/IN S12 ... 189 H
Jermyn Crs HACK/IN S12 ... 189 H
Jermyn Cft DOD/DAR S75 ... 54 E
Jermyn Dr HACK/IN S12 ... 189 H
Jermyn Wy HACK/IN S12 ... 189 H
Jersey Rd SHEFP/MNR S2 ... 171 G8
Jesmond Av BSLYN/ROY S71 ... 30 C
Jesop Ct DIN S25 ...
Jessamine Rd SHEFN S5 ... 153 F
Jessell St DARN/MH S9 ... 172 E
Jessop St SHEF S1 ... 9 D4
Jewitt Rd KIMB S61 ... 132 E
Joan Croft La BTLY DN5 ... 39 F
Joan La MALT S66 ... 159 F
Joan Royd La STKB/PEN S36 ... 77
Job La BWTY DN10 ... 165
Jockell Dr RAW S62 ... 133
Jockey Rd STKB/PEN S36 ... 78 E
John Calvert Rd HAN/WDH S13 ... 190 E1
John Hibbard Av HAN/WDH S13 ... 174 D8
John Hibbard Crs HAN/WDH S13 ... 174 C
John Hibbard Ri HAN/WDH S13 ... 174 C
Johnny Moor Long La GLE DN14 ... 14
  THNE DN8 ... 14
Johnson Ct CONI DN12 ... 115 K4
Johnson La CHPT/GREN S35 ... 130 C
  OWL S3 ... 9 E2
Johnson St DOD/DAR S75 ... 2 A3
  OWL S3 ... 9
  STKB/PEN S36 ... 104 E6
Johnston's Rd HTFD DN7 ... 42 C
John St AWLS/ASK DN6 ... 63
  SHEFN S5 ... 7
  BSLY S70 ... 82 B2
  CUD/GR S72 ... 59
  DEARNE S63 ... 60
  ECK/KIL S21 ... 204
  HEM/SK/SE WF9 ... 34
  MALT S66 ... 157
  MEX/SWTN S64 ... 113
  RHAM S60 ... 6
  SHEFP/MNR S2 ... 9
  WMB/DAR S73 ... 83
  WRKS S80 ... 210
John Ward St HAN/WDH S13 ... 174
John West St STKB/PEN S36 ... 104
Joiner St OWL S3 ... 9 E2
Jones Av WMB/DAR S73 ... 83
Jordan Crs KIMB S61 ... 154
Jordanthorpe Gn SHEFS S8 ... 201
Jordanthorpe Pkwy SHEFS S8 ... 201
Jordanthorpe Vw SHEFS S8 ... 187 J8
Josephine Rd KIMB S61 ... 154
Joseph La STKB/PEN S36 ... 102
Joseph Rd FUL S10 ... 170 C2
Joseph St BSLY S70 ... 2
  CUD/GR S72 ... 58
  ECK/KIL S21 ... 204
  RHAM S60 ... 6
Joshua Rd ABRD S7 ... 170
Josselin Ct CHPT/GREN S35 ... 130 A2 1
Jossey La BTLY DN5 ... 64
Jowett House La DOD/DAR S75 ... 52
Jowitt Cl MALT S66 ... 159
Jowitt Rd ECC S11 ... 186
Jubb Cl RHAM/THRY S65 ... 156
Jubilee Cl BWTY DN10 ... 143
Jubilee Crs ECK/KIL S21 ... 191
Jubilee Rd DARN/MH S9 ... 172
  DON DN1 ... 5
Jubilee St RHAM S60 ... 6
Judd Field La STKB/PEN S36 ... 101
Judith Rd AU/AST/KP S26 ... 191
Judy Rw BSLYN/ROY S71 ... 3
Julian Rd DARN/MH S9 ... 153
Julian Wy DARN/MH S9 ... 153
Jumble La KIMB S61 ... 131
Jumble Rd ECC S11 ... 184
Junction Cl WMB/DAR S73 ... 84
Junction Rd ECC S11 ... 170
  HAN/WDH S13 ... 174
  HTFD DN7 ... 41
  NROS/TKH DN11 ... 118
Junction St BSLY S70 ... 3
  WMB/DAR S73 ... 84 C6
June Rd HAN/WDH S13 ... 190
Juniper Ri ECK/KIL S21 ... 205

K

Kashmir Gdns *DARN/MH* S9 .... 172 D2 🖸
Catherine Rd *MALT* S66 .... 157 K8
Catherine Gv *DEARNE* S63 .... 86 E1
Cay Crs *RAW* S62 .... 111 F7
Kaye Pl *FUL* S10 .... 8 A2
Kay's Ter *BSLY* S70 .... 57 F8
Cay St *HOY* S74 .... 108 C2
Kea Park Cl *MALT* S66 .... 158 B2
Kearsley La *CONI* DN12 .... 114 C7
Kearsley Rd *SHEFP/MNR* S2 .... 9 D6
Keats Crs *WRKN* S81 .... 211 F3
Keats Gv *STKB/PEN* S36 .... 78 A3
Keats Rd *DONS/BSCR* DN4 .... 116 E1 🖸
ST/HB/BR S6 .... 151 J1
Keble Martin Wy *DEARNE* S63 .... 111 G1
Kedleston Rd *WRKN* S81 .... 210 D1
Keenan Av *HEM/SK/SE* WF9 .... 34 D6
Keeper La *HOR/CROF* WF4 .... 29 J1
Keepers Cl *NROS/TKH* DN11 .... 119 C5
Keeton Hall Rd *AU/AST/KP* S26 .... 193 F4
Keeton's Hl *SHEFP/MNR* S2 .... 8 C5 🖸
Keir Pl *RAW* S62 .... 134 A1
Keir St *BSLY* S70 .... 2 A1
Keir Ter *BSLY* S70 .... 2 A3 🖸
Kelgate *MOS* S20 .... 204 B1
Kelham Island *OWL* S3 .... 9 D1
Kelham St *DON* DN1 .... 4 C5
Kelly St *DEARNE* S63 .... 86 D1
Kelsey Gdns *DONS/BSCR* DN4 .... 118 D2
Kelsey Ter *BSLY* S70 .... 2 C6 🖸
Kelso Dr *DONS/BSCR* DN4 .... 90 A8
Kelvin Gv *WMB/DAR* S73 .... 84 B5
Kelvin St *MEX/SWTN* S64 .... 113 F2
RHAM/THRY S65 .... 134 C6
Kemp Cl *ECK/KIL* S21 .... 205 G1 🖸
Kemps Wy *HOLM/MEL* HD7 .... 48 D5
Kempton Dr *HTFD* DN7 .... 67 K3
Kempton Gdns *MEX/SWTN* S64 .... 113 H1
Kempton Park Rd *BTLY* DN5 .... 90 A2
Kempwell Dr *RAW* S62 .... 111 J7
Kenbourne Gv *ABRD* S7 .... 170 E8 🖸
Kenbourne Rd *ABRD* S7 .... 170 E8
Kendal Av *DIN* S25 .... 194 A1
Kendal Cl *BTLY* DN5 .... 89 H6 🖸
WRKN S81 .... 196 C7
Kendal Crs *BSLY* S70 .... 82 B3 🖸
CONI DN12 .... 114 E5
Kendal Dr *DEARNE* S63 .... 86 B6
DRON S18 .... 200 E6
Kendal Green Rd *BSLY* S70 .... 81 K3
Kendal Gv *BSLYN/ROY* S71 .... 57 H7
Kendal Rd *BTLY* DN5 .... 64 D8
ST/HB/BR S6 .... 151 J2
Kendal V *BSLY* S70 .... 82 B3
Kendon Gdns *THNE* DN8 .... 23 K7
Kendray St *BSLY* S70 .... 2 C4
Kenilworth Cl *BTLY* DN5 .... 90 A1 🖸
WRKN S80 .... 210 E6
Kenilworth Dr *WRKN* S81 .... 196 D1
Kenilworth Pl *ECC* S11 .... 170 C7 🖸
Kenilworth Rd *DONS/BSCR* DN4 .... 90 B8
Kenley Cl *WRKN* S81 .... 196 B1
Kenmare Crs *WHHL* DN2 .... 91 K3
Kennedy Cl *STKB/PEN* S36 .... 76 E4
Kennedy Dr *DEARNE* S63 .... 86 C4
Kennedy Rd *SHEFS* S8 .... 186 C5
Kenneth Av *HTFD* DN7 .... 41 K3
HTFD DN7 .... 68 A3
Kenneth St *RHAM/THRY* S65 .... 7 D5 🖸
Kenning Hall Cl
  SHEFP/MNR S2 .... 171 K8 🖸
Kenninghall Dr *SHEFP/MNR* S2 .... 171 K8
Kenninghall Mt
  SHEFP/MNR S2 .... 171 K8 🖸
Kenninghall Pl *SHEFP/MNR* S2 .... 171 K8
Kenninghall Rd *SHEFP/MNR* S2 .... 171 K8
Kennington Av *AWLS/ASK* DN6 .... 63 C2
Kennington Gv *CONI* DN12 .... 115 K4
Kenrock Cl *BTLY* DN5 .... 65 H6
Kensington Av *STKB/PEN* S36 .... 77 H3
Kensington Rd *DOD/DAR* S75 .... 2 A2
Kent Av *RAW* S62 .... 111 H8
Kent Cl *BSLYN/ROY* S71 .... 30 D3 🖸
WRKN S81 .... 210 D1
Kent House Cl *HAN/WDH* S13 .... 189 G7
Kentmere Cl *DRON* S18 .... 200 E6 🖸
Kent Rd *DONS/BSCR* DN4 .... 116 E1
KIMB S61 .... 132 B6 🖸
SHEFS S8 .... 187 H1
Kents Gdns *THNE* DN8 .... 24 A4
Kenwell Dr *TOT/DORE* S17 .... 200 E6 🖸
Kenwood Av *ABRD* S7 .... 170 E8 🖸
Kenwood Bank *ECC* S11 .... 8 A6
Kenwood Cl *BSLY* S70 .... 56 E7 🖸
Kenwood Park Rd *ABRD* S7 .... 8 B6
Kenwood Ri *MALT* S66 .... 157 H1 🖸
Kenwood Rd *ABRD* S7 .... 170 D8
ECC S11 .... 8 B6
Kenworthy Rd *BSLY* S70 .... 2 C6 🖾
STKB/PEN S36 .... 104 E1 🖸
Kenyon St *HEM/SK/SE* WF9 .... 35 F4
OWL S3 .... 8 C2
Keppel Dr *KIMB* S61 .... 131 J5
Keppel Pl *SHEFN* S5 .... 153 G1

Keppel Rd *KIMB* S61 .... 131 J5
SHEFN S5 .... 153 G1
Keppel View Rd *KIMB* S61 .... 132 A7
Kepple Cl *NROS/TKH* DN11 .... 118 E8
Keresforth Cl *BSLY* S70 .... 55 H7
Keresforth Hall Rd *BSLY* S70 .... 55 H7
Keresforth Ct *BSLY* S70 .... 55 H7
Keresforth Hall Rd *BSLY* S70 .... 2 A6
Keresforth Hill Rd *BSLY* S70 .... 55 H8 🖸
Keresforth Rd *DOD/DAR* S75 .... 80 E1
Kerwin Cl *TOT/DORE* S17 .... 185 G7
Kerwin Dr *TOT/DORE* S17 .... 185 G7
Kerwin Rd *TOT/DORE* S17 .... 185 G7
Kestrel Av *KIMB* S61 .... 131 H2
Kestrel Cl *ECK/KIL* S21 .... 191 F8 🖸
Kestrel Dr *AWLS/ASK* DN6 .... 63 J1
  ECK/KIL S21 .... 203 K4
Kestrel Gn *SHEFP/MNR* S2 .... 172 A5 🖸
Kestrel Ms *WRKN* S81 .... 196 B8
Kestrel Ri *BSLY* S70 .... 82 A7 🖸
Keswick Cl *BTLY* DN5 .... 64 D7
Keswick Cl *ST/HB/BR* S6 .... 150 D7
Keswick Crs *RHAM* S60 .... 154 E8
Keswick Pl *DRON* S18 .... 200 D6
Keswick Rd *DOD/DAR* S75 .... 29 F5
  WRKN S81 .... 196 C7
Keswick Wk *BSLYN/ROY* S71 .... 57 J7
Kettle *DIN* S25 .... 194 B1 🖸
Kettlebridge Rd *DARN/MH* S9 .... 172 C4
Ketton Av *SHEFS* S8 .... 187 G4
Ketton Wk *DOD/DAR* S75 .... 55 H4 🖸
Kevin Gv *MALT* S66 .... 158 C3
Kew Crs *HACK/IN* S12 .... 188 B5
Kexbrough Dr *DOD/DAR* S75 .... 28 B7
Key Av *HOY* S74 .... 109 F1
Keyes Ri *BWTY* DN10 .... 165 C7
Keyworth Pl *HAN/WDH* S13 .... 189 J1
Keyworth Rd *ST/HB/BR* S6 .... 151 H6 🖸
Khartoum Rd *ECC* S11 .... 8 A6
Kilbroyd Dr *DOD/DAR* S75 .... 28 B6
Kid La *WRKN* S81 .... 179 J2
Kieran Cl *DIN* S25 .... 177 J5
Kier Hardie Av
  NROS/TKH DN11 .... 119 F7 🖸
Kilburn Rd *DRON* S18 .... 200 C6
Kildale Gdns *MOS* S20 .... 190 B8 🖸
Kildonan Gv *HACK/IN* S12 .... 188 E4
Kilham La *ARMTH* DN3 .... 94 A6
Killamarsh La *ECK/KIL* S21 .... 206 A1
Kiln Bent Rd *HOLM/MEL* HD7 .... 72 D1
Kilner Wy *SHEFN* S5 .... 153 H5
Kilnhouse Bank La
  HOLM/MEL HD7 .... 46 E6
Kilnhurst Rd *CONI* DN12 .... 112 E8
  RAW S62 .... 133 K1
  RHAM/THRY S65 .... 113 F8
Kiln La *KBTN* HD8 .... 26 C2
Kiln Rd *KIMB* S61 .... 132 C7
Kilton Cl *WRKN* S81 .... 210 E3
Kilton Crs *WRKN* S81 .... 210 E3
Kilton Gld *WRKN* S81 .... 211 F3
Kilton Hl *OWL* S3 .... 171 H1 🖸
  WRKN S81 .... 210 E2
  WRKS S80 .... 210 E4
Kilton Rd *WRKN* S81 .... 210 E4
Kilton Ter *WRKS* S80 .... 210 E4
Kilvington Av *HAN/WDH* S13 .... 172 D8 🖸
Kilvington Crs *HAN/WDH* S13 .... 172 D8
Kilvington Rd *HAN/WDH* S13 .... 172 D8
Kimberley St *DARN/MH* S9 .... 172 B1
Kimberworth Park Rd
  KIMB S61 .... 132 C2 🖸
Kimberworth Rd *KIMB* S61 .... 132 C8
Kinder Gdns *SHEFN* S5 .... 152 C2
Kine Moor La *STKB/PEN* S36 .... 79 G1
King Av *MALT* S66 .... 159 J3
  NROS/TKH DN11 .... 118 D6
King Ecgbert Rd *TOT/DORE* S17 .... 199 J2
King Edward Crs *THNE* DN8 .... 23 K6 🖸
King Edward Rd *DONS/BSCR* DN4 .... 4 B8
  THNE DN8 .... 23 J7
King Edwards Rd
  NROS/TKH DN11 .... 139 J3
King Edward St *BSLYN/ROY* S71 .... 56 E1
  HEM/SK/SE WF9 .... 33 H1 🖸
Kingfield Rd *ECC* S11 .... 170 D8
Kingfisher Cl *WHHL* DN2 .... 66 A8 🖸
Kingfisher Dr *NROS/TKH* DN11 .... 119 F6
Kingfisher Ri *KIMB* S61 .... 131 H1 🖸
Kingfisher Rd *AWLS/ASK* DN6 .... 63 J1
Kingfisher Wk *WRKN* S81 .... 196 A8
  WRKN S81 .... 210 A1
King Georges Cl
  NROS/TKH DN11 .... 118 C7 🖸
King Georges Ct *HTFD* DN7 .... 41 K5
King George Sq *ARMTH* DN3 .... 66 E3
King George's Rd
  NROS/TKH DN11 .... 118 C6
King James St *ST/HB/BR* S6 .... 170 D1
King's Cl *HTFD* DN7 .... 42 C7
Kings Coppice *TOT/DORE* S17 .... 199 H1
Kings Ct *BSLY* S70 .... 82 D3
Kings Court Rd *THNE* DN8 .... 23 K6 🖸
King's Crs *CONI* DN12 .... 115 J4
Kings Cft *HEM/SK/SE* WF9 .... 34 A5
Kingscroft Cl *TOT/DORE* S17 .... 185 J7
Kingsdale *WRKN* S81 .... 197 F7
Kingsforth La *MALT* S66 .... 157 K7
Kingsforth Rd *MALT* S66 .... 157 K8
Kingsley Av *BTLY* DN5 .... 90 C3

Kingsley Cl *BSLYN/ROY* S71 .... 56 B1 🖸
Kingsley Crs *ARMTH* DN3 .... 93 G1
Kingsley Park Av *ABRD* S7 .... 186 B5
Kingsley Park Gv *ECC* S11 .... 186 B5
Kingsley Rd *AWLS/ASK* DN6 .... 63 H2
Kingsmead Dr *ARMTH* DN3 .... 93 J7
Kings Ms *ECC/KIL* S21 .... 204 C4
King's Rd *AWLS/ASK* DN6 .... 18 E7
  CUD/GR S72 .... 31 K6
  DON DN1 .... 5 E2
  MEX/SWTN S64 .... 113 G2
  WMB/DAR S73 .... 84 A5 🖸
King's St *CUD/GR* S72 .... 58 D1
King's Ter *AWLS/ASK* DN6 .... 18 E7
Kingston Cl *ARMTH* DN3 .... 93 K6 🖸
  WRKS S80 .... 211 G7
Kingstone Pl *BSLY* S70 .... 2 A6 🖸
Kingston Rd *WHHL* DN2 .... 92 A3
  WRKN S81 .... 196 C1
  WRKS S80 .... 211 F7
Kingston St *ATT* S4 .... 152 D8
King St *AU/AST/KP* S26 .... 175 G7
  BSLY S70 .... 2 C5
  CHPT/GREN S35 .... 130 B1
  DEARNE S63 .... 60 D8
  DEARNE S63 .... 86 D2
  DON DN1 .... 5 D3 🖸
  HOY S74 .... 109 G1
  MEX/SWTN S64 .... 112 C4 🖸
  SHEF S1 .... 9 E2
  THNE DN8 .... 23 J8
  WRKS S80 .... 210 C4
Kings Wy *RHAM* S60 .... 155 K5
Kingsway *DEARNE* S63 .... 60 B7
  DOD/DAR S75 .... 28 E6
  HTFD DN7 .... 41 K4
  WMB/DAR S73 .... 84 A5
  WRKN S81 .... 210 E3
Kingsway Cl *NROS/TKH* DN11 .... 119 F8 🖸
Kingsway Gv *DEARNE* S63 .... 60 B7 🖸
Kingswood Av *DIN* S25 .... 178 A3
  MOS S20 .... 189 J5
Kingswood Cl *MOS* S20 .... 189 J5 🖸
  WRKN S81 .... 179 J1
Kingswood Crs *HOY* S74 .... 83 F8
Kingswood Cft *MOS* S20 .... 189 J5 🖸
Kingswood Gv *MOS* S20 .... 189 J5
King's Wood La *DIN* S25 .... 178 E1
Kingwell Crs *BSLY* S70 .... 82 A1 🖸
Kingwell Cft *BSLY* S70 .... 82 B2 🖸
Kingwell Ms *BSLY* S70 .... 82 B2 🖸
Kingwell Rd *BSLY* S70 .... 82 B7
Kinharvie Rd *SHEFN* S5 .... 152 A4
Kinnaird Av *SHEFN* S5 .... 152 D2 🖸
Kinnaird Pl *SHEFN* S5 .... 152 D2
Kinnaird Rd *SHEFN* S5 .... 152 D2
Kinsbourne Gn *HTFD* DN7 .... 42 B8
Kinsey Rd *CHPT/GREN* S35 .... 107 H8
Kipling Av *DONS/BSCR* DN4 .... 116 C1
Kipling Cl *DRON* S18 .... 201 J8
  WRKN S81 .... 211 F2
Kipling Rd *ARMTH* DN3 .... 80 E7 🖸
Kirby La *KIMB* S61 .... 108 E8
Kirby St *MEX/SWTN* S64 .... 113 F2
Kirk Balk *HOY* S74 .... 108 E1
Kirkbridge Wy *HEM/SK/SE* WF9 .... 34 E3 🖸
Kirkby Rd *HACK/IN* S12 .... 188 C3 🖸
  HACK/IN S12 .... 188 C3 🖸
Kirkby Cl *HEM/SK/SE* WF9 .... 34 B4
Kirkby Dr *HACK/IN* S12 .... 188 C3
Kirkbygate *HEM/SK/SE* WF9 .... 33 H2
Kirkby Rd *HACK/IN* S12 .... 188 C3
  HEM/SK/SE WF9 .... 33 H1
Kirkby Vw *HACK/IN* S12 .... 188 C4
Kirkcroft Av *ECK/KIL* S21 .... 191 H8
  KIMB S61 .... 131 H2
Kirkcroft Cl *KIMB* S61 .... 131 G2 🖸
Kirkcroft Dr *ECK/KIL* S21 .... 205 H1
Kirkcroft La *ECK/KIL* S21 .... 205 H1
Kirk Cross Crs *BSLYN/ROY* S71 .... 30 D5
Kirkdale Crs *HAN/WDH* S13 .... 173 K6
Kirkdale Dr *HAN/WDH* S13 .... 173 K6
Kirk Edge Av *CHPT/GREN* S35 .... 150 C3
Kirk Edge Dr *CHPT/GREN* S35 .... 150 B3
Kirk Edge Rd *ST/HB/BR* S6 .... 149 F1
Kirkfield Cl *DOD/DAR* S75 .... 53 J3
Kirkfield Wy *BSLYN/ROY* S71 .... 30 D5
Kirkgate La *CUD/GR* S72 .... 31 K1
Kirkham Cl *BSLYN/ROY* S71 .... 3 F2
Kirkham Pl *BSLYN/ROY* S71 .... 30 E8 🖸
Kirkhouse Green Rd *HTFD* DN7 .... 21 F7
Kirklands Dr *RAW* S62 .... 133 H1
Kirk La *GLE* DN14 .... 21 J1
Kirklees Wy *HOLM/MEL* HD7 .... 48 E4
Kirkpatrick Dr *WRKN* S81 .... 195 K8
Kirkstall Cl *BTLY* DN5 .... 90 A2
  DIN S25 .... 193 K4 🖸
  RHAM S60 .... 154 D6
Kirkstall Rd *BSLYN/ROY* S71 .... 29 K8
  ECC S11 .... 170 C7
Kirkstead Abbey Ms *HAN* S11 .... 131 H4
Kirkstead Gdns *HAN/WDH* S13 .... 174 C8
Kirkstead Rd *KIMB* S61 .... 131 H8
Kirkstone Cl *BTLY* DN5 .... 64 D7
Kirkstone Rd *ST/HB/BR* S6 .... 151 H4
Kirk St *ATT* S4 .... 171 J1
  DONS/BSCR DN4 .... 4 B4
Kirk Wy *BSLYN/ROY* S71 .... 56 E4

Kirton La HTFD DN7 .... 42 C3
Kirton Rd ATT S4 .... 152 D8
Kitchin Rd WMB/DAR S73 .... 83 J4
Kitson Dr BSLYN/ROY S71 .... 56 E4
Kiveton Gdns AU/AST/KP S26 .... 193 F4
Kiveton La AU/AST/KP S26 .... 193 G5
Knabbs La STKB/PEN S36 .... 79 K3
Knab Cl ECC S11 .... 186 C2
Knab Cft ECC S11 .... 186 C2
Knab Ri ECC S11 .... 186 C2
Knab Rd ECC S11 .... 186 C2
Knapton Av RAW S62 .... 133 H1
Knaresboro Rd ABRD S7 .... 186 C4
Knaresborough Cl AU/AST/KP S26 .... 175 G8
Knaresborough Rd CONI DN12 .... 114 A6
Knaton Rd WRKN S81 .... 180 C8
Knavesmire Gdns DONS/BSCR DN4 .... 92 C5
Knightscroft Pde HEM/SK/SE WF9 .... 35 F5
Knollbeck Av WMB/DAR S73 .... 84 D7
Knoll Beck Cl DEARNE S63 .... 86 B3
Knoll Beck Crs WMB/DAR S73 .... 84 D7
Knollbeck La WMB/DAR S73 .... 84 D7
Knoll Cl STKB/PEN S36 .... 105 F6
The Knoll DRON S18 .... 201 K4
Knott End WRKN S81 .... 180 C4
Knowle Cl ST/HB/BR S6 .... 169 G1
Knowle Cft ECC S11 .... 186 A2
Knowle La ECC S11 .... 185 K2
Knowle Rd BSLY S70 .... 82 C1
SHEFS S5 .... 152 C1
Knowles Av STKB/PEN S36 .... 105 G7
Knowles St STKB/PEN S36 .... 78 C5
Knowle Top MOS S20 .... 190 C8
Knowl Rd HOLM/MEL HD7 .... 46 A3
Knowsley St BSLY S70 .... 2 A4
Knutton Crs SHEFN S5 .... 151 K1
Knutton Ri SHEFN S5 .... 129 K8
Knutton St SHEFN S5 .... 151 K1
Knutton Rd SHEFN S5 .... 151 K1
Kye La AU/AST/KP S26 .... 206 E1
Kyle Cl SHEFS S5 .... 151 K3
Kyle Crs SHEFN S5 .... 151 K3
Kynance Crs RHAM S60 .... 154 E8

L

Laburnam BSLY S70 .... 82 C3
Laburnum Av MALT S66 .... 157 G1
THNE DN8 .... 23 K5
Laburnum Cl CHPT/GREN S35 .... 130 E3
DIN S25 .... 193 K3
WRKS S80 .... 210 B6
Laburnum Dr ARMTH DN3 .... 67 H8
Laburnum Gv CONI DN12 .... 114 B6
ECK/KIL S21 .... 205 G2
EPW DN9 .... 120 C3
STKB/PEN S36 .... 104 E7
Laburnum Pde MALT S66 .... 158 E2
Laburnum Pl BTLY DN5 .... 64 E5
MALT S66 .... 158 E2
MEX/SWTN S64 .... 112 E1
WRKN S81 .... 180 D3
Laburnum Rd DONS/BSCR DN4 .... 116 C3
MALT S66 .... 158 E2
MEX/SWTN S64 .... 112 E1
WRKN S81 .... 180 D3
Laceby Cl RHAM/THRY S65 .... 135 J8
Laceby Ct BSLY S70 .... 55 H8
Ladies Spring Gv TOT/DORE S17 .... 186 A8
Ladock Cl BSLYN/ROY S71 .... 33 J2
Ladybank Av MOS S20 .... 204 B1
Ladybank Vw ECK/KIL S21 .... 204 B3
Ladycroft DEARNE S63 .... 86 B5
Lady Cft DEARNE S63 .... 111 H1
Lady Croft La WMB/DAR S73 .... 83 K8
Ladycroft Rd ARMTH DN3 .... 93 C3
Lady Field Rd AU/AST/KP S26 .... 193 J6
Lady Gap La AWLS/ASK DN6 .... 37 K2
Lady Ida's Dr ECK/KIL S21 .... 203 J3
MOS S20 .... 204 A2
Ladylea Cl WRKS S80 .... 209 K5
Lady Mary Vw BTLY DN5 .... 64 A5
Lady Oak Rd RHAM/THRY S65 .... 134 B6
Ladyroyd Cft CUD/GR S72 .... 57 J1
Lady's Br OWL S3 .... 9 E2
Ladysmith Av ABRD S7 .... 186 D1
Lady Wk WRKN S81 .... 196 A8
Lady Wharncliffe's Rd CHPT/GREN S35 .... 128 C2
Ladywood Rd CUD/GR S72 .... 58 E1
Laird Av ST/HB/BR S6 .... 151 F6
Laird Dr ST/HB/BR S6 .... 151 F6
Laird Rd ST/HB/BR S6 .... 151 F6
Laithe Av HOLM/MEL HD7 .... 47 F5
Laithe Bank Dr HOLM/MEL HD7 .... 47 F5
Laithe Cft DOD/DAR S75 .... 54 E8
Laithes Cl BSLYN/ROY S71 .... 30 C8
Laithes Crs BSLYN/ROY S71 .... 30 A8
Laithes La BSLYN/ROY S71 .... 30 B8
Lake Cl CONI DN12 .... 115 H6
Lakeen Rd WHHL DN2 .... 31 K5
Lakeland Cl CUD/GR S72 .... 57 K2
Lakeland Dr DIN S25 .... 194 A1
Lake Rd AWLS/ASK DN6 .... 63 K4
Lakeside Bvd DONS/BSCR DN4 .... 91 K8
Lambcote Wy MALT S66 .... 159 J1

Lambcroft Vw HAN/WDH S13 .... 190 A1
Lamb Dr SHEFN S5 .... 151 J4
Lambecroft BSLYN/ROY S71 .... 30 D6
Lambe Flatt DOD/DAR S75 .... 28 B7
Lambert Fold DOD/DAR S75 .... 55 F8
Lambert Rd BSLY S70 .... 3 F6
Lamberts La RHAM/THRY S65 .... 134 D4
Lambert St OWL S3 .... 9 D2
Lambert Wk BSLY S70 .... 3 F5
Lambeth Rd DONS/BSCR DN4 .... 90 E8
Lamb Hl ST/HB/BR S6 .... 148 E3
Lamb Hill Cl HAN/WDH S13 .... 175 F8
Lamb La BSLYN/ROY S71 .... 56 D2
DIN S25 .... 178 E4
Lambra Rd BSLY S70 .... 2 C4
Lambrell Av AU/AST/KP S26 .... 192 C5
Lambrell Gn AU/AST/KP S26 .... 192 C5
Lamb Rd SHEFN S5 .... 151 J4
Lamma Well Rd HOLM/MEL HD7 .... 87 H8
Lanark Dr MEX/SWTN S64 .... 87 H8
Lanark Gdns WHHL DN2 .... 92 B2
Lancaster Av ARMTH DN3 .... 66 E3
WHHL DN2 .... 92 B3
Lancaster Cl NROS/TKH DN11 .... 140 A8
Lancaster Crs NROS/TKH DN11 .... 140 A8
Lancaster Dr BWTY DN10 .... 142 A7
HTFD DN7 .... 69 H7
Lancaster Ga BSLY S70 .... 2 B3
Lancaster Rd STKB/PEN S36 .... 104 E6
Lancaster St BSLY S70 .... 60 D6
DEARNE S63 .... 60 D6
OWL S3 .... 8 C1
Lancaster Wk WRKN S81 .... 196 C7
Lancastrian Wy WRKN S81 .... 210 E1
Lancing Rd SHEFP/MNR S2 .... 9 E6
Land Ends Rd THNE DN8 .... 23 C5
Landsdown Av HEM/SK/SE WF9 .... 33 K6
Landseer Cl DRON S18 .... 200 E7
SHEFS S8 .... 187 K5
Landseer Ct MALT S66 .... 157 G1
Landseer Dr SHEFS S8 .... 187 K5
Landseer Pl GLV S14 .... 188 A5
Lane End CHPT/GREN S35 .... 108 A8
Lane End Rd RHAM S60 .... 155 K4
Laneham Cl DONS/BSCR DN4 .... 118 C1
Lane Head Cl RAW S62 .... 133 K1
Lane Head Ri DOD/DAR S75 .... 29 F5
Lane Head Rd DOD/DAR S75 .... 53 G4
ST/HB/BR S6 .... 147 H3
TOT/DORE S17 .... 199 G3
Laneside Cl DONS/BSCR DN4 .... 4 A5
The Lanes RHAM/THRY S65 .... 134 A8
The Lane ECK/KIL S21 .... 205 H6
Lang Av BSLYN/ROY S71 .... 57 F5
Langcliffe Cl DOD/DAR S75 .... 29 F5
Lang Crs BSLYN/ROY S71 .... 57 F5
Langdale Cl NROS/TKH DN11 .... 140 A7
Langdale Dr BTLY DN5 .... 64 C7
DRON S18 .... 201 J4
NROS/TKH DN11 .... 140 A7
Langdale Rd AWLS/ASK DN6 .... 37 J6
BSLYN/ROY S71 .... 57 F5
DOD/DAR S75 .... 54 D2
SHEFS S8 .... 186 E2
WRKN S81 .... 196 D8
Langdale Wy DIN S25 .... 178 B8
Langdon Dr KIMB S61 .... 132 B7
Langdon St ECC S11 .... 8 C6
Langer St DONS/BSCR DN4 .... 4 A5
Langford Cl DOD/DAR S75 .... 55 F8
Langhdale Cl RHAM/THRY S65 .... 135 F8
Langley La KBTN HD8 .... 26 B5
Langleys Rd AWLS/ASK DN6 .... 18 A6
Langley St WRKS S80 .... 210 D3
Langsett Av ST/HB/BR S6 .... 151 F5
Langsett Crs ST/HB/BR S6 .... 151 J8
Langsett Gv ST/HB/BR S6 .... 170 D1
Langsett Ri ST/HB/BR S6 .... 170 D1
Langsett Rd BSLYN/ROY S71 .... 29 K8
ST/HB/BR S6 .... 151 H7
Langsett Rd North CHPT/GREN S35 .... 128 B7
Langsett Rd South CHPT/GREN S35 .... 150 D1
Langthwaite La BTLY DN5 .... 64 A5
HEM/SK/SE WF9 .... 34 D5
Langthwaite Rd BTLY DN5 .... 64 D5
HEM/SK/SE WF9 .... 34 D5
Langton Gdns ARMTH DN3 .... 93 K7
Lansbury Av CHPT/GREN S35 .... 130 A2
MALT S66 .... 159 J4
NROS/TKH DN11 .... 119 F6
Lansbury Pl RAW S62 .... 134 B1
Lansbury Rd ECK/KIL S21 .... 204 B4
Lansdowne Cl DEARNE S63 .... 60 B8
Lansdowne Crs DOD/DAR S75 .... 28 C8
MEX/SWTN S64 .... 112 C5
Lansdowne Rd WHHL DN2 .... 92 B2
Lanyon Wy BSLYN/ROY S71 .... 3 E2
Lapwater Rd KIMB S61 .... 132 C4
Lapwing V KIMB S61 .... 131 H1
Larch Av ECK/KIL S21 .... 205 G2
EPW DN9 .... 120 A4
MALT S66 .... 157 H2
Larch Cl WMB/DAR S73 .... 84 D2
The Larches MEX/SWTN S64 .... 112 B5
Larchfield Pl BSLYN/ROY S71 .... 56 A8
Larchfield Rd DONS/BSCR DN4 .... 90 C8

Larch Gv CHPT/GREN S35 .... 130 B
CONI DN12 .... 114 B
Larch Hl DARN/MH S9 .... 173 C
Larch Pl BSLY S70 .... 82 D
Larch Rd ECK/KIL S21 .... 203 K
MALT S66 .... 158 E
Larkhill Cl RAW S62 .... 133 K
Lark Spinney WRKN S81 .... 210 A1
Larkspur Cl ARMTH DN3 .... 66 E
MEX/SWTN S64 .... 112 B
Lark St ST/HB/BR S6 .... 170 B
Larwood WRKN S81 .... 211 F1
Larwood Gv CONI DN12 .... 115 K4
Latham Sq ECC S11 .... 185 J
Lathe Rd RHAM S60 .... 156 B
Lathkill Cl HAN/WDH S13 .... 172 E
Lathkill Rd HAN/WDH S13 .... 172 E
Latimer Cl AU/AST/KP S26 .... 193 F
Latin Gdns BTLY DN5 .... 63 K
Lauder Rd BTLY DN5 .... 90 D
Lauder St ATT S4 .... 152 E
Laudsdale Cl RHAM/THRY S65 .... 134 C8
Laudsdale Rd RHAM/THRY S65 .... 134 B
Laughton Common Rd MALT S66 .... 177 C
Laughton Rd DARN/MH S9 .... 153 J5
DIN S25 .... 178 D7
DONS/BSCR DN4 .... 4 E
MALT S66 .... 177 F
Launce Rd SHEFN S5 .... 152 A
Laurel Av BSLY S70 .... 56 E
BTLY DN5 .... 90 E
MALT S66 .... 157 J
THNE DN8 .... 23 K
Laurel Cl DIN S25 .... 193 K
ECK/KIL S21 .... 204 A
Laurel Dr ECK/KIL S21 .... 205 C
Laurel Rd ARMTH DN3 .... 67 C
Laurel Sq EPW DN9 .... 120 C
Laurel Ter AWLS/ASK DN6 .... 37 F
DONS/BSCR DN4 .... 90 D8
Laurold Av HTFD DN7 .... 69 H
Lavender Cl CONI DN12 .... 114 E
Lavenham Pl AWLS/ASK DN6 .... 37 F
Laverack St HAN/WDH S13 .... 173 H
Laverdene Av TOT/DORE S17 .... 199 H
Laverdene Cl TOT/DORE S17 .... 199 J3
Laverdene Dr TOT/DORE S17 .... 199 K
Laverdene Rd TOT/DORE S17 .... 199 J
Laverdene Wy TOT/DORE S17 .... 199 K3
Laverock Wy SHEFN S5 .... 152 E
Lavinia Rd CHPT/GREN S35 129
Law Common Rd HOLM/MEL HD7 .... 74 C
Lawn Av AWLS/ASK DN6 .... 63 C
DON DN1 .... 5 E3
Lawndale AWLS/ASK DN6 .... 37 C
Lawndale Fold DOD/DAR S75 .... 28 E7
Lawn Garth BTLY DN5 .... 64 C
Lawn La AWLS/ASK DN6 .... 20 E
Lawn Rd DON DN1 .... 5 F
WRKN S81 .... 180 C
The Lawns ECC S11 .... 186 E
The Lawn DRON S18 .... 201 H
Lawrence Cl DOD/DAR S75 .... 54 C
MALT S66 .... 157 C
Lawrence Dr MEX/SWTN S64 .... 112 E
Law Slack Rd HOLM/MEL HD7 .... 74 C
Lawson Rd FUL S10 .... 170 E
Lawton La RHAM S60 .... 155 I
Laxey Rd ST/HB/BR S6 .... 169 J2
Laxton Cl MALT S66 .... 158 E
Laxton Rd BSLYN/ROY S71 .... 30 A
Laycock Av AU/AST/KP S26 .... 175 C
Layden Dr BTLY DN5 .... 63 K
Leabrook Rd DRON S18 .... 200 C
Leach La MEX/SWTN S64 .... 113 F
Lea Ct WRKS S80 .... 210 A
Leadbeater Dr HACK/IN S12 .... 188 C2
Leadbeater Rd HACK/IN S12 .... 188 E
Leader Rd ST/HB/BR S6 .... 151 C
Lead Hl WRKS S80 .... 210 C
Leadley St DEARNE S63 .... 86 D2
Leadmill Rd SHEF S1 .... 9 E4
SHEFP/MNR S2 .... 9 E5
Leadmill St SHEF S1 .... 9 F
Leaf Cl MALT S66 .... 159 H
Leake Rd ST/HB/BR S6 .... 151 H5
Leak Hall Crs KBTN HD8 .... 51 C
Leak Hall La KBTN HD8 .... 51 C
Leamington Gdns WHHL DN2 .... 92 B2
WHHL DN2 .... 92 B2
Leamington St FUL S10 .... 170 C3
Leapings La STKB/PEN S36 .... 77 C
Lea Rd BSLYN/ROY S71 .... 30 B
DRON S18 .... 201 H
Lease Gate Rd RHAM S60 .... 156 B
Leas Gdns HOLM/MEL HD7 .... 48 C
The Leas BTLY DN5 .... 90 C
The Lea MEX/SWTN S64 .... 112 A
MOS S20 .... 190 B
Leaton Cl ST/HB/BR S6 .... 150 E
Leavygreave Rd OWL S3 .... 8 B3
Leawood Pl ST/HB/BR S6 .... 169 H1
Le Brun Sq WRKN S81 .... 196 C
Ledbury Gdns BTLY DN5 .... 90 C
Ledbury Rd BSLYN/ROY S71 .... 56 A
Ledger Cl AU/AST/KP S26 .... 192 E
Ledger Ct HOY S74 .... 109 J2
Ledsham Cl RHAM/THRY S65 .... 7 C
Ledsham Rd RHAM/THRY S65 .... 7 C
Ledstone Rd SHEFS S8 .... 186 C

ee Av STKB/PEN S36 .... 105 G6
ee Brook La RAW S62 .... 110 B5
ee Cft MALT S66 .... 159 K3
SHEF S1 .... 9 D2 🖫
eedham Cl SHEFN S5 .... 153 G3
eedham Rd RHAM/THRY S65 .... 156 B3
SHEFN S5 .... 153 G3
eeds Av DIN S25 .... 178 A8
eeds Rd DARN/MH S9 .... 172 C1
WRKN S81 .... 195 H8
ee La DOD/DAR S75 .... 25 K5
STKB/PEN S36 .... 76 A3
STKB/PEN S36 .... 126 A4
eeming Ct BWTY DN10 .... 164 A1
ee Moor La ST/HB/BR S6 .... 149 J7
ee Rd ST/HB/BR S6 .... 150 C6
ees Av STKB/PEN S36 .... 78 A4
ees Hall Av SHEFS S8 .... 187 H6
ees Hall Pl SHEFS S8 .... 187 H2
ees Hall Rd SHEFS S8 .... 187 H2
ees House Ct SHEFS S8 .... 187 G3 🖫
eger Wy DONS/BSCR DN4 .... 91 K4
WHHL DN2 .... 66 B8
egion Rd AU/AST/KP S26 .... 175 J8 🖫
eicester Av WHHL DN2 .... 91 K4
eicester Rd DIN S25 .... 178 C6
eigh St DARN/MH S9 .... 153 H8
eighton Cl BSLYN/ROY S71 .... 2 C2 🖫
eighton Dr GLV S14 .... 188 B4
eighton Pl GLV S14 .... 188 B4
eighton Rd GLV S14 .... 188 A2
eighton Vw SHEFP/MNR S2 .... 188 A2
einster Av WHHL DN2 .... 91 K2
emont Rd TOT/DORE S17 .... 199 J5
ennox Rd BSLYN/ROY S71 .... 151 G6
WHHL DN2 .... 92 A2
enny Balk AWLS/ASK DN6 .... 35 K8
enton St SHEFP/MNR S2 .... 9 E5 🖫
eonard Cl SHEFP/MNR S2 .... 172 C8
eopold Av DIN S25 .... 178 B7 🖫
eopold St BSLY S70 .... 2 A5 🖫
DIN S25 .... 178 B6
SHEF S1 .... 9 D5
eppings La ST/HB/BR S6 .... 151 H5
epton Gdns BSLY S70 .... 82 C1 🖫
escar La ECC S11 .... 170 C7
esley Rd DEARNE S63 .... 86 D2
eslie Av CONI DN12 .... 114 B5
eslie Rd MALT S66 .... 158 E3
ST/HB/BR S6 .... 151 F6
esmond Crs CUD/GR S72 .... 85 H1
estermoor Av AU/AST/KP S26 ... 192 C5 🖫
etard Dr RHAM S60 .... 155 F6
evels La EPW DN9 .... 95 G7
everick Dr RAW S62 .... 112 B8
everstock Gn HTFD DN7 .... 42 B8
everton Dr ECC S11 .... 8 C5
everton Gdns SHEFP/MNR S2 .... 8 C5 🖫
everton Wy RHAM/THRY S65 ... 134 D6 🖫
eveson St ATT S4 .... 171 K2
evet Rd DONS/BSCR DN4 .... 92 E6
ewdendale BSLY S70 .... 82 B3
ewes Rd CONI DN12 .... 114 C6
ewis Rd BSLYN/ROY S71 .... 57 F3
HAN/WDH S13 .... 172 E3
eybourne Cl KIMB S61 .... 132 B6
eyburn Cl DONS/BSCR DN4 .... 92 E8
eyburn Dr AU/AST/KP S26 .... 175 G7
eyburn Gv CHPT/GREN S35 .... 130 B1 🖫
eyburn Rd AWLS/ASK DN6 .... 37 G5
SHEFS S8 .... 187 F1
ey End BSLY S70 .... 82 A3
eyfield Ct ARMTH DN3 .... 93 H2
eyfield Vw TOT/DORE S17 .... 185 H8
eyland Av HTFD DN7 .... 42 D8
The Leylands DOD/DAR S75 .... 55 F3
eys Cl DONS/BSCR DN4 .... 116 C3
eys La AWLS/ASK DN6 .... 36 E6
DIN S25 .... 178 D6
The Leys HEM/SK/SE WF9 .... 33 K6
iberty Cl ST/HB/BR S6 .... 169 J2 🖫
iberty Dr ST/HB/BR S6 .... 169 J1
iberty Hl ST/HB/BR S6 .... 169 J2
iberty La CHPT/GREN S35 .... 106 C4
iberty Pl ST/HB/BR S6 .... 169 J1
iberty Ri ST/HB/BR S6 .... 169 J2
ibrary Cl KIMB S61 .... 132 D4
ichen Cl ARMTH DN3 .... 86 E6
ichfield Cl WRKN S81 .... 195 G8
ichfield Gdns CONI DN12 .... 115 H6
ichfield Rd HTFD DN7 .... 42 D7 🖫
WHHL DN2 .... 91 J1
ichfield Wy RHAM S60 .... 155 G6
ichford Rd SHEFP/MNR S2 .... 187 J1
idgate Crs HEM/SK/SE WF9 .... 34 C5
idgate La CUD/GR S72 .... 31 J4
idget Cl DONS/BSCR DN4 .... 92 D8
idget La DEARNE S63 .... 60 E8
MALT S66 .... 158 B7
MALT S66 .... 157 K1
idgett La DIN S25 .... 178 B7
DOD/DAR S75 .... 107 J2
idgett Wy BSLYN/ROY S71 .... 30 D3
iffey Av WHHL DN2 .... 91 K2
ifford Pl HOY S74 .... 109 J2
ifford Rd WHHL DN2 .... 5 F1
ifford St DARN/MH S9 .... 154 B4

Lightwood Rd ECK/KIL S21 .... 203 G5
Lilac Av STKB/PEN S36 .... 104 C7
Lilac Cl DIN S25 .... 193 K3 🖫
Lilac Crs CONI DN12 .... 115 J6
.... 83 F8
Lilac Gv BWTY DN10 .... 142 A8
CONI DN12 .... 114 B6
DONS/BSCR DN4 .... 92 E7
EPW DN9 .... 120 B3
MALT S66 .... 157 H2
MALT S66 .... 158 C2
WRKN S81 .... 180 C8
Lilac Rd ARMTH DN3 .... 67 M8
MOS S20 .... 190 D4
SHEFN S5 .... 153 F4
Liley La STKB/PEN S36 .... 76 D6
Lilian St South RHAM/THRY S65 .... 7 D5
Lillee Ct WRKN S81 .... 211 F2
Lilley St HEM/SK/SE WF9 .... 33 G1
Lilley Ter HEM/SK/SE WF9 .... 34 A5
Lilford Rd ARMTH DN3 .... 93 K7
Lilly Hall Cl MALT S66 .... 158 E1
Lilly Hall Rd MALT S66 .... 159 F2
Lilydene Av CUD/GR S72 .... 32 C8
Limb La TOT/DORE S17 .... 185 H7
Limbreck Ct BTLY DN5 .... 64 D6
Limbrick Cl ST/HB/BR S6 .... 151 G8
Limbrick Rd ST/HB/BR S6 .... 151 H8
Lime Av EPW DN9 .... 120 D3
WRKN S81 .... 179 J1
Lime Cl RHAM/THRY S65 .... 135 J5
Lime Ct BTLY DN5 .... 90 A6 🖫
Lime Crs HEM/SK/SE WF9 .... 34 D6
Limedale Vw ARMTH DN3 .... 67 F1 🖫
Lime Gv BSLYN/ROY S71 .... 30 D6
CHPT/GREN S35 .... 130 B3
HEM/SK/SE WF9 .... 34 D6
MALT S66 .... 159 J2
MEX/SWTN S64 .... 112 C6
Limegrove RHAM S60 .... 7 F6
Lime Gv STKB/PEN S36 .... 104 D7
NROS/TKH DN11 .... 138 D8
Limekiln La MALT S66 .... 138 D8
NROS/TKH DN11 .... 138 D5
Limekilns DIN S25 .... 193 K1
Limelands Rd DIN S25 .... 178 A7
Lime Rd ECK/KIL S21 .... 203 K6
Limes Av DOD/DAR S75 .... 29 H5
DOD/DAR S75 .... 55 G4
Limes Cl DOD/DAR S75 .... 29 H5
Limestone Cl WRKN S81 .... 194 B1
Limestone Cottage La
ST/HB/BR S6 .... 151 G3
Lime St MOS S20 .... 190 D5
ST/HB/BR S6 .... 170 C1
Limesway DOD/DAR S75 .... 55 G4
MALT S66 .... 159 G2
Lime Tree Av ARMTH DN3 .... 67 G8
Limetree Av AU/AST/KP S26 .... 192 C4
Lime Tree Av ECK/KIL S21 .... 205 G2
Limetree Av MALT S66 .... 177 F1
Lime Tree Av WRKN S81 .... 180 C8
Lime Tree Court Ct
HEM/SK/SE WF9 .... 33 F1 🖫
Lime Tree Gv BWTY DN10 .... 142 A8
NROS/TKH DN11 .... 119 F7
RAW S62 .... 134 A1
Limpool Cl DONS/BSCR DN4 .... 92 E8
Limpsfield Rd DARN/MH S9 .... 154 A5
Linaker Rd ST/HB/BR S6 .... 170 B2
Linburn Cl BSLYN/ROY S71 .... 30 B3 🖫
Linburn Rd SHEFS S8 .... 187 F5
Linby Rd BSLYN/ROY S71 .... 30 A7
Lincoln Crs HEM/SK/SE WF9 .... 35 F3
Lincoln Gdns DEARNE S63 .... 86 C2 🖫
Lincoln Rd HTFD DN7 .... 69 H8
WHHL DN2 .... 91 J1
Lincoln St DARN/MH S9 .... 153 J5 🖫
MALT S66 .... 159 H3
NROS/TKH DN11 .... 119 F1
RHAM S60 .... 6 C2
WRKS S80 .... 210 E6
Lincoln Vw WRKS S80 .... 210 E5
Lincroft Dr RAW S62 .... 133 J4
Lindale Cl DIN S25 .... 194 B2
Lindale Gdns DEARNE S63 .... 86 E3
The Lindales DOD/DAR S75 .... 55 H5 🖫
Linden Av DRON S18 .... 201 H4
MALT S66 .... 158 B7
SHEFS S8 .... 186 E5
Linden Cl HTFD DN7 .... 42 C7 🖫
Linden Ct CHPT/GREN S35 .... 130 C6
Linden Crs STKB/PEN S36 .... 104 C8
Linden Gv CONI DN12 .... 115 J6
MALT S66 .... 158 E2
Linden Rd CHPT/GREN S35 .... 130 C6
DEARNE S63 .... 110 E1
Linden Wk BTLY DN5 .... 64 D1
Lindholme Bank Rd HTFD DN7 .... 69 K5
Lindholme Dr NROS/TKH DN11 ...... 119 G6
Lindholme Gdns MOS S20 .... 190 A5 🖫
Lindhurst Rd BSLYN/ROY S71 .... 29 K7
Lindisfarne Rd DRON S18 .... 201 H7 🖫
Lindley Cl EPW DN9 .... 121 F4
Lindley Crs DEARNE S63 .... 60 C8
Lindley Rd EPW DN9 .... 121 F4
SHEFN S5 .... 152 E5 🖫
Lindley's Cft AU/AST/KP S26 .... 193 F2

Lindley St RHAM/THRY S65 .... 7 D3
Lindrick NROS/TKH DN11 .... 161 K1
Lindrick Av MEX/SWTN S64 .... 112 D5
Lindrick Cl CUD/GR S72 .... 31 K6
DONS/BSCR DN4 .... 118 B2
NROS/TKH DN11 .... 161 J1
WRKN S81 .... 180 D8
WRKN S81 .... 210 D2
Lindrick Dl WRKN S81 .... 194 E5
Lindrick Dr ARMTH DN3 .... 93 G2 🖫
Lindrick La NROS/TKH DN11 .... 161 J2
Lindrick Rd HTFD DN7 .... 69 G1
WRKN S81 .... 195 G4
Lindsay Av SHEFN S5 .... 152 C3
Lindsay Cl SHEFN S5 .... 152 C2
Lindsay Crs SHEFN S5 .... 152 C2
Lindsay Dr SHEFN S5 .... 152 C2
Lindsay Pl AU/AST/KP S26 .... 175 H8
Lindsay Rd SHEFN S5 .... 152 C2
Lindsey Cl DONS/BSCR DN4 .... 92 D8
Lindsey Rd NROS/TKH DN11 .... 163 F2
Lindum Dr MALT S66 .... 157 H3
Lindum St DONS/BSCR DN4 .... 4 B4
Lindwall Ct WRKN S81 .... 211 F2 🖫
Lingamore Leys DEARNE S63 .... 60 C6
Lingard St DOD/DAR S75 .... 2 A3 🖫
Lingard St DOD/DAR S75 .... 2 A2 🖫
Lingfield Cl MALT S66 .... 157 K5
Lingfield Dr BTLY DN5 .... 90 A2
Ling Field Rd AWLS/ASK DN6 .... 62 C4
BTLY DN5 .... 62 C4
Lingfoot Av SHEFS S8 .... 201 H1
Lingfoot Cl SHEFS S8 .... 201 H1 🖫
Lingfoot Crs SHEFS S8 .... 201 H1 🖫
Lingfoot Dr SHEFS S8 .... 201 J1 🖫
Lingfoot Pl SHEFS S8 .... 201 H1
Ling House La HTFD DN7 .... 41 G5
Lingmoor Cl DONS/BSCR DN4 .... 116 B3
Lingodell Cl DIN S25 .... 178 A3
Lings La HTFD DN7 .... 68 C2
MALT S66 .... 157 H3
PONT WF8 .... 16 B7
The Lings ARMTH DN3 .... 93 J2
MALT S66 .... 157 J3
Lingthwaite DOD/DAR S75 .... 55 F8 🖫
Link Rd RHAM/THRY S65 .... 135 F5
Links Rd DRON S18 .... 201 H7
Links Vw DOD/DAR S75 .... 29 G5
Linkswood Av WHHL DN2 .... 66 B8
The Link DOD/DAR S75 .... 81 F1
Linkway AWLS/ASK DN6 .... 18 A4 🖫
WHHL DN2 .... 92 A1
Linley La HACK/IN S12 .... 189 G2 🖫
Linnet Mt HACK/IN S12 .... 131 G2
The Linnets WRKN S81 .... 196 B8
Linscott Rd SHEFS S8 .... 186 E5
Linshaws Rd HOLM/MEL HD7 .... 73 J2
Linthwaite La HOY S74 .... 109 K2
RAW S62 .... 109 K4
Linton St HACK/IN S12 .... 55 G7
Liphill Bank Rd HOLM/MEL HD7 ...... 47 F2
Lipp Av ECK/KIL S21 .... 191 G8
Liquorice La WRKN S81 .... 196 E5
Liskeard Rd AWLS/ASK DN6 .... 63 H2 🖫
Lisle Rd RHAM/THRY S65 .... 7 F6
Lismore Rd SHEFS S8 .... 187 H2
Lister Av DONS/BSCR DN4 .... 4 B6
HACK/IN S12 .... 188 D3
RAW S62 .... 111 H8
Lister Cl HACK/IN S12 .... 188 D4 🖫
RAW S62 .... 91 K2
Lister Crs HACK/IN S12 .... 188 D4
Lister Dr HACK/IN S12 .... 188 D4
Lister La OWL S3 .... 8 C1 🖫
Lister Pl HACK/IN S12 .... 188 D4 🖫
Lister Rd ST/HB/BR S6 .... 170 C1
Lister St RHAM/THRY S65 .... 7 E4
Lister Wy HACK/IN S12 .... 188 D3
Little Cake HOLM/MEL HD7 .... 48 B5
Little Common La ECC S11 .... 185 K4
CLE DN14 .... 10 D5
KIMB S61 .... 132 A8
RHAM S60 .... 156 D6
Littledale Rd DARN/MH S9 .... 172 D5
Littlefield La WMB/DAR S73 .... 84 A4
Littlefield Rd DIN S25 .... 178 A6
Little Haynooking La MALT S66 ...... 159 G2
Little Hemsworth HEM/SK/SE WF9 .. 33 H1
Littlehey Cl MALT S66 .... 158 E1
Little La ATT S4 .... 153 G6 🖫
BTLY DN5 .... 89 H3
HACK/IN S12 .... 188 D1
HEM/SK/SE WF9 .... 34 E4
HOLM/MEL HD7 .... 47 J2 🖫
HOLM/MEL HD7 .... 48 B1
KIMB S61 .... 131 F1
WHHL DN2 .... 66 B6
WRKS S80 .... 208 D1
Little Leeds HOY S74 .... 109 K1
Little London Dr SHEFS S8 .... 187 F1 🖫
Little London Rd SHEFS S8 .... 186 E2
Little Matlock Gdns ST/HB/BR S6 .. 169 H1
Little Matlock Wy ST/HB/BR S6 .. 169 H1 🖫
Littlemoor ECK/KIL S21 .... 204 C3
Littlemoor Av AU/AST/KP S26 ...... 192 C5
Littlemoor La DONS/BSCR DN4 .... 4 B5
Littlemoor St DONS/BSCR DN4 ...... 4 B5 🖫
Little New Cl DOD/DAR S75 .... 55 C4 🖫
Little Norton Av SHEFS S8 .... 187 G8

Little Norton Dr SHEFS S8 .... 187 G7
Little Norton La SHEFS S8 .... 187 G7
Little Norton Wy SHEFS S8 .... 187 G8
Little Wood Dr GLV S14 .... 188 B4
Little Wood La AU/AST/KP S26 .... 208 A2
Little Wood Rd GLV S14 .... 188 C4 ⬛
Littlewood Rd THNE DN8 .... 23 K8
Littlewood St DONS/BSCR DN4 .... 4 B4 ⬛
Littlewood Wy MALT S66 .... 159 J1
Littleworth Cl NROS/TKH DN11 .... 119 G6 ⬛
Littleworth La BSLYN/ROY S71 .... 56 E4
NROS/TKH DN11 .... 119 G6 ⬛
Littondale WRKN S81 .... 196 E8 ⬛
Liverpool Av WHHL DN2 .... 91 J1
Liverpool St DARN/MH S9 .... 153 G6 ⬛
Livesey St ST/HB/BR S6 .... 151 J7
Livingstone Av WHHL DN2 .... 66 C6
Livingstone Crs BSLYN/ROY S71 .... 56 C2
Livingstone Rd CHPT/GREN S35 .... 129 K1
Livingston Rd DARN/MH S9 .... 172 A1 ⬛
Llewelyn Crs AWLS/ASK DN6 .... 18 B8
Lloyd St ATT S4 .... 152 E6
RAW S62 .... 133 J4
Load Field Rd ST/HB/BR S6 .... 126 C6
Loakfield Dr SHEFN S5 .... 130 A8
Lobelia Ct DIN S25 .... 193 K2
Lobelia Crs ARMTH DN3 .... 66 E4
Lobwood BSLY S70 .... 82 B2
Lobwood La BSLY S70 .... 82 C2 ⬛
Locarno Rd THNE DN8 .... 24 A4
Lock Cl GLE DN14 .... 11 J3
Lockeaflash Crs BSLY S70 .... 82 E1 ⬛
Locke Av BSLY S70 .... 82 A1 ⬛
Locke Rd DOD/DAR S75 .... 81 F1
Lockesley Av CONI S12 .... 114 B5
Locke St BSLY S70 .... 2 A6
Lockgate Rd GLE DN14 .... 10 D7
Lock Hl THNE DN8 .... 23 H8
Lock House Rd DARN/MH S9 .... 153 K6
Locking Dr ARMTH DN3 .... 93 H2
Lock La DARN/MH S9 .... 154 B4
THNE DN8 .... 23 H8
Locksley Av ARMTH DN3 .... 66 E5
Locksley Dr MALT S66 .... 176 D1
Lock St ST/HB/BR S6 .... 170 C1
Lockton Cl CHPT/GREN S35 .... 107 H7
Lockwood Av DIN S25 .... 193 K4
Lockwood Cl RHAM/THRY S65 .... 156 D1
THNE DN8 .... 24 A8
Lockwood La BSLY S70 .... 2 C6
Lockwood Rd DEARNE S63 .... 86 D1
DON DN1 .... 5 E1
RHAM/THRY S65 .... 134 B8
Lodge Dr RAW S62 .... 108 E6
Lodge Farm Cl DIN S25 .... 193 K1
Lodge Hill Dr AU/AST/KP S26 .... 192 B2
Lodore Rd WRKN S81 .... 196 D8
Logan Rd DARN/MH S9 .... 173 F3
Loicher La CHPT/GREN S35 .... 130 E6
Lomas Cl ST/HB/BR S6 .... 150 B8
Lombard Cl DOD/DAR S75 .... 2 B2 ⬛
Lombard Crs WMB/DAR S73 .... 84 B2
London La AWLS/ASK DN6 .... 20 A5
London Rd SHEFS S8 .... 8 C5
London Rd South SHEFS S8 .... 171 G8
London Wy KIMB S61 .... 131 F3
Longacre Ct MOS S20 .... 190 E6
Longacre Rd DRON S18 .... 201 C8
Longacre Vw MOS S20 .... 190 E7
Longacre Wy MOS S20 .... 190 E7
Longcar La BSLY S70 .... 2 A5
Long Cswy BSLYN/ROY S71 .... 3 F2
HATH/EY S32 .... 182 E3
Long Cl DONS/BSCR DN4 .... 118 C2
Long Close La HOLM/MEL HD7 .... 49 C1
Long Cft DOD/DAR S75 .... 29 C6
Longcroft Av DRON S18 .... 200 B5
Longcroft Dr DRON S18 .... 200 C5
Long Croft Rd DRON S18 .... 200 C5
Longdale Dr HEM/SK/SE WF9 .... 34 D3
Longdendale Trail GLSP SK13 .... 98 B3
STKB/PEN S36 .... 99 K2
Long Edge La BTLY DN5 .... 38 A7
Longfellow Dr RHAM/THRY S65 .... 156 A2
WRKN S81 .... 211 F3
Longfellow Dr DONS/BSCR DN4 .... 117 F1
Longfield Cl WMB/DAR S73 .... 83 J3
Longfield Dr DOD/DAR S75 .... 29 C6
DONS/BSCR DN4 .... 118 C1
RHAM/THRY S65 .... 135 J7
Long Field Rd ARMTH DN3 .... 67 H4
Longfield Rd FUL S10 .... 170 B2
Longfields Crs HOY S74 .... 108 E1
Longford Cl TOT/DORE S17 .... 200 A2 ⬛
Longford Crs TOT/DORE S17 .... 200 A2
Longford Dr TOT/DORE S17 .... 199 K3
Longford Rd TOT/DORE S17 .... 199 K3
Longford Spinney TOT/DORE S17 .... 199 K3
Long Ga NROS/TKH DN11 .... 138 C2
Longhurst WRKN S81 .... 211 F2

Long Ing Rd HOLM/MEL HD7 .... 47 K8
Longlands Av AU/AST/KP S26 .... 192 C5
Longlands Dr DOD/DAR S75 .... 29 G7 ⬛
RHAM/THRY S65 .... 135 F4
Long Lands La AWLS/ASK DN6 .... 62 E3
Long La BTLY DN5 .... 89 J3
CHPT/GREN S35 .... 128 B8
CHPT/GREN S35 .... 150 B3
ECK/KIL S21 .... 202 E6
ECK/KIL S21 .... 205 J1
FUL S10 .... 169 K3
GLE DN14 .... 12 A3
KBTN HD8 .... 26 C4
PONT WF8 .... 16 D6
RHAM S60 .... 174 D1
ST/HB/BR S6 .... 150 B6
ST/HB/BR S6 .... 169 H2
ST/HB/BR S6 .... 169 H2
STKB/PEN S36 .... 78 C6
STKB/PEN S36 .... 104 A7
WRKN S81 .... 196 C1
Longley Av West SHEFN S5 .... 152 A5
Longley Cl DOD/DAR S75 .... 54 D5 ⬛
SHEFN S5 .... 152 C5
Longley Crs SHEFN S5 .... 152 C4
Longley Dr SHEFN S5 .... 152 C5
Longley Edge La HOLM/MEL HD7 .... 48 A6
Longley Edge Rd HOLM/MEL HD7 .... 48 A6
Longley Farm Vw SHEFN S5 .... 152 C5
Longley Hall Gv SHEFN S5 .... 152 C5
Longley Hall Ri SHEFN S5 .... 152 C5
Longley Hall Rd SHEFN S5 .... 152 C5
Longley Hall Wy SHEFN S5 .... 152 D4
Longley La HOLM/MEL HD7 .... 47 K6
SHEFN S5 .... 152 C5
Long Leys La CONI S12 .... 137 H2
Longley St DOD/DAR S75 .... 54 D3
Long Line ECC S11 .... 185 F5
Longman Rd BSLY S70 .... 2 B2
Long Mdw BWTY DN10 .... 165 J4
Longridge Rd BSLYN/ROY S71 .... 56 E1 ⬛
Long Rd MALT S66 .... 176 E5
Longside Wy DOD/DAR S75 .... 55 F5
Longsight Rd DOD/DAR S75 .... 29 F6
Longstone Crs HACK/IN S12 .... 139 F3
Longthwaite Dr DIN S25 .... 178 A3 ⬛
Longton Rd ARMTH DN3 .... 67 F3 ⬛
Lonsdale Av BSLYN/ROY S71 .... 57 J7
WHHL DN2 .... 92 A4
Lonsdale Cl DIN S25 .... 194 B1 ⬛
Lonsdale Rd ST/HB/BR S6 .... 151 H4
Loosemore Dr HACK/IN S12 .... 188 B2
Lopham Cl OWL S3 .... 9 E1 ⬛
Lopham St OWL S3 .... 9 E1 ⬛
OWL S3 .... 171 H1 ⬛
Lordens Hi DIN S25 .... 178 C6
Lords Cl CONI S12 .... 115 K5
Lord's Head La DONS/BSCR DN4 .... 116 A3
Lord St BSLYN/ROY S71 .... 57 G3 ⬛
HTFD DN7 .... 41 K4 ⬛
RHAM/THRY S65 .... 7 F3
Lorna Rd MEX/SWTN S64 .... 113 F2
Lorne Cl DRON S18 .... 200 D5
Lorne Rd DEARNE S63 .... 60 A7
Lothian Rd WHHL DN2 .... 92 B2
Louden Cl KIMB S61 .... 131 J5
Louden Rd KIMB S61 .... 131 J5
Lound Cl BTLY DN5 .... 62 A2
Lound Rd DARN/MH S9 .... 173 F4
Lound Side CHPT/GREN S35 .... 130 B1
Louth Rd ECC S11 .... 170 B8
Lovell St ATT S4 .... 171 K2
Loversall Cl DONS/BSCR DN4 .... 116 E2
Love St OWL S3 .... 9 D2
Lovetot Av AU/AST/KP S26 .... 175 H7
Lovetot Rd DARN/MH S9 .... 172 A2 ⬛
KIMB S61 .... 132 B5
Lowburn Rd HAN/WDH S13 .... 172 E8
Low Common ECK/KIL S21 .... 205 H8
Low Cft BSLYN/ROY S71 .... 30 C4
Low Cudworth CUD/GR S72 .... 57 J2
Lowedges Crs SHEFS S8 .... 201 F1 ⬛
Lowedges Dr SHEFS S8 .... 201 F1 ⬛
Lowedges Pl SHEFS S8 .... 201 G1 ⬛
Lowedges Rd SHEFS S8 .... 201 F1
Lowe La DOD/DAR S75 .... 80 E4
Lowell Av DONS/BSCR DN4 .... 116 E1 ⬛
Lower Boundary Rd BTLY DN5 .... 40 A7
Lower Castlereagh St BSLY S70 .... 2 B4 ⬛
Lower Common La KBTN HD8 .... 26 C4
Lower Denby La KBTN HD8 .... 51 H4
Lower Dolcliffe Rd
MEX/SWTN S64 .... 112 A2
Lower High Royds DOD/DAR S75 .... 29 F7
Lower Kenyon St THNE DN8 .... 23 J7
Lower Malton Rd BTLY DN5 .... 64 B8
Lower Maythorn La
HOLM/MEL HD7 .... 49 H1
Lower Mdw HOLM/MEL HD7 .... 47 G2 ⬛
Lower Mill Cl DEARNE S63 .... 86 B3
Lower Northcroft
HEM/SK/SE WF9 .... 35 H4
Lower Northfield La
HEM/SK/SE WF9 .... 34 B4
Lower Thomas St BSLY S70 .... 2 B5 ⬛
Lower Unwin St STKB/PEN S36 .... 78 A5
Lower York St WMB/DAR S73 .... 84 A4 ⬛
Lowfield Av HACK/IN S12 .... 189 G6

KIMB S61 .... 133 F4
Lowfield Cl ARMTH DN3 .... 67 G1 ⬛
Low Field Gv DEARNE S63 .... 86 D6
Low Field La BWTY DN10 .... 142 D1
Lowfield Mdw DEARNE S63 .... 86 C6
Lowfield Rd DEARNE S63 .... 86 C6
WHHL DN2 .... 66 B8
Low Fisher Ga DON DN1 .... 4 C2
Lowgate BTLY DN5 .... 64 B8
GLE DN14 .... 11 F6
Low Ga HEM/SK/SE WF9 .... 35 F4
HOLM/MEL HD7 .... 48 A3
Low Grange Rd DEARNE S63 .... 60 B3
Low Grange Sq DEARNE S63 .... 60 B3
Lowhill THNE DN8 .... 23 G6
Lowhouse Rd SHEFN S5 .... 131 F6
Low Laithes Vw WMB/DAR S73 .... 83 J3 ⬛
Lowlands Cl BSLYN/ROY S71 .... 56 E4
BTLY DN5 .... 64 E4
Low La HTFD DN7 .... 40 E2
KIMB S61 .... 132 D1
RHAM S60 .... 158 D8
Low Levels Bank HTFD DN7 .... 44 A2
THNE DN8 .... 71 F7
Low Moor La STKB/PEN S36 .... 102 D4
Low Pasture Cl DOD/DAR S75 .... 55 F8
Low Rd BWTY DN10 .... 164 B8
CHPT/GREN S35 .... 128 C8
CONI DN12 .... 114 D4
DONS/BSCR DN4 .... 90 D8
ST/HB/BR S6 .... 170 A6
STKB/PEN S36 .... 79 G6
Low Rd East DONS/BSCR DN4 .... 116 A4
Low Rd West DONS/BSCR DN4 .... 115 K4
Lowry Dr DRON S18 .... 201 F1 ⬛
Low St DOD/DAR S75 .... 81 G7
WRKN S81 .... 196 E2
Lowther Rd DON DN1 .... 5 F1 ⬛
ST/HB/BR S6 .... 151 J6
Lowther Sq WRKN S81 .... 180 C8 ⬛
Lowton Wy MALT S66 .... 158 C8
Lowtown Cl WRKS S80 .... 210 E5 ⬛
Lowtown St WRKS S80 .... 210 E6
Lowtown Vw WRKS S80 .... 210 E5 ⬛
Low Vw DOD/DAR S75 .... 54 D8
Low Wood Cl MEX/SWTN S64 .... 112 B6 ⬛
Loxley Av WMB/DAR S73 .... 83 K5
Loxley Mt AWLS/ASK DN6 .... 17 K7
Loxley Rd BSLYN/ROY S71 .... 57 G4
ST/HB/BR S6 .... 149 F3
Loxley View Rd FUL S10 .... 170 B2
Loy Cl KIMB S61 .... 132 C4
Lucas St ATT S4 .... 152 D8 ⬛
Ludgate Cl NROS/TKH DN11 .... 119 F6
Ludwell Hl BTLY DN5 .... 87 K5
Lugano Gv WMB/DAR S73 .... 84 B1 ⬛
Luke La ST/HB/BR S6 .... 150 E6
Lulworth Cl BSLY S70 .... 3 E5 ⬛
Lumb La CHPT/GREN S35 .... 127 K7
Lumley Crs MALT S66 .... 159 G3
Lumley Dr DIN S25 .... 177 J5
NROS/TKH DN11 .... 140 A8
Lumley St ATT S4 .... 171 K3
DARN/MH S9 .... 172 B3 ⬛
Lump La CHPT/GREN S35 .... 129 H6
Luna Cft HACK/IN S12 .... 188 E5
Lunbreck Rd DONS/BSCR DN4 .... 115 K2
Lund Av BSLYN/ROY S71 .... 57 G4
Lund Cl BSLYN/ROY S71 .... 57 G4
Lund Crs BSLYN/ROY S71 .... 57 G4
Lundhill Cl WMB/DAR S73 .... 84 B6
Lundhill Gv WMB/DAR S73 .... 84 B7
Lund Hill La BSLYN/ROY S71 .... 31 G8
Lundhill Rd WMB/DAR S73 .... 84 B7
Lund La BSLYN/ROY S71 .... 57 G4
Lund Rd CHPT/GREN S35 .... 150 C2
Lundwood Cl MOS S20 .... 190 A5 ⬛
Lundwood Dr MOS S20 .... 190 A5
Lundwood Gv MOS S20 .... 190 A5
Lundy Rd DRON S18 .... 201 F2
Lunn Rd CUD/GR S72 .... 57 J7
Lupton Cls SHEFS S8 .... 201 F1
Lupton Dr SHEFS S8 .... 201 F1
Lupton Rd SHEFS S8 .... 201 F1
Luterel Dr AU/AST/KP S26 .... 175 H7
Lutterworth Dr AWLS/ASK DN6 .... 63 H1
Lvy Ct CUD/GR S72 .... 57 J1
Lych Gate Cl DONS/BSCR DN4 .... 93 F8 E
Lydgate Cl FUL S10 .... 170 B4
Lydgate Ct FUL S10 .... 170 A4
Lydgate Hall Crs FUL S10 .... 170 A4
Lydgate La FUL S10 .... 170 A4
Lydgetts HOLM/MEL HD7 .... 47 G2 ⬛
Lyme St RHAM S60 .... 6 B4
Lyminster Rd ST/HB/BR S6 .... 151 H2
Lyminton La RHAM S60 .... 174 C3
Lymister Av RHAM S60 .... 155 J5
Lyncroft Cl RHAM S60 .... 155 G7 ⬛
Lyndale Av ARMTH DN3 .... 66 D6
Lynden Av AWLS/ASK DN6 .... 63 H2
Lyndhurst Cl AWLS/ASK DN6 .... 188 E4
ECC S11 .... 23 G7 ⬛
THNE DN8 .... 23 G7 ⬛
Lyndhurst Crs ARMTH DN3 .... 66 D4
Lyndhurst Rd AWLS/ASK DN6 .... 18 A4
Lyndhurst Ri AWLS/ASK DN6 .... 18 A4
Lyndhurst Rd ECC S11 .... 186 C1 ⬛
Lynmouth Rd ABRD S7 .... 186 E2
Lynn Pl DARN/MH S9 .... 153 J7 ⬛

.ynton Av *RHAM* S60 ...... **155** K4
.ynton Dr *ARMTH* DN3 ...... **66** D2
.ynton Pl *DOD/DAR* S75 ...... **28** C7
.ynwood Cl *ECC* S11 ...... **8** A6 🔟
.ynwood Dr *BSLYN/ROY* S71 ...... **30** D6
  MEX/SWTN S64 ...... **112** E2
.yons Cl *ATT* S4 ...... **152** D8
.yons St *ATT* S4 ...... **152** D8 🔟
.ytham Av *BSLYN/ROY* S71 ...... **56** E2
  DIN S25 ...... **178** B8
.yttleton Crs *STKB/PEN* S36 ...... **77** K6
.ytton Av *SHEFN* S5 ...... **151** K3
.ytton Cl *DONS/BSCR* DN4 ...... **116** E1
.ytton Crs *SHEFN* S5 ...... **151** K2
.ytton Dr *SHEFN* S5 ...... **151** K2
.ytton Rd *SHEFN* S5 ...... **151** K2

M

Mabel St *RHAM/THRY* S65 ...... **7** E5 🔟
Mable St *WRKS* S80 ...... **209** K3
Macaulay Cl *WRKN* S81 ...... **211** G3
Machin Dr *RAW* S62 ...... **111** F7
Machin Gv *WRKN* S81 ...... **196** A8
Machin La *STKB/PEN* S36 ...... **104** A5
Machins Ct *DRON* S18 ...... **201** C5 🔟
Machon Bank *ABRD* S7 ...... **186** E1
  FUL S10 ...... **8** B4 🔟
Machon Bank Rd *ECC* S11 ...... **186** D1
Mackenzie Crs *CHPT/GREN* S35 ...... **129** J3
  FUL S10 ...... **8** B4 🔟
Mackenzie St *ECC* S11 ...... **8** B6 🔟
Mackenzie Wy *AU/AST/KP* S26 ...... **192** D5
Macmanus Av *RAW* S62 ...... **111** J7
Macnaghten Rd *DOD/DAR* S75 ...... **108** A2 🔟
Macro Rd *WMB/DAR* S73 ...... **84** B6
Madam La *ARMTH* DN3 ...... **40** D7
Madehurst Gdns
  SHEFP/MNR S2 ...... **171** H8
Madehurst Ri *SHEFP/MNR* S2 ...... **171** H8 🔟
Madehurst Rd *SHEFP/MNR* S2 ...... **171** H8
Madehurst Vw *SHEFP/MNR* S2 ...... **171** H8 🔟
Madingley Cl *DONS/BSCR* DN4 ...... **116** F2
Madison Dr *BWTY* DN10 ...... **164** A1
Mafeking Pl *CHPT/GREN* S35 ...... **130** B1
Magellan Rd *MALT* S66 ...... **48** D5
Maggot La *KIMB* S61 ...... **79** G5
Magna Cl *MALT* S66 ...... **157** F1
Magna Crs *MALT* S66 ...... **157** F1
Magna La *RHAM/THRY* S65 ...... **134** C6
Magnolia Cl *ARMTH* DN3 ...... **66** E4 🔟
  CUD/GR S72 ...... **32** A5 🔟
  DIN S25 ...... **193** K4
Magpie Cl *WRKN* S81 ...... **196** A8 🔟
Magpie Gv *SHEFP/MNR* S2 ...... **172** A5 🔟
Mahon Av *RAW* S62 ...... **133** J1
Maidstone Rd *ST/HB/BR* S6 ...... **151** J3
Maidwell Wy *ARMTH* DN3 ...... **66** D3
Main Av *CONI* DN12 ...... **115** J4
  TOT/DORE S17 ...... **199** J3
Main Ga *HOLM/MEL* HD7 ...... **48** D5
Main Rd *CHPT/GREN* S35 ...... **128** A4
  DARN/MH S9 ...... **172** E5 🔟
  DRON S18 ...... **200** A7
  DRON S18 ...... **202** A8
  ECK/KIL S21 ...... **203** F8
  ECK/KIL S21 ...... **203** G4
  ECK/KIL S21 ...... **205** F6
  HACK/IN S12 ...... **189** G8
Main St *ARMTH* DN3 ...... **93** G6
  AU/AST/KP S26 ...... **175** G8
  AU/AST/KP S26 ...... **175** G8
  AU/AST/KP S26 ...... **175** J3
  AWLS/ASK DN6 ...... **36** C6
  BTLY DN5 ...... **89** J7
  BWTY DN10 ...... **165** J8
  CHPT/GREN S35 ...... **129** H7
  CUD/GR S72 ...... **32** A1
  DEARNE S63 ...... **86** D2
  DIN S25 ...... **193** K2
  EPW DN9 ...... **94** A8
  GLE DN14 ...... **11** K3
  GLE DN14 ...... **12** A3
  HACK/IN S12 ...... **189** G3
  HTFD DN7 ...... **22** B8
  HTFD DN7 ...... **69** F1
  KIMB S61 ...... **133** F4
  MALT S66 ...... **157** J2
  MEX/SWTN S64 ...... **112** E3
  NROS/TKH DN11 ...... **116** E8
  NROS/TKH DN11 ...... **162** C6
  NROS/TKH DN11 ...... **162** D3
  PONT WF8 ...... **16** E1
  RAW S62 ...... **109** H6
  RAW S62 ...... **133** K1
  RHAM S60 ...... **6** B4
  RHAM/THRY S65 ...... **135** J4
  WMB/DAR S73 ...... **83** K4
  WRKN S81 ...... **180** D1
Makin St *MEX/SWTN* S64 ...... **113** H2
Malcolm Cl *BSLY* S70 ...... **56** E7 🔟
Malham Cl *BWTY* DN10 ...... **142** A7
  CUD/GR S72 ...... **31** K4
Malham Gdns *MOS* S20 ...... **190** B8
Malham Gv *MOS* S20 ...... **190** C8
Malham Pl *CHPT/GREN* S35 ...... **130** A1

Malham Tarn Ct
  DONS/BSCR DN4 ...... **92** A7 🔟
Malincroft *DOD/DAR* S75 ...... **29** G7
Malinda St *OWL* S3 ...... **8** C3 🔟
Malin Rd *RHAM/THRY* S65 ...... **134** C7
  ST/HB/BR S6 ...... **151** F8
Mallard Av *ARMTH* DN3 ...... **66** E1
Mallard Cl *DONS/BSCR* DN4 ...... **116** C1
  KIMB S61 ...... **131** H2
Mallard Dr *ECK/KIL* S21 ...... **191** F8 🔟
The Mallards *WRKN* S81 ...... **196** A8 🔟
Mallin Dr *CONI* DN12 ...... **115** J7
Mallory Av *RAW* S62 ...... **133** H1
Mallory Dr *MEX/SWTN* S64 ...... **113** J1
Mallory Rd *RHAM/THRY* S65 ...... **134** B7
Mallory Wy *CUD/GR* S72 ...... **31** K8
Malpas Hl *NROS/TKH* DN11 ...... **161** J6
Maltby La *MALT* S66 ...... **137** G8
Maltby Rd *WRKN* S81 ...... **180** C1
Maltby St *DARN/MH* S9 ...... **153** H8
Malthouse Rd *BSLYN/ROY* S71 ...... **2** C4 🔟
Malting La *ATT* S4 ...... **9** F2 🔟
The Maltings *RHAM* S60 ...... **6** C5 🔟
Maltkiln St *RHAM* S60 ...... **6** C5
Malton Dr *AU/AST/KP* S26 ...... **175** J8
Malton Pl *BSLYN/ROY* S71 ...... **29** K8 🔟
  WHHL DN2 ...... **92** A2
Malton St *ATT* S4 ...... **152** D8
Maltravers Cl *SHEFP/MNR* S2 ...... **172** A5 🔟
Maltravers Crs *SHEFP/MNR* S2 ...... **171** K4
Maltravers Pl *SHEFP/MNR* S2 ...... **172** A3 🔟
  SHEFP/MNR S2 ...... **172** A4 🔟
Maltravers Rd *SHEFP/MNR* S2 ...... **172** A4
Maltravers Ter *SHEFP/MNR* S2 ...... **172** A5
Maltravers Wy *SHEFP/MNR* S2 ...... **172** A5 🔟
Malvern Av *BTLY* DN5 ...... **90** B2 🔟
Malvern Cl *DOD/DAR* S75 ...... **55** C5 🔟
  THNE DN8 ...... **43** H1 🔟
Malvern Rd *DARN/MH* S9 ...... **172** D2
  WHHL DN2 ...... **92** B3
Malwood Wy *MALT* S66 ...... **159** J1
Manchester Rd *FUL* S10 ...... **169** J4
  ST/HB/BR S6 ...... **167** F3
  STKB/PEN S36 ...... **76** D6
  STKB/PEN S36 ...... **104** D8
  STKB/PEN S36 ...... **105** K8
Mandeville St *DARN/MH* S9 ...... **172** E2
Mangham Rd *KROS/TKH* DN11 ...... **139** K7 🔟
Mangham Rd *KIMB* S61 ...... **6** C1
Mangham Wy *KIMB* S61 ...... **6** C1
Mannering Rd *DONS/BSCR* DN4 ...... **116** B1 🔟
Manners St *OWL* S3 ...... **171** F1
Manor Ap *KIMB* S61 ...... **132** C8
Manor Av *DEARNE* S63 ...... **86** D2
Manor Cl *ARMTH* DN3 ...... **40** D8
  AU/AST/KP S26 ...... **193** F2 🔟
  AWLS/ASK DN6 ...... **18** C3 🔟
  BWTY DN10 ...... **143** K4
  DEARNE S63 ...... **84** E8 🔟
  MALT S66 ...... **159** G2
  PONT WF8 ...... **16** E2
  RAW S62 ...... **111** F7
  WRKS S80 ...... **210** A5
Manor Cft *RHAM/THRY* S65 ...... **134** C7
Manor Crs *CUD/GR* S72 ...... **32** C7
  DRON S18 ...... **201** F6
  RHAM S60 ...... **154** E7
Manor Cft *CUD/GR* S72 ...... **32** A2
Manor Dr *AU/AST/KP* S26 ...... **193** F2
  BTLY DN5 ...... **114** E2
  CUD/GR S72 ...... **32** C7
  RHAM S60 ...... **156** B6
  WHHL DN2 ...... **5** F3
Manor End *BSLY* S70 ...... **55** C5
Manor Est *BTLY* DN5 ...... **64** C3
Manor Farm *AU/AST/KP* S26 ...... **175** H5 🔟
  BSLYN/ROY S71 ...... **30** E7
Manor Farm Ct *MOS* S20 ...... **190** E4 🔟
  RHAM/THRY S65 ...... **134** C3
Manor Farm Dr *MEX/SWTN* S64 ...... **112** B5
Manor Farm Gdns *DIN* S25 ...... **193** K3 🔟
Manor Farm La *GLE* DN14 ...... **21** F2
Manor Farm Ms *MOS* S20 ...... **190** E4 🔟
Manor Flds *KIMB* S61 ...... **132** B7
Manor Gdns *BSLYN/ROY* S71 ...... **57** H7
  BTLY DN5 ...... **89** J6
  HTFD DN7 ...... **42** D8 🔟
Manor Garth *AWLS/ASK* DN6 ...... **18** B3
Manor Gv *BSLYN/ROY* S71 ...... **30** C4
  CUD/GR S72 ...... **32** C7
  HEM/SK/SE WF9 ...... **33** K6
  STV/CWN S43 ...... **206** A8
  WRKS S80 ...... **210** A5
Manor House Cl *HOY* S74 ...... **109** F1
Manor House Ct *BTLY* DN5 ...... **64** C6 🔟
Manor House Rd *KIMB* S61 ...... **132** B7
Manor Laith Rd *SHEFP/MNR* S2 ...... **171** K5
Manor La *DIN* S25 ...... **178** C5
  MEX/SWTN S64 ...... **87** F7
  SHEFP/MNR S2 ...... **172** A3
  STKB/PEN S36 ...... **79** F6
Manor Oaks Cl *SHEFP/MNR* S2 ...... **9** F3
Manor Oaks Ct *SHEFP/MNR* S2 ...... **171** K4 🔟
Manor Oaks Dr *SHEFP/MNR* S2 ...... **9** F3 🔟
Manor Oaks Gdns *SHEFP/MNR* S2 ...... **9** F3 🔟
Manor Oaks Pl *SHEFP/MNR* S2 ...... **172** A5 🔟
Manor Oaks Rd *SHEFP/MNR* S2 ...... **9** F3

Manor Occupation Rd
  BSLYN/ROY S71 ...... **30** C3
Manor Pk *DOD/DAR* S75 ...... **53** J8
Manor Park Av *SHEFP/MNR* S2 ...... **172** B6
Manor Park Centre
  SHEFP/MNR S2 ...... **172** C5 🔟
Manor Park Cl *SHEFP/MNR* S2 ...... **172** B6
Manor Park Ct *SHEFP/MNR* S2 ...... **172** B6 🔟
Manor Park Crs *SHEFP/MNR* S2 ...... **172** B6
Manor Park Dr *SHEFP/MNR* S2 ...... **172** B5
Manor Park Pl *SHEFP/MNR* S2 ...... **172** B5
Manor Park Ri *SHEFP/MNR* S2 ...... **172** B5
Manor Park Rd *SHEFP/MNR* S2 ...... **172** B5
Manor Park Wy *SHEFP/MNR* S2 ...... **172** B6
Manor Pl *RAW* S62 ...... **133** K2 🔟
Manor Ri *NROS/TKH* DN11 ...... **139** F1
Manor Rd *ARMTH* DN3 ...... **40** D7
  AU/AST/KP S26 ...... **192** B3
  AU/AST/KP S26 ...... **193** G6
  AWLS/ASK DN6 ...... **18** C8
  AWLS/ASK DN6 ...... **38** C1
  BTLY DN5 ...... **64** D3 🔟
  BTLY DN5 ...... **87** H6
  BWTY DN10 ...... **164** B5
  CUD/GR S72 ...... **32** C7
  DEARNE S63 ...... **60** B7
  DEARNE S63 ...... **84** D8
  DIN S25 ...... **178** B5
  ECK/KIL S21 ...... **205** H2
  HTFD DN7 ...... **42** D8
  KBTN HD8 ...... **26** D3
  MALT S66 ...... **159** H2
  MEX/SWTN S64 ...... **112** C5
  RHAM S60 ...... **154** E7
  STV/CWN S43 ...... **206** A8
Manor Sq *DEARNE* S63 ...... **60** A7
Manor St *BSLYN/ROY* S71 ...... **30** E7
Manor Vw *CUD/GR* S72 ...... **31** K5
  MOS S20 ...... **190** C8 🔟
Manor Wy *AU/AST/KP* S26 ...... **193** F2
  AWLS/ASK DN6 ...... **38** C1
  HOY S74 ...... **109** F1
  SHEFP/MNR S2 ...... **172** A4
Manse Cl *DONS/BSCR* DN4 ...... **93** F7
  AWLS/ASK DN6 ...... **37** J5
Mansel Av *SHEFN* S5 ...... **151** K1
Mansel Crs *SHEFN* S5 ...... **151** J1
Mansel Rd *SHEFN* S5 ...... **151** K1
Mansfield Crs *ARMTH* DN3 ...... **66** E8
  AWLS/ASK DN6 ...... **37** J5
Mansfield Dr *HACK/IN* S12 ...... **188** D1
Mansfield Rd *AU/AST/KP* S26 ...... **191** H3
  AU/AST/KP S26 ...... **191** K4
  BSLYN/ROY S71 ...... **30** A7
  DONS/BSCR DN4 ...... **4** B5
  ECK/KIL S21 ...... **205** K1
  HACK/IN S12 ...... **188** D1
  RHAM S60 ...... **7** D4
  RHAM S60 ...... **209** H8
  WRKS S80 ...... **210** A5
Mansion Court Gdns *THNE* DN8 ...... **23** J7
Manston Wy *WRKN* S81 ...... **196** A7
Manton Crs *WRKS* S80 ...... **211** F6
Manton Dl *WRKS* S80 ...... **211** F6
Manton St *SHEFP/MNR* S2 ...... **9** E5 🔟
Manton Vls *WRKS* S80 ...... **211** G6
Manvers Cl *AU/AST/KP* S26 ...... **175** H8 🔟
  DIN S25 ...... **178** A8 🔟
Manvers Pk *DEARNE* S63 ...... **112** B1
Manvers Rd *AU/AST/KP* S26 ...... **175** H8
  MEX/SWTN S64 ...... **112** D2
  MOS S20 ...... **190** D3
  ST/HB/BR S6 ...... **151** H8
Manvers St *WRKS* S80 ...... **210** C4 🔟
Manvers Wy *DEARNE* S63 ...... **85** G7
Maori Av *DEARNE* S63 ...... **85** K5
Maple Av *DONS/BSCR* DN4 ...... **92** E7
  EPW DN9 ...... **120** B3
  MALT S66 ...... **158** E2
Maplebeck Dr *DARN/MH* S9 ...... **154** B5
Maplebeck Rd *DARN/MH* S9 ...... **154** B6
Maple Cl *BSLY* S70 ...... **3** E6
Maple Croft Crs *SHEFN* S5 ...... **153** G4
Maple Croft Rd *SHEFN* S5 ...... **153** G4
Maple Dr *ECK/KIL* S21 ...... **205** G2
  EPW DN9 ...... **94** D8
  MALT S66 ...... **157** C1
  WRKN S81 ...... **196** D8
Maple Gv *AU/AST/KP* S26 ...... **175** K7
  BWTY DN10 ...... **142** K8
  CONI DN12 ...... **114** A7
  DARN/MH S9 ...... **173** G4
  STKB/PEN S36 ...... **104** E7
Maple Rd *CHPT/GREN* S35 ...... **130** B3
Maple Rd *AU/AST/KP* S26 ...... **192** C4
  DOD/DAR S75 ...... **29** F6
  DOD/DAR S75 ...... **107** J4
  MEX/SWTN S64 ...... **112** E2
  THNE DN8 ...... **23** K6
Mapperley Rd *DRON* S18 ...... **200** C6 🔟
Mappin's Rd *RHAM* S60 ...... **174** B2 🔟
Mappin St *SHEF* S1 ...... **8** C3
Mapplebeck Rd *CHPT/GREN* S35 ...... **107** K8
Maran Av *WMB/DAR* S73 ...... **85** F2
Marbeck Cl *DIN* S25 ...... **177** K6
Marcham Dr *MOS* S20 ...... **190** E3 🔟
March Bank *RHAM/THRY* S65 ...... **135** F4
March Flatts Rd *RHAM/THRY* S65 ...... **135** F5
March Ga *CONI* DN12 ...... **114** D6
March St *CONI* DN12 ...... **114** D5
  DARN/MH S9 ...... **153** J3

March Vale Ri *CONI* DN12 .... 114 C6
Marchwood Av *ST/HB/BR* S6 .... 169 J1
Marchwood Dr *ST/HB/BR* S6 .... 150 D8
Marchwood Rd *ST/HB/BR* S6 .... 150 D8
Marcliff Cl *MALT* S66 .... 156 C5
Marcliff La *MALT* S66 .... 156 C3
Marcliff Crs *MALT* S66 .... 156 E3
Marcliff La *MALT* S66 .... 156 E3
Marden Rd *ABRD* S7 .... 186 E1 🔢
Margaret Cl *AU/AST/KP* S26 .... 191 H1 🔢
   WMB/DAR S73 .... 84 C2
Margaret Rd *WMB/DAR* S73 .... 84 B5
   WMB/DAR S73 .... 84 C2
Margaret St *MALT* S66 .... 159 J4
   SHEF S1 .... 9 D5
Margate Dr *ATT* S4 .... 152 E7
Margate St *CUD/GR* S72 .... 32 D8
Margetson Crs *SHEFN* S5 .... 152 A1
Margetson Dr *SHEFN* S5 .... 151 K1
Margetson Rd *SHEFN* S5 .... 152 A1
Marian Crs *AWLS/ASK* DN6 .... 63 G2
Marigold Cl *SHEFN* S5 .... 153 F4
Marina Rd *WMB/DAR* S73 .... 84 B2
Marina Vw *THNE* DN8 .... 43 J2
Marion Cl *HEM/SK/SE* WF9 .... 33 K5
Marion Rd *ST/HB/BR* S6 .... 151 G5
Marjorie St *WRKS* S80 .... 209 J3
Mark Bottoms La *HOLM/MEL* HD7 ... 47 J1
Markbrook Dr *CHPT/GREN* S35 ...... 107 H7
Market Cl *BSLYN/ROY* S71 .... 3 D4 🔢
Market Hl *BSLY* S70 .... 2 B4
Market Pl *AWLS/ASK* DN6 .... 18 D7
   CONI DN12 .... 115 J5
   CUD/GR S72 .... 31 J8
   DON DN1 .... 4 C3
Market Rd *DON* DN1 .... 5 D2 🔢
Market Sq *AWLS/ASK* DN6 .... 63 J5
   BSLY S70 .... 2 B4
   CHPT/GREN S35 .... 130 C2
   CUD/GR S72 .... 31 J8
   DEARNE S63 .... 60 B7
   DEARNE S63 .... 86 D2
   ECK/KIL S21 .... 204 B4
   HAN/WDH S13 .... 190 A1 🔢
   HOY S74 .... 83 F8
   MEX/SWTN S64 .... 112 D4
   MEX/SWTN S64 .... 113 F5 🔢
   RHAM S60 .... 6 C4
   STKB/PEN S36 .... 78 A4
   WRKS S80 .... 210 D4
Markfield Dr *MALT* S66 .... 157 F1
Markham Av *ARMTH* DN3 .... 67 F8
   AWLS/ASK DN6 .... 37 K7
   CONI DN12 .... 114 B5
Markham Ct *CONI* DN12 .... 114 B5 🔢
Markham Rd *CONI* DN12 .... 115 J5
   WRKS S80 .... 180 C4
Markham Sq *CONI* DN12 .... 115 K5
Markham St *SHEFS* S8 .... 187 F1 🔢
Mark La *FUL* S10 .... 184 E1
Mark St *BSLY* S70 .... 2 B4 🔢
Marlborough Av *BTLY* DN5 .... 90 C4
Marlborough Cl *DEARNE* S63 ...... 60 B7 🔢
   DIN S25 .... 177 K8 🔢
Marlborough Crs *AWLS/ASK* DN6 .. 18 E8
Marlborough Cft
   HEM/SK/SE WF9 .... 34 E3 🔢
Marlborough Ri *AU/AST/KP* S26 ... 191 J1
Marlborough Rd *AWLS/ASK* DN6 ... 18 E7
   FUL S10 .... 170 C4
   THNE DN8 .... 43 K1 🔢
   WHHL DN2 .... 5 F2
Marlcliffe Rd *ST/HB/BR* S6 .... 151 F5
Marley Rd *SHEFP/MNR* S2 .... 172 A6
Marlfield Cft *CHPT/GREN* S35 ..... 130 C7
Marlow Cl *MALT* S66 .... 157 J5
   WHHL DN2 .... 92 B2 🔢
Marlowe Dr *RHAM/THRY* S65 ...... 156 A2
Marlowe Gdns *WRKS* S81 .... 211 F3
Marlowe Rd *ARMTH* DN3 .... 40 B8
   RHAM/THRY S65 .... 156 A2
Marlow Rd *WHHL* DN2 .... 92 B2
Marmion Rd *ECC* S11 .... 170 B8 🔢
Marples Cl *SHEFS* S8 .... 171 F8 🔢
Marples Dr *SHEFS* S8 .... 171 F8 🔢
Marquis Gdns *ARMTH* DN3 .... 40 E8
Marr Grange La *BTLY* DN5 .... 63 F3
Marrick Ct *CHPT/GREN* S35 .... 130 A2 🔢
Marrion Rd *RAW* S62 .... 133 K1
Marriott La *SHEFS* S8 .... 186 D4
Marriott Pl *RAW* S62 .... 111 G8
Marriott Rd *MEX/SWTN* S64 ...... 112 D3
   SHEFS S8 .... 186 D4
Marrison Dr *ECK/KIL* S21 .... 205 G1
Marr Ter *FUL* S10 .... 169 K6
Marsala Wk *WMB/DAR* S73 .... 84 C1
Marsden Gv *THNE* DN8 .... 23 H7
Marsden La *OWL* S3 .... 8 C2
Marsden Rd *STKB/PEN* S36 .... 105 F6 🔢
Marshall Av *DONS/BSCR* DN4 ..... 90 D8 🔢
Marshall Cl *RAW* S62 .... 133 J3
Marshall Gr *HEM/SK/SE* WF9 ...... 34 D4
Marshall Gv *DEARNE* S63 .... 111 J2 🔢
Marshall Mill Ct *KBTN* HD8 .... 26 A6
Marshall Rd *SHEFS* S8 .... 187 F5
Marsh Av *DRON* S18 .... 201 H4
Marsh Cl *MOS* S20 .... 204 A3

Marshfield *BSLY* S70 .... 82 A6 🔢
Marsh Ga *BTLY* DN5 .... 4 B2
Marsh Hl *MALT* S66 .... 136 D6
Marsh Hill La *GLE* DN14 .... 13 F8
Marsh House Rd *ECC* S11 .... 185 H2
Marshland Rd *THNE* DN8 .... 23 K6
Marsh La *ARMTH* DN3 .... 40 B8
   ARMTH DN3 .... 40 B5
   ARMTH DN3 .... 66 B1
   BTLY DN5 .... 65 F3
   FUL S10 .... 169 K4
   KBTN HD8 .... 49 H1
   THNE DN8 .... 23 H3
Marsh Rd *AWLS/ASK* DN6 .... 40 B3
   BTLY DN5 .... 4 B1
   HOLM/MEL HD7 .... 48 C4
Marsh St *RHAM* S60 .... 6 B5
   STKB/PEN S36 .... 105 G6 🔢
   WMB/DAR S73 .... 84 A4
Marsh Vw *ECK/KIL* S21 .... 203 K5
Marson Av *AWLS/ASK* DN6 .... 63 G2
Marston Cl *DRON* S18 .... 200 D7
Marston Crs *TOT/DORE* S17 ...... 199 J2
Marstone Crs *TOT/DORE* S17 .... 199 J2
Marston Rd *FUL* S10 .... 170 B3
Martin Beck La *NROS/TKH* DN11 .. 141 F7
Martin Cl *AU/AST/KP* S26 .... 175 G6
   BSLY S70 .... 82 A7
Martin Crs *ECK/KIL* S21 .... 204 A4
Martin Crs *SHEFN* S5 .... 152 C1
Martin Cft *DOD/DAR* S75 .... 53 J7 🔢
Martindale Wk *AWLS/ASK* DN6 .. 37 K7 🔢
Martin La *BWTY* DN10 .... 141 K7
   BWTY DN10 .... 141 J5
   BWTY DN10 .... 142 B1
   HOY S74 .... 82 E6
Martin Ri *ECK/KIL* S21 .... 204 A4
   KIMB S61 .... 131 H1
Martin's Rd *BSLYN/ROY* S71 ...... 57 F4
Martin St *ST/HB/BR* S6 .... 8 B1
Martin Wells Rd *CONI* DN12 ..... 115 K6
Martlet Wy *WRKS* S80 .... 210 E7 🔢
Marton Av *HEM/SK/SE* WF9 ...... 33 F1 🔢
Marton Dr *HTFD* DN7 .... 42 C8
Marton Rd *BTLY* DN5 .... 64 C2
Marvell Rd *BTLY* DN5 .... 90 A1 🔢
Mary Ann Cl *BSLYN/ROY* S71 ..... 56 E5
Mary La *WMB/DAR* S73 .... 84 E2
Mary Rd *AWLS/ASK* DN6 .... 18 C8
Mary's Pl *DOD/DAR* S75 .... 55 D7
Mary St *CUD/GR* S72 .... 85 H1
   DOD/DAR S75 .... 54 C3
   ECK/KIL S21 .... 204 B4
   RHAM S60 .... 6 B3 🔢
   SHEF S1 .... 9 D5
   WRKS S80 .... 209 K3
Masbrough St *RHAM* S60 .... 6 B4
Masefield Ct *DIN* S25 .... 178 C7 🔢
Masefield Pl *WRKN* S81 .... 211 F3
Masefield Rd *DEARNE* S63 .... 85 F8 🔢
   HAN/WDH S13 .... 172 E8
   WHHL DN2 .... 66 B8
Masham Ct *DONS/BSCR* DN4 ...... 92 D7 🔢
Mason Av *AU/AST/KP* S26 .... 175 H4
Mason Crs *HAN/WDH* S13 .... 173 F8
Mason Dr *AU/AST/KP* S26 .... 175 G6
Mason Gv *HAN/WDH* S13 .... 189 F1
Mason Lathe Rd *SHEFN* S5 .... 153 F2
Mason St *DEARNE* S63 .... 86 D2 🔢
Masons Wy *BSLY* S70 .... 82 D1
Massey Rd *HAN/WDH* S13 .... 190 B2
Mastall La *BTLY* DN5 .... 65 H5
Masters Crs *SHEFN* S5 .... 152 C2
Masters Rd *SHEFN* S5 .... 152 C2
Mather Av *DARN/MH* S9 .... 172 D5
Mather Ct *DARN/MH* S9 .... 172 D4
Mather Crs *DARN/MH* S9 .... 172 D4
Mather Dr *DARN/MH* S9 .... 172 D4
Mather Rd *DARN/MH* S9 .... 172 D4
Matilda La *SHEF* S1 .... 9 E4
Matilda St *SHEF* S1 .... 9 D4
Matilda Wy *SHEF* S1 .... 9 D4 🔢
Matlock Rd *BSLYN/ROY* S71 ...... 56 C1
   FUL S10 .... 170 C2
Mattersey Cl *DONS/BSCR* DN4 .. 118 D2 🔢
Mattersey Rd *BWTY* DN10 .... 165 J3
Matthews Av *DEARNE* S63 .... 111 G1
Matthews Dr *DEARNE* S63 .... 111 G2
Matthews Dr *MALT* S66 .... 157 G4 🔢
Matthews Fold *SHEFS* S8 .... 187 J6 🔢
Matthews La *SHEFS* S8 .... 187 J6
Matthew St *OWL* S3 .... 8 C1 🔢
Maud's Br *THNE* DN8 .... 44 E2
Mauncer Crs *HAN/WDH* S13 ...... 173 K8
Mauncer Dr *HAN/WDH* S13 .... 173 K8
Mauncer La *HAN/WDH* S13 .... 189 K1
Maun Wy *SHEFN* S5 .... 152 D4
Maurice St *RAW* S62 .... 133 J4
Mawfa Av *SHEFS* S8 .... 187 K5
Mawfa Crs *SHEFS* S8 .... 187 K5 🔢
Mawfa Dr *SHEFS* S8 .... 187 K5
Mawfa Rd *SHEFS* S8 .... 187 K5 🔢
Mawfield Rd *DOD/DAR* S75 .... 54 E3
Mawson Green La *GLE* DN14 ...... 22 A1
Maxey Pl *SHEFS* S8 .... 187 G1 🔢
Maxfield Av *FUL* S10 .... 170 C4
Maxwell St *ATT* S4 .... 171 J1
Maxwell Wy *ATT* S4 .... 171 J1

May Av *DONS/BSCR* DN4 .... 116 D'
Mayberry Dr *DOD/DAR* S75 .... 53 J6
Maycock Av *KIMB* S61 .... 132 A5
May Day Gn *BSLY* S70 .... 2 C4 🔢
Mayfair Cl *NROS/TKH* DN11 ...... 162 E5
Mayfield *AWLS/ASK* DN6 .... 18 D
   BSLYN/ROY S71 .... 3 E
   STKB/PEN S36 .... 78 E6
Mayfield Av *HTFD* DN7 .... 42 C
Mayfield Crs *BSLY* S70 .... 81 K1 🔢
   NROS/TKH DN11 .... 118 E2
Mayfield Rd *BTLY* DN5 .... 4 A
   FUL S10 .... 168 E8
Mayfields *BTLY* DN5 .... 64 A6
Mayfields Wy *HEM/SK/SE* WF9 ... 34 A6
Mayflower Av *BWTY* DN10 .... 164 B5
Mayflower Cl *BWTY* DN10 .... 142 B3
Mayflower Rd *DONS/BSCR* DN4 .. 115 K3
Maynard Rd *RHAM* S60 .... 156 B4
May Rd *ST/HB/BR* S6 .... 151 G2
May Ter *BSLY* S70 .... 55 H6
Maythorne Cl *DOD/DAR* S75 ...... 29 H7
May Tree Cl *MOS* S20 .... 190 C6
Maytree Cl *WMB/DAR* S73 .... 84 D5
May Tree Cft *MOS* S20 .... 190 C6
May Tree La *MOS* S20 .... 190 C6
Mcconnel Crs *NROS/TKH* DN11 .. 118 C6
Mcintyre Rd *STKB/PEN* S36 ...... 104 E7
Mclaren Crs *MALT* S66 .... 159 H
Mclintock Wy *BSLY* S70 .... 2 A4 🔢
Meaburn Cl *DONS/BSCR* DN4 ...... 92 E8
Meade Dr *WRKN* S81 .... 196 E6
Meadow Av *CUD/GR* S72 .... 58 A3 🔢
   RAW S62 .... 111 G2
Meadow Bank *HOLM/MEL* HD7 ... 48 B
Meadow Bank Av *ABRD* S7 .... 170 D8
Meadowbank Cl *KIMB* S61 .... 154 D1
Meadow Bank Rd *ABRD* S7 .... 170 D8
   DARN/MH S9 .... 153 K5
   KIMB S61 .... 154 A2
Meadow Cl *AU/AST/KP* S26 .... 192 E4
   DRON S18 .... 201 J5
   RHAM/THRY S65 .... 134 D6
Meadow Ct *BSLYN/ROY* S71 .... 30 E4
Meadowcourt *DARN/MH* S9 ..... 153 J5
Meadow Ct *HEM/SK/SE* WF9 ..... 35 G4
Meadow Crs *BSLYN/ROY* S71 ..... 30 E4
   CUD/GR S72 .... 32 D8
   MOS S20 .... 189 K8
Meadow Cft *ARMTH* DN3 .... 67 F
   BTLY DN5 .... 89 K7
   CUD/GR S72 .... 31 K4
   HEM/SK/SE WF9 .... 33 G
   MEX/SWTN S64 .... 112 B
Meadowcroft Cl *RHAM* S60 ..... 156 A
Meadowcroft Gdns *MOS* S20 ... 190 C7
Meadowcroft Gld *MOS* S20 ..... 190 C7
Meadowcroft Ri *MOS* S20 .... 190 C7
Meadow Dirve *NROS/TKH* DN11 .. 140 B6
Meadow Dr *BSLYN/ROY* S71 .... 56 E
   CHPT/GREN S35 .... 129 K2
   MEX/SWTN S64 .... 112 B5
   WRKS S80 .... 210 A5
Meadowfield Dr *HOY* S74 .... 109 F3
Meadow Field Rd *ARMTH* DN3 ... 67 F
Meadow Gate Av *MOS* S20 ...... 191 F4
Meadow Gate Cl *MOS* S20 ...... 191 F5 🔢
Meadow Gate La *MOS* S20 ...... 191 F6
Meadowgates *DEARNE* S63 .... 86 B4
Meadow Gv *TOT/DORE* S17 ...... 199 H3
Meadow Grove Rd *TOT/DORE* S17. 199 H3
Meadowhall Rd *DARN/MH* S9 .... 153 J5
   KIMB S61 .... 154 A2
Meadowhall Wy *DARN/MH* S9 ... 153 K4
Meadow Head *SHEFS* S8 .... 186 E8
Meadow Head Av *SHEFS* S8 ..... 186 E8
Meadow Head Dr *SHEFS* S8 ..... 187 F7
Meadow House Dr *FUL* S10 ...... 169 H6
Meadowland Ri *CUD/GR* S72 ..... 57 K2
Meadow La *DOD/DAR* S75 .... 28 D
   MALT S66 .... 159 H3
   MEX/SWTN S64 .... 113 F4
   RAW S62 .... 111 G8
   WMB/DAR S73 .... 84 E2
   WRKN S81 .... 181 J5
Meadow Lea *WRKS* S80 .... 210 A5
Meadowpark Cft *DIN* S25 .... 178 A7
Meadow Ri *ARMTH* DN3 .... 33 F1
   HEM/SK/SE WF9 .... 33 F1
   NROS/TKH DN11 .... 139 F
Meadow Rd *BSLYN/ROY* S71 ...... 30 E4
   WRKS S80 .... 210 A5
The Meadows *AU/AST/KP* S26 ... 192 E2
   KBTN HD8 .... 51 G2 🔢
Meadow St *BSLYN/ROY* S71 .... 2 C5
   DIN S25 .... 177 J5
   KIMB S61 .... 154 D7
   OWL S3 .... 8 C2
Meadow Ter *ECC* S11 .... 170 C7 🔢
The Meadow *BTLY* DN5 .... 89 K6
Meadow Vw *BSLY* S70 .... 82 B2
   STKB/PEN S36 .... 78 C4
Meadow View Cl *HOY* S74 .... 108 E2
Meadow View Rd *MEX/SWTN* S64. 112 C7
   SHEFS S8 .... 187 J6
Meadow Wk *ARMTH* DN3 .... 67 F4
Meadow Wy *MEX/SWTN* S64 .... 112 E4
   NROS/TKH DN11 .... 162 E2
Meadstead Dr *BSLYN/ROY* S71 ... 30 C4

The Meads SHEFS S8 .... 187 H7
The Meadway TOT/DORE S17 .... 185 H8
Meal Hill La HOLM/MEL HD7 ...... 48 E5
Meal Hill Rd HOLM/MEL HD7 ...... 46 C6
Mears Cl STKB/PEN S36 .... 78 B4
Measham Dr HTFD DN7 .... 42 B2
The Mede AWLS/ASK DN6 .... 65 G2
Medina Wy DOD/DAR S75 .... 54 D2
Medley Vw CONI DN12 .... 114 E6
Medlock Cl HAN/WDH S13 .... 173 J5
Medlock Crs HAN/WDH S13 ...... 173 J5
Medlock Cft HAN/WDH S13 ...... 173 J5
Medlock Dr HAN/WDH S13 .... 173 J6
Medlock Rd HAN/WDH S13 ...... 173 J6 🔢
Medlock Wy HAN/WDH S13 ...... 173 J5
Medway Cl DOD/DAR S75 .... 54 E2
Medway Pl WMB/DAR S73 .... 84 C6 🔢
Meersbrook Av SHEFS S8 .... 187 H7
Meersbrook Park Rd SHEFS S8 .. 187 G1
Meersbrook Rd SHEFS S8 .... 187 H2
Meetinghouse Cft HAN/WDH S13 . 190 A1
Meetinghouse La HAN/WDH S13 .. 190 A1
SHEF S1 .... 9 E2 🔢
Mekyll Cl MALT S66 .... 157 G1 🔢
Melbeck Ct CHPT/GREN S35 ...... 129 K2 🔢
Melbourne Av AU/AST/KP S26 .... 175 J7
DEARNE S63 .... 86 A5
DRON S18 .... 200 B6
FUL S10 .... 170 C2
Melbourne Gv NROS/TKH DN11 .. 162 E3 🔢
Melbourne Rd DONS/BSCR DN4 .. 116 B1
STKB/PEN S36 .... 104 D6
Melbourn Rd FUL S10 .... 170 C2
Melciss Rd ATT S4 .... 157 F3
Melford Cl DOD/DAR S75 .... 29 G6 🔢
Melford Dr DONS/BSCR DN4 ...... 116 D3
Melfort Gln FUL S10 .... 169 K4 🔢
Mell Av HOY S74 .... 108 E1
Mellinder La BTLY DN5 .... 88 D1
Melling Av BTLY DN5 .... 90 C4
Mellington St SHEFS S8 .... 187 J5
Mellish Rd WRKN S81 .... 180 C5
Mellor La HOLM/MEL HD7 .... 46 E3
Mellor Lea Farm Cha
  CHPT/GREN S35 .... 130 C5
Mellor Lea Farm Dr
  CHPT/GREN S35 .... 130 C5
Mellor Lea Farm Garth
  CHPT/GREN S35 .... 130 C5
Mellor Rd WMB/DAR S73 .... 84 B5
Mellow Fields Rd DIN S25 ...... 177 K3
Mellwood Gv WMB/DAR S73 ...... 83 K7 🔢
Mellwood La HEM/SK/SE WF9 ...... 34 D4
Melrose Cl DONS/BSCR DN4 ...... 90 B8
  MALT S66 .... 176 D1
Melrose Gv RHAM S60 .... 155 K5
Melrose Rd ATT S4 .... 171 H1
Melrose Wy BSLYN/ROY S71 ...... 56 E5
Meltham House La
  HOLM/MEL HD7 .... 48 E3
Melton Av DEARNE S63 .... 86 D2 🔢
  WMB/DAR S73 .... 84 E7
Melton Cl HEM/SK/SE WF9 .... 35 F2 🔢
Meltonfield Cl ARMTH DN3 ...... 93 H2 🔢
Melton Gdns BTLY DN5 .... 89 J6
Melton Gn DEARNE S63 .... 111 F1
Melton Gv HACK/IN S12 .... 189 J5
Melton High St DEARNE S63 .... 111 F1
Melton Mill La BTLY DN5 .... 88 A7
Melton Rd BTLY DN5 .... 89 F6
Melton St MEX/SWTN S64 .... 113 H3
  WMB/DAR S73 .... 84 E7 🔢
Melton Ter BSLY S70 .... 82 D2 🔢
Melton Wood Gv BTLY DN5 ...... 89 J6 🔢
Melville St WMB/DAR S73 .... 84 A4 🔢
Melvinia Crs DOD/DAR S75 ...... 2 A1
Melwood Cft ARMTH DN3 .... 93 H5
Memorial Av WRKS S80 .... 210 D5
Mendip Cl BTLY DN5 .... 90 B2 🔢
  DOD/DAR S75 .... 55 G5 🔢
Mendip Ri RHAM S60 .... 155 G7 🔢
Menson Dr HTFD DN7 .... 42 C7
Merbeck Dr CHPT/GREN S35 ...... 107 K6
Merbeck Gv CHPT/GREN S35 ...... 107 K7 🔢
Mercel Av ARMTH DN3 .... 67 H7
Mercia Cl WRKN S81 .... 196 E6 🔢
Mercia Dr TOT/DORE S17 .... 199 J1
Meredith Crs DONS/BSCR DN4 .. 116 E1
Meredith Rd ST/HB/BR S6 ...... 151 F2
Mere La ARMTH DN3 .... 67 F6
Merlin Cl AWLS/ASK DN6 .... 63 J1
  BSLY S70 .... 82 A7
Merlin Wy KIMB S61 .... 131 H1
  SHEFN S5 .... 152 D4
Merrill Rd DEARNE S63 .... 60 B6
Merton La DARN/MH S9 .... 153 J3
Merton Ri DARN/MH S9 .... 153 J3
Merton Rd DARN/MH S9 .... 153 J3 🔢
Metcalfe Av ECK/KIL S21 .... 205 C1
Methley Cl SHEFP/MNR S2 ...... 188 B1
Methley St CUD/GR S72 .... 57 J1
Mexborough Rd DEARNE S63 .... 86 C6
Meynell Crs SHEFN S5 .... 151 J3
Meynell Rd SHEFN S5 .... 151 J3
Meyrick Dr DOD/DAR S75 .... 28 C3
Michael Crt DEARNE S63 .... 111 G1
Michael Rd BSLYN/ROY S71 ...... 57 F5
Michael's Cl CUD/GR S72 .... 32 D8
Mickelden Wy DOD/DAR S75 .... 55 F6 🔢

Micklebring Gv CONI DN12 ...... 114 B7
Micklebring La MALT S66 .... 137 G5
Micklebring Wy MALT S66 ...... 136 C8
Mickleden Edge STKB/PEN S36 .. 101 K6
Micklethwaite Gv THNE DN8 .... 23 K3 🔢
Micklethwaite Rd THNE DN8 .... 23 K3
Mickley La TOT/DORE S17 ...... 199 K3
Middle Av RAW S62 .... 133 J1
Middle Bank DONS/BSCR DN4 .... 5 E6
Middlebrook La THNE DN8 ...... 23 J8
Middleburn Cl BSLY S70 .... 3 D6
Middlecliff Cl MOS S20 .... 190 C6 🔢
Middlecliff Ct MOS S20 .... 190 C6 🔢
Middlecliff La CUD/GR S72 ...... 58 E7
  CUD/GR S72 .... 59 F7
Middlecliff Ri MOS S20 .... 190 C6
Middle Dr RHAM S60 .... 155 J6
Middlefield Cl TOT/DORE S17 .. 185 G8
Middlefield Cft TOT/DORE S17 .. 199 G1
Middle Field La HOR/CROF WF4 .. 28 D1
Middle Field La PONT WF8 ...... 16 D2
Middle Field Rd DOD/DAR S75 .. 54 C7
Middlefield Rd DONS/BSCR DN4 . 92 D8
  RHAM S60 .... 155 K5
Middlefields Dr RHAM S60 ...... 156 B6
Middlegate BTLY DN5 .... 64 B9 🔢
Middle Hay Cl HACK/IN S12 .... 188 A2
Middle Hay Pl HACK/IN S12 .... 188 A2
Middle Hay Ri HACK/IN S12 .... 188 A2
Middle Hay Vw GLV S14 .... 188 A3
Middle La BTLY DN5 .... 39 F4
  CHPT/GREN S35 .... 129 G6
  RHAM/THRY S65 .... 7 E3
  ST/HB/BR S6 .... 170 A1 🔢
Middle La South RHAM/THRY S65 . 7 F4
Middle Ox Cl MOS S20 .... 204 D1
Middle Ox Gdns MOS S20 .... 204 D1
Middle Pl RHAM/THRY S65 ...... 134 A8
Middlesex St BSLY S70 .... 2 C5
Middle St BWTY DN10 .... 143 K4
Middleton La DIN S25 .... 178 A7
Middleton Rd CHPT/GREN S35 .. 129 J7
Middlewood Rd ST/HB/BR S6 .... 151 F4
Middlewood Rd North
  CHPT/GREN S35 .... 150 E2
Middlewoods DOD/DAR S75 ...... 55 F8 🔢
Midfield Rd FUL S10 .... 170 A3
Midhill Rd SHEFP/MNR S2 ...... 171 H8
Midhope Cliff La STKB/PEN S36 . 102 D2
Midhope Hall La STKB/PEN S36 . 103 G3
Midhope La STKB/PEN S36 ...... 102 E3
Midhope Wy DOD/DAR S75 ...... 55 F6
Midhurst Gv DOD/DAR S75 ...... 54 D2
Midhurst Rd ST/HB/BR S6 ...... 151 G2
Midland Rd BSLYN/ROY S71 .... 30 C5
  KIMB S61 .... 154 D7
  MEX/SWTN S64 .... 112 D4
Midland St BSLY S70 .... 2 C4 🔢
  RAW S62 .... 133 H5
  SHEF S1 .... 9 D5 🔢
Midvale Av ST/HB/BR S6 .... 170 E1
Midvale Cl ST/HB/BR S6 .... 8 B1
Milano Ri WMB/DAR S73 .... 84 C2
Milbanke St DON DN1 .... 5 D2 🔢
Milburn Ct MOS S20 .... 190 E6 🔢
Milburn Gv MOS S20 .... 190 E6
Milcroft Crs HTFD DN7 .... 42 C7 🔢
Milden Pl BSLY S70 .... 3 D6
Milden Rd ST/HB/BR S6 .... 151 F5
Mile End Av HTFD DN7 .... 68 D2
Milefield La CUD/GR S72 .... 32 B8
Milefield Vw CUD/GR S72 ...... 32 C8 🔢
Mile Oak Rd RHAM S60 .... 155 J4
Miles Cl SHEFN S5 .... 152 B6
Miles La CHPT/GREN S35 .... 107 K8
  SHEFN S5 .... 152 A6
Mileswood Cl CUD/GR S72 ...... 59 G4 🔢
Milethorn La DON DN1 .... 5 D1
Milford Av HOY S74 .... 109 J1
Milford St DARN/MH S9 .... 153 J7
Milgate St BSLYN/ROY S71 ...... 30 C3
Milgrove Crs CHPT/GREN S35 .. 107 J7
Millais Ri MALT S66 .... 135 G8
Millard Av HTFD DN7 .... 42 B7
Millard La MALT S66 .... 159 H3
Millars Wk HEM/SK/SE WF9 ...... 33 K6
Mill Cl AU/AST/KP S26 .... 193 F3
  DIN S25 .... 177 K1
  HEM/SK/SE WF9 .... 33 K5
  RHAM S60 .... 6 B6
Mill Ct BSLY S70 .... 82 B2 🔢
Milldale Rd TOT/DORE S17 ...... 199 K2
Milldyke Cl RHAM S60 .... 156 C6 🔢
Miller Cl THNE DN8 .... 43 K1
Miller Cft HAN/WDH S13 .... 189 J1
Miller Dale Dr RHAM S60 ...... 155 C8 🔢
Miller La STKB/PEN S36 .... 103 J3
  THNE DN8 .... 43 K1
Miller Rd SHEFS S8 .... 171 F8 🔢
Millers Dl BSLY S70 .... 82 B3
Miller St STKB/PEN S36 .... 105 J6 🔢
Mill Field Ct ARMTH DN3 ...... 67 F1 🔢
Millfield Rd BTLY DN5 .... 65 F7
Mill Field Rd HTFD DN7 .... 22 A7
Millfield Rd THNE DN8 .... 23 J7

Mill Flds AU/AST/KP S26 .... 192 E3
Millfield Vw WRKS S80 .... 210 A5
Mill Gdns WRKS S80 .... 210 A5
Mill Ga BTLY DN5 .... 64 E7
Mill Hvn DIN S25 .... 193 K2
Mill Hill Rd RHAM S60 .... 156 B6
Mill Hl RHAM S60 .... 83 J5
  WMB/DAR S73 .... 85 G8 🔢
Mill Hill Cl BTLY DN5 .... 90 C4
Mill Hill Rd HTFD DN7 .... 68 D2
Mill Hills AU/AST/KP S26 ...... 193 F2
Millhouse La STKB/PEN S36 .... 76 E4
Millhouses Ct ECC S11 .... 186 B5
Millhouses Gln ECC S11 .... 186 B5 🔢
Millhouses La ABRD S7 .... 186 C4
Millhouses St HOY S74 .... 109 F2
Millicent Sq MALT S66 .... 159 H4 🔢
Millindale MALT S66 .... 159 H3
Mill La AWLS/ASK DN6 .... 37 G5
  AWLS/ASK DN6 .... 63 J1
  BTLY DN5 .... 87 H6
  DEARNE S63 .... 111 F2
  DIN S25 .... 193 K2
  DOD/DAR S75 .... 28 D6
  DONS/BSCR DN4 .... 89 J8
  DRON S18 .... 201 H6
  ECK/KIL S21 .... 204 E5
  HATH/EY S32 .... 182 B8
  HEM/SK/SE WF9 .... 33 K6
  HEM/SK/SE WF9 .... 35 C3
  RAW S62 .... 109 G5
  RHAM S60 .... 174 B3
  STKB/PEN S36 .... 50 E7
  STKB/PEN S36 .... 77 C4
  STKB/PEN S36 .... 105 J6
  STKB/PEN S36 .... 126 C3
  TOT/DORE S17 .... 199 K2
Mill Lee La ST/HB/BR S6 ...... 148 D4
Mill Lee Rd ST/HB/BR S6 ...... 148 D4
Mill Meadow Gdns MOS S20 .... 191 F6
Millmoor La RHAM S60 .... 6 A4
Millmoor Rd WMB/DAR S73 ...... 84 C3
Millmount Rd HOY S74 .... 109 G1
  SHEFS S8 .... 187 F2
Millrace Dr DEARNE S63 .... 86 B3
Mill Rd CHPT/GREN S35 .... 130 C6
  ECK/KIL S21 .... 204 B3
  RHAM S60 .... 174 B3
Mill Road Cl CHPT/GREN S35 .. 130 B6 🔢
Millsands OWL S3 .... 9 E2
Mills Dr HTFD DN7 .... 69 H7
Mill Shaw La HOLM/MEL HD7 .... 49 F6
Millside CUD/GR S72 .... 31 K4
Millside Ct BTLY DN5 .... 64 E7 🔢
Millside Wk CUD/GR S72 .... 31 K4
Millstone Cl DRON S18 .... 200 D5 🔢
Millstone Dr AU/AST/KP S26 .. 175 H8
Millstones STKB/PEN S36 ...... 79 F6
Millstream Cl BTLY DN5 .... 90 B6
Mill St ARMTH DN3 .... 93 G1
  HEM/SK/SE WF9 .... 33 K5
  KIMB S61 .... 132 E3
  RHAM S60 .... 6 C5
  WRKS S80 .... 210 C3
Millthorpe Rd SHEFN S5 .... 152 E3
Mill Vw DEARNE S63 .... 86 A6
  HEM/SK/SE WF9 .... 35 A1
Millwood Rd DONS/BSCR DN4 .. 116 C2 🔢
Mill Wood Vw ST/HB/BR S6 .... 150 B8
Milne Av NROS/TKH DN11 .... 163 H3
Milne Dr NROS/TKH DN11 .... 163 J3
Milne Gv NROS/TKH DN11 .... 163 H3
Milner Av STKB/PEN S36 .... 77 J4
Milner Cl MALT S66 .... 157 K1
Milner Ga CONI DN12 .... 115 F4
Milner Gate Ct CONI DN12 .... 114 C5
Milner Rd DONS/BSCR DN4 ...... 90 C8 🔢
Milnes St BSLY S70 .... 3 D5 🔢
Milnes St DOD/DAR S75 .... 54 D3
Milnrow Crs SHEFN S5 .... 152 A1
Milnrow Dr SHEFN S5 .... 152 A1
Milnrow Rd SHEFN S5 .... 152 A1
Milton Av BTLY DN5 .... 90 C3
Milton Cl DEARNE S63 .... 84 E7
  HOY S74 .... 83 G8
  KIMB S61 .... 132 E3
Milton Ct MEX/SWTN S64 .... 112 B4
Milton Crs HOY S74 .... 109 F2
Milton Dr WRKN S81 .... 211 F3
Milton Gv ARMTH DN3 .... 66 E5 🔢
  ARMTH DN3 .... 93 G1
  WMB/DAR S73 .... 84 B5
Milton La SHEF S1 .... 8 C4
Milton Rd ABRD S7 .... 170 E8
  ARMTH DN3 .... 93 K6
  AWLS/ASK DN6 .... 37 K6
  CHPT/GREN S35 .... 129 J2
  DIN S25 .... 178 C7
  HOY S74 .... 109 F1 🔢
  MEX/SWTN S64 .... 113 F2
  RHAM/THRY S65 .... 7 E2
Milton St CUD/GR S72 .... 59 G5
  MALT S66 .... 159 G3
  MEX/SWTN S64 .... 112 B4
  OWL S3 .... 8 C4
  RHAM S60 .... 6 B3
Milton Wk DON DN1 .... 5 D4
  WRKN S81 .... 211 F3

Minden Cl MALT S66 ... 157 G3
Minden Cl BTLY DN5 ... 64 E7
Minna Rd OWL S3 ... 152 C8
Minneymoor La CONI DN12 ... 114 E4
Minneymoor La CONI DN12 ... 114 E5
Minster Rd CHPT/GREN S35 ... 130 D7
DONS/BSCR DN4 ... 93 F8
Minster Wy BSLYN/ROY S71 ... 56 E4
Minsthorpe La HEM/SK/SE WF9 ... 35 F1
Minto Rd ST/HB/BR S6 ... 151 G6
Mission Fld WMB/DAR S73 ... 84 D7
Mitchell Cl BSLY S70 ... 82 E2
HTFD DN7 ... 42 B6
WRKN S81 ... 196 C6
Mitchell Rd SHEFS S8 ... 187 F5
WMB/DAR S73 ... 83 K2
Mitchell's St BSLY S70 ... 83 F2
Mitchell St OWL S3 ... 8 B2
Mitchelson Av DOD/DAR S75 ... 54 D8
Moat Cft BTLY DN5 ... 64 C6
Moat Hills Ct BTLY DN5 ... 64 D6
Moat La MALT S66 ... 157 J6
Modda La HOLM/MEL HD7 ... 47 J3
Modena Ct WMB/DAR S73 ... 84 B1
Moffat Gdns WHHL DN2 ... 66 C6
Moffatt Rd SHEF/MNR S2 ... 171 H8
Moira Cl HTFD DN7 ... 42 C2
Molineaux Cl SHEFN S5 ... 152 E2
Molineaux Rd SHEFN S5 ... 152 D1
Molloy Pl SHEFS S8 ... 187 G1
Molloy St SHEFS S8 ... 187 G1
Mona Av FUL S10 ... 170 C3
Mona Rd DONS/BSCR DN4 ... 4 B6
FUL S10 ... 170 C2
Monckton Rd NROS/TKH DN11 ... 163 H3
SHEFN S5 ... 153 G4
Moncrieffe Rd ABRD S7 ... 186 E1
Monksbridge La DIN S25 ... 177 J6
Monks Cl KIMB S61 ... 131 K5
Monkspring BSLY S70 ... 82 D2
Monks Wy BSLYN/ROY S71 ... 56 E4
WRKN S81 ... 195 H8
Monk Ter BSLYN/ROY S71 ... 57 F2
Monkton Wy BSLYN/ROY S71 ... 30 D2
Monkwood Rd RAW S62 ... 111 G8
Monmouth St WHHL DN2 ... 91 K1
WRKN S81 ... 210 E1
Monmouth St OWL S3 ... 8 D4
Monsal Cres BSLYN/ROY S71 ... 30 B8
Monsal St DEARNE S63 ... 60 B7
Montague Av CONI DN12 ... 114 B4
Montague St CUD/GR S72 ... 31 K7
DON DN1 ... 5 D2
ECC S11 ... 8 B5
Montagu Rd BTLY DN5 ... 90 B5
Montagu St MEX/SWTN S64 ... 113 C8
Monteney Crs SHEFN S5 ... 130 B7
Monteney Gdns SHEFN S5 ... 130 B8
Monteney Rd SHEFN S5 ... 130 B8
Montfort Dr OWL S3 ... 171 H1
Montgomery Av ABRD S7 ... 170 E8
Montgomery Dr ABRD S7 ... 170 E8
Montgomery Rd ABRD S7 ... 170 E8
DEARNE S63 ... 111 H1
Montgomery Terrace Rd
ST/HB/BR S6 ... 8 C1
Montrose WRKN S81 ... 211 F2
Montrose Av DOD/DAR S75 ... 28 E6
WHHL DN2 ... 92 A2
Montrose Pl DRON S18 ... 200 D5
Montrose Rd ECC S11 ... 186 C2
Moonpenny Wy DRON S18 ... 201 G6
Moonshine La SHEFN S5 ... 152 A4
Moorbank Cl DOD/DAR S75 ... 55 H3
WMB/DAR S73 ... 83 J3
Moorbank Dr FUL S10 ... 169 J4
Moorbank Rd FUL S10 ... 169 H4
WMB/DAR S73 ... 83 J2
Moorbank Vw WMB/DAR S73 ... 83 J2
Moorbridge Crs WMB/DAR S73 ... 84 E6
Moorbrow HOLM/MEL HD7 ... 48 B5
Moor Crs MOS S20 ... 190 A8
Moorcrest Rd DOD/DAR S75 ... 29 C5
Moorcroft Av FUL S10 ... 169 F7
Moorcroft Cl FUL S10 ... 169 F8
Moorcroft Dr FUL S10 ... 169 F8
Moorcroft Rd FUL S10 ... 169 F8
Moordale Vw RAW S62 ... 112 B8
Moor Dike Rd HTFD DN7 ... 69 H8
HTFD DN7 ... 69 J3
Moor Edges Rd THNE DN8 ... 24 D8
Moorend La DOD/DAR S75 ... 79 K2
Moor End Rd FUL S10 ... 170 C3
Moorends Rd THNE DN8 ... 23 K1
Moore St SHEFP/MNR S2 ... 8 C4
Moore Street Rbt OWL S3 ... 8 C4
Moor Farm Av MOS S20 ... 189 K7
Moor Farm Garth MOS S20 ... 190 A7
Moor Farm Ri MOS S20 ... 189 K7
Moorfield Av RHAM/THRY S65 ... 135 J8
Moorfield Cl RHAM/THRY S65 ... 135 J8
Moorfield Crs HEM/SK/SE WF9 ... 33 F1
Moorfield Dr ARMTH DN3 ... 93 G2
Moorfield Gv RHAM/THRY S65 ... 135 J8
Moorfield Pl HEM/SK/SE WF9 ... 33 F1
Moor Gap ARMTH DN3 ... 93 J7
Moorgate Av FUL S10 ... 8 A2

RHAM S60 ... 7 D6
Moorgate Cha RHAM S60 ... 7 D6
Moorgate Crs DRON S18 ... 201 H7
Moorgate Gv RHAM S60 ... 7 D6
Moorgate Rd RHAM S60 ... 7 D6
Moorgate St RHAM S60 ... 7 D5
Moor Green Cl DOD/DAR S75 ... 55 F5
Moor Head SHEF S1 ... 9 D4
Moorhouse Cl RHAM S60 ... 156 C6
Moorhouse Ct HEM/SK/SE WF9 ... 35 F6
Moorhouse Gap AWLS/ASK DN6 ... 36 A6
Moorhouse La AWLS/ASK DN6 ... 35 H7
DOD/DAR S75 ... 28 B2
RHAM S60 ... 156 C6
Moorhouse Vw HEM/SK/SE WF9 ... 35 C5
Moorland Av BSLY S70 ... 55 G7
DOD/DAR S75 ... 29 C5
Moorland Crs DOD/DAR S75 ... 29 C5
Moorland Dr STKB/PEN S36 ... 104 D6
Moorland Gv DONS/BSCR DN4 ... 92 B6
Moorland Pl ST/HB/BR S6 ... 169 C1
Moorland Rd HAN/WDH S13 ... 182 B8
Moorlands HOLM/MEL HD7 ... 48 B4
MALT S66 ... 156 E3
Moorlands Crs RHAM S60 ... 156 B6
Moorland Ter CUD/GR S72 ... 57 K2
Moorland Vw AU/AST/KP S26 ... 175 J8
DEARNE S63 ... 85 F7
DRON S18 ... 202 C6
HACK/IN S12 ... 188 C5
KBTN HD8 ... 26 D5
Moor La ARMTH DN3 ... 66 D2
BSLY S70 ... 108 A2
CONI DN12 ... 136 C6
CUD/GR S72 ... 59 H3
EPW DN9 ... 96 C2
GLE DN14 ... 12 B8
STKB/PEN S36 ... 125 K3
THNE DN8 ... 24 A5
THNE DN8 ... 70 D1
Moor La North RHAM/THRY S65 ... 135 J7
Moor La South RHAM/THRY S65 ... 135 J8
Moor Oaks Rd FUL S10 ... 170 C4
Moor Owners Rd THNE DN8 ... 24 E8
Moor Rd DEARNE S63 ... 111 J1
GLE DN14 ... 14 E1
GLE DN14 ... 15 J4
GLE DN14 ... 15 C2
RHAM/THRY S65 ... 156 A1
ST/HB/BR S6 ... 149 J3
THNE DN8 ... 44 B2
Moorshutt Rd HEM/SK/SE WF9 ... 33 F1
Moorside FUL S10 ... 168 E7
Moorside Av STKB/PEN S36 ... 77 K5
Moorside La DOD/DAR S75 ... 29 C7
MOS S20 ... 190 A7
Moorsyde Av FUL S10 ... 170 B2
Moorsyde Crs FUL S10 ... 170 B2
Moorthorpe Gdns MOS S20 ... 189 J5
Moorthorpe Gn HACK/IN S12 ... 189 J5
Moorthorpe Wy MOS S20 ... 189 J5
MOS S20 ... 190 A5
Moor Top Dr HEM/SK/SE WF9 ... 33 C2
Moor Top Rd MOS S20 ... 202 D6
Moor Top Rd NROS/TKH DN11 ... 162 E2
Moortown Av DIN S25 ... 178 C8
Moor Va MOS S20 ... 189 H5
Moor Valley Cl HACK/IN S12 ... 189 J6
Moor Vw ARMTH DN3 ... 93 J7
Moorview KIMB S61 ... 154 A1
Moor View Dr SHEFS S8 ... 186 E5
Moor View Rd SHEFS S8 ... 187 G4
Moor View Ter ECC S11 ... 185 J2
Moorwinstow Cft
TOT/DORE S17 ... 185 J8
Moorwood La ST/HB/BR S6 ... 168 B3
TOT/DORE S17 ... 199 F5
Moorwoods Av CHPT/GREN S35 ... 130 A2
Moorwoods La CHPT/GREN S35 ... 130 A2
Moray Pl DRON S18 ... 200 D5
Mordaunt Rd SHEFP/MNR S2 ... 188 B1
More Hall La STKB/PEN S36 ... 127 K3
Morgan Av SHEFN S5 ... 151 K4
Morgan Cl SHEFN S5 ... 152 A4
Morgan Rd SHEFN S5 ... 151 K5
Morland Cl GLV S14 ... 188 B4
Morland Dr GLV S14 ... 188 B4
Morland Pl GLV S14 ... 188 B4
Morland Rd GLV S14 ... 188 A4
Morley Cl DRON S18 ... 200 C6
Morley Fold KBTN HD8 ... 51 G2
Morley Pl CONI DN12 ... 114 C6
Morley St KIMB S61 ... 132 B6
WHHL DN2 ... 5 E1
Morley St RAW S62 ... 133 J3
ST/HB/BR S6 ... 151 C8
Morpeth St OWL S3 ... 8 C2
RHAM/THRY S65 ... 7 D4
Morrall Rd SHEFF S5 ... 130 A8
Morrell St MALT S66 ... 159 H3
Morris Av RAW S62 ... 111 J7
Morrison Av MALT S66 ... 159 H1
Morrison Dr NROS/TKH DN11 ... 118 E7
Morrison Pl WMB/DAR S73 ... 84 D1
Morrison Rd WMB/DAR S73 ... 84 C1
Morris Rd DONS/BSCR DN4 ... 116 B3
Mortain Rd RHAM S60 ... 155 J6

Mortains AU/AST/KP S26 ... 193 F1
Morthen Hall La MALT S66 ... 157 G8
Morthen La MALT S66 ... 157 F7
RHAM S60 ... 175 H1
Morthen Rd MALT S66 ... 157 J7
Mortimer Dr STKB/PEN S36 ... 77 K6
Mortimer Rd MALT S66 ... 159 K3
ST/HB/BR S6 ... 147 J3
STKB/PEN S36 ... 103 K2
STKB/PEN S36 ... 103 J6
Mortlake Rd SHEFN S5 ... 152 E5
Mortomley Cl CHPT/GREN S35 ... 107 K8
Mortomley La CHPT/GREN S35 ... 107 K8
Morton Cl BSLYN/ROY S71 ... 56 E7
Morton Gv WRKN S81 ... 196 C6
Morton La ECK/KIL S21 ... 202 E6
Morton Pl CHPT/GREN S35 ... 129 H7
Morton Rd MEX/SWTN S64 ... 113 G2
Morton Wood Gv HOLM/MEL HD7 ... 48 C4
Mosborough Hall Dr MOS S20 ... 204 C2
Mosborough Moor MOS S20 ... 188 K7
Mosborough Rd HAN/WDH S13 ... 172 D8
Moscar Cross Rd ST/HB/BR S6 ... 166 D2
Moses Vw WRKN S81 ... 195 G8
Mosgrove Cl WRKN S81 ... 196 A8
Mosham Cl EPW DN9 ... 120 E1
Mosham Rd EPW DN9 ... 120 C2
Moss Cl MALT S66 ... 157 G3
Mosscroft La HTFD DN7 ... 68 E5
Mossdale WRKN S81 ... 196 E7
Mossdale Av MOS S20 ... 190 B8
Mossdale Cl BTLY DN5 ... 64 B8
Moss Dr ECK/KIL S21 ... 205 H2
Moss Edge Rd HOLM/MEL HD7 ... 47 F7
Moss Gv HACK/IN S12 ... 190 B3
Moss Hvn AWLS/ASK DN6 ... 20 A6
Moss La AWLS/ASK DN6 ... 40 B2
Mossley Rd STKB/PEN S36 ... 105 K1
Moss Rd HOLM/MEL HD7 ... 47 H2
Moss Rd AWLS/ASK DN6 ... 19 F7
AWLS/ASK DN6 ... 20 B6
TOT/DORE S17 ... 199 F3
Moss Vw MOS S20 ... 203 K1
Moss Wy HACK/IN S12 ... 190 B4
MOS S20 ... 190 B8
Motehall Dr SHEFP/MNR S2 ... 172 C6
Motehall Pl SHEFP/MNR S2 ... 172 D6
Motehall Rd SHEFP/MNR S2 ... 172 C6
Motehall Wy SHEFP/MNR S2 ... 172 C6
The Motte KIMB S61 ... 132 C7
Mottram St BSLYN/ROY S71 ... 2 C3
Mount Av CUD/GR S72 ... 32 D7
CUD/GR S72 ... 59 H6
WRKN S81 ... 210 C2
Mountbatten Dr CHPT/GREN S35 ... 129 J2
Mount Cl BSLY S70 ... 2 C6
Mount Crs HOY S74 ... 108 E1
Mountenoy Rd RHAM S60 ... 6 C6
Mountfields Wk
HEM/SK/SE WF9 ... 34 A6
Mountford Cft TOT/DORE S17 ... 199 J2
Mount Pleasant BSLY S70 ... 82 C3
CUD/GR S72 ... 32 D7
DONS/BSCR DN4 ... 90 D8
Mount Pleasant Cl
CHPT/GREN S35 ... 130 B1
Mount Pleasant Rd DEARNE S63 ... 111 J3
KIMB S61 ... 6 A3
SHEFP/MNR S2 ... 8 C6
THNE DN8 ... 23 H5
Mount Rd CHPT/GREN S35 ... 129 H5
CUD/GR S72 ... 32 D7
OWL S3 ... 152 A8
Mount Scar Vw HOLM/MEL HD7 ... 48 C3
Mount St BSLY S70 ... 2 B5
BSLYN/ROY S71 ... 57 G7
ECC S11 ... 6 A3
KIMB S61 ... 6 A3
Mount Ter DEARNE S63 ... 111 F1
WMB/DAR S73 ... 83 K4
The Mount ARMTH DN3 ... 67 F6
Mount Vernon Av BSLY S70 ... 2 C6
Mount Vernon Crs BSLY S70 ... 82 B1
Mount Vernon Rd BSLY S70 ... 82 A1
Mount Vw CONI DN12 ... 115 J6
Mount View Av SHEFS S8 ... 187 G4
Mount View Gdns SHEFS S8 ... 187 G4
Mount View Rd HOLM/MEL HD7 ... 48 D5
SHEFS S8 ... 187 G5
Mousehole Cl RHAM/THRY S65 ... 134 D6
Mousehole La RHAM/THRY S65 ... 134 D6
Mouse Park Ga CHPT/GREN S35 ... 128 E4
Mowbray Gdns RHAM/THRY S65 ... 134 B7
Mowbray Pl RHAM/THRY S65 ... 134 B7
Mowbray Rd THNE DN8 ... 43 J3
Mowbray St OWL S3 ... 9 D1
RHAM/THRY S65 ... 134 A7
Mowson Crs CHPT/GREN S35 ... 150 C2
Mowson La CHPT/GREN S35 ... 150 C2
Moxon Cl STKB/PEN S36 ... 105 G2
Mucky La BSLYN/ROY S71 ... 57 H6
STKB/PEN S36 ... 104 D3
Muglet La MALT S66 ... 159 J3
Mugup La HOLM/MEL HD7 ... 48 D6
Muirfield WRKN S81 ... 211 F1
Muirfield Av DONS/BSCR DN4 ... 119 C1
MEX/SWTN S64 ... 112 D5
Mulberry Av THNE DN8 ... 23 K3
Mulberry Cl BTLY DN5 ... 90 C4

RAW S62 .... 133 J4 🄱
Mulberry Crs *WRKN* S81 .... 180 D8
Mulberry Rd *DIN* S25 .... 194 A1
ECK/KIL S21 .... 205 K5
Mulberry St *SHEF* S1 .... 9 E3 🄱
Mulberry Wy *ARMTH* DN3 .... 95 C3 🄱
ECK/KIL S21 .... 205 F2 🄱
Mulehouse Rd *FUL* S10 .... 170 A3
Mundella Pl *SHEFS* S8 .... 187 C4
Munro Cl *ECK/KIL* S21 .... 205 H1
Munsbrough La *KIMB* S61 .... 132 D5
Munsbrough Ri *KIMB* S61 .... 132 E4
Murdoch Pl *BSLYN/ROY* S71 ...... 29 K8 🄱
Murdock Rd *DARN/MH* S9 .... 152 A5
Murrayfield Dr *MOS* S20 .... 204 C1 🄱
Murray Rd *ECC* S11 .... 186 B1
ECK/KIL S21 .... 191 J8 🄱
RAW S62 .... 133 K1
Musgrave Crs *SHEFN* S5 .... 152 B6
Musgrave Dr *SHEFN* S5 .... 152 B6
Musgrave Pl *SHEFN* S5 .... 152 B6
Musgrave Rd *SHEFN* S5 .... 152 A6
Musgrove Av *RHAM/THRY* S65 .... 135 F5
Mushroom La *FUL* S10 .... 8 A3
Muskoka Av *ECC* S11 .... 185 J2
Muskoka Dr *ECC* S11 .... 185 J1
Mutual St *DONS/BSCR* DN4 .... 4 B4
Myers Av *CHPT/GREN* S35 .... 128 C7
Myers Grove La *ST/HB/BR* S6 ...... 150 E8
Myers La *CHPT/GREN* S35 .... 149 K4
Myers St *WMB/DAR* S73 .... 83 K3
Mylnhurst Rd *ECC* S11 .... 186 B3
Mylor Ct *BSLYN/ROY* S71 .... 3 F2 🄱
Mylor Rd *ECC* S11 .... 186 A1
Myrtle Crs *MALT* S66 .... 157 H2
Myrtle Gv *AU/AST/KP* S26 .... 192 C5
EPW DN9 .... 94 B8
Myrtle Rd *HTFD* DN7 .... 42 A7
SHEFP/MNR S2 .... 9 D6
WMB/DAR S73 .... 83 K4
Myrtle Springs *HACK/IN* S12 ...... 188 B2
Myrtle St *DOD/DAR* S75 .... 55 H5 🄱
Myton Rd *DARN/MH* S9 .... 172 C3

N

Nab La *HTFD* DN7 .... 22 A8
Nairn Dr *DRON* S18 .... 200 D6 🄱
Nairn St *FUL* S10 .... 170 B4
Nancy Crs *CUD/GR* S72 .... 58 E1 🄱
Nancy Rd *CUD/GR* S72 .... 58 E1
Nanny Hl *SHEFP* S36 .... 105 F6
Nanny Marr Rd *WMB/DAR* S73 ...... 84 E1
Nan Sampson Bank *EPW* DN9 ...... 96 A7
Napier Mt *BSLY* S70 .... 82 A1
Napier St *ECC* S11 .... 8 B5
Narrow La *BTLY* DN5 .... 39 G2
BWTY DN10 .... 80 A1
DIN S25 .... 194 A2
NROS/TKH DN11 .... 139 H5
Naseby Av *BTLY* DN5 .... 90 A1
Naseby Cl *HTFD* DN7 .... 68 B2 🄱
Naseby Dr *DARN/MH* S9 .... 153 H5
Nash La *WRKN* S81 .... 211 C3
Nathan Ct *MOS* S20 .... 190 D6
Nathan Dr *MOS* S20 .... 190 D5
Nathan Gv *MOS* S20 .... 190 C5
Navan Rd *SHEFP/MNR* S2 .... 172 C8
Naylor Gv *CHPT/GREN* S35 .... 150 B1 🄱
DOD/DAR S75 .... 54 E8
Naylor Rd *CHPT/GREN* S35 .... 128 B8
CHPT/GREN S35 .... 150 B1
Naylor St *RAW* S62 .... 133 J4
Neale Rd *WHHL* DN2 .... 66 A7
Nearcroft Rd *KIMB* S61 .... 132 C7
Nearfield Rd *DONS/BSCR* DN4 .... 118 C1
Needham Wy *ECC* S11 .... 186 C2
Needlewood *DOD/DAR* S75 .... 80 E1 🄱
Neepsend La *OWL* S3 .... 9 D1 🄱
Neild Rd *HOY* S74 .... 109 G1
Neill Rd *ECC* S11 .... 170 C7
Nelson Av *BSLYN/ROY* S71 .... 3 D1
Nelson Cl *RHAM* S60 .... 155 C7
Nelson Pl *CHPT/GREN* S35 .... 129 J2
Nelson Rd *CONI* DN12 .... 115 J5
MALT S66 .... 159 J2
ST/HB/BR S6 .... 169 K1
Nelson St *BSLY* S70 .... 2 B4 🄱
CUD/GR S72 .... 32 B3
RHAM/THRY S65 .... 7 D4
Nemesia Cl *DIN* S25 .... 193 J3 🄱
Nene Gv *EPW* DN9 .... 94 B8
Nene Wk *WRKN* S81 .... 196 C8
Nesfield Wy *SHEFN* S5 .... 152 E5
Nether Av *CHPT/GREN* S35 .... 129 J6
ECK/KIL S21 .... 205 C1
Nether Cantley La *ARMTH* DN3 .... 95 C5
Nether Crs *CHPT/GREN* S35 .... 129 J6
Nethercroft *DOD/DAR* S75 .... 54 D2
Netherdene Rd *DRON* S18 .... 201 C6
Nether Edge Rd *ABRD* S7 .... 186 E2
Netherfield Cl *STKB/PEN* S36 ...... 105 J6 🄱
Netherfield La *RAW* S62 .... 133 J3
Netherfield Rd *FUL* S10 .... 170 B2
Netherfields Crs *DRON* S18 .... 201 C7
Netherfield Vw *RHAM/THRY* S65 .. 134 C7
Nethergate *ST/HB/BR* S6 .... 169 F2

Nethergreen Av *ECK/KIL* S21 ...... 191 H8
Nethergreen Ct *ECK/KIL* S21 ...... 191 H8 🄱
Nethergreen Gdns *ECK/KIL* S21 .. 191 H8 🄱
Nethergreen Rd *ECC* S11 .... 169 J7
Nether Hall Rd *DON* DN1 .... 5 D3
Nether House La *STKB/PEN* S36 .... 76 E8
Netherhouses *HOLM/MEL* HD7 .... 47 G2 🄱
Nether La *CHPT/GREN* S35 .... 130 C5
Nether Ley Av *CHPT/GREN* S35 .. 130 B2
Nether Ley Ct *CHPT/GREN* S35 .. 130 B2 🄱
Nether Ley Cft *CHPT/GREN* S35 .. 130 B2 🄱
Nether Ley Gdns
CHPT/GREN S35 .... 130 B2 🄱
Nethermoor Av *ECK/KIL* S21 ...... 191 H8 🄱
Nethermoor Cl *ECK/KIL* S21 .... 191 H8
Nethermoor Dr *ECK/KIL* S21 .... 191 H8
MALT S66 .... 157 H5
Nethermoor La *ECK/KIL* S21 ...... 191 H8
Nether Oak Cl *MOS* S20 .... 191 F5 🄱
Nether Oak Dr *MOS* S20 .... 191 F5
Nether Oak Vw *MOS* S20 .... 191 F5 🄱
Nether Rd *DOD/DAR* S75 .... 53 K6
Nether Shire La *SHEFN* S5 .... 130 D8
Netherthorpe Rd *ECK/KIL* S21 .... 205 C1
Netherthorpe Rd *OWL* S3 .... 8 B3
Nether Thorpe Rd *WRKS* S80 ...... 208 C3
Netherthorpe St *OWL* S3 .... 8 C2 🄱
Netherthorpe Wy *DIN* S25 .... 178 A8
Netherton Pl *WRKS* S80 .... 210 C6
Netherton Rd *WRKS* S80 .... 210 E6
Netherwood Rd *WMB/DAR* S73 .... 84 A2
Nettle Cft *NROS/TKH* DN11 .... 140 B8
Nettleham Rd *SHEFS* S8 .... 187 F4
Nettleholme *HTFD* DN7 .... 42 C7
Neville Av *BSLY* S70 .... 3 F6
Neville Cl *BSLY* S70 .... 56 E8 🄱
HEM/SK/SE WF9 .... 34 B4
OWL S3 .... 9 E1
WMB/DAR S73 .... 83 J3
Neville Ct *WMB/DAR* S73 .... 83 J3
Neville Crs *BSLY* S70 .... 56 E8
Neville Dr *OWL* S3 .... 171 H1
Neville La *HTFD* DN7 .... 21 F7
Neville Pits La *GLE* DN14 .... 10 B6
Neville Rd *KIMB* S61 .... 132 C6
Neville St *RHAM* S60 .... 6 C3
Newall Dr *BWTY* DN10 .... 165 H1
Newark Cl *DOD/DAR* S75 .... 29 C5
Newark Rd *MEX/SWTN* S64 .... 112 D2
Newark St *DARN/MH* S9 .... 153 H8 🄱
Newbiggin Cl *RAW* S62 .... 133 H3
Newbiggin Dr *RAW* S62 .... 133 H3
Newbold Ter *RAW* S62 .... 133 H3
Newbolt Rd *DONS/BSCR* DN4 .... 116 E1
Newbould Crs *MOS* S20 .... 190 E4
Newbould La *FUL* S10 .... 170 C5
Newbridge Gv *CONI* DN12 .... 115 K5 🄱
Newburn Dr *DARN/MH* S9 .... 154 B5
Newbury Rd *HEM/SK/SE* WF9 ...... 35 F2
Newbury Rd *FUL* S10 .... 170 B3 🄱
Newbury Wy *BTLY* DN5 .... 90 A1 🄱
Newby Crs *DONS/BSCR* DN4 ...... 116 D2
Newcastle Av *WRKS* S80 .... 210 B5
Newcastle Cl *DIN* S25 .... 178 A8 🄱
WRKS S80 .... 210 C5
Newcastle St *SHEF* S1 .... 8 C3
New Chapel Av *STKB/PEN* S36 .... 77 K6
New Cl *DOD/DAR* S75 .... 53 J7
New Close La *AWLS/ASK* DN6 ...... 17 F8
Newcomen Rd *BTLY* DN5 .... 4 A1
Newcroft Cl *MOS* S20 .... 191 F4
New Cross Dr *HAN/WDH* S13 ...... 189 J1
New Cross Wy *HAN/WDH* S13 .... 189 J1
Newdale Av *CUD/GR* S72 .... 57 H2 🄱
Newell Av *MALT* S66 .... 157 H5
Newent La *FUL* S10 .... 170 B3
Newfield Av *BSLYN/ROY* S71 ...... 56 E3
Newfield Crs *DEARNE* S63 .... 111 G2
TOT/DORE S17 .... 185 G8
Newfield Cft *TOT/DORE* S17 ...... 185 G7
Newfield Farm Cl
SHEFP/MNR S2 .... 188 A2 🄱
Newfield Green Rd
SHEFP/MNR S2 .... 187 K1
Newfield La *TOT/DORE* S17 .... 185 G8
Newfields Av *THNE* DN8 .... 23 K5
Newfields Cl *THNE* DN8 .... 23 K5
Newfields Dr *THNE* DN8 .... 23 K5
New Fold *HOLM/MEL* HD7 .... 47 J3
New Ga *HOLM/MEL* HD7 .... 48 B6
Newgate Cl *CHPT/GREN* S35 ...... 107 J8
Newgate St *WRKS* S80 .... 210 D5
New Gn *HTFD* DN7 .... 41 K3
Newhall Av *MALT* S66 .... 157 H5
New Hall Crs *STKB/PEN* S36 ...... 104 C5 🄱
Newhall La *MALT* S66 .... 158 B4
New Hall La *STKB/PEN* S36 .... 104 B6
Newhall Rd *ARMTH* DN3 .... 67 F4
ATT S4 .... 153 F7
DARN/MH S9 .... 153 G8
New Hi *CONI* DN12 .... 114 D5
Newhill Rd *BSLYN/ROY* S71 .... 56 B2
DEARNE S63 .... 111 G2
New Holles Ct *WRKS* S80 .... 210 D6
Newholme Dr *THNE* DN8 .... 23 K4 🄱
New Ings *ARMTH* DN3 .... 93 F1
New Ings La *ARMTH* DN3 .... 40 C5

Newington Av *CUD/GR* S72 .... 31 J7 🄱
Newington Dr *AU/AST/KP* S26 .... 175 J8
Newington Rd *BWTY* DN10 .... 142 D7
ECC S11 .... 170 C7
New Inn La *HTFD* DN7 .... 41 K2 🄱
New Laithe La *HOLM/MEL* HD7 .... 48 A3
Newland Av *CUD/GR* S72 .... 57 H2
MALT S66 .... 159 C1
Newland Rd *BSLYN/ROY* S71 ...... 29 K8
HACK/IN S12 .... 188 C1
KBTN HD8 .... 26 C5
Newlands Cl *DONS/BSCR* DN4 .. 118 E1
Newlands Dr *BTLY* DN5 .... 90 C2
HACK/IN S12 .... 188 C1
Newlands Gv *HACK/IN* S12 .... 188 D1
Newlands Rd *HACK/IN* S12 .... 188 C1
New La *BTLY* DN5 .... 89 H6
HEM/SK/SE WF9 .... 35 F1
NROS/TKH DN11 .... 119 F6
New Lodge Crs *BSLYN/ROY* S71 .. 29 K8
Newlyn Dr *BSLYN/ROY* S71 .... 3 F2
Newlyn Pl *SHEFS* S8 .... 187 F4
Newlyn Rd *SHEFS* S8 .... 187 F4
Newman Av *BSLYN/ROY* S71 ...... 30 D6
Newman Cl *DARN/MH* S9 .... 153 J3 🄱
Newman Ct *RHAM* S60 .... 155 K5
Newman Dr *DARN/MH* S9 .... 153 H3
Newman Rd *DARN/MH* S9 .... 153 H4
RHAM S60 .... 155 K4
Newmarche Dr *AWLS/ASK* DN6 .. 19 F7
Newmarch St *DARN/MH* S9 .... 154 B4
Newmarket Ct *DONS/BSCR* DN4 .. 92 C5
New Mdw *RAW* S62 .... 111 G2
New Mill Bank *STKB/PEN* S36 .... 127 F2
New Mill Field Rd *HTFD* DN7 .... 42 E8
HTFD DN7 .... 68 E1
New Mill Rd *HOLM/MEL* HD7 .... 48 A1
New Orchard La *MALT* S66 .... 158 A8
New Orchard Rd *MALT* S66 .... 157 K8
New Park Est *HTFD* DN7 .... 42 B2
HTFD DN7 .... 68 B1
New Row La *STKB/PEN* S36 .... 51 F7
New Royd *STKB/PEN* S36 .... 76 E4
Newsam Rd *MEX/SWTN* S64 ...... 112 C6
Newsham Dr *SHEFS* S8 .... 187 F2
New Smithy Av *STKB/PEN* S36 .... 77 H3 🄱
New Smithy Dr *STKB/PEN* S36 .... 77 H3
Newsome Av *WMB/DAR* S73 .... 83 J4
New Station Rd *MEX/SWTN* S64 .. 112 D4
Newstead Av *CHPT/GREN* S35 .. 128 C7
HACK/IN S12 .... 189 C5
Newstead Cl *DRON* S18 .... 200 C6 🄱
HACK/IN S12 .... 189 G4 🄱
Newstead Dr *HACK/IN* S12 .... 189 C5
Newstead Gv *HACK/IN* S12 .... 189 G4 🄱
Newstead Pl *HACK/IN* S12 .... 189 C5
Newstead Ri *HACK/IN* S12 .... 189 C5
Newstead Rd *BSLYN/ROY* S71 .... 29 K7
BTLY DN5 .... 64 C6
HACK/IN S12 .... 189 G4
Newstead Wy *HACK/IN* S12 .... 189 C5
New St *AWLS/ASK* DN6 .... 38 A6
BSLY S70 .... 2 C4
BSLY S70 .... 82 D3
BSLY S70 .... 82 E5 🄱
BSLYN/ROY S71 .... 30 D4
BSLYN/ROY S71 .... 57 F7 🄱
BTLY DN5 .... 64 D7
CHPT/GREN S35 .... 107 J7
CUD/GR S72 .... 32 A1
CUD/GR S72 .... 58 D1
CUD/GR S72 .... 59 H6
DEARNE S63 .... 86 C6 🄱
DIN S25 .... 178 A3
DIN S25 .... 178 B6
DOD/DAR S75 .... 29 G6
DOD/DAR S75 .... 80 E1
DON DN1 .... 4 C5
EPW DN9 .... 121 F2
HEM/SK/SE WF9 .... 34 D4 🄱
KBTN HD8 .... 26 A6
KIMB S61 .... 131 C3
KIMB S61 .... 132 E3
MEX/SWTN S64 .... 113 J2
MOS S20 .... 190 E5

RAW S62 .... 133 J2
RHAM S60 .... 174 B1
SHEF S1 .... 9 D2
WMB/DAR S73 .... 83 J8
WMB/DAR S73 .... 84 B4 🔲
WMB/DAR S73 .... 84 D2
New Street Bus Link MOS S20 ... 190 E7
New Street La SHEFP/MNR S2 ... 9 F2 🔲
Newthorpe Rd AWLS/ASK DN6 .... 17 K3
Newton Av STKB/PEN S36 .... 104 C5
Newton Cl WRKN S81 .... 196 A8
Newton Dr BTLY DN5 .... 90 C4
RHAM/THRY S65 .... 7 F4
Newton La BTLY DN5 .... 90 C4
SHEF S1 .... 9 D4 🔲🔲
STKB/PEN S36 .... 104 C5
Newton Pl KIMB S61 .... 131 G4
Newton Rd BSLY S70 .... 2 A3 🔲
RHAM/THRY S65 .... 7 F4
Newtown Av BSLYN/ROY S71 .... 30 C5
CUD/OR S72 .... 57 J2
Newtown Gn CUD/OR S72 .... 57 J2 🔲
Newtree Dr NROS/TKH DN11 ... 138 E1
New Wortley Rd KIMB S61 .... 6 B3
Niagara Rd ST/HB/BR S6 .... 151 H4
Nicholas La DEARNE S63 .... 86 B2
Nicholas St BSLY S70 .... 2 A4 🔲
Nicholson Av DEARNE S63 ...... 111 G2
DOD/DAR S75 .... 54 D3
Nicholson Pl SHEFS S8 .... 187 H1 🔲
SHEFS S8 .... 187 H1
Nicholson Rd DONS/BSCR DN4 .... 4 A5
SHEFS S8 .... 187 H1
Nichols Rd BTLY DN5 .... 170 A2
Nickerwood Dr AU/AST/KP S26 .. 191 H1
Nidderdale Cl MALT S66 .... 157 H1
Nidderdale Rd KIMB S61 .... 132 C4
Nidd Rd DARN/MH S9 .... 172 C2
Nidd Rd East DARN/MH S9 ...... 172 C2
Nightingale Cl RHAM S60 .... 6 C5
Nightingale Cft RHAM S60 .... 6 C5
Nightingale Cft KIMB S61 .... 131 H1
Nightingale Gv WRKN S81 .... 196 A8
Nightingale Rd CHPT/GREN S35 .. 129 J7 🔲
Nile St FUL S10 .... 170 C5 🔲
Ninelands Rd HATH/EY S32 ...... 182 C8
Ninescores La EPW DN9 .... 96 A7
Ninian Gv RHAM S60 .... 6 C5
Noble La HOY S74 .... 109 G2
Nodder Rd HAN/WDH S13 .... 172 E8
Noehill Pl SHEFP/MNR S2 .... 172 D6 🔲
Noehill Rd SHEFP/MNR S2 .... 172 D6
Nookery Cl MALT S66 .... 159 J1 🔲
Nooking Cl ARMTH DN3 .... 93 H1
Nook La ST/HB/BR S6 .... 169 G1
STKB/PEN S36 .... 78 B6
The Nook FUL S10 .... 8 A2
STKB/PEN S36 .... 78 D1
Nora St DEARNE S63 .... 86 E1
Norborough Rd DARN/MH S9 ... 154 B5
WHHL DN2 .... 5 F1
Norbreck Rd AWLS/ASK DN6 .... 19 F6 🔲
DONS/BSCR DN4 .... 115 K2
Norbrook Wy RHAM S60 .... 156 C6
Norburn Dr ECK/KIL S21 .... 205 H1
Norbury Cl DRON S18 .... 200 D6 🔲
Norcroft BSLY S70 .... 82 A1
Norcroft La DOD/DAR S75 .... 53 H4
Norfolk Av NROS/TKH DN11 .... 163 J3
Norfolk Cl BSLYN/ROY S71 .... 3 E1
Norfolk Dr DIN S25 .... 194 A1
NROS/TKH DN11 .... 163 H3
Norfolk Gv NROS/TKH DN11 .... 163 H3
Norfolk Hl CHPT/GREN S35 ...... 129 H6
Norfolk La SHEF S1 .... 9 D3 🔲🔲
Norfolk Park Av SHEFP/MNR S2 .. 171 K7
Norfolk Park Dr SHEFP/MNR S2 .... 9 F5
Norfolk Park Rd SHEFP/MNR S2 .... 9 F5
Norfolk Rd MALT S66 .... 159 H2
Norfolk Rd CUD/OR S72 .... 59 H6
DONS/BSCR DN4 .... 116 E1 🔲
NROS/TKH DN11 .... 163 H3
SHEFP/MNR S2 .... 9 F4
Norfolk Rw SHEF S1 .... 9 D3
Norfolk St RHAM/THRY S65 .... 7 D3
SHEF S1 .... 9 D3
WRKS S80 .... 210 C5
Norfolk Wy RHAM S60 .... 155 K5
Norgreave Wy MOS S20 .... 190 C8
Norman Cl BSLY S70 .... 82 B2 🔲
BSLYN/ROY S71 .... 3 E1
Norman Crs BTLY DN5 .... 64 A8
NROS/TKH DN11 .... 118 D6
Normancroft Crs
  SHEFP/MNR S2 .... 172 E6 🔲
Normancroft Dr
  SHEFP/MNR S2 .... 172 D6 🔲
Normancroft Wy SHEFP/MNR S2 .. 172 D6 🔲
Normandale Av ST/HB/BR S6 .... 150 C7
Normandale Rd CUD/OR S72 .... 59 H5
  ST/HB/BR S6 .... 151 J8 🔲
Norman Dr HTFD DN7 .... 68 C1
Norman Rd HTFD DN7 .... 68 B1
  KBTN HD8 .... 51 G2
Norman St DARN/MH S9 .... 153 H8
  DEARNE S63 .... 60 D7
Normanton Gdns ATT S4 .... 152 B6
Normanton Gv HAN/WDH S13 .. 189 H1
Normanton Hl HACK/IN S12 ..... 188 E1

Normanton Spring Ct
  HAN/WDH S13 .... 189 G1
Normanton Spring Rd
  HAN/WDH S13 .... 189 G2
Normanville Av RHAM S60 .... 154 E6
Norrel's Cft RHAM S60 .... 172 A8
Norridge Bottom
  HOLM/MEL HD7 .... 47 K2 🔲
Norris Rd ST/HB/BR S6 .... 155 H1
Norroy St ATT S4 .... 171 K1 🔲
Norstead Crs MALT S66 .... 157 K1
Northampton Rd WHHL DN2 ...... 92 B2
North Av BWTY DN10 .... 142 B7
  HEM/SK/SE WF9 .... 34 E5
North Bridge La BTLY DN5 .... 4 B2
North Church St SHEF S1 .... 9 D2 🔲
North Cliff Rd CONI DN12 .... 114 C4
North Cl BSLYN/ROY S71 .... 30 D4
North Common Rd THNE DN8 .... 23 G3
Northcote Av SHEFS S8 .... 187 H1
Northcote Rd SHEFS S8 .... 187 H1
North Crs ECK/KIL S21 .... 165 J7
  HEM/SK/SE WF9 .... 35 G3
  RHAM/THRY S65 .... 7 F3
Northcroft HEM/SK/SE WF9 ...... 35 F4
Northcroft HEM/SK/SE WF9 ...... 35 F5
North Dr BTLY DN5 .... 6 C2
North Eastern Rd THNE DN8 ..... 23 H7
North End Dr BTLY DN5 .... 87 H5
Northern Av SHEFP/MNR S2 .... 172 A8
Northern Common DRON S18 ... 200 B4
North Farm Cl AU/AST/KP S26 .. 192 E8
North Farm Ct AU/AST/KP S26 .. 175 K8
North Fld DOD/DAR S75 .... 53 J7
Northfield Cl FUL S10 .... 170 C2 🔲
Northfield Ct MALT S66 .... 157 G3 🔲
Northfield Dr WRKN S81 .... 195 G3
Northfield Gv HEM/SK/SE WF9 .. 34 A4
Northfield La HEM/SK/SE WF9 .. 34 A4
  MALT S66 .... 157 F2
North Field AWLS/ASK DN6 ...... 35 K7
Northfield Rd BTLY DN5 .... 4 A1
  FUL S10 .... 170 B3
  RHAM S60 .... 6 C5
Northfield St HEM/SK/SE WF9 .. 34 A4
Northgate CUD/OR S72 .... 32 B1
  DOD/DAR S75 .... 55 H4
North Ga MEX/SWTN S64 .... 113 H2
NROS/TKH DN11 .... 139 K7
Northgate THNE DN8 .... 24 A3
North Hill Rd SHEFS S8 .... 152 A3
North Ings Rd HTFD DN7 .... 42 E7
Northlands AU/AST/KP S26 ...... 192 E8
  BSLYN/ROY S71 .... 30 D3
Northlands Rd SHEFN S5 .... 152 A3
North La GLE DN14 .... 12 B8
  GLE DN14 .... 12 E7
  STKB/PEN S36 .... 52 C5
North Park La AWLS/ASK DN6 ... 38 A4
North Pitt St KIMB S61 .... 154 C1
North Pl DOD/DAR S75 .... 55 G4
  RHAM/THRY S65 .... 7 F3
North Qd SHEFN S5 .... 152 E3
North Royds Wd BSLYN/ROY S71 .. 30 A6
Northside Rd DEARNE S63 .... 111 J1
North St CONI DN12 .... 115 K5
  DONS/BSCR DN4 .... 5 D5
  HEM/SK/SE WF9 .... 34 A4
  KIMB S61 .... 6 B3
  MEX/SWTN S64 .... 112 D4
  RAW S62 .... 112 A8
  WMB/DAR S73 .... 84 D1
North Swaithe Cl BTLY DN5 ...... 64 D5
Northumberland Av HOY S74 .... 83 F8
  WHHL DN2 .... 92 A2
  WRKN S81 .... 180 C8
Northumberland Rd FUL S10 .... 170 C4
Northumberland Wy
  BSLYN/ROY S71 .... 57 G7
Northumbria Cl WRKN S81 ...... 210 E1 🔲
North Wy WRKN S81 .... 180 D8 🔲
Northwood WRKN S81 .... 210 E1 🔲
Norton & Kirk Smeaton Rd
  PONT WF8 .... 16 E2
Norton Av HACK/IN S12 .... 188 B3
  SHEFS S8 .... 187 K6
Norton Church Glebe SHEFS S8 .. 187 H6 🔲
Norton Church Rd SHEFS S8 .... 187 H6
Norton Common La
  AWLS/ASK DN6 .... 18 C4
Norton Common Rd
  AWLS/ASK DN6 .... 18 E5
Norton Green Cl SHEFS S8 .... 187 J6
Norton Hammer La SHEFS S8 ... 186 E5 🔲
Norton La SHEFS S8 .... 187 G8
Norton Lees Cl SHEFS S8 .... 187 G4 🔲
Norton Lees Crs SHEFS S8 .... 187 G3
Norton Lees La SHEFS S8 .... 187 F3
Norton Lees Rd SHEFS S8 .... 187 F2
Norton Lees Sq SHEFS S8 .... 187 G3
Norton Ms SHEFS S8 .... 187 J6
Norton Mill La AWLS/ASK DN6 .. 17 K3
Norton Park Av SHEFS S8 .... 187 H7 🔲

Norton Park Crs SHEFS S8 .... 187 G7
Norton Park Dr SHEFS S8 .... 187 G7
Norton Park Rd SHEFS S8 .... 187 G8
Norton Park Vw SHEFS S8 .... 187 G7
Norton Rd DEARNE S63 .... 85 G8
  SHEFS S8 .... 188 A5
  WHHL DN2 .... 92 A2 🔲
Norville Crs WMB/DAR S73 .... 84 E1
Norwich Rd WHHL DN2 .... 65 K8
Norwith Rd DONS/BSCR DN4 ... 118 C3
Norwood Av EPW DN9 .... 94 B8
  MALT S66 .... 159 G1
  SHEFN S5 .... 152 C6
Norwood Cl MALT S66 .... 159 G1 🔲
  SHEFN S5 .... 152 C6
Norwood Crs AU/AST/KP S26 ... 192 C6
  ECK/KIL S21 .... 191 K8
Norwood Dr BTLY DN5 .... 64 D4
  DOD/DAR S75 .... 54 D2
  SHEFN S5 .... 152 C6
Norwood Grange Dr SHEFN S5 .. 152 C5
Norwood La STKB/PEN S36 .... 77 G2
Norwood Pl ECK/KIL S21 .... 191 K8
Nor Wood Rd HEM/SK/SE WF9 .. 33 G2
Norwood Rd CONI DN12 .... 114 C5
  HTFD DN7 .... 42 A6
  SHEFN S5 .... 152 C6
Nostell Fold DOD/DAR S75 .... 80 E1 🔲
Nostell Pl DONS/BSCR DN4 ...... 118 C1
Nottingham Cliff OWL S3 .... 171 G1
Nottingham Cl BSLYN/ROY S71 .. 57 H8
  BTLY DN5 .... 90 A1 🔲
  DIN S25 .... 193 K4 🔲
Nottingham St OWL S3 .... 152 C8
  RHAM/THRY S65 .... 7 D3 🔲
  RHAM/THRY S65 .... 7 D5 🔲
Novello St MALT S66 .... 159 K3
Nowill Ct SHEFS S8 .... 187 G1 🔲
Nowill Pl SHEFS S8 .... 187 G1 🔲
Nunnery Crs RHAM S60 .... 174 A1
Nunnery Dr SHEFP/MNR S2 ...... 172 B3
Nunnery Ter SHEFP/MNR S2 ..... 172 A4
Nunthorpe Cl HTFD DN7 .... 42 C8 🔲
Nursery Crs DIN S25 .... 193 K1
Nursery Dr CHPT/GREN S35 ..... 130 C7
  RHAM S60 .... 174 A1
Nursery Gdns BSLY S70 .... 57 F8 🔲
Nursery Gv CHPT/GREN S35 ..... 130 C7
Nursery La BTLY DN5 .... 89 H8
  OWL S3 .... 9 E1 🔲
Nursery Rd AU/AST/KP S26 ...... 175 C7
  DIN S25 .... 178 A8
Nursery St BSLY S70 .... 2 B5
  OWL S3 .... 9 E1 🔲
Nutfields Gv HTFD DN7 .... 42 A3 🔲
Nuttall Pl SHEFP/MNR S2 .... 171 K4
Nutwell Cl DONS/BSCR DN4 ..... 118 C1
Nutwell La ARMTH DN3 .... 93 G1

O

Oak Av DEARNE S63 .... 111 K2
Oakbank Cl MEX/SWTN S64 ..... 112 C7
Oakbank Ct TOT/DORE S17 ...... 199 J2 🔲
Oakbrook Rd ECC S11 .... 169 K7
Oak Cl ECK/KIL S21 .... 205 G2
  HOY S74 .... 108 D2
  MALT S66 .... 157 C1
  MEX/SWTN S64 .... 112 C6
  WRKS S80 .... 210 C6
Oak Ct BTLY DN5 .... 90 A6
  MEX/SWTN S64 .... 112 D2
Oak Crs THNE DN8 .... 23 J6
Oakcrest DONS/BSCR DN4 .... 114 D3
Oakdale BSLY S70 .... 82 C2
Oakdale Cl ARMTH DN3 .... 66 E6 🔲
Oakdale Pl KIMB S61 .... 154 C1
Oak Dale Rd DONS/BSCR DN4 .. 115 K3
Oakdale Rd DIN S25 .... 194 A2
  ECC S11 .... 186 D1
  KIMB S61 .... 154 C2
Oakdell DRON S18 .... 201 K4
Oakdene NROS/TKH DN11 .... 118 E7
Oaken Wood Cl KIMB S61 .... 131 H2
Oaken Wood Rd KIMB S61 .... 131 G1
Oakes Gn DARN/MH S9 .... 172 B1
Oakes Park Vw SHEFS S8 .... 187 K6 🔲
Oakes St DARN/MH S9 .... 153 J3 🔲
Oakfern Gv CHPT/GREN S35 ..... 107 J7
Oakfield Wk DOD/DAR S75 .... 55 G5
Oak Gv CONI DN12 .... 114 C6
Oak Grove Gn TOT/DORE S17 ... 199 J3
Oakham Dr OWL S3 .... 171 F1
Oakham Pl DOD/DAR S75 .... 55 H4
Oak Haven Av CUD/OR S72 .... 59 H6 🔲
Oakhill Rd ABRD S7 .... 186 D1
  DRON S18 .... 201 J4
  WHHL DN2 .... 92 A1
Oakholme Av WRKN S81 .... 210 D2
Oakholme Ms ECC S11 .... 170 C6 🔲
Oakholme Ri WRKN S81 .... 210 D2
Oakholme Rd ECC S11 .... 170 C6
Oakland Av HTFD DN7 .... 42 B8
Oakland Cl WRKN S81 .... 195 G2
Oakland Rd ST/HB/BR S6 .... 151 G7
Oaklands ARMTH DN3 .... 119 H3

Oaklands Av *BSLYN/ROY* S71........ 56 E3
Oaklands Dr *DONS/BSCR* DN4 ...... 92 C7
NROS/TKH DN11..................... 162 C5
Oaklands Gdns *DONS/BSCR* DN4 .. 92 C8
Oaklands Pl *DEARNE* S63............ 111 H2
Oak La *GLE* DN14....................... 13 J4
Oak Lea *KIMB* S61..................... 132 E4
Oak Lea Av *DEARNE* S63............. 85 F8
Oaklea Gv *BSLY* S70.................. 29 C5
Oak Leigh *DOD/DAR* S75............ 53 H5
Oakley Rd *HAN/WDH* S13............ 175 G5
Oak Lodge *CHPT/GREN* S35........ 107 H8
Oakmoor Rd *THNE* DN8............... 24 A3
Oak Pk *FUL* S10........................ 170 B5
Oak Rd *ARMTH* DN3................... 67 F7
CUD/GR S72............................ 32 A5
DEARNE S63............................ 60 C7
DEARNE S63............................ 111 K2
HACK/IN S12........................... 188 C5
MALT S66............................... 158 E2
MEX/SWTN S64........................ 112 D2
MOS S20................................. 190 D3
THNE DN8............................... 23 J6
Oaks *STKB/PEN* S36.................. 104 D6
Oak Scar La *HOLM/MEL* HD7 .... 48 C5
Oaks Cl *DEARNE* S63................. 111 K3
Oaks Crs *BSLY* S70................... 3 F5
Oaks Farm Dr *DOD/DAR* S75....... 28 E7 🟩
Oaks Fold *SHEFN* S5.................. 153 F1
Oaks Fold Av *SHEFN* S5.............. 153 F1
Oaks Fold Rd *SHEFN* S5............. 153 F2
Oaks La *BSLY* S70.................... 3 F5
BSLYN/ROY S71....................... 3 F4
KIMB S61............................... 131 K6
SHEFN S5.............................. 153 F2
ST/HB/BR S6.......................... 149 F5
STKB/PEN S36........................ 103 K4
Oak St *BSLY* S70..................... 2 A4
CUD/GR S72........................... 58 E2
HEM/SK/SE WF9...................... 34 D6
MOS S20................................ 190 A7
SHEFS S8.............................. 171 G8
Oaks Wood Dr *DOD/DAR* S75...... 28 E7 🟩
DONS/BSCR DN4...................... 4 C5
Oak Ter *AU/AST/KP* S26............ 175 F7
DONS/BSCR DN4...................... 4 C5
Oak Tree Av *CUD/GR* S72........... 31 J8
Oak Tree Cl *DOD/DAR* S75.......... 28 C7 🟩
Oak Tree Gv *HEM/SK/SE* WF9 ..... 33 J1
Oak Tree Ri *WRKN* S80.............. 180 C8
Oak Tree Rd *ARMTH* DN3........... 93 K6
EWTY DN10............................ 142 A8
Oakwell Cl *MALT* S66................ 159 H1
Oakwell Dr *AWLS/ASK* DN6......... 19 F7
Oak Well La *BSLY* S70............... 3 D5
Oakwell Ter *BSLYN/ROY* S71...... 3 D5 🟩
Oakwell Vw *BSLYN/ROY* S71....... 3 D5 🟩
Oakwood *ARMTH* DN3................ 93 J7 🟩
Oakwood Cl *BSLY* S70............... 82 D3
Oakwood Crs *BSLYN/ROY* S71..... 30 C3
CHPT/GREN S35...................... 150 C2
RAW S62............................... 111 H8
Oakwood Dr East *RHAM* S60....... 155 K4
Oakwood Dr West *RHAM* S60....... 155 J4
Oakwood Sq *DOD/DAR* S75........ 28 A7 🟩
Oakworth Cl *DOD/DAR* S75........ 55 G4 🟩
MOS S20................................ 204 C7 🟩
Oakworth Dr *MOS* S20.............. 204 B1 🟩
Oakworth Gv *MOS* S20.............. 204 B1
Oakworth Vw *MOS* S20............. 204 B1
Oates Av *RAW* S62.................. 133 K2
Oates Cl *KIMB* S61.................. 132 D1
Oates St *KIMB* S61.................. 132 D8
Oats Orch *MOS* S20................. 204 B1 🟩
Oberon Crs *WMB/DAR* S73........ 84 C1
Oborne Cl *RHAM/THRY* S65....... 135 K7
Occupation La *HACK/IN* S12....... 189 H4
Occupation Rd *RAW* S62........... 108 E6
RAW S62............................... 133 H3
Ochre Dike Cl *MOS* S20............ 190 C5 🟩
Ochre Dike La *MOS* S20............ 190 B5
Octavia Cl *RHAM* S60............... 155 F5 🟩
Oddfellows Rd *HATH/EY* S32...... 182 C8
Oddy La *NROS/TKH* DN11.......... 161 J2
Odom Ct *SHEFS* S8.................. 187 H1
Ogden Rd *WHHL* DN2................ 66 C7
Oil Mill Fold *RHAM* S60............. 6 C4
Oldale Cl *HAN/WDH* S13........... 190 A2
Oldale Ct *HAN/WDH* S13........... 190 A1
Oldale Gv *HAN/WDH* S13........... 190 A1
Old Anna Lane or Long La
STKB/PEN S36........................ 77 H3
Old Bar La *HOLM/MEL* HD7........ 49 C7
Old Bawtry Rd *EPW* DN9........... 120 E6
Old Carpenter's Yd *HTFD* DN7..... 41 J2
Old Coach Rd *WRKS* S80........... 211 K8
Oldcoates Cl *DIN* S25............... 178 B5 🟩
Oldcoates Rd *DIN* S25.............. 178 C4
Old Cross La *DEARNE* S63......... 111 J1
Old Epworth Rd (East) *HTFD* DN7 ... 43 F8

Old Farm Ct *MEX/SWTN* S64...... 112 D1
Oldfield Av *CONI* DN12.............. 114 A5
ST/HB/BR S6.......................... 169 H1
Oldfield Cl *ARMTH* DN3............. 41 C8 🟩
HOY S74................................ 109 F1
HTFD DN7.............................. 41 J4
Oldfield Crs *HTFD* DN7.............. 41 K4
Oldfield La *HTFD* DN7............... 41 K4
Old Field La *HTFD* DN7.............. 41 G5
Oldfield La *KBTN* HD8............... 26 C5
Oldfield Rd *RHAM/THRY* S65...... 134 C8
ST/HB/BR S6.......................... 169 H2
THNE DN8.............................. 43 K1
Oldfield Ter *ST/HB/BR* S6.......... 169 H2
Old Fulwood Rd *ECC* S11........... 169 H8
Old Ga *HOLM/MEL* HD7............. 46 B8
Old Garden Dr *RHAM/THRY* S65 ... 7 E3
Oldgate La *RHAM/THRY* S65...... 134 D6
Old Hall Cl *BTLY* DN5............... 89 K7
DIN S25................................. 177 K3
MALT S66............................... 157 J2 🟩
Old Hall Dr *MALT* S66............... 157 J2
Old Hall La *MALT* S66............... 26 B2
Old Hall Pl *BTLY* DN5............... 64 E7
Old Hall Rd *AWLS/ASK* DN6....... 37 H6 🟩
BTLY DN5.............................. 64 E7
Old Hall Wk *CUD/GR* S72.......... 59 H6 🟩
Oldhay Cl *TOT/DORE* S17.......... 199 H1
Old Hay Gdns *TOT/DORE* S17..... 199 G1
Old Hay La *TOT/DORE* S17........ 199 G1
Old Hexthorpe *DONS/BSCR* DN4 ... 4 A5 🟩
Old House Cl *WMB/DAR* S73...... 83 K8 🟩
Old La *CHPT/GREN* S35............ 149 K1
MOS S20................................ 190 E8
Old Manchester Rd *STKB/PEN* S36 ... 75 K7
Old Manor Dr *STKB/PEN* S36..... 78 E6
Old Mill La *BSLY* S70................ 2 B3
BSLYN/ROY S71...................... 3 D2
CHPT/GREN S35...................... 105 G1
Old Mill Rd *CONI* DN12............. 114 E6
Old Park Av *SHEFS* S8............. 186 D8
Old Park Rd *SHEFS* S8............. 186 D8
Old Post Office Sq *EWTY* DN10 ... 165 K4 🟩
Old Quarry La *AU/AST/KP* S26 ... 192 B4
The Old Railway Yd *SHEFS* S8.... 186 D4
Old Retford Rd *HAN/WDH* S13.... 174 A6
CONI DN12............................. 114 A7
HOLM/MEL HD7....................... 47 F5
Oldroyd Av *CUD/GR* S72........... 58 D1
Old School Cl *HOY* S74.............. 83 F8 🟩
Old School La *NROS/TKH* DN11 ... 116 E8
RHAM S60.............................. 174 B1
Old Scotch Spring La *MALT* S66 ... 138 D7 🟩
Old Sheffield Rd *RHAM* S60........ 6 B5
Old St *AWLS/ASK* DN6.............. 36 A8
SHEFP/MNR S2....................... 9 F2
Old Thorne Rd *HTFD* DN7.......... 42 E7
Old Village Rd *AWLS/ASK* DN6 ... 37 H3
Old Warren V *RAW* S62............. 108 B8
Oldwell Cl *TOT/DORE* S17......... 199 H5
Old Wortley Rd *KIMB* S61.......... 132 B7
Old Yew Ga *CHPT/GREN* S35...... 128 C5
Old Yew La *HOLM/MEL* HD7....... 47 H5
Olive Cl *AU/AST/KP* S26............ 175 H8
Olive Crs *HACK/IN* S12............. 188 C5
Olive Grove Rd *SHEFP/MNR* S2 ... 9 E6
Olive Rd *MOS* S20................... 190 B8
Oliver Rd *ABRD* S7.................. 186 C5
DONS/BSCR DN4...................... 90 D8
Olivers Crs *DARN/MH* S9........... 173 F3
Olivers Mt *DARN/MH* S9............ 173 G3
Oliver St *MEX/SWTN* S64.......... 112 C2
Olivers Wy *RHAM* S60.............. 154 E8
Olivet Rd *SHEFS* S8................. 187 F5
Ollerton Rd *BSLYN/ROY* S71...... 30 A7
Omega Bvd *THNE* DN8.............. 25 K3
Onchan Rd *ST/HB/BR* S6.......... 169 J2 🟩
Onesacre Rd *ST/HB/BR* S6........ 127 F4
Onesmoor Bottom *ST/HB/BR* S6 ... 127 H8
Onslow Rd *ECC* S11................. 170 B8
Orange Cft *NROS/TKH* DN11...... 140 D8 🟩
Orange St *SHEF* S1.................. 8 C3 🟩🟩
Orchard Av *DIN* S25................. 178 A8
AWLS/ASK DN6....................... 18 A4 🟩
BSLYN/ROY S71...................... 56 D2
CHPT/GREN S35...................... 130 C5
DIN S25................................. 178 A2 🟩
DOD/DAR S75......................... 29 G6
DOD/DAR S75......................... 79 K2 🟩
HTFD DN7.............................. 68 A2
RHAM S60.............................. 174 B1
STV/CWN S43......................... 206 A8 🟩
Orchard Crs *SHEFN* S5............. 130 C8
Orchard Cft *AU/AST/KP* S26...... 192 B4
BWTY DN10............................ 142 B8
DOD/DAR S75......................... 81 F1
Orchard Dr *AWLS/ASK* DN6....... 18 A4
CUD/GR S72........................... 32 A1
HTFD DN7.............................. 68 A2
Orchard Flatts Crs *KIMB* S61..... 132 D5
Orchard Gdns *DIN* S25............. 193 K3
Orchard Gv *HTFD* DN7.............. 42 B6
MALT S66............................... 158 E1
Orchard La *AU/AST/KP* S26....... 192 B5
MOS S20................................ 190 D5

Orchard Lea Dr *AU/AST/KP* S26 ... 175 H8 🟩
Orchard Lee *AU/AST/KP* S26...... 206 E1
Orchard Pl *CUD/GR* S72............ 57 K2
DEARNE S63........................... 111 G1
ECK/KIL S21.......................... 205 H1
RHAM S60.............................. 6 B4
Orchard Rd *ST/HB/BR* S6.......... 170 C1
Orchard Sq *DRON* S18............. 200 D5
Orchard St *DEARNE* S63........... 86 D3
DONS/BSCR DN4...................... 4 B5
SHEF S1................................ 9 D3 🟩
STKB/PEN S36........................ 105 J7 🟩
THNE DN8.............................. 23 J8
WMB/DAR S73........................ 84 A4
Orchard Ter *DOD/DAR* S75........ 53 J3
The Orchard *AWLS/ASK* DN6..... 17 K7
DIN S25................................. 194 A1
Orchard Wk *EPW* DN9............... 94 B8
Orchard Wy *DEARNE* S63.......... 60 C7
RHAM S60.............................. 155 F8
Orchid Wy *DIN* S25.................. 193 J3
Oregreave Dr *HAN/WDH* S13..... 174 A6
Oregreave La *HAN/WDH* S13..... 173 J6
Oregreave Pl *HAN/WDH* S13...... 173 K5
Oregreave Rd *RHAM* S60.......... 174 A2
Oregreave Wy *HAN/WDH* S13.... 174 A7
Oriel Rd *FUL* S10.................... 169 G8
Oriel Wy *BSLYN/ROY* S71.......... 56 E4
Ormesby Cl *DRON* S18............. 200 C6 🟩
Ormesby Crs *BTLY* DN5............ 90 B2
Ormesby Wy *MALT* S66............ 157 K2
Ormes Meadow *MOS* S20.......... 190 A5
Ormond Cl *SHEFS* S8............... 201 H1
Ormond Dr *SHEFS* S8.............. 201 H1
Ormond Rd *SHEFS* S8.............. 201 H1
Ormond Wy *SHEFS* S8............. 187 H8
Ormsby Cl *CHPT/GREN* S35....... 105 J2
DONS/BSCR DN4...................... 116 D3
Orpen Dr *SHEFS* S8................. 188 A5
Orpen Wy *SHEFS* S8................ 188 A5 🟩
Orwell Cl *WMB/DAR* S73........... 84 C6
Osbert Dr *MALT* S66................ 157 K8
Osberton Pl *ECC* S11............... 170 C7
Osberton St *NROS/TKH* DN11.... 117 H8
RAW S62............................... 134 A1
RHAM/THRY S65...................... 134 B6
Osbert Rd *RHAM* S60............... 156 A4
Osborne Av *AU/AST/KP* S26....... 175 J7
AWLS/ASK DN6....................... 33 C2 🟩
Osborne Cl *ECC* S11................ 170 C8 🟩
Osborne Cft *AU/AST/KP* S26...... 207 F1
Osborne Dr *AU/AST/KP* S26...... 193 F2
Osborne Ms *BSLY* S70.............. 3 D5 🟩
Osborne Rd *AU/AST/KP* S26...... 193 F5
ECC S11................................ 170 C8
WHHL DN2.............................. 5 F2
Osborne St *BSLY* S70............... 3 D5
Osgathorpe Crs *ATT* S4............ 152 D7 🟩
Osgathorpe Dr *ATT* S4............. 152 E7
Osgathorpe Rd *ATT* S4............ 152 D7
Osmaston Rd *SHEFS* S8........... 187 F5 🟩
Osmond Dr *BSLY* S70............... 82 B2
Osmond Pl *BSLY* S70............... 82 B2 🟩
Osmond Wy *BSLY* S70.............. 82 B2 🟩
Osmund Rd *ECK/KIL* S21.......... 203 K4
Osprey Av *BSLY* S70................ 82 A7
Osprey Cl *AWLS/ASK* DN6......... 63 J1
Osprey Gdns *SHEFP/MNR* S2 ..... 172 A5 🟩
Osprey Rd *AU/AST/KP* S26........ 191 J7 🟩
Oswestry Rd *SHEFN* S5............ 152 D3
Oswin Av *DONS/BSCR* DN4........ 90 C7
Otley Cl *CONI* DN12................. 114 E5
Otter St *DARN/MH* S9.............. 172 B1
Oughtibridge La *CHPT/GREN* S35 ... 128 D8
Oughton Wy *ATT* S4................. 152 E8
Oulton Av *MALT* S66................ 157 K1
Oulton Dr *CUD/GR* S72............. 31 K8
Oulton Ri *MEX/SWTN* S64......... 113 J1
Ouseburn Cft *DARN/MH* S9....... 172 C2
Ouseburn Rd *DARN/MH* S9........ 172 C2 🟩
Ouseburn St *DARN/MH* S9........ 172 C2 🟩
Ouse Rd *DARN/MH* S9.............. 172 C2
Ouslethwaite Ct *BSLY* S70........ 81 K1
Outgang La *DIN* S25................ 177 J4
MALT S66............................... 159 J4
Outram Rd *SHEFP/MNR* S2....... 172 A5
Oval Rd *RHAM/THRY* S65.......... 134 A8
The Oval *AWLS/ASK* DN6.......... 63 G1 🟩
CONI DN12............................. 114 D4
DIN S25................................. 194 A1
DONS/BSCR DN4...................... 92 B6
HOR/CROF WF4....................... 30 C1
HTFD DN7.............................. 42 A6
NROS/TKH DN11...................... 140 A7
SHEFN S5.............................. 152 D4
WRKN S80............................. 210 E3
Overcroft Ri *TOT/DORE* S17...... 199 J3
Overdale Av *BSLY* S70.............. 82 C1
Overdale Gdns *TOT/DORE* S17 ... 199 J3
Overdale Ri *TOT/DORE* S17....... 199 J3 🟩
Overdale Rd *WMB/DAR* S73....... 84 B6
Overend Cl *GLV* S14................. 187 K3
Overend Dr *GLV* S14................ 187 K3
Overend Rd *GLV* S14................ 187 K3
WRKS S80.............................. 210 C3
Overend Wy *GLV* S14............... 187 K3
Oversley Rd *WHHL* DN2............ 91 J1

Oversley St *DARN/MH* S9 .... 154 B4
Overton Rd *ST/HB/BR* S6 .... 151 G5
Owday La *WRKN* S81 .... 195 K5
Owen Cl *RHAM/THRY* S65 .... 7 D2 ⊟
  ST/HB/BR S6 .... 151 J1 ⊟
Owen Pl *ST/HB/BR* S6 .... 151 J1
Owler Car La *DRON* S18 .... 202 A3
  SHEFS S8 .... 202 A2
Owler Ga *CHPT/GREN* S35 .... 128 A7
Owler La *ATT* S4 .... 152 E6
Owlings Pl *ST/HB/BR* S6 .... 151 F7
Owlings Rd *ST/HB/BR* S6 .... 151 F7
Owlthorpe Av *MOS* S20 .... 189 K7
Owlthorpe Cl *MOS* S20 .... 189 K7 ⊟
Owlthorpe Dr *MOS* S20 .... 189 K7
Owlthorpe Greenway *MOS* S20 .... 190 C6
Owlthorpe Gv *MOS* S20 .... 189 K7
Owlthorpe La *MOS* S20 .... 189 K7
Owlthorpe Ri *MOS* S20 .... 189 K7
Owram St *WMB/DAR* S73 .... 84 D2 ⊟
Owston La *AWLS/ASK* DN6 .... 38 A5
Owston Rd *AWLS/ASK* DN6 .... 37 K7
Ox Carr *ARMTH* DN3 .... 93 F1
Ox Close Av *KIMB* S61 .... 132 B6
  TOT/DORE S17 .... 200 A2
Oxclose Dr *DRON* S18 .... 200 C6 ⊡⊡
Oxclose La *DRON* S18 .... 200 C6
Oxclose Park Rd *MOS* S20 .... 190 D8
Oxclose Park Rd North *MOS* S20 .... 204 D1
Oxford Cl *ARMTH* DN3 .... 93 F1
Oxford Dr *NROS/TKH* DN11 .... 162 E2
Oxford Pl *BSLYN/ROY* S71 .... 57 F7 ⊟
  DON DN1 .... 4 C3
Oxford Rd *WRKN* S81 .... 196 D1
Oxford St *BSLY* S70 .... 3 D6
  BSLYN/ROY S71 .... 57 F7
  HEM/SK/SE WF9 .... 34 E5
  MEX/SWTN S64 .... 112 D2
  NROS/TKH DN11 .... 118 D6
  RHAM/THRY S65 .... 7 F3
  ST/HB/BR S6 .... 8 A2
Ox Hl *MOS* S20 .... 204 E2
Ox Lee La *HOLM/MEL* HD7 .... 48 D7
Oxley Cl *STKB/PEN* S36 .... 104 D6
Oxley Gv *RHAM* S60 .... 7 E6
Oxspring Bank *SHEFN* S5 .... 151 J5
Oxspring La *STKB/PEN* S36 .... 78 E4
Oxspring Rd *STKB/PEN* S36 .... 78 A7
Oxted Rd *DARN/MH* S9 .... 153 H5
Oxton Dr *DONS/BSCR* DN4 .... 116 A1
Oxton Rd *BSLYN/ROY* S71 .... 30 B7

P

Pack Horse Cl *KBTN* HD8 .... 26 D3
Pack Horse Gn *DOD/DAR* S75 .... 53 J7
Pack Horse La *CHPT/GREN* S35 .... 107 K7
Packington Rd *DONS/BSCR* DN4 .... 93 F8
Packman La *AU/AST/KP* S26 .... 193 H6
  AU/AST/KP S26 .... 207 J3
Packman Rd *DEARNE* S63 .... 84 E8
Packman Wy *DEARNE* S63 .... 110 E1
Packwood Cl *BTLY* DN5 .... 90 B2
  DOD/DAR S75 .... 29 H6
Paddock Cl *BTLY* DN5 .... 90 A2
  BTLY DN5 .... 114 E1 ⊟
  EPW DN9 .... 120 B1 ⊟
  RHAM/THRY S65 .... 135 F5
  WRKN S81 .... 197 F8
The Paddock *ARMTH* DN3 .... 40 D7 ⊟
  AWLS/ASK DN6 .... 63 K1 ⊟
  KIMB S61 .... 131 J3
  NROS/TKH DN11 .... 140 A8
  WMB/DAR S73 .... 83 K7
  WMB/DAR S73 .... 84 D1
Paddock Wy *DRON* S18 .... 201 H5
Padley Cl *DOD/DAR* S75 .... 54 D8 ⊟
Padley Wy *SHEFN* S5 .... 152 D3
Padua Ri *WMB/DAR* S73 .... 84 C2
Pagdin Dr *NROS/TKH* DN11 .... 162 D5
Page Hall Rd *SHEFN* S5 .... 152 E6
Pagenall Dr *AU/AST/KP* S26 .... 175 H7
Paget St *DARN/MH* S9 .... 153 G8
Pagnell Av *DEARNE* S63 .... 60 A8
Palermo Fold *WMB/DAR* S73 .... 84 C1 ⊟
Palgrave Crs *SHEFN* S5 .... 151 K3
Palgrave Rd *SHEFN* S5 .... 151 J3
Pall Ml *BSLY* S70 .... 2 C4 ⊟
Palm Av *ARMTH* DN3 .... 67 H8
Palmer Cl *STKB/PEN* S36 .... 77 K6 ⊟
Palmer Crs *DRON* S18 .... 201 H6
Palmer Rd *DARN/MH* S9 .... 172 E1
Palmer's Av *HEM/SK/SE* WF9 .... 35 F5
Palmerston Av *MALT* S66 .... 159 F1
Palmerston Rd *FUL* S10 .... 8 A3 ⊟
Palmer St *DARN/MH* S9 .... 172 B2 ⊟
  DONS/BSCR DN4 .... 5 E5
Palmers Wy *MALT* S66 .... 176 D1
Palm Gv *CONI* DN12 .... 114 B7
Palm Hollow Cl *MALT* S66 .... 156 E3
Palm La *ST/HB/BR* S6 .... 170 C1 ⊟

Palm St *DOD/DAR* S75 .... 55 H4
  ST/HB/BR S6 .... 170 C1
Pamela Dr *DONS/BSCR* DN4 .... 115 K1
Pangbourne Rd *DEARNE* S63 .... 60 B6
Pantry Gn *BSLY* S70 .... 82 D3 ⊟
Pantry Hl *BSLY* S70 .... 82 D2
Pantry Well *BSLY* S70 .... 82 D3 ⊟
Paper Mill La *NROS/TKH* DN11 .... 140 B7
Paper Mill Rd *SHEFN* S5 .... 130 E8
The Parade *RAW* S62 .... 111 H8 ⊟
Paradise La *SHEF* S1 .... 9 D2 ⊟
Paradise Sq *SHEF* S1 .... 9 D2 ⊟
Paradise St *SHEF* S1 .... 9 D2 ⊟
Parish Wy *BSLYN/ROY* S71 .... 56 E4
Paris Rd *HOLM/MEL* HD7 .... 48 B3
Park Av *ARMTH* DN3 .... 66 E8
  AWLS/ASK DN6 .... 37 K7
  BSLY S70 .... 2 B4
  BSLYN/ROY S71 .... 30 A8
  BSLYN/ROY S71 .... 30 E4
  BTLY DN5 .... 89 K6
  CHPT/GREN S35 .... 106 C4
  CHPT/GREN S35 .... 130 B3
  CONI DN12 .... 114 D6
  CUD/GR S72 .... 31 J8
  CUD/GR S72 .... 32 D7
  CUD/GR S72 .... 32 E4
  DIN S25 .... 178 A8
  DRON S18 .... 199 K7
  DRON S18 .... 201 H5
  ECC S11 .... 170 D7
  HEM/SK/SE WF9 .... 34 A5
  KBTN HD8 .... 26 C4
  MEX/SWTN S64 .... 113 F5
  RHAM S60 .... 156 B5
  STKB/PEN S36 .... 77 K4
Park Ct *DEARNE* S63 .... 60 C7
Park Crs *BSLYN/ROY* S71 .... 30 E4
  CHPT/GREN S35 .... 130 C7
  DONS/BSCR DN4 .... 115 K2
  FUL S10 .... 8 A4
  THNE DN8 .... 43 J1
Park Crest *HEM/SK/SE* WF9 .... 33 C1
Park Dr *AU/AST/KP* S26 .... 175 F8
  AWLS/ASK DN6 .... 18 A6
  BTLY DN5 .... 89 K6
Parkdrive *DOD/DAR* S75 .... 81 G3
Park Dr *STKB/PEN* S36 .... 104 E6
Park Drive Wy *STKB/PEN* S36 .... 104 E5 ⊟
Park Edge *HATH/EY* S12 .... 182 B7
Park End Rd *DEARNE* S63 .... 60 C7
Parker's La *FUL* S10 .... 170 C4
  TOT/DORE S17 .... 185 C7
Parker's Rd *FUL* S10 .... 170 C4
Parker St *BSLY* S70 .... 2 A4
Park Farm *DRON* S18 .... 200 C5
Park Farm Ms *ECK/KIL* S21 .... 205 H6
Parkfield Ct *RAW* S62 .... 133 J4 ⊟
Parkfield Rd *RHAM/THRY* S65 .... 7 E4
Parkgate *HEM/SK/SE* WF9 .... 34 A6
Parkgate Av *CONI* DN12 .... 114 B5
Parkgate Cl *MOS* S20 .... 189 J7 ⊟
Parkgate Cft *MOS* S20 .... 189 J7 ⊟
Parkgate Dr *HACK/IN* S12 .... 189 J6
Park Grange Cl *SHEFP/MNR* S2 .... 9 F6
Park Grange Cft *SHEFP/MNR* S2 .... 9 F5
Park Grange Dr *SHEFP/MNR* S2 .... 9 F6
Park Grange Mt *SHEFP/MNR* S2 .... 9 F6
Park Grange Rd *SHEFP/MNR* S2 .... 9 E5
Park Grange Vw *SHEFP/MNR* S2 .... 171 K8
Park Gv *BSLY* S70 .... 2 B5
  MALT S66 .... 157 J2
  RAW S62 .... 111 J8
  STKB/PEN S36 .... 104 E5 ⊡
Parkhall La *ECK/KIL* S21 .... 205 H5
Parkhead Cl *BSLYN/ROY* S71 .... 30 B3
Parkhead Ct *ECC* S11 .... 185 K3
Parkhead Crs *ECC* S11 .... 185 K3
Park Head Rd *HOLM/MEL* HD7 .... 47 H3
  KBTN HD8 .... 49 K2
Parkhead Rd *ECC* S11 .... 185 K4
Park Hl *AU/AST/KP* S26 .... 175 F8
  DOD/DAR S75 .... 28 A5
  ECK/KIL S21 .... 204 C4
Parkhill Crs *ARMTH* DN3 .... 41 F8 ⊟
Park Hill Dr *WRKN* S81 .... 179 J3
Parkhill Rd *ARMTH* DN3 .... 41 F8
Park Hill Rd *WMB/DAR* S73 .... 84 B4
Park Hollow *WMB/DAR* S73 .... 84 C5
Park House La *DARN/MH* S9 .... 154 C6
Parkin House La *STKB/PEN* S36 .... 76 E5
Parkland Dr *NROS/TKH* DN11 .... 119 G6
Parklands *ARMTH* DN3 .... 66 E6
Parklands Av *DIN* S25 .... 178 A7
Parklands Cl *NROS/TKH* DN11 .... 119 F6
Parkland Wk *EPW* DN9 .... 121 G1
Park La *CHPT/GREN* S35 .... 105 J4
  CONI DN12 .... 136 B2
  CONI DN12 .... 136 B5
  CUD/GR S72 .... 58 E4
  DIN S25 .... 177 J5
  DONS/BSCR DN4 .... 92 B5
  EPW DN9 .... 121 F1
  FUL S10 .... 8 A4
  GLE DN14 .... 10 C5

GLE DN14 .... 12 E3
  KBTN HD8 .... 50 B2
  RHAM/THRY S65 .... 134 E6
  STKB/PEN S36 .... 78 A4
  STKB/PEN S36 .... 78 E7
Park Lane Cl *HTFD* DN7 .... 68 A3
Park Lane Ct *RHAM/THRY* S65 .... 134 E4
Park Lane Rd *HTFD* DN7 .... 67 K3
Park Mill Wy *KBTN* HD8 .... 26 C4
Park Mt *RHAM/THRY* S65 .... 7 D4
Park Nook *RHAM/THRY* S65 .... 134 D5
Park Pl *RHAM/THRY* S65 .... 134 A6
  WRKS S80 .... 210 D6
Park Ri *DRON* S18 .... 200 A7
Park Rd *AWLS/ASK* DN6 .... 18 C3
  BSLY S70 .... 2 B6
  BSLY S70 .... 82 B3
  BTLY DN5 .... 64 D5 ⊟
  BWTY DN5 .... 142 A8
  CONI DN12 .... 114 C6
  CUD/GR S72 .... 32 D9
  CUD/GR S72 .... 32 E4
  DEARNE S63 .... 60 B7
  DEARNE S63 .... 111 H2
  DON DN1 .... 5 D3
  KBTN HD8 .... 26 C4
  MEX/SWTN S64 .... 112 A5
  MEX/SWTN S64 .... 113 F2
  RHAM/THRY S65 .... 7 F5
  ST/HB/BR S6 .... 169 K1
  THNE DN8 .... 24 A4
Park Side *HOLM/MEL* HD7 .... 48 D3
Parkside La *ST/HB/BR* S6 .... 169 H1
Parkside Ms *BSLY* S70 .... 82 B2 ⊡⊡
Parkside Rd *HOY* S74 .... 108 C3
Park Side Rd *ST/HB/BR* S6 .... 151 H6
Parkson Rd *RHAM* S60 .... 156 A5
Park Spring Dr *SHEFP/MNR* S2 .... 9 F6
Park Spring Gv *SHEFP/MNR* S2 .... 9 F6
Park Spring Pl *SHEFP/MNR* S2 .... 9 F6
Park Spring Rd *CUD/GR* S72 .... 58 C3
Park Spring Wy *SHEFP/MNR* S2 .... 9 F6
Park Square Rbt *ATT* S4 .... 9 F2
Parks Rd *HTFD* DN7 .... 42 A7
Parkstone Crs *MALT* S66 .... 158 C3
Parkstone Delph *HACK/IN* S12 .... 188 C5
Parkstone Gv *HTFD* DN7 .... 42 C7 ⊟
Parkstone Wy *WHHL* DN2 .... 66 B8 ⊟
Park St *AU/AST/KP* S26 .... 175 G8
  BSLY S70 .... 2 B5
  KIMB S61 .... 6 A3
  RAW S62 .... 133 J1
  STV/CWN S43 .... 206 D8 ⊟
  WMB/DAR S73 .... 84 B5
  WRKS S80 .... 210 C5
Park Ter *CHPT/GREN* S35 .... 130 C3
  DON DN1 .... 5 D3
The Park *DOD/DAR* S75 .... 53 H3
Park Vale Dr *RHAM/THRY* S65 .... 134 E5
Park Vw *AU/AST/KP* S26 .... 192 E4
  AWLS/ASK DN6 .... 63 K2
Parkview *BSLY* S70 .... 82 C2
Park Vw *BSLYN/ROY* S71 .... 30 E3
  CUD/GR S72 .... 31 K4 ⊟
  CUD/GR S72 .... 32 A5
  CUD/GR S72 .... 32 E4
  DOD/DAR S75 .... 54 E8
  HOLM/MEL HD7 .... 47 J2
  MALT S66 .... 159 J2
  STV/CWN S43 .... 206 B8
  THNE DN8 .... 43 J1
Park View Av *MOS* S20 .... 190 C8
Park View Rd *CHPT/GREN* S35 .... 130 B3
  DOD/DAR S75 .... 29 H6
  KIMB S61 .... 153 K2
  ST/HB/BR S6 .... 151 H6
Parkway *ARMTH* DN3 .... 93 G2 ⊟
Park Wy *AWLS/ASK* DN6 .... 63 J1
Parkway Av *DARN/MH* S9 .... 172 B3
Parkway Dr *DARN/MH* S9 .... 172 B3
Parkway Dr *DARN/MH* S9 .... 172 C3
Parkway North *WHHL* DN2 .... 91 J1
Parkways *HTFD* DN7 .... 42 C8
Parkway South *WHHL* DN2 .... 91 K1
Parkwood Ri *ARMTH* DN3 .... 67 F2
Parkwood Rd *OWL* S3 .... 151 K8
Parkwood Rd North *SHEFN* S5 .... 152 A6
  SHEFN S5 .... 152 A6
Parliament St *ECC* S11 .... 8 B5 ⊟
Parma Ri *WMB/DAR* S73 .... 84 B2
Parsley Hay Cl *HAN/WDH* S13 .... 173 H6 ⊟
Parsley Hay Dr *HAN/WDH* S13 .... 173 H6 ⊟
Parsley Hay Gdns *HAN/WDH* S13 .... 173 H6
Parsley Hay Rd *HAN/WDH* S13 .... 173 H6
Parsonage Cl *MOS* S20 .... 204 D1 ⊟
Parsonage Crs *ST/HB/BR* S6 .... 170 C1
Parsonage St *ST/HB/BR* S6 .... 170 C1
Parson Cross Rd *ST/HB/BR* S6 .... 151 H3
Partridge Cl *ECK/KIL* S21 .... 203 K4
Partridge Flatt Rd
  DONS/BSCR DN4 .... 118 C1
Partridge Pl *AU/AST/KP* S26 .... 191 J1
Partridge Ri *DONS/BSCR* DN4 .... 118 E1
Partridge Rd *ARMTH* DN3 .... 40 E8
Partridge Vw *SHEFP/MNR* S2 .... 172 A5 ⊟
Pashley Cft *WMB/DAR* S73 .... 83 J5
Pashley Rd *THNE* DN8 .... 43 K1
Passfield Rd *NROS/TKH* DN11 .... 119 F7
Passhouses Rd *ATT* S4 .... 152 C7 ⊟

Pasture Cl *ARMTH* DN3 .... 93 F2
WRKN S81 .... 180 E8
WRKS S80 .... 210 A5
Pasture Gv *ECK/KIL* S21 .... 204 A4
Pasture La *BTLY* DN5 .... 114 C1
BWTY DN10 .... 165 H2
DEARNE S63 .... 85 G3
The Pastures *AU/AST/KP* S26 .... 192 E2
BWTY DN10 .... 164 H1 🔲
Paternoster Rw *SHEF* S1 .... 9 E4
Paterson Ct *STKB/PEN* S36 .... 104 D5
Paterson Ct *STKB/PEN* S36 .... 104 D5 🔲
Paterson Cft *STKB/PEN* S36 .... 104 D5 🔲
Paterson Gdns *STKB/PEN* S36 ...... 104 D5
Paterson Rd *DIN* S25 .... 178 C6
Patmore Rd *SHEF* S5 .... 152 E3
Patrick Stirling Ct
DONS/BSCR DN4 .... 4 A5 🔲
Patterdale Cl *HACK/IN* S12 .... 138 D2
Patterdale Wy *DIN* S25 .... 194 B1
Patte Roale Cl *AWLS/ASK* DN6 ...... 37 K6
Pavilion Cl *CUD/GR* S72 .... 32 D4 🔲
Pavilion La *RHAM* S60 .... 154 C5
Pavillion Cl *CONI* DN12 .... 115 K4
Paw Hill La *STKB/PEN* S36 .... 76 D7
Paxton Av *AWLS/ASK* DN6 .... 38 A6
Paxton Crs *ARMTH* DN3 .... 66 E8
Paxton La *FUL* S10 .... 8 A4 🔲
Payler Cl *SHEFP/MNR* S2 .... 172 C7
Payne Crs *RAW* S62 .... 111 H8
Peacock Cl *ECK/KIL* S21 .... 205 C1
KIMB S61 .... 131 G1
Pea Fields La *CHPT/GREN* S35 .... 106 E5
Peakdale Crs *HACK/IN* S12 .... 138 G2
Peake Av *CONI* DN12 .... 114 B5
Peake's Cft *BWTY* DN10 .... 142 B8
Peak La *MALT* S66 .... 159 F4
Peak Rd *BSLYN/ROY* S71 .... 30 B8 🔲
Peaks Mt *MOS* S20 .... 190 C6
Pearce Rd *DARN/MH* S9 .... 172 E4
Pearce Wk *DARN/MH* S9 .... 172 E4
Pearl St *ECC* S11 .... 8 B6
Pearmain Dr *MALT* S66 .... 136 E8
Pea Royd La *STKB/PEN* S36 .... 105 F5
Pearson Crs *WMB/DAR* S73 .... 83 J3
Pearson Pl *SHEFS* S8 .... 187 F3
Pearson's Cl *RHAM/THRY* S65 ...... 156 B3
Pearson's Fld *WMB/DAR* S73 .... 84 A4
Pearson St *STKB/PEN* S36 .... 104 E5 🔲
Pear St *ECC* S11 .... 8 B5
Peartree Av *DEARNE* S63 .... 60 B7
Pear Tree Av *MALT* S66 .... 157 H2
Pear Tree Cl *CUD/GR* S72 .... 59 G5
ECK/KIL S21 .... 205 G2
RHAM S60 .... 155 G7
WRKN S81 .... 195 G3 🔲
Pear Tree La *HTFD* DN7 .... 21 F8
Pear Tree Rd *SHEFS* S5 .... 152 E1
Pearwood Crs *DONS/BSCR* DN4 .... 116 C2
Peasehill Cl *RAW* S62 .... 2 B5
Peashill St *RAW* S62 .... 133 J2
Peastack La *NROS/TKH* DN11 ...... 139 J1
Peatfield Rd *ECK/KIL* S21 .... 191 K8
Peat Pits La *CHPT/GREN* S35 .... 127 J7
Peck Hall La *ST/HB/BR* S6 .... 149 F3
Peck Mill Vw *AU/AST/KP* S26 .... 193 H6
Peckham Rd *CHPT/GREN* S35 ...... 130 A1 🔲
Pedley Av *MOS* S20 .... 190 C6
Pedley Cl *MOS* S20 .... 190 C6 🔲
Pedley Dr *MOS* S20 .... 190 C7 🔲
Pedley Gv *MOS* S20 .... 190 C6
Peel Castle Rd *THNE* DN8 .... 43 K1
Peel Hill Rd *THNE* DN8 .... 43 K1
Peel Pde *BSLYN/ROY* S71 .... 2 B4
Peel Sq *BSLY* S70 .... 2 B4 🔲
Peel St *BSLY* S70 .... 2 B4 🔲
FUL S10 .... 170 C5 🔲
Pelham St *WRKS* S80 .... 210 E6
Pell La *HOLM/MEL* HD7 .... 48 B1
Pell's Cl *DON* DN1 .... 4 C3 🔲
Pembrey Ct *MOS* S20 .... 190 E5
Pembroke Av *DONS/BSCR* DN4 .... 116 D1
Pembroke Crs *CHPT/GREN* S35 .... 129 J1
Pembroke Dr *WRKN* S81 .... 196 C5
Pembroke Ri *BTLY* DN5 .... 193 K3 🔲
DIN S25 .... 193 K3 🔲
Pembroke St *ECC* S11 .... 8 B5 🔲
KIMB S61 .... 154 C1
Pendeen Rd *ECC* S11 .... 169 K7 🔲
Pendennis Av *HEM/SK/SE* WF9 .... 34 D3
Pendlebury Gv *HOY* S74 .... 108 D2 🔲
Pendle Cft *MOS* S20 .... 191 F6 🔲
Pengeston Rd *STKB/PEN* S36 .... 77 J5
Penistone Boundary Wk
STKB/PEN S36 .... 53 F7
STKB/PEN S36 .... 76 C2
STKB/PEN S36 .... 76 E2
STKB/PEN S36 .... 78 D2
Penistone La *STKB/PEN* S36 .... 102 E2
Penistone Rd *CHPT/GREN* S35 .... 129 J4
HOLM/MEL HD7 .... 48 D6
HOLM/MEL HD7 .... 48 E1
KBTN HD8 .... 49 K1
KBTN HD8 .... 50 D5

ST/HB/BR S6 .... 126 B6
ST/HB/BR S6 .... 151 K8
Penistone St *DON* DN1 .... 5 D2 🔲
Penley St *ECC* S11 .... 8 C6 🔲
Penlington Cl *HEM/SK/SE* WF9 .... 33 G2 🔲
Pennine Cl *HOLM/MEL* HD7 .... 47 G2
Pennine Dr *KBTN* HD8 .... 26 A5
Pennine Gdns *MALT* S66 .... 158 E1 🔲
Pennine Ri *ARMTH* DN3 .... 26 A5
Pennine Rd *THNE* DN8 .... 43 H1
Pennine Vw *DOD/DAR* S75 .... 29 F5
STKB/PEN S36 .... 104 E8
Pennine Wy *DOD/DAR* S75 .... 55 C5
KBTN HD8 .... 26 A5
Pen Nook Cl *STKB/PEN* S36 .... 105 G8
Pen Nook Ct *STKB/PEN* S36 .... 105 H8 🔲
Pen Nook Dr *STKB/PEN* S36 .... 105 H8
Pen Nook Gdns *STKB/PEN* S36 .... 105 H8
Penns Rd *SHEFP/MNR* S2 .... 187 J1
Penny Engine La *ECK/KIL* S21 ...... 204 C3
Penny Hi *WRKN* S81 .... 179 G3
Penny Hill La *AU/AST/KP* S26 .... 175 K3
Pennyholme Cl *AU/AST/KP* S26 ... 193 F5
Penny La *TOT/DORE* S17 .... 199 C2
Penny Piece La *DIN* S25 .... 193 K1
Penny Piece Pl *DIN* S25 .... 193 K1
Penrhyn Rd *ECC* S11 .... 170 C8
Penrhyn Wk *BSLYN/ROY* S71 .... 57 H7
Penrith Cl *SHEFN* S5 .... 151 K5
Penrith Crs *SHEFN* S5 .... 151 K5
Penrith Gv *BSLYN/ROY* S71 .... 57 G7
Penrith Rd *SHEFN* S5 .... 151 K5
Penrose Pl *HAN/WDH* S13 .... 189 J1
Penthorpe Cl *HACK/IN* S12 .... 188 D1 🔲
Pentland Dr *WRKN* S81 .... 180 C8 🔲
Pentland Gdns *MOS* S20 .... 190 B5
Pentland Rd *DRON* S18 .... 200 D6
Penton St *SHEF* S1 .... 9 D3 🔲
Penyghent Cl *CHPT/GREN* S35 ..... 130 A1 🔲
Pepper Cl *FUL* S10 .... 120 A1
Pepper St *HOY* S74 .... 83 F7
Percival Av *WRKN* S81 .... 210 C3
Percy St *HEM/SK/SE* WF9 .... 34 A5
OWL S3 .... 8 C1 🔲
RHAM/THRY S65 .... 7 D4 🔲
Peregrine Dr *BSLY* S70 .... 82 A7
Peregrine Wy *AU/AST/KP* S26 .... 206 D2 🔲
AU/AST/KP S26 .... 206 E2 🔲
Perigree Rd *SHEFS* S8 .... 186 D4
Periwood Av *SHEFS* S8 .... 186 D4
Periwood Cl *SHEFS* S8 .... 186 E4 🔲
Periwood Dr *SHEFS* S8 .... 186 E4 🔲
Periwood Gv *SHEFS* S8 .... 186 E4 🔲
Perkyn Rd *SHEFN* S5 .... 130 D8
Perkyn Ter *SHEFN* S5 .... 130 D8
Perran Gv *BTLY* DN5 .... 90 C2
Perseverance St *BSLY* S70 .... 2 A4 🔲
Persimmon Cl *NROS/TKH* DN11 ... 118 E8
Perth Cl *MEX/SWTN* S64 .... 113 H1
Petal Cl *MALT* S66 .... 159 J1
Peterborough Cl *FUL* S10 .... 168 E6
Peterborough Dr *FUL* S10 .... 168 E6
Peterborough Rd *FUL* S10 .... 168 E6
Petergate *BTLY* DN5 .... 64 C7
Peter's Cl *CONI* DN12 .... 115 J6
Peter St *KIMB* S61 .... 132 B8
MALT S66 .... 176 E1
Petre Dr *ATT* S4 .... 153 F7
Petre St *ATT* S4 .... 152 E8
Petworth Cft *BSLYN/ROY* S71 .... 30 C5 🔲
Petworth Dr *ECC* S11 .... 185 K5
Peveril Cl *AU/AST/KP* S26 .... 192 E4
Peveril Crs *BSLYN/ROY* S71 .... 30 B8 🔲
Peveril Rd *ECC* S11 .... 170 B8
ECK/KIL S21 .... 204 C3
Pexton Rd *ATT* S4 .... 152 D7
Philadelphia Dr *ST/HB/BR* S6 .... 8 B1 🔲
Philadelphia Gdns *ST/HB/BR* S6 .... 8 B1 🔲
Philadelphia Gv *ST/HB/BR* S6 .... 8 B1 🔲
Philip Rd *BSLY* S70 .... 56 E8
Phillimore Rd *DARN/MH* S9 .... 172 D1
Phillips Rd *ST/HB/BR* S6 .... 150 C6
Phoenix Av *HACK/IN* S12 .... 189 G6
Phoenix Gv *RHAM* S60 .... 154 E6
Phoenix La *DEARNE* S63 .... 60 D8
Phoenix Rd *DARN/MH* S9 .... 154 B4
HACK/IN S12 .... 189 G6
Piccadilly *BTLY* DN5 .... 64 D7
Piccadilly Rd *MEX/SWTN* S64 ...... 112 B6
Pickburn La *BTLY* DN5 .... 62 D4
Pickering Crs *AU/AST/KP* S26 .... 191 G1
Pickering Gv *THNE* DN8 .... 43 J1
Pickering Rd *BTLY* DN5 .... 64 D4
OWL S3 .... 152 A8
Pickering St *DARN/MH* S9 .... 153 J7 🔲
Pickhill's Av *DEARNE* S63 .... 86 E1
Pickmere Rd *FUL* S10 .... 170 B5
Pickup Crs *WMB/DAR* S73 .... 84 A6
Pickwick Dr *RHAM* S60 .... 173 K1
Piece End *CHPT/GREN* S35 .... 107 J7
Piece End Cl *CHPT/GREN* S35 ...... 107 J7 🔲
The Pieces North *RHAM* S60 .... 156 A7
The Pieces South *RHAM* S60 .... 156 A7
Pighills La *DRON* S18 .... 29 J7
Pike Lowe Gv *DOD/DAR* S75 .... 29 F5
Pike Rd *RHAM* S60 .... 155 F6
Pilgrim Cl *WRKN* S81 .... 195 H8 🔲
Pilgrim Ri *BWTY* DN10 .... 142 C6

Pilgrim St *OWL* S3 .... 152 C8
Pilgrims Wy *WRKS* S80 .... 210 D5
Pilley Gn *DOD/DAR* S75 .... 107 J2
Pilley Hi *DOD/DAR* S75 .... 80 E1 🔲
Pilley La *DOD/DAR* S75 .... 107 J1
Pincheon Green La *GLE* DN14 .... 13 G8
Pinchfield Ct *MALT* S66 .... 157 G4
Pinchfield Holt *MALT* S66 .... 157 G4
Pinchfield La *MALT* S66 .... 157 G4
Pinchmill Hollow *MALT* S66 .... 157 G5
Pinch Mill La *RHAM* S60 .... 156 D6
Pindar Oaks Cottages *BSLY* S70 ..... 3 E5 🔲
Pindar Oaks St *BSLY* S70 .... 3 D5
Pindar St *BSLY* S70 .... 3 E5 🔲
Pine Av *DIN* S25 .... 193 K4
Pine Cl *BSLY* S70 .... 82 D1
BWTY DN10 .... 165 K4
ECK/KIL S21 .... 205 C2
HOY S74 .... 109 F2
MALT S66 .... 157 H1
Pine Cft *CHPT/GREN* S35 .... 130 B3
Pinecroft Wy *CHPT/GREN* S35 .... 130 B3
Pinefield Av *ARMTH* DN3 .... 67 F1
Pinefield Rd *ARMTH* DN3 .... 67 F1
Pine Gv *CONI* DN12 .... 114 B7
Pinehall Dr *BSLYN/ROY* S71 .... 56 E5
Pine Hall Rd *ARMTH* DN3 .... 67 H1
Pinehurst Ri *MEX/SWTN* S64 .... 112 C5
Pine Rd *DONS/BSCR* DN4 .... 92 E7
The Pines *FUL* S10 .... 168 E7
Pine St *HEM/SK/SE* WF9 .... 34 D6
Pine Tree Cl *WRKS* S80 .... 210 C6
Pine Tree Wy *MEX/SWTN* S64 ...... 112 C7
Pine Wk *MEX/SWTN* S64 .... 112 C7
Pinewood Av *ARMTH* DN3 .... 67 C7
DONS/BSCR DN4 .... 116 B2 🔲
Pinewood Cl *CUD/GR* S72 .... 59 G4
Pinfold Cl *CUD/GR* S72 .... 59 H5
Pinfold Cl *BSLYN/ROY* S71 .... 57 F7 🔲
EPW DN9 .... 121 F4 🔲
MEX/SWTN S64 .... 112 B5
Pinfold Ct *ARMTH* DN3 .... 66 E1 🔲
Pinfold Dr *WRKN* S81 .... 180 D8
Pinfold Hi *BSLY* S70 .... 82 B1
Pinfold Lands *MEX/SWTN* S64 .... 113 G3
Pinfold La *AWLS/ASK* DN6 .... 18 A4
AWLS/ASK DN6 .... 20 A7
BSLYN/ROY S71 .... 30 D5
CHPT/GREN S35 .... 79 J5
GLE DN14 .... 11 J3
HTFD DN7 .... 22 B5
NROS/TKH DN11 .... 161 J1
NROS/TKH DN11 .... 162 C5
OWL S3 .... 152 B8
PONT WF8 .... 16 E2
RHAM/THRY S65 .... 7 D5 🔲
THNE DN8 .... 23 H7
WMB/DAR S73 .... 84 E2
Pinfold Pl *NROS/TKH* DN11 .... 139 J8
Pinfold St *ECK/KIL* S21 .... 204 B4
The Pinfold *BTLY* DN5 .... 87 J5
Pinfold Vw *GLE* DN14 .... 11 J3 🔲
Pingle Av *ABRD* S7 .... 186 C4
Pingle La *RHAM/THRY* S65 .... 135 H5
Pingle Rd *ABRD* S7 .... 186 C4
ECK/KIL S21 .... 191 J8
Pingles Crs *RHAM/THRY* S65 .... 134 D5
Pinner Rd *ECC* S11 .... 170 C8
Pinstone St *SHEF* S1 .... 9 D5
Pipe House La *RAW* S62 .... 111 J8 🔲
Piper Cl *SHEFN* S5 .... 152 B4
Piper Ct *SHEFN* S5 .... 152 B4 🔲
Piper Crs *SHEFN* S5 .... 152 B4
Pipering La (East) *BTLY* DN5 .... 64 C8
Pipering La (West) *BTLY* DN5 .... 64 B8
Piper La *AU/AST/KP* S26 .... 175 K8
Piper Rd *SHEFN* S5 .... 152 C4
Piper Well La *KBTN* HD8 .... 49 K1
Pipeyard La *ECK/KIL* S21 .... 204 A4
Pippin Ct *MALT* S66 .... 158 E1
Pipworth Gv *SHEFP/MNR* S2 .... 172 E6
Pipworth La *ECK/KIL* S21 .... 204 D3
Pisgah House Rd *FUL* S10 .... 170 C4 🔲
Pitchford La *FUL* S10 .... 169 H6
Pithouse La *AU/AST/KP* S26 .... 191 C4
Pit La *HAN/WDH* S13 .... 188 C1
KIMB S61 .... 131 C4
RHAM S60 .... 174 D3
Pitman Rd *CONI* DN12 .... 113 K4
Pitsmoor Rd *ATT* S4 .... 152 C8
OWL S3 .... 171 C1
Pittam Cl *ARMTH* DN3 .... 93 C1
Pitt Cl *SHEF* S1 .... 8 C3 🔲
Pitt La *SHEF* S1 .... 8 C3 🔲
Pitt St *BSLY* S70 .... 2 B4
ECK/KIL S21 .... 204 A5
KIMB S61 .... 154 C1
MEX/SWTN S64 .... 113 H2
SHEF S1 .... 8 C3
WMB/DAR S73 .... 84 B2
Pitt St West *BSLY* S70 .... 2 A4 🔲
Plains La *THNE* DN8 .... 25 H1
Plane Dr *MALT* S66 .... 157 H5 🔲
Plane Tree Wy *EPW* DN9 .... 120 A4
Planet Rd *AWLS/ASK* DN6 .... 37 K8
Plank Ga *CHPT/GREN* S35 .... 128 E5
STKB/PEN S36 .... 105 K8
Plantation Av *BSLYN/ROY* S71 ...... 30 E4
DIN S25 .... 178 B6

DIN S25 .... 194 A1
DONS/BSCR DN4 .... 119 G3
Plantation Cl AWLS/ASK DN6 .... 19 F8
MALT S66 .... 159 G1
Plantation Dr DIN S25 .... 178 B6
Plantation Dr BWTY DN10 .... 165 G6
Plantation Hl WRKN S81 .... 210 E2
WRKN S81 .... 211 F4
Plantation Rd BTLY DN5 .... 39 K8
SHEFS S8 .... 187 G1
THNE DN8 .... 23 J8
Plantin Ri MOS S20 .... 190 C8
The Plantin MOS S20 .... 190 C8
Plants Yd WRKS S80 .... 210 C5
Platts Dr MOS S20 .... 190 B8
Platts La CHPT/GREN S35 .... 128 D8
ST/HB/BR S6 .... 148 C7
Platt St OWL S3 .... 171 G1
Pleasant Av CUD/GR S72 .... 59 H5
Pleasant Cl HACK/IN S12 .... 188 D1
Pleasant Rd HACK/IN S12 .... 188 D1
Pleasant Vw CUD/GR S72 .... 57 K3
Pleasley Rd RHAM S60 .... 155 K6
Plough Dr WRKN S81 .... 180 D8
Plover Ct DONS/TKH DN11 .... 119 F6
SHEFP/MNR S2 .... 172 A5
Plover Cft S61 .... 131 H1
Plover Dene WRKN S81 .... 196 A8
Plover Dr BSLY S70 .... 82 A7
Plowright Dr SHEFP/MNR S2 .... 187 K2
Plowright Mt SHEFP/MNR S2 .... 187 K2
Plowright Wy SHEFP/MNR S2 ...... 187 K2
Plumber St BSLY S70 .... 2 B4
Plumbley Hall Ms MOS S20 .... 204 A1
Plumbley Hall Rd MOS S20 .... 190 A8
Plumbley La MOS S20 .... 203 K1
Plum La OWL S3 .... 9 D2
Plumper's Rd DARN/MH S9 .... 154 A5
Plumpton Av MEX/SWTN S64 .... 113 H1
Plumpton Gdns DONS/BSCR DN4 . 119 F1
Plumpton La ST/HB/BR S6 .... 148 D3
Plumpton Park Rd
DONS/BSCR DN4 .... 119 F2
Plum St OWL S3 .... 9 D2
Plumtree Hill Rd HTFD DN7 .... 41 K1
Plumtree Rd BWTY DN10 .... 163 H1
Plunket Rd WHHL DN2 .... 5 F2
Plymouth Rd ABRD S7 .... 186 E2
Poffinder Wood Rd HTFD DN7 ...... 42 E2
Pog La CHPT/GREN S35 .... 106 A1
Pogmoor La DOD/DAR S75 .... 55 F5
Pogmoor Rd DOD/DAR S75 .... 55 G6
Pog Well La DOD/DAR S75 .... 54 C5
Pole Hi SHEFS S6 .... 187 G5
Poles Bank EPW DN9 .... 97 G4
Polka Ct OWL S3 .... 171 G1
Pollard Cl ST/HB/BR S6 .... 169 H1
Pond Common La STKB/PEN S36 . 104 E1
Pond Hi SHEF S1 .... 9 E3
Pond Rd ST/HB/BR S6 .... 169 H1
Pond St BSLY S70 .... 2 B5
SHEF S1 .... 9 E3
Pontefract Rd CUD/GR S72 .... 31 K6
DEARNE S63 .... 84 E8
Pontefract Ter HEM/SK/SE WF9 .... 33 H7
Pool Av AWLS/ASK DN6 .... 18 D7
Pool Dr DONS/BSCR DN4 .... 119 J3
Poole Pl DARN/MH S9 .... 172 E3
Poole Rd DARN/MH S9 .... 172 E3
Pool Hill La KBTN N8 .... 51 K2
Pools La BSLYN/ROY S71 .... 31 F4
ECK/KIL S21 .... 202 E3
Pool Sq SHEF S1 .... 9 D3
Pope Av CONI DN12 .... 114 A5
Poplar Av CUD/GR S72 .... 31 K5
DEARNE S63 .... 86 D2
MOS S20 .... 190 D2
RHAM/THRY S65 .... 134 D5
STKB/PEN S36 .... 104 E7
Poplar Cl ARMTH DN3 .... 93 J7
DRON S18 .... 201 J8
ECK/KIL S21 .... 202 D6
MEX/SWTN S64 .... 112 E1
WRKS S80 .... 210 B6
Poplar Dr DEARNE S63 .... 111 J3
RHAM S60 .... 154 E7
Poplar Gld MALT S66 .... 157 G3
Poplar Gv BSLYN/ROY S71 .... 18 D7
BSLYN/ROY S71 .... 57 F3
CONI DN12 .... 114 C6
DONS/BSCR DN4 .... 115 K3
MEX/SWTN S64 .... 112 C4
RHAM/THRY S65 .... 135 K7
Poplar Pl ARMTH DN3 .... 93 G1
Poplar Ri MALT S66 .... 158 E1
Poplar Rd AWLS/ASK DN6 .... 37 J6
CHPT/GREN S35 .... 128 B8
ECK/KIL S21 .... 204 A5
HTFD DN7 .... 42 A7
WMB/DAR S73 .... 84 B6

Poplars Rd BSLY S70 .... 3 E6
The Poplars BTLY DN5 .... 87 H4
CONI DN12 .... 114 C6
Poplar St CUD/GR S72 .... 58 E2
Poplar Ter BSLYN/ROY S71 .... 30 E3
BTLY DN5 .... 64 E7
HEM/SK/SE WF9 .... 35 F5
Poplar Wy RHAM S60 .... 173 G3
Popple St KIMB S61 .... 153 F6
Poppyfields Wy ARMTH DN3 .... 93 H8
Porter Brook Vw ECC S11 .... 8 A6
Porter Ter DOD/DAR S75 .... 55 C5
Portland Av AU/AST/KP S26 .... 175 J8
Portland Cl DIN S25 .... 178 A7
Portland Ct ST/HB/BR S6 .... 170 E1
Portland La SHEF S1 .... 8 C3
Portland Pl DON DN1 .... 4 C3
MALT S66 .... 159 H2
WRKS S80 .... 210 D3
Portland Rd MOS S20 .... 190 E5
NROS/TKH DN11 .... 118 E8
Portland St BSLY S70 .... 3 E5
MEX/SWTN S64 .... 112 C4
ST/HB/BR S6 .... 8 B1
ST/HB/BR S6 .... 8 B1
WRKS S80 .... 210 C4
Portobello OWL S3 .... 8 C3
Portobello St SHEF S1 .... 8 C3
Portsea Rd ST/HB/BR S6 .... 151 G7
Pot House La STKB/PEN S36 .... 104 E7
Potterdyke Av RAW S62 .... 111 J7
Potter Hill KIMB S61 .... 133 F4
Potter Hill La CHPT/GREN S35 .... 107 H8
Potteric Carr Rd DONS/BSCR DN4 . 5 E5
Potters Ga CHPT/GREN S35 .... 107 H8
HOLM/MEL HD7 .... 49 J7
Potters Nook WRKN S81 .... 195 H8
Potter St WRKS S80 .... 210 D5
Pottery Cl RAW S62 .... 133 J2
Potts Crs CUD/GR S72 .... 59 H5
Poucher St KIMB S61 .... 153 K1
Poulton St BSLYN/ROY S71 .... 56 E1
Powder Mill La BSLY S70 .... 82 D4
Powell Dr ECK/KIL S21 .... 205 G1
Powell St BSLY S70 .... 82 C3
HEM/SK/SE WF9 .... 34 C4
OWL S3 .... 8 B2
Power Station Rd BTLY DN5 .... 4 B2
Powley Rd ST/HB/BR S6 .... 151 H2
Poxton Gv HEM/SK/SE WF9 .... 34 D6
Poynton Av AU/AST/KP S26 .... 175 J4
Poynton Dr DIN S25 .... 178 B5
Poynton Wy AU/AST/KP S26 .... 175 J4
Poynton Wood Crs
TOT/DORE S17 .... 200 A1
Poynton Wood Gld
TOT/DORE S17 .... 200 A1
Prescott Gv HTFD DN7 .... 42 B7
Prescott Rd ST/HB/BR S6 .... 151 F5
President Wy ATT S4 .... 9 F1
Preston Av HOY S74 .... 83 H8
Preston St SHEFP/MNR S2 .... 171 G8
Preston Wy BSLYN/ROY S71 .... 56 A1
Prestwich St DARN/MH S9 .... 153 J3
Priest Croft La BSLYN/ROY S71 ..... 58 C7
Priestley Av DOD/DAR S75 .... 28 B7
RAW S62 .... 112 A8
Priestley Cl DONS/BSCR DN4 ...... 116 C2
Priestley St SHEFP/MNR S2 .... 9 E5
Priest Royd DOD/DAR S75 .... 29 F6
Primrose Av RHAM S60 .... 155 G8
SHEFN S5 .... 153 F3
WMB/DAR S73 .... 84 C7
Primrose Cir NROS/TKH DN11 .... 119 F6
Primrose Cl ECK/KIL S21 .... 191 J8
Primrose Crs MOS S20 .... 190 D4
Primrose Dr CHPT/GREN S35 ...... 130 C7
Primrose Hl KIMB S61 .... 6 B2
RHAM S60 .... 6 C2
ST/HB/BR S6 .... 170 E1
Primrose La ECK/KIL S21 .... 191 J7
Primrose Wy HOY S74 .... 109 F3
WRKN S81 .... 210 E1
Primulas Cl DIN S25 .... 193 J3
Prince Arthur St DOD/DAR S75 ...... 2 A3
Prince Charles Rd ATT S4 .... 196 B8
Prince of Wales Rd DARN/MH S9 . 172 E4
ATT S4 .... 172 D6
Prince's Crs CONI DN12 .... 115 J4
Prince's Rd DONS/BSCR DN4 ...... 92 B6
Princess Anne Rd WRKN S81 .... 210 C1
Princess Av HEM/SK/SE WF9 .... 34 E5
HTFD DN7 .... 41 K3
Princess Cl DEARNE S63 .... 86 A5
Princess Ct SHEFP/MNR S2 .... 172 D7
Princess Dr DEARNE S63 .... 60 D8
STKB/PEN S36 .... 105 F8
Princess Gdns WMB/DAR S73 .... 84 A5
Princess Gv DOD/DAR S75 .... 107 H2
Princess Sq ARMTH DN3 .... 66 E5
Princess Rd DEARNE S63 .... 86 D2
DRON S18 .... 201 C5
MEX/SWTN S64 .... 113 C2
Princess St ATT S4 .... 171 K2
AWLS/ASK DN6 .... 63 J3
BSLY S70 .... 2 B4
CUD/GR S72 .... 58 D1
DEARNE S63 .... 85 C8
DIN S25 .... 177 J5

DOD/DAR S75 .... 29 F6
HOY S74 .... 108 C2
WMB/DAR S73 .... 83 K4
Prince's St DON DN1 .... 5 D3
RHAM S60 .... 6 A4
Prince St HEM/SWTN S64 .... 112 C3
Pringle Rd RHAM S60 .... 154 E6
Printing Office St DON DN1 .... 4 C3
Prior Rd CONI DN12 .... 114 C6
Priorswell Rd WRKS S80 .... 210 D5
Priory Av ECC S11 .... 8 A6
Priory Cl BSLY S70 .... 82 A5
CHPT/GREN S35 .... 130 B6
CONI DN12 .... 114 D4
Priory Ct AU/AST/KP S26 .... 206 E2
Priory Crs BSLYN/ROY S71 .... 57 F4
Priory Pl ABRD S7 .... 170 E8
BSLYN/ROY S71 .... 57 F5
CHPT/GREN S35 .... 130 B6
Priory Rd Or Hall La AWLS/ASK DN6 . 17 K3
Priory Wy AU/AST/KP S26 .... 175 J8
Pritchard Cl HACK/IN S12 .... 189 K4
Probert Av DEARNE S63 .... 86 C2
Proctor Pl ST/HB/BR S6 .... 151 H7
Progress Dr MALT S66 .... 157 J3
Prospect Cl MALT S66 .... 157 J3
Prospect Dr TOT/DORE S17 .... 199 K2
WRKN S81 .... 210 D1
Prospect Pl TOT/DORE S17 .... 200 A1
Prospect Prec WRKN S81 .... 210 E1
Prospect Rd BTLY DN5 .... 64 D3
DEARNE S63 .... 86 B4
DRON S18 .... 201 J4
SHEFP/MNR S2 .... 171 G8
SHEFS S8 .... 171 G8
TOT/DORE S17 .... 200 A2
Prospect St BSLY S70 .... 2 A4
CUD/GR S72 .... 31 J8
Providence Ct BSLY S70 .... 2 C5
Providence Rd ST/HB/BR S6 .... 170 B1
Providence St KIMB S61 .... 133 F4
RHAM S60 .... 6 B4
WMB/DAR S73 .... 83 H5
Pryor Mede AU/AST/KP S26 .... 206 E2
Psalter La ECC S11 .... 170 E8
Psalters Dr STKB/PEN S36 .... 78 D6
Psalters La KIMB S61 .... 132 C8
Purbeck Ct MOS S20 .... 190 B5
Purbeck Gv MOS S20 .... 190 B5
Purbeck Rd MOS S20 .... 190 B5
Purcell Cl MALT S66 .... 159 K3
Purslove Cl MALT S66 .... 157 K5
Pye Av DOD/DAR S75 .... 29 F7
Pye Bank Cl OWL S3 .... 171 G1
Pye Bank Dr OWL S3 .... 171 G1
Pye Bank Rd OWL S3 .... 171 G1
Pym Rd MEX/SWTN S64 .... 113 F2

Q

The Quadrant TOT/DORE S17 .... 199 J2
Quail Ri SHEFP/MNR S2 .... 172 A5
Quaker Cl DEARNE S63 .... 111 G2
Quaker La BSLYN/ROY S71 .... 57 G7
DONS/BSCR DN4 .... 116 A1
Quantock Cl THNE DN8 .... 43 H2
Quarry Bank DEARNE S63 .... 110 E1
Quarry Bank Rd CUD/GR S72 .... 57 J1
Quarry Cl DOD/DAR S75 .... 28 C7
RHAM S60 .... 154 D7
Quarryfield La MALT S66 .... 157 G8
Quarry Field La MALT S66 .... 157 G5
Quarry Flds MALT S66 .... 157 C4
Quarry Gv WRKN S81 .... 196 A8
Quarry Hl ECK/KIL S21 .... 203 F5
HACK/IN S12 .... 189 J7
RHAM S60 .... 6 C4
Quarry Hill Rd DEARNE S63 .... 111 H3
Quarry La ARMTH DN3 .... 93 J7
AWLS/ASK DN6 .... 63 H3
DIN S25 .... 195 K1
ECC S11 .... 7 G8
KIMB S61 .... 6 B2
Quarry Pl DIN S25 .... 178 C6
Quarry Rd AWLS/ASK DN6 .... 18 C4
DRON S18 .... 202 C6
ECK/KIL S21 .... 191 C8
HAN/WDH S13 .... 173 C4
HOY S74 .... 82 E6
TOT/DORE S17 .... 199 J2
Quarry St BSLY S70 .... 2 C5
BSLYN/ROY S71 .... 56 E2
CUD/GR S72 .... 31 J8
MEX/SWTN S64 .... 113 C3
RAW S62 .... 133 J1
Quarry Vale Gv HACK/IN S12 .... 188 E3
Quarry Vale Rd HACK/IN S12 .... 188 E3
Quay Rd THNE DN8 .... 23 C6
Quayside THNE DN8 .... 23 F6
Queen Av MALT S66 .... 159 H3
NROS/TKH DN11 .... 118 D6
Queen Elizabeth Crs WRKS S80 .. 209 J3
Queen Gdns WMB/DAR S73 .... 84 A5
Queen Mary Cl SHEFP/MNR S2 .. 172 C8

Queen Mary Crs ARMTH DN3 66 E3
SHEFP/MNR S2 172 C7
Queen Mary Gv SHEFP/MNR S2 172 B8 2
Queen Mary Ms SHEFP/MNR S2 172 C8 2
Queen Mary Rd SHEFP/MNR S2 172 B7
Queen Mary's Rd
NROS/TKH DN11 118 D6
Queen Mary St MALT S66 159 H4 2
Queens Av AU/AST/KP S26 192 C5
CUD/GR S72 59 G8
DOD/DAR S75 2 A3
MEX/SWTN S64 112 C3
Queensberry Rd WHHL DN2 92 B3
Queen's Ct BTLY DN5 90 D1 1
THNE DN8 23 H8
Queen's Crs BWTY DN10 142 B8
CONI DN12 115 J4
HOY S74 108 B2 1
HTFD DN7 41 K4 3
Queen's Dr BTLY DN5 90 D1
CUD/GR S72 31 K6
CUD/GR S72 31 J4
DOD/DAR S75 54 E8
DOD/DAR S75 55 H4
Queens Gdns DOD/DAR S75 55 H4
HOY S74 108 C2 6
Queensgate CHPT/GREN S35 129 J7 2
Queens Rd AU/AST/KP S26 175 G8
AWLS/ASK DN6 18 E7
AWLS/ASK DN6 37 K7
BSLYN/ROY S71 2 C4
CUD/GR S72 31 K6
CUD/GR S72 58 E1
DON DN1 5 E2
MOS S20 190 D3
SHEFP/MNR S2 9 D6
WRKN S81 180 C8
Queen's Rw OWL S3 8 C2 9
Queen's Ter MEX/SWTN S64 113 F2
Queen St BSLY S70 2 C4
CHPT/GREN S35 130 B1
DEARNE S63 60 D8
DEARNE S63 86 D2
DIN S25 178 B5
DONS/BSCR DN4 4 B6 4
ECK/KIL S21 204 C4
HEM/SK/SE WF9 34 E5
HOY S74 108 B2
MEX/SWTN S64 112 C4
MOS S20 204 A1
RAW S62 111 K8
RHAM/THRY S65 7 F3
SHEF S1 9 D2
STKB/PEN S36 78 B4
THNE DN8 23 H8
WMB/DAR S73 84 E1
WRKS S80 210 D5
Queensway BSLY S70 82 C3
BSLYN/ROY S71 30 D3 2
DOD/DAR S75 55 H4 4
HOY S74 109 G1
RHAM S60 155 J5
WRKN S81 210 D3
Queen Victoria Rd TOT/DORE S17 199 K2
Quern Wy WMB/DAR S73 84 D1
Quest Av WMB/DAR S73 83 J7
Quiet La ECC S11 185 F1
Quilter Rd MALT S66 159 K3
Quintec Ct RAW S62 7 D1
Quoit Gn DRON S18 201 H6

R

Raby Rd WHHL DN2 5 F1
Raby St DARN/MH S9 154 B4
Race Common Av STKB/PEN S36 77 K7
Racecommon La BSLY S70 2 A6
Racecommon Rd BSLY S70 2 A5
Racecourse Rd MEX/SWTN S64 111 K4
Race La STKB/PEN S36 127 F2
Race St BSLY S70 2 B4
Racker Wy ST/HB/BR S6 151 G8
Rackford Rd DIN S25 194 A2
Radburn Rd NROS/TKH DN11 118 D8
Radcliffe La BTLY DN5 64 B6
Radcliffe Rd BSLYN/ROY S71 30 A7
BTLY DN5 64 D5
Radford Cl RHAM/THRY S65 135 K7
Radford Park Av HEM/SK/SE WF9 34 A6
Radford St OWL S3 8 C2
WRKS S80 210 E6
Radley Av MALT S66 157 F2
Radnor Cl MOS S20 190 E5
Radnor Wy WHHL DN2 92 B2
Raeburn Cl GLV S14 188 A5
Raeburn Pl GLV S14 188 A4
Raeburn Rd GLV S14 188 A4
Raeburn Wy SHEFS S8 188 A5
Rag La CHPT/GREN S35 79 H8
Ragusa Dr NROS/TKH DN11 118 E8
Rail Mill Wy RAW S62 133 J5
Rails Rd ST/HB/BR S6 168 E3
Railway Av RHAM S60 174 A2
Railway Ter RHAM S60 6 B4 4
Railway Vw DEARNE S63 86 D2
Rainborough Ms DEARNE S63 84 E8 3
Rainborough Rd DEARNE S63 110 E1
Rainbow Av HACK/IN S12 189 K3
Rainbow Crs HACK/IN S12 190 A3
Rainbow Dr HACK/IN S12 190 A3
Rainbow Gv HACK/IN S12 190 A3
Rainbow Pl HACK/IN S12 190 A3
Rainbow Rd HACK/IN S12 190 A3
Rainbow Wy HACK/IN S12 189 K3
Raines Av WRKN S81 210 C1
Raines Park Rd WRKN S81 196 C8
Rainford Dr BSLYN/ROY S71 56 E1
Rainford Sq ARMTH DN3 66 E2 1
Rainton Gv DOD/DAR S75 55 G4
Raintree Ct BTLY DN5 90 C2
Raisen Hall Pl SHEFN S5 152 B5
Raisen Hall Rd SHEFN S5 152 A4
Rake Bridge Bank HTFD DN7 68 C5
Rake Head Rd HOLM/MEL HD7 46 B8
Rakes La CONI DN12 137 K3
NROS/TKH DN11 117 G5
Raleigh Ct WHHL DN2 92 A4
Raleigh Dr CHPT/GREN S35 129 J2
Raleigh Rd SHEFS S8 187 H1
Raleigh Ter DONS/BSCR DN4 116 B1
Raley St BSLY S70 2 A5
Ralph Ellis Dr STKB/PEN S36 104 E7
Ralston Ct MOS S20 204 B1 5
Ralston Cft MOS S20 204 C1 8
Ralston Gv MOS S20 204 B1
Ramper Rd MALT S66 158 C6
WRKN S81 179 J4
Rampton Rd ABRD S7 171 F8 12
Ramsden Av WRKN S81 180 C4
Ramsden Crs WRKN S81 180 D8 4
Ramsden Rd HOLM/MEL HD7 47 F7
RHAM S60 7 D5
Ramsey Rd FUL S10 170 C3
Ramsker Dr ARMTH DN3 93 G2
Ramskir La HTFD DN7 42 A2
Ramsworth Cl BTLY DN5 90 B2 5
Ranby Rd ECC S11 170 B8
Randall Pl SHEFP/MNR S2 8 C6
Randall St ECK/KIL S21 203 K5 1
SHEFP/MNR S2 9 D5
Randerson Dr MEX/SWTN S64 112 D6
Rands La ARMTH DN3 67 H8
Ranelagh Dr ECC S11 186 B2
Ranfield Ct RHAM/THRY S65 135 K7 1
Rangeley Rd ST/HB/BR S6 170 A2
Ranmoor Cliffe Rd FUL S10 169 J6
Ranmoor Crs FUL S10 169 K6
Ranmoor Hl HATH/EY S32 182 A7
Ranmoor Park Rd FUL S10 169 K6
Ranmoor Ri FUL S10 169 K6 2
Ranmoor Rd FUL S10 169 K6
Ranskill Ct DARN/MH S9 153 K8
Ranworth Rd MALT S66 157 K2
Ranyard Rd DONS/BSCR DN4 90 C8 5
Raseby Av MOS S20 190 C5
Raseby Cl MOS S20 190 C5
Raseby Pl MOS S20 190 C5 2
Rasen Cl MEX/SWTN S64 113 G1
Ratcliffe Rd ECC S11 8 A6
Ratten Rw DOD/DAR S75 80 D1
NROS/TKH DN11 117 F8
Ravencar Rd ECK/KIL S21 203 K4
Ravencarr Pl SHEFP/MNR S2 172 C6
Ravencarr Rd SHEFP/MNR S2 172 C6
Raven Dr KIMB S61 131 H1
Ravenfield Cl MOS S20 189 J5
Ravenfield Dr BSLYN/ROY S71 56 B1
Ravenfield La RHAM/THRY S65 135 H2
Ravenfield Rd ARMTH DN3 93 H2
Ravenfield St CONI DN12 114 A4
Ravenholt BSLY S70 82 B3
Raven La CUD/GR S72 31 H1
Raven Mdw MEX/SWTN S64 112 B7
Raven Rd ABRD S7 186 D1
Raven Royd BSLYN/ROY S71 30 A6
Ravenscar Cl CONI DN12 114 A4
Ravens Cl DOD/DAR S75 29 G7 3
Ravenscourt BSLY S70 82 C3
WRKN S81 210 E1 7
Ravenscroft Av HAN/WDH S13 173 G7
Ravenscroft Cl HAN/WDH S13 173 G7 1
Ravenscroft Ct HAN/WDH S13 173 G7 2
Ravenscroft Crs HAN/WDH S13 173 G7
Ravenscroft Dr HAN/WDH S13 173 G7
Ravenscroft Ov HAN/WDH S13 173 G7 3
Ravenscroft Pl HAN/WDH S13 173 G7 4
Ravenscroft Rd HAN/WDH S13 173 G8
Ravenscroft Wy HAN/WDH S13 173 G8
Ravensdale Rd DRON S18 200 C6
Ravenshaw Cl DOD/DAR S75 55 G4 3
Ravensmead Ct DEARNE S63 86 B5
Ravens Wk CONI DN12 115 F5
Ravens Wy HOLM/MEL HD7 48 D3
Ravenswood Dr EPW DN9 94 B8
Ravensworth Rd DON DN1 5 E4 1
The Ravine SHEFN S5 131 F8
Raw La MALT S66 138 B6
Rawmarsh Hl RAW S62 133 J3
Rawmarsh Rd RHAM S60 6 C3
Rawson Cl DONS/BSCR DN4 92 E6 2
Rawson Rd NROS/TKH DN11 139 J8
RHAM/THRY S65 7 D3 7
Rawsons Bank CHPT/GREN S35 130 C7
Rawson Spring Rd ST/HB/BR S6 151 J5
Rawson Spring Wy SHEFN S5 151 J5
Raybould Rd KIMB S61 132 C6 2
Rayls Ri AU/AST/KP S26 193 F2
Rayls Rd AU/AST/KP S26 193 F2
Raymond Av CUD/GR S72 58 D1
Raymond Rd BSLY S70 56 E8
BTLY DN5 90 C1
Raymoth La WRKN S81 196 C8
Raynald Rd SHEFP/MNR S2 172 C6
Raynor Sike La CHPT/GREN S35 127 K7
Rayton Ct NROS/TKH DN11 163 F3
Rayton La WRKN S81 211 H4
Rayton Sp WRKN S81 211 F4
Reader Crs MEX/SWTN S64 112 C3
Reading Room La
CHPT/GREN S35 106 C4
Reaper Crs CHPT/GREN S35 129 K1
Reasbeck Ter BSLYN/ROY S71 56 A2 1
Reasby Av RHAM/THRY S65 135 J7
Rebecca Ms BSLY S70 2 C5 10
Rebecca Rw BSLY S70 2 C5
Recreation Av MALT S66 177 F1
Recreation La NROS/TKH DN11 118 D6
Recreation Rd AWLS/ASK DN6 63 J3 1
DEARNE S63 85 J8
Rectory Cl BSLYN/ROY S71 30 E6
DEARNE S63 60 A7
ECK/KIL S21 204 C3
STKB/PEN S36 105 F6
WMB/DAR S73 84 A5
Rectory Gdns AU/AST/KP S26 193 F3
AU/AST/KP S26 206 E1
CONI DN12 115 H8
DON DN1 5 E2
ECK/KIL S21 205 H1
Rectory La DEARNE S63 60 A7
EPW DN9 120 E4
Rectory Ms BTLY DN5 89 J7 4
Rectory Rd ECK/KIL S21 205 H1
Rectory St RAW S62 133 J3
Rectory Wy BSLYN/ROY S71 56 E4 2
Redbourne Rd BTLY DN5 64 E6
Redbrook Ct DOD/DAR S75 55 H3 3
Redbrook Cft HACK/IN S12 189 J4 4
Redbrook Gv MOS S20 189 J4 5
Redbrook Rd DOD/DAR S75 55 F3
Redbrook Vw DOD/DAR S75 55 H3
Redbrook Wk DOD/DAR S75 55 H3
Redcar Cl CONI DN12 113 K5
Redcar Rd FUL S10 170 C4
Redcliffe Cl DOD/DAR S75 55 G3
Redfearn St BSLYN/ROY S71 2 C3 4
Redfern Av MOS S20 190 B6
Redfern Ct MOS S20 190 B6 1
Redfern Dr MOS S20 190 B6
Redfern Gv MOS S20 190 B6
Red Fern Gv STKB/PEN S36 104 E7
Redgrave Pl MALT S66 157 G1
Redhall Cl ARMTH DN3 67 F3
Red Hl AU/AST/KP S26 193 F5
SHEF S1 8 C3 15
Redhill Av BSLY S70 3 F6
Redhill Ct NROS/TKH DN11 116 E8
Red Hill La BTLY DN5 61 H8
Red House La AWLS/ASK DN6 37 H8
AWLS/ASK DN6 62 E1
Redland Crs THNE DN8 23 K6
Redland Gv DOD/DAR S75 29 G5
Redland Wy MALT S66 159 F1
Red La ECC S11 170 C6
WRKN S81 196 E5
Redmarsh Av RAW S62 111 H8
Redmires La FUL S10 168 B6
Redmires Rd FUL S10 167 J7
FUL S10 169 G5
Red Oak La ST/HB/BR S6 150 B8 1
Red Quarry La DIN S25 179 G7
Redrock Rd RHAM S60 155 K5
Redscope Crs KIMB S61 132 A5
Redscope Rd KIMB S61 132 A6
Redthorne Wy CUD/GR S72 31 J4
Redthorn Rd HAN/WDH S13 173 H7
Redthorpe Crest DOD/DAR S75 55 F3 2
Redwing Cl WRKN S81 210 A1
Redwood Av BSLYN/ROY S71 30 D4
ECK/KIL S21 205 G2
Redwood Cl HOY S74 108 E2
Redwood Dr MALT S66 158 D2
Redwood Gln CHPT/GREN S35 130 A3
Reedham Dr MALT S66 157 K2
Reedholme La THNE DN8 14 A7
Regent Av ARMTH DN3 93 H2
Regent Crs BSLYN/ROY S71 30 A8
Regent Crescent CUD/GR S72 32 B2
Regent Gdns BSLY S70 2 B3
Regent Gv BTLY DN5 90 C2
NROS/TKH DN11 118 E8
Regent Sq DON DN1 5 E3 2
Regent St BSLY S70 2 B3
CUD/GR S72 32 B2
DONS/BSCR DN4 90 D8
HEM/SK/SE WF9 34 D4
HOY S74 108 B2
KIMB S61 154 C1
SHEF S1 8 C3 16
Regents Wy AU/AST/KP S26 175 J8 4
Regent Ter OWL S3 8 C3
Regina Crs CUD/GR S72 32 B4
Reginald Rd BSLY S70 56 E8
WMB/DAR S73 84 C5 2
Rembrandt Dr DRON S18 200 E6

Remington Av *SHEFN* S5 .... **130** A8
Remington Dr *SHEFN* S5 .... **130** A8 ☒
Remount Av *KIMB* S61 .... **132** A5
Remount Rd *KIMB* S61 .... **132** A5 ☒
Remple Av *HTFD* DN7 .... **69** H1
Remple Common Rd *HTFD* DN7 .... **69** G3
Remple La *HTFD* DN7 .... **69** H1
Renald La *STKB/PEN* S36 .... **52** B8
Renathorpe Rd *SHEFN* S5 .... **152** E1
Rencliffe Av *RHAM* S60 .... **155** J4
Reneville Cl *RHAM* S60 .... **6** C6
Reneville Ct *SHEFN* S5 .... **130** B7
Reneville Crs *SHEFN* S5 .... **130** B7
Reneville Dr *SHEFN* S5 .... **130** B7 ☒
Reney Av *SHEFS* S8 .... **200** D1
Reney Dr *SHEFS* S8 .... **200** D1
Reney Rd *SHEFS* S8 .... **186** E8
Renishaw Av *RHAM* S60 .... **156** A5
Renishaw Cl *CHPT/GREN* S35 .... **107** H7
Renshaw Rd *ECC* S11 .... **186** A1
Renville Cl *RAW* S62 .... **111** H8
Renway Rd *RHAM* S60 .... **7** F6
Repton Cl *DRON* S18 .... **200** C6 ☒
Repton Rd *AWLS/ASK* DN6 .... **37** J7
Reresby Crs *RHAM* S60 .... **156** B5
Reresby Dr *RHAM* S60 .... **156** B5
Reresby Rd *RHAM* S60 .... **156** B5
   RHAM/THRY S65 .... **155** K5
Reservoir Rd *AU/AST/KP* S26 .... **175** G3
   FUL S10 .... **170** C4
Retford Rd *HAN/WDH* S13 .... **173** J6
   WRKN S81 .... **211** K5
   WRKS S80 .... **210** E5
Retford Wk *NROS/TKH* DN11 .... **119** G6
Revel Garth *KBTN* HD8 .... **51** H2
Revell Cl *RHAM/THRY* S65 .... **134** D8
Revill Cl *MALT* S66 .... **159** C1
Revill Ct *DIN* S25 .... **178** B5 ☒
Revill La *HAN/WDH* S13 .... **190** A1
Rex Av *ABRD* S7 .... **186** B3
Reynard Crs *ECK/KIL* S21 .... **205** F7
Reynard La *ST/HB/BR* S6 .... **169** F2
Reynolds Cl *DRON* S18 .... **200** E7
   MALT S66 .... **157** G2
Rhodes Av *KIMB* S61 .... **132** B5
Rhodes Dr *RHAM* S60 .... **156** B5
Rhodes St *SHEFP/MNR* S2 .... **9** F3 ☒
Ribble Cft *CHPT/GREN* S35 .... **130** A1
Ribblesdale *WRKN* S81 .... **196** E7 ☒
Ribblesdale Dr *HACK/IN* S12 .... **189** H6
Ribble Wy *SHEFN* S5 .... **152** D4
Riber Av *BSLYN/ROY* S71 .... **30** E8
Riber Cl *ST/HB/BR* S6 .... **150** C8
Ribston Ct *DARN/MH* S9 .... **172** D3 ☒
Ribston Pl *DARN/MH* S9 .... **172** D3 ☒
Ribston Pl *DARN/MH* S9 .... **172** D3 ☒
Ribston Rd *DARN/MH* S9 .... **172** C3
Richard Av *BSLYN/ROY* S71 .... **56** B1
Richard La *NROS/TKH* DN11 .... **118** D6
Richard Rd *BSLYN/ROY* S71 .... **56** B1
   DOD/DAR S75 .... **28** C7
   RHAM S60 .... **7** D5
Richards Ct *SHEFP/MNR* S2 .... **187** H1 ☒
Richards Rd *SHEFP/MNR* S2 .... **171** G8
Richard St *BSLY* S70 .... **2** A4 ☒
Richards Wy *RAW* S62 .... **133** K1
Rich Farm Cl *BTLY* DN5 .... **65** G4
Rich Ga *HOLM/MEL* HD7 .... **48** A5
Richmond Av *DOD/DAR* S75 .... **28** C8 ☒
   HAN/WDH S13 .... **173** G2
Richmond Cl *AWLS/ASK* DN6 .... **19** F7
Richmond Dr
   HAN/WDH S13 .... **173** F8 ☒
Richmond Farm Ms
   HAN/WDH S13 .... **173** F8 ☒
Richmond Gv *HAN/WDH* S13 .... **173** G7 ☒
Richmond Hall Av *HAN/WDH* S13.. **173** F7
Richmond Hall Crs
   HAN/WDH S13 .... **173** F8 ☒
Richmond Hall Dr
   HAN/WDH S13 .... **173** F7 ☒
Richmond Hall Rd
   HAN/WDH S13 .... **173** F7
Richmond Hall Wy
   HAN/WDH S13 .... **173** F8 ☒
Richmond Hill Rd *BTLY* DN5 .... **90** B5 ☒
   HAN/WDH S13 .... **173** F8 ☒
Richmond La *DN10 .... **164** A1
Richmond Park Av *HAN/WDH* S13.. **173** G5
   KIMB S61 .... **154** A1
Richmond Park Cl
   HAN/WDH S13 .... **173** G6 ☒
Richmond Park Crs
   HAN/WDH S13 .... **173** G6
Richmond Park Cft
   HAN/WDH S13 .... **173** F5
Richmond Park Dr
   HAN/WDH S13 .... **173** G6
Richmond Park Gv
   HAN/WDH S13 .... **173** F6
Richmond Park Ri
   HAN/WDH S13 .... **173** F5
Richmond Park Rd
   HAN/WDH S13 .... **173** G6
Richmond Park Vw
   HAN/WDH S13 .... **173** G6
Richmond Park Wy
   HAN/WDH S13 .... **173** G6 ☒
Richmond Pl *HAN/WDH* S13 .... **173** F8 ☒

Richmond Rd *BTLY* DN5.................... **64** A8
   DEARNE S63 .... **60** B7
   HAN/WDH S13 .... **173** G7
   HAN/WDH S13 .... **188** E1
   KIMB S61 .... **154** B1
   THNE DN8 .... **24** A3
   WRKN S81 .... **196** D1
Richmond St *BSLY* S70 .... **2** A4 ☒
   OWL S3 .... **171** H1
Richworth Rd *HAN/WDH* S13 .... **173** H7
Ricknald Cl *AU/AST/KP* S26 .... **175** H5
Ridal Av *STKB/PEN* S36 .... **104** D5
Ridal Cl *STKB/PEN* S36 .... **104** D5
Ridal Cft *STKB/PEN* S36 .... **104** D5 ☒
Riddell Av *WRKN* S81 .... **180** C4
Riddings Cl *HEM/SK/SE* WF9 .... **33** C2
   MALT S66 .... **177** F1 ☒
   SHEFP/MNR S2 .... **172** C8
Riddings La *BWTY* DN10 .... **142** C4
Rider Rd *ST/HB/BR* S6 .... **151** H7
Ridge Balk La *AWLS/ASK* DN6 .... **63** G2
Ridgehill Av *HACK/IN* S12 .... **188** C2
Ridge Rd *AWLS/ASK* DN6 .... **63** J5
   ECK/KIL S21 .... **203** C5
   RHAM/THRY S65 .... **7** D3
The Ridge *FUL* S10 .... **169** G6
Ridge View Cl *DARN/MH* S9 .... **153** H4
Ridge View Dr *DARN/MH* S9 .... **153** H4
Ridgewalk Wy *BSLY* S70 .... **82** A1
Ridgeway *DRON* S18 .... **201** K4
   RHAM/THRY S65 .... **134** B8
   WRKN S81 .... **210** F1 ☒
Ridgeway Cescent *HACK/IN* S12 .. **188** C2
Ridgeway Cl *MALT* S66 .... **158** B3
   RHAM/THRY S65 .... **134** C8
Ridgeway Crs *BSLYN/ROY* S71 .... **30** C6
   HACK/IN S12 .... **188** C1
Ridgeway Dr *HACK/IN* S12 .... **188** C1
Ridgeway Moor *HACK/IN* S12 .... **203** G1
Ridgeway Rd *HACK/IN* S12 .... **188** C2
   RHAM S60 .... **154** E7
   SHEFP/MNR S2 .... **188** C1 ☒
Ridgewood Av *ARMTH* DN3 .... **66** E6
Ridgill Av *AWLS/ASK* DN6 .... **37** H6
Ridgway Av *WMB/DAR* S73 .... **84** D1
Riding Cl *DONS/BSCR* DN4 .... **119** C1
   MALT S66 .... **157** F2
Ridings Av *BSLYN/ROY* S71 .... **56** C2
The Ridings *BSLYN/ROY* S71 .... **56** D2 ☒
Ridingwood Ri *KBTN* HD8 .... **26** B5 ☒
Rig Cl *KIMB* S61 .... **132** C6
Rig Dr *MEX/SWTN* S64 .... **111** K4
Riggs High Rd *ST/HB/BR* S6 .... **168** D2
Riggs Low Rd *ST/HB/BR* S6 .... **168** D2
Riley Av *DONS/BSCR* DN4 .... **116** C1
Riley Rd *DEARNE* S63 .... **111** J2
Rimington Rd *WMB/DAR* S73 .... **84** A4
Rimini Ri *WMB/DAR* S73 .... **84** B2
Ringinglow Rd *ECC* S11 .... **185** F3
Ringstead Av *FUL* S10 .... **169** J5
Ringstead Crs *FUL* S10 .... **169** K5
Ringstone Gv *CUD/GR* S72 .... **32** D4
Ringway *DEARNE* S63 .... **86** B5
Ringwood *WRKN* S81 .... **210** F1 ☒
Ringwood Crs *MOS* S20 .... **190** E5
Ringwood Dr *MOS* S20 .... **190** E5
Ringwood Gv *MOS* S20 .... **190** E5
Ringwood Rd *MOS* S20 .... **190** E5 ☒
Ripley Gv *DOD/DAR* S75 .... **55** G3
Ripley St *ST/HB/BR* S6 .... **151** H8
Ripon Av *WHHL* DN2 .... **91** J1
Ripon St *DARN/MH* S9 .... **172** B2
Ripon Wy *AU/AST/KP* S26 .... **175** G8
Rippon Ct *RAW* S62 .... **111** J8
Rippon Crs *ST/HB/BR* S6 .... **151** G7
Rippon Rd *ST/HB/BR* S6 .... **151** G7
Risedale Rd *DEARNE* S63 .... **86** E3 ☒
The Rise *DIN* S25 .... **194** A2
   RHAM S60 .... **112** A5
Rishworth Av *KBTN* HD8 .... **26** A1
Rising Gr *OWL* S3 .... **171** H1
Rivelin Bank *ST/HB/BR* S6 .... **151** G8
Rivelin Mill Br *ST/HB/BR* S6 .... **168** E4
Rivelin Park Crs *ST/HB/BR* S6 .... **169** K1
Rivelin Park Dr *ST/HB/BR* S6 .... **169** K2
Rivelin Park Rd *ST/HB/BR* S6 .... **170** A2
Rivelin Rd *ST/HB/BR* S6 .... **170** A1
Rivelin St *ST/HB/BR* S6 .... **170** A1
Rivelin Ter *ST/HB/BR* S6 .... **170** A1
Rivelin Valley Rd *ST/HB/BR* S6 ..... **168** E4
Riverdale Av *ECC* S11 .... **169** K7
Riverdale Dr *FUL* S10 .... **170** A6
Riverdale Rd *BTLY* DN5 .... **64** B7
   ECC S11 .... **170** A7
Riverhead *BTLY* DN5 .... **89** J6
River La *BWTY* DN10 .... **143** K5
   HTFD DN7 .... **22** C8 ☒
Riverside *KBTN* HD8 .... **26** B5
Riverside Cl *ST/HB/BR* S6 .... **150** E7
   WMB/DAR S73 .... **85** F1 ☒
Riverside Dr *BTLY* DN5 .... **89** K6
Riverside Gdns *DEARNE* S63 .... **86** C6 ☒
   EPW DN9 .... **94** A8
Riverside Wy *RHAM* S60 .... **6** B5
River Ter *ST/HB/BR* S6 .... **151** H7
River Vw Rd *CHPT/GREN* S35 .... **128** C8
River Wy *EPW* DN9 .... **94** A8

Riviera Pde *BTLY* DN5.......................... **4** B1
Rix Rd *MEX/SWTN* S64 .... **112** C7
Roache Dr *DEARNE* S63 .... **86** B3
Roach Rd *ECC* S11 .... **170** C7
Roaine Dr *HOLM/MEL* HD7 .... **48** A4
Robert Av *BSLYN/ROY* S71 .... **56** E5
Robert Rd *SHEFS* S8 .... **187** F8
Roberts Av *CONI* DN12 .... **114** E6
Robertshaw Crs *STKB/PEN* S36 ... **105** C6 ☒
Robertson Dr *ST/HB/BR* S6 .... **170** A1
Robertson Rd *ST/HB/BR* S6 .... **170** A2
Roberts Rd *CONI* DN12 .... **115** K6
   DONS/BSCR DN4 .... **4** B5
Roberts St *CUD/GR* S72 .... **31** J8 ☒
   WMB/DAR S73 .... **83** K5 ☒
Robert St *BSLY* S70 .... **82** B3 ☒
   RHAM S60 .... **6** A4 ☒
Robey St *ATT* S4 .... **152** E6
Robinets Rd *KIMB* S61 .... **132** D4
Robin Hood Av *BSLYN/ROY* S71 ...... **30** E3 ☒
Robin Hood Cha *ST/HB/BR* S6 ...... **150** B8
Robin Hood Crs *ARMTH* DN3 .... **67** F6 ☒
Robin Hood Rd *ARMTH* DN3 .... **67** F6
   DARN/MH S9 .... **153** H3 ☒
Robin La *BSLYN/ROY* S71 .... **30** E3
   HEM/SK/SE WF9 .... **32** D2
   MOS S20 .... **190** D3
Robin Pl *AU/AST/KP* S26 .... **191** J1
Robins Cl *AU/AST/KP* S26 .... **175** J8
Robinson Dr *WRKS* S80 .... **210** C6
Robinson Rd *SHEFP/MNR* S2 .... **9** FA ☒
Robinson St *RHAM* S60 .... **6** C6
Rob Royd *DOD/DAR* S75 .... **80** E1 ☒
Rob Royd La *BSLY* S70 .... **81** J1
Roche Cl *BSLYN/ROY* S71 .... **3** E2 ☒
Roche End *AU/AST/KP* S26 .... **192** E2
Roche Av *SHEFN* S5 .... **129** K8
Rocher Cl *SHEFN* S5 .... **129** K8
Rocher Gv *SHEFN* S5 .... **129** K8
Rocher La *CHPT/GREN* S35 .... **127** F4
Rochester Cl *FUL* S10 .... **168** E6 ☒
   WRKN S81 .... **196** E8
Rochester Dr *FUL* S10 .... **168** E6
Rochester Rd *BSLYN/ROY* S71 .... **3** E1
   DIN S25 .... **193** K4
   FUL S10 .... **168** E6
Rochester Rw *BTLY* DN5 .... **90** A2
Rockcliffe Dr *NROS/TKH* DN11 ...... **116** E8
Rockcliffe Rd *RAW* S62 .... **133** J3
Rockfield Dr *WRKN* S81 .... **195** G4
Rockingham Cl *BSLY* S70 .... **107** K1
   DRON S18 .... **200** C6 ☒
   SHEF S1 .... **9** D4 ☒
Rockingham Ga *SHEF* S1 .... **9** D4 ☒
Rockingham La *SHEF* S1 .... **8** C3
Rockingham Rd *DOD/DAR* S75 .... **81** F2
   MEX/SWTN S64 .... **111** K5
   RAW S62 .... **133** K1
Rockingham Rw *BSLY* S70 .... **108** A1
Rockingham St *BSLY* S70 .... **108** A1
   BSLYN/ROY S71 .... **2** B1
   CUD/GR S72 .... **32** D8 ☒
   RHAM S60 .... **108** B1
   SHEF S1 .... **8** C3
Rockingham Wy *SHEF* S1 .... **9** D4 ☒
Rocklea Cl *MEX/SWTN* S64 .... **112** B5 ☒
Rockley Av *BSLY* S70 .... **81** K6
   WMB/DAR S73 .... **83** J6
Rockley Crs *BSLY* S70 .... **81** K8
Rockley La *BSLY* S70 .... **81** J7
   BTLY DN5 .... **38** C4
   DOD/DAR S75 .... **81** H4
Rockley Mdw *BSLY* S70 .... **81** K6
Rockley Nook *WHHL* DN2 .... **66** A8 ☒
Rockley Rd *ST/HB/BR* S6 .... **151** C5
Rockley Vw *DOD/DAR* S75 .... **107** J3
Rock Mt *HOY* S74 .... **109** G1 ☒
Rock Mount Rd *DARN/MH* S9 .... **153** J3
Rock Side Rd *STKB/PEN* S36 .... **77** H4
Rock St *BSLY* S70 .... **2** A3 ☒
   OWL S3 .... **9** E1
Rockwood Cl *CHPT/GREN* S35 ...... **129** K2 ☒
   DOD/DAR S75 .... **28** E7 ☒
Roddis Cl *DIN* S25 .... **177** K6 ☒
Roden Wy *RAW* S62 .... **111** F7
Rodes Av *CUD/GR* S72 .... **59** H5
Rodger Rd *HAN/WDH* S13 .... **174** B8
Rodger St *KIMB* S61 .... **6** A3
Rodman Dr *HAN/WDH* S13 .... **174** B7
Rodman St *HAN/WDH* S13 .... **174** B7
Rod Moor Rd *TOT/DORE* S17 .... **200** B3
Rodney Hl *ST/HB/BR* S6 .... **150** C7
Rod Side *ST/HB/BR* S6 .... **167** K2
Rodwood Av *STV/CWN* S43 .... **206** A8
Roebuck Hl *HOY* S74 .... **83** C7
Roebuck Rd *ST/HB/BR* S6 .... **8** A2
Roebuck St *WMB/DAR* S73 .... **84** B6
Roeburn Cl *DOD/DAR* S75 .... **29** F5 ☒
Roe Croft Cl *BTLY* DN5 .... **89** J5
Roehampton Ri *BSLYN/ROY* S71 ..... **57** C7
   BTLY DN5 .... **90** B2 ☒
Roe La *DOD **154** D6
Roe La *ATT* S4 .... **152** C7
Roger Rd *BSLYN/ROY* S71 .... **57** F5
Rojean Rd *CHPT/GREN* S35 .... **129** J7
Rokeby Dr *SHEFN* S5 .... **152** B1
Rokeby Rd *SHEFN* S5 .... **152** B1
Rolleston Av *MALT* S66 .... **159** F2
Rolleston Rd *AWLS/ASK* DN6 .... **37** J7

SHEFN S5 .... 152 D3
Rollet Cl SHEFF/MNR S2 ... 172 C7
Rollin Dr ST/HB/BR S6 .... 151 G6
Rolling Dales Cl MALT S66 .. 137 F8
Rolls Crs RAW S62 .... 111 F7
Roman Ct KIMB S61 .... 154 B1
Roman Crs RAW S62 .... 133 H1
  RHAM S60 .... 155 F6
Romandale Gdns SHEFF/MNR S2 .. 172 E6
Roman Rdg AWLS/ASK DN6 ... 37 F8
  AWLS/ASK DN6 .... 63 G3
Roman Ridge Rd DARN/MH S9 .. 153 J4
Roman Rd DOD/DAR S75 ..... 28 C8
  DONS/BSCR DN4 .... 5 E4
Roman St DEARNE S63 ...... 60 D6
Romney Cl MALT S66 .... 157 C1
Romney Dr DRON S18 .... 200 E6
Romsdal Rd FUL S10 .... 170 C3
Romwood Av NROS/SWTN S64 .. 111 K4
Ronald Rd DARN/MH S9 ..... 172 E3
  DONS/BSCR DN4 .... 90 D8
Ronksley Crs SHEFN S5 .... 152 E1
Ronksley La ST/HB/BR S6 .. 168 A4
Ronksley Rd SHEFN S5 ..... 152 E1
Roods La HOLM/MEL HD7 .... 46 D4
Rookdale Cl DOD/DAR S75 .. 55 G3
Rookery Bank STKB/PEN S36 .. 105 J7
Rookery Cha STKB/PEN S36 .. 105 J7
Rookery Ct AU/AST/KP S26 .. 192 C4
  STKB/PEN S36 .... 105 J7
Rookery Dell STKB/PEN S36 .. 105 J7
Rookery Ri STKB/PEN S36 .. 105 J8
Rookery Rd MEX/SWTN S64 .. 112 A5
The Rookery STKB/PEN S36 .. 105 J7
Rookery V STKB/PEN S36 ... 105 J7
Rook HI BSLY S70 .... 82 D2
Roper House La CHPT/GREN S35 .. 105 H1
Roper La CHPT/GREN S35 ... 79 J8
Rope Wk THNE DN8 .... 23 H8
Rosamond Av TOT/DORE S17 .. 200 A1
Rosamond Cl TOT/DORE S17 .. 200 A1
Rosamond Dr TOT/DORE S17 .. 200 A2
Rosamond Gld TOT/DORE S17 .. 200 A1
Rosamond Pl TOT/DORE S17 .. 200 A1
Rosa Rd FUL S10 .... 170 C3
Roscoe Bank ST/HB/BR S6 .. 169 J2
Roscoe Dr ST/HB/BR S6 .... 169 K2
Roscoe Mt ST/HB/BR S6 .... 169 K2
Roscoe Rd OWL S3 .... 8 C1
Rose Av DONS/BSCR DN4 .... 4 B6
  MOS S20 .... 190 D4
  WMB/DAR S73 .... 58 C8
Roseberry Av HTFD DN7 .... 42 C8
Roseberry Cl HOY S74 ..... 109 F3
Roseberry St KIMB S61 .... 134 D7
Roseberry Ter BSLY S70 ... 2 C5
Rose Cl RHAM S60 .... 155 G8
Rose Ct DONS/BSCR DN4 .... 4 A6
  MALT S66 .... 157 F3
Rose Crs BTLY DN5 .... 64 B8
  RAW S62 .... 134 A1
Rosedale Av RAW S62 ...... 133 J1
Rosedale Cl RAW S62 ...... 55 H6
Rosedale Gdns BSLY S70 ... 8 A6
  ECC S11 .... 8 A6
Rosedale Rd AU/AST/KP S26 .. 175 J7
  BTLY DN5 .... 64 A8
  BTLY DN5 .... 64 D5
  ECC S11 .... 8 A6
Rosedale Wy MALT S66 ..... 157 H1
Rose Dr MALT S66 .... 157 G2
Rose Garth Av AU/AST/KP S26 .. 175 J7
Rosegarth Cl BTLY DN5 .... 64 B8
Rose Gv WMB/DAR S73 ...... 83 J3
Rose HI DONS/BSCR DN4 .... 92 B6
  MOS S20 .... 189 K7
Rosehill Av HEM/SK/SE WF9 .. 33 F1
Rose Hill Av RAW S62 ..... 111 K8
Rose Hill Cl MOS S20 ..... 189 K7
  STKB/PEN S36 .... 78 A5
Rosehill Ct BSLY S70 ..... 8 C1
Rose Hill Dr DOD/DAR S75 .. 54 E8
  MOS S20 .... 189 J7
Rose Hill Rl DONS/BSCR DN4 .. 92 B5
Rosehill Rd RAW S62 ...... 133 J1
Rose La AWLS/ASK DN6 ..... 38 C1
  DIN S25 .... 177 H1
Roselle St ST/HB/BR S6 ... 151 H7
Rosemary Gv BTLY DN5 ..... 114 E2
Rosemary Rd MALT S66 ..... 157 F2
Rosemary St SHEFP/MNR S2 .. 9 E5
Rosexby Cl DONS/BSCR DN4 .. 118 C2
Rose Pl WMB/DAR S73 ...... 83 K3
Rose Tree Av CUD/GR S72 .. 31 J3
Rose Tree Cl CUD/GR S72 .. 31 J8
Rose Wy ECK/KIL S21 ...... 205 H2
Rosewood Dr ARMTH DN3 .... 40 D8
Roslin Rd FUL S10 .... 170 C4
Roslyn Crs HATH/EY S32 ... 182 C8
Roslyn Rd HATH/EY S32 .... 182 C8
Rosser Av HACK/IN S12 .... 188 B5
Rossetti Gdns WRKN S81 ... 211 G4
Rossetti Mt MALT S66 ..... 157 C1
Rossington Br DONS/BSCR DN4 .. 119 G3
Rossington Rd ECC S11 .... 170 C7
Rossington St CONI DN12 .. 114 A3

Rossiter Rd KIMB S61 ..... 133 F3
Rosslyn Av AU/AST/KP S26 .. 175 J7
Rosslyn Crs BTLY DN5 ..... 64 E5
Rossmoor Cl EPW DN9 ...... 94 B8
Ross St DARN/MH S9 .... 173 F3
Rosston Rd MALT S66 ...... 159 J2
Roston Cl DRON S18 .... 200 D6
Rotcher Rd HOLM/MEL HD7 .. 47 K3
Rothay Cl DRON S18 .... 200 E7
Rothay Rd ATT S4 .... 153 G6
Rothbury Cl MOS S20 ...... 190 E5
Rothbury Ct MOS S20 ...... 190 E5
Rothbury Wy RHAM S60 ..... 155 F6
Rother Crs RHAM S60 ...... 174 C3
Rotherham Baulk WRKN S81 .. 179 H8
Rotherham Cl ECK/KIL S21 .. 191 K7
Rotherham La DIN S25 ..... 177 J2
Rotherham Rd AU/AST/KP S26 .. 190 E3
  BSLYN/ROY S71 .... 56 B1
  CUD/GR S72 .... 59 H8
  CUD/GR S72 .... 85 G2
  DEARNE S63 .... 110 E1
  DIN S25 .... 177 J5
  ECK/KIL S21 .... 191 K7
  HAN/WDH S13 .... 173 K5
  MALT S66 .... 158 D2
  MOS S20 .... 190 D8
  NROS/TKH DN11 .... 161 H1
  RAW S62 .... 7 D1
  RHAM S60 .... 155 F6
  RHAM/THRY S65 .... 7 D1
Rotherham Rd North MOS S20 .. 190 D8
Rotherham Roundwalk KIMB S61 .. 6 C1
  RAW S62 .... 110 A7
  RHAM S60 .... 174 D1
Rotherham St DARN/MH S9 .. 153 H8
Rothermoor Av AU/AST/KP S26 .. 192 C5
Rother Rd RHAM S60 .... 155 C4
Rotherside Rd ECK/KIL S21 .. 204 D3
Rotherstoke Cl RHAM S60 .. 7 D6
Rother St WMB/DAR S73 .... 84 C7
Rother Ter RHAM S60 ...... 155 C4
Rothervale Cl MOS S20 .... 190 E3
Rother Valley Wy MOS S20 .. 191 F7
Rother View Rd RHAM S60 .. 155 G4
Rother Wy MALT S66 .... 158 B1
Rotherway RHAM S60 .... 155 J8
Rotherwood Av HAN/WDH S13 .. 174 B7
Rotherwood Cl BTLY DN5 ... 90 A1
Rotherwood Crs MALT S66 .. 176 E1
Rotherwood Rd ECK/KIL S21 .. 191 J8
Rothesay Cl BTLY DN5 ..... 90 C2
Roughbirchworth La
  STKB/PEN S36 .... 78 D7
Rough La CHPT/GREN S35 ... 106 B7
  CHPT/GREN S35 .... 105 J8
Roughwood Rd KIMB S61 .... 132 B5
Round Close Rd HOLM/MEL HD7 .. 74 A1
Roundel St DARN/MH S9 .... 172 B2
Round Green La DOD/DAR S75 .. 81 G3
Roundwood Ct BSLY S70 .... 82 B3
Roundwood Gv RAW S62 ..... 133 K2
Roundwood Wy WMB/DAR S73 .. 84 C2
Rowan Cl BSLY S70 .... 2 C6
  CHPT/GREN S35 .... 150 B3
  EPW DN9 .... 120 B3
  THNE DN8 .... 23 K5
Rowan Crs WHHL DN2 .... 92 B1
Rowan Ct DOD/DAR S75 ..... 55 G4
  MALT S66 .... 157 H2
Rowan Garth BTLY DN5 ..... 90 D1
Rowan Mt WHHL DN2 .... 92 A1
Rowan Rd ECK/KIL S21 ..... 204 A6
Rowan Tree Dell TOT/DORE S17 .. 199 J4
Rowan Tree Rd ECK/KIL S21 .. 205 F1
Rowborn Dr CHPT/GREN S35 .. 150 E3
Rowdale Crs HACK/IN S12 .. 189 F2
Rowel La ST/HB/BR S6 ..... 150 A8
Rowena Av ARMTH DN3 ...... 66 E6
Rowena Dr BTLY DN5 .... 89 J3
  MALT S66 .... 157 K8
Rowena Rd CONI DN12 ...... 114 C5
Rowgate KBTN HD8 .... 50 B1
Rowland Rd DOD/DAR S75 ... 55 H4
  SHEFP/MNR S2 .... 9 D6
Rowland St BSLYN/ROY S71 .. 30 E3
  OWL S3 .... 9 D1
Rowley La HEM/SK/SE WF9 .. 35 F6
Rowms La MEX/SWTN S64 .... 112 E4
Rowsley St SHEFP/MNR S2 .. 9 E5
Roxby Cl DONS/BSCR DN4 ... 118 C2
Roxton Av SHEFS S8 .... 187 F7
Roxton Rd SHEFS S8 .... 186 E6
Royal Av DON DN1 .... 5 E2
Royal Ct DOD/DAR S75 ..... 54 D1
  HOY S74 .... 109 G1
Royal Crs WRKN S81 .... 210 C1
Royale Cl ECK/KIL S21 .... 204 C4
Royal St BSLY S70 .... 2 B4
Royd Av CUD/GR S72 .... 57 J1
  DOD/DAR S75 .... 29 G6
  STKB/PEN S36 .... 76 E4
Royd Cl BSLY S70 .... 82 A3
Roydfield Cl MOS S20 ..... 190 B5
Roydfield Dr MOS S20 ..... 190 B5

Roydfield Gv MOS S20 ..... 190 B5
Royd Field La STKB/PEN S36 .. 78 A7
Royd La DOD/DAR S75 ...... 54 B4
  HOLM/MEL HD7 .... 47 H5
  STKB/PEN S36 .... 76 E3
  STKB/PEN S36 .... 105 G8
Royd Moor Rd STKB/PEN S36 .. 76 E2
Royd Mt HOLM/MEL HD7 ..... 47 K3
Royds Av HOLM/MEL HD7 .... 48 C1
  RHAM S60 .... 156 B5
Royds Cl HOLM/MEL HD7 .... 48 C1
Royds Crs WRKS S80 .... 209 J2
Royds Close Crs RHAM/THRY S65 .. 134 D5
Royds Dr HOLM/MEL HD7 .... 48 C1
Rubens Cl DRON S18 .... 201 F6
Rud Broom La STKB/PEN S36 .. 77 J4
Ruddle La MALT S66 .... 137 G3
Ruddle Mill La CONI DN12 .. 138 A6
Rudgate La GLE 13 J8
Rudyard Rd ST/HB/BR S6 ... 151 H7
Rufford Av BSLYN/ROY S71 .. 30 B7
Rufford Cl MOS S20 .... 190 E5
Rufford Ri DEARNE S63 .... 86 B3
  MOS S20 .... 190 E5
Rufford Rd DONS/BSCR DN4 .. 5 F5
  WRKS S80 .... 211 F7
Rufus La NROS/TKH DN11 ... 118 C6
Rugby St OWL S3 .... 171 G1
Rugged Butts La BWTY DN10 .. 143 H4
Rundle Dr ABRD S7 .... 170 E8
Rundle Rd ABRD S7 .... 170 E8
  STKB/PEN S36 .... 104 E6
Runnymede Rd WHHL DN2 .... 92 A4
Rupert Rd ABRD S7 .... 186 E2
Rural Crs ARMTH DN3 ...... 93 J7
Rural La ST/HB/BR S6 ..... 150 E5
Rushby St ATT S4 .... 153 F6
Rushdale Av SHEFS S8 ..... 187 G2
Rushdale Mt SHEFS S8 ..... 187 G2
Rushdale Rd SHEFS S8 ..... 187 G2
Rushdale Ter SHEFS S8 .... 187 G2
Rushey Cl RAW S62 .... 111 H7
  WRKS S80 .... 211 F5
Rushley Av TOT/DORE S17 .. 185 H7
Rushley Cl EPW DN9 .... 120 B1
  TOT/DORE S17 .... 185 H7
Rushley Dr TOT/DORE S17 .. 185 H7
Rushley Rd TOT/DORE S17 .. 185 H8
Rushworth Cl DOD/DAR S75 .. 28 E7
Rushy La STKB/PEN S36 .... 126 C3
Rushy Moor Av AWLS/ASK DN6 .. 18 E7
Rushy Moor La AWLS/ASK DN6 .. 18 E7
Rushy Moor Rd AWLS/ASK DN6 .. 39 F1
Ruskin Av MEX/SWTN S64 ... 113 C1
Ruskin Cl DEARNE S63 ..... 85 F8
Ruskin Dr ARMTH DN3 ...... 93 H1
Ruskin Rd DONS/BSCR DN4 .. 116 D1
Ruskin Sq SHEFS S8 .... 187 C1
Russell Av NROS/TKH DN11 .. 162 E5
Russell Cl BSLYN/ROY S71 .. 56 C2
Russell Ct ECC S11 .... 186 A5
Russell Pl MALT S66 ...... 159 H1
Russell Rd MEX/SWTN S64 .. 112 D8
Russell St OWL S3 .... 9 D1
  RHAM/THRY S65 .... 7 D2
Russet Gv BWTY DN10 ...... 142 B8
Russett Ct MALT S66 ...... 158 E1
Rustlings Rd ECC S11 ..... 170 A7
Ruthin St ATT S4 .... 153 F7
Ruth Sq FUL S10 .... 8 B4
Ruthven Dr DONS/BSCR DN4 .. 90 A1
Ruthyn Av STV/CWN S43 .... 206 A8
Rutland Av DIN S25 .... 177 K8
Rutland Crs NROS/TKH DN11 .. 162 E2
Rutland Dr NROS/TKH DN11 .. 118 C6
Rutland Pk FUL S10 .... 170 C5
Rutland Pl WMB/DAR S73 ... 83 J5
Rutland Rd OWL S3 .... 171 C1
Rutland St DON DN1 .... 5 E2
  OWL S3 .... 171 C1
Rutland Wy DOD/DAR S75 ... 55 H4
  OWL S3 .... 8 C1
Ryan Dr HAN/WDH S13 ...... 174 C8
Ryan Pl RAW S62 .... 133 J3
Rydal Cl DEARNE S63 ...... 86 B6
  DRON S18 .... 200 D6
  STKB/PEN S36 .... 78 A3
Rydal Dr WRKN S81 .... 196 C2
Rydalhurst Av ST/HB/BR S6 .. 150 E5
Rydall Pl BTLY DN5 .... 64 C7
Rydal Rd AWLS/ASK DN6 .... 37 K6
  DIN S25 .... 178 B8

SHEFS S8 .... 186 E2
Rydal Wy MEX/SWTN S64 .... 113 H1
Ryebank HOLM/MEL HD7 .... 48 A3
Rye Bank Rd MOS S20 .... 156 C6
Rye Close La HOLM/MEL HD7 .... 46 A3
Rye Cft BSLYN/ROY S71 .... 56 B1
CONI DN12 .... 115 F5
NROS/TKH DN11 .... 139 K7
Ryecroft Av AWLS/ASK DN6 .... 17 K4
Ryecroft Glen Rd TOT/DORE S17 .... 185 K8
Ryecroft La HOLM/MEL HD7 .... 48 B4
Ryecroft Rd AWLS/ASK DN6 .... 17 K4
RAW S62 .... 134 B1
Ryecroft Vw TOT/DORE S17 .... 185 H7
Ryefield Gdns ECC S11 .... 186 A2
Ryefields HOLM/MEL HD7 .... 48 C3
Ryegate Crs FUL S10 .... 170 B4
Ryegate Rd FUL S10 .... 170 B5
Rye La ST/HB/BR S6 .... 149 H8
Ryeview Gdns KIMB S61 .... 132 E5
Ryhill Dr HACK/IN S12 .... 189 J5
Ryle Rd ABRD S7 .... 186 E1
Rylstone Ct HACK/IN S12 .... 189 K5
Rylstone Gv HACK/IN S12 .... 189 K5
Rylstone Wk BSLY S70 .... 82 E1
Ryton Av WMB/DAR S73 .... 84 C6
Ryton Cl MALT S66 .... 159 H2
Ryton Pl WRKS S80 .... 210 C4
Ryton Rd DIN S25 .... 193 K2
Ryton Wy DONS/BSCR DN4 .... 119 F1

S

Sackerville Ter ECK/KIL S21 .... 191 F8
Sackup La DOD/DAR S75 .... 28 E6
Sackville Rd FUL S10 .... 170 D3
Sackville St BSLY S70 .... 2 A3
Saddler Av MOS S20 .... 190 B6
Saddler Cl MOS S20 .... 190 B6
Saddler Gn MOS S20 .... 190 B6
Saddler La BSLY S70 .... 2 B3
Sadler's Ga WMB/DAR S73 .... 83 K3
Saffron Cl NROS/TKH DN11 .... 139 J8
Saffron Crs NROS/TKH DN11 .... 139 J8
Saffron Rd NROS/TKH DN11 .... 139 J8
St Agnes' Rd DONS/BSCR DN4 .... 91 K5
St Aidan's Av SHEFP/MNR S2 .... 171 K7
St Aidan's Cl SHEFP/MNR S2 .... 172 A6
St Aidan's Dr SHEFP/MNR S2 .... 172 A6
St Aidan's Mt SHEFP/MNR S2 .... 172 A7
St Aidan's Pl SHEFP/MNR S2 .... 172 A7
St Aidan's Rd SHEFP/MNR S2 .... 172 A7
St Aidan's Wy SHEFP/MNR S2 .... 172 A7
St Albans Cl FUL S10 .... 169 G6
St Albans Ct MALT S66 .... 157 H8
St Albans Dr FUL S10 .... 169 F6
St Albans Pl FUL S10 .... 169 F6
St Albans Rd MALT S66 .... 157 G3
St Alban's Wy MALT S66 .... 157 G3
St Andrew Rd STKB/PEN S36 .... 105 H7
St Andrew's Cl ABRD S7 .... 170 D8
MALT S66 .... 157 H8
MEX/SWTN S64 .... 112 C5
St Andrews Dr HOY S74 .... 109 F1
St Andrews Dr DONS/BSCR DN4 .... 5 E5
St Andrews Gv HTFD DN7 .... 42 C8
St Andrew's Rd ARMTH DN3 .... 170 D8
CONI DN12 .... 114 C6
HOY S74 .... 109 F1
St Andrew's Sq DEARNE S63 .... 86 B5
St Andrew's Ter DONS/BSCR DN4 .... 5 E5
St Andrew's Wk RHAM S60 .... 154 D6
St Andrew's Wy ARMTH DN3 .... 67 J1
BSLYN/ROY S71 .... 57 H8
St Annes Cl WRKS S80 .... 210 A4
St Anne's Dr BSLYN/ROY S71 .... 30 E8
WRKS S80 .... 210 A5
St Annes Rd DONS/BSCR DN4 .... 91 K5
St Annes Vw WRKS S80 .... 210 A4
St Annes Wy WRKS S80 .... 210 A5
St Ann's Rd RHAM/THRY S65 .... 7 D3
STKB/PEN S36 .... 105 G8
St Anthony Rd FUL S10 .... 170 A4
St Augustine's Rd DONS/BSCR DN4 .... 92 C6
St Austell Dr DOD/DAR S75 .... 54 D3
St Barbara's Cl MALT S66 .... 159 F3
St Barbara's Rd WMB/DAR S73 .... 84 C2
St Barnabas La SHEFP/MNR S2 .... 9 D6
St Barnabas Rd SHEFP/MNR S2 .... 9 D6
St Bartholomew's Cl MALT S66 .... 159 F3
St Bartholomews Ri DONS/BSCR DN4 .... 92 C6
St Bede's Rd RHAM S60 .... 6 B4
St Catherine's Av DONS/BSCR DN4 .... 4 B6
St Catherine Dr HTFD DN7 .... 67 K3
St Catherines Wy DONS/BSCR DN4 .... 55 G6
St Cecilia's Rd DONS/BSCR DN4 .... 91 K6
St Chad's Wy BTLY DN5 .... 89 K7
St Charles St DARN/MH S9 .... 172 A1
St Christophers Cl BSLYN/ROY S71 .... 57 H8
St Christopher's Crs BTLY DN5 .... 90 B1
St Clements Cl BSLYN/ROY S71 .... 57 H8
BTLY DN5 .... 90 A1
St Cuthbert St WRKS S80 .... 210 D5
St David Rd STKB/PEN S36 .... 105 H7

St David's Cl WRKN S81 .... 210 E1
St David's Dr BSLYN/ROY S71 .... 57 G7
BTLY DN5 .... 90 A1
DIN S25 .... 193 K4
RHAM S60 .... 154 D6
St David's Rd CONI DN12 .... 114 C5
St Dominic's Cl BTLY DN5 .... 89 J7
St Edmund's Av MALT S66 .... 176 E2
St Edwards Av BSLY S70 .... 2 A5
St Edwins Cl HTFD DN7 .... 42 B8
St Elizabeth Cl SHEFP/MNR S2 .... 9 E6
St Eric's Rd DONS/BSCR DN4 .... 92 C7
St Francis Bvd BSLYN/ROY S71 .... 30 E8
St Francis Cl MALT S66 .... 135 H8
St George Rd STKB/PEN S36 .... 105 H7
St George's Av HTFD DN7 .... 68 A3
MEX/SWTN S64 .... 112 A4
St George's Cl OWL S3 .... 8 B2
THNE DN8 .... 44 A2
St Georges Dr RHAM S60 .... 154 D6
St George's Ter OWL S3 .... 8 C5
St Giles Ga BTLY DN5 .... 90 A2
St Giles Sq CHPT/GREN S35 .... 130 A2
St Helen Rd STKB/PEN S36 .... 105 H8
St Helen's Av BSLYN/ROY S71 .... 56 C5
Saint Helens Rd DEARNE S63 .... 60 A7
St Helens Rd RHAM S60 .... 174 D4
St Helen's Rd DONS/BSCR DN4 .... 91 K5
St Helen's Sq ARMTH DN3 .... 66 E3
St Helen's St HOY S74 .... 109 H1
St Helens Wy BSLYN/ROY S71 .... 56 E2
St Helier Dr DOD/DAR S75 .... 55 G5
St Hilda Av BSLY S70 .... 55 H6
St Hilda Cl STKB/PEN S36 .... 105 H8
St Hildas Dr DEARNE S63 .... 60 D6
St Hilda's Rd DONS/BSCR DN4 .... 91 K5
St James Av DIN S25 .... 193 K3
St James Cl HTFD DN7 .... 67 K2
St James Cl ARMTH DN3 .... 66 E3
DEARNE S63 .... 111 K1
St James' Dr RHAM/THRY S65 .... 135 J5
St James Gdns DONS/BSCR DN4 .... 4 B5
St James' Br DON DN1 .... 4 C4
St James' St SHEF S1 .... 9 D3
St James' Vw RHAM/THRY S65 .... 135 J4
St James Wk HAN/WDH S13 .... 174 B7
St Joan Av STKB/PEN S36 .... 105 H8
St Johns Cft STKB/PEN S36 .... 78 C1
St John's Av DOD/DAR S75 .... 54 D3
MALT S66 .... 157 H1
RHAM S60 .... 6 A4
St John's Cl DOD/DAR S75 .... 80 D1
RHAM/THRY S65 .... 7 F2
STKB/PEN S36 .... 77 K5
St John's Ct DIN S25 .... 178 A3
MALT S66 .... 157 H1
St Johns Cft NROS/TKH DN11 .... 138 E1
St John's Rd BSLY S70 .... 2 B5
CONI DN12 .... 115 J5
CUD/GR S72 .... 57 J1
DIN S25 .... 178 A3
DONS/BSCR DN4 .... 4 A6
DRON S18 .... 202 A7
MEX/SWTN S64 .... 112 B4
RHAM/THRY S65 .... 7 F2
SHEFP/MNR S2 .... 171 K3
STKB/PEN S36 .... 105 J7
St John's Wk BSLYN/ROY S71 .... 30 E4
St Joseph's Cl DIN S25 .... 178 B6
St Joseph's Rd HAN/WDH S13 .... 173 H5
St Julien's Mt DOD/DAR S75 .... 53 H3
St Julien's Wy DOD/DAR S75 .... 53 H3
St Lawrence Rd DARN/MH S9 .... 154 B4
HTFD DN7 .... 42 A8
St Leger Av DIN S25 .... 177 J5
St Leger Wy DIN S25 .... 178 B5
St Leonards NROS/TKH DN11 .... 139 K8
St Leonard's Av RHAM/THRY S65 .... 135 F5
St Leonard's Cl DIN S25 .... 178 A7
St Leonards Ct SHEFN S5 .... 152 C4
Saint Leonard's Cft RHAM/THRY S65 .... 134 E4
St Leonard's La RHAM/THRY S65 .... 7 E3
RHAM/THRY S65 .... 7 E3
St Leonard's Lea BTLY DN5 .... 90 B1
St Leonard's Pl RHAM/THRY S65 .... 7 E3
St Leonard's Rd RHAM/THRY S65 .... 7 D3
St Leonards Wy BSLYN/ROY S71 .... 57 H8
St Luke's Cl HTFD DN7 .... 67 K3
St Lukes Wy BSLYN/ROY S71 .... 57 F2
St Margaret Av STKB/PEN S36 .... 105 H7
St Margarets Av BTLY DN5 .... 87 H4
St Margaret's Dr MEX/SWTN S64 .... 112 A4
St Margaret's Rd CHPT/GREN S35 .... 130 C7
DONS/BSCR DN4 .... 91 K6
St Mark Rd STKB/PEN S36 .... 105 H7
St Mark's Cl WRKN S81 .... 196 B7
St Mark's Crs FUL S10 .... 8 A4
St Martin Cl STKB/PEN S36 .... 105 H7
St Martin's Av BTLY DN5 .... 90 C2
BWTY DN10 .... 142 A8
St Martins Cl DOD/DAR S75 .... 55 G5
WRKN S81 .... 179 J1
St Mary Crs STKB/PEN S36 .... 105 H8

St Mary's Cl CHPT/GREN S35 .... 130 B6
HEM/SK/SE WF9 .... 35 F5
St Mary's Crs MEX/SWTN S64 .... 112 B3
NROS/TKH DN11 .... 139 J8
St Mary's Dr ARMTH DN3 .... 93 H1
HTFD DN7 .... 67 K3
RHAM S60 .... 174 A1
St Mary's Gdn BSLY S70 .... 82 B5
St Mary's Ga BSLY S70 .... 2 D3
NROS/TKH DN11 .... 139 K8
SHEFP/MNR S2 .... 8 C5
St Mary's La CHPT/GREN S35 .... 130 B6
St Mary's Pl BSLY S70 .... 2 B3
St Mary's Rd CONI DN12 .... 115 K6
DEARNE S63 .... 86 E1
DON DN1 .... 5 E1
HTFD DN7 .... 67 K2
NROS/TKH DN11 .... 139 K8
RAW S62 .... 133 K2
SHEF S1 .... 9 D5
WMB/DAR S73 .... 83 K5
WMB/DAR S73 .... 84 E2
St Mary's Sq SHEFP/MNR S2 .... 8 C5
St Mary's St STKB/PEN S36 .... 78 A4
St Mary's Vw KIMB S61 .... 132 E4
St Matthews Wy BSLYN/ROY S71 .... 3 F2
St Matthias Rd STKB/PEN S36 .... 105 H8
St Michael's Av BSLYN/ROY S71 .... 56 E1
MEX/SWTN S64 .... 112 C3
NROS/TKH DN11 .... 119 F5
St Michael's Cl CHPT/GREN S35 .... 130 C7
DEARNE S63 .... 86 C2
THNE DN8 .... 44 A1
St Michael's Crs CHPT/GREN S35 .... 130 C7
St Michael's Dr THNE DN8 .... 44 A1
St Michael's Rd CHPT/GREN S35 .... 130 C7
DONS/BSCR DN4 .... 92 A6
St Nicholas Cl ARMTH DN3 .... 66 D5
St Nicholas Rd THNE DN8 .... 23 J7
St Nicholas Wy BWTY DN10 .... 164 B1
St Nicolas Rd RAW S62 .... 133 K1
St Oswald's Cl EPW DN9 .... 120 E4
St Oswald's Dr ARMTH DN3 .... 66 D5
EPW DN9 .... 121 F4
St Owens Dr DOD/DAR S75 .... 55 G5
St Patrick Rd STKB/PEN S36 .... 105 H7
St Patrick's Rd WHHL DN2 .... 91 K3
St Patrick's Wy BTLY DN5 .... 90 A1
St Paul Cl AU/AST/KP S26 .... 192 E2
STKB/PEN S36 .... 105 H7
St Paul's Pde BSLYN/ROY S71 .... 57 G7
BTLY DN5 .... 90 A2
St Peter Av STKB/PEN S36 .... 105 J7
St Peter's Cl BTLY DN5 .... 87 H3
RHAM S60 .... 154 D7
SHEF S1 .... 9 D2
St Peter's Ga DEARNE S63 .... 60 B6
St Peter's Rd CONI DN12 .... 114 C6
DONS/BSCR DN4 .... 90 B8
WRKS S80 .... 194 A8
St Peter's Ter BSLY S70 .... 3 D5
St Philip's Rd OWL S3 .... 8 C1
St Phillip's Cl MALT S66 .... 159 F3
St Quentin Cl TOT/DORE S17 .... 200 B2
St Quentin Dr TOT/DORE S17 .... 200 B2
St Quentin Mt TOT/DORE S17 .... 200 B2
St Quentin Ri TOT/DORE S17 .... 200 B2
St Quentin Vw TOT/DORE S17 .... 200 B2
St Ronan's Rd ABRD S7 .... 171 F8
St Sepulchre Ga DON DN1 .... 4 C3
St Sepulchre Ga West DON DN1 .... 4 C4
St Stephen's Dr AU/AST/KP S26 .... 175 H7
St Stephen's Rd RHAM/THRY S65 .... 7 D3
St Stephens Wk BTLY DN5 .... 90 B2
OWL S3 .... 8 B2
St Thomas Rd FUL S10 .... 170 B4
St Thomas's Cl DONS/BSCR DN4 .... 116 B1
St Thomas's Rd DOD/DAR S75 .... 55 F5
St Thomas St SHEF S1 .... 8 C3
St Ursula's Rd DONS/BSCR DN4 .... 91 K5
St Veronica Rd STKB/PEN S36 .... 105 H8
St Vincent Av AWLS/ASK DN6 .... 63 G1
DON DN1 .... 5 E2
St Vincent's Av ARMTH DN3 .... 93 H8
St Wandrilles Cl CHPT/GREN S35 .... 130 C6
St Wilfrid's Rd DONS/BSCR DN4 .... 92 B6
SHEFP/MNR S2 .... 9 D6
St Withold Av MALT S66 .... 176 E1
Salcombe Cl DOD/DAR S75 .... 29 H7
Salcombe Gv BWTY DN10 .... 142 A7
Sale Hl FUL S10 .... 170 B5
Salerno Wy WMB/DAR S73 .... 84 B1
Sales La GLE DN14 .... 21 J2
Sale St HOY S74 .... 108 B2
Salisbury Av DRON S18 .... 201 C7
Salisbury Rd DONS/BSCR DN4 .... 4 A5
DRON S18 .... 201 H8
FUL S10 .... 170 B4
MALT S66 .... 159 G1
Salisbury St DOD/DAR S75 .... 2 A2
Salmon St ECC S11 .... 8 A6
Salt Box Gv CHPT/GREN S35 .... 129 H7
Salt Box La CHPT/GREN S35 .... 129 H8
Salter Hill La STKB/PEN S36 .... 104 B1
Salterbrook DEARNE S63 .... 86 C2
Saltersbrook Rd WMB/DAR S73 .... 58 C8
Salter's Wy STKB/PEN S36 .... 78 A5
Salt Hl WRKN S81 .... 179 K2
Salt Hill Rd WRKN S81 .... 180 A4

amson St *SHEFP/MNR* S2 .... 9 F4 🔲
andall Beat Rd *WHHL* DN2 .... 92 C1
andall Beat Rd *DONS/BSCR* DN4 ... 92 A4
andall Carr Rd *ARMTH* DN3 .... 66 C3
andall La *ARMTH* DN3 .... 66 C3
andall Park Dr *WHHL* DN2 .... 66 B8
andall Ri *WHHL* DN2 .... 92 A1
andall Stones Rd *ARMTH* DN3 .... 66 C4
andal Vw *DIN* S25 .... 177 J4
andal Rd *CONI* DN12 .... 114 B6
andalwood Cl *WHHL* DN2 .... 66 B7 🔲
andalwood Ri *MEX/SWTN* S64 ...... 112 C7
andbeck Cl *BSLYN/ROY* S71 .... 2 C1 🔲
andbeck Ct *NROS/TKH* DN11 .... 119 F7 🔲
andbeck La *NROS/TKH* DN11 .... 160 E4
andbeck Pl *ECC* S11 .... 170 D8
andbeck Rd *DONS/BSCR* DN4 .... 5 F4
andbeck Wy *MALT* S66 .... 158 B2
andbed Rd *OWL* S3 .... 151 K8
andbergh Rd *KIMB* S61 .... 152 B5
andby Ct *SHEFS* S8 .... 188 A5 🔲
andby Cft *SHEFS* S8 .... 188 A5 🔲
andby Dr *SHEFS* S8 .... 188 A5
andcliffe Rd *WHHL* DN2 .... 92 A1
andcroft St *HOY* S74 .... 108 D2 🔲
andeby Dr *RHAM/THRY* S65 .... 135 J8
anderson St *DARN/MH* S9 .... 153 C8
andford Ct *BSLY* S70 .... 2 A5 🔲
andford Grove Rd *ABRD* S7 .... 186 E1
andford Rd *DONS/BSCR* DN4 .... 116 D1
HEM/SK/SE WF9 .... 35 F2
andhill Cl *RAW* S62 .... 112 A3
andhill Gv *CUD/GR* S72 .... 32 C6
andhill Ri *EPW* DN9 .... 94 A8
andhill Rd *RAW* S62 .... 134 A1
andhill Rd *WRKS* S80 .... 210 C4
andhurst Rd *DONS/BSCR* DN4 .... 93 F8
and La *EPW* DN9 .... 96 C3
andmartins *WRKN* S81 .... 196 A8
andown Cl *ECK/KIL* S21 .... 203 K4 🔲
andown Gdns *DONS/BSCR* DN4 .... 92 C5
andown Rd *MEX/SWTN* S64 .... 113 C1
andpiper Rd *KIMB* S61 .... 131 C1
andpit Hl *ARMTH* DN3 .... 93 J7
andringham Av *RHAM* S60 .... 156 A6
andringham Cl *STKB/PEN* S36 ...... 77 H3 🔲
andringham Crs *WRKN* S81 .... 196 B8
andringham Pl *RHAM/THRY* S65 ... 135 J7
andringham Rd *DARN/MH* S9 ... 153 H3 🔲
WHHL DN2 .... 91 K4
androck Dr *DONS/BSCR* DN4 .... 92 D8
androck Rd *NROS/TKH* DN11 .... 162 E2
ands Cl *GLV* S14 .... 188 A3
ne Sands *ST/HB/BR* S6 .... 148 D2
andstone Av *DARN/MH* S9 .... 153 C5
andstone Dr *DARN/MH* S9 .... 153 H4
andstone Dr *DARN/MH* S9 .... 153 C5
andstone Rd *DARN/MH* S9 .... 153 C5
andtoft Rd *HTFD* DN7 .... 43 J7
andwith Rd *AU/AST/KP* S26 .... 192 E2
andy Acres Cl *MOS* S20 .... 190 D6
andy Acres Dr *MOS* S20 .... 190 C6
andybridge La *CUD/GR* S72 .... 31 J3
andycroft's
DONS/BSCR DN4 .... 116 B1 🔲
andyfields Vw *AWLS/ASK* DN6 ...... 37 J6
andy Flat La *MALT* S66 .... 157 G5
andygate *DEARNE* S63 .... 111 J1
andygate Ga *HOLM/MEL* HD7 .... 48 B3
andygate Grange Dr *FUL* S10 ...... 169 J5
andygate Cv *FUL* S10 .... 169 H5 🔲
andygate Pk *FUL* S10 .... 169 G5
andygate Park Crs *FUL* S10 .... 169 H5
andygate Park Rd *FUL* S10 .... 169 H4
andygate Rd *FUL* S10 .... 169 H5
andy La *DONS/BSCR* DN4 .... 91 K6
MALT S66 .... 157 K4
MALT S66 .... 158 A3
WMB/DAR S73 .... 83 F5
WRKS S80 .... 210 C3
andymount *NROS/TKH* DN11 ...... 163 F2
andymount East
NROS/TKH DN11 .... 163 F3 🔲
andymount Rd *DEARNE* S63 .... 111 K2
andymount West
NROS/TKH DN11 .... 163 F3 🔲
ankey Sq *DEARNE* S63 .... 86 C2
aracens La *BWTY* DN10 .... 164 A5
arah St *KIMB* S61 .... 6 A4
MEX/SWTN S64 .... 113 F3
ark Rd *SHEFP/MNR* S2 .... 171 G8 🔲
aundby Cl *DONS/BSCR* DN4 .... 92 B8
aunderson St *STKB/PEN* S36 .... 77 J3
aunders Rd *SHEFP/MNR* S2 ... 172 A4 🔲
aunders Rd *SHEFP/MNR* S2 .... 172 A4
aunders Rw *WMB/DAR* S73 .... 83 K5
avage La *TOT/DORE* S17 .... 185 H8
avile St *ATT* S4 .... 9 F1
avile St East *ATT* S4 .... 171 K1
avile Wk *CUD/GR* S72 .... 32 C4
aville Hall La *DOD/DAR* S75 .... 80 E1 🔲

Saville La *STKB/PEN* S36 .... 77 G4
Saville Rd *DEARNE* S63 .... 111 H2
DOD/DAR S75 .... 81 F7
RHAM S60 .... 156 A6
Saville St *CUD/GR* S72 .... 31 J8
KBTN HD8 .... 26 A6 🔲
RHAM/THRY S65 .... 134 B6
Sawdon Rd *ECC* S11 .... 8 B5 🔲
Sawn Moor Av *MALT* S66 .... 177 F1
Sawn Moor Rd *MALT* S66 .... 177 F2
Sawston Cl *DONS/BSCR* DN4 .... 116 D5
Saxon Av *HEM/SK/SE* WF9 .... 33 J5
Saxon Crs *BSLY* S70 .... 82 B2
Saxon Gv *HEM/SK/SE* WF9 .... 33 K6
Saxonlea Av *SHEFP/MNR* S2 .... 172 E6
Saxonlea Ct *SHEFP/MNR* S2 .... 172 E6
Saxonlea Crs *SHEFP/MNR* S2 .... 172 E6
Saxonlea Dr *SHEFP/MNR* S2 .... 172 D6 🔲
Saxon Mt *HEM/SK/SE* WF9 .... 33 J5
Saxon Rd *AU/AST/KP* S26 .... 193 F5
KIMB S61 .... 154 A1
SHEFS S8 .... 187 G1
Saxon Rw *CONI* DN12 .... 115 F6
Saxon St *CUD/GR* S72 .... 57 J1
DEARNE S63 .... 60 D7
Saxon Wy *NROS/TKH* DN11 .... 162 E3
Saxton Av *DONS/BSCR* DN4 .... 92 B7
Saxton Cl *HOY* S74 .... 83 J8
WRKS S80 .... 210 D5
Saxton Dr *RHAM* S60 .... 155 J6
Sayers Cl *BTLY* DN5 .... 87 H5
Scafell Pl *DIN* S25 .... 194 B1
Scaftworth Cl *DONS/BSCR* DN4 ... 118 B1
Scaly Ga *HOLM/MEL* HD7 .... 49 F5
HOLM/MEL HD7 .... 49 F2
Scammadine Cl *RHAM* S60 .... 155 F7
Scarborough Cl *DIN* S25 .... 178 A8 🔲
Scarborough La *NROS/TKH* DN11 . 118 C6
Scarborough Rd *DARN/MH* S9 ...... 172 E2
MALT S66 .... 157 G2
Scarbrough Crs *MALT* S66 .... 159 H3 🔲
Scarfield Cl *BSLYN/ROY* S71 ...... 57 G7 🔲
Scarfold *HOLM/MEL* HD7 .... 47 K2
Scargill Cft *SHEF* S1 .... 9 D2
Scar Hole La *HOLM/MEL* HD7 .... 49 F3
Scar La *BSLYN/ROY* S71 .... 57 G7
Scarlett Oak Meadow
ST/HB/BR S6 .... 169 G1 🔲
Scarll Rd *DONS/BSCR* DN4 .... 4 A5
Scarsdale Cl *DRON* S18 .... 201 H7
Scarsdale Cross *DRON* S18 .... 201 H6 🔲
Scarsdale Rd *DRON* S18 .... 201 H6
SHEFS S8 .... 187 F4
Scarsdale St *DIN* S25 .... 178 C6
Scarth Av *DONS/BSCR* DN4 .... 4 B6
Scawsby La *BTLY* DN5 .... 63 J7
Scawthorpe Av *BTLY* DN5 .... 64 A6
Sceptone Gv *CUD/GR* S72 .... 31 K4
Schofield Dr *WMB/DAR* S73 .... 84 D1
Schofield Pl *WMB/DAR* S73 .... 84 D1 🔲
Schofield Rd *STKB/PEN* S36 .... 105 G6
WMB/DAR S73 .... 84 C1
Scholefield Dr *MEX/SWTN* S64 .... 112 E2
Schole Av *STKB/PEN* S36 .... 77 K4
Schole Hill La *STKB/PEN* S36 .... 77 J5
Scholes Gn *KIMB* S61 .... 131 K4
Scholes La *KIMB* S61 .... 131 H4
Scholes Moor Rd *HOLM/MEL* HD7 .. 48 B3
Scholes Rd *HOLM/MEL* HD7 .... 48 D3
Scholes Vw *CHPT/GREN* S35 .... 130 C6
Scholey Av *WRKN* S81 .... 195 G4
Scholey Rd *MALT* S66 .... 157 G2
Scholey St *OWL* S3 .... 9 E1 🔲
Scholfield Crs *MALT* S66 .... 159 J3 🔲
School Av *MOS* S20 .... 190 C8
School Cl *AU/AST/KP* S26 .... 192 B4
MOS S20 .... 190 D8
Schoolfield Dr *RAW* S62 .... 111 J8
School Green La *FUL* S10 .... 169 F8
School Gv *AU/AST/KP* S26 .... 175 J8
School Hl *CUD/GR* S72 .... 31 J8 🔲
RHAM S60 .... 156 A6
School La *ARMTH* DN3 .... 93 G7
CHPT/GREN S35 .... 129 H6
DRON S18 .... 201 G6
ECK/KIL S21 .... 203 G4
EPW DN9 .... 120 B1
HSH/HY S32 .... 182 C7
KBTN HD8 .... 51 H1
MALT S66 .... 138 B7
RAW S62 .... 133 H4
RHAM/THRY S65 .... 134 E4
SHEFP/MNR S2 .... 9 F3
SHEFS S8 .... 187 F8 🔲
ST/HB/BR S6 .... 169 G2
School Lane Cl *SHEFS* S8 .... 187 J6
School Rd *AU/AST/KP* S26 .... 192 A5
CHPT/GREN S35 .... 107 K8
DIN S25 .... 177 K3
FUL S10 .... 170 B4
MALT S66 .... 177 F1
MOS S20 .... 191 H5 🔲
WRKN S81 .... 180 C4
School Wy *AU/AST/KP* S26 .... 175 G8
BSLY S70 .... 56 E7
CUD/GR S72 .... 31 J7 🔲
CUD/GR S72 .... 59 G5
DEARNE S63 .... 60 C7
DEARNE S63 .... 86 B5

DIN S25 .... 178 B6
DOD/DAR S75 .... 2 A2
DOD/DAR S75 .... 28 D6
DOD/DAR S75 .... 29 H6
ECK/KIL S21 .... 204 B4
HOLM/MEL HD7 .... 47 K2
MOS S20 .... 190 B8
RHAM/THRY S65 .... 134 D5
WMB/DAR S73 .... 83 K8
WMB/DAR S73 .... 84 A4
WMB/DAR S73 .... 84 E1
School Wk *BWTY* DN10 .... 142 B8
CONI DN12 .... 114 A3
CONI DN12 .... 115 H8
MALT S66 .... 159 G2
Scorcher Hills La *AWLS/ASK* DN6 ... 37 G3
Scotch Spring La *MALT* S66 .... 160 C1
Scotia Cl *SHEFP/MNR* S2 .... 172 B7 🔲
Scotia Dr *SHEFP/MNR* S2 .... 172 B7 🔲
Scotland St *OWL* S3 .... 8 C2
Scot La *BWTY* DN10 .... 142 B8
DON DN1 .... 5 D3
Scott Av *BTLY* DN5 .... 87 H5
CONI DN12 .... 114 B6
Scott Cl *MALT* S66 .... 176 C1 🔲
WRKN S81 .... 211 G3
Scott Crs *ARMTH* DN3 .... 66 D4
Scott Hl *BTLY* DN5 .... 89 J7
KBTN HD8 .... 26 C4
Scott Rd *ATT* S4 .... 152 D7
Scott St *ATT* S4 .... 153 F7
Scott Wk *MALT* S66 .... 158 E1
Scovell Av *RAW* S62 .... 111 H8
Scowerdons La *HACK/IN* S12 ...... 189 H2
Scowerdons Dr *HACK/IN* S12 ...... 189 H2
Scraith Wood Dr *SHEFN* S5 .... 151 J5
Scratta La *WRKS* S80 .... 208 E5
Scrooby Cl *NROS/TKH* DN11 ...... 163 F3
Scrooby Dr *RAW* S62 .... 133 G4
Scrooby La *RAW* S62 .... 133 G4
Scrooby Pl *RAW* S62 .... 133 F4
Scrooby Rd *NROS/TKH* DN11 ..... 163 G3
Scrooby St *KIMB* S61 .... 133 F4
Seabrook Rd *SHEFP/MNR* S2 .... 171 K5
Seagrave Av *HACK/IN* S12 .... 188 D3
Seagrave Crs *HACK/IN* S12 .... 188 C3
Seagrave Dr *HACK/IN* S12 .... 188 C3
Seagrave Rd *HACK/IN* S12 .... 188 C3
Searby Rd *RHAM/THRY* S65 .... 135 J8
Seaton Cl *SHEFP/MNR* S2 .... 172 B5
Seaton Crs *SHEFP/MNR* S2 .... 172 B5
Seaton Gdns *NROS/TKH* DN11 .... 118 E8
Seaton Pl *SHEFP/MNR* S2 .... 172 B5
Seaton Wy *SHEFP/MNR* S2 .... 172 B5
Sebastion Vw *RHAM* S60 .... 155 F5
Second Av *AWLS/ASK* DN6 .... 63 K3
HEM/SK/SE WF9 .... 33 J6
Second La *DIN* S25 .... 194 A4
MALT S66 .... 157 H5
Sedan St *ATT* S4 .... 152 D8
Sedge Cl *MALT* S66 .... 157 J3
Sedgefield Wy *MEX/SWTN* S64 .... 113 C1
Sedgley Rd *ST/HB/BR* S6 .... 151 J7
Sefton Rd *ECC* S11 .... 169 J8
Selborne Rd *FUL* S10 .... 170 A4
Selborne St *RHAM/THRY* S65 .... 7 D2
Selbourne Cl *DOD/DAR* S75 ...... 54 D2 🔲
Selby Cl *AU/AST/KP* S26 .... 175 G8
Selby Rd *BSLYN/ROY* S71 .... 30 A8 🔲
GLE DN14 .... 13 K6
SHEFN S5 .... 152 E6
THNE DN8 .... 23 G7
WHHL DN2 .... 91 K2 🔲
Selhurst Crs *DONS/BSCR* DN4 .... 92 D8
Selkirk Rd *WHHL* DN2 .... 92 B1
Sellars Rd *KIMB* S61 .... 132 B6
Sellers St *SHEFS* S8 .... 171 F8 🔲🔲
Selly Oak Gv *SHEFS* S8 .... 201 J1
Selly Oak Rd *SHEFS* S8 .... 201 J1 🔲
Selvage La *GLE* DN14 .... 12 A4
Selwyn St *RHAM/THRY* S65 .... 7 D2 🔲
RHAM/THRY S65 .... 7 D2 🔲
Senior Rd *DARN/MH* S9 .... 172 E3
DONS/BSCR DN4 .... 4 A3
Sennen Cft *BSLYN/ROY* S71 .... 3 E2 🔲
Serlby Dr *AU/AST/KP* S26 .... 207 F2
Serlby La *AU/AST/KP* S26 .... 206 E1
Serlby Rd *NROS/TKH* DN11 .... 163 G3
Setcup La *ECK/KIL* S21 .... 204 A5
Seth Ter *BSLY* S70 .... 3 D5 🔲
Sevenairs Rd *MOS* S20 .... 190 C4
Sevenfields Ct *ST/HB/BR* S6 .... 151 F6
Sevenfields La *ST/HB/BR* S6 .... 151 F6
Severn Ct *FUL* S10 .... 8 A3 🔲
Severn Rd *FUL* S10 .... 8 A3 🔲
Severnside Dr *HAN/WDH* S13 ...... 173 J8
Severnside Gdns *HAN/WDH* S13 .. 173 J8
Severnside Rd *HAN/WDH* S13 ...... 173 J8
Sewell Rd *MOS* S20 .... 204 D1
Sexton Dr *MALT* S66 .... 157 J3
Seymore Rd *AU/AST/KP* S26 .... 191 H1
Seymour Rd *MALT* S66 .... 159 J2 🔲
Shackleton Rd *WHHL* DN2 .... 66 C6
Shackleton Vw *STKB/PEN* S36 .... 78 A5
Shady Side *DONS/BSCR* DN4 .... 4 A5
Shaftesbury Av *WHHL* DN2 .... 92 A4
Shaftesbury Dr *HOY* S74 .... 108 E2
Shaftesbury St *BSLY* S70 .... 56 E7

Shaftholme La *BTLY* DN5 .... 65 F1
Shaftholme Rd *BTLY* DN5 .... 65 G2
Shafton Hall Dr *CUD/GR* S72 .... 31 J4
Shafton Rd *RHAM* S60 .... 156 A6
Shaftsbury Av *AWLS/ASK* DN6 .... 63 G2
Shaftsbury Sq *RHAM/THRY* S65 .... 7 J3
Shakespeare Av *AWLS/ASK* DN6 .... 17 K5
　BTLY DN5 .... 90 K1
Shakespeare Crs *DRON* S18 .... 201 J7
Shakespeare Dr *DIN* S25 .... 178 C2
Shakespeare Rd *BTLY* DN5 .... 64 E6 回
　DEARNE S63 .... 85 G8
　RHAM/THRY S65 .... 7 H3
Shakespeare St *WRKN* S81 .... 211 F3
Shaldon Av *AU/AST/KP* S26 .... 175 H8
Shalesmoor *OWL* S3 .... 8 C1
Shambles St *BSLY* S70 .... 2 B4
Shardlow Gdns *DONS/BSCR* DN4 .... 118 E1
Sharlston Gdns *NROS/TKH* DN11 .... 119 G6
Sharman Cl *DRON* S18 .... 202 C6
Sharpe Av *SHEFS* S8 .... 186 E7
Sharpfield Av *RAW* S62 .... 81 H7
Sharp Royd Nook *STKB/PEN* S36 .... 104 E2
Sharrard Cl *HACK/IN* S12 .... 188 D2
Sharrard Dr *HACK/IN* S12 .... 188 D2
Sharrard Gv *HACK/IN* S12 .... 188 D1
Sharrard Rd *HACK/IN* S12 .... 188 D2
Sharrow La *ECC* S11 .... 8 B6
Sharrow St *ECC* S11 .... 8 C6
Sharrow Vale Rd *ECC* S11 .... 170 C7
Sharrow Vw *ABRD* S7 .... 8 B6
Shaw Ct *ARMTH* DN3 .... 93 H2
Shawfield Av *HOLM/MEL* HD7 .... 47 G3
Shawfield Cl *ARMTH* DN3 .... 67 F1
Shawfield Rd *BSLYN/ROY* S71 .... 30 D8
　BSLYN/ROY S71 .... 56 D1
Shaw La *AWLS/ASK* DN6 .... 19 K2
　BSLY S70 .... 55 H6
　BSLYN/ROY S71 .... 31 F6
　DOD/DAR S75 .... 29 H6
　HOLM/MEL HD7 .... 47 G3
　STKB/PEN S36 .... 102 E4
　WHHL DN2 .... 66 C7
Shaw Rd *CONI* DN12 .... 115 J4
　RHAM/THRY S65 .... 7 F2
Shawsfield Rd *RHAM* S60 .... 7 F6
Shaw St *BSLY* S70 .... 2 A5
　WRKS S80 .... 210 C4 回
Shaw Wood Wy *WHHL* DN2 .... 66 C8
Shay House La *STKB/PEN* S36 .... 104 E7
Shay La *HOLM/MEL* HD7 .... 46 B4
Shay Rd *STKB/PEN* S36 .... 104 E6
The Shay *DONS/BSCR* DN4 .... 92 D8
Sheaf Bank *SHEFP/MNR* S2 .... 171 G8 回
Sheaf Cl *CONI* DN12 .... 114 E6
Sheaf Ct *BSLY* S70 .... 56 E8
Sheaf Crs *DEARNE* S63 .... 86 C6
Sheaf Pl *WRKN* S81 .... 196 C8
Sheaf St *SHEF* S1 .... 9 E3
Sheards Cl *DRON* S18 .... 201 F6
Sheards Dr *DRON* S18 .... 200 E6 回
Sheards Wy *DRON* S18 .... 200 E6
Shearman Av *KIMB* S61 .... 132 B5
Shear Square Rbt *SHEF* S1 .... 9 E4
Shearwood Rd *FUL* S10 .... 8 A3 回
Sheep Bridge La *NROS/TKH* DN11 .. 119 C5
Sheep Cote La *HTFD* DN7 .... 68 C4
Sheepcote Rd *ECK/KIL* S21 .... 205 C1
Sheep Cote Rd *RHAM/THRY* S65 ... 156 C4
Sheep Dike La *MALT* S66 .... 157 H7
Sheep Dip La *HTFD* DN7 .... 42 A8
Sheephill Rd *ECC* S11 .... 184 D6
Sheep La *BTLY* DN5 .... 88 D6
Sheepwash La *NROS/TKH* DN11 .... 140 D6
Sheerien Cl *BSLYN/ROY* S71 .... 29 K7
Sheffield La *RHAM* S60 .... 174 A2
Sheffield Pkwy *HAN/WDH* S13 .... 173 G4
　SHEFP/MNR S2 .... 171 K3
　SHEFP/MNR S2 .... 173 F5
Sheffield Rd *BSLY* S70 .... 2 C5
　BSLY S70 .... 82 A8
　CONI DN12 .... 114 A7
　CONI DN12 .... 115 G4
　DARN/MH S9 .... 153 K6
　DIN S25 .... 193 J2
　DIN S25 .... 194 A3
　DONS/BSCR DN4 .... 115 J2
　DRON S18 .... 201 F4
　ECK/KIL S21 .... 191 G8
　ECK/KIL S21 .... 205 H7
　HACK/IN S12 .... 189 H5
　HAN/WDH S13 .... 174 E7
　HAN/WDH S13 .... 189 J1 回
　HATH/EY S32 .... 182 C8
　HOLM/MEL HD7 .... 48 D1
　MOS S20 .... 204 B2
　RHAM S60 .... 6 C5
　STKB/PEN S36 .... 78 C5
　WRKN S81 .... 181 K4
Sheldon Av *CONI* DN12 .... 114 E6
Sheldon La *ST/HB/BR* S6 .... 169 C1 回
Sheldon Rd *ABRD* S7 .... 186 E1
　STKB/PEN S36 .... 104 E6
Sheldon St *SHEFP/MNR* S2 .... 9 D5
Sheldrake Cl *KIMB* S61 .... 131 G2
Shelley Av *DONS/BSCR* DN4 .... 116 E1
Shelley Cl *STKB/PEN* S36 .... 78 A3
Shelley Dr *ARMTH* DN3 .... 93 H2

Sheldon La *BSLYN/ROY* S71 .... 3 E2
　DIN S25 .... 178 D7
　DRON S18 .... 201 J8
　RHAM/THRY S65 .... 156 A2
Shelley Gv *BTLY* DN5 .... 90 C3 回
Shelley Rd *AWLS/ASK* DN6 .... 63 H2
Shelley Rd *RHAM/THRY* S65 .... 156 A1
Shelley St *WRKS* S80 .... 210 E4
Shelley Wy *DEARNE* S63 .... 85 F8 回
Shenstone Cl *RHAM/THRY* S65 ...... 156 A3
Shenstone Rd *ST/HB/BR* S6 .... 151 G5
　ST/HB/BR S6 .... 151 C5
Shepcote La *DARN/MH* S9 .... 153 K8
Shepcote Wy *DARN/MH* S9 .... 153 K8
Shephard's Cl *CONI* DN12 .... 114 A4
Shepherd Dr *CHPT/GREN* S35 ..... 129 K1 回
Shepherd La *DEARNE* S63 .... 60 C8
Shepherd's Av *WRKN* S81 .... 210 D2
Shepherds Cft *EPW* DN9 .... 121 G1
Shepherd St *OWL* S3 .... 8 C2
Shepley Cft *CHPT/GREN* S35 .... 129 C1 回
Sheppard Rd *DONS/BSCR* DN4 .... 90 D8
Shepperson Rd *ST/HB/BR* S6 .... 151 G6
Sherbourne Av *MALT* S66 .... 157 K4
Sherburn Cl *AWLS/ASK* DN6 .... 37 F5
Sherburn Ga *CHPT/GREN* S35 ...... 130 A1
Sherburn Rd *BSLYN/ROY* S71 .... 29 K8
Sherde Rd *ST/HB/BR* S6 .... 170 D1
Sheridan Av *DONS/BSCR* DN4 .... 117 F1
Sheridan Ct *BSLYN/ROY* S71 .... 3 E2 回
Sheridan Dr *RHAM/THRY* S65 .... 156 B1
Sheridan Rd *ARMTH* DN3 .... 40 E7 回
Sheringham Cl *CHPT/GREN* S35 ... 107 J8
Sherwood Av *ARMTH* DN3 .... 66 E5 回
　AWLS/ASK DN6 .... 18 B8
　BTLY DN5 .... 90 A1
　CONI DN12 .... 114 D6
Sherwood Cl *AWLS/ASK* DN6 .... 17 K6 回
Sherwood Crs *RHAM/THRY* S65 ...... 7 D4
Sherwood Dr *AWLS/ASK* DN6 .... 37 F5
　DONS/BSCR DN4 .... 116 B2
Sherwood Gln *SHEFS* S8 .... 186 B6
Sherwood Rd *DRON* S18 .... 200 D6
　ECK/KIL S21 .... 191 J8
　NROS/TKH DN11 .... 119 F7
　NROS/TKH DN11 .... 162 E2
　WRKS S80 .... 210 D3
Sherwood St *BSLYN/ROY* S71 ...... 2 C4 回
Sherwood Wy *CUD/GR* S72 .... 31 H6
Shetland Rd *DRON* S18 .... 201 H7
Shield Av *BSLY* S70 .... 82 A2
Shildon Gv *THNE* DN8 .... 24 B4
Shining Cliff Ct *BWTY* DN10 .... 142 A7
Ship Hl *RHAM* S60 .... 6 C4
Shipman Balk *MALT* S66 .... 137 F2
Shipman Ct *MOS* S20 .... 190 B8 回
Shipton St *ST/HB/BR* S6 .... 8 B1 回
Shirburn Gdns *DONS/BSCR* DN4 ..... 92 B6
Shirebrook Rd *SHEFS* S8 .... 187 G1
Shirecliffe Cl *OWL* S3 .... 152 B5
Shirecliffe La *OWL* S3 .... 152 B8
Shirecliffe Rd *SHEFN* S5 .... 152 B5
Shiregreen La *SHEFN* S5 .... 153 F3
Shiregreen Ter *SHEFN* S5 .... 152 E8
Shirehall Crs *SHEFN* S5 .... 135 C8
Shirehall Rd *SHEFN* S5 .... 152 E1
Shireoaks Common *WRKN* S81 .... 195 J8
Shireoaks Rd *DRON* S18 .... 201 J5
　WRKN S81 .... 209 K2
　WRKS S80 .... 209 K3
Shires Cl *BTLY* DN5 .... 89 J6
Shirland Av *BSLYN/ROY* S71 .... 56 B1
Shirland Ct *DARN/MH* S9 .... 172 D2 回
Shirland La *DARN/MH* S9 .... 172 B1
Shirland Ms *DARN/MH* S9 .... 172 D2 回
Shirland Pl *DARN/MH* S9 .... 172 D2 回
Shirley La *AWLS/ASK* DN6 .... 39 F2
Shirley Rd *DONS/BSCR* DN4 ...... 4 A5 回
Shore Hall La *STKB/PEN* S36 .... 77 F5
Shoreham Av *RHAM* S60 .... 155 K6
Shoreham Dr *RHAM* S60 .... 155 J6
Shoreham St *SHEF* S1 .... 9 E4
　SHEFP/MNR S2 .... 9 D6
Shore La *FUL* S10 .... 170 A5
Shortbrook Bank *MOS* S20 .... 190 C7 回
Shortbrook Cl *MOS* S20 .... 190 C7
Shortbrook Cft *MOS* S20 .... 190 D7 回
Shortbrook Dr *MOS* S20 .... 190 C7
Shortbrook Rd *MOS* S20 .... 190 C7
Shortbrook Wy *MOS* S20 .... 190 C7
Shortfield Ct *BSLYN/ROY* S71 .... 29 K7
Short Ga *NROS/TKH* DN11 .... 138 D1
Short La *DONS/BSCR* DN4 .... 92 A8
　ST/HB/BR S6 .... 168 C2
Shortridge St *DARN/MH* S9 .... 172 B1
Short Rd *WHHL* DN2 .... 92 B3
Shorts La *TOT/DORE* S17 .... 199 F1
Short Wood Cl *BSLY* S70 .... 82 A6
Shortwood La *BTLY* DN5 .... 59 K3
Shrewsbury Cl *MEX/SWTN* S64 .. 112 E2 回
Shrewsbury Rd *NROS/TKH* DN11 .. 163 G3
　SHEFP/MNR S2 .... 9 E4
　STKB/PEN S36 .... 78 A4
　WRKS S80 .... 211 F6
Shrewsbury Ter *KIMB* S61 .... 154 C1
Shroggs Head Cl *WMB/DAR* S73 .. 84 E1 回
Shrogswood Rd *RHAM/THRY* S65 .. 156 C4
Shubert Cl *HAN/WDH* S13 .... 173 K7

Shude HI *SHEF* S1 .... 9 E2
Sicey Av *SHEFN* S5 .... 130 E1
Sicey La *SHEFN* S5 .... 152 E1
Sicklebrook La *DRON* S18 .... 202 A4
Sidcop Rd *CUD/GR* S72 .... 31 J3
Siddall St *OWL* S3 .... 8 C3 回
Sidings Ct *DONS/BSCR* DN4 .... 5 E
Sidling Hollow *ST/HB/BR* S6 .... 149 F7
Sidney Rd *WHHL* DN2 .... 92 A
Sidney St *MEX/SWTN* S64 .... 112 C
　SHEF S1 .... 9 D
Sidons Cl *KIMB* S61 .... 132 B5
Siemens Cl *DARN/MH* S9 .... 154 B5
Siena Cl *WMB/DAR* S73 .... 84 B
Sike Cl *DOD/DAR* S75 .... 28 C6
Sike La *HOLM/MEL* HD7 .... 48 C
　STKB/PEN S36 .... 77 H
Sikes Rd *DIN* S25 .... 193 H
Silkstone Cl *DOD/DAR* S75 .... 190 C7
　HACK/IN S12 .... 189 C
Silkstone Crs *HACK/IN* S12 .... 189 C
Silkstone Dr *HACK/IN* S12 .... 189 F1
Silkstone La *DOD/DAR* S75 .... 53 J
Silkstone Ov *THNE* DN8 .... 24 A
Silkstone Pl *HACK/IN* S12 .... 189 C
Silkstone Rd *HACK/IN* S12 .... 189 C
Silkstone Vw *HOY* S74 .... 83 F
Silver Birch Av *FUL* S10 .... 169 G8
Silver Birch Gv *EPW* DN9 .... 121 G4
Silverdale Cl *ARMTH* DN3 .... 93 K
　ECC S11 .... 186 A5
Silverdale Crs *ECC* S11 .... 186 A
Silverdale Cft *ECC* S11 .... 186 A
Silverdale Dr *BSLYN/ROY* S71 .... 56 E
Silverdale Gdns *ECC* S11 .... 186 B3
　ECC S11 .... 186 A3
Silverdale Gld *ECC* S11 .... 186 A
Silverdale Rd *ECC* S11 .... 186 A
Silverdales *DIN* S25 .... 178 C
Silver Hill Rd *ECC* S11 .... 186 E
Silver Jubilee Cl *WHHL* DN2 .... 92 E
Silver Mill Rd *SHEFP/MNR* S2 .... 9 D6
Silvermoor Dr *RHAM/THRY* S65 ... 135 J
Silverstone Av *CUD/GR* S72 .... 31 H
Silver St *BSLY* S70 .... 2 E
　DOD/DAR S75 .... 80 E
　DON DN1 .... 5 D3
　HTFD DN7 .... 41 H
　RHAM/THRY S65 .... 134 C
　SHEF S1 .... 9 D
　THNE DN8 .... 23 J
Silver Street Head *SHEF* S1 .... 9 D2 回
Simcrest Av *ECK/KIL* S21 .... 205 H
Sime St *WRKS* S80 .... 210 C
Simmonite Rd *KIMB* S61 .... 132 C2
Simons Wy *WMB/DAR* S73 .... 83 C
Simpson Pl *MEX/SWTN* S64 .... 112 E
Simpson Rd *HEM/SK/SE* WF9 .... 35 G3
Sim Royd La *STKB/PEN* S36 .... 52 A
Sims St *SHEF* S1 .... 9 C
Singleton Crs *ST/HB/BR* S6 .... 151 H8
Singleton Gv *ST/HB/BR* S6 .... 151 H8
Singleton Rd *ST/HB/BR* S6 .... 151 H
Siskin Ct *WRKN* S81 .... 196 A
Sitka Cl *BSLYN/ROY* S71 .... 30 C
Sitwell Av *STKB/PEN* S36 .... 104 C2
Sitwell Cl *WRKN* S81 .... 211 F
Sitwell Dr *RHAM* S60 .... 155 G
Sitwell Gv *MEX/SWTN* S64 .... 112 C
　RHAM S60 .... 155 F
Sitwell La *MALT* S66 .... 157 C4
Sitwell Park Rd *RHAM/THRY* S65 . 156 C
Sitwell Pl *SHEFP/MNR* S2 .... 8 C6
Sitwell Rd *ABRD* S7 .... 8 C
　WRKN S81 .... 211 F
Sitwell St *ECK/KIL* S21 .... 204 E
Sitwell V *RHAM* S60 .... 155 C
Sitwell Vw *RHAM* S60 .... 156 C
Sivilla Rd *MEX/SWTN* S64 .... 112 C
Sixrood La *AWLS/ASK* DN6 .... 37 H
Skellow Hall Gdns *AWLS/ASK* DN6 .. 37 C
Skellow Rd *AWLS/ASK* DN6 .... 37 H
Skelton Av *DOD/DAR* S75 .... 29 C
Skelton Dr *HAN/WDH* S13 .... 190 A
Skelton Gv *HAN/WDH* S13 .... 189 K
Skelton La *HAN/WDH* S13 .... 189 K
　MOS S20 .... 190 C
Skelton Ri *CHPT/GREN* S35 .... 150 C
Skelton Rd *SHEFS* S8 .... 197 G8
Skelwith Cl *ATT* S4 .... 153 C
Skelwith Dr *ATT* S4 .... 153 C
Skelwith Rd *ATT* S4 .... 153 C
Skew Hill La *CHPT/GREN* S35 .... 129 C
Skiers View Rd *HOY* S74 .... 108 C
Skiers Wy *HOY* S74 .... 108 C
Skinnerthorpe Rd *ATT* S4 .... 152 E
Skinpit La *STKB/PEN* S36 .... 78 C
Skipton Cl *CONI* DN12 .... 113 K
Skipton Rd *ATT* S4 .... 152 D
　AU/AST/KP S26 .... 175 C
Skipwith Cl *NROS/TKH* DN11 .... 117 H
Skipwith Gdns *NROS/TKH* DN11 .. 118 D7
Skye Edge Av *SHEFP/MNR* S2 .... 171 J
Skye Edge Rd *SHEFP/MNR* S2 ...... 171 J
Slack Fields La *CHPT/GREN* S35 .... 128 C
Slack La *CUD/GR* S72 .... 31 J
　HOLM/MEL HD7 .... 47 H
Slacks La *MALT* S66 .... 157 J
Slack Top La *HOLM/MEL* HD7 .... 49 H
Slack Wk *WRKS* S80 .... 210 C

lade Rd *MEX/SWTN* S64 .... **112** B5
lade Vw *DIN* S25 .... **159** F8
laidburn La *CHPT/GREN* S35 .... **130** A1
lant Ga *STKB/PEN* S36 .... **76** E3
late St *STKB/PEN* S2 .... **171** H8 🔟
layleigh Av *FUL* S10 .... **169** G7
layleigh Delph *FUL* S10 .... **169** G7
layleigh Dr *FUL* S10 .... **169** H7
layleigh La *FUL* S10 .... **169** G7
laynes La *BWTY* DN10 .... **143** F7
lay Pit La *HTFD* DN7 .... **69** F1
laypit La *WRKS* S80 .... **207** K1
leaford St *DARN/MH* S9 .... **172** B1 🔟
ledbrook La *STKB/PEN* S36 .... **75** H1
ledgate Dr *MALT* S66 .... **156** E4
ledgate La *MALT* S66 .... **156** E4
ledmere Rd *BTLY* DN5 .... **90** B1
leep Hill La *AWLS/ASK* DN6 .... **36** C1
linn St *FUL* S10 .... **170** C3
litting Mill La *DARN/MH* S9 .... **172** B1 🔟
lloade La *HACK/IN* S12 .... **189** F8
lmallage La *HAN/WDH* S13 .... **174** E6
lmaldale Rd *HACK/IN* S12 .... **189** F3
lmalfield La *ST/HB/BR* S6 .... **126** B7
lmall La *STKB/PEN* S36 .... **53** E2
lmeaton Cl *RHAM/THRY* S65 .... **135** J7
lmeaton St *ECC* S11 .... **8** C6 🔟
lmelter Wood Av *HAN/WDH* S13 ... **173** G8
lmelter Wood Cl *HAN/WDH* S13 ... **173** G8 🔟
lmelter Wood Crs *HAN/WDH* S13 .. **173** H8
lmelter Wood La *HAN/WDH* S13 ... **173** G8
lmelter Wood Pl *HAN/WDH* S13 ... **173** H8
lmelter Wood Ri *HAN/WDH* S13 ... **173** H8
lmelter Wood Rd *HAN/WDH* S13 ... **189** H1
lmelter Wood Wy *HAN/WDH* S13 ... **173** G8
lmillie Rd *NROS/TKH* DN11 .... **119** F7
lmithey Cl *CHPT/GREN* S35 .... **129** J1
lmithfield *OWL* S3 .... **8** C2
lmith La *HACK/IN* S12 .... **188** C5
lmithies La *BSLYN/ROY* S71 .... **2** B1
lmithies Rd *MEX/SWTN* S64 .... **112** B3
lmithies St *BSLYN/ROY* S71 .... **2** B1
lmithley La *WMB/DAR* S73 .... **83** H3
lmith Rd *STKB/PEN* S36 .... **104** D6
lmith Sq *DONS/BSCR* DN4 .... **90** C8
                                 NROS/TKH DN11 .... **162** E2
lmith St *CHPT/GREN* S35 .... **130** B2
                     DONS/BSCR DN4 .... **90** C8
                     WMB/DAR S73 .... **84** G4 🔟
lmithy Bridge La *WMB/DAR* S73 ...... **84** A8
lmithy Bridge Rd *ST/HB/BR* S6 ...... **148** D3
lmithy Carr Av *CHPT/GREN* S35 ..... **130** A2
lmithy Carr Cl *CHPT/GREN* S35 ..... **130** A2
lmithy Cl *CHPT/GREN* S35 .... **106** C3
                     KIMB S61 .... **132** C6
lmithy Cft *DRON* S18 .... **200** C5
lmithy Fold La *CHPT/GREN* S35 ..... **106** C3
lmithy Hl *CHPT/GREN* S35 .... **79** K8
                     KBTN HD8 .... **51** G4
lmithy Mdw *HATH/EY* S32 .... **182** C7
lmithy Moor La *STKB/PEN* S36 ..... **104** B4
lmithy Moor La *STKB/PEN* S36 ..... **104** B4
lmithy Wood Crs *SHEFS* S8 .... **187** F3 🔟
lmithy Wood La *DOD/DAR* S75 .... **80** C1
lmithy Wood Rd *CHPT/GREN* S35 .. **130** D3
                     SHEFS S8 .... **186** E3
lnail Hl *RHAM* S60 .... **6** C4 🔟
lnailsden Wy *DOD/DAR* S75 .... **29** J7
lnaithing La *FUL* S10 .... **169** J6
lnaithing Park Cl *FUL* S10 .... **169** J6 🔟
lnaithing Park Rd *FUL* S10 .... **169** J6 🔟
lnaith Rd *GLE* DN14 .... **11** K1
                     GLE DN14 .... **12** A1
lnake La *CONI* DN12 .... **114** E6
lnape Hl *DRON* S18 .... **201** G5
lnapehill Cl *DRON* S18 .... **201** G4 🔟
lnapehill Crs *DRON* S18 .... **201** G4
lnape Hill Dr *DRON* S18 .... **201** H4 🔟
lnape Hill La *DRON* S18 .... **201** G5
lnape Hill Rd *WMB/DAR* S73 .... **84** E2
lnape La *NROS/TKH* DN11 .... **163** F5
lnatchells La *GLE* DN14 .... **21** K3
lnelston Cl *DRON* S18 .... **200** C6 🔟🔟
lnetterton Cl *CUD/GR* S72 .... **31** K8 🔟
lnig Hl *SHEF* S1 .... **9** E2
lnipe Park Rd *NROS/TKH* DN11 ...... **163** C3
lnittle Rd *HOLM/MEL* HD7 .... **48** A8
lnowberry Cl *MEX/SWTN* S64 .... **112** B7
lnowden Ter *WMB/DAR* S73 .... **84** A4
lnowdon La *ECK/KIL* S21 .... **202** D4
lnowdon Wy *RHAM* S60 .... **155** G8
lnow La *OWL* S3 .... **9** D2
lnug La *HOLM/MEL* HD7 .... **49** F6
lnydale Rd *CUD/GR* S72 .... **31** J8
lpaper La *DRON* S18 .... **201** G5
lpap House La *HAN/WDH* S13 .... **174** C8
lpa Rd *WMB/DAR* S73 .... **83** K5
lpally St *SHEF* S1 .... **8** C2
lpolway Rd *DRON* S18 .... **200** D5
lpomercotes Rd *HACK/IN* S12 .... **189** F2
lpomersby Av *BTLY* DN5 .... **90** C3
lpomerset Rd *DON* DN1 .... **5** D4
                     OWL S3 .... **171** H1
lpomerset St *BSLY* S70 .... **2** A3 🔟
                     CUD/GR S72 .... **57** J1 🔟
                     MALT S66 .... **159** J3 🔟
                     OWL S3 .... **171** H1 🔟

Somerton Dr *DONS/BSCR* DN4 .... **92** D8
                     HTFD DN7 .... **69** G1
Somerville Ter *ST/HB/BR* S6 .... **170** D1
Sorby Rd *AU/AST/KP* S26 .... **175** F8
Sorby St *ATT* S4 .... **9** F1
Sorby Wy *MALT* S66 .... **157** G4
Sorrell La *HTFD* DN7 .... **22** B5
Sorrel Rd *MALT* S66 .... **157** H1
Sorreisykes Cl *RHAM* S60 .... **156** A7 🔟
Sorrento Vw *WMB/DAR* S73 .... **84** C1
Sothall Cl *MOS* S20 .... **190** D4
Sothall Ct *MOS* S20 .... **190** D4 🔟
Sothall Gn *MOS* S20 .... **190** D4
Sothall Ms *MOS* S20 .... **190** D4 🔟
Sough Hall Av *KIMB* S61 .... **131** G2
Sough Hall Cl *KIMB* S61 .... **131** G2
Sough Hall Crs *KIMB* S61 .... **131** G2
Sough Hall Rd *KIMB* S61 .... **131** G3
Soughley La *CHPT/GREN* S35 .... **105** K5
                     FUL S10 .... **168** C7
Sour La *HTFD* DN7 .... **22** C8
Sousa St *MALT* S66 .... **159** K3
Southall St *SHEFS* S8 .... **187** G1 🔟🔟
Southard's La *AU/AST/KP* S26 ..... **208** A3
South Av *BWTY* DN10 .... **142** B7
                     HEM/SK/SE WF9 .... **34** D5
                     MEX/SWTN S64 .... **112** A5
                     WRKS S80 .... **211** F6
Southbourne Rd *ECC* S11 .... **170** C5
Southbreck Ri *WRKS* S80 .... **211** F6
South Cl *BSLYN/ROY* S71 .... **30** D5
Southcote Dr *DRON* S18 .... **200** D6
South Crs *DOD/DAR* S75 .... **54** E8
                     ECK/KIL S21 .... **191** J8
                     RHAM/THRY S65 .... **134** A8
South Cft *CUD/GR* S72 .... **31** K4
                     KBTN HD8 .... **51** G4
Southcroft Gdns *SHEFS* S8 .... **187** F1 🔟
Southdene *WRKN* S81 .... **210** E1
South Dr *BSLYN/ROY* S71 .... **30** D5
                     DEARNE S63 .... **86** A6
South Drive Farm *AWLS/ASK* DN6 .. **37** H6
South End *THNE* DN8 .... **43** K2
South End La *GLE* DN14 .... **10** B7
Southend Pl *SHEF/MNR* S2 .... **172** A6 🔟
Southend Rd *SHEF/MNR* S2 .... **172** A6 🔟
Southern Wd *WRKS* S80 .... **210** A2
Southey Av *SHEFN* S5 .... **152** B4
Southey Cl *SHEFN* S5 .... **152** A4 🔟
Southey Crs *MALT* S66 .... **159** H2
                     SHEFN S5 .... **152** A4
Southey Dr *SHEFN* S5 .... **152** B4
Southey Green Cl *SHEFN* S5 .... **152** A4 🔟
Southey Green Rd *SHEFN* S5 .... **151** J3
Southey Hall Dr *SHEFN* S5 .... **152** A4
Southey Hall Rd *SHEFN* S5 .... **152** A4
Southey Hl *SHEFN* S5 .... **152** A4
Southey Ri *SHEFN* S5 .... **152** A4
Southey Rd *MALT* S66 .... **159** H2 🔟
South Farm Av *AU/AST/KP* S26 .... **206** E1
Southfield Cl *THNE* DN8 .... **43** K2 🔟
Southfield Dr *DRON* S18 .... **201** J7
Southfield La *DEARNE* S63 .... **60** A8
Southfield Mt *DRON* S18 .... **201** J7 🔟
Southfield Rd *ARMTH* DN3 .... **93** G1
                     CUD/GR S72 .... **57** K3
                     THNE DN8 .... **23** K8
Southgate *CUD/GR* S72 .... **32** B1
                     DOD/DAR S75 .... **55** H4
                     ECK/KIL S21 .... **204** C4
                     HOY S74 .... **109** F2
                     STKB/PEN S36 .... **78** B5
Southgate Ct *ECK/KIL* S21 .... **204** C4
South Grimesthorpe Rd *ATT* S4 ... **171** J1 🔟
Southgrove Rd *FUL* S10 .... **8** A5
Southlands Wy *AU/AST/KP* S26 .... **175** J8
South La *DOD/DAR* S75 .... **52** E6
                     SHEF S1 .... **9** D5
Southlea Av *HOY* S74 .... **109** G1
Southlea Cl *HOY* S74 .... **109** G2 🔟
Southlea Dr *HOY* S74 .... **109** G1
Southlea Rd *HOY* S74 .... **109** F1
Southmoor Av *ARMTH* DN3 .... **93** F2
Southmoor La *ARMTH* DN3 .... **93** F2
Southmoor Rd *CUD/GR* S72 .... **33** G5
                     WRKS S80 .... **211** F6
South Pde *BWTY* DN10 .... **164** B2
                     OWL S3 .... **9** D1
                     THNE DN8 .... **43** J1
                     WHHL DN2 .... **5** E3
                     WRKN S81 .... **210** D3
South Pl *DOD/DAR* S75 .... **55** G4
South Precipitator Rd
                     ARMTH DN3 .... **40** B7
South Rd *ARMTH* DN3 .... **40** B7
                     CHPT/GREN S35 .... **107** J8
                     DOD/DAR S75 .... **54** E7
                     KIMB S61 .... **132** B8
                     ST/HB/BR S6 .... **170** C1
                     THNE DN8 .... **24** A4
South Sea Rd *HAN/WDH* S13 .... **189** J1
South St *AWLS/ASK* DN6 .... **63** J5
                     BSLY S70 .... **55** H6 🔟
                     DIN S25 .... **178** B6
                     DOD/DAR S75 .... **80** E1
                     DONS/BSCR DN4 .... **5** D5

HEM/SK/SE WF9 .... **33** H1
HOLM/MEL HD7 .... **48** B1
KIMB S61 .... **133** F4
KIMB S61 .... **154** B2
MALT S66 .... **177** F1 🔟
MOS S20 .... **204** B1
RAW S62 .... **133** K1
WMB/DAR S73 .... **84** D2 🔟
South Street Pk *SHEF/MNR* S2 .... **9** F3
South Vale Dr *RHAM/THRY* S65 .... **134** E5
South Vw *BWTY* DN10 .... **142** D6
                     HOLM/MEL HD7 .... **48** E4
                     MOS S20 .... **190** E8
                     WMB/DAR S73 .... **84** D2
                     WRKN S81 .... **210** D2
South View Cl *ST/HB/BR* S6 .... **150** D6
South View Crs *ABRD* S7 .... **171** F8 🔟🔟
South View Ri *ST/HB/BR* S6 .... **150** D6
                     HOY S74 .... **8** C6
South View Ter *RHAM* S60 .... **174** A2 🔟
Southwell Cl *WRKS* S80 .... **210** E5
Southwell Ri *MEX/SWTN* S64 .... **113** G1 🔟
Southwell Rd *ATT* S4 .... **153** G6 🔟
                     RAW S62 .... **134** A1
                     WHHL DN2 .... **91** J1
Southwell St *DOD/DAR* S75 .... **2** A5 🔟🔟
Southwood Av *DRON* S18 .... **201** G8
South Wood Dr *THNE* DN8 .... **43** J2
Spa Brook Cl *HACK/IN* S12 .... **189** H3
Spa Brooke Dr *HACK/IN* S12 .... **189** H2
Spa La *HAN/WDH* S13 .... **190** A2
Spa Lane Cft *HAN/WDH* S13 .... **190** A1
Spalton Rd *RAW* S62 .... **133** J3
Spansyke St *DONS/BSCR* DN4 .... **4** B4
Sparken Cl *WRKS* S80 .... **210** C7
Sparken Dl *WRKS* S80 .... **210** C7
Sparken Hl *WRKS* S80 .... **210** D6
Sparkfields *DOD/DAR* S75 .... **29** G7
Spark La *DOD/DAR* S75 .... **29** G7 🔟
Spartan Vw *MALT* S66 .... **136** E8 🔟
Sparth La *HOLM/MEL* HD7 .... **46** E3
Spa Ter *AWLS/ASK* DN6 .... **18** D7
Spa View Av *HACK/IN* S12 .... **189** H4
Spa View Dr *HACK/IN* S12 .... **189** H4
Spa View Pl *HACK/IN* S12 .... **189** H4
Spa View Rd *HACK/IN* S12 .... **189** H4
Spa View Ter *HACK/IN* S12 .... **189** H4 🔟
Spa View Wy *HACK/IN* S12 .... **189** H4
Spa Well Crs *RHAM* S60 .... **174** C2
Spa Well Gv *CUD/GR* S72 .... **32** D4
Speedwell Pl *WRKS* S80 .... **210** C3
Speetley Vw *STV/CWN* S43 .... **206** B8
Speeton Rd *ST/HB/BR* S6 .... **151** H8 🔟
Spencer Dr *RHAM/THRY* S65 .... **135** J7
Spencer Gn *RHAM* S60 .... **156** C6 🔟
Spencer Rd *SHEF/MNR* S2 .... **171** G8
Spencer St *BSLY* S70 .... **2** B5
                     MEX/SWTN S64 .... **112** D2
Spennithorne Rd *AWLS/ASK* DN6 .. **37** F5
Spenser Rd *RHAM/THRY* S65 .... **7** F5
Spey Cl *DOD/DAR* S75 .... **29** H8
Spey Dr *EPW* DN9 .... **94** B8
Spicer House La *STKB/PEN* S36 ...... **50** C8
Spilsby Cl *DONS/BSCR* DN4 .... **119** F1
Spink Hall Cl *STKB/PEN* S36 .... **105** F7 🔟
Spink Hall La *STKB/PEN* S36 .... **104** E7
Spinkhill Av *HAN/WDH* S13 .... **172** E7
Spinkhill Dr *HAN/WDH* S13 .... **173** F7
Spinkhill La *ECK/KIL* S21 .... **205** G5
Spinkhill Rd *ECK/KIL* S21 .... **205** J5
                     HAN/WDH S13 .... **173** F8
Spinney Cl *RHAM* S60 .... **155** K4
Spinneyfield *RHAM* S60 .... **155** K5
Spinney Hl *BTLY* DN5 .... **89** J7
The Spinney *ARMTH* DN3 .... **67** F1
                     DONS/BSCR DN4 .... **116** C2 🔟
Spitalfields *OWL* S3 .... **9** E1 🔟
Spital Gv *NROS/TKH* DN11 .... **119** F8
Spital Hl *ATT* S4 .... **9** F1
Spital La *OWL* S3 .... **9** F1
Spital St *OWL* S3 .... **9** E1
Spittlerush La *PONT* WF8 .... **17** H3
Spofforth Rd *DARN/MH* S9 .... **172** C2 🔟
Spooner Dr *ECK/KIL* S21 .... **205** G1
Spooner Rd *FUL* S10 .... **170** C4
Spoon Cl *ST/HB/BR* S6 .... **169** G1 🔟
Spoonhill Rd *ST/HB/BR* S6 .... **169** H1
Spoon La *ST/HB/BR* S6 .... **168** E1
Spoon Ms *ST/HB/BR* S6 .... **169** G1
Spoon Wy *ST/HB/BR* S6 .... **169** G1
Spotswood Cl *DRON* S18 .... **188** A3 🔟
Spotswood Dr *SHEF/MNR* S2 .... **188** A2 🔟
Spotswood Mt *GLV* S14 .... **188** A2 🔟
Spotswood Pl *GLV* S14 .... **187** K3
Spotswood Rd *SHEFS* S8 .... **187** K3
Spout La *ST/HB/BR* S6 .... **169** F1
Spout Spinney *ST/HB/BR* S6 .... **169** F1
Springbank *WMB/DAR* S73 .... **84** D2 🔟
Springbank Cl *BSLYN/ROY* S71 ...... **30** D7 🔟
                     EPW DN9 .... **121** G1
Spring Bank Cft *HOLM/MEL* HD7 .... **47** G3
Spring Bank Rd *CONI* DN12 .... **114** C7
Spring Cl *ECK/KIL* S21 .... **205** G8
Spring Close Dell *GLV* S14 .... **188** B3
Spring Close Mt *GLV* S14 .... **188** B3
Spring Close Wy *GLV* S14 .... **188** A3
                     HACK/IN S12 .... **188** D2
                     SHEFP/MNR S2 .... **9** D5

Spring Crs BTLY DN5 .... 89 J6
Spring Cft KIMB S61 .... 132 C6
Springcroft Dr BTLY DN5 .... 64 B7
Spring Dr WMB/DAR S73 .... 84 D7
Springgate DEARNE S63 .... 85 K5 ☐
Springfield Av ECC S11 .... 186 C2
　HEM/SK/SE WF9 .... 33 H1
　HTFD DN7 .... 42 D8
　KBTN HD8 .... 26 B5
Springfield Cl ABRD S7 .... 186 C3
　ARMTH DN3 .... 93 H2 ☐
　ECK/KIL S21 .... 204 A4
　KBTN HD8 .... 26 B5
　KIMB S61 .... 6 C1
　WMB/DAR S73 .... 84 E2
　WRKN S81 .... 195 G3
Springfield Ct BTLY DN5 .... 90 B2 ☐
Springfield Crs HOY S74 .... 108 C2
　PONT WF8 .... 17 F2
　WMB/DAR S73 .... 84 E2
Springfield Dr KBTN HD8 .... 50 B3
　RHAM/THRY S65 .... 135 F5
Springfield Gln ECC S11 .... 186 B3
Springfield Mt HEM/SK/SE WF9 .... 34 D6 ☐
Springfield Pl BSLY S70 .... 2 A4 ☒
Springfield Rd ABRD S7 .... 186 C3
　CONI DN12 .... 115 K5
　CUD/GR S72 .... 32 C8
　MALT S66 .... 157 F2
　MEX/SWTN S64 .... 112 D8
Springfield St BSLY S70 .... 55 H6
Spring Gdns BSLYN/ROY S71 .... 3 F1 ☐
　BWTY DN10 .... 142 B7
　DON DN1 .... 4 C3
　HOLM/MEL HD7 .... 47 H2
　HOY S74 .... 109 H3
Spring Grove Gdns
　CHPT/GREN S35 .... 128 A6
Spring Hl FUL S10 .... 170 C3
Springhill Av WMB/DAR S73 .... 84 D7
Spring Hill Cl BTLY DN5 .... 89 J6 ☐
Spring Hill Rd FUL S10 .... 170 C3
Spring House Rd FUL S10 .... 170 C3 ☒
Spring La BSLYN/ROY S71 .... 30 D7
　BTLY DN5 .... 89 J3
　DOD/DAR S75 .... 29 H3
　HOLM/MEL HD7 .... 47 G5
　HOLM/MEL HD7 .... 48 D2
　SHEFP/MNR S2 .... 172 A7
　WRKN S81 .... 209 G3
　WRKS S80 .... 209 H3
Spring St BSLY S70 .... 2 B5
　OWL S3 .... 9 D2
　RHAM/THRY S65 .... 7 D3
Spring Vale Av BSLY S70 .... 82 A3 ☐
Springvale Rd CUD/GR S72 .... 59 H5
　MALT S66 .... 157 H5
Spring Vale Rd HEM/SK/SE WF9 .... 34 B4 ☐
Springvale Rd ST/HB/BR S6 .... 8 A2
Spring View Rd FUL S10 .... 170 C3 ☒
Spring Wk WRKS S80 .... 210 C6
Spring Water Av HACK/IN S12 .... 189 H4
Spring Water Cl HACK/IN S12 .... 189 J4 ☐
Spring Water Dr HACK/IN S12 .... 189 H3
Springwell Av MOS S20 .... 190 C3
Springwell Cl MALT S66 .... 159 J1
Springwell Crs MOS S20 .... 190 C3
Springwell Gdns
　DONS/BSCR DN4 .... 116 C1 ☐
Springwell Gv MOS S20 .... 190 C3
Springwell La DONS/BSCR DN4 .... 116 C2
　NROS/TKH DN11 .... 116 D5
Springwood Av AU/AST/KP S26 .... 175 G6
Springwood Rd ARMTH DN3 .... 93 J7 ☒
　CHPT/GREN S35 .... 105 K1
Springwood La CHPT/GREN S35 .... 129 H1
Springwood Rd BTLY DN5 .... 64 B7
　HOY S74 .... 108 D2
　SHEFS S8 .... 187 G1 ☐
Springwood Vw STKB/PEN S36 .... 78 C5
Sprotbrough La BTLY DN5 .... 62 E8
Sprotbrough Rd BTLY DN5 .... 90 C4
Spruce Av BSLYN/ROY S71 .... 30 C4
　MALT S66 .... 157 G2
Spruce Crs EPW DN9 .... 120 B5
Spruce Ri ECK/KIL S21 .... 205 G2
Spry La CUD/GR S72 .... 59 K4
Spur Crs WRKS S80 .... 211 F6
Spurley Hey Gv STKB/PEN S36 .... 105 F7
Spurr St SHEFP/MNR S2 .... 9 E6
The Square East MALT S66 .... 135 H8
The Square AU/AST/KP S26 .... 192 B5
　BSLY S70 .... 2 A5
　CUD/GR S72 .... 58 E1
　RAW S62 .... 108 E6
The Square West MALT S66 .... 135 H8
Stable Cl WRKN S81 .... 196 E8 ☐
Stables La BTLY DN5 .... 87 H3
The Stables MEX/SWTN S64 .... 112 A3
Stacey Crs CUD/GR S72 .... 32 C8
Stacey Dr RHAM/THRY S65 .... 134 D4 ☐
Stacey La ST/HB/BR S6 .... 149 J6
Stacye Av HAN/WDH S13 .... 190 B1
Stacye Ri HAN/WDH S13 .... 190 B1
Stadium Cl WRKN S81 .... 210 A1

Stadium Ct RAW S62 .... 133 H5
Stadium Wy DARN/MH S9 .... 172 B2
　HEM/SK/SE WF9 .... 35 C2
　RHAM/THRY S65 .... 7 E1
Stafford Cl DRON S18 .... 200 C5 ☐
Stafford Crs RHAM S60 .... 155 J6
Stafford Dr RHAM S60 .... 155 J6
Stafford La SHEFP/MNR S2 .... 171 K5 ☒
　SHEFP/MNR S2 .... 171 K5
Staffordshire Cl MALT S66 .... 159 J2 ☐
Stafford Wy CHPT/GREN S35 .... 130 A2 ☒
Stag Cl RHAM S60 .... 156 B4
Stag Crs RHAM/THRY S65 .... 156 B4
Stag La RHAM S60 .... 156 A4
Stainborough Cl DOD/DAR S75 .... 80 E1
Stainborough La DOD/DAR S75 .... 80 D7
Stainborough Rd DOD/DAR S75 .... 80 D1
Stainborough Vw BSLY S70 .... 82 A2 ☐
　DOD/DAR S75 .... 107 J1 ☐
Staincross Common
　DOD/DAR S75 .... 29 G5
Staindrop Vw CHPT/GREN S35 .... 130 A5
Stainforth Moor Rd HTFD DN7 .... 69 J2
　THNE DN8 .... 70 D2
Stainforth Rd ARMTH DN3 .... 41 F7
　HTFD DN7 .... 41 F6
Stanley Cl DOD/DAR S75 .... 55 C5 ☐
Stainmore Av MOS S20 .... 190 E5
Stainmore Cl DOD/DAR S75 .... 53 J7 ☐
Stainton Cl BSLYN/ROY S71 .... 55 K1
Stainton La MALT S66 .... 137 J8
　NROS/TKH DN11 .... 138 C3
Stainton Rd ECC S11 .... 170 B7
Stainton St CONI DN12 .... 114 A4
Stair Rd ATT S4 .... 152 D7
Stake Hill Rd ST/HB/BR S6 .... 147 K8
Stake Lane Bank HOLM/MEL HD7 .... 48 A2
Stalker Lees Rd ECC S11 .... 8 A6
Stalley Royd La HOLM/MEL HD7 .... 48 E4
Stambers Cl WRKN S81 .... 195 G4
Stamford St DARN/MH S9 .... 153 G8 ☐
Stampers Hl DOD/DAR S75 .... 81 J5
Stanage Ri HACK/IN S12 .... 189 F2
Stanbury Cl DOD/DAR S75 .... 55 C4
Stancil La NROS/TKH DN11 .... 117 K8
　NROS/TKH DN11 .... 139 K3
Standhill Crs BSLYN/ROY S71 .... 29 K8
Standish Av SHEFN S5 .... 152 B6
Standish Cl SHEFN S5 .... 152 B6
Standish Crs HEM/SK/SE WF9 .... 34 B3
Standish Dr SHEFN S5 .... 152 B6
Standish Rd SHEFN S5 .... 152 B6
Standon Crs DARN/MH S9 .... 153 G2
Standon Dr DARN/MH S9 .... 153 G2
Standon Rd DARN/MH S9 .... 153 H2
Staneford Ct MOS S20 .... 190 B6
Stanford Cl MALT S66 .... 159 K3
Stanford Rd DRON S18 .... 200 C6 ☐
Stanhope Av DOD/DAR S75 .... 53 J2
Stanhope Gdns DOD/DAR S75 .... 55 J4
Stanhope Rd DON DN1 .... 5 L1
　HACK/IN S12 .... 188 E2
Stanhope St BSLY S70 .... 2 A4 ☐☐
　KBTN HD8 .... 26 A6 ☐
Stanhurst La HTFD DN7 .... 43 H5
Staniforth Av ECK/KIL S21 .... 203 K4
Staniforth Crs AU/AST/KP S26 .... 192 E2
Staniforth Rd DARN/MH S9 .... 172 C2
Stannington Gdns DONS/BSCR DN4 .... 41 K4
　HTFD DN7 .... 41 K4
Stanley Gv AU/AST/KP S26 .... 175 K7 ☐
Stanley La OWL S3 .... 9 E1 ☐
Stanley Rd BSLY S70 .... 57 F7
　BTLY DN5 .... 64 A8
　CHPT/GREN S35 .... 129 K5
　HTFD DN7 .... 41 K4 ☐
　SHEFS S8 .... 187 H2
　STKB/PEN S36 .... 97 K4
Stanley Sq ARMTH DN3 .... 66 E3 ☐
Stanley St BSLY S70 .... 57 K2
　CUD/GR S72 .... 59 K2
　ECK/KIL S21 .... 191 H4
　OWL S3 .... 9 E1 ☐☐
　RHAM S60 .... 6 C4 ☐
　WRKN S81 .... 210 C2
Stanley Ter MALT S66 .... 158 C5
Stannington Gln ST/HB/BR S6 .... 169 J1
Stannington Ri ST/HB/BR S6 .... 151 F8 ☐
Stannington Rd ST/HB/BR S6 .... 169 F1
Stannington View Rd FUL S10 .... 170 A3
Stanton Crs HACK/IN S12 .... 189 F3 ☐
Stan Va PONT WF8 .... 17 F1
Stanwell Av DARN/MH S9 .... 153 H3
Stanwell St DARN/MH S9 .... 153 H3
Stanwood Av ST/HB/BR S6 .... 169 K1
Stanwood Crs ST/HB/BR S6 .... 169 K1
Stanwood Dr ST/HB/BR S6 .... 169 K1 ☐
Stanwood Ms ST/HB/BR S6 .... 169 K1
Stanwood Rd ST/HB/BR S6 .... 169 K1
Staple Gn RHAM/THRY S65 .... 135 F5
Stapleton Rd DONS/BSCR DN4 .... 116 A2
Starkbridge La GLE DN14 .... 21 F1
Star La BSLY S70 .... 2 B4
Starling Gv WRKN S81 .... 210 A1
Starling Md SHEFP/MNR S2 .... 172 A5 ☐
Starnhill Cl CHPT/GREN S35 .... 130 D5

Statham Ct WRKN S81 .... 211 F2 ☐
Station Ap HATH/EY S32 .... 182 C8
Station Cl EPW DN9 .... 120 E5
Station La CHPT/GREN S35 .... 128 C8
　DARN/MH S9 .... 153 H5
Station Rd ARMTH DN3 .... 66 E7
　AU/AST/KP S26 .... 192 D5
　AWLS/ASK DN6 .... 18 D2
　AWLS/ASK DN6 .... 18 B6
　AWLS/ASK DN6 .... 38 A3
　BSLY S70 .... 2 A3
　BSLY S70 .... 82 D7
　BSLYN/ROY S71 .... 30 C3
　BSLYN/ROY S71 .... 57 G2
　BTLY DN5 .... 65 G5
　BWTY DN10 .... 142 B3
　BWTY DN10 .... 143 J4
　BWTY DN10 .... 164 B5
　CHPT/GREN S35 .... 130 C7
　CHPT/GREN S35 .... 130 D6
　CONI DN12 .... 114 D2
　DARN/MH S9 .... 172 E3 ☐
　DEARNE S63 .... 60 C2
　DEARNE S63 .... 85 K3
　DEARNE S63 .... 86 B5
　DEARNE S63 .... 111 J3
　DIN S25 .... 177 J4
　DOD/DAR S75 .... 28 D6
　DOD/DAR S75 .... 54 D8
　ECK/KIL S21 .... 204 C4
　ECK/KIL S21 .... 204 D5
　ECK/KIL S21 .... 205 H1
　ECK/KIL S21 .... 205 F7
　EPW DN9 .... 121 F2
　EPW DN9 .... 121 F1
　HAN/WDH S13 .... 174 B8
　HATH/EY S32 .... 182 C6
　HEM/SK/SE WF9 .... 35 F4
　HOLM/MEL HD7 .... 47 K2
　HTFD DN7 .... 41 K5
　HTFD DN7 .... 42 C2
　MEX/SWTN S64 .... 113 F7
　MOS S20 .... 190 D7
　MOS S20 .... 190 B8 ☐
　NROS/TKH DN11 .... 119 F4
　RHAM S60 .... 6 A1
　RHAM S60 .... 174 C3
　RHAM S60 .... 174 A4
　STKB/PEN S36 .... 105 K1
　WMB/DAR S73 .... 84 B6
Station St MEX/SWTN S64 .... 112 C4
Station Wy DIN S25 .... 177 J4
Staton Av MOS S20 .... 190 E8
Staton La DRON S18 .... 202 C6
The Statutes RHAM S60 .... 6 C4 ☐
Staunton Rd DONS/BSCR DN4 .... 93 F3
Staveley La ECK/KIL S21 .... 203 J8
　ECK/KIL S21 .... 204 C1
Staveley Rd SHEFS S8 .... 171 G8 ☐
Staveley St CONI DN12 .... 115 J4
Steade Rd ABRD S7 .... 171 F8
Steadfield Rd HOY S74 .... 108 C5 ☐
Steadfolds Cl MALT S66 .... 177 G2
Steadfolds La DIN S25 .... 177 G2
　MALT S66 .... 177 F1
Steadfolds Ri MALT S66 .... 177 G2
The Steadlands RAW S62 .... 111 G8 ☐
Stead La HOY S74 .... 108 C2
Stead St ECK/KIL S21 .... 204 B2
Steele St HOY S74 .... 108 B5
Steel Hl CHPT/GREN S35 .... 129 H1
Steel Rd ECC S11 .... 170 C7
Steel St RHAM S60 .... 154 D2
Steep La STKB/PEN S36 .... 78 C5
Steetley La WRKS S80 .... 208 E8
Steeton Rd HOY S74 .... 109 H1
Stemp St ECC S11 .... 8 C6 ☐
Stenton Rd SHEFS S8 .... 187 F1
Stephen Dr CHPT/GREN S35 .... 129 G1
　FUL S10 .... 169 K6
Stephen Hl FUL S10 .... 169 K6
Stephen Hill Rd FUL S10 .... 169 K6
Stephen La CHPT/GREN S35 .... 129 G1
Stepney St SHEFP/MNR S2 .... 9 F2 ☐
Stepping La CHPT/GREN S35 .... 129 G1
Sterndale Rd ABRD S7 .... 186 C4
Steven Cl CHPT/GREN S35 .... 130 A1
Steven Crs CHPT/GREN S35 .... 130 A1
Steven Pl CHPT/GREN S35 .... 130 A1
Stevenson Dr DOD/DAR S75 .... 54 D7
　RHAM/THRY S65 .... 156 A2
Stevenson Rd DARN/MH S9 .... 172 A1
　DONS/BSCR DN4 .... 116 C2
　WRKN S81 .... 211 F3 ☐
Stevenson Wy DARN/MH S9 .... 172 A1
Stevens Rd DONS/BSCR DN4 .... 4 B5 ☐
Steventon Rd RHAM/THRY S65 .... 135 F1
Stewart Cl WRKN S81 .... 196 C5 ☐
Stewart Rd ECC S11 .... 8 A4
　WRKN S81 .... 196 C5
Stewarts Rd RAW S62 .... 133 K1
Stewart St DON DN1 .... 4 C2
Sticking La MEX/SWTN S64 .... 86 D7
Stirling Av BWTY DN10 .... 142 B7
Stirling Cl HOY S74 .... 109 H1
　WRKN S81 .... 196 C7 ☐
Stirling Dr WRKN S81 .... 196 C7
Stirling St DON DN1 .... 4 C2
Stockarth Cl CHPT/GREN S35 .... 150 E1

Stockarth La CHPT/GREN S35 ...... 150 D3
Stockbridge Av BTLY DN5 .... 64 D8 ⓫
Stockbridge La AWLS/ASK DN6 ...... 38 B4
BTLY DN5 .... 65 F5
Stockil Rd DONS/BSCR DN4 .... 5 E4
Stockingate HEM/SK/SE WF9 .... 34 A6
Stock Rd SHEFP/MNR S2 .... 172 A6
Stocks Green Ct TOT/DORE S17 .... 199 G3
Stocks Green Dr TOT/DORE S17 .... 199 H3 ⓫
Stocks Hi CHPT/GREN S35 .... 150 B6
Stock's La DOD/DAR S75 .... 2 A3
RAW S62 .... 133 J2
STKB/PEN S36 .... 102 D3
Stockton Cl OWL S3 .... 9 E1 ⓫
Stockwell Av BTLY DN5 .... 64 D8 ⓫
Stockwell La AU/AST/KP S26 .... 192 B6
Stocthorn Gap CHPT/GREN S35 ...... 128 B5
Stoke St DARN/MH S9 .... 172 A2
Stoket La AU/AST/KP S26 .... 175 K2
Stokewell Rd DEARNE S63 .... 58 F8
Stoneacre Av HACK/IN S12 .... 189 K4
Stoneacre Cl HACK/IN S12 .... 189 K4 ⓫
Stoneacre Dr HACK/IN S12 .... 189 K5
Stoneacre Rd HACK/IN S12 .... 189 K4
Stonebridge La CUD/GR S72 .... 59 J5
Stonecliffe Cl SHEFP/MNR S2 .... 172 C6
Stonecliffe Dr STKB/PEN S36 .... 104 E8
Stonecliffe Pl SHEFP/MNR S2 .... 172 C6
Stonecliffe Rd SHEFP/MNR S2 ...... 172 C6
Stonedale Cl MOS S20 .... 190 B8 ⓫
Stone Delf FUL S10 .... 169 G6
Stone Font Gv DONS/BSCR DN4 ..... 92 E8
Stonegarth Cl CUD/GR S72 .... 57 J1 ⓫
Stonegate THNE DN8 .... 23 J8
Stonegravels Wy MOS S20 .... 204 A4
Stone Grey Rd NROS/TKH DN11 ..... 161 J1
RHAM/THRY S65 .... 157 J2
Stone Gv FUL S10 .... 8 A4
Stone Hl HTFD DN7 .... 43 H8
Stone Hill Dr DN7 .... 43 C8
Stonehill Ri BTLY DN5 .... 64 B7 ⓫
CUD/GR S72 .... 57 J1
STKB/PEN S36 .... 77 K6
Stone Hill Rd HTFD DN7 .... 43 C8
Stone La HAN/WDH S13 .... 189 J2
Stonelea Cl DOD/DAR S75 .... 53 J7 ⓫
Stone Lea Gv HEM/SK/SE WF9 ...... 35 F5 ⓫
Stoneleigh Cft BSLY S70 .... 2 C6 ⓫
Stoneley Cl HACK/IN S12 .... 188 C6
Stoneley Crs HACK/IN S12 .... 188 D6
Stoneley Dell HACK/IN S12 .... 188 D6
Stoneley Dr HACK/IN S12 .... 188 D6
Stonelow Gv DRON S18 .... 201 K5
Stonelow Rd DRON S18 .... 201 J5
Stonely Brook RHAM/THRY S65 .... 157 J2
Stone Moor Rd STKB/PEN S36 ...... 104 D8
Stone Park Cl MALT S66 .... 159 J2 ⓫
Stone Riding CONI DN12 .... 115 H6
Stone Rd DRON S18 .... 201 J3
Stone St BSLYN/ROY S71 .... 2 B1
MOS S20 .... 190 B8
Stonewood Cl FUL S10 .... 169 H5 ⓫
Stonewood Gv FUL S10 .... 169 H5
Stoney Bank Dr AU/AST/KP S26 .... 192 E5
Stoney Ga CHPT/GREN S35 .... 107 J7
Stoney La MALT S66 .... 160 B3
Stoney Royd BSLYN/ROY S71 .... 30 A6
Stoney Well La MALT S66 .... 160 B3
Stony Croft La AWLS/ASK DN6 ...... 37 H5
STKB/PEN S36 .... 103 H4
Stonyford Rd WMB/DAR S73 .... 84 C3
Stony Ga HOLM/MEL HD7 .... 47 H5
Stony La NROS/TKH DN11 .... 139 H5
ST/HB/BR S6 .... 149 J4
Stoops La DONS/BSCR DN4 .... 92 A8
Stoops Rd DONS/BSCR DN4 .... 92 C8
Stopes Rd ST/HB/BR S6 .... 168 E1 ⓫
Store St SHEFP/MNR S2 .... 9 E5
Storey's Ga WMB/DAR S73 .... 83 J4
Storey St MEX/SWTN S64 .... 112 B4
Storrs Br ST/HB/BR S6 .... 149 K6
Storrs Bridge La ST/HB/BR S6 ...... 149 K6
Storrs Carr ST/HB/BR S6 .... 149 J7
Storrs Hall Rd ST/HB/BR S6 .... 170 B1
Storrs La BTLY DN5 .... 39 F3
CHPT/GREN S35 .... 107 C5
ST/HB/BR S6 .... 150 A8
STKB/PEN S36 .... 79 F5
Storrs Mill La BSLYN/ROY S71 ...... 58 B5
Storrs Road Vw CUD/GR S72 .... 58 A3
Storth Av FUL S10 .... 169 J7
Storth La AU/AST/KP S26 .... 192 C4
AU/AST/KP S26 .... 192 E2
CHPT/GREN S35 .... 127 J4
FUL S10 .... 169 J6
Storthholme Ms FUL S10 .... 169 K6 ⓫
Stotfold Dr DEARNE S63 .... 60 B7
Stotfold Rd BTLY DN5 .... 60 C4
Stothard Rd FUL S10 .... 170 B3

Stottercliffe Rd STKB/PEN S36 ..... 77 J4
Stour La ST/HB/BR S6 .... 150 E5
Stovin Cl DARN/MH S9 .... 172 D1
Stovin Dr DARN/MH S9 .... 172 D1
Stow Bridge La RHAM S60 .... 175 J1
Stowe Av ABRD S7 .... 186 C3
Stradbroke Av HAN/WDH S13 ...... 173 F8
Stradbroke Cl HAN/WDH S13 .... 173 G8
Stradbroke Crs HAN/WDH S13 ..... 173 G8
Stradbroke Dr HAN/WDH S13 ...... 173 G8
Stradbroke Pl HAN/WDH S13 ...... 173 F8
Stradbroke Rd HAN/WDH S13 ...... 173 F8
Stradbroke Wy HAN/WDH S13 .... 173 G8
Strafford Cl BSLY S70 .... 82 A1
HOY S74 .... 109 H1
Strafford Pl KIMB S61 .... 131 F2
Strafford Rd KIMB S61 .... 132 B5
Strafford St DEARNE S63 .... 28 B7
Strafford Wk DOD/DAR S75 .... 80 E1
Straight La AWLS/ASK DN6 .... 36 C3
DEARNE S63 .... 86 D2
Stratford Rd FUL S10 .... 169 H6
Stratford Wy MALT S66 .... 157 K3
Strathavon Rd WRKN S81 .... 196 D1
Strathmore Dr WRKN S81 .... 196 D1
Strathmore Gdns
HEM/SK/SE WF9 .... 35 G3 ⓫
Strathmore Gv DEARNE S63 .... 111 J1
Strathtay Rd ECC S11 .... 170 B8
Strauss Crs MALT S66 .... 159 J5
Strawberry Av SHEFN S5 .... 152 C1
Strawberry Gdns BSLYN/ROY S71 . 30 D5
Strawberry Lee La TOT/DORE S17 . 199 F7 ⓫
Straw La ST/HB/BR S6 .... 8 B1 ⓫
Streatfield Crs NROS/TKH DN11 .... 118 D7
Street Farm Cl AU/AST/KP S26 ..... 206 E1
Streetfield Crs MOS S20 .... 204 B1 ⓫
Streetfields MOS S20 .... 204 C1
Street La BTLY DN5 .... 62 A5
RAW S62 .... 110 B5
Strelley Av SHEFS S8 .... 186 E6
Strelley Rd BSLYN/ROY S71 .... 29 K7 ⓫
SHEFS S8 .... 186 D6
Stretton Cl DONS/BSCR DN4 .... 93 F7
Stretton Rd BSLYN/ROY S71 .... 56 B2
ECC S11 .... 170 C8
Strines Moor Rd HOLM/MEL HD7 .. 48 B8
Stringers Cft RHAM S60 .... 156 C6 ⓫
Stripe Rd BWTY DN10 .... 141 F5
Struan Rd ECC S11 .... 186 C2
Strutt Rd OWL S3 .... 152 B8
Stuart Gv CHPT/GREN S35 .... 130 B3
Stuart La CHPT/GREN S35 .... 130 C3
Stuart St DEARNE S63 .... 60 D7
Stubbin Cl RAW S62 .... 111 G8
Stubbin Fold HOLM/MEL HD7 ...... 47 F4
Stubbing Ct RAW S62 .... 111 G8
Stubbing House La
CHPT/GREN S35 .... 129 F8
Stubbing La CHPT/GREN S35 .... 150 A3 ⓫
WRKS S80 .... 210 B4
Stubbin La HOLM/MEL HD7 .... 47 H4
KBTN HD8 .... 51 J1
RAW S62 .... 111 G7
SHEFN S5 .... 152 D3
Stubbin Rd RAW S62 .... 110 E8
Stubbins Hl CONI DN12 .... 115 K6
Stubbs Br AWLS/ASK DN6 .... 36 B5
Stubbs Crs KIMB S61 .... 132 C6
Stubbs La AWLS/ASK DN6 .... 18 A2
Stubbs Rd PONT WF8 .... 17 H2
WMB/DAR S73 .... 83 K5
Stubley Cl DRON S18 .... 200 D5
Stubley Crs DRON S18 .... 200 D5
Stubley Dr DRON S18 .... 200 E5
Stubley Hollow DRON S18 .... 200 D5
Stubley La DRON S18 .... 200 D5
Stubley Pl DRON S18 .... 200 E5
Studfield Crs ST/HB/BR S6 .... 150 E7
Studfield Dr ST/HB/BR S6 .... 150 E7
Studfield Gv ST/HB/BR S6 .... 150 E7
Studfield Hl ST/HB/BR S6 .... 150 E6
Studfield Ri ST/HB/BR S6 .... 150 E6
Studfield Rd ST/HB/BR S6 .... 150 E7
Studley Ct DARN/MH S9 .... 172 E3 ⓫
Studmoor Rd KIMB S61 .... 132 A5
Stump Cross Gdns DEARNE S63 ... 86 A5
Stump Cross Rd DEARNE S63 ...... 111 H2
Stumperlowe Av FUL S10 .... 169 H6
Stumperlowe Cl FUL S10 .... 169 J7 ⓫
Stumperlowe Crescent Rd
FUL S10 .... 169 H7
Stumperlowe Hall Cha FUL S10 .... 169 H6 ⓫
Stumperlowe Hall Rd FUL S10 ..... 169 H8
Stumperlowe La FUL S10 .... 169 H7
Stumperlowe Park Rd FUL S10 ..... 169 H7
Stumperlowe Vw FUL S10 .... 169 H7
Stupton Rd DARN/MH S9 .... 153 H5
Sturge Cft SHEFP/MNR S2 .... 187 H1 ⓫
Sturton Cl DONS/BSCR DN4 .... 118 B1
Sturton Cft RHAM/THRY S65 .... 134 D6
Sturton Rd ATT S4 .... 152 D7
Stygate La AWLS/ASK DN6 .... 17 K5
Styrrup La NROS/TKH DN11 .... 162 C5
Styrrup Rd NROS/TKH DN11 .... 162 C5
Sudbury Dr AU/AST/KP S26 .... 175 J8
Sudbury St OWL S3 .... 8 C1 ⓫

Sude Hl HOLM/MEL HD7 .... 48 D1
Sude Hill Ter HOLM/MEL HD7 ...... 48 E1 ⓫
Suffolk Av NROS/TKH DN11 .... 163 J3
Suffolk Cl DIN S25 .... 194 A1 ⓫
Suffolk Gv NROS/TKH DN11 .... 163 J3
Suffolk Rd DONS/BSCR DN4 .... 116 E1 ⓫
NROS/TKH DN11 .... 163 H3
SHEFP/MNR S2 .... 9 E4
Sugworth Rd ST/HB/BR S6 .... 147 H8
Sulby Gv BSLY S70 .... 82 E1
Sullivan Gv HEM/SK/SE WF9 .... 34 A6
Summerdale Rd CUD/GR S72 .... 57 H2
Summerfield RHAM/THRY S65 ..... 7 D4 ⓫
Summerfield Rd DRON S18 .... 201 H4
Summerfields Dr EPW DN9 .... 121 F1
Summerfield St FUL S10 .... 8 B5
Summer La BSLY S70 .... 2 A3
BSLYN/ROY S71 .... 30 C3
KBTN HD8 .... 26 A1
TOT/DORE S17 .... 199 G3
WMB/DAR S73 .... 83 H5
Summerley Lower Rd DRON S18 ... 202 A5
Summerley Rd DRON S18 .... 202 A5
Summer Rd BSLYN/ROY S71 .... 30 C3 ⓫
Summer St BSLY S70 .... 2 A5 ⓫
OWL S3 .... 8 A4
Summervale HOLM/MEL HD7 ...... 47 K1 ⓫
Summerwood La DRON S18 .... 201 F4
Summerwood Pl DRON S18 .... 201 F5
Sumner Rd RHAM/THRY S65 .... 7 E3
Sunderland Pl NROS/TKH DN11 .... 140 A8
Sunderland St ECC S11 .... 8 B5 ⓫
NROS/TKH DN11 .... 139 K8
Sunderland Ter BSLY S70 .... 3 D5 ⓫
Sundew Cft CHPT/GREN S35 .... 107 J7 ⓫
Sundew Gdns CHPT/GREN S35 ..... 107 J6
Sundown Pl HAN/WDH S13 .... 173 H7
Sundown Rd HAN/WDH S13 .... 173 H7
Sunfield Av WRKN S81 .... 210 E3
Sunningdale Av DOD/DAR S75 ..... 29 F6 ⓫
Sunningdale Cl ARMTH DN3 .... 119 G1 ⓫
MEX/SWTN S64 .... 57 J6
Sunningdale Dr CUD/GR S72 .... 31 K6
Sunningdale Mt ECC S11 .... 186 B2
Sunningdale Rd DIN S25 .... 178 B8
HTFD DN7 .... 69 G1
WHHL DN2 .... 91 K2 ⓫
Sunny Av HEM/SK/SE WF9 .... 35 G5
Sunny Bank FUL S10 .... 8 B5
HOY S74 .... 83 G8
Sunnybank KBTN HD8 .... 51 C2
Sunny Bank WRKN S81 .... 210 D3
Sunnybank Crs RHAM S60 .... 155 F7 ⓫
Sunny Bank Dr CUD/GR S72 .... 57 J3
Sunny Bank Ri HOY S74 .... 109 H1 ⓫
Sunny Bank Rd DOD/DAR S75 ...... 53 J7
STKB/PEN S36 .... 127 F1
Sunny Bar DON DN1 .... 5 D3 ⓫
Sunnybrook Cl HOY S74 .... 109 F5
Sunnymead ABTN HD8 .... 26 A5
Sunnymede WRKN S81 .... 210 E1 ⓫
Sunnymede Av AWLS/ASK DN6 .... 18 E2
Sunnymede Crs AWLS/ASK DN6 ... 18 E6
Sunnymede Ter AWLS/ASK DN6 ... 18 E7
Sunnyside ARMTH DN3 .... 66 D5
ARMTH DN3 .... 93 K7 ⓫
WRKN S81 .... 210 D1
WRKS S80 .... 208 C8
Sunnyside Cl DIN S25 .... 194 A1
Sunnyvale Av TOT/DORE S17 ...... 199 H3
Sunnyvale Mt HEM/SK/SE WF9 .... 34 D4
Sunnyvale Rd TOT/DORE S17 ...... 199 H3
Surbiton St DARN/MH S9 .... 153 J7
Surrey Cl BSLY S70 .... 2 C6
Surrey La SHEF S1 .... 9 E4
Surrey St DONS/BSCR DN4 .... 90 E8
SHEF S1 .... 9 D3
Surtees Cl MALT S66 .... 157 F8 ⓫
Sussex Rd ATT S4 .... 9 F1
CHPT/GREN S35 .... 130 B2
Sussex St ATT S4 .... 9 F1
Suthard Cross Rd FUL S10 .... 170 B3 ⓫
Sutherland Cl WRKN S81 .... 180 D7 ⓫
Sutherland Rd ATT S4 .... 171 J1
Sutherland St ATT S4 .... 171 J2
Sutton Av BSLYN/ROY S71 .... 30 A7
Sutton Rd ARMTH DN3 .... 66 E2
AWLS/ASK DN6 .... 17 K7
AWLS/ASK DN6 .... 38 B2
Sutton St OWL S3 .... 8 B3
Suzanne Crs HEM/SK/SE WF9 ...... 34 D4
Swaith Av BTLY DN5 .... 64 C8
Swaithedale BSLY S70 .... 82 D2
Swaithe Vw BSLY S70 .... 82 E2
Swale Gdns DEARNE S63 .... 86 C5
Swaledale WRKN S81 .... 196 E6
Swaledale Rd ABRD S7 .... 186 D2
Swale Dr CHPT/GREN S35 .... 129 K2
Swale Gdns DARN/MH S9 .... 172 E3 ⓫
Swale Rd KIMB S61 .... 132 D4
Swallow Cl BSLY S70 .... 82 A7
DOD/DAR S75 .... 28 C7
Swallow Ct NROS/TKH DN11 .... 119 F6
Swallow Gv WRKN S81 .... 196 B8 ⓫
Swallow Hill Rd DOD/DAR S75 ..... 29 F8
Swallow La AU/AST/KP S26 .... 191 J1
Swallow Wood Ct HAN/WDH S13 . 189 J4 ⓫
Swamp Wk ST/HB/BR S6 .... 151 J8
Swan Bank Ct HOLM/MEL HD7 .... 47 K3

Swan Bank La *HOLM/MEL* HD7 ...... **47** K3
Swanbourne Pl *SHEFN* S5 .... **152** D3 🔳
Swanbourne Rd *SHEFN* S5 .... **152** D2
Swan Ct *WRKN* S81 .... **195** K8
Swanee Rd *BSLY* S70 .... **82** C1
Swannington Cl *DONS/BSCR* DN4 ...... **93** F8
Swan Rd *AU/AST/KP* S26 .... **191** J1
Swan St *BTLY* DN5 .... **64** E6 🔳
  BWTY DN10 .... **164** B1
  RHAM S60 .... **6** C5
Swan Syke Dr *AWLS/ASK* DN6 ...... **18** B4
Swarcliffe Rd *DARN/MH* S9 ...... **172** C2
Sweep La *HOLM/MEL* HD7 .... **48** A4
Sweyn Cft *BSLY* S70 .... **82** B2 🔳🔳
Swifte Ri *KIMB* S61 .... **131** H1
Swift Cl *DOD/DAR* S75 .... **2** A3
Swift Rd *CHPT/GREN* S35 .... **129** J7
Swift St *DOD/DAR* S75 .... **2** A3
Swift Wy *SHEFP/MNR* S2 .... **172** A5
Swinburne Av *AWLS/ASK* DN6 ...... **63** H7
  DONS/BSCR DN4 .... **116** E1 🔳🔳
Swinburne Cl *ARMTH* DN3 .... **40** E7 🔳
Swinburne Pl *RHAM/THRY* S65 ...... **156** A2
Swinburne Rd *RHAM/THRY* S65 ...... **156** A2
Swinnock La *CHPT/GREN* S35 ...... **127** K5
Swinnow Rd *NROS/TKH* DN11 ...... **163** H3
Swinston Hill Rd *DON* S5 .... **178** C7
Swinton Rd *MEX/SWTN* S64 ...... **112** E3
Swinton St *OWL* S3 .... **9** D1
Swithen Hl *DOD/DAR* S75 .... **28** A3
Sycamore Av *ARMTH* DN3 .... **67** H8
  AU/AST/KP S26 .... **192** B5
  CUD/GR S72 .... **31** J8 🔳
  CUD/GR S72 .... **58** E2 🔳
  DRON S18 .... **201** G4
  MALT S66 .... **157** H2
Sycamore Crs *BWTY* DN10 .... **142** A8
  DEARNE S63 .... **111** J2 🔳
Sycamore Dr *BSLY/ROY* S71 ...... **30** B4
  ECK/KIL S21 .... **205** G2
  EPW DN9 .... **120** B3
Sycamore Farm Cl *MALT* S66 ...... **157** G4 🔳
Sycamore Gv *CONI* DN12 .... **114** B6 🔳
  DONS/BSCR DN4 .... **92** E7
Sycamore House Rd *SHEFN* S5 ...... **153** G1
Sycamore Rd *ARMTH* DN3 .... **40** D8
  CHPT/GREN S35 .... **130** C7
  HEM/SK/SE WF9 .... **33** F1
  MEX/SWTN S64 .... **112** D2
  RHAM/THRY S65 .... **134** A6
  STKB/PEN S36 .... **104** D7
  WRKN S81 .... **180** C8
The Sycamores *BTLY* DN5 .... **64** A6 🔳
Sycamore Vw *BTLY* DN5 .... **90** A6
Sycamore Wk *STKB/PEN* S36 ...... **78** A4 🔳
Syday La *ECK/KIL* S21 .... **205** H6
Sydney Rd *ST/HB/BR* S6 .... **8** A2
Syke Cft *BSLYN/ROY* S71 .... **30** D2
Sykehouse La *ST/HB/BR* S6 ...... **149** G8
Sykehouse Rd *GLE* DN14 .... **12** D8
Sykes Av *DOD/DAR* S75 .... **2** A3
Sykes Ct *MEX/SWTN* S64 .... **112** C6
Sykes St *BSLY* S70 .... **2** A6
Sylvan Cl *MALT* S66 .... **159** J1
Sylvester Av *DONS/BSCR* DN4 ...... **4** C5
Sylvester Gdns *SHEF* S1 .... **9** D4
Sylvester St *SHEF* S1 .... **9** D5
Sylvestria Ct *NROS/TKH* DN11 ...... **119** F6
Sylvia Cl *HAN/WDH* S13 .... **174** B8 🔳
Symes Gdns *DONS/BSCR* DN4 ...... **92** E6
Symonds Av *RAW* S62 .... **111** F7
Symons Crs *SHEFN* S5 .... **152** A2

Tadcaster Cl *CONI* DN12 .... **113** K5
Tadcaster Crs *SHEFS* S8 .... **187** F3
Tadcaster Rd *SHEFS* S8 .... **187** F3
Tadcaster Wy *SHEFS* S8 .... **187** F3 🔳
Tait Av *CONI* DN12 .... **115** J7
Talbot Av *ARMTH* DN3 .... **40** E8
Talbot Crs *SHEFP/MNR* S2 .... **9** F4 🔳
Talbot Gdns *SHEFP/MNR* S2 ...... **9** F4 🔳
Talbot Pl *SHEFP/MNR* S2 .... **9** F4 🔳
Talbot Rd *MEX/SWTN* S64 .... **112** E4
  NROS/TKH DN11 .... **163** G3
  SHEFP/MNR S2 .... **9** F5 🔳
  STKB/PEN S36 .... **77** K4
  WRKS S80 .... **210** E5
Talbot St *SHEFP/MNR* S2 .... **9** F4
Talmont Rd *ECC* S11 .... **186** B1
Tamar Cl *DOD/DAR* S75 .... **54** D2
Tanfield Cl *BSLYN/ROY* S71 ...... **30** B3
Tanfield Rd *ST/HB/BR* S6 .... **151** J6
Tanfield Wy *MALT* S66 .... **157** G3
Tankersley La *HOY* S74 .... **108** A3
Tank Rw *BSLY* S70 .... **56** E6
Tannery Cl *HAN/WDH* S13 ...... **189** K1
Tannery St *HAN/WDH* S13 ...... **189** K1
Tan Pit Cl *BTLY* DN5 .... **60** C3
Tanpit La *AWLS/ASK* DN6 .... **18** A2
Tan Pit La *BTLY* DN5 .... **60** C3
Tansley Dr *DARN/MH* S9 .... **153** J3

Tansley St *DARN/MH* S9 .... **153** J3
Tanyard Cft *CUD/GR* S72 .... **32** D4 🔳
Taplin Rd *ST/HB/BR* S6 .... **151** G7
Tapton Bank *FUL* S10 .... **170** A5 🔳
Tapton Crescent Rd *FUL* S10 ...... **170** B5
Tapton Hill Rd *FUL* S10 .... **170** A4
Tapton House Rd *FUL* S10 .... **170** B5
Tapton Ms *FUL* S10 .... **170** B4
Tapton Park Rd *FUL* S10 .... **169** K6
Taptonville Crs *FUL* S10 .... **170** C5 🔳
Taptonville Rd *FUL* S10 .... **170** C4
Tarleton Cl *ARMTH* DN3 .... **67** F3 🔳
Tasker Rd *FUL* S10 .... **170** B4
Tasman Gv *MALT* S66 .... **159** F1
Tatenhill Gdns *DONS/BSCR* DN4 ...... **119** F1
Taunton Av *DARN/MH* S9 .... **153** J4
Taunton Gdns *MEX/SWTN* S64 ...... **113** H1
Taunton Gv *DARN/MH* S9 .... **153** J4 🔳
Taverner Cl *CHPT/GREN* S35 ...... **107** J6
Taverner Cft *CHPT/GREN* S35 ...... **107** K7 🔳
Taverner Wy *CHPT/GREN* S35 ...... **107** K7
Tavistock Rd *SHEFS* S8 .... **187** F1
Tavy Cl *DOD/DAR* S75 .... **54** D2 🔳
Tay Cl *DRON* S18 .... **200** D5
Taylor Crs *CUD/GR* S72 .... **58** D2
  WRKN S81 .... **195** G4
Taylor Dr *WRKN* S81 .... **195** G4
Taylor Rw *BSLY* S70 .... **2** C5 🔳🔳
Taylors Cl *RAW* S62 .... **133** H5
Taylors La *RAW* S62 .... **133** H4
Taylor St *CONI* DN12 .... **114** E5
T Benedict Ct *SHEFP/MNR* S2 ...... **171** K7 🔳
Teague Pl *WRKS* S80 .... **210** B4
Teal Ct *WRKN* S81 .... **196** B8
Teapot Cnr *BTLY* DN5 .... **90** C3
Teasdale Rd *HACK/IN* S12 .... **189** H6
  KIMB S61 .... **132** C4
Teeside Cl *BTLY* DN5 .... **90** A2
Telford Rd *BTLY* DN5 .... **90** C2
Telson Cl *MEX/SWTN* S64 .... **111** K4
Temperance St *MEX/SWTN* S64 ...... **112** C4 🔳
Tempest Av *WMB/DAR* S73 ...... **58** D8
Tempest Rd *HEM/SK/SE* WF9 ...... **34** B3
Templar Cl *MALT* S66 .... **176** D1 🔳
Temple Crs *MALT* S66 .... **157** J3
Temple Gdns *DONS/BSCR* DN4 ...... **92** E8
Temple Rd *RHAM* S60 .... **154** C4
Templestowe Ga *CONI* DN12 ...... **115** F5 🔳
Ten Acre Rd *KIMB* S61 .... **132** C7
Tenby Gdns *DONS/BSCR* DN4 ...... **90** D8
Tenby Gv *WRKS* S80 .... **210** E5
Tennyson Av *ARMTH* DN3 .... **93** G1
  AWLS/ASK DN6 .... **17** K6
  BTLY DN5 .... **90** C3
  MEX/SWTN S64 .... **113** G4
  THNE DN8 .... **23** K8 🔳
Tennyson Cl *DIN* S25 .... **178** C7 🔳
  STKB/PEN S36 .... **78** A5
Tennyson Wk *DARN/MH* S9 ...... **211** F3
Tennyson Ri *DEARNE* S63 .... **85** F8
Tennyson Rd *BTLY* DN5 .... **64** E6
  MALT S66 .... **159** H8
  RHAM/THRY S65 .... **156** A1
  ST/HB/BR S6 .... **170** D1
Ten Pound Wk *DONS/BSCR* DN4 ...... **5** H2
Tenter Balk La *AWLS/ASK* DN6 ...... **63** H7
Tenter Cl *SHEFN* S5 .... **153** G4 🔳
Tenter Hl *HOLM/MEL* HD7 .... **48** E4
Tenter La *DONS/BSCR* DN4 .... **115** K1
  STKB/PEN S36 .... **104** D1
Tenter Rd *DONS/BSCR* DN4 .... **115** K1
Tenters Gn *BSLY* S70 .... **82** A3
Tenter St *KIMB* S61 .... **6** B3
  SHEF S1 .... **9** D2
Terminus Rd *ABRD* S7 .... **186** C4 🔳
Terrace Rd *RAW* S62 .... **133** J5
Terrey Rd *TOT/DORE* S17 .... **199** J2
Terry St *DARN/MH* S9 .... **153** J8
Tetney Rd *FUL* S10 .... **169** K6
Tewitt Rd *BTLY* DN5 .... **64** D3 🔳
Teynham Dr *SHEFN* S5 .... **152** A5
Teynham Rd *SHEFN* S5 .... **151** K5
Thackeray Av *RAW* S62 .... **112** A8
Thackeray Cl *WRKN* S81 .... **211** F5
Thames St *RHAM* S60 .... **6** B3
Thealby Gdns *DONS/BSCR* DN4 ...... **92** B8
Thellusson Av *BTLY* DN5 .... **89** K1
Theobald Av *DONS/BSCR* DN4 ...... **5** F4
Theobald Cl *DONS/BSCR* DN4 ...... **5** E5 🔳
Theodore Rd *AWLS/ASK* DN6 ...... **18** B8
Thicket Dr *MALT* S66 .... **159** J1
Thickett La *STKB/PEN* S36 .... **78** B7
Thickwoods La *STKB/PEN* S36 ...... **102** C5
Thievesdale Av *WRKN* S81 ...... **196** D8 🔳
Thievesdale Cl *WRKN* S81 ...... **196** E8
Thievesdale La *WRKN* S81 ...... **196** E8
  WRKN S81 .... **197** H6
Third Av *AWLS/ASK* DN6 .... **63** K3
Thirlmere Dr *DIN* S25 .... **194** B1
  DRON S18 .... **201** G5
Thirlmere Gdns *ARMTH* DN3 ...... **66** E4 🔳
Thirlmere Rd *BSLYN/ROY* S71 ...... **3** D4 🔳
  SHEFS S8 .... **186** E2 🔳
Thirlwall Av *CONI* DN12 .... **114** B5
Thirlwell Rd *SHEFS* S8 .... **187** G1
Thirsk Cl *CONI* DN12 .... **113** K5
Thomas Rd *HTFD* DN7 .... **42** A4
Thomas St *AU/AST/KP* S26 ...... **192** D5

BSLY S70 .... **2** B5
BSLY S70 .... **82** B3 🔳
CONI DN12 .... **115** J6
HEM/SK/SE WF9 .... **33** H1
MEX/SWTN S64 .... **112** D6
MEX/SWTN S64 .... **112** C6
SHEF S1 .... **8** C4
WMB/DAR S73 .... **84** E2 🔳
Thompson Av *CONI* DN12 .... **115** H5
  NROS/TKH DN11 .... **162** E2
Thompson Cl *MALT* S66 .... **137** F8
  RAW S62 .... **111** F7 🔳
Thompson Dr *HTFD* DN7 .... **42** C8 🔳
  MEX/SWTN S64 .... **112** B6
Thompson Gdns
  CHPT/GREN S35 .... **107** H7 🔳
Thompson Hl *CHPT/GREN* S35 ...... **107** H8
Thompson House Gn
  ST/HB/BR S6 .... **147** J3
Thompson Nook *HTFD* DN7 ...... **42** C7 🔳
Thompson Rd *FUL* S10 .... **8** A5
  WMB/DAR S73 .... **84** A5
Thompson Ter *AWLS/ASK* DN6 ...... **18** E7
Thomson Av *DONS/BSCR* DN4 ...... **90** C6
Thomson Cl *DEARNE* S63 .... **111** J9
Thoresby Av *BSLYN/ROY* S71 ...... **3** E1
  DONS/BSCR DN4 .... **5** F5
Thoresby Cl *AU/AST/KP* S26 ...... **175** K8
Thoresby Rd *ST/HB/BR* S6 ...... **151** H6
Thorn Bank *EPW* DN9 .... **97** F7
Thornborough Cl
  SHEFP/MNR S2 .... **171** J8 🔳
Thornborough Pl
  SHEFP/MNR S2 .... **171** J8 🔳
Thornborough Rd
  SHEFP/MNR S2 .... **171** H6
Thornbridge Av *HACK/IN* S12 ...... **189** F4
Thornbridge Cl *HACK/IN* S12 ...... **189** F4
Thornbridge Crs *HACK/IN* S12 ...... **189** G4
Thornbridge Dr *HACK/IN* S12 ...... **189** G4
Thornbridge Gv *HACK/IN* S12 ...... **189** F4 🔳
Thornbridge La *HACK/IN* S12 ...... **189** G4 🔳
Thornbridge Pl *HACK/IN* S12 ...... **189** F4 🔳
Thornbridge Ri *HACK/IN* S12 ...... **189** G4
Thornbridge Rd *HACK/IN* S12 ...... **189** G4
Thornbridge Wy *HACK/IN* S12 ...... **189** G4
Thornbrook Cl *CHPT/GREN* S35 ...... **130** C7
Thornbrook Gdns
  CHPT/GREN S35 .... **130** B7
Thornbrook Ms
  CHPT/GREN S35 .... **130** B1 🔳
Thornbury Hill La *MALT* S66 ...... **161** G7
Thorncliffe Gdns *EPW* DN9 ...... **94** B8 🔳
Thorncliffe La *CHPT/GREN* S35 ...... **108** A1
Thorndale Ri *RHAM* S60 .... **155** C7 🔳
Thorne & Dikesmarsh Rd
  THNE DN8 .... **23** H4
Thorne Cl *BSLYN/ROY* S71 ...... **29** K8
Thorne End Rd *DOD/DAR* S75 ...... **29** G2
Thornely Av *DOD/DAR* S75 ...... **54** E2
Thorne Rd *ABRD* S7 .... **186** E2 🔳
  ARMTH DN3 .... **66** D6
  BWTY DN10 .... **142** C2
  DON DN1 .... **5** E1
  EPW DN9 .... **121** F7
  HTFD DN7 .... **41** K3
  HTFD DN7 .... **42** A3
Thorne Round Wk *HTFD* DN7 ...... **22** C1
Thorne Waste Drain Rd *THNE* DN8 ...... **24** E1
Thorn Garth *BTLY* DN5 .... **90** D1
Thornham Cl *ARMTH* DN3 .... **93** G2 🔳
Thornham La *ARMTH* DN3 .... **94** A1
Thornhill Av *RHAM* S60 .... **154** E8
  WHHL DN2 .... **92** A4
Thornhill Edge *RHAM* S60 .... **6** B3 🔳
Thornhill Pl *DEARNE* S63 .... **111** H1 🔳
Thornhill Rd *NROS/TKH* DN11 ...... **162** C7
Thorn House La *CHPT/GREN* S35 ...... **127** J7
Thorn La *WHHL* DN2 .... **66** C7
Thornlea Ct *CONI* DN12 .... **115** H6
Thornley Sq *DEARNE* S63 .... **60** A7 🔳
Thorn Rd *MEX/SWTN* S64 .... **112** C6
Thornseat Rd *ST/HB/BR* S6 ...... **147** H1
Thornsett Gdns *TOT/DORE* S17 ...... **185** K6 🔳
Thornsett Rd *ECC* S11 .... **8** B3
Thornton Cl *HEM/SK/SE* WF9 ...... **33** G2 🔳
Thornton Dl *WRKN* S81 .... **197** F8 🔳
Thorntondale Rd *BTLY* DN5 ...... **90** A4
Thornton Pl *DRON* S18 .... **200** C6 🔳
Thornton Rd *BSLY* S70 .... **3** E1
Thornton St *KIMB* S61 .... **154** B0
Thornton Ter *BSLY* S70 .... **3** F6
Thorntree Cl *KIMB* S61 .... **131** G3
Thorntree La *DOD/DAR* S75 ...... **2** A2 🔳
  GLE DN14 .... **10** D6
Thorntree Rd *KIMB* S61 .... **131** G3
Thornwell Gv *CUD/GR* S72 ...... **57** H1 🔳
Thornwell La *KIMB* S61 .... **131** G3
Thorogate *RAW* S62 .... **111** J2
Thorold Pl *ARMTH* DN3 .... **66** E6
Thorp Av *HOLM/MEL* HD7 .... **48** A3
Thorpe Cl *SHEFP/MNR* S2 .... **9** J2
Thorpe Av *DRON* S18 .... **201** J3
Thorpe Bank *ARMTH* DN3 .... **40** C5
Thorpe Dr *MOS* S20 .... **190** C5
Thorpefield Cl *KIMB* S61 .... **131** H1
Thorpefield Dr *KIMB* S61 .... **131** G2
Thorpe Grange La *BTLY* DN5 ...... **39** G8
Thorpe Gn *MOS* S20 .... **190** B5

Thorpehall Rd *ARMTH* DN3 .... 67 F4
Thorpe House Av *SHEFS* S8 .... 187 H3
Thorpe House Ri *SHEFS* S8 .... 187 G3
Thorpe House Rd *SHEFS* S8 .... 187 G3
Thorpe la *AWLS/ASK* DN6 .... 39 K5
  BTLY DN5 .... 89 J6
  WRKS S80 .... 208 E1
Thorpe Mere Rd *BTLY* DN5 .... 39 K7
Thorpe Mere Vw *BTLY* DN5 .... 39 K7
Thorpe Rd *AU/AST/KP* S26 .... 193 F6
  BWTY DN10 .... 165 H7
Thorpe St *KIMB* S61 .... 131 H7
Three Hills La *RHAM/THRY* S65 .... 134 E4 2
Three Nooks La *CUD/GR* S72 .... 31 J6
Threshfield Wy *HACK/IN* S12 .... 189 K4 5
Thrislington Sq *THNE* DN8 .... 24 A3 8
Thrumpton Rd *BSLYN/ROY* S71 ...... 30 A6 5
Thrush Av *RHAM* S60 .... 155 G7 10
Thrush St *ST/HB/BR* S6 .... 170 B1
Thruxton Cl *CUD/GR* S72 .... 31 K7 2
Thrybergh Ct *CONI* DN12 .... 114 C4 1
Thrybergh Hall Rd *RAW* S62 .... 134 A1
Thrybergh La *RHAM/THRY* S65 .... 135 G4
Thundercliffe Rd *KIMB* S61 .... 131 J8
Thurgoland Bank *STKB/PEN* S36 .... 79 G7
Thurgoland Hall La
  GLE DN14 .... 79 J8
Thuristone Rd *STKB/PEN* S36 .... 77 J3
Thurnscoe Bridge Rd *DEARNE* S63 .... 86 C1
Thurnscoe La *CUD/GR* S72 .... 59 J6
Thurnscoe Rd *DEARNE* S63 .... 86 B5
Thurstan Av *SHEFS* S8 .... 186 E7
Tiber Vw *RHAM* S60 .... 155 F5 3
Tickhill Back La *NROS/TKH* DN11 .... 138 C5
Tickhill Rd *BWTY* DN10 .... 142 A8
  DONS/BSCR DN4 .... 116 D1
  MALT S66 .... 159 J3
  NROS/TKH DN11 .... 162 D2
Tickhill Sq *CONI* DN12 .... 114 A4
Tickhill St *CONI* DN12 .... 114 A3
Tickhill Wy *NROS/TKH* DN11 .... 119 C7
Tideswell Rd *SHEFN* S5 .... 152 D4
Tideworth Hague La *GLE* DN14 .... 21 K1
Tiercel Ms *DIN* S25 .... 178 A6
Tilford Rd *HAN/WDH* S13 .... 190 A1
Tillotson Cl *SHEFS* S8 .... 187 G1 13
Tillotson Ri *SHEFS* S8 .... 187 G1 14
Tiltshills La *BTLY* DN5 .... 38 D8
Tilts La *BTLY* DN5 .... 39 F8
  BTLY DN5 .... 39 F8
Timothy Wood Av *BSLY* S70 .... 82 A7
Tingle Bridge Av *WMB/DAR* S73 ..... 83 K8
Tingle Bridge Crs *WMB/DAR* S73 .... 83 K8 8
Tingle Bridge La *WMB/DAR* S73 ..... 83 K8
Tingle Cl *WMB/DAR* S73 .... 83 K8
Tinker Bottom *ST/HB/BR* S6 .... 148 C5
Tinker La *HOY* S74 .... 108 B1
  ST/HB/BR S6 .... 170 B2
Tinker Rd *RAW* S62 .... 133 K1
Tinker's HI *WRKN* S81 .... 197 J2
Tinsley Park Cl *DARN/MH* S9 .... 153 K8
Tinsley Park Rd *DARN/MH* S9 .... 153 K8
Tinsley Rd *HOY* S74 .... 82 E8
Tippit la *CUD/GR* S72 .... 57 K2
Tipton St *DARN/MH* S9 .... 153 H5
Tithe Barn Av *HAN/WDH* S13 .... 173 K8
Tithe Barn Cl *HAN/WDH* S13 .... 174 A8
Tithe Barn Ct *MEX/SWTN* S64 .... 86 E7 1
Tithe Barn La *HAN/WDH* S13 .... 190 A1
  THNE DN8 .... 23 K8 1
Tithe Barn Wy *HAN/WDH* S13 ...... 173 K8
Tithe Laithe *HOY* S74 .... 109 F1 1
Titterton Cl *DARN/MH* S9 .... 172 C1
Titterton St *DARN/MH* S9 .... 172 C1 2
Tiverton Cl *MEX/SWTN* S64 .... 112 C5 2
Tivy Dl *DOD/DAR* S75 .... 53 H3
Tivy Dale Cl *DOD/DAR* S75 .... 53 H3
Tivydale Dr *DOD/DAR* S75 .... 28 D8
Tivy Dale Dr *DOD/DAR* S75 .... 53 H3
Toadham La *GLE* DN14 .... 10 C6
Toad La *MALT* S66 .... 176 D2
Toby Wood La *KBTN* H08 .... 50 E2
Tockwith Rd *DARN/MH* S9 .... 172 D2 1
Todmorden Cl *CONI* DN12 .... 113 K4
Todwick Ct *AU/AST/KP* S26 .... 193 K4
Todwick Rd *AU/AST/KP* S26 .... 177 G7
  SHEFS S8 .... 186 E3
Toecroft La *BTLY* DN5 .... 89 G6
Tofield Rd *NROS/TKH* DN11 .... 116 D7
Tofts La *ST/HB/BR* S6 .... 169 G3
  STKB/PEN S36 .... 104 C2
Toftstead *ARMTH* DN3 .... 93 G2
Toftwood Av *FUL* S10 .... 170 A3 1
Toftwood Rd *FUL* S10 .... 170 B3
Togo St *DEARNE* S63 .... 60 B8 1
Toll Bar Av *HACK/IN* S12 .... 188 A2 1
Toll Bar Cl *HACK/IN* S12 .... 188 A2
Tolibar Cl *ST/HB/BR* S36 .... 78 E7
Toll Bar Dr *HACK/IN* S12 .... 188 A2
Toll Bar Rd *MEX/SWTN* S64 .... 112 A4
  RHAM/THRY S65 .... 156 D3
Toll House Md *MOS* S20 .... 190 A8
Tom La *FUL* S10 .... 169 H6
Tomlinson Rd *HOY* S74 .... 109 G1
Tompson HI *CHPT/GREN* S35 ...... 107 G8
Tooker Rd *RHAM* S60 .... 7 D5
Topcliffe Rd *BSLYN/ROY* S71 .... 56 B2
Top Field La *RHAM/THRY* S65 ..... 134 C7
Top Hall Rd *DONS/BSCR* DN4 .... 118 E2

Top La *BTLY* DN5 .... 60 A3
  HTFD DN7 .... 41 F3
Toppham Dr *SHEFS* S8 .... 201 F1
Toppham Rd *SHEFS* S8 .... 201 F1
Toppham Wy *SHEFS* S8 .... 201 F1
Top Rd *ARMTH* DN3 .... 40 E8
  BWTY DN10 .... 143 K4
  CHPT/GREN S35 .... 150 C3
Top Side *CHPT/GREN* S35 .... 129 G6
Top St *BWTY* DN10 .... 142 B8
Top Tree Wy *RHAM/THRY* S65 .... 134 E4
Top View Crs *CONI* DN12 .... 115 J7
Torbay Rd *ATT* S4 .... 152 E8
Tor Cl *BSLYN/ROY* S71 .... 56 B2
Torksey Cl *DONS/BSCR* DN4 .... 118 D2 2
Torksey Rd *SHEFN* S5 .... 152 E3
Torne Cl *DONS/BSCR* DN4 .... 119 F1
Torne Vw *EPW* DN9 .... 94 B7
Torry Ct *HAN/WDH* S13 .... 190 A1
Tortmayns *AU/AST/KP* S26 .... 192 E2
Torver Dr *DEARNE* S63 .... 86 B6
Tor Wy *RHAM* S60 .... 155 G8
Torwood Dr *SHEFS* S8 .... 186 E8 2
Totley Brook Cft
  TOT/DORE S17 .... 199 H2 1
Totley Brook Gln
  TOT/DORE S17 .... 199 H2 2
Totley Brook Gv *TOT/DORE* S17 .... 199 H2
Totley Brook Rd *TOT/DORE* S17 ... 199 H1
Totley Brook Wy
  TOT/DORE S17 .... 199 H2 2
Totley Cl *BSLYN/ROY* S71 .... 30 C8
Totley Grange Cl
  TOT/DORE S17 .... 199 H1 3
Totley Grange Rd *TOT/DORE* S17 .... 199 H3
Totley Hall La *TOT/DORE* S17 .... 199 H1
Totley La *TOT/DORE* S17 .... 200 B2
Totties La *HOLM/MEL* HD7 .... 48 C2
Towcester Rd *MEX/SWTN* S64 ..... 113 H1
Tower Cl *BTLY* DN5 .... 64 A6
  SHEFP/MNR S2 .... 9 F6 1
Tower Dr *SHEFP/MNR* S2 .... 9 F6
Towers La *HATH/EY* S32 .... 197 K7
Tower St *BSLY* S70 .... 2 B6
Town End *DRON* S18 .... 202 B6
Town End Av *AU/AST/KP* S26 ...... 175 H7
  HOLM/MEL HD7 .... 48 B1
Townend Av *RHAM/THRY* S65 ..... 134 D5
Townend Cl *RHAM* S60 .... 174 C3
Townend La *STKB/PEN* S36 .... 105 H8
Town End Rd *CHPT/GREN* S35 .... 130 A7
  HOLM/MEL HD7 .... 48 A1
Townend St *FUL* S10 .... 170 C3
Town End Vw *HOLM/MEL* HD7 .... 48 A1
Town Field La *CHPT/GREN* S35 .... 127 J4
Town Fields Av *CHPT/GREN* S35 .... 130 C7
Town Ga *HOLM/MEL* HD7 .... 47 G2
  HOLM/MEL HD7 .... 47 K2
Towngate *DOD/DAR* S75 .... 29 G6
  DOD/DAR S75 .... 53 J7
  STKB/PEN S36 .... 77 H3
Towngate Rd *CHPT/GREN* S35 .... 150 B2
Town Hall St *HOLM/MEL* HD7 .... 47 K2 1
Townhead Rd *TOT/DORE* S17 .... 199 G1
Townhead St *SHEF* S1 .... 9 D3
Town La *KIMB* S61 .... 132 A5
Town Moor Wr *WHHL* DN2 .... 5 F2
Towns St *DARN/MH* S9 .... 154 A4
  RHAM S60 .... 6 C6
Town View Av *BTLY* DN5 .... 63 H7
Toyne St *FUL* S10 .... 170 B3
Trafalgar Rd *ST/HB/BR* S6 .... 151 H3
Trafalgar St *AWLS/ASK* DN6 .... 37 K6
  SHEF S1 .... 8 C3
Trafford Ct *DON* DN1 .... 4 C3 7
Trafford Rd *AWLS/ASK* DN6 .... 18 A4
Trafford Wy *DON* DN1 .... 4 C5
Tranker La *WRKN* S81 .... 209 K1
Tranmoor Av *DONS/BSCR* DN4 ...... 92 D8
Tranmoor Ct *HOY* S74 .... 108 C2 4
Tranmoor La *ARMTH* DN3 .... 93 G2
Trans Pennine Trail *AWLS/ASK* DN6 .... 40 D2
  BSLYN/ROY S71 .... 31 F8
  CHPT/GREN S35 .... 105 J2
  CHPT/GREN S35 .... 106 A3
  CHPT/GREN S35 .... 106 D4
  CONI DN12 .... 131 J8
  DARN/MH S9 .... 153 G8
  ECK/KIL S21 .... 205 F6
  HAN/WDH S13 .... 173 G6
  KIMB S61 .... 154 C2
  RAW S62 .... 108 A4
Trap La *ECC* S11 .... 185 J1
Travey Rd *SHEFP/MNR* S2 .... 172 C8 3
Travis Av *THNE* DN8 .... 23 K8
Travis Cl *THNE* DN8 .... 23 K8
Travis Gdns *DONS/BSCR* DN4 .... 90 C6
Travis Gv *THNE* DN8 .... 23 K8
Travis Pl *FUL* S10 .... 8 B4
Tredis Cl *BSLYN/ROY* S71 .... 3 E2
Treecrest Ri *DOD/DAR* S75 .... 2 B1
Treefield Cl *KIMB* S61 .... 132 D4
Treelands *DOD/DAR* S75 .... 55 C4
Tree Root Wk *FUL* S10 .... 8 A5 3
Treeton La *AU/AST/KP* S26 .... 175 F4
  RHAM S60 .... 174 B2
Treetown Crs *RHAM* S60 .... 174 C2 1
Treherne Rd *RHAM/THRY* S65 .... 7 E5

Trelawney Wk *BSLY* S70 .... 82 A2 2
Trent Cl *CONI* DN12 .... 115 K4
Trent Gv *DRON* S18 .... 201 H4
Trentham Cl *RHAM* S60 .... 155 G7 8
Trenton Cl *HAN/WDH* S13 .... 190 B1
Trenton St *HAN/WDH* S13 .... 190 B1
Trent St *DARN/MH* S9 .... 172 A1
  WRKS S80 .... 210 C3
Treswell Crs *ST/HB/BR* S6 .... 151 H7 3
Trewan Ct *BSLYN/ROY* S71 .... 3 E2 3
Tricket Rd *CHPT/GREN* S35 .... 107 H7
Trickett Rd *ST/HB/BR* S6 .... 151 H8
Trinity Dr *KBTN* HD8 .... 51 C2
Trinity Mdw *CHPT/GREN* S35 .... 79 J8 3
Trinity Rd *AU/AST/KP* S26 .... 193 F5 1
Trinity St *OWL* S3 .... 9 D2
Trippet La *SHEF* S1 .... 9 D3
Tristford Cl *RHAM* S60 .... 174 B1
Troon Rd *HTFD* DN7 .... 42 C8
Troon Wk *DIN* S25 .... 178 B7
Trouble Wood La *ST/HB/BR* S6 .... 149 F5
Trough Dr *RHAM/THRY* S65 .... 135 F5
Trough La *HEM/SK/SE* WF9 .... 35 H4
Troutbeck Cl *DEARNE* S63 .... 60 B8
Troutbeck Rd *SHEFS* S8 .... 186 E3
Trowell Wy *BSLYN/ROY* S71 .... 30 A7
Trueman Ct *WHHL* DN2 .... 211 F2 1
Trueman Gn *MALT* S66 .... 159 F1
Trueman Rd *BSLYN/ROY* S71 .... 57 F5 2
Truman Gv *STKB/PEN* S36 .... 105 J6 1
Truman St *BTLY* DN5 .... 64 D6
Trumfleet La *AWLS/ASK* DN6 .... 20 A6
  AWLS/ASK DN6 .... 40 A1
Trundle la *HTFD* DN7 .... 22 B8
Truro Av *WHHL* DN2 .... 66 B7
Truro Ct *BSLYN/ROY* S71 .... 3 E2
Truswell Av *FUL* S10 .... 170 A3
Truswell Rd *FUL* S10 .... 170 A4
Tudor Ct *HEM/SK/SE* WF9 .... 34 E4
Tudor Rd *AWLS/ASK* DN6 .... 63 K4
  WHHL DN2 .... 92 A3
Tudor St *DEARNE* S63 .... 60 D7
  NROS/TKH DN11 .... 118 E7
Tudor Wy *BSLY* S70 .... 82 B2
Tudworth Field Rd *HTFD* DN7 .... 43 H5
Tudworth Rd *HTFD* DN7 .... 43 H7
  THNE DN8 .... 43 J3
Tuffolds Cl *SHEFP/MNR* S2 .... 172 C8
Tulip Tree Cl *MOS* S20 .... 190 E2
Tullibardine Rd *ECC* S11 .... 186 B1
Tumbling La *BSLYN/ROY* S71 .... 57 G1
Tummon Rd *SHEFP/MNR* S2 .... 172 A5
Tummon St *KIMB* S61 .... 6 A4 8
Tune St *BSLY* S70 .... 3 G5
  WMB/DAR S73 .... 83 K5
Tunwell Av *SHEFN* S5 .... 130 C8
Tunwell Dr *SHEFN* S5 .... 130 C8
Tunwell Greave *SHEFN* S5 .... 130 C8
Tunwell Rd *MALT* S66 .... 158 D6
Turf Moor Rd *HTFD* DN7 .... 69 J2
Turie Av *SHEFN* S5 .... 152 B1
Turie Crs *SHEFN* S5 .... 152 B1
Turnberry *WRKN* S81 .... 211 F1
Turnberry Cl *BTLY* DN5 .... 64 D7 3
Turnberry Gv *CUD/GR* S72 .... 31 K6 2
Turnberry Wy *DIN* S25 .... 178 B8
Turner Av *WMB/DAR* S73 .... 83 J4
Turner Cl *DRON* S18 .... 201 F6 3
  RAW S62 .... 133 K3
Turner Dr *WRKN* S81 .... 210 D3
Turner La *RHAM* S60 .... 156 A6
Turner Rd *WRKN* S81 .... 210 C3
Turner's Cl *HOY* S74 .... 83 G8
Turners La *FUL* S10 .... 170 C5 10
  SHEFP/MNR S2 .... 9 E4
Turnesc Gv *DEARNE* S63 .... 60 D8
Turnpike Cft *CHPT/GREN* S35 ..... 129 H6 1
Turnshaw Av *AU/AST/KP* S26 ...... 175 G6
Turnshaw Rd *AU/AST/KP* S26 ...... 175 K4
Tutbury Gdns *DONS/BSCR* DN4 ..... 93 F8
Tuxford Crs *BSLYN/ROY* S71 .... 56 E5
The Twenty Lands *RHAM* S60 ...... 174 C4
Twentywell Dr *TOT/DORE* S17 ..... 200 B3 1
Twentywell La *TOT/DORE* S17 ..... 186 A8
Twentywell Ri *TOT/DORE* S17 ..... 186 B8
Twentywell Rd *TOT/DORE* S17 .... 200 B2
Twentywell Vw *TOT/DORE* S17 .... 200 B2
Twibell St *BSLYN/ROY* S71 .... 3 J1
Twickenham Cl *MOS* S20 .... 204 C1 3
Twickenham Ct *MOS* S20 .... 204 C1 4
Twickenham Crs *MOS* S20 .... 204 C2
Twickenham Gld *MOS* S20 .... 204 C1 1
Twickenham Gln *MOS* S20 .... 204 D2 2
Twickenham Gv *MOS* S20 .... 204 C1 2
Twitchill Dr *HAN/WDH* S13 .... 189 K1
Twyford Cl *MEX/SWTN* S64 .... 111 K4
Tyas Pl *MEX/SWTN* S64 .... 113 G2 1
Tyas Rd *SHEFN* S5 .... 130 B8
Tye Rd *MOS* S20 .... 190 E4
Tylden Rd *WRKS* S80 .... 209 K2 1
Tylden Wy *WRKS* S80 .... 209 J2 1
Tyler St *DARN/MH* S9 .... 153 J4
Tyler Wy *DARN/MH* S9 .... 153 J4
Tylney Rd *SHEFP/MNR* S2 .... 171 K6
Tynedale Ct *ARMTH* DN3 .... 67 F3 3
Tynker Av *MOS* S20 .... 190 E4
Tyzack Rd *SHEFS* S8 .... 186 E5

U

Ughill Rd ST/HB/BR S6 ...... 148 C5
Ulley Crs HAN/WDH S13 ...... 172 D8
Ulley La AU/AST/KP S26 ...... 175 J4
Ulley Rd HAN/WDH S13 ...... 172 D8
Ulley Vw AU/AST/KP S26 ...... 175 H5
Ullswater Av MOS S20 ...... 204 C1
Ullswater CI DEARNE S63 ...... 86 B6
   DIN S25 ...... 178 A8
   DRON S18 ...... 200 E5
   MOS S20 ...... 204 C1
Ullswater Dr DRON S18 ...... 200 E6
Ullswater PI DRON S18 ...... 200 E5
Ullswater Rd BSLYN/ROY S71 57 J7
   MEX/SWTN S64 ...... 113 J1
Ulrica Dr MALT S66 ...... 176 E1
Ulverston Av AWLS/ASK DN6 ...... 19 F7
Ulverston Rd SHEFS S8 ...... 186 E3
Underbank La STKB/PEN S36 ...... 104 C3
Underbank Old Rd HOLM/MEL HD7.. 48 A3
Undercliffe Rd ST/HB/BR S6 ...... 169 K1
Undergate Rd DIN S25 ...... 178 A5
Underhill BSLY S70 ...... 82 C5
Underhill La ST/HB/BR S6 ...... 151 G2
Underhill Rd BSLY S70 ...... 82 C1
Underwood Av BSLY S70 ...... 82 C1
Underwood Gdns WRKS S80 ...... 210 A4
Underwood Rd SHEFS S8 ...... 187 F3
Union Ct BSLY S70 ...... 2 C5
Union La SHEF S1 ...... 9 D4
Union Rd ECC S11 ...... 186 D1
   THNE DN8 ...... 23 H8
Union St AU/AST/KP S26 ...... 192 E8
   BSLY S70 ...... 2 C5
   DON DN1 ...... 4 C4
   HEM/SK/SE WF9 ...... 33 H1
   KIMB S61 ...... 6 A4
   SHEF S1 ...... 9 D4
Unity PI RHAM S60 ...... 6 C4
Unsliven Rd STKB/PEN S36 ...... 104 B4
Unstone-dronfield By-pass
   DRON S18 ...... 201 F4
Unstone HI DRON S18 ...... 201 K7
Unstone St SHEFP/MNR S2 ...... 9 D5
Unwin Crs STKB/PEN S36 ...... 78 A5
Unwin St STKB/PEN S36 ...... 78 A5
Uplands Av DOD/DAR S75 ...... 28 B7
Uplands Rd ARMTH DN3 ...... 93 H1
Uplands Wy RAW S62 ...... 133 H1
Upper Albert Rd SHEFS S8 ...... 187 F2
Upper Clara St KIMB S61 ...... 154 C1
Upper Cliffe Rd DOD/DAR S75 ...... 54 D7
Upper Common La KBTN HD8 ...... 26 C7
Upperfield CI MALT S66 ...... 159 G1
Upper Field La DOD/DAR S75 ...... 27 G6
Upperfield Rd MALT S66 ...... 137 F8
Upper Folderings DOD/DAR S75 .. 54 E8
Upper Forest Rd BSLYN/ROY S71..... 30 A7
Upper Ga GA HOLM/MEL HD7 ...... 48 D5
Upper Gate Rd ST/HB/BR S6...... 169 F2
Upper Hanover St OWL S3 ...... 8 B4
Upper High Royds DOD/DAR S75 ... 29 F7
Upper House Rd HOLM/MEL HD7 ... 48 B7
Upper Hoyland Rd HOY S74 ...... 82 D8
Upper Kenyon St THNE DN8 ...... 23 J7
Upper La KBTN HD8 ...... 26 A1
Upper Ley Ct CHPT/GREN S35 ... 130 B2
Upper Ley Dell CHPT/GREN S35 .. 130 B2
Upper Maythorn La
   HOLM/MEL HD7 ...... 49 J7
Upper Mdw HOLM/MEL HD7...... 2 C5
Upper New St BSLY S70 ...... 2 C5
Upper Rye CI RHAM S60...... 156 C6
Upper School La DRON S18 ...... 201 H7
Upper Sheffield Rd BSLY S70 ...... 82 B1
Upperthong La HOLM/MEL HD7.... 47 H2
Upperthorpe ST/HB/BR S6 ...... 8 A1
Upperthorpe Gln ST/HB/BR S6 ... 8 A1
Upperthorpe Rd ECK/KIL S21 ...... 205 H2
   ST/HB/BR S6 ...... 8 B1
Upper Valley Rd SHEFS S8...... 187 H2
Upper Whiston La RHAM S60 ...... 156 B8
Upperwood Rd WMB/DAR S73 ...... 84 B1
Upper Wortley Rd KIMB S61 ...... 131 G4
Upton CI MALT S66 ...... 137 F8
   WMB/DAR S73 ...... 83 J3
Upwell HI ATT S4 ...... 153 F1
Upwell La ATT S4 ...... 153 F6
Upwell St ATT S4 ...... 153 F6
Upwood Rd ST/HB/BR S6 ...... 151 G6
Urban Rd DONS/BSCR DN4 ...... 4 A5
Urch CI CONI DN12 ...... 114 D6
Uttley CI DARN/MH S9 ...... 172 D1
Uttley Cft DARN/MH S9 ...... 172 D1
Uttley Dr DARN/MH S9 ...... 172 D1
Uttoxeter Av MEX/SWTN S64 ...... 113 H1

V

Vaal St BSLY S70 ...... 3 E5

Vainor Rd ST/HB/BR S6 ...... 151 F5
Vale Av RHAM/THRY S65 ...... 134 E5
Vale CI DRON S18 ...... 201 H6
Vale Crs RHAM/THRY S65 ...... 134 E5
Vale Gv ST/HB/BR S6 ...... 150 D7
Valentine CI SHEFN S5 ...... 152 D2
Valentine Crs SHEFN S5 ...... 152 D2
Valentine Rd SHEFN S5 ...... 152 D2
Vale Rd OWL S3 ...... 152 A8
   RHAM/THRY S65 ...... 134 E5
Valiant Gdns BTLY DN5 ...... 90 B4
Valley Av HEM/SK/SE WF9 ...... 35 G4
Valley Dr ARMTH DN3 ...... 93 J7
   DEARNE S63 ...... 111 G1
Valley Rd CHPT/GREN S35 ...... 129 K1
   DOD/DAR S75 ...... 29 F6
   ECK/KIL S21 ...... 191 H8
   HACK/IN S12 ...... 190 A5
   MEX/SWTN S64 ...... 112 A5
   SHEFS S8 ...... 187 G1
   WMB/DAR S73 ...... 84 B3
   WRKN S81 ...... 196 C8
   WRKN S81 ...... 210 C2
Valley St HEM/SK/SE WF9 ...... 34 E5
Valley Vw HEM/SK/SE WF9 ...... 35 G4
Valley View CI ECK/KIL S21 ...... 204 A5
Valley Wy HOY S74 ...... 109 F1
Vancouver Dr DEARNE S63 ...... 86 A5
Varley Gdns MALT S66 ...... 157 G1
Varney Rd DEARNE S63 ...... 111 H2
Varsity Ct HTFD DN7 ...... 69 H8
Vaughan Av DON DN1 ...... 5 D2
Vaughan Rd AWLS/ASK DN6 ...... 18 A6
   DOD/DAR S75 ...... 55 G4
Vaughton HI STKB/PEN S36 ...... 105 K6
Vauxhall CI DARN/MH S9 ...... 153 J3
Vauxhall Rd DARN/MH S9 ...... 153 J3
Velvet Wood CI DOD/DAR S75 ...... 55 F4
Venetian Crs WMB/DAR S73 ...... 84 C2
Ventnor CI DONS/BSCR DN4 ...... 90 C8
Ventnor PI ABRD S7 ...... 8 C6
Venus Ct RHAM S60 ...... 155 F5
Verdant Wy SHEFN S5 ...... 152 E2
Verdon St OWL S3 ...... 9 E1
Verelst Av AU/AST/KP S26 ...... 175 H6
Vere Rd ST/HB/BR S6 ...... 151 H5
Verger CI NROS/TKH DN11 ...... 119 F6
Vermuyden Rd THNE DN8 ...... 24 A4
Vernon CI BSLY S70 ...... 2 C6
Vernon Crs BSLY S70...... 82 A2
Vernon Delph FUL S10 ...... 169 K4
Vernon Dr CHPT/GREN S35 ...... 130 A1
Vernon Rd BSLY S70 ...... 82 A1
   RHAM/THRY S65 ...... 156 A4
   TOT/DORE S17 ...... 199 J1
Vernon St BSLY S70 ...... 108 A1
   BSLYN/ROY S71 ...... 2 C3
   HOY S74 ...... 108 D2
Vernon St North BSLYN/ROY S71 .. 2 C3
Vernon Ter FUL S10 ...... 170 A5
Vernon Wy DOD/DAR S75 ...... 55 G4
   MALT S66 ...... 159 F1
Verona Ri WMB/DAR S73 ...... 84 D2
Vesey St RAW S62 ...... 133 J3
Vessey Rd WRKN S81 ...... 196 C8
Vicarage CI CHPT/GREN S35 ...... 129 H7
   DONS/BSCR DN4 ...... 93 F8
   DRON S18 ...... 200 A7
   HEM/SK/SE WF9 ...... 34 B4
Vicarage Crs CHPT/GREN S35 ...... 129 H7
Vicarage Dr NROS/TKH DN11 ...... 116 E8
Vicarage La BSLYN/ROY S71 ...... 30 D4
   TOT/DORE S17 ...... 185 H6
Vicarage Rd CHPT/GREN S35 ...... 129 H7
   DARN/MH S9 ...... 153 G8
Vicarage Wk STKB/PEN S36 ...... 78 A4
Vicarage Wy BTLY DN5 ...... 65 G5
Vicar Crs WMB/DAR S73 ...... 84 E2
Vicar La BWTY DN10 ...... 143 K4
   HAN/WDH S13 ...... 173 K8
   SHEF S1 ...... 9 D3
Vicar Rd DEARNE S63 ...... 85 G8
   WMB/DAR S73 ...... 84 E2
Vicar's Wk WRKS S80 ...... 210 D5
Vicar's Well HEM/SK/SE WF9 ...... 34 D6
Vickers Av SHEFN S5 ...... 152 E4
Vickers Dr SHEFN S5 ...... 152 E4
Vickers Rd CHPT/GREN S35 ...... 107 J8
   SHEFN S5 ...... 152 E5
Victoria Av HTFD DN7 ...... 42 C7
   RHAM/THRY S65 ...... 7 E4
Victoria CI AU/AST/KP S26 ...... 192 E5
   HTFD DN7 ...... 42 A5
   STKB/PEN S36 ...... 104 E6
Victoria Ct AU/AST/KP S26 ...... 192 E5
   BTLY DN5 ...... 64 E4
Victoria Crs BSLY S70 ...... 2 A3
   BSLY S70 ...... 81 K8
Victoria Crs West DOD/DAR S75...... 2 A3
Victoria La NROS/TKH DN11 ...... 118 D6
Victorian Crs WHHL DN2 ...... 5 F2
Victoria Quays Rbt ATT S4 ...... 9 F2
Victoria Rd AWLS/ASK DN6 ...... 38 C1
   AWLS/ASK DN6 ...... 64 A1
   BSLY S70 ...... 2 A3
   BSLYN/ROY S71 ...... 30 E3
   BTLY DN5 ...... 64 E5
   CONI DN12 ...... 115 J4
   DEARNE S63 ...... 85 G8
   DONS/BSCR DN4 ...... 4 B6
   FUL S10 ...... 8 B5
   MEX/SWTN S64 ...... 113 F2
   MOS S20 ...... 190 D3
   RAW S62 ...... 133 J2
   STKB/PEN S36 ...... 105 F6
   WMB/DAR S73 ...... 84 D5
   WRKS S80 ...... 210 D5
Victoria Springs HOLM/MEL HD7 ..... 47 H3
Victoria Station Rd ATT S4 ...... 9 E2
Victoria St BSLY S70 ...... 2 B3
   BSLY S70 ...... 56 E7
   CUD/CR S72 ...... 31 J5
   DEARNE S63 ...... 86 D2
   DIN S25 ...... 178 C6
   DRON S18 ...... 201 F5
   HEM/SK/SE WF9 ...... 33 H1
   HOLM/MEL HD7 ...... 47 K2
   HOY S74 ...... 109 G1
   KBTN HD8 ...... 26 B5
   MALT S66 ...... 159 H2
   MEX/SWTN S64 ...... 112 D1
   MEX/SWTN S64 ...... 112 D8
   RHAM S60 ...... 6 A4
   RHAM S60 ...... 174 B1
   STKB/PEN S36 ...... 78 A4
   STKB/PEN S36 ...... 104 E6
   WMB/DAR S73 ...... 84 E1
Victoria Ter BSLY S70 ...... 3 D5
   KBTN HD8 ...... 26 C5
Victoria Wy MALT S66 ...... 158 E1
Victor Rd HEM/SK/SE WF9 ...... 34 B5
   TOT/DORE S17 ...... 185 K6
Victor St AWLS/ASK DN6 ...... 37 J1
   HEM/SK/SE WF9 ...... 34 E5
   ST/HB/BR S6 ...... 151 J1
Viewland CI CUD/CR S72 57
   KBTN HD8 ...... 79 K
Viewlands DOD/DAR S75 ...... 79 K
Viewlands CI MALT S66 ...... 157 K3
   STKB/PEN S36 ...... 78 A
View Rd RHAM/THRY S65 ...... 7 F
   SHEFS S8 ...... 171 C8
   STKB/PEN S36 ...... 77 H
Viewtree CI RAW S62 ...... 108 E6
Viking CI KBTN HD8 ...... 26 A
Vikinglea CI SHEFP/MNR S2 ...... 172 D7
Vikinglea Dr SHEFP/MNR S2 ...... 172 D
Vikinglea Gld SHEFP/MNR S2 ...... 172 D6
Vikinglea Rd SHEFP/MNR S2 ...... 172 D
Viking Wy AU/AST/KP S26 ...... 193 F4
Villa Gdns BTLY DN5 ...... 64 D
Village St AWLS/ASK DN6 ...... 63 J
Villa Park Rd DONS/BSCR DN4 ...... 92 D
Villa Rd AWLS/ASK DN6 ...... 63 J
Villiers CI SHEFP/MNR S2 ...... 188 A
Villiers Dr SHEFP/MNR S2 ...... 188 A
Vincent Rd BSLYN/ROY S71 ...... 57 G4
   ECC S11 ...... 8 C
   RHAM/THRY S65 ...... 135 H
Vine CI BSLYN/ROY S71...... 3 F
   RHAM S60 ...... 6 B4
Vine Rd NROS/TKH DN11 ...... 140 B
Vinery CI KBTN HD8 ...... 26 C
Vineyard Ct NROS/TKH DN11 ...... 139 J
Viola Bank STKB/PEN S36 ...... 104 E
Violet Av CONI DN12 ...... 115 J
   MOS S20 ...... 190 C
Violet Bank Rd ABRD S7 ...... 186 E1
Vissett CI HEM/SK/SE WF9 ...... 32 E
Vissitt La HEM/SK/SE WF9 ...... 32 D
Vivian Rd SHEFN S5 ...... 152 E
Vizard Rd HOY S74 ...... 109 C
Vulcan PI WRKS S80 ...... 210 D
Vulcan Rd DARN/MH S9 ...... 153 J
Vulcan Wy HTFD DN7 ...... 69 H

W

Wadbrough Rd FUL S10 ...... 8 A
Waddington Rd DOD/DAR S75 ...... 55 C
Wade CI RHAM S60 ...... 7 F6
Wade Meadow ST/HB/BR S6 ...... 151 F6
Wade St ATT S4 ...... 153 F6
   DOD/DAR S75 ......
Wadman Rd HOLM/MEL HD7 ...... 48 C
Wadsley La ST/HB/BR S6 ...... 151 F5
Wadsley Park Crs ST/HB/BR S6 .... 151 F
Wadsworth Av HACK/IN S12 ...... 188 F2
Wadsworth Dr HACK/IN S12 ...... 189 F
   RAW S62 ...... 111 F
Wadsworth Rd HACK/IN S12 ...... 188 E2
   MALT S66 157
Wadworth Av NROS/TKH DN11 ...... 119 C
Wadworth CI BTLY DN5 ...... 87 H
Wadworth Hall La
   NROS/TKH DN11 ...... 116 D
Wadworth HI NROS/TKH DN11 ...... 117 F
Wadworth Ri RHAM/THRY S65 ...... 134 D
Wadworth St CONI DN12 ...... 114 D
Wagon Rd KIMB S61 ...... 132 E
Wain Ct WRKN S81 197
Waingate SHEF S1 ...... 9 E2
Wainwright Av HAN/WDH S13 ...... 173 F

WMB/DAR S73 ... 83 J4
Wainwright Rd HAN/WDH S13 ... 172 E7
Wainwright Pl WMB/DAR S73 ... 83 J4 ⬛
Wainwright Rd DONS/BSCR DN4 ... 5 E4
  KIMB S61 ... 132 C6 ⬛
Wakefield Rd BSLYN/ROY S71 ... 29 K7
  BSLYN/ROY S71 ... 30 A8
  BSLYN/ROY S71 ... 56 A1
  DOD/DAR S75 ... 29 J6
  KBTN HD8 ... 26 C4
  KBTN HD8 ... 51 F2
Wake Rd ABRD S7 ... 170 E8
Walbank Rd ARMTH DN3 ... 93 H1
Walbert Av DEARNE S63 ... 60 B8
Walbrook BSLY S70 ... 82 C5
Walden Av BTLY DN5 ... 64 B6
Walden Rd SHEFP/MNR S2 ... 171 H8
Walden Stubbs Rd AWLS/ASK DN6... 18 A3
Walders Av ST/HB/BR S6 ... 151 F5
Walders La STKB/PEN S36 ... 127 F1
Walesmoor Av AU/AST/KP S26 ... 192 C3
Wales Pl FUL S10 ... 170 D1
Wales Rd AU/AST/KP S26 ... 193 B5
Waleswood Av AU/AST/KP S26 ... 191 G3
Waleswood Vw AU/AST/KP S26 ... 191 H1
Walford Rd ECK/KIL S21 ... 205 K1
Walker Cl CHPT/GREN S35 ... 129 H7
Walker Edge ST/HB/BR S6 ... 126 D4
Walker La RHAM/THRY S65 ... 7 D4
Walker Rd DOD/DAR S75 ... 108 A2 ⬛
  KIMB S61 ... 132 C6
Walkers La ECK/KIL S21 ... 205 J1
Walker St MEX/SWTN S64 ... 112 D4
  OWL S3 ... 9 E1
  RAW S62 ... 134 A1
Walker Vw RAW S62 ... 134 A1
Walkley Bank Cl ST/HB/BR S6 ... 170 C1
Walkley Bank Rd ST/HB/BR S6 ... 170 B1
Walkley Crescent Rd
  ST/HB/BR S6 ... 170 B1
Walkley La ST/HB/BR S6 ... 151 H7
Walkley Rd ST/HB/BR S6 ... 170 C1
Walkley St ST/HB/BR S6 ... 8 A1
Walkley Ter FUL S10 ... 170 A1
Walk Royd Hl DOD/DAR S75 ... 28 A5
The Walk BSLY S70 ... 107 K1
Wallace Rd DONS/BSCR DN4 ... 116 B1
  OWL S3 ... 171 F1
Waller Rd ST/HB/BR S6 ... 170 A2
Wallingbrook Ri WRKS S80 ... 209 K5
Walling Rd DARN/MH S9 ... 153 J5
Walling Rd DARN/MH S9 ... 153 J5 ⬛
Wallingwells La WRKN S81 ... 195 J1
Wall Nook La KBTN HD8 ... 49 J1
Wallroyds KBTN HD8 ... 51 F2
Walls La STV/CWN S43 ... 206 E7
  WRKS S80 ... 207 G7
Wall St BSLY S70 ... 2 B5
Walney Fold BSLYN/ROY S71 ... 56 E1 ⬛
Walnut Av EPW DN9 ... 120 B3
  NROS/TKH DN11 ... 140 A8
  WRKN S81 ... 195 H8
Walnut Dr DIN S25 ... 178 B7
  ECK/KIL S21 ... 205 G2 ⬛
Walnut Gv MEX/SWTN S64 ... 112 C1
Walnut Pl CHPT/GREN S35 ... 133 J6
Walnut Rd THNE DN8 ... 23 J8
Walnut St HEM/SK/SE WF9 ... 34 E6
Walnut Tree Hl NROS/TKH DN11 ... 117 F2
Walpole Cl DONS/BSCR DN4 ... 116 C2
Walpole Gv AU/AST/KP S26 ... 175 H6
Walseker La AU/AST/KP S26 ... 192 C8
Walsham Dr BTLY DN5 ... 90 B2
Walshaw Rd CHPT/GREN S35 ... 150 C2
Walters Rd MALT S66 ... 159 J2
Walter St RHAM S60 ... 6 B3
  ST/HB/BR S6 ... 151 J8 ⬛
Waltham Dr AWLS/ASK DN6 ... 37 F5
Waltham Gdns MOS S20 ... 190 E5 ⬛
Waltham St BSLY S70 ... 2 C5
Waltheof Rd SHEFP/MNR S2 ... 172 C7
Waitin Rd HOLM/MEL HD7 ... 47 J6
Walton Cl FUL S10 ... 8 A5
Walton St DOD/DAR S75 ... 55 H4
Walton St North DOD/DAR S75 ... 55 G4
Wannop St RAW S62 ... 133 J4
Wansfell Rd ATT S4 ... 153 G6
The Wapping RHAM/THRY S65 ... 113 J8
Warburton Cl SHEFP/MNR S2 ... 171 J8 ⬛
Warburton Gdns
  SHEFP/MNR S2 ... 171 J8 ⬛
Warburton Rd SHEFP/MNR S2 ... 171 J8
Ward Bank Rd HOLM/MEL HD7 ... 47 K3
Warde-aldam Crs MALT S66 ... 157 F2
Warde Av DONS/BSCR DN4 ... 116 C1
Warden Cl DONS/BSCR DN4 ... 93 J7
Warden St RHAM S60 ... 155 G4
Ward La STV/CWN S43 ... 206 B4
Wardlow Rd HACK/IN S12 ... 188 E2
Ward Pl SHEFP/MNR S2 ... 8 C6 ⬛
Ward Place La HOLM/MEL HD7 ... 47 J4
Wardsend Rd SHEFN S5 ... 151 J5
Wardsend Rd North ST/HB/BR S6.. 151 H4
Ward St OWL S3 ... 9 D1 ⬛
  STKB/PEN S36 ... 78 A5
Wareham Ct MOS S20 ... 190 E5 ⬛
Wareham Gv DOD/DAR S75 ... 55 F7

Warehouse La DEARNE S63 ... 111 H1
Warminster Crs SHEFS S8 ... 187 G3
Warminster Dr SHEFS S8 ... 187 H3
Warminster Dr SHEFS S8 ... 187 H4 ⬛
Warminster Pl SHEFS S8 ... 187 H5
Warminster Rd SHEFS S8 ... 187 G3
Warmsworth Halt CONI DN12... 115 J5
Warmsworth Rd DONS/BSCR DN4.. 116 B1
Warner Av DOD/DAR S75 ... 55 G5
Warner Pl DOD/DAR S75 ... 55 H5
Warner Rd DOD/DAR S75 ... 55 G5
  ST/HB/BR S6 ... 151 G6
Warnington Dr ARMTH DN3 ... 119 G3
  DONS/BSCR DN4 ... 119 F2
Warning Tongue La ARMTH DN3 ... 93 G8
Warren Av RAW S62 ... 111 H8
Warren Cl BSLYN/ROY S71 ... 30 E2
  DONS/BSCR DN4 ... 115 K1
  WHHL DN2 ... 91 K3
  WRKN S81 ... 195 G3
Warren Crs BSLY S70 ... 2 C6
  ECK/KIL S21 ... 203 G5
Warren Dr KIMB S61 ... 132 C7
Warreners Dr RHAM/THRY S65... 134 E5
Warren Gdns CHPT/GREN S35 ... 108 B7
Warren Hl KIMB S61 ... 132 C7
Warren House La MALT S66 ... 157 J1
Warren La CHPT/GREN S35 ... 108 C7
  DOD/DAR S75 ... 29 H5
  DONS/BSCR DN4 ... 118 C2
  HOY S74 ... 108 A6
Warren Mt KIMB S61 ... 132 C7
Warrenne Cl HTFD DN7 ... 42 B8 ⬛
Warrenne Rd HTFD DN7 ... 42 B8
Warren Pl BSLY S70 ... 2 C6 ⬛
Warren Quarry La BSLY S70 ... 2 C5
Warren Ri DRON S18 ... 201 J4
Warren Rd MALT S66 ... 157 G2
  THNE DN8 ... 43 K1
Warren St ATT S4 ... 171 K2
Warren V MEX/SWTN S64 ... 111 K6
  RAW S62 ... 111 K8
Warren Vale Rd MEX/SWTN S64 ... 111 K4
Warren Vw HOY S74 ... 108 D3
Warrington Rd FUL S10 ... 8 A2 ⬛
Warris Cl KIMB S61 ... 132 B6
Warris Pl SHEFP/MNR S2 ... 171 K4
Warsop Rd BSLYN/ROY S71 ... 29 K6
Warwick Av WRKN S81 ... 196 D1
Warwick Cl HTFD DN7 ... 69 G1
Warwick Rd BSLYN/ROY S71 ... 3 E2
  WHHL DN2 ... 92 A2
Warwick St FUL S10 ... 170 C3 ⬛
  RHAM/THRY S65 ... 7 D5
Warwick Ter FUL S10 ... 170 C3 ⬛
Warwick Wy DIN S25 ... 194 A1
Wasdale Av MOS S20 ... 204 C1 ⬛
Wasdale Cl MOS S20 ... 204 C1
Washfield Crs RHAM S60 ... 174 C3
Washfield La RHAM S60 ... 174 C4
Washford Rd DARN/MH S9 ... 172 A1
Washington Av CONI DN12 ... 114 A5
  WMB/DAR S73 ... 83 J5
Washington Dr DIN S25 ... 178 A7 ⬛
Washington Gv BTLY DN5 ... 64 D8
Washington Rd AWLS/ASK DN6 ... 63 J2
  CHPT/GREN S35 ... 130 C6
  DEARNE S63 ... 86 C3
  ECC S11 ... 8 C6
Washington St MEX/SWTN S64 ... 113 G2
Washpit New Rd HOLM/MEL HD7 ... 47 K6
Wasteneys Rd AU/AST/KP S26 ... 193 F2
Watch House La BTLY DN5 ... 90 C1
Watchley La BTLY DN5 ... 61 G5
Watch St HAN/WDH S13... 174 B7
Water Bank EPW DN9 ... 97 F5
Waterdale Dr DIN S25 ... 5 D5
Waterdale Cl BTLY DN5 ... 90 A7 ⬛
Waterdale Rd BSLY S70 ... 82 A3
Waterfield Ms MOS S20 ... 190 C6 ⬛
Waterfield Pl BSLYN/ROY S71 ... 57 F7 ⬛
Waterford Rd OWL S3 ... 151 K8
Water Hall La STKB/PEN S36 ... 78 A3
Waterhouse Cl RHAM/THRY S65... 134 D6
Watering Place Rd STKB/PEN S36 77 H4 ⬛
Water La HEM/SK/SE WF9 ... 33 J3
  HTFD DN7 ... 41 K2
  NROS/TKH DN11 ... 161 K2
  PONT WF8 ... 17 F1
  RAW S62 ... 109 H4
  RHAM S60 ... 6 C5
  TOT/DORE S17 ... 185 K8
  WRKN S81 ... 196 E1
Waterloo Rd BSLY S70 ... 2 A4 ⬛
Waterloo Wk OWL S3 ... 8 C1 ⬛
Watermead DEARNE S63 ... 86 C6
Watermeade ECK/KIL S21 ... 203 K5
Mdw Mdw WRKS S80 ... 210 B6
Water Rw HOLM/MEL HD7 ... 48 D1 ⬛
Water Royd Dr DOD/DAR S75 ... 54 E8
Waterside THNE DN8 ... 23 J8
Waterside Gdns CHPT/GREN S35 ... 128 C8
Waterside Rd THNE DN8 ... 23 C6 ⬛
Waterslack Rd NROS/TKH DN11 ... 163 C3
Water Slacks Cl HAN/WDH S13 ... 189 K1 ⬛
Water Slacks Dr HAN/WDH S13 ... 189 K1
Water Slacks Rd HAN/WDH S13 ... 189 K1
Watersmeet Rd ST/HB/BR S6... 151 G8

Water St HOLM/MEL HD7 ... 47 G4
  KBTN HD8 ... 26 A6 ⬛
  OWL S3 ... 9 D2 ⬛
  RHAM S60 ... 6 C3
Waterthorpe Cl MOS S20 ... 190 D7 ⬛
Waterthorpe Crs MOS S20 ... 190 D7
Waterthorpe Gdns MOS S20... 190 C7
Waterthorpe Cld MOS S20 ... 190 C7
Waterthorpe Gln MOS S20 ... 190 D7 ⬛
Waterthorpe Greenway MOS S20.. 190 B4
Waterthorpe Ri MOS S20 ... 190 D7
Waterton Cl HEM/SK/SE WF9 ... 34 C4 ⬛
Waterton La HTFD DN7 ... 68 D5
Water Way Garth GLE DN14 ... 11 J3 ⬛
Watery La HOLM/MEL HD7 ... 46 C7
Watery St OWL S3 ... 8 C1
Wath Rd ABRD S7 ... 186 E1 ⬛
  DEARNE S63 ... 86 A6
  HOY S74 ... 109 H3
  MEX/SWTN S64 ... 112 C1
  WMB/DAR S73 ... 84 C6
Wath Wood Bottom DEARNE S63 .. 111 H4
Wath Wood Dr DEARNE S63 ... 111 J4
Wath Wood Rd DEARNE S63 ... 111 J3
Watkinson Gdns MOS S20 ... 190 C5
Watnall Rd BSLYN/ROY S71 ... 30 A7 ⬛
Watson Cl KIMB S61 ... 132 C7
Watson Gln KIMB S61 ... 131 K7
Watson Rd FUL S10 ... 170 C5 ⬛
  KIMB S61 ... 132 C7
  WRKS S80 ... 210 D4
Watsons Cft HTFD DN7 ... 42 C5 ⬛
Watson St HOY S74 ... 108 C2 ⬛
Watt La FUL S10 ... 169 K5
Wavell Crs BWTY DN10 ... 165 H6
Waveney Dr DOD/DAR S75 ... 54 D4 ⬛
Waverley Av AU/AST/KP S26 ... 192 E4
  CONI DN12 ... 114 D5
  DONS/BSCR DN4 ... 90 B8
  MALT S66 ... 177 F1
Waverley Ct BTLY DN5 ... 64 D3
Waverley Pl WRKS S80 ... 210 E7
Waverley Rd DARN/MH S9 ... 172 E3 ⬛
Waverley Vw RHAM S60 ... 174 A2
Waverley Wy WRKS S80 ... 210 E7
Waycliffe BSLYN/ROY S71 ... 3 F2
Wayford Av BSLY S70 ... 157 K1
Wayland Av BSLY S70 ... 82 A2
Wayland Rd ECC S11 ... 8 A6
Weakland Cl HACK/IN S12 ... 189 H5
Weakland Crs HACK/IN S12 ... 189 H4
Weakland Dr HACK/IN S12... 189 H4
Weakland Wy HACK/IN S12 ... 189 H4 ⬛
Weatherall Pl AWLS/ASK DN6 ... 37 G5
Weather Hill La HOLM/MEL HD7... 47 H7
Weaver Cl DOD/DAR S75 ... 54 D4
Weavers Cl CHPT/GREN S35 ... 129 H6
Webb Av STKB/PEN S36 ... 105 H7
Webbs Av ST/HB/BR S6 ... 169 J1
Webster Cl KIMB S61 ... 132 A7 ⬛
Webster Crs KIMB S61 ... 132 A7
Webster St DARN/MH S9 ... 153 J6 ⬛
Wedgewood Cl RAW S62 ... 133 J2
Weedon St DARN/MH S9 ... 153 J5
Weet Shaw La CUD/GR S72 ... 31 H6
Weetwood Dr ECC S11 ... 186 B2 ⬛
Weetwood Rd RHAM S60 ... 155 K5
Weigh La SHEFP/MNR S2 ... 9 F5 ⬛
Weir Head DARN/MH S9 ... 153 J6
Weirside WRKN S81 ... 180 D1
Welbeck Dr DRON S18 ... 200 C5
Welbeck Dr AU/AST/KP S26 ... 175 K8
Welbeck Rd DONS/BSCR DN4 ... 5 F4
  NROS/TKH DN11 ... 163 F2 ⬛
Welbeck St DOD/DAR S75 ... 2 A3
  WRKS S80 ... 210 D5
Welbury Gdns MOS S20 ... 204 C1
Welby Pl SHEFS S8 ... 187 F3
Welfare Av CONI DN12 ... 114 B5
Welfare Rd AWLS/ASK DN6 ... 63 J4
  DEARNE S63 ... 60 B7
Welfare Vw DEARNE S63 ... 86 C3
Welham Dr RHAM S60 ... 7 D6
Welland Cl OWL S3 ... 171 F1
  WRKN S81 ... 196 C8
Welland Ct DOD/DAR S75 ... 54 D4
Welland Crs HOY S74 ... 109 H1
Wellbeck Rd ST/HB/BR S6 ... 170 B1
Wellbourne Cl CHPT/GREN S35... 130 D3
Wellcarr Rd SHEFS S8 ... 187 G5
Wellcliffe Cl MALT S66 ... 157 H1
Wellcroft Cl WHHL DN2 ... 92 B1
Well Dr RHAM/THRY S65 ... 135 F5
Wellesley Cl WRKN S81 ... 196 B7
Wellesley Rd FUL S10 ... 8 A3
Wellfield Cl HACK/IN S12 ... 189 C6
  ST/HB/BR S6 ... 8 A1
Wellfield Crs WRKN S81 ... 195 G4
Wellfield Gv STKB/PEN S36 ... 78 A2
Wellfield Rd DOD/DAR S75 ... 2 A1
  KIMB S61 ... 132 B5
  ST/HB/BR S6 ... 8 A1
Wellgate CONI DN12 ... 114 D5
  DOD/DAR S75 ... 29 G6
  RHAM/THRY S65 ... 6 C4
Wellgate Mt RHAM/THRY S65 ... 7 D4
Well Green Rd ST/HB/BR S6 ... 169 F2
Wellhead Rd SHEFS S8 ... 187 G1 ⬛
Well Hill Gv BSLYN/ROY S71 ... 30 D3 ⬛

Well Hill Rd *CHPT/GREN* S35 .... 105 J3
  HOLM/MEL HD7 .... 48 A4
Well House La *STKB/PEN* S36 .... 77 J1
Well Houses La *CHPT/GREN* S35 .... 106 C2
Wellhouse Wy *STKB/PEN* S36 .... 78 A2
Wellingley La *NROS/TKH* DN11 ...... 139 J5
Wellington Av *DIN* S25 .... 177 K8
Wellington Cl *BSLYN/ROY* S71 .... 3 E1
Wellington Crs *BSLY* S70 .... 82 D2
Wellington Gv *BTLY* DN5 .... 64 D8
  BWTY DN10 .... 142 A7 🔟
Wellington Dr *CONI* DN12 .... 115 J5
Wellington Rd *CONI* DN12 .... 115 J5
  HTFD DN7 .... 69 H7
  ST/HB/BR S6 .... 169 J2
Wellington St *BSLY* S70 .... 86 D2 🔢
  MEX/SWTN S64 .... 115 F2
  SHEF S1 .... 9 D3 🔢
Welling Wy *KIMB* S61 .... 132 B8
Well La *AU/AST/KP* S26 .... 175 G5
  BSLYN/ROY S71 .... 56 D2
  NROS/TKH DN11 .... 117 H8
  RHAM S60 .... 156 C6
  RHAM S60 .... 156 A6 🔢
  RHAM S60 .... 174 C5
  ST/HB/BR S6 .... 150 E5
Well Meadow Dr *OWL* S3 .... 8 C2 🔢
Well Meadow St *OWL* S3 .... 8 C2 🔢
Well Pl *SHEFS* S8 .... 187 G1 🔢
Well Rd *SHEFS* S8 .... 187 G1 🔢
Wells Mt *KBTN* HD8 .... 50 B1
Wells Rd *WHHL* DN2 .... 91 J1
Wells St *CUD/GR* S72 .... 28 D7 🔢
  DOD/DAR S75 .... 28 D7 🔢
The Wells *DIN* S25 .... 193 K2
Well St *BSLY* S70 .... 2 A4 🔢
Wellsyke Rd *AWLS/ASK* DN6 .... 38 A8
Wellthorne Av *STKB/PEN* S36 .... 51 F6
Wellthorne La *STKB/PEN* S36 .... 50 E6
Well View Rd *KIMB* S61 .... 132 A7
The Wellway *MALT* S66 .... 135 G8
Welney Pl *ST/HB/BR* S6 .... 151 H3
Welton Cl *DONS/BSCR* DN4 .... 118 B1
Welwyn Cl *HACK/IN* S12 .... 188 D3 🔢
Welwyn Rd *HACK/IN* S12 .... 188 D3
Wembley Av *CONI* DN12 .... 114 B5
Wembley Cl *WHHL* DN2 .... 92 B2 🔢
Wembley Rd *THNE* DN8 .... 23 K4
  WRKN S81 .... 180 D4 🔢
Wenchrist La *GLE* DN14 .... 22 B4
Wendan Rd *THNE* DN8 .... 43 J1
Wendel Gv *HOY* S74 .... 109 J1 🔢
Wenlock St *HAN/WDH* S13 .... 175 H6 🔢
Wensley Cl *ATT* S4 .... 153 F6
Wensley Crs *DONS/BSCR* DN4 .... 92 E8
Wensley Cft *ATT* S4 .... 153 F5
Wensleydale *WRKN* S81 .... 196 F7
Wensley Dale Dr *RHAM* S60 .... 155 G8
Wensleydale Rd *BTLY* DN5 .... 64 A8
  KIMB S61 .... 132 C4
Wensley Gdns *ATT* S4 .... 155 F5
Wensley Gn *ATT* S4 .... 155 F5
Wensley Rd *BSLYN/ROY* S71 .... 29 K8
Wensley St *ATT* S4 .... 155 F5
  DEARNE S63 .... 60 A7
Went Br *AWLS/ASK* DN6 .... 18 E2
Wentdale *PONT* WF8 .... 17 F1
Wentdale Cl *KIMB* S61 .... 131 F2
Wentworth Cl *KIMB* S61 .... 131 F2
Wentworth Ct *BWTY* DN10 .... 164 B1
  RAW S62 .... 132 E3
Wentworth Crs *DOD/DAR* S75 ...... 29 H7 🔢
  STKB/PEN S36 .... 78 A4
Wentworth Dr *DOD/DAR* S75 ...... 29 H7 🔢
  HEM/SK/SE WF9 .... 34 B4
  RAW S62 .... 133 J3
Wentworth Gdns *MEX/SWTN* S64 .. 112 B7
Wentworth Mdw *STKB/PEN* S36 .... 77 K3
Wentworth Ms *STKB/PEN* S36 .... 78 A4 🔢
Wentworth Pl *KIMB* S61 .... 131 K5
Wentworth Rd *DOD/DAR* S75 .... 28 E7
  DOD/DAR S75 .... 200 C6
  DRON S18 .... 82 E6
  HOY S74 .... 83 H3
  HOY S74 .... 109 H4
  KIMB S61 .... 131 G2
  RAW S62 .... 111 G2
  STKB/PEN S36 .... 77 K3
  WHHL DN2 .... 5 E1
Wentworth St *BSLY* S70 .... 81 K8
  BSLYN/ROY S71 .... 2 B2 🔢
Wentworth Vw *HOY* S74 .... 109 G2 🔢
  WMB/DAR S73 .... 84 A6
Wentworth Wy *DIN* S25 .... 178 C8
  DOD/DAR S75 .... 80 E1
  DOD/DAR S75 .... 107 J3
Wescoe Av *CUD/GR* S72 .... 59 H6
Wesley Av *AU/AST/KP* S26 .... 175 K5
Wesley Ct *KIMB* S61 .... 131 G2
Wesley La *FUL* S10 .... 121 J5
Wesley Pl *DIN* S25 .... 193 K3 🔢
Wesley Rd *AU/AST/KP* S26 .... 192 D4
  CHPT/GREN S35 .... 107 H8
Wesley St *BSLY* S70 .... 2 C4 🔢
  HEM/SK/SE WF9 .... 34 D5
Wesley Ter *KBTN* HD8 .... 51 G1

Wessenden Cl *DOD/DAR* S75 .... 55 F6 🔢
Wessex Cl *WRKN* S81 .... 210 E1 🔢
Wessex Gdns *TOT/DORE* S17 .... 199 H2
Wessex Rd *WRKN* S81 .... 210 E1
West Av *AWLS/ASK* DN6 .... 63 C3
  DEARNE S63 .... 86 A6
  DONS/BSCR DN4 .... 90 D8
  HEM/SK/SE WF9 .... 35 C3
  HTFD DN7 .... 42 A3
  RAW S62 .... 133 J1
  WMB/DAR S73 .... 83 J4
West Bank *HTFD* DN7 .... 41 J2
Westbank Cl *DRON* S18 .... 201 H3
Westbank Dr *DIN* S25 .... 193 J3
West Bank Ri *DIN* S25 .... 193 K5
West Bar *SHEF* S1 .... 9 D2
West Bawtry Rd *RHAM* S60 .... 155 C6
Westbourne Gdns
  DONS/BSCR DN4 .... 116 C1 🔢
Westbourne Gv *DOD/DAR* S75 ...... 2 A2 🔢
Westbourne Ter *DOD/DAR* S75 ...... 55 H6
Westbridge Rd *STV/CWN* S43 ...... 206 A8
Westbrook Bank *ECC* S11 .... 8 A6
Westbrook Rd *CHPT/GREN* S35 ... 130 B2
Westbury Av *CHPT/GREN* S35 ..... 130 B5
Westbury Cl *DOD/DAR* S75 .... 55 C3
Westbury St *DARN/MH* S9 .... 172 B2
Westby Cl *RHAM/THRY* S65 .... 135 K7
Westby La *RHAM* S60 .... 156 A6
West Circuit *ARMTH* DN3 .... 40 B7
West Cl *KIMB* S61 .... 132 B7
West Ct *THNE* DN8 .... 43 J1
West Crs *STKB/PEN* S36 .... 78 D5
  STKB/PEN S36 .... 104 D6
Westcroft Crs *MOS* S20 .... 190 C7
Westcroft Dr *MOS* S20 .... 190 C7
Westcroft Gdns *MOS* S20 .... 190 C7
Westcroft Gln *MOS* S20 .... 190 C8 🔢
Westcroft Gv *MOS* S20 .... 190 C8
West Don St *ST/HB/BR* S6 .... 107 K4
West Dr *GLE* DN14 .... 11 J3
  STV/CWN S43 .... 206 A8
West End Av *BSLYN/ROY* S71 .... 30 B4
  BTLY DN5 .... 64 D8
  HOLM/MEL HD7 .... 48 B1
  STKB/PEN S36 .... 76 E4
West End Crs *BSLYN/ROY* S71 .... 30 B4
West End Gdns *GLE* DN14 .... 11 J3
Westend La *GLE* DN14 .... 10 B4
West End La *NROS/TKH* DN11 ..... 118 C5
  DEARNE S63 .... 110 E1
West End Vw *ECK/KIL* S21 .... 204 A5
Westerdale *WRKN* S81 .... 196 E7
Westerdale Rd *BTLY* DN5 .... 90 A1
Western Av *DIN* S25 .... 178 B7
Western Bank *FUL* S10 .... 8 B5 🔢
Western Rd *FUL* S10 .... 170 B3
  RHAM/THRY S65 .... 7 F3
Western St *BSLY* S70 .... 2 B3
Western Ter *WMB/DAR* S73 .... 83 K4
Westerton Dr *MALT* S66 .... 157 K3
Westfield Av *AU/AST/KP* S26 ...... 191 K1
  ECC S11 .... 186 A5 🔢
Westfield Centre *MOS* S20 .... 190 C7
Westfield Crs *AWLS/ASK* DN6 .... 18 D7
  DEARNE S63 .... 60 B7
  MOS S20 .... 190 B7
Westfield Dr *WRKN* S81 .... 210 E2
Westfield Gv *HACK/IN* S12 .... 189 K4 🔢
Westfield La *BTLY* DN5 .... 87 G4
  ECK/KIL S21 .... 203 F7
  HEM/SK/SE WF9 .... 34 E6
West Field La *HOLM/MEL* HD7 ...... 48 B1
Westfield La *HTFD* DN7 .... 21 H6
  PONT WF8 .... 17 F4
  STKB/PEN S36 .... 77 H3
  STV/CWN S43 .... 205 K8
Westfield Northway *MOS* S20 ..... 190 C7
Westfield Rd *ARMTH* DN3 .... 93 F1 🔢
  DEARNE S63 .... 84 D8 🔢
  DONS/BSCR DN4 .... 4 B5
  DRON S18 .... 201 J7
  ECK/KIL S21 .... 205 G2
  HTFD DN7 .... 21 H7
  HTFD DN7 .... 42 D8
  MALT S66 .... 139 J3
  NROS/TKH DN11 .... 139 J8
  RAW S62 .... 133 H3
Westfields *BSLY* S70 .... 82 B3
  BSLYN/ROY S71 .... 30 B3
Westfield Southway *MOS* S20 ..... 190 C7
Westfield St *BSLY* S70 .... 2 A4 🔢
Westfield Ter *SHEF* S1 .... 8 C5
Westfield Vls *HTFD* DN7 .... 42 D7 🔢
West Garth Cl *DIN* S25 .... 178 E6 🔢
Westgate *BSLY* S70 .... 2 B4
  BSLYN/ROY S71 .... 3 E1
  HEM/SK/SE WF9 .... 33 F1
  STKB/PEN S36 .... 78 A5

Westgate Vw *WRKS* S80 .... 210 C5
Westgate *WRKS* S80 .... 210 C5 🔢
West Green Dr *ARMTH* DN3 .... 66 D3
West Gv *BSLYN/ROY* S71 .... 30 B3
  WHHL DN2 .... 91 K2
West Hl *KIMB* S61 .... 153 K1
Westhill La *SHEF* S1 .... 8 C3 🔢
Westholme Rd *DONS/BSCR* DN4 .... 4 B5
West Kirk La *CUD/GR* S72 .... 59 H8
West Laith Ga *DON* DN1 .... 4 C3 🔢
Westland Cl *MOS* S20 .... 190 C6
Westland Gdns *MOS* S20 .... 190 B6
Westland Gv *MOS* S20 .... 190 C7 🔢
Westland Rd *MOS* S20 .... 190 C6
West La *AU/AST/KP* S26 .... 175 F6
  GLE DN14 .... 20 E2
  MALT S66 .... 158 B6
  ST/HB/BR S6 .... 148 C6
  ST/HB/BR S6 .... 149 J5
Westminster Cl *FUL* S10 .... 169 F6 🔢
  WRKN S81 .... 196 E8
Westminster Crs *FUL* S10 .... 169 F6
  WHHL DN2 .... 92 B2 🔢
Westminster Dr *HTFD* DN7 .... 67 K3
West Moor Crs *DOD/DAR* S75 .... 55 K5
West Moor La *ARMTH* DN3 .... 67 J8
Westmoreland St *ST/HB/BR* S6 ... 8 B1 🔢
Westmorland Dr *WRKN* S81 .... 180 C7
Westmorland St *DONS/BSCR* DN4 116 C0
Westmorland Wy *BTLY* DN5 .... 89 H6
Westmount Av *DEARNE* S63 .... 85 F7
Westnall Rd *SHEFN* S5 .... 130 E8
Westnall Ter *SHEFN* S5 .... 130 E8
Westongales Wy *BTLY* DN5 .... 64 D7 🔢
Weston Rd *DONS/BSCR* DN4 .... 116 E9
Westover Rd *FUL* S10 .... 169 J5
West Park Dr *AU/AST/KP* S26 ..... 175 F8
West Pinfold *BSLYN/ROY* S71 .... 30 C4
Westpit Hl *DEARNE* S63 .... 84 D8
West Pl *BTLY* DN5 .... 64 E6
West Qd *SHEFN* S5 .... 152 E4
West Rd *DOD/DAR* S75 .... 55 H6
  MEX/SWTN S64 .... 112 C2
  THNE DN8 .... 24 A4
West Service Rd *ARMTH* DN3 .... 40 E7
Westside Gra *DONS/BSCR* DN4 ..... 4 A6
West St *BSLY* S70 .... 82 C3
  BSLYN/ROY S71 .... 30 E3
  BWTY DN10 .... 143 J5
  CONI DN12 .... 114 D3
  CUD/GR S72 .... 32 B3
  DEARNE S63 .... 86 D1 🔢
  DEARNE S63 .... 111 J5
  DIN S25 .... 193 K3
  DON DN1 .... 4 C3
  DRON S18 .... 201 F5 🔢
  ECK/KIL S21 .... 204 A3
  HEM/SK/SE WF9 .... 33 J1
  HEM/SK/SE WF9 .... 35 G3
  HOY S74 .... 108 D7
  MALT S66 .... 158 A4
  MEX/SWTN S64 .... 112 C2
  MOS S20 .... 190 D6
  NROS/TKH DN11 .... 163 F1
  SHEF S1 .... 8 C5
  THNE DN8 .... 43 J1
  WMB/DAR S73 .... 83 K4
  WMB/DAR S73 .... 84 D2
  WRKS S80 .... 210 C5
West Street La *SHEF* S1 .... 9 D3 🔢
Westthorpe Fields Rd *ECK/KIL* S21... 205 G3
Westthorpe Rd *ECK/KIL* S21 .... 205 H4
West Vale Gv *RHAM/THRY* S65 .... 134 E1
West Vw *CUD/GR* S72 .... 57 K2
  STV/CWN S43 .... 206 A7
West View *TOT/DORE* S17 .... 199 K1
  DEARNE S63 .... 86 B3
West View La *TOT/DORE* S17 ..... 199 K1 🔢
West View Rd *KIMB* S61 .... 153 K1
  MEX/SWTN S64 .... 115 F7
West Wy *BSLY* S70 .... 2 B3
Westway *WRKN* S81 .... 196 E8
Westwell Pl *MOS* S20 .... 204 B3
Westwick Crs *TOT/DORE* S17 ...... 186 D1
Westwick Gv *SHEFS* S8 .... 186 D1
Westwick Rd *SHEFS* S8 .... 186 D1
Westwood Ct *BSLY* S70 .... 2 B3 🔢
  CHPT/GREN S35 .... 107 G6
Westwood Dr *WRKS* S80 .... 209 K4
Westwood La *CHPT/GREN* S35 .... 107 G6
Westwood New Rd *DOD/DAR* S75... 107 J3
Westwood Rd *ECC* S11 .... 169 K4
Wetherby Cl *BTLY* DN5 .... 90 A1
Wetherby Dr *DARN/MH* S9 .... 172 E3
Wetherby Dr *AU/AST/KP* S26 ...... 175 C3
  MEX/SWTN S64 .... 113 G3
Wet Moor La *DEARNE* S63 .... 85 J7
Wet Shaw La *ST/HB/BR* S6 .... 148 A4
Whaley Rd *DOD/DAR* S75 .... 54 E5
Whams Rd *STKB/PEN* S36 .... 75 K5
Wharf Cl *MEX/SWTN* S64 .... 112 D4 🔢
Wharfedale *WRKN* S81 .... 196 F7
Wharfedale Dr *CHPT/GREN* S35 .. 129 J6
Wharfedale Rd *DOD/DAR* S75 ...... 55 F6
Wharf Rd *DARN/MH* S9 .... 154 A2
  DON DN1 .... 5 D1
  MEX/SWTN S64 .... 113 J2

Wharf St *ATT* S4 .... 9 E2 🔟
  BSLYN/ROY S71 .... 3 D2 🔟
  BWTY DN10 .... 142 B8
  MEX/SWTN S64 .... 112 D4
Wharncliffe *DOD/DAR* S75 .... 81 F1 🔟
Wharncliffe Av *AU/AST/KP* S26 .... 175 J7 🔟
  CHPT/GREN S35 .... 128 A4
  DEARNE S63 .... 111 J1 🔟
Wharncliffe Cl *HOY* S74 .... 108 C3
  RAW S62 .... 111 G7 🔟
Wharncliffe Rd *CHPT/GREN* S35 .. 107 J8 🔟
  FUL S10 .... 8 B4
Wharncliffe St *BSLY* S70 .... 2 A4
  BSLYN/ROY S71 .... 30 E7 🔟
  DONS/BSCR DN4 .... 4 A4 🔟
  RHAM/THRY S65 .... 7 D3
Wharton Av *AU/AST/KP* S26 .... 175 H6
Wheatacre Rd *STKB/PEN* S36 .... 105 F6
Wheata Dr *SHEFN* S5 .... 130 B8
Wheata Pl *SHEFN* S5 .... 130 B8
Wheata Rd *SHEFN* S5 .... 152 B1
Wheat Cft *CONI* S62 .... 99 J7
Wheatcroft *SHEF* S1 .... 197 F8 🔟
Wheatcroft Rd *RAW* S62 .... 134 A1
Wheatfield Cl *ARMTH* DN3 .... 67 F1
Wheatfield Crs *SHEFN* S5 .... 152 E1
Wheatfield Dr *DEARNE* S63 .... 60 C8 🔟
  NROS/TKH DN11 .... 140 A7
Wheathill St *RHAM* S60 .... 6 C5 🔟
Wheatley Av *HAN/WDH* S13 .... 173 G6
Wheatley Gv *HAN/WDH* S13 .... 173 G6
Wheatley Hall Rd *WHHL* DN2 .... 66 C6
  WHHL DN2 .... 91 J1
Wheatley Hill La *KBTN* HD8 .... 26 B7
Wheatley Pl *CONI* DN12 .... 114 A4 🔟
Wheatley Ri *DOD/DAR* S75 .... 29 G5 🔟
Wheatley Rd *BSLY* S70 .... 57 F8 🔟
  BTLY DN5 .... 64 D5
  KIMB S61 .... 132 B6
  MEX/SWTN S64 .... 112 D8
Wheatley St *CONI* DN12 .... 114 A4
Wheeldon St *SHEF* S1 .... 8 C5 🔟🔟
Wheel La *CHPT/GREN* S35 .... 129 J7
  CHPT/GREN S35 .... 150 J1
The Wheel *CHPT/GREN* S35 .... 129 K7
Wheldrake Rd *SHEFN* S5 .... 152 E5
Whernside Av *CHPT/GREN* S35 .... 130 A1 🔟
Whinacre Cl *SHEFS* S8 .... 201 H1 🔟
Whinacre Pl *SHEFS* S8 .... 201 H1
Whinby Cft *DOD/DAR* S75 .... 55 F6
Whinby Rd *DOD/DAR* S75 .... 54 C7
Whin Cl *HEM/SK/SE* WF9 .... 33 G2
Whinfell Cl *AWLS/ASK* DN6 .... 63 J1
Whinfell Ct *ECC* S11 .... 185 J5
Whin Gdns *DEARNE* S63 .... 60 C6
Whin Hill Rd *DONS/BSCR* DN4 .... 92 C7
Whinmoor Cl *DOD/DAR* S75 .... 53 J6
Whinmoor Dr *DOD/DAR* S75 .... 53 J6
Whinmoor Rd *CHPT/GREN* S35 .... 107 H8
  SHEFN S5 .... 153 C4 🔟
Whinmoor Vw *DOD/DAR* S75 .... 53 J6
Whinmoor Wy *DOD/DAR* S75 .... 53 J7
Whinny Haugh La
  NROS/TKH DN11 .... 162 A2
Whinside Crs *DEARNE* S63 .... 60 B6
The Whins *RAW* S62 .... 133 F2
Whiphill Cl *DONS/BSCR* DN4 .... 92 D8 🔟
Whiphill La *ARMTH* DN3 .... 93 H2
Whiphill Top La *ARMTH* DN3 .... 93 K7
Whirlow Court Rd *ECC* S11 .... 185 K5
Whirlowdale Cl *ECC* S11 .... 185 K5 🔟
Whirlowdale Crs *ECC* S11 .... 186 B4
Whirlowdale Ri *ECC* S11 .... 185 K5 🔟
Whirlowdale Rd *ABRD* S7 .... 186 A5
  ECC S11 .... 185 K5
Whirlow Gv *ECC* S11 .... 185 K5
Whirlow La *ECC* S11 .... 185 K5
Whirlow Ms *ECC* S11 .... 185 K4 🔟
Whirlow Park Rd *ABRD* S7 .... 185 K6
Whisperwood Dr
  DONS/BSCR DN4 .... 116 E3
Whiston Brook Vw *RHAM* S60 .... 156 B6
Whiston Gra *RHAM* S60 .... 155 K6
Whiston Gn *RHAM* S60 .... 156 A7 🔟
Whiston Gv *RHAM* S60 .... 7 E6
Whiston V *RHAM* S60 .... 156 A7
Whitaker Cl *NROS/TKH* DN11 .... 118 E8
Whitbeck Cl *NROS/TKH* DN11 .... 116 E8
Whitbourne Cl *BSLYN/ROY* S71 .... 56 A2 🔟
Whitburn Rd *DON* DN1 .... 5 E4 🔟
Whitby Rd *DARN/MH* S9 .... 172 D3 🔟
  DARN/MH S9 .... 172 D3 🔟
  NROS/TKH DN11 .... 163 F2
Whitcomb Dr *NROS/TKH* DN11 .... 119 F1
White Apron St *HEM/SK/SE* WF9 .... 34 A5
White Av *WRKN* S81 .... 180 C4
White Cft *SHEF* S1 .... 9 D2
Whitecroft Crs *RHAM* S60 .... 155 F7
White Cross Av *CUD/GR* S72 .... 57 J2
White Cross Ct *CUD/GR* S72 .... 57 K2 🔟
White Cross Gdns *CUD/GR* S72 .... 32 A1
White Cross La *BSLY* S70 .... 82 E2
  NROS/TKH DN11 .... 116 D6
White Cross Mt *CUD/GR* S72 .... 57 K2 🔟
White Cross Ri *BSLY* S70 .... 82 E2
White Cross Rd *CUD/GR* S72 .... 57 J2
White Ga *DIN* S25 .... 194 B1 🔟
White Gate Rd *HOLM/MEL* HD7 .... 47 G6

Whitehall Rd *KIMB* S61 .... 132 C3
White Hart Fold
  HEM/SK/SE WF9 .... 35 G1 🔟
White Hart Yd *WRKS* S80 .... 210 C5 🔟
Whitehead Av *STKB/PEN* S36 .... 105 G7
Whitehead Cl *DIN* S25 .... 178 A7
White Hill Av *BSLY* S70 .... 55 F6
Whitehill Av *RHAM* S60 .... 155 F7
Whitehill Dr *RHAM* S60 .... 155 F8
White Hill Gv *BSLY* S70 .... 55 G6 🔟
Whitehill La *RHAM* S60 .... 155 F6
Whitehill Rd *RHAM* S60 .... 155 F7
White Hill Ter *BSLY* S70 .... 55 F6 🔟
Whitehouse Ct *NROS/TKH* DN11 .... 163 H3
White House Dr *NROS/TKH* DN11 .... 163 H3
Whitehouse La *ST/HB/BR* S6 .... 170 D1
White House Rd *NROS/TKH* DN11 .... 163 H3
Whitehouse Rd *ST/HB/BR* S6 .... 170 D1
White House Vw *ARMTH* DN3 .... 40 D7
White La *BTLY* DN5 .... 61 K3
  CHPT/GREN S35 .... 108 C8
  HACK/IN S12 .... 188 C4
  THNE DN8 .... 23 G8
Whitelea Gv *MEX/SWTN* S64 .... 112 E3
White Lee La *CHPT/GREN* S35 .... 126 E4
Whitelee Rd *MEX/SWTN* S64 .... 112 D3
Whiteley La *ECC* S11 .... 169 G8
White Ley Rd *CONI* S40 .... 16 F6
Whiteley Wood Cl *ECC* S11 .... 169 J8
Whiteley Wood Rd *ECC* S11 .... 185 J1
Whitelow La *TOT/DORE* S17 .... 184 E8
White Rose Ct *BTLY* DN5 .... 65 F6
White Rose Wy *DONS/BSCR* DN4 .... 5 E6
  DONS/BSCR DN4 .... 117 J1
White's La *SHEFP/MNR* S2 .... 171 K4
White Thorns Cl *SHEFS* S8 .... 201 H3 🔟
White Thorns Dr *SHEFS* S8 .... 201 H2
White Thorns Vw *SHEFS* S8 .... 201 H1
White Walls La *HOLM/MEL* HD7 .... 46 C4
Whitewater La *NROS/TKH* DN11 .... 162 B8
  WRKN S81 .... 181 J2
Whiteways Cl *ATT* S4 .... 152 E7
Whiteways Dr *ATT* S4 .... 152 E7 🔟
Whiteways Gv *ATT* S4 .... 152 E7
Whiteways Rd *ATT* S4 .... 152 E7
White Wells Gdns *HOLM/MEL* HD7 .. 48 C4
White Wells Rd *HOLM/MEL* HD7 .... 48 C4
Whitewood Cl *BSLYN/ROY* S71 .... 30 C4 🔟
Whitfield Gdns *WRKN* S81 .... 195 F3
Whitfield Rd *FUL* S10 .... 169 G8
  RAW S62 .... 111 F7
Whiting St *SHEFS* S8 .... 187 G1 🔟🔟
Whitley Carr *CHPT/GREN* S35 .... 129 K5
Whitley La *CHPT/GREN* S35 .... 129 J6
Whitley Rd *STKB/PEN* S36 .... 76 A1
Whitley Vw *CHPT/GREN* S35 .... 130 C5
Whitley View Rd *KIMB* S61 .... 153 J2
Whitney Cl *DONS/BSCR* DN4 .... 116 B2 🔟
Whitsun Dl *WRKN* S81 .... 197 F8
Whittier Rd *DONS/BSCR* DN4 .... 116 D1
Whittington St *DON* DN1 .... 5 D1
Whitton Ct *DONS/BSCR* DN4 .... 118 B1
Whitwell Crs *STKB/PEN* S36 .... 104 E6
Whitwell La *STKB/PEN* S36 .... 104 D7
Whitwell Rd *AU/AST/KP* S26 .... 208 C4
  WRKS S80 .... 208 C3
Whitwell St *DARN/MH* S9 .... 173 F3
Whitwell Vw *NROS/TKH* DN11 .... 119 G6 🔟
Whitworth La *DARN/MH* S9 .... 153 H8
Whitworth Rd *FUL* S10 .... 169 J6
Whitworth St *DEARNE* S63 .... 86 D2 🔟
Whitworth Wy *DEARNE* S63 .... 85 H8
Whybourne Gv *RHAM* S60 .... 7 D4 🔟
Whyn Vw *DEARNE* S63 .... 60 B7 🔟
Wicker *DON* DN1 .... 9 E2
Wicker La *OWL* S3 .... 9 E2
Wickersley Rd *RHAM/THRY* S65 .... 7 F6
Wickett Hern Rd *ARMTH* DN3 .... 93 J1
Wicket Wy *CONI* DN12 .... 115 K4
Wickfield Cl *HACK/IN* S12 .... 189 H2
Wickfield Dr *HACK/IN* S12 .... 189 G3
Wickfield Gv *HACK/IN* S12 .... 189 G2
Wickfield Pl *HACK/IN* S12 .... 189 G2
Wickfield Rd *HACK/IN* S12 .... 189 H3
Wickins La *HOLM/MEL* HD7 .... 47 G1
Wickleden Ga *HOLM/MEL* HD7 .... 48 C4
Wicklow La *WHHL* DN2 .... 91 K2
Widdop Cl *HAN/WDH* S13 .... 173 F7
Widdop Cft *HAN/WDH* S13 .... 173 F7
Widford La *RHAM* S60 .... 155 K7
Widgeon Dr *WHHL* DN2 .... 91 K2
Wigfield Dr *BSLY* S70 .... 82 A2
Wigfull Rd *ECC* S11 .... 170 C6
Wignall Av *MALT* S66 .... 156 E5
Wigthorpe La *WRKN* S81 .... 196 E3
Wike Gate Cl *THNE* DN8 .... 44 A1 🔟
Wike Gate Gv *THNE* DN8 .... 44 A1 🔟
Wike Gate Rd *THNE* DN8 .... 24 A8
Wike Rd *BSLYN/ROY* S71 .... 57 F5
Wilberforce Rd *DIN* S25 .... 193 K2
  WHHL DN2 .... 66 C6
Wilbrook Ri *DOD/DAR* S75 .... 55 F5
Wilby La *BSLY* S70 .... 3 D5 🔟
Wilcox Cl *ST/HB/BR* S6 .... 151 J2
Wilcox Rd *ST/HB/BR* S6 .... 151 H2
Wild Av *RAW* S62 .... 111 F8
Wildene Dr *MEX/SWTN* S64 .... 113 F1
Wildflower Cl *NROS/TKH* DN11 .... 118 D8

Wilding Cl *KIMB* S61 .... 132 B7
Wilding Wy *KIMB* S61 .... 132 B7
Wildspur Gv *HOLM/MEL* HD7 .... 48 D3
Wilford Rd *BSLYN/ROY* S71 .... 29 K6
Wilfred Cl *DARN/MH* S9 .... 172 C2 🔟
Wilfred Dr *DARN/MH* S9 .... 172 C2
Wilfred Rd *RHAM* S60 .... 6 C4
Wilfrid Rd *DARN/MH* S9 .... 172 C2 🔟
Wilkinson Av *NROS/TKH* DN11 .... 119 F7 🔟
  THNE DN8 .... 23 K5
Wilkinson La *OWL* S3 .... 8 B3 🔟
  OWL S3 .... 8 B3 🔟
Wilkinson Rd *HOY* S74 .... 109 H2
Wilkinson St *BSLY* S70 .... 2 C5 🔟
  FUL S10 .... 8 B3
  OWL S3 .... 8 B3 🔟
Willan Dr *RHAM* S60 .... 174 A2
Willbury Dr *HACK/IN* S12 .... 188 C3
Willey St *OWL* S3 .... 9 E2 🔟🔟
William Bradford Cl *BWTY* DN10 .. 142 D6
William Cl *MOS* S20 .... 204 B1 🔟
William Crs *MOS* S20 .... 190 B8
William La *NROS/TKH* DN11 .... 118 C6
Williamson Rd *ECC* S11 .... 170 D8
Williams Rd *BTLY* DN5 .... 90 C1
Williams St *WRKN* S81 .... 180 C4
William St *BSLY* S70 .... 82 B2
  DEARNE S63 .... 86 B2
  DEARNE S63 .... 111 J1
  ECK/KIL S21 .... 204 B4
  FUL S10 .... 8 B4
  MEX/SWTN S64 .... 112 D4
  RAW S62 .... 133 K3
  RHAM/THRY S65 .... 7 D4
  WMB/DAR S73 .... 83 K4 🔟
Willingham Cl *MOS* S20 .... 190 E6
Willingham Gdns *MOS* S20 .... 190 E5 🔟🔟
Willington Rd *AWLS/ASK* DN6 .... 37 H6
  SHEFN S5 .... 152 D3
Willis Rd *ST/HB/BR* S6 .... 151 G6
Willman Rd *BSLYN/ROY* S71 .... 57 G4
Willoughby St *ATT* S4 .... 152 E5
Willow Av *DONS/BSCR* DN4 .... 92 E7
  RAW S62 .... 133 K2
  THNE DN8 .... 23 J5
  WRKN S81 .... 180 C3
Willow Bank *BSLYN/ROY* S71 .... 2 A1
Willow Bridge La *HTFD* DN7 .... 40 D1
Willowbrook *AWLS/ASK* DN6 .... 37 C5
Willow Brook Rd *DOD/DAR* S75 .... 29 F7
Willow Cl *CUD/GR* S72 .... 31 J8 🔟
  DIN S25 .... 193 K4
  GLE DN14 .... 12 A3
  HOY S74 .... 108 D2
  MALT S66 .... 157 H1
  RHAM S60 .... 155 G8
  WRKS S80 .... 210 C6
Willow Ct *MALT* S66 .... 157 G2
Willow Crs *CHPT/GREN* S35 .... 130 B3
  EPW DN9 .... 120 A3
  MALT S66 .... 137 H5
  THNE DN8 .... 23 J6
Willowdale Cl *BTLY* DN5 .... 90 A7
Willow Dene Rd *CUD/GR* S72 .... 32 D8 🔟
Willow Dr *CONI* DN12 .... 115 K4
  DARN/MH S9 .... 173 C4
  HEM/SK/SE WF9 .... 33 F2
  MALT S66 .... 157 H1
  MEX/SWTN S64 .... 112 E2
Willow Garth *GLE* DN14 .... 12 A4 🔟
  HEM/SK/SE WF9 .... 35 G5
  RAW S62 .... 133 K1
Willowgarth Av *RHAM* S60 .... 155 F8
Willow Garth La *AWLS/ASK* DN6 .... 18 E6
Willow Gv *AU/AST/KP* S26 .... 175 K7 🔟
  GLE DN14 .... 12 A4 🔟
  THNE DN8 .... 23 K5
Willow La *DEARNE* S63 .... 86 C6
  GLE DN14 .... 12 A4
  NROS/TKH DN11 .... 119 F6
Willowlees Ct *DONS/BSCR* DN4 .... 92 D8 🔟
Willow Pl *MALT* S66 .... 137 H5
Willow Rd *ARMTH* DN3 .... 67 H8
  AWLS/ASK DN6 .... 18 A6
  DEARNE S63 .... 60 C7
  ECK/KIL S21 .... 111 K3
  MALT S66 .... 205 C2
  STKB/PEN S36 .... 158 E2
  THNE DN8 .... 104 E8
The Willows *KIMB* S61 .... 23 J6
Willow St *CONI* DN12 .... 132 A5
Willow Wk *BTLY* DN5 .... 114 E5
Wilmington Dr *DONS/BSCR* DN4 .... 64 D4 🔟
Wilsden Gv *DOD/DAR* S75 .... 91 J8
Wilsic La *NROS/TKH* DN11 .... 55 G3 🔟
Wilsic Rd *NROS/TKH* DN11 .... 139 G5
Wilson Av *RAW* S62 .... 138 D1
  STKB/PEN S36 .... 133 H1
Wilson Cl *BWTY* DN10 .... 78 A5 🔟
Wilson Dr *RHAM/THRY* S65 .... 165 H7
Wilson Gv *BSLYN/ROY* S71 .... 134 D6
Wilson Pl *SHEFS* S8 .... 57 F3
Wilson St *DRON* S18 .... 187 C1 🔟
  ECC S11 .... 201 J3
  STKB/PEN S36 .... 170 C7
Wilson St *DRON* S18 .... 105 J7
  OWL S3 .... 201 H7 🔟
  WMB/DAR S73 .... 171 G1
   .... 83 J4

Wilthorpe Av *DOD/DAR* S75 .... 55 H3
Wilthorpe Cl *DOD/DAR* S75 .... 55 H3
Wilthorpe Farm Rd *DOD/DAR* S75 ... 55 H3
Wilthorpe Gdns *HACK/IN* S12 .... 189 J4 🔢
Wilthorpe Gn *DOD/DAR* S75 .... 55 H3 🔢
Wilthorpe La *DOD/DAR* S75 .... 55 G3 🔢
Wilthorpe Rd *DOD/DAR* S75 .... 55 F3
Wilton Cl *RAW* S62 .... 133 J2
Wilton Ct *KIMB* S61 .... 132 D8
Wilton Gdns *KIMB* S61 .... 132 D8
Wilton La *KIMB* S61 .... 154 D1
Wilton Pl *FUL* S10 .... 8 B4
Wiltshire Rd *WHHL* DN2 .... 92 B3
Winberry Av *DIN* S25 .... 194 A2
Wincanton Cl *MEX/SWTN* S64 .... 113 G1
Winchester Av *FUL* S10 .... 169 F7
.... *WHHL* DN2 .... 91 K1
Winchester Cl *WRKN* S81 .... 196 E8
Winchester Cres *FUL* S10 .... 169 F7
Winchester Dr *FUL* S10 .... 169 F7 🔢
Winchester Ms *NROS/TKH* DN11 .... 163 F1
Winchester Rd *FUL* S10 .... 169 F7
.... *HTFD* DN7 .... 42 B7
Winchester Wy *BSLYN/ROY* S71 .... 57 H8 🔢
.... *BTLY* DN5 .... 90 A1
.... *RHAM* S60 .... 154 D6
Wincobank Av *SHEFN* S5 .... 153 F4
Wincobank Cl *SHEFN* S5 .... 153 G4 🔢
Wincobank La *ATT* S4 .... 153 G6
Wincobank La *SHEFN* S5 .... 153 G4
Windam *DARNTH* DN3 .... 40 E7
Windermere Av *DRON* S18 .... 200 E6
.... *NROS/TKH* DN11 .... 162 E5 🔢
.... *WHHL* DN2 .... 92 D3 🔢
Windermere Cl *AWLS/ASK* DN6 ...... 37 H6 🔢
.... *WRKN* S81 .... 196 C7 🔢
Windermere Ct *DIN* S25 .... 194 A1
Windermere Crs *ARMTH* DN3 .... 66 E3 🔢
Windermere Gra *CONI* DN12 .... 115 J6 🔢
Windermere Rd *BSLYN/ROY* S71 .... 3 D4 🔢
.... *SHEFS* S8 .... 186 E2 🔢
.... *STKB/PEN* S36 .... 78 A5
Winders Pl *WMB/DAR* S73 .... 84 A5 🔢
Windgate Hl *CONI* DN12 .... 114 C4
Windham Cl *BSLYN/ROY* S71 .... 2 C2 🔢
Windhill Av *DOD/DAR* S75 .... 29 F4
.... *MEX/SWTN* S64 .... 113 H1
Windhill Crs *DOD/DAR* S75 .... 29 F4
.... *MEX/SWTN* S64 .... 113 H1
Windhill Dr *DOD/DAR* S75 .... 29 F4
Windhill La *DOD/DAR* S75 .... 29 F4
Wind Hill La *STKB/PEN* S36 .... 103 J7
Windhill Mt *DOD/DAR* S75 .... 28 E4
Windhill Ter *MEX/SWTN* S64 .... 113 H1
The Windings *DEARNE* S63 .... 60 D8
Windle Edge *STKB/PEN* S36 .... 99 K1
Windle Rd *DONS/BSCR* DN4 .... 4 A5
Windle Sq *ARMTH* DN3 .... 66 E3 🔢
Windlestone Sq *THNE* DN8 .... 24 B3
Windmere Av *DEARNE* S63 .... 86 D3
Windmill Av *CONI* DN12 .... 114 E6
.... *CUD/GR* S72 .... 32 C7
Windmill Balk La *AWLS/ASK* DN6 .. 63 J3
Windmill Dr *NROS/TKH* DN11 .... 138 E1
Windmill Greenway *MOS* S20 .... 204 C2
Windmill Hill La *CHPT/GREN* S35 .. 129 K3
Windmill La *AWLS/ASK* DN6 .... 17 J5
.... *KBTN* HD8 .... 49 J4
.... *SHEFN* S5 .... 153 F4
.... *WRKS* S80 .... 210 E7
Windmill Rd *DIN* S25 .... 194 A1
.... *WMB/DAR* S73 .... 83 J3
Windmill Vw *HOLM/MEL* HD7 .... 48 B4
Windsor Av *DOD/DAR* S75 .... 28 B7
.... *STKB/PEN* S36 .... 77 H3
Windsor Cl *AWLS/ASK* DN6 .... 19 F7
.... *BTLY* DN5 .... 87 H5
.... *MALT* S66 .... 157 J1
Windsor Ct *HTFD* DN7 .... 67 K3
Windsor Crs *BSLYN/ROY* S71 .... 3 E2
.... *CUD/GR* S72 .... 59 G8
Windsor Dr *BTLY* DN5 .... 87 H4
.... *DOD/DAR* S75 .... 54 E8 🔢
.... *DRON* S18 .... 200 C6
.... *MEX/SWTN* S64 .... 113 H1
Windsor Gdns *WRKN* S81 .... 196 C1
Windsor Rd *AU/AST/KP* S26 .... 191 J1
Windsor Ri *CONI* DN12 .... 114 C4 🔢
.... *HEM/SK/SE* WF9 .... 33 J1
.... *KIMB* S61 .... 131 G3
.... *SHEFS* S8 .... 187 F1
.... *WHHL* DN2 .... 5 F2
.... *WRKN* S81 .... 196 B8
.... *WRKN* S81 .... 196 C1
Windsor Sq *DEARNE* S63 .... 60 D7
Windsor St *ATT* S4 .... 171 K1 🔢
.... *DEARNE* S63 .... 60 D7
.... *HEM/SK/SE* WF9 .... 35 F5
.... *HOY* S74 .... 82 E8
Windsor Wk *BTLY* DN5 .... 90 B1
.... *DIN* S25 .... 193 J4
Windy Bank *ST/HB/BR* S6 .... 148 B1
Windy House La *SHEFP/MNR* S2 ... 172 B8
Windy Rdg *AU/AST/KP* S26 .... 175 G6
Windyridge *BWTY* DN10 .... 165 K4
Winfield Rd *DEARNE* S63 .... 111 J2
Wingerworth Av *SHEFS* S8 .... 186 D8
Wingfield Av *WRKN* S81 .... 210 D1
Wingfield Cl *DRON* S18 .... 200 C7

KIMB S61 .... 132 D4
Wingfield Crs *HACK/IN* S12 .... 188 E2
Wingfield Rd *BSLYN/ROY* S71 .... 56 B1
.... *KIMB* S61 .... 132 B4
Winifred St *RHAM* S60 .... 6 B3
.... *WRKS* S80 .... 209 J3
Winkley Ter *SHEFN* S5 .... 153 F2
Winlea Av *RHAM/THRY* S65 .... 156 D3
Winn Cl *ST/HB/BR* S6 .... 151 G4
Winn Dr *ST/HB/BR* S6 .... 151 G4
Winnery Cl *NROS/TKH* DN11 .... 139 K7 🔢
Winney Bank La *HOLM/MEL* HD7 ... 48 A2
Winney Hl *AU/AST/KP* S26 .... 206 E2
Winney La *AU/AST/KP* S26 .... 206 E3
Winn Gdns *ST/HB/BR* S6 .... 151 G4
Winn Gv *ST/HB/BR* S6 .... 151 G4
Winnipeg Rd *BTLY* DN5 .... 64 E6
Winsford Rd *ST/HB/BR* S6 .... 151 H2
Winster Cl *BSLY* S70 .... 82 A7
Winster Gv *WRKN* S81 .... 196 D7
Winster Rd *ST/HB/BR* S6 .... 151 H6
Winston Av *STKB/PEN* S36 .... 104 C5
Winston Gn *BWTY* DN10 .... 165 C6
Winter Av *BSLYN/ROY* S71 .... 30 D7
.... *DOD/DAR* S75 .... 55 H5
Winter Hill La *KIMB* S61 .... 132 B8
Winterhill Rd *KIMB* S61 .... 154 A1
Winter Rd *DOD/DAR* S75 .... 55 H5
Winter St *OWL* S3 .... 8 B2
Winter Ter *DOD/DAR* S75 .... 55 H5
Winterton Cl *DONS/BSCR* DN4 ...... 118 C1 🔢
Winterton Gdns *HACK/IN* S12 .... 190 A4
Winterwell Rd *DEARNE* S63 .... 85 F8
Winton Cl *BSLY* S70 .... 5 D6 🔢
Winton Rd *WHHL* DN2 .... 92 A3
Wiseton Rd *ECC* S11 .... 170 C6
Wisewood Av *ST/HB/BR* S6 .... 151 F1
Wisewood La *ST/HB/BR* S6 .... 151 F7
Wisewood Pl *ST/HB/BR* S6 .... 151 F7
Wisewood Rd *ST/HB/BR* S6 .... 151 F7
Witham Ct *DOD/DAR* S75 .... 54 D4
Witham Rd *FUL* S10 .... 170 C5
Withens Av *ST/HB/BR* S6 .... 151 C5
Withens Ct *DOD/DAR* S75 .... 29 F6
Withyside *KBTN* HD8 .... 51 H1
Witmore St *HEM/SK/SE* WF9 .... 35 F4
Witney St *SHEFP/MNR* S2 .... 9 D6 🔢
Wivelsfield Rd *DONS/BSCR* DN4 ... 90 A8
Woburn Cl *DONS/BSCR* DN4 .... 116 B2
Woburn Pl *DOD/DAR* S75 .... 80 E1 🔢
.... *ECC* S11 .... 185 K5
Wolfe Dr *ST/HB/BR* S6 .... 151 J2 🔢
Wolfe Rd *ST/HB/BR* S6 .... 151 J2
Wolfstones Rd *HOLM/MEL* HD7 .... 47 F1
Wollaton Av *TOT/DORE* S17 .... 200 A3
Wollaton Cl *BSLYN/ROY* S71 .... 29 K7
Wollaton Dr *TOT/DORE* S17 .... 200 A2 🔢
Wollaton Rd *TOT/DORE* S17 .... 199 K3
Wolseley Rd *SHEFS* S8 .... 171 FB
Wolsey Av *WHHL* DN2 .... 92 A3
Wolverley Rd *HAN/WDH* S13 .... 189 J1
Wombwell Av *DEARNE* S63 .... 111 G2 🔢
Wombwell La *BSLY* S70 .... 57 G8
.... *WMB/DAR* S73 .... 82 E5
Wombwell Rd *HOY* S74 .... 83 F8
Wong La *NROS/TKH* DN11 .... 139 J8
.... *NROS/TKH* DN11 .... 161 J1
Wood Acres *DOD/DAR* S75 .... 55 F5
Woodall La *AU/AST/KP* S26 .... 206 C1
Woodall Rd *ECK/KIL* S21 .... 205 K2
.... *RHAM/THRY* S65 .... 156 B2
Woodall Rd South
.... *RHAM/THRY* S65 .... 156 B2
Woodbank Crs *SHEFS* S8 .... 187 F2
Woodbank Rd *ST/HB/BR* S6 .... 168 D3
Woodbine Rd *DARN/MH* S9 .... 153 G8
Woodbourn Hl *DARN/MH* S9 .... 172 B3
Woodbourn Rd *DARN/MH* S9 .... 172 B3
Woodburn Dr *CHPT/GREN* S35 ...... 130 C2
Woodbury Cl *DARN/MH* S9 .... 153 H2
Woodbury Rd *DARN/MH* S9 .... 153 H2
Wood Cliffe *ECC* S11 .... 185 F1
Wood Cl *CHPT/GREN* S35 .... 130 D3
.... *RAW* S62 .... 111 H6
.... *RHAM/THRY* S65 .... 133 H7
Woodcock Cl *KIMB* S61 .... 132 C5
Woodcock Pl *SHEFP/MNR* S2 .... 171 K4
Woodcock Rd *HOY* S74 .... 109 F2
Woodcock Wy *AWLS/ASK* DN6 ...... 37 J8 🔢
Wood Cft *SHEFS* S8 .... 132 C6
Woodcross Av *DONS/BSCR* DN4 ... 93 F8
Wood End Av *STKB/PEN* S36 .... 77 K6
Woodend Cl *ST/HB/BR* S6 .... 151 F8
Woodend Dr *ST/HB/BR* S6 .... 151 F8
Woodfall La *ST/HB/BR* S6 .... 151 H6
Woodfarm Av *ST/HB/BR* S6 .... 169 K1
Woodfarm Cl *ST/HB/BR* S6 .... 169 J1
Woodfarm Dr *ST/HB/BR* S6 .... 169 J1
Woodfarm Pl *ST/HB/BR* S6 .... 169 J1
Woodfield Av *MEX/SWTN* S64 .... 113 G2
Woodfield Cl *WMB/DAR* S73 .... 84 D1
Woodfield Rd *ARMTH* DN3 .... 93 H2
.... *AWLS/ASK* DN6 .... 17 C7
.... *DEARNE* S63 .... 110 E1
.... *DONS/BSCR* DN4 .... 116 E1
.... *FUL* S10 .... 170 B3
.... *PONT* WF8 .... 16 C7
Wood Flds *MALT* S66 .... 157 K3
Wood Fold *OWL* S3 .... 152 B3

Woodfoot Rd *RHAM* S60 .... 155 J6
Woodford Rd *ARMTH* DN3 .... 40 E7
Woodgarth Ct *AWLS/ASK* DN6 ...... 17 K7
Woodgrove Rd *DARN/MH* S9 .... 153 J2
.... *RHAM/THRY* S65 .... 134 B8
Woodhall Cl *WMB/DAR* S73 .... 84 D1
Woodhall Ri *MEX/SWTN* S64 .... 112 C5 🔢
Woodhall Rd *WMB/DAR* S73 .... 84 D2
Woodhead Dr *HOY* S74 .... 82 E6
Woodhead La *HOY* S74 .... 83 F6
Woodhead Rd *CHPT/GREN* S35 ..... 106 C6
.... *HOLM/MEL* HD7 .... 72 A2
.... *SHEFP/MNR* S2 .... 9 D6
Woodholm Pl *ECC* S11 .... 186 B2 🔢
Woodholm Rd *ECC* S11 .... 186 B2
Woodhouse Av *MOS* S20 .... 190 D3
Woodhouse Cl *RAW* S62 .... 111 G7 🔢
Woodhouse Ct *MOS* S20 .... 190 C2
Woodhouse Crs *MOS* S20 .... 190 D3
Woodhouse Gn *MALT* S66 .... 157 K8
Woodhouse Green Rd *HTFD* DN7 .. 21 J8
Woodhouse La *DOD/DAR* S75 .... 29 G3
.... *HOLM/MEL* HD7 .... 47 G6
.... *HTFD* DN7 .... 68 B3
.... *MOS* S20 .... 190 D2
.... *WRKN* S81 .... 180 E7
Woodhouse Rd *HACK/IN* S12 .... 188 D7
.... *HOY* S74 .... 108 E2
.... *WHHL* DN2 .... 91 H1
Woodland Av *DIN* S25 .... 194 A2 🔢
.... *WRKS* S80 .... 211 F6 🔢
Woodland Cl *MALT* S66 .... 157 G4
.... *RHAM* S60 .... 173 K2
Woodland Dr *BSLY* S70 .... 55 G7
.... *DIN* S25 .... 194 A2
.... *HACK/IN* S12 .... 188 D5 🔢
.... *WRKN* S81 .... 210 C1
Woodland Gdns *MALT* S66 .... 159 J2
Woodland Gv *DEARNE* S63 .... 111 J8
Woodland Pl *TOT/DORE* S17 .... 199 K2
Woodland Ri *STKB/PEN* S36 .... 79 K2
Woodland Rd *DEARNE* S63 .... 111 J3
.... *SHEFS* S8 .... 187 G1
Woodlands Av *MOS* S20 .... 190 D2
Woodlands Cl *AU/AST/KP* S26 ...... 175 H6 🔢
.... *KBTN* HD8 .... 51 H1
Woodlands Crs *MEX/SWTN* S64 .... 113 J1
Woodlands Ri *AWLS/ASK* DN6 ...... 17 K6
Woodlands Rd *AWLS/ASK* DN6 ..... 63 J3
.... *HOY* S74 .... 83 F7
Woodlands Vw *CUD/GR* S72 .... 59 H5
.... *HOY* S74 .... 83 F6
.... *WMB/DAR* S73 .... 83 H7
Woodland Ter *CUD/GR* S72 .... 58 E2
Woodland Vw *CUD/GR* S72 .... 57 J2
.... *HACK/IN* S12 .... 188 D7
.... *MEX/SWTN* S64 .... 113 H3 🔢
.... *STKB/PEN* S36 .... 79 K2
Woodland View Rd
.... *ST/HB/BR* S6 .... 170 A1
Woodland Wy *RHAM/THRY* S65 .... 156 B3
Wood La *BSLYN/ROY* S71 .... 30 D6
.... *CONI* DN12 .... 115 J3
.... *CUD/GR* S72 .... 58 D7
.... *DOD/DAR* S75 .... 29 K4
.... *HOLM/MEL* HD7 .... 47 F4
.... *HTFD* DN7 .... 22 C7
.... *KBTN* HD8 .... 51 F2
.... *MALT* S66 .... 138 B8
.... *MALT* S66 .... 157 H1
.... *MALT* S66 .... 176 C2
.... *NROS/TKH* DN11 .... 116 C5
.... *RHAM* S60 .... 154 D1
.... *RHAM* S60 .... 174 D6
.... *ST/HB/BR* S6 .... 169 K1
.... *THNE* DN8 .... 22 E3
Wood Lane Cl *ST/HB/BR* S6 .... 169 J1
Woodlea Gdns *DONS/BSCR* DN4 ... 92 E7
Woodlea Gv *ARMTH* DN3 .... 93 G1
Woodlea Wy *WHHL* DN2 .... 66 B8 🔢
Woodleys Av *RAW* S62 .... 111 H7
Woodman Dr *MEX/SWTN* S64 .... 113 H1
Woodmoor St *BSLYN/ROY* S71 ..... 30 E7
Woodnook Gv *ECK/KIL* S21 .... 203 G3
Woodpecker Cl *AU/AST/KP* S26 ... 191 J7
Wood Rd *KIMB* S61 .... 132 C5
.... *ST/HB/BR* S6 .... 151 G1
Woodrove Av *HAN/WDH* S13 .... 172 D5
Woodrove Cl *HAN/WDH* S13 .... 172 D5
Woodroyd Av *BSLYN/ROY* S71 ..... 30 D5
Woodroyd Cl *BSLYN/ROY* S71 ..... 30 D5
Wood Royd Hill La *HOLM/MEL* HD7 . 49 C5
Wood Royd Rd *STKB/PEN* S36 ...... 105 G6
Wood Seats *CHPT/GREN* S35 .... 129 J3
Woodseats Cl *SHEFS* S8 .... 186 E4
Woodseats House Rd *SHEFS* S8 ... 187 F1
Woodseats Rd *SHEFS* S8 .... 186 E4
Woodsetts La *WRKN* S81 .... 195 J3
Woodsetts Rd *DIN* S25 .... 194 A3
.... *WRKN* S81 .... 195 H3
Woodsett Wk *CONI* DN12 .... 115 J3
Woodside *KBTN* HD8 .... 51 H1
Woodside Av *DEARNE* S63 .... 111 J4
.... *DRON* S18 .... 200 A2
.... *ECK/KIL* S21 .... 191 K2
Woodside Ct *AWLS/ASK* DN6 .... 63 H3 🔢
.... *MALT* S66 .... 157 J2
Woodside La *CHPT/GREN* S35 ...... 129 J2
.... *EPW* DN9 .... 96 E1

OWL S3	171	G1 ☑
Woodside Rd AWLS/ASK DN6	63	H3
BTLY DN5	64	B7
WRKN S81	195	H8
Woodside Vw DRON S18	200	A7
HOLM/MEL HD7	47	G3
NROS/TKH DN11	165	G3
Woodside Wk KIMB S61	132	D5
Wood Spring Ct ATT S4	153	F7
Wood's Riding DONS/BSCR DN4	92	C3
Woodstock Rd ABRD S7	186	E1
DOD/DAR S75	2	A1
DONS/BSCR DN4	116	B1
ST/HB/BR S6	150	D6
Wood St BSLY S70	2	C5
CUD/GR S72	32	B1
DON DN1	5	D3
KBTN HD8	26	A6
MEX/SWTN S64	112	E2
RHAM/THRY S65	134	D5
ST/HB/BR S6	170	E1
WMB/DAR S73	83	K5
Wood Syke DOD/DAR S75	55	F8
Wood Ter RHAM S60	115	G4
Woodthorpe Cl SHEFP/MNR S2	172	C7
Woodthorpe Crs HAN/WDH S13	172	E7 ☑
Woodthorpe Rd HAN/WDH S13	172	E8
Woodvale Rd ECC S11	170	B6
Woodview BTLY DN5	89	J6 ☑
CONI DN12	115	F6
HOY S74	109	H2
Woodview La DOD/DAR S75	55	G4 ☑
Wood View Pl RHAM S60	155	G4
Woodview Rd ST/HB/BR S6	151	H8
Woodview Ter ECC S11	169	J7 ☑
Woodview Wk ECC S11	30	D2
HOY S74	83	F7
MEX/SWTN S64	112	E1
WMB/DAR S73	83	H7
The Woodway MALT S66	135	G8
Woofindin Av ECC S11	169	J8
Woofindin Rd ECC S11	169	H8
Woolcroft Dr HOLM/MEL HD7	48	B1
Wooldale Cliff Rd HOLM/MEL HD7	48	A1
Wooldale Cl MOS S20	189	J5
Wooldale Cft MOS S20	189	J5
Wooldale Dr MOS S20	189	J5
Wooldale Gdns MOS S20	189	J5
Wooley Av WHHL DN2	83	K5
Woolley Colliery Rd DOD/DAR S75	28	D4
Woolley Edge La DOD/DAR S75	28	D2
Woolley Rd STKB/PEN S36	104	D6
Woolley Wood Rd SHEFN S5	131	F8
Woolstocks La DOD/DAR S75	53	H4
Wootton Ct RHAM/THRY S65	134	D5 ☑
Worcester Ct FUL S10	169	F6 ☑
WRKN S81	196	E3 ☑
Worcester Dr FUL S10	169	F6
Worcester Rd FUL S10	168	E6
Wordsworth Av AWLS/ASK DN6	17	K6
DIN S25	178	C7 ☑
DONS/BSCR DN4	116	E1
SHEFN S5	151	K4
STKB/PEN S36	77	K5
Wordsworth Cl SHEFN S5	151	K1
Wordsworth Crs SHEFN S5	151	K3
Wordsworth Dr BTLY DN5	90	C3
RHAM/THRY S65	7	F4
SHEFN S5	151	K3
Wordsworth Pl DRON S18	201	J8
Wordsworth Rd BSLYN/ROY S71	3	E1
DEARNE S63	85	F8
Work Bank La STKB/PEN S36	77	J3

Workhouse La OWL S3	9	D2 ☑
Worksop Rd AU/AST/KP S26	175	H8
DARN/MH S9	172	C1
DIN S25	194	B4
NROS/TKH DN11	161	J2
WRKN S81	195	G3 ☑
WRKS S80	194	A8
WRKS S80	208	C8
Wormley Hill La GLE DN14	22	E3
Worral Av RHAM S60	174	C3
Worral Cl BSLY S70	82	A1
Worral Ct ARMTH DN3	67	F5 ☑
Worrall Dr CHPT/GREN S35	150	C2
Worrall Rd CHPT/GREN S35	129	K1
CHPT/GREN S35	150	C3
Worry Goose La RHAM S60	156	B5
Worsborough Vw DOD/DAR S75	107	J1
Worsbrough Rd BSLY S70	82	A7
HOY S74	82	E6
Worsley Cl BSLY S70	82	C1
Worsley Pl AWLS/ASK DN6	37	G5
Worthing Crs CONI DN12	114	E5
Worthing Rd DARN/MH S9	172	A3
Wortley Av MEX/SWTN S64	112	C5
WMB/DAR S73	83	J3
Wortley Dr CHPT/GREN S35	128	D8
Wortley Ms KIMB S61	131	F3
Wortley Rd CHPT/GREN S35	105	K5
CHPT/GREN S35	107	H7
KIMB S61	132	B7
KIMB S61	132	D8 ☑
STKB/PEN S36	105	J6
Wortley St BSLY S70	2	B4 ☑
Wortley Vw HOY S74	82	E6
Wostenholm Rd ABRD S7	171	F8
Wragby Rd ECC S11	170	A7
Wragg La AU/AST/KP S26	191	F2
Wragg Rd SHEFP/MNR S2	172	A5
Wrancarr La AWLS/ASK DN6	39	K1
Wrangbrook La HEM/SK/SE WF9	35	H1
Wreakes La DRON S18	201	F5
Wrelton Cl BSLYN/ROY S71	30	C4
Wren Bank SHEFP/MNR S2	172	A5 ☑
Wren Ct WRKN S81	196	A8
Wren Park Cl HACK/IN S12	189	G7
Wrens Wy BSLY S70	82	A7
Wright Crs WMB/DAR S73	84	A5
Wright's Hl SHEFP/MNR S2	8	C5
Wrightson Av DONS/BSCR DN4	115	K2 ☑
Wrightson Ter BTLY DN5	90	E1 ☑
Wright St DIN S25	194	A1
Wroot Rd EPW DN9	121	J1
Wroxham Cl MALT S66	157	K2 ☑
Wroxham Dr MALT S66	157	K2
Wroxham Wy BTLY DN5	90	B2
MALT S66	157	K2
Wulfric Cl SHEFP/MNR S2	172	B7
Wulfric Pl SHEFP/MNR S2	172	B7
Wulfric Rd ECK/KIL S21	204	A4
SHEFP/MNR S2	172	C1
Wyatt Av ECC S11	186	C1
Wybourn House Rd		
SHEFP/MNR S2	172	A4 ☑
Wybourn Ter SHEFP/MNR S2	172	A4 ☑
Wychwood Cl DONS/BSCR DN4	116	C3
Wychwood Cft MOS S20	190	E5 ☑
Wychwood Gln MOS S20	190	E5 ☑
Wychwood Gv MOS S20	190	E5 ☑
Wycombe St BSLYN/ROY S71	57	F5 ☑
Wyedale Cft MOS S20	190	D3
Wyming Brook Dr FUL S10	167	K5
The Wynd ECK/KIL S21	205	F8
Wynford Dr HEM/SK/SE WF9	35	F4
Wyn Gv WMB/DAR S73	84	D8
Wynlea Dr WRKN S81	180	D1

Wynmoor Crs WMB/DAR S73	84	D7
Wynyard Rd ST/HB/BR S6	151	G6 ☑
Wyvern Gdns TOT/DORE S17	199	J1

Y

Yarborough Ter BTLY DN5	4	B1
Yardley Sq OWL S3	8	B2 ☑
Yarmouth St DARN/MH S9	153	J6 ☑
Yarwell Dr MALT S66	159	F1
Yates Cl MALT S66	157	F4
Yealand Cl AWLS/ASK DN6	63	J1
Yearling Cha MEX/SWTN S64	112	A4
Yeoman Cl WRKS S80	210	E6
Yeomans Rd ST/HB/BR S6	8	B1 ☑
Yeomans Wy DIN S25	193	K3
Yewdale BSLY S70	82	C2
Yew Greave Crs SHEFN S5	130	A6
Yew La CHPT/GREN S35	130	B7
SHEFN S5	130	A8
Yews Av BSLY S70	82	C2
Yews Cl CHPT/GREN S35	150	C3
Yews La BSLY S70	82	C1
ST/HB/BR S6	149	G7
Yews Pl BSLY S70	3	E6
Yew Tree Av DIN S25	194	B2
Yew Tree Crs NROS/TKH DN11	119	F5
Yew Tree Dr BWTY DN10	142	A8
DARN/MH S9	154	C6
ECK/KIL S21	205	G2 ☑
EPW DN9	120	C3
Yew Tree La HOLM/MEL HD7	47	F4
Yew Tree Rd MALT S66	158	D1
Yewtrees La STKB/PEN S36	126	E2
Yoredale Av CHPT/GREN S35	130	A1
York Gdns DONS/BSCR DN4	92	C6
York La MALT S66	157	G8
York Ms WRKN S81	195	H8 ☑
York Pl MEX/SWTN S64	112	E2
York Ri AU/AST/KP S26	175	G8
York Rd BTLY DN5	64	A7
DARN/MH S9	172	E2
HTFD DN7	42	B7
NROS/TKH DN11	140	A8
NROS/TKH DN11	163	F3
RHAM/THRY S65	7	D3
STKB/PEN S36	104	E6 ☑
York St BSLY S70	2	B4 ☑
CUD/GR S72	57	H1
DEARNE S63	60	D6
HEM/SK/SE WF9	33	H2
HOY S74	83	F8
MEX/SWTN S64	112	E2
NROS/TKH DN11	118	D5
SHEF S1	9	D2
WMB/DAR S73	84	A4
Youlgreave Dr HACK/IN S12	189	F2
Young St DON DN1	5	D3 ☑
SHEF S1	8	C4
Yvonne Gv WMB/DAR S73	83	J4

Z

Zamor Crs MALT S66	176	E2
Zetland Rd HOY S74	109	J2
WHHL DN2	5	F2
Zion Dr DOD/DAR S75	29	G6
Zion Pl DARN/MH S9	172	B1

Abbeydale Grange School
ABRD S7 .... **186** D3
Abbeydale Park Sports Club
TOT/DORE S17 .... **186** A8
Abbeydale Primary School
ABRD S7 .... **187** F1
Abbey Lane Primary School
SHEFS S8 .... **186** E5
Abbey School
KIMB S61 .... **132** A8
A C E Business Centre
ATT S4 .... **9** E1
Acorn Business Park
SHEFS S8 .... **186** E3
Acres Hill Primary School
DARN/MH S9 ...... **172** D4
Adwick Comprehensive School
AWLS/ASK DN6 ... **63** J2
Adwick Leisure Centre
AWLS/ASK DN6 ... **63** J3
Adwick Park Junior School
AWLS/ASK DN6 ... **63** J2
Adwick Road Surgery
MEX/SWTN S64 ... **113** G2
Adwick Washington First School
AWLS/ASK DN6 ... **63** K3
Akwaaba Surgery
CHPT/GREN S35 ... **130** C3

The Alhambra Shopping Centre
BSLY S70 .... **2** C4
All Saints Church of
England School
DIN S25 .... **177** K2
All Saints RC School
SHEFP/MNR S2 .... **9** F5
All Saints School
BTLY DN5 .... **61** H2
Amber Business Centre
RHAM S60 .... **6** C3
Ambergate Clinics
KIMB S61 .... **6** A4
Ambler Junior School
DONS/BSCR DN4 ... **116** C1
Anchorage School
BTLY DN5 .... **90** B1
Anns Grove Primary School
SHEFS S8 .... **171** G8
Anston Brook Junior School
DIN S25 .... **193** K2
Anston Park Junior &
Infant School
DIN S25 .... **178** A8
Apperknowle County
Primary School
DRON S18 .... **202** B6

Arbourthorne Junior School
SHEFP/MNR S2 .... **187** K1
Ardsley Oaks Junior &
Infant School
BSLY S70 .... **57** G7
Arksey County Junior &
Infant School
BTLY DN5 .... **65** G5
Armthorpe High School
ARMTH DN3 .... **67** F8
Armthorpe Southfield Infant &
Junior School
ARMTH DN3 .... **93** G2
The Armthorpe Surgery
ARMTH DN3 .... **93** F1
Art Gallery & Museum
RHAM/THRY S65 ... **7** E4
Ashdell Preparatory School
FUL S10 .... **170** B5
Ash Hill Middle School
HTFD DN7 .... **42** B8
Ashley Industrial Estate
RHAM S60 .... **6** C3
Ashville Medical Centre
BSLY S70 .... **56** E7
Ashwood Road Junior &
Infant School
RAW S62 .... **133** J4

Asian Mosque Centre
SHEFP/MNR S2 .... 171 G8
Askern CP School
BTLY DN5 .... 64 D2
Askern Health Centre
AWLS/ASK DN6 .... 18 D7
Askern Spa Junior School
AWLS/ASK DN6 .... 38 C1
Askern Swimming Pool
AWLS/ASK DN6 .... 18 B7
Aston Comprehensive School
AU/AST/KP S26 .... 175 G6
Aston Fence Junior &
Infant School
HAN/WDH S13 .... 174 E7
Aston Hall Cricket Club
AU/AST/KP S26 .... 176 A8
Aston Lodge School
AU/AST/KP S26 .... 191 J1
Aston Springwood Junior School
AU/AST/KP S26 .... 175 J7
Aston Swallownest Junior &
Infant School
AU/AST/KP S26 .... 175 F7
Athersley North Primary School
BSLYN/ROY S71 .... 29 K7
Athersley South Junior School
BSLYN/ROY S71 .... 30 A8
Athron Industrial Estate
DON DN1 .... 5 D2
Atlas Business Park
CHPT/GREN S35 .... 130 D6
Auckley County Primary School
EPW DN9 .... 120 B1
Aughton Junior & Infant School
AU/AST/KP S26 .... 175 H6
Austerfield Park Golf Club Ltd
BWTY DN10 .... 142 C1
The Avenue Medical Practice
SHEFS S8 .... 186 D8
Badsley Moor Lane Jmi Centre
RHAM/THRY S65 .... 156 A1
Balby Carr School
DONS/BSCR DN4 .... 117 F1
Balby Waverley First School
DONS/BSCR DN4 .... 116 B1
Ballifield Primary School
HAN/WDH S13 .... 173 J7
Bank End Junior & Infant School
BSLY S70 .... 82 D1
Bankwood Lane Industrial Estate
NROS/TDH DN11 .... 118 C5
Bankwood Primary School
SHEFS S8 .... 187 K2
Barlborough Hall School
STV/CWN S43 .... 206 B6
Barlborough Primary School
STV/CWN S43 .... 206 B8
Barnburgh Primary School
BTLY DN5 .... 87 H5
Barnby Dun Primary School
ARMTH DN3 .... 40 E8
Barnsley Borough Council
BSLY S70 .... 2 C4
Barnsley Christian School
BSLY S70 .... 2 B4
Barnsley College
BSLY S70 .... 2 B3
Barnsley College
DOD/DAR S75 .... 2 A1
Barnsley County Court
BSLY S70 .... 2 B3
Barnsley District General Hospital
BSLY S70 .... 55 H4
Barnsley Football Club
BSLYN/ROY S71 .... 3 D4
Barnsley Magistrates Court
BSLY S70 .... 2 B3
Barnsley Metropolitan
Borough Council
BSLY S70 .... 2 A6
Barnsley Metropolitan
Borough Council
BSLY S70 .... 2 C3
Barnsley Metropolitan
Borough Council
BSLY S70 .... 82 B3
Barnsley Metropolitan
Borough Council
BSLYN/ROY S71 .... 3 D2
Barnsley Metropolitan
Borough Council
BSLYN/ROY S71 .... 30 A8
Barnsley Metropolitan
Borough Council
BSLYN/ROY S71 .... 30 D3
Barnsley Metropolitan
Borough Council
DEARNE S63 .... 86 D3
Barnsley Metropolitan
Borough Council
DOD/DAR S75 .... 28 C7
Barnsley Metropolitan
Borough Council
DOD/DAR S75 .... 107 H1
Barnsley Metropolitan
Borough Council
WMB/DAR S73 .... 84 C4
Barnsley Municipal Golf Club
DOD/DAR S75 .... 29 H5

Barnsley Private Clinic
DOD/DAR S75 .... 2 A2
The Basement Gallery
FUL S10 .... 169 B3
Baslow Road Surgery
TOT/DORE S17 .... 199 J2
Bassetlaw District
General Hospital
WRKN S81 .... 210 E2
Bassetlaw Leisure Centre
WRKS S80 .... 210 E3
Bawtry Health Centre
BWTY DN10 .... 142 B8
Beauchief Golf Club House
SHEFS S8 .... 186 B6
Beevor Industrial Estate
BSLYN/ROY S71 .... 3 E3
Beighton Health Centre
MOS S20 .... 190 D3
Belgrave Medical Centre
SHEFP/MNR S2 .... 9 D6
Bentley Colliery Cricket Club
BTLY DN5 .... 64 E5
Bentley Health Centre
BTLY DN5 .... 64 D6
Bentley High Street
Primary School
BTLY DN5 .... 64 E7
Bentley Sunnyfields Infant School
BTLY DN5 .... 64 B8
Bentley Sunnyfields Junior School
BTLY DN5 .... 64 C8
Bents Green Special School
ECC S11 .... 185 J2
Bircotes Sports Centre
NROS/TDH DN11 .... 163 G2
Birdsedge First School
KBTN HD8 .... 50 B3
Birdwell Health Centre
BSLY S70 .... 108 A1
Birdwell Primary School
BSLY S70 .... 82 A8
Birkdale Preparatory School
ECC S11 .... 8 A5
Birkdale School
ECC S11 .... 170 C6
Birkhill Primary School
ECK/KIL S21 .... 203 K5
Birkwood First School
CUD/GR S72 .... 57 K2
Birley First School
HACK/IN S12 .... 189 F4
Birley Health Centre
HACK/IN S12 .... 189 F5
Birley Middle School
HACK/IN S12 .... 189 F4
Birley Primary School
HACK/IN S12 .... 189 F4
Birley Spa Primary School
HACK/IN S12 .... 189 H3
Blackburn County
Junior Mixed School
KIMB S61 .... 153 J1
Bluebell Medical Centre
SHEFN S5 .... 153 G4
Bluestone Middle School
SHEFP/MNR S2 .... 171 K7
Bluestone Primary School
SHEFP/MNR S2 .... 171 K7
Bolton Medical Centre
DEARNE S63 .... 86 A5
Bolton Upon Dearne
Infant School
DEARNE S63 .... 86 B5
Bootham Lane Industrial Estate
HTFD DN7 .... 42 B6
Bracken Moor Sports Club
STKB/PEN S36 .... 105 F7
Bradfield Dungworth
Primary School
ST/HB/BR S6 .... 149 H6
Bradfield School
CHPT/GREN S35 .... 150 B2
Bradmarsh Business Park
RHAM S60 .... 6 B5
Bramley Grange Jmi School
MALT S66 .... 157 J1
Bramley Sunnyside Jmi School
MALT S66 .... 157 H1
Brampton Ellis Infant School
DEARNE S63 .... 111 F1
Brampton Health Centre
WMB/DAR S73 .... 84 D7
Brantwood Independent
School for Girls
ABRD S7 .... 8 A6
Brierley C of E Junior &
Infant School
CUD/GR S72 .... 32 D4
Brinsworth Clinic
RHAM S60 .... 154 E6
Brinsworth Comprehensive School
RHAM S60 .... 154 D7
Brinsworth Medical Centre
RHAM S60 .... 154 D6
Brinsworth Whitehill Jm School
RHAM S60 .... 155 F8
Broad Elms School
ECC S11 .... 185 K3

Broadway School
BSLY S70 .... 55 G7
Brodsworth Hall
BTLY DN5 .... 62 C4
Brook House Junior School
MOS S20 .... 191 F4
Broomhill Clinic
FUL S10 .... 170 C5
Broomhill Infant School
FUL S10 .... 170 C5
Broomhill Medical Centre
FUL S10 .... 8 A4
Broomhill Medical Surgery
FUL S10 .... 170 B5
Broom Lane Medical Centre
RHAM S60 .... 155 K4
Broom Valley Junior &
Infant School
RHAM S60 .... 7 D6
Brunswick Primary School
HAN/WDH S13 .... 174 B8
Bumcross Surgery
CHPT/GREN S35 .... 130 A2
Burns Medical Centre
DONS/BSCR DN4 .... 92 D7
The Burns Practice
WHHL DN2 .... 5 E3
Burntwood School
HEM/SK/SE WF9 .... 34 B5
Burntwood Sports &
Leisure Centre
CUD/GR S72 .... 33 F5
Burton Road Junior &
Infant School
BSLYN/ROY S71 .... 3 D2
The Business Centre
RHAM S60 .... 6 C4
The Business Centre
RHAM S60 .... 6 B6
Byron Wood Primary School
ATT S4 .... 152 C8
Camms Endowed C of E
Primary School
MOS S20 .... 204 B3
Campsmount School
AWLS/ASK DN6 .... 17 J5
Canklow Meadows
Industrial Estate
RHAM S60 .... 155 G6
Canklow Woods Junior &
Infant School
RHAM S60 .... 155 G5
Cannon Hall Museum &
Country Park
DOD/DAR S75 .... 53 F2
Cantley Hawthorn First School
DONS/BSCR DN4 .... 92 D6
Cantley Hawthorn Junior School
DONS/BSCR DN4 .... 92 D6
Cantley Health Centre
DONS/BSCR DN4 .... 92 E8
Carbrook Hall Industrial Estate
DARN/MH S9 .... 153 J6
Carcroft Health Centre
AWLS/ASK DN6 .... 37 K7
Carcroft Industrial Estate
AWLS/ASK DN6 .... 38 A8
Carfield Primary School
SHEFS S8 .... 187 G2
Caribbean Sports Club
CHPT/GREN S35 .... 130 D7
Carlton Industrial Estate
BSLYN/ROY S71 .... 30 D7
Carlton Junior & Infant School
BSLYN/ROY S71 .... 30 E7
Carlton Phoenix Industrial Estate
WRKS S80 .... 210 E3
Carrfield Junior & Infant School
DEARNE S63 .... 86 B4
Carrfield Medical Centre
SHEFP/MNR S2 .... 187 H1
Carterknowle & Dore Medical Practice
ABRD S7 .... 186 E2
Carter Knowle Junior School
ABRD S7 .... 186 D2
Castle Market
SHEF S1 .... 9 E2
Cathedral Church of St Peter & St. Paul
SHEF S1 .... 9 D2
Cawthorne C of E Junior & Infant School
DOD/DAR S75 .... 53 H3
Cawthorne Victoria Jubilee Museum
DOD/DAR S75 .... 53 H2
Cedar Special School
DONS/BSCR DN4 .... 116 C1
Central Business Park
RHAM S60 .... 6 B4
Central Sheffield University Hospitals
FUL S10 .... 8 A3
Chapeltown Surgery
CHPT/GREN S35 .... 130 C3
Charnock Hall Primary School
HACK/IN S12 .... 188 D5
Charter Gallery Museum
CONI DN12 .... 114 C5
Chaucer School
SHEFN S5 .... 151 K2
Chestnut House Surgery
THNE DN8 .... 23 J7
Childrens Hospital N H S Trust
FUL S10 .... 8 A3

Child Welfare & School Clinic
RHAM/THRY S65 .... 7 E2

Church Drive Surgery
CUD/GR S72 .... 32 C4

Clifford C of E Grammar School
ECC S11 .... 8 A6

City Museum & Mappin Art Gallery
FUL S10 .... 8 A3

Civic Building
RHAM/THRY S65 .... 6 C3

Civic Theatre
BSLY S70 .... 2 C4

Claremont Hospital
FUL S10 .... 169 H5

Claycliffe Business Park
DOD/DAR S75 .... 54 D2

Clayfield Industrial Estate
DONS/BSCR DN4 .... 116 D1

Clifford Lister Business Centre
MALT S66 .... 157 F3

Clifton Comprehensive School
RHAM/THRY S65 .... 7 E2

Clough House Medical Centre
SHEFP/MNR S2 .... 9 E5

Club House
AWLS/ASK DN6 .... 37 H3

Coit Primary School
CHPT/GREN S35 .... 130 B3

Coleridge Road Jmi School
RHAM/THRY S65 .... 7 F2

College of Technology
RHAM/THRY S65 .... 6 C4

College Pines Golf Club
WRKS S80 .... 210 E8

Colonnades Centre
DON DN1 .... 4 C3

Concord Middle School
SHEFN S5 .... 153 G3

Conisbrough Castle
CONI DN12 .... 115 F4

Contour Health Centre
RHAM S60 .... 6 C5

Cooper Gallery
BSLY S70 .... 2 B3

Cope Street Surgery
BSLY S70 .... 3 D6

Copley School
BTLY DN5 .... 89 J7

Coroners Court
DON DN1 .... 4 C4

Cortonwood County
  Primary School
WMB/DAR S73 .... 84 D7

Costhorpe Industrial Estate
WRKN S81 .... 180 C6

County Primary School
ARMTH DN3 .... 67 F5

County Primary School
BWTY DN10 .... 143 J5

The Crookes Practice
FUL S10 .... 170 C3

Crown Court
OWL S3 .... 9 D2

Crucible Theatre
SHEF S1 .... 9 E3

Cudworth Churchfield School
CUD/GR S72 .... 31 J8

The Culvert Surgery
ECC S11 .... 8 A6

Cumberworth C of E First School
KBTN HD8 .... 50 C1

Cupola Gallery
ST/HB/BR S6 .... 151 H5

Curlew Junior School
WHHL DN2 .... 66 E5

The Curtain Gallery
ECC S11 .... 8 A6

Cusworth Hall
BTLY DN5 .... 90 A3

Dalton Foljambe Infant School
RHAM/THRY S65 .... 134 D6

Dalton Health Centre
RHAM/THRY S65 .... 134 C6

Danum Grammar School
WHHL DN2 .... 92 C2

Darfield C of E Junior School
WMB/DAR S73 .... 84 E1

Darfield Cricket Club
WMB/DAR S73 .... 84 E2

Darfield Health Centre
WMB/DAR S73 .... 84 E2

Darfield Valley Primary School
WMB/DAR S73 .... 84 C3

Darnall Health Centre
DARN/MH S9 .... 172 E2

Darnall Road Surgery
DARN/MH S9 .... 172 D2

Davy Gallery
NROS/TKH DN11 .... 139 K8

Dead Earnest Theatre
ST/HB/BR S6 .... 170 C1

Dearne Goldthorpe Junior &
  Infant School
DEARNE S63 .... 86 D2

Dearne Highgate Junior &
  Infant School
DEARNE S63 .... 86 B2

Dearne High School
DEARNE S63 .... 86 D3

Dearne Valley Health Centre
KBTN HD8 .... 26 A6

Deepcar Junior School
STKB/PEN S36 .... 105 H7

Deerlands Special School
SHEFN S5 .... 152 C2

Deer Park Surgery
ST/HB/BR S6 .... 169 J1

Denaby Lane Industrial Estate
CONI DN12 .... 113 K4

Denby C of E First School
KBTN HD8 .... 51 F4

Denby Dale Industrial Park
KBTN HD8 .... 51 G1

Dental Health Centre
BSLY S70 .... 2 B4

Derbyshire County Council
ECK/KIL S21 .... 204 C4

Devonshire Green Medical Centre
OWL S3 .... 8 A5

Dinnington Business Centre
DIN S25 .... 178 A3

Dinnington Clinic
DIN S25 .... 178 B7

Dinnington Comprehensive School
DIN S25 .... 178 B5

Dinnington Rugby Club
DIN S25 .... 178 D6

Dinnington St Josephs RC School
DIN S25 .... 178 B6

Dobcroft Infant School
ECC S11 .... 186 B3

Dobcroft Junior School
ECC S11 .... 186 B4

Dodworth C of E School
DOD/DAR S75 .... 80 D1

Dodworth Health Centre
DOD/DAR S75 .... 54 E8

Dodworth Junior School
DOD/DAR S75 .... 54 E8

Doncaster Area
  Health Authority
CONI DN12 .... 114 C5

Doncaster Area
  Health Authority
DON DN1 .... 5 D3

Doncaster Area
  Health Authority
MEX/SWTN S64 .... 113 G3

Doncaster Balby Central
  First School
DONS/BSCR DN4 .... 5 B5

Doncaster Civic Theatre
DON DN1 .... 5 D3

Doncaster College
BTLY DN5 .... 88 C7

Doncaster College
DON DN1 .... 4 C2

Doncaster Crown Court
DON DN1 .... 5 D4

Doncaster Golf Course
DONS/BSCR DN4 .... 119 F3

Doncaster Health Authority
DONS/BSCR DN4 .... 5 D6

Doncaster Health Authority
DONS/BSCR DN4 .... 116 E2

Doncaster Magistrates Court
DON DN1 .... 4 C4

Doncaster Metropolitan
  Borough Council
ARMTH DN3 .... 66 D5

Doncaster Metropolitan
  Borough Council
CONI DN12 .... 114 D5

Doncaster Metropolitan
  Borough Council
DON DN1 .... 5 D2

Doncaster Metropolitan
  Borough Council
DONS/BSCR DN4 .... 92 D7

Doncaster Metropolitan
  Borough Council
MEX/SWTN S64 .... 113 H2

Doncaster Metropolitan
  Borough Council
NROS/TKH DN11 .... 118 C6

Doncaster Metropolitan
  District Council
DON DN1 .... 5 D3

Doncaster Museum & Art Gallery
DON DN1 .... 5 E3

Doncaster Road Infant School
MEX/SWTN S64 .... 113 H3

Doncaster Road Jmi School
RHAM/THRY S65 .... 7 F2

Doncaster Road Junior School
MEX/SWTN S64 .... 113 H3

Doncaster Road Primary School
BSLY S70 .... 3 D5

Doncaster Rovers Football Club
DONS/BSCR DN4 .... 91 K5

Doncaster Royal Infirmary &
  Montagu Hospital NHS Trust
WHHL DN2 .... 5 F1

Doncaster & South Humber
  Healthcare NHS Trust
DONS/BSCR DN4 .... 116 E2

Doncaster Town Cricket Club
WHHL DN2 .... 5 E3

Don Valley High School
BTLY DN5 .... 64 A7

Dore Junior & Infant School
TOT/DORE S17 .... 199 H1

Dovercourt Surgery
SHEFP/MNR S2 .... 172 A6

Dr Chambers & Partners
CHPT/GREN S35 .... 107 J7

Dr John Bingham Junior &
  Infant School
SHEFS S8 .... 201 G2

Dr John Worrall School
DARN/MH S9 .... 153 H8

Dronfield County Junior School
DRON S18 .... 201 G6

Dronfield Health Centre
DRON S18 .... 201 G6

Dronfield Infant School
DRON S18 .... 201 G6

The Dronfield School
DRON S18 .... 200 E5

Dronfield Sports Centre
DRON S18 .... 201 F6

Dukeries Art Gallery
WRKS S80 .... 210 C3

Dukeries Clinic
WRKS S80 .... 210 D5

Dukeries Industrial Estate
WRKN S81 .... 210 A1

Dunsville Health Centre
HTFD DN7 .... 67 K3

Dykeshall Medical Centre
ST/HB/BR S6 .... 151 G6

Eastwood Trading Estate
RHAM/THRY S65 .... 7 F1

Ecclesall Infant School
ECC S11 .... 185 K1

Ecclesall Medical Centre
ECC S11 .... 186 A2

Ecclesfield
  Comprehensive School
CHPT/GREN S35 .... 130 B4

Ecclesfield Health Centre
CHPT/GREN S35 .... 130 C6

Ecclesfield Parish Council
CHPT/GREN S35 .... 107 K8

Eckington Health Centre
ECK/KIL S21 .... 204 C4

Eckington Junior School
ECK/KIL S21 .... 204 B4

Eckington School
ECK/KIL S21 .... 203 J4

Edenthorpe Surgery
ARMTH DN3 .... 66 E5

Edlington School
CONI DN12 .... 115 J7

Edlington Victoria
  Primary School
CONI DN12 .... 115 H4

Edward Sheerien School
BSLYN/ROY S71 .... 56 C1

Ellers Middle School
DONS/BSCR DN4 .... 92 A7

Ellesmere Teaching School
ATT S4 .... 171 J1

Emmett Carr Surgery
ECK/KIL S21 .... 205 F7

Eppic Theatre
CHPT/GREN S35 .... 129 H6

Falkland House Surgery
ECC S11 .... 186 A1

Far Lane Medical Centre
ST/HB/BR S6 .... 151 G6

Ferham House Clinic
KIMB S61 .... 154 D1

Fernbank Special School
AWLS/ASK DN6 .... 63 K1

Fernham Junior & Infant School
KIMB S61 .... 154 D1

Finningley Airfield
EPW DN9 .... 120 C5

Finningley C of E School
EPW DN9 .... 121 G4

Fire Police Museum
SHEF S1 .... 9 D2

Firs Hill Junior School
ATT S4 .... 152 C7

Firth Park Medical Centre
SHEFN S5 .... 152 E4

Firth Park School
SHEFN S5 .... 152 D4

Flanderwell Junior &
  Infant School
MALT S66 .... 157 G1

The Foulstone School
WMB/DAR S73 .... 84 E1

Foxhill Medical Centre
ST/HB/BR S6 .... 151 J1

Fox Hill Primary School
ST/HB/BR S6 .... 151 J1

Frame Gallery
RHAM S60 .... 6 C3

Frenchgate Centre
DONS/BSCR DN4 .... 4 B3

Fullerton House School
CONI DN12 .... 114 A4

The Gables School
WMB/DAR S73 .... **84** A5
The Gallery
DON DN1 .... **5** D3
Gawber Junior & Infant School
DOD/DAR S75 .... **55** F4
Gladys Buxton School
DRON S18 .... **201** J5
Gleadless Clinic
HACK/IN S12 .... **188** D4
Gleadless Primary School
HACK/IN S12 .... **188** D2
Globe Business Centre
OWL S3 .... **8** C1
Goldthorpe Health Centre
DEARNE S63 .... **86** C3
Goldthorpe Industrial Estate
DEARNE S63 .... **86** A3
Goldthorpe RC Jmi School
DEARNE S63 .... **86** D1
Gooseacre Primary School
DEARNE S63 .... **60** B6
Grange Gate Junior School
BSLYN/ROY S71 .... **57** F5
Grange Lane Industrial Estate
BSLYN/ROY S71 .... **57** F7
Graves Art Gallery
SHEF S1 .... **9** E3
Greasborough Health Centre
KIMB S61 .... **132** E4
Greasborough Junior &
Infant School
KIMB S61 .... **132** E4
Great Houghton Clinic
CUD/GR S72 .... **59** H6
Green Arbour School
MALT S66 .... **176** E1
Greengate Lane Primary School
CHPT/GREN S35 .... **107** K8
Greenhill Health Centre
SHEFS S8 .... **200** E1
Greenhill Primary School
SHEFS S8 .... **186** E8
Greenlands Junior School
DARN/MH S9 .... **172** E5
Green Lane Middle School
THNE DN8 .... **44** A1
Greenside Surgery
KIMB S61 .... **132** E4
Green Top First School
THNE DN8 .... **43** J1
Greenway Natural Health Centre
TOT/DORE S17 .... **199** H3
Grenoside Primary School
CHPT/GREN S35 .... **129** H6
Greystones First School
ECC S11 .... **170** A8
Greystones Medical Centre
ECC S11 .... **170** B8
Greystones Primary School
ECC S11 .... **170** B8
Grimethorpe Hall
CUD/GR S72 .... **32** C7
Grimethorpe Ladywood
First School
CUD/GR S72 .... **58** E1
Grove Street Junior &
Infant School
BSLYN/ROY S71 .... **3** D4
Guildhall Industrial Estate
ARMTH DN3 .... **66** D4
Gunthwaite Hall
STKB/PEN S36 .... **51** J5
Hackenthorpe Medical Centre
HACK/IN S12 .... **189** J4
Hade Edge Primary School
HOLM/MEL HD7 .... **48** A7
Haggonfields County
Primary School
WRKS S80 .... **209** J3
Halfway Infant School
MOS S20 .... **190** C8
Halfway Junior School
MOS S20 .... **190** C8
Hallam Primary School
FUL S10 .... **169** G6
Hallamshire Business Park
FUL S10 .... **8** B5
The Hallamshire Gallery
ECC S11 .... **170** B8
Hallamshire Natural Health Centre
ECC S11 .... **170** C7
Hall Cross Comprehensive School
DON DN1 .... **5** E3
Handsworth Branch Clinic
HAN/WDH S13 .... **173** H6
Handsworth Road Medical Centre
HAN/WDH S13 .... **173** H6
Hanover Medical Centre
FUL S10 .... **8** B4
Harrison Drive Business Centre
WRKN S81 .... **180** C3
Harthill Junior & Infant School
AU/AST/KP S26 .... **206** E2
Harworth C of E Primary School
NROS/TKH DN11 .... **162** E3
Harworth Medical Centre
NROS/TKH DN11 .... **163** F2
Harworth Park Industrial Estate
NROS/TKH DN11 .... **163** F5

Hatfield Comprehensive School
HTFD DN7 .... **42** C8
Hatfield County Primary School
HTFD DN7 .... **42** B7
Hatfield & Dunsville County
Primary School
HTFD DN7 .... **68** B2
Hatfield Primary School
SHEFN S5 .... **152** E2
Hatfield Woodhouse County
Primary School
HTFD DN7 .... **69** H1
Hathersage Swimming Pool
HATH/EY S32 .... **182** C8
Hayfield Comprehensive School
EPW DN9 .... **120** A3
Healthcare Surgery
SHEFN S5 .... **151** J3
The Health Centre
CONI DN12 .... **115** J5
Heather Garth Junior &
Infant School
DEARNE S63 .... **86** A4
Heeley Business Centre
SHEFP/MNR S2 .... **9** D6
Heeley Green Surgery
SHEFP/MNR S2 .... **187** H1
Heeley Retail Park
SHEFP/MNR S2 .... **187** F4
Hellaby Industrial Estate
MALT S66 .... **158** B1
Hemingfield Ellis C of E
Junior & Infant School
WMB/DAR S73 .... **83** D7
Hemsworth Primary School
GLV S14 .... **187** K5
Hepworth Junior & Infant School
HOLM/MEL HD7 .... **48** D6
Herdings Primary School
GLV S14 .... **188** A5
Herries School
SHEFN S5 .... **151** K5
Herringthorpe Junior &
Infant School
RHAM/THRY S65 .... **156** A3
Hesley Hall School
NROS/TKH DN11 .... **140** E3
Hexthorpe First School
DONS/BSCR DN4 .... **4** A4
Hexthorpe Primary School
DONS/BSCR DN4 .... **4** A5
Hickleton Golf Club
DEARNE S63 .... **61** G7
Highfields County Primary School
AWLS/ASK DN6 .... **63** J5
Highfields Junior School
WMB/DAR S73 .... **83** K4
High Greave Jmi School
RHAM/THRY S65 .... **134** B3
High Green Health Centre
CHPT/GREN S35 .... **107** J7
High Green Primary School
CHPT/GREN S35 .... **107** J7
High School
HTFD DN7 .... **42** C8
High Storrs School
ECC S11 .... **185** K1
Highwoods Infant School
MEX/SWTN S64 .... **112** D1
Hill Brow Surgery
DOD/DAR S75 .... **29** F6
Hill House Preparatory School
DON DN1 .... **5** E2
Hill Primary School
DEARNE S63 .... **60** E6
Hillsborough Health Centre
ST/HB/BR S6 .... **151** H8
Hillsborough Primary School
ST/HB/BR S6 .... **151** H6
Hill Top Junior & Infant School
CONI DN12 .... **115** H6
Hinchliffe Mill County School
HOLM/MEL HD7 .... **47** F5
Hinde House School
SHEFN S5 .... **153** F3
Hm Prison
BTLY DN5 .... **4** B3
Holgate School
BSLY S70 .... **55** H6
Hollies Medical Centre
ECC S11 .... **170** D8
Hollis Hospital
TOT/DORE S17 .... **185** J5
Hollywood Bowling
DARN/MH S9 .... **153** K7
Holmescarr Junior Mixed School
NROS/TKH DN11 .... **118** D6
Holme School
HOLM/MEL HD7 .... **46** B6
Holmfirth Craft Market
HOLM/MEL HD7 .... **47** J2
Holt House Industrial Estate
ABRD S7 .... **186** D3
Holy Cross Deanery C of E
Junior & Infant School
BSLYN/ROY S71 .... **56** C1
Holy Family CP School
HTFD DN7 .... **42** A3
Holy Family RC Primary School
WRKS S80 .... **210** E7

Holyrood RC Junior &
Infant School
BSLY S70 .... **2** A5
Houghton Main Welfare &
Sports Club
DEARNE S63 .... **59** H8
Howarth Junior & Infant School
RHAM S60 .... **155** F8
Hoyland Common
Primary School
HOY S74 .... **108** B2
Hoyland Elsecar C of E Junior &
Infant School
HOY S74 .... **109** J2
Hoyland Greenfield Junior &
Infant School
HOY S74 .... **109** G1
Hoyland St Helens RC Junior &
Infant School
HOY S74 .... **108** E1
Hoyland Sports Centre
HOY S74 .... **108** D1
H S B C Sports Club
TOT/DORE S17 .... **185** H6
Hucklow Primary School
SHEFN S5 .... **152** D5
Huddersfield Technical College
HOLM/MEL HD7 .... **47** K1
Hungerhill Comprehensive School
ARMTH DN3 .... **66** E5
Humingley Junior & Infant School
BSLY S70 .... **57** F8
Hunters Bar Junior & Infant School
ECC S11 .... **170** C7
I B T E Museum of
Telecommunications
WRKS S80 .... **210** D5
Industrial Centre
MEX/SWTN S64 .... **113** F3
Industrial Estate
HEM/SK/SE WF9 .... **34** C5
Intake High School
WHHL DN2 .... **92** C2
Intake Junior & Infant School
HACK/IN S12 .... **188** D1
Ironbridge Industrial Estate
HAN/WDH S13 .... **174** A7
Ivanhoe Junior & Infant School
CONI DN12 .... **114** B6
Jamiyat Tablig Ul Islam Mosque
DARN/MH S9 .... **172** C1
Jaunty Springs Health Centre
HACK/IN S12 .... **188** D3
Jessop Hospital for Women
OWL S3 .... **8** B3
Jordanthorpe Health Centre
SHEFS S8 .... **201** H1
Junction 34 Industrial Estate
DARN/MH S9 .... **154** A6
Kayes First School
KBTN HD8 .... **26** C5
Kelham Island Museum
OWL S3 .... **9** D1
Kelvin Grove Surgery
WMB/DAR S73 .... **84** B5
Kendray Hospital
BSLY S70 .... **3** F5
Kendray Infant School
BSLY S70 .... **3** F6
Kendray Primary School
BSLY S70 .... **3** E6
Keresforth Primary School
DOD/DAR S75 .... **81** F1
Kexborough Junior School
DOD/DAR S75 .... **28** A7
Khan Medical Centre
NROS/TKH DN11 .... **163** F3
Killamarsh County Junior &
Infant School
ECK/KIL S21 .... **191** J8
Killamarsh Leisure Centre
ECK/KIL S21 .... **191** H8
Killamarsh Medical Centre
ECK/KIL S21 .... **191** G8
Kilnhurst Business Park
MEX/SWTN S64 .... **134** D1
Kilnhurst Junior & Infants School
MEX/SWTN S64 .... **112** E1
Kilton Forest Golf Club
WRKN S81 .... **211** F1
Kilton Industrial Estate
WRKS S80 .... **210** E4
Kimberworth
Comprehensive School
KIMB S61 .... **154** C1
Kimberworth Infants School
KIMB S61 .... **132** C8
Kimberworth Park Clinic
KIMB S61 .... **132** B6
Kimberworth Park Medical Centre
KIMB S61 .... **132** B7
King Egbert Secondary School
TOT/DORE S17 .... **199** H1
King Edward First School
THNE DN8 .... **23** K7
King Edward Vii School
FUL S10 .... **8** A4
Kingfisher First School
WHHL DN2 .... **65** K8
Kingthorne Group Practice
ARMTH DN3 .... **66** E5

Kingthorne Group Practice
DON DN1....................................... 5 E2

Kirk Balk School
HOY S74..................................... 108 D1

Kirkby Avenue Primary School
BTLY DN5...................................... 90 D1

Kirk Sandall Infant School
ARMTH DN3..................................... 66 E4

Kirk Sandall Junior School
ARMTH DN3..................................... 66 E4

Kirk Smeaton C of E Primary School
PONT WF8...................................... 16 E1

Kirton Lane Primary School
HTFD DN7...................................... 42 B3

Kitchen Gallery
RHAM S60.. 6 C4

Kiveton Park Group Practice
AU/AST/KP S26................................ 192 D5

Kiveton Park Infant School
AU/AST/KP S26................................ 192 D5

Lacewood Primary School
DEARNE S63.................................... 86 C5

Lakeside First School
DONS/BSCR DN4.................................. 5 F5

The Lakeside Surgery
WRKN S81.................................... 180 D5

Langold Dyscarr Junior School
WRKN S81.................................... 180 B4

Langold Health Centre
WRKN S81.................................... 180 D4

Lantern Theatre
ABRD S7.. 8 B6

Larwood Health Centre
WRKN S81.................................... 211 H1

Laughton Junior & Infant School
DIN S25...................................... 177 K3

Lawn Road Industrial Estate
WRKN S81.................................... 180 C7

Lecture Theatre
SHEF S1.. 8 C3

Lenthall School
DRON S18.................................... 201 H4

Lilly Hall Junior & Middle School
MALT S66.................................... 159 F2

Limpsfield Junior School
DARN/MH S9.................................. 153 H5

Lindrick Golf Club
WRKN S81.................................... 195 F5

Listerdale Shopping Centre
RHAM/THRY S65................................ 156 D3

The Little Gallery
RAW S62...................................... 109 J6

Littlemoor First School
AWLS/ASK DN6................................. 38 B1

Little Theatre
DEARNE S63.................................... 60 B8

Littleworth Lane Infant School
BSLYN/ROY S71................................ 56 E4

Lobwood Junior & Infant School
BSLY S70...................................... 82 B2

Lodge Moor Medical Centre
FUL S10...................................... 168 E6

Longcar Junior & Infant School
BSLY S70.. 2 A5

Lound Infant School
CHPT/GREN S35............................... 130 A1

Lound Junior School
CHPT/GREN S35............................... 130 B1

Lowedges Primary School
SHEFS S8.................................... 201 F1

Loxley Primary School
ST/HB/BR S6................................. 150 C6

Lundwood Medical Centre
BSLYN/ROY S71................................ 56 E5

The Lyceum Theatre
SHEF S1.. 9 E3

Lydgate Infant School
FUL S10...................................... 170 A4

Lydgate Junior School
FUL S10...................................... 170 A5

Makki Mosque
SHEFS S8.................................... 187 G1

Malin Bridge Primary School
ST/HB/BR S6................................. 151 G7

Maltby Comprehensive School
MALT S66.................................... 159 G2

Maltby Crags Junior & Infant School
MALT S66.................................... 159 G3

Maltby Hall Infant School
MALT S66.................................... 159 G2

Maltby Health Centre
MALT S66.................................... 159 G2

Maltby Manor Junior & Infant School
MALT S66.................................... 159 H2

Maltby Redwood Jmi School
MALT S66.................................... 158 D2

Maltby Sports Centre
MALT S66.................................... 159 G2

Manor Clinic
SHEFP/MNR S2................................ 188 B1

Manor Lodge Middle School
SHEFP/MNR S2................................ 172 A6

Manor Lodge Primary School
SHEFP/MNR S2................................ 172 A6

Manor Middle School
HTFD DN7...................................... 42 D7

Manor Park Medical Centre
SHEFP/MNR S2................................ 172 C5

Manor Top Medical Centre
HACK/IN S12.................................. 188 C1

Manton Infant School
WRKS S80.................................... 211 G6

Manton Junior School
WRKS S80.................................... 211 F6

Maple Industrial Estate
DOD/DAR S75................................... 29 J7

Mapplewell Health Centre
DOD/DAR S75................................... 29 G7

Market Hall
DON DN1.. 5 D2

Market Junior School
HOY S74....................................... 83 F8

Marlcliffe Primary School
ST/HB/BR S6................................. 151 G5

Marshgate Industrial Estate
BTLY DN5....................................... 4 B2

Marsh Lane Primary School
ECK/KIL S21................................. 203 G4

Mattersey Primary School
BWTY DN10................................... 165 J8

Mayflower Junior & Infant School
BWTY DN10................................... 142 B8

Mayflower Junior School
BWTY DN10................................... 142 B7

The Mcauley School
DONS/BSCR DN4................................ 93 F7

Meadow Bank Industrial Estate
KIMB S61.................................... 154 C1

Meadowhall Centre
DARN/MH S9.................................. 153 K4

Meadowhall Junior School
KIMB S61.................................... 154 D1

Meadowhall Retail Park
DARN/MH S9.................................. 153 K7

Meadowhead School
SHEFS S8.................................... 187 G8

Meadows Junior School
AU/AST/KP S26............................... 192 C4

Meadowview Industrial Estate
ARMTH DN3..................................... 67 J8

Meersbrook Bank Primary School
SHEFS S8.................................... 187 F2

Melrose Surgery
OWL S3...................................... 171 H1

Merlin Theatre
ABRD S7...................................... 170 D8

Merlin Theatre
ST/HB/BR S6................................. 150 D6

Metronomesports & leisurecomplex
BSLYN/ROY S71................................. 3 D3

Mexborough Business Centre
MEX/SWTN S64................................ 113 G2

Mexborough Comprehensive School
MEX/SWTN S64................................ 112 E1

Mexborough Windhill Junior & Infant School
MEX/SWTN S64................................ 113 H1

Mill Road Surgery
HEM/SK/SE WF9................................ 34 E3

Mill Trading Estate
BSLYN/ROY S71................................. 3 E4

Minsterthorpe Community College
HEM/SK/SE WF9................................ 34 E3

Minsterthorpe Swimming Pool
HEM/SK/SE WF9................................ 35 F3

Monk Bretton Health Centre
BSLYN/ROY S71................................. 3 F1

Monksbridge Trading Estate
DIN S25..................................... 177 J5

Monkwood Health Centre
RAW S62..................................... 111 H8

Montagu Hospital
MEX/SWTN S64................................ 113 F1

Monteney Middle & Primary School
SHEFN S5.................................... 130 B8

Montgomery House Medical Centre
ST/HB/BR S6................................... 8 B1

Montgomery Theatre
SHEF S1.. 9 D3

Moorends Clinic
THNE DN8...................................... 23 K4

Moorends Marshland First School
THNE DN8...................................... 24 A4

Moorgate Business Centre
RHAM S60....................................... 7 D5

Moorgate Mosque & Community Centre
RHAM S60....................................... 6 C4

Morley Place Junior School
CONI DN12................................... 114 B5

Mosborough Medical Centre
MOS S20..................................... 190 A8

Mosborough Primary School
MOS S20..................................... 190 B8

Mosque
OWL S3...................................... 171 H1

Mosque
RHAM S60....................................... 6 B4

Mossbrook Special School
SHEFS S8.................................... 187 J7

Moss Road Industrial Estate
AWLS/ASK DN6................................. 18 E7

The Mount Group Practice
DON DN1.. 5 E2

Mount Osborne Industrial Park
BSLYN/ROY S71................................. 3 E4

Mount St Marys College
ECK/KIL S21................................. 205 G5

Mount Vernon Hospital
BSLY S70...................................... 82 A1

Museum
ECC S11..................................... 170 C7

Myers Grove School
ST/HB/BR S6................................. 151 F8

National Music Centre
SHEF S1.. 9 E4

The Nelson Practice
BTLY DN5...................................... 64 B8

Nether Edge Hospital
ECC S11..................................... 186 D1

Nether Green Infant School
FUL S10..................................... 169 H7

Nether Green Junior School
FUL S10..................................... 169 J7

Netherthorpe Primary School
OWL S3... 8 C2

Newfield School
SHEFS S8.................................... 187 J4

The New Indoor Market
MALT S66.................................... 159 H2

Newman Special School
RHAM S60.................................... 155 K6

New Street Health Centre
BSLY S70....................................... 2 B5

New Surgery
MEX/SWTN S64................................ 113 G3

Newton Business Centre
BTLY DN5...................................... 90 C4

New Village Primary School
BTLY DN5...................................... 64 E5

Nightingale Primary School
DONS/BSCR DN4............................... 116 B1

Nook Lane Junior School
ST/HB/BR S6................................. 150 B8

Norfolk Middle School
SHEFP/MNR S2................................ 172 A7

Norfolk Park Health Centre
SHEFP/MNR S2.................................. 9 F6

North Anston Business Centre
DIN S25..................................... 177 J7

North Border County Secondary School
NROS/TKH DN11............................... 163 G2

North Border Infant School
NROS/TKH DN11............................... 163 G3

North Border Junior School
NROS/TKH DN11............................... 163 G3

Northcliffe School
CONI DN12................................... 114 B4

North East Derbyshire District Council
DRON S18.................................... 201 G6

North East Derbyshire District Council
DRON S18.................................... 201 H6

Northfield Junior School
DRON S18.................................... 201 J4

Northfield School
HEM/SK/SE WF9................................ 34 B4

Northlands Community Health Centre
SHEFN S5.................................... 152 A3

North Notts College of Further Education
WRKN S81.................................... 210 D2

Northstead Surgery
BWTY DN10................................... 142 A8

Norton County Junior & Infant School
AWLS/ASK DN6................................. 17 K4

Norton Free Primary School
SHEFS S8.................................... 187 J6

Norton Oakes Cricket Club
SHEFS S8.................................... 187 K6

Nortonthorpe Hall School
KBTN HD8...................................... 26 A6

Nortonthorpe Industrial Estate
KBTN HD8...................................... 26 A6

Notre Dame School
FUL S10..................................... 170 A6

Nottingham County Health Clinic
WRKN S81.................................... 196 D1

Oakes Park Special School
SHEFS S8.................................... 187 J5

Oakfield Junior School
WMB/DAR S73.................................. 84 A5

Oakwell Business Centre
BSLYN/ROY S71................................. 3 E4

Oakwood Garden
DONS/BSCR DN4................................ 92 D8

Oakwood Swimming Baths
RHAM S60.................................... 155 J4

Odeon Cinema
BSLY S70....................................... 2 C3

Odeon Cinema
DON DN1.. 5 D3

Odeon Cinema
SHEF S1.. 9 E3

Old College of Technology
BSLY S70....................................... 2 B3

Old Forge Business Park
SHEFP/MNR S2................................ 171 G8

Old Hall Comprehensive School
KIMB S61.................................... 132 B8

Ora Gallery
ECC S11 .... 8 A6
Orchard Infant School
BTLY DN5 .... 89 J7
Oughtibridge Primary School
CHPT/GREN S35 .... 128 C8
Our Lady of Sorrows RC School
ARMTH DN3 .... 67 F8
Our Lady RC Primary School
BTLY DN5 .... 64 E6
Our Ladys & St Josephs RC
Jmi School
DEARNE S63 .... 111 J1
Owlthorpe Surgery
MOS S20 .... 189 J5
Owston Skellow First School
AWLS/ASK DN6 .... 37 J5
Oxspring Junior & Infant School
STKB/PEN S36 .... 78 E6
Parkgate Business Park
RAW S62 .... 133 J5
Parkgate Medical Centre
RAW S62 .... 133 J3
Park Health Centre
SHEFP/MNR S2 .... 9 F3
Park Hill Primary School
SHEFP/MNR S2 .... 9 F3
Park Infant School
WHHL DN2 .... 91 J1
Park Primary School
WHHL DN2 .... 91 J1
Park Road Infant School
MEX/SWTN S64 .... 113 F1
Park Street Junior &
Infant School
WMB/DAR S73 .... 84 B5
Parson Cross C of E
Primary School
ST/HB/BR S6 .... 151 J3
Peacock Trading Estate
ST/HB/BR S6 .... 151 K7
Penistone Grammar School
STKB/PEN S36 .... 77 K2
Penistone Group Practice
STKB/PEN S36 .... 78 A4
Penistone Sports Centre
STKB/PEN S36 .... 77 K3
Penistone Springvale Jmi School
STKB/PEN S36 .... 78 C4
Penistone Thurlstone Jmi School
STKB/PEN S36 .... 77 H3
The Petersgate Medical Centre
BTLY DN5 .... 64 B7
Peveril School of Art
ECC S11 .... 170 B7
Pheasant Bank Junior School
NROS/TKH DN11 .... 118 D6
Phillimore Park Primary School
DARN/MH S9 .... 172 D1
Phoenix Surgery
DON DN1 .... 5 D3
Phoenix Theatre
BWTY DN10 .... 142 B8
Picture Drome Cinema Museum
HOLM/MEL HD7 .... 47 J2
Pipworth Junior School
SHEFP/MNR S2 .... 172 D6
Pitsmoor Dental Health Centre
ATT S4 .... 152 C8
Pitsmoor Surgery
OWL S3 .... 152 B8
Platts Common Industrial Estate
HOY S74 .... 82 E8
Plumb Estates
ARMTH DN5 .... 66 C5
Plumtree Farm Estate
NROS/TKH DN11 .... 163 H2
Pollington Balne C of E School
GLE DN14 .... 11 J4
Ponds Forge International
Sports Centre
SHEF S1 .... 9 E3
Pontefract Road Junior &
Infant School
CUD/GR S72 .... 31 J7
Porter Croft School
ECC S11 .... 8 B5
Portland Business Park
HAN/WDH S13 .... 173 G6
Primary School
HTFD DN7 .... 42 B8
Prince Edward Middle School
SHEFP/MNR S2 .... 172 C8
Prince Edward Primary School
SHEFP/MNR S2 .... 172 C8
Prince of Wales Road
Medical Centre
DARN/MH S9 .... 172 E4
Priory School
DONS/BSCR DN4 .... 92 D8
Prospect Hill Junior &
Infant School
WRKN S81 .... 210 E1
Public Baths
DEARNE S63 .... 111 J1
Public Baths
ST/HB/BR S6 .... 8 B1
Public Swimming Baths
ECK/KIL S21 .... 204 C4

Pye Bank Trinity C of E
Junior School
OWL S3 .... 171 H1
Queens Medical Centre
MALT S66 .... 159 H2
Queens Road Clinic
BSLYN/ROY S71 .... 2 C4
Queen Street Junior &
Infant School
MEX/SWTN S64 .... 112 C4
Railwaymens Sports Club
BSLYN/ROY S71 .... 31 F3
Ravenfield Junior &
Infant School
RHAM/THRY S65 .... 135 J6
Rawmarsh Leisure Centre
RAW S62 .... 133 K3
Rawmarsh Monkwood
Jmi School
RAW S62 .... 111 H8
Rawmarsh Thorogate Junior &
Infant School
RAW S62 .... 111 J8
Redbrook Business Park
DOD/DAR S75 .... 55 G2
Redscope Junior & Infant School
KIMB S61 .... 132 B6
Reflex Theatre
SHEFS S8 .... 187 G1
Regent Square Group Practice
DON DN1 .... 5 E3
Register Office
DON DN1 .... 5 E4
Reighead Primary School
MOS S20 .... 190 D4
Renishaw Primary School
ECK/KIL S21 .... 205 F7
Richard Newman Infant School
BSLYN/ROY S71 .... 30 A8
The Richmond Fellowship
MEX/SWTN S64 .... 112 C4
Richmond Hill Junior & Infant School
BTLY DN5 .... 90 B4
Richmond Medical Centre
HAN/WDH S13 .... 173 F8
Ridgeway Medical Centre
RHAM/THRY S65 .... 134 B8
Ridgeway Primary School
HACK/IN S12 .... 189 G7
Ridgewood
Comprehensive School
BTLY DN5 .... 89 K1
Rivelin Primary School
ST/HB/BR S6 .... 151 G8
Riverside Business Park
KBTN HD8 .... 26 A5
Robin Hood Golf Club
AWLS/ASK DN6 .... 38 B4
Rockingham Business Park
BSLY S70 .... 108 A1
Rockingham College of Further
Education
DEARNE S63 .... 111 H1
Rockingham Junior &
Infant School
KIMB S61 .... 132 C4
Rockley Mount School
BSLY S70 .... 55 H8
Rose Court Surgery
MALT S66 .... 157 F3
Rosedale Middle School
BTLY DN5 .... 64 A8
Rosedale Road Infant School
BTLY DN5 .... 64 A8
Rossington
Comprehensive School
NROS/TKH DN11 .... 119 F8
Rossington Hall School
NROS/TKH DN11 .... 141 J1
Rossington Parish Council
NROS/TKH DN11 .... 118 C6
Rossington Swimming Pool
NROS/TKH DN11 .... 118 E5
Rotherham Borough Council
MALT S66 .... 176 E1
Rotherham Civic Theatre
RHAM/THRY S65 .... 7 D4
Rotherham College of
Arts & Technology
RHAM/THRY S65 .... 7 D3
Rotherham County Court
RHAM/THRY S65 .... 7 D4
Rotherham District
General Hospital
RHAM S60 .... 155 J5
Rotherham Health Authority
RHAM S60 .... 6 C4
Rotherham Health Authority
RHAM S60 .... 155 H5
Rotherham Health Authority
RHAM/THRY S65 .... 7 F4
Rotherham Metropolitan
Borough Council
MALT S66 .... 157 J2
Rotherham Metropolitan
Borough Council
MALT S66 .... 176 E1
Rotherham Metropolitan
Borough Council
RAW S62 .... 133 H2

Rotherham Metropolitan
Borough Council
RHAM S60 .... 6 C³
Rotherham Metropolitan
Borough Council
RHAM/THRY S65 .... 7 D4
Rotherham Metropolitan
Borough Council
RHAM/THRY S65 .... 7 D3
Rotherham Priority Health Trust
RHAM/THRY S65 .... 7 D4
Rotherham Road Medical Centre
BSLYN/ROY S71 .... 56 B4
Rotherham Rugby Club
RHAM/THRY S65 .... 7 E5
Rotherham Town Cricket Club
RHAM/THRY S65 .... 7 E5
Rotherham Town Hall
RHAM S60 .... 6 C4
Rotherham United Football Club
RHAM S60 .... 6 A5
Rotunda Business Centre
CHPT/GREN S35 .... 108 A8
Roughwood Junior School
KIMB S61 .... 132 B5
Rowan School
TOT/DORE S17 .... 199 J¹
Rowena Infant School
CONI DN12 .... 114 C5
Royal Hallamshire Hospital
FUL S10 .... 8 A4
Royston Clinic
BSLYN/ROY S71 .... 30 D4
Royston Comprehensive School
BSLYN/ROY S71 .... 30 D3
Royston Meadstead
Junior School
BSLYN/ROY S71 .... 30 C4
Royston Midland Junior &
Infant School
BSLYN/ROY S71 .... 30 D3
Royston St John Baptist C E (A)
Primary School
BSLYN/ROY S71 .... 30 D4
Rspca Centre
BWTY DN10 .... 141 K1
Rudston Preparatory School
RHAM/THRY S65 .... 7 E5
Ruskin Gallery
SHEF S1 .... 9 D3
Rustlings Road Medical Centre
ECC S11 .... 170 A7
Rutland Business Park
OWL S3 .... 171 F¹
Ryecroft Infant School
RAW S62 .... 133 K¹
Ryton Park Primary School
WRKS S80 .... 210 D¹
Sacred Heart R C Primary School
ST/HB/BR S6 .... 151 H8
St Albans Junior & Infant School
MALT S66 .... 157 G¹
St Ann RC School
CONI DN12 .... 114 B¹
St Andrews C of E Methodist
Aided School
DRON S18 .... 200 D¹
St Annes Infant School
WRKS S80 .... 210 B¹
St Anns Medical Centre
RHAM/THRY S65 .... 7 D¹
St Anns Surgery
KIMB S61 .... 132 B¹
St Augustines County
Junior School
WRKN S81 .... 211 F¹
St Bedes Primary School
KIMB S61 .... 132 B¹
St Bernards RC School
RHAM/THRY S65 .... 134 B¹
St Catherines RC Primary School
OWL S3 .... 152 B¹
St Francis Xavier RC School
DONS/BSCR DN4 .... 4 C¹
St Georges Church
SHEF S1 .... 8 C¹
St Georges Hospital
ST/HB/BR S6 .... 8 A¹
St Giles C of E (Aided)
Primary School
ECK/KIL S21 .... 205 G¹
St Helens Junior & Infant School
BSLYN/ROY S71 .... 56 E¹
St James Swimming Pool
DON DN1 .... 5 D¹
St John Fisher RC Junior &
Infants School
HACK/IN S12 .... 189 J¹
St Johns C of E Infants School
STKB/PEN S36 .... 77 K¹
St Johns C of E (Park)
Primary School
SHEFP/MNR S2 .... 171 K¹
St Johns C of E Primary School
WRKN S81 .... 196 C¹
St Johns C of E School
MEX/SWTN S64 .... 113 G¹
St John the Baptist C of E (Aided)
Junior School
STKB/PEN S36 77

St Josephs Junior & Infants School
RAW S62 .... 133 J2
St Josephs School
NROS/TKH DN11 .... 118 E6
St Lukes C of E School
WRKN S81 .... 195 H7
St Maries R C Primary School
FUL S10 .... 170 A6
St Marys Catholic School
CONI DN12 .... 115 H5
St Mary School
FUL S10 .... 170 C2
St Marys C of E Junior &
Infant School
DOD/DAR S75 .... 55 H5
St Marys C of E Junior &
Infant School
RAW S62 .... 133 J2
St Marys C of E Primary School
ST/HB/BR S6 .... 170 D1
St Marys High Green RC
Primary School
CHPT/GREN S35 .... 107 K7
St Marys RC School
RHAM/THRY S65 .... 156 B1
St Marys School
DONS/BSCR DN4 .... 92 C7
St Marys School
DRON S18 .... 202 B7
St Matthews Infant School
DOD/DAR S75 .... 55 H5
St Michaels C of E School
HATH/EY S32 .... 182 C7
St Michaels C of E School
NROS/TKH DN11 .... 119 G6
St Michaels RC
Comprehensive School
BSLYN/ROY S71 .... 30 C8
St Michaels RC Junior &
Infant School
WMB/DAR S73 .... 84 C3
St Oswalds RC Primary School
SHEFP/MNR S2 .... 172 A5
St Patricks Primary School
NROS/TKH DN11 .... 163 G3
St Patricks RC School
SHEFN S5 .... 152 D3
St Peters RC Primary School
DONS/BSCR DN4 .... 91 K6
St Theresas School
SHEFP/MNR S2 .... 172 D8
St Thomas More R C
Primary School
CHPT/GREN S35 .... 129 J8
St Thomas of Canterbury R C
Primary School
SHEFS S8 .... 187 F7
Saint Vincent Medical Centre
DON DN1 .... 5 E3
St Wilfreds C of E (A) Junior &
Infant School
ARMTH DN3 .... 93 J7
St Wilfrids RC Primary School
ABRD S7 .... 186 C3
Sandall Wood School
WHHL DN2 .... 92 C2
Sandhill J M I School
RAW S62 .... 134 B1
Sandhill Primary School
CUD/GR S72 .... 59 H6
The Sandringham Practice
WHHL DN2 .... 92 A2
Sarans Gallery
NROS/TKH DN11 .... 139 K8
Scawsby College
BTLY DN5 .... 89 K1
Scawsby Health Centre
BTLY DN5 .... 90 B1
Scawthorpe Clinic
BTLY DN5 .... 64 B8
Scholes Cricket Club
HOLM/MEL HD7 .... 48 C4
Scholes Junior & Infant School
HOLM/MEL HD7 .... 48 C4
Scissett Middle School
KBTN HD8 .... 26 A5
Scissett Swimming Baths
KBTN HD8 .... 26 B5
Scofton Golf Course
BWTY DN10 .... 163 K8
Shafton Two Gates Junior &
Infant School
CUD/GR S72 .... 31 K5
Shardlows Sports Club
CHPT/GREN S35 .... 130 C5
Sharrow Lane Surgery
ECC S11 .... 8 C6
Shaw Lane Industrial Estate
WHHL DN2 .... 66 D7
Shaw Wood Junior &
Infant School
ARMTH DN3 .... 67 F7
Sheaf Heaf Gardens
Industrial Estate
SHEFP/MNR S2 .... 9 E5
Sheffield Area Health
Authority Sports & Social Club
ECC S11 .... 169 H8
Sheffield Area Health
Authority (Teaching)
FUL S10 .... 8 B3

Sheffield City Council
ATT S4 .... 9 F1
Sheffield City Council
ATT S4 .... 152 D7
Sheffield City Council
ATT S4 .... 152 C8
Sheffield Cantley Middle School
CHPT/GREN S35 .... 129 J8
Sheffield City Council
DARN/MH S9 .... 153 K6
Sheffield City Council
DARN/MH S9 .... 172 E3
Sheffield City Council
HACK/IN S12 .... 189 G4
Sheffield City Council
HAN/WDH S13 .... 189 K1
Sheffield City Council
MOS S20 .... 190 C5
Sheffield City Council
OWL S3 .... 8 C1
Sheffield City Council
OWL S3 .... 171 G1
Sheffield City Council
SHEF S1 .... 9 D3
Sheffield City Council
SHEFN S5 .... 131 F8
Sheffield City Council
SHEFP/MNR S2 .... 9 E6
Sheffield City Council
SHEFP/MNR S2 .... 172 A4
Sheffield City Council
SHEFP/MNR S2 .... 172 C8
Sheffield City Council
SHEFP/MNR S2 .... 187 K2
Sheffield City Council
SHEFS S8 .... 187 G2
Sheffield City Council
SHEFS S8 .... 200 E1
Sheffield City Council
ST/HB/BR S6 .... 151 H7
The Sheffield College
MOS S20 .... 190 D7
The Sheffield College
SHEFN S5 .... 130 A8
The Sheffield College
SHEFP/MNR S2 .... 9 E5
The Sheffield College
SHEFS S8 .... 187 H8
Sheffield County Court
OWL S3 .... 9 D2
Sheffield Eagles R L F C
DARN/MH S9 .... 172 C1
Sheffield Hallam University
FUL S10 .... 8 A4
Sheffield Hallam University
SHEF S1 .... 9 E3
Sheffield Health Authority
CHPT/GREN S35 .... 128 C8
Sheffield Health Authority
FUL S10 .... 8 B3
Sheffield Health Authority
SHEFN S5 .... 152 D3
Sheffield High School
ECC S11 .... 170 C5
Sheffield Magistrates Court
SHEF S1 .... 9 E2
Sheffield Medical Centre
OWL S3 .... 9 F1
Sheffield Natural Health Centre
SHEFS S8 .... 171 F8
Sheffield Sports Stadium Ltd
ST/HB/BR S6 .... 151 J6
Sheffield Technology Park
DARN/MH S9 .... 172 B1
Sheffield United AFC
SHEFP/MNR S2 .... 9 D5
Sheffield United Cricket Club
DARN/MH S9 .... 154 C6
Sheffield Wednesday
Football Club
ST/HB/BR S6 .... 151 H5
Shirecliffe Junior School
SHEFN S5 .... 151 K5
Shire Green Medical Centre
SHEFN S5 .... 153 F1
Shireoaks Business Centre
WRKN S81 .... 209 J1
Shireoaks Miners Welfare &
Sports Club
WRKN S81 .... 209 H1
Shooters Grove Primary School
ST/HB/BR S6 .... 150 E8
Shortbrook Primary School
MOS S20 .... 190 D7
Shrewsbury Hospital
SHEFP/MNR S2 .... 9 F4
Sikh Temple
ATT S4 .... 152 D8
Silverdale School
ECC S11 .... 185 J2
Sir Edmund Hillary County Primary
School
WRKN S81 .... 210 E3
Sir Harold Jackson
Primary School
TOT/DORE S17 .... 200 B2
Sitwell Junior & Infants School
RHAM S60 .... 156 A4

The Sloan Practice
SHEFS S8 .... 187 K5
Sothall Medical Centre
MOS S20 .... 190 D5
Sothall Snooker & Leisure Centre
MOS S20 .... 190 D4
South Cantley Middle School
DONS/BSCR DN4 .... 118 E1
South Elmsall Ash Grove
Junior & Infant School
HEM/SK/SE WF9 .... 35 F3
South Elmsall Health Centre
HEM/SK/SE WF9 .... 34 E4
Southey Green Medical Centre
SHEFN S5 .... 152 A4
Southey Hill Surgery
SHEFN S5 .... 152 A3
South Kirkby Common
Road School
HEM/SK/SE WF9 .... 33 K6
South Kirkby First School
HEM/SK/SE WF9 .... 34 D4
South Yorkshire Business Centre
RAW S62 .... 133 H5
Springfield Primary School
OWL S3 .... 8 C4
Springwood Junior &
Infant School
HOY S74 .... 108 E2
Sprotbrough Health Centre
BTLY DN5 .... 90 B5
Stag Medical Centre
RHAM/THRY S65 .... 156 B4
Stainforth Middle School
HTFD DN7 .... 41 K3
Stairfoot Health Centre
BSLY S70 .... 56 E8
Stanilamd Yacht Club
THNE DN8 .... 23 G8
Stanley Street County
Primary School
WRKN S81 .... 210 C2
Stannington Health Centre
ST/HB/BR S6 .... 169 G1
Stannington Infant School
ST/HB/BR S6 .... 169 G1
Station Road Industrial Estate
WMB/DAR S73 .... 84 B4
Station Road Junior &
Infant School
CONI DN12 .... 114 D4
Stirling Junior School
DON DN1 .... 4 C4
Stockingate First School
HEM/SK/SE WF9 .... 33 K6
Stockingate Surgery
HEM/SK/SE WF9 .... 34 A5
Stocksbridge Golf Club
STKB/PEN S36 .... 105 G8
Stocksbridge High School
STKB/PEN S36 .... 104 E6
Stocksbridge Junior School
STKB/PEN S36 .... 104 E7
Stocksbridge Leisure Centre
STKB/PEN S36 .... 104 D6
Stocksbridge Rugby Club
STKB/PEN S36 .... 104 E5
Stonelow Junior School
DRON S18 .... 201 H5
Storm House School
DEARNE S63 .... 86 B8
Stradbroke Primary School
HAN/WDH S13 .... 173 F8
Sues Health Centre
BSLYN/ROY S71 .... 30 B7
Summerfields Junior &
Infants School
BSLYN/ROY S71 .... 30 B3
Sunday School
DEARNE S63 .... 60 A7
Superbowl Two Thousand
KIMB S61 .... 132 B7
Superintendent Swimming Baths
CHPT/GREN S35 .... 130 B2
Swallownest Health Centre
AU/AST/KP S26 .... 175 H8
Swinton Brookfield
Primary School
MEX/SWTN S64 .... 112 C5
Swinton Comprehensive School
MEX/SWTN S64 .... 112 B5
Swinton Fitzwilliam
Infants School
MEX/SWTN S64 .... 112 A5
Swinton Meadows Business Park
MEX/SWTN S64 .... 112 E4
Swinton Meadows
Industrial Estate
MEX/SWTN S64 .... 112 E4
Swinton Milton Special School
MEX/SWTN S64 .... 112 B4
Swinton Swimming Pool
MEX/SWTN S64 .... 112 C4
Sycamore Hall Preparatory School
DONS/BSCR DN4 .... 90 D8
Tapton Secondary School
FUL S10 .... 170 A5
Tates Gallery
DARN/MH S9 .... 172 E3
Tates Gallery
ST/HB/BR S6 .... 151 H7

Technical College
WRKN S81 .... 196 E4
Templeborough Business Centre
RHAM S60 .... 6 B6
Tertiary College
ECK/KIL S21 .... 204 B4
Thomas Rotherham College
RHAM S60 .... 7 D6
Thornbridge School
HACK/IN S12 .... 189 F5
Thorne Golf Club
THNE DN8 .... 43 G2
Thorne Grammar School
THNE DN8 .... 23 K7
Thorne Health Centre
THNE DN8 .... 23 J8
Thorne South Common
First School
THNE DN8 .... 43 K1
Thorne Swimming Baths
THNE DN8 .... 23 K8
Thornhill Industrial Estate
KIMB S61 .... 6 B2
Thornhill Jmi School
RHAM S60 .... 6 B3
Thorpe Hesley Clinic
KIMB S61 .... 131 G3
Thorpe Hesley Infant School
KIMB S61 .... 131 F3
Thorpe Hesley Junior School
KIMB S61 .... 131 G3
Thrybergh Comprehensive School
RHAM/THRY S65 .... 134 E4
Thrybergh Fullerton Church of
England J & I School
RHAM/THRY S65 .... 134 E4
Thrybergh Medical Centre
RHAM/THRY S65 .... 134 E5
Thrybergh St Gerards RC
M & I School
RHAM/THRY S65 .... 134 C5
Thurcroft Infant School
MALT S66 .... 176 E1
Thurcroft Junior Mixed School
MALT S66 .... 177 F1
Thurgoland C of E
Primary School
CHPT/GREN S35 .... 79 J8
Thurnscoe Business Centre
DEARNE S63 .... 60 D8
Thurnscoe Business Park
DEARNE S63 .... 60 D8
Thurnscoe Gooseacre J M School
DEARNE S63 .... 60 B6
Tickfield Eastfield Primary School
NROS/TKH DN11 .... 139 K7
Tickhill C of E School
NROS/TKH DN11 .... 139 J8
Tinsley Junior School
DARN/MH S9 .... 154 B5
Todwick Jmi School
AU/AST/KP S26 .... 192 E2
Tornedale Infant School
NROS/TKH DN11 .... 118 E6
Totley All Saints C of E
Primary School
TOT/DORE S17 .... 199 G3
Totley Primary School
TOT/DORE S17 .... 199 H3
Town Fields Primary School
WHHL DN2 .... 5 E2
Trafalgar House Medical Centre
ST/HB/BR S6 .... 151 J3
Tramways Medical Centre
ST/HB/BR S6 .... 151 H7
Travis County Primary School
HTFD DN7 .... 42 D7
Treeton C of E Junior &
Infant School
RHAM S60 .... 174 C3
U C I Cinema
MOS S20 .... 190 C4
University of Sheffield
ECC S11 .... 170 B6
University of Sheffield
FUL S10 .... 8 A3
University of Sheffield
FUL S10 .... 170 C4
University of Sheffield
OWL S3 .... 8 B3
Unstone Junior School
DRON S18 .... 202 A8
Untitled Gallery
SHEF S1 .... 9 E4
Upperthong Junior &
Infant School
HOLM/MGL HD7 .... 47 H3
Upperwood Junior &
Infant School
WMB/DAR S73 .... 84 C1

Valley Medical Centre
STKB/PEN S36 .... 104 E5
Verdon Recreation Centre
OWL S3 .... 9 E1
Victoria Middle School
CONI DN12 .... 115 J4
Victoria Primary School
DEARNE S63 .... 111 K1
Wadworth County Primary School
NROS/TKH DN11 .... 139 F1
Wakefield Metropolitan
District Council
HEM/SK/SE WF9 .... 34 E5
Wales High School
AU/AST/KP S26 .... 192 C4
Wales Junior & Infant School
AU/AST/KP S26 .... 192 B5
Walkley Medical Centre
FUL S10 .... 170 C1
Walk Talk Galleries
ECC S11 .... 170 B7
Waltheof School
SHEFP/MNR S2 .... 172 D5
Ward Green Junior School
BSLY S70 .... 82 A2
Warmsworth Primary School
DONS/BSCR DN4 .... 115 K1
Warren House Surgery
BSLY S70 .... 2 C5
Wath C of E Jmi School
DEARNE S63 .... 85 H8
Wath Park Infant School
DEARNE S63 .... 111 H2
Wath Pope Pius R C
Secondary School
DEARNE S63 .... 111 K3
Wath R U F C
DEARNE S63 .... 85 J8
Wath Upon Dearne
Comprehensive School
DEARNE S63 .... 111 J2
Wath West Industrial Estate
DEARNE S63 .... 85 F7
Waverley Junior School
DONS/BSCR DN4 .... 116 B1
Welfare Clinic
ECK/KIL S21 .... 204 B4
Wellgate Infant School
DOD/DAR S75 .... 29 G6
Wentworth Castle College of
Education
DOD/DAR S75 .... 80 E4
Wentworth C of E School
RAW S62 .... 109 H6
Westfield Health Centre
MOS S20 .... 190 C7
West Melton J & I School
DEARNE S63 .... 85 F8
Weston Park Hospital N H S Trust
FUL S10 .... 8 A3
West Road First School
THNE DN8 .... 24 A4
Westside Gallery
FUL S10 .... 8 A5
Westways Middle Primary School
FUL S10 .... 170 C3
Wharncliffe Side Primary School
CHPT/GREN S35 .... 127 K5
Wheatley Hall Business Centre
WHHL DN2 .... 65 K8
Whiston Grange School
RHAM S60 .... 155 K6
Whiston Junior & Infant School
RHAM S60 .... 156 A6
Whiston Worry Goose Jmi School
RHAM S60 .... 156 C6
White House Surgery
SHEFP/MNR S2 .... 172 D7
Whitelea Grove Trading Estate
MEX/SWTN S64 .... 112 D3
Whiteley Wood Clinic
ECC S11 .... 169 J8
White Rose Surgery
HEM/SK/SE WF9 .... 34 E4
Whiteways Junior School
ATT S4 .... 152 E7
Whitley Hall Cricket Club
CHPT/GREN S35 .... 129 K6
Wickersley Comprehensive School
MALT S66 .... 157 H3
Wickersley Health Centre
MALT S66 .... 157 G2
William Levick Infant School
DRON S18 .... 200 C5
William Levick Primary School
DRON S18 .... 200 C5
Wilsic Hall School
NROS/TKH DN11 .... 138 D3
Wilthorpe Junior School
DOD/DAR S75 .... 55 H3

Wincobank Surgery
DARN/MH S9 .... 153 J3
Windmill Hill Primary School
CHPT/GREN S35 .... 130 A1
Wingfield Comprehensive School
KIMB S61 .... 132 D5
Wisewood Secondary School
ST/HB/BR S6 .... 150 E6
Wombwell Aldham Junior &
Infant School
WMB/DAR S73 .... 83 H4
Wombwell Clinic
WMB/DAR S73 .... 83 K4
Wombwell Cricket Club
WMB/DAR S73 .... 83 J4
Wombwell High School
WMB/DAR S73 .... 84 B6
Wombwell Jump Junior &
Infant School
HOY S74 .... 83 G4
Wombwell Public Baths
WMB/DAR S73 .... 84 A4
Woodfield First School
DONS/BSCR DN4 .... 116 E5
Woodgrove Surgery
DEARNE S63 .... 111 J4
Woodhouse Clinic
HAN/WDH S13 .... 189 K2
Woodhouse Medical Centre
HAN/WDH S13 .... 189 K3
Woodlands East RC School
AWLS/ASK DN6 .... 63 K4
Woodlands First School
AWLS/ASK DN6 .... 63 H4
Woodlands Middle School
AWLS/ASK DN6 .... 63 H4
Woodseats Medical Centre
SHEFS S8 .... 187 F4
Woodseats Primary School
SHEFS S8 .... 187 F4
Woodsetts Infant School
WRKN S81 .... 195 G4
Woodsetts Junior & Infant School
WRKN S81 .... 195 G4
Woodside Surgery
AWLS/ASK DN6 .... 63 H4
Woodstock Bower Group Practice
KIMB S61 .... 154 D6
Woodthorpe Community
Primary School
HAN/WDH S13 .... 172 E3
Works
ARMTH DN3 .... 66 C4
Works
RHAM/THRY S65 .... 134 B4
Worksop College
WRKS S80 .... 211 F4
Worksop Cricket & Sports Club
WRKS S80 .... 210 C5
Worksop Leisure Centre
WRKN S81 .... 210 C4
Worksop Hartland
Comprehensive School
WRKS S80 .... 210 D5
Worksop Portland
Comprehensive School
WRKS S80 .... 210 C4
Worksop Redlands County Primary
School
WRKS S80 .... 210 E5
Worksop Valley
Comprehensive School
WRKN S81 .... 210 C4
Worsbrough Bridge RC School
BSLY S70 .... 82 C5
Worsbrough C of E Junior &
Infant School
BSLY S70 .... 82 A5
Worsbrough Common
County Primary School
BSLY S70 .... 82 A4
Worsbrough Health Centre
BSLY S70 .... 82 C5
Worsbrough High School
BSLY S70 .... 82 E5
Worsbrough Mill Museum
BSLY S70 .... 82 B6
W R C C Clinic
HTFD DN7 .... 41 K4
Wybourn Primary School
SHEFP/MNR S2 .... 171 K3
Yewlands School
CHPT/GREN S35 .... 129 K2
Yews Day Hospital
CHPT/GREN S35 .... 150 C6
York House Medical Centre
SHEFP/MNR S2 .... 172 E6
Yorkshire Neurology Clinic
MALT S66 .... 157 F3

Page 2

A4
1 Dean St
2 Hindle St
3 Knowsley St
4 McIntock Wy
5 Nicholas St
6 Perseverance St
7 Pitt St West
8 Richard St
9 Richmond St
10 Springfield Pl
11 Stanhope St
12 Stanley St
13 Waterloo Rd
14 Well St
15 Westfield St

B4
1 Beaconsfield St
2 Fenton St
3 George Sq
4 Graham's Orch
5 Holden Ct
6 Lower Castlereagh St
7 Mark St
8 Nelson St
9 Peel Sq
10 Plumber St
11 Royal St
12 Wortley St
13 York St

C4
1 Burleigh Ct
2 Burlington Ar
3 Cheapside
4 Freemans Wy
5 Hayes Crt
6 Malthouse Rd
7 May Day Grn
8 Midland St
9 Pall Mall
10 Sherwood St
11 Wesley St

C5
1 Britannia Cl
2 Buckley St
3 Copper Cl
4 Denison Ct
5 Duke Crs
6 Duke St
7 Freeman St
8 Providence Ct
9 Quarry St
10 Rebecca St
11 Rosebery Ter
12 Taylor Rw
13 Upper New St
14 Wilkinson St

C6
1 California Crs
2 Chestnut Ct
3 Dickinson Pl
4 Dickinson Rd
5 Essex Rd
6 Frederic Pl
7 Hornby St
8 Howard St
9 Kelsey Ter
10 Kenworthy Rd
11 Stoneleigh Cft
12 Warren Pl

Page 8

A2
1 Barber Crs
2 Barber Pl
3 The Coach Houses
4 Crookesmoor Dr
5 Elliot Rd
6 Ivy Gr
7 Ivy Cv
8 Moorgate Av
9 Warrington Rd

B1
1 Blake Grove Rd
2 Brandreth Rd
3 Brandreth Ct
4 Burlington Ct
5 Carnarvon St
6 Daniel Hill Ter
7 Gilpin La
8 Philadelphia Dr
9 Philadelphia Gv
10 Portland St
11 Shipton St
12 Straw La
13 Westmoreland St
14 Yeomans Rd

B4
1 Broomspring Cl
2 Broomsprings La
3 Exeter Wy
4 Gloucester Crs
5 Hanover St
6 Holberry Cl
7 Holberry Gdns
8 Mackenzie Crs
9 Monmouth St
10 Ruth Sq
11 Upper Hanover St

C2
1 Blue Boy St
2 Brocco St
3 Brownell St
4 Burnt Tree La
5 Craven St
6 Ellison St
7 Morpeth St
8 Netherthorpe St
9 Queen's Rw
10 Well Meadow Dr
11 Well Meadow St

C3
1 Abney St
2 Boden La
3 Broad Lane Ct
4 Canning St
5 Charlotte La
6 Chester St
7 Congress St
8 Convent Pl
9 Devonshire La
10 Devonshire St
11 Orange St
12 Pitt Cl
13 Pitt La
14 Portland La
15 Red Hl
16 Regent St
17 St George's Ter
18 St Thomas St
19 Siddall St
20 Westhill La
21 Wheeldon St

C4
1 Bath St
2 Broomhall St
3 Broomspring La
4 Cavendish St
5 Chester La
6 Evans St
7 Exeter Pl
8 Headford Ms
9 Headford St

C6
1 Asher Rd
2 Bennett St
3 Crowther Pl
4 Croydon St
5 Grosvenor Sq
6 Mount Pleasant Rd
7 Penley St
8 Salmon St
9 Sitwell Pl
10 Smeaton St
11 Stemp St
12 Ventnor Pl
13 Ward Pl

Page 9

D1
1 Cotton Mill Rw
2 Ebenezer Pl
3 Ebenezer St
4 Neepsend La
5 Rowland St
6 Ward St

D3
1 Barker's Pool
2 Bells Sq
3 Cambridge St
4 Chapel Wk
5 Charles La
6 Cross Burgess St
7 East Pde
8 Fargate
9 Holly La
10 Norfolk La
11 Orchard La
12 Orchard St
13 Penton St
14 Pool Sq
15 St James' St
16 Wellington St
17 West Street La

D5
1 Ascot St
2 Baron St
3 Countess Rd
4 Forge La
5 Hereford St
6 Midland St

E1
1 Andrew La
2 Andrew St
3 Denholme Cl
4 Lopham Cl
5 Lopham St
6 Nursery La
7 Scholey St
8 Spitalfields
9 Stanley La
10 Stanley St
11 Stockton Cl

E3
1 Bakers Hl
2 Cadman La
3 Esperanto Pl
4 Fitzalan Sq
5 Gilbert St
6 High St
7 Mulberry St

F2
1 Blast La
2 Cadman St
3 Effingham La
4 Malting La
5 New Street La
6 Stepney St

F3
1 Anson St
2 Blackwell Cl
3 Blackwell Ct
4 Crown Pl
5 High Street La
6 Manor Oaks Dr
7 Manor Oaks Gdns
8 Rhodes St
9 Talbot Rd
10 Weigh La

F4
1 Coates St
2 Glencoe Dr
3 Glencoe Pl
4 Robinson Rd
5 Samson St
6 Talbot Crs
7 Talbot Gdns
8 Talbot Pl

F5
1 Claywood Rd

F6
1 Tower Cl

Page 30

C8
1 Blackheath Cl
2 Carlton Rd
3 Derwent Cl

Page 33

H1
1 Baylee St
2 Bush St
3 George St
4 Grove Lea Cl
5 The Haverlands
6 King Edward St
7 Pontefract Ter
8 Union St

Page 55

F6
1 Ancote Cl
2 Crowden Wk
3 Drury Farm Ct
4 Mickelden Wy
5 Wessenden Cl
6 White Hill Ter

F8
1 Cinder Hills Wy
2 Cramlands
3 Far Townend
4 Hannas Royd
5 Heather Knowle
6 Lambert Fold
7 Lingthwaite
8 Middlewoods

G4
1 Little New Cl
2 Oakworth Cl
3 Ravenshaw Cl
4 Samuel Sq
5 Vaughan Rd
6 Woodview La

G5
1 Birchfield Wk
2 Cotswold Cl
3 Gramsian Cl
4 Greaves Fold
5 Hambleton Cl
6 Malvern Cl
7 Mary's Pl
8 Mendip Cl
9 Porter Ter
10 St Owens Dr

H3
1 Huddersfield Rd
2 Moorbank Cl
3 Redbrook Ct
4 Wilthorpe Gn

H5
1 Helensburgh Cl
2 The Lindales
3 Myrtle St

J4
1 Carrington St
2 Lingard St
3 Thorntree La
4 Westbourne Sq

J6
1 Dean St
2 Hindle St
3 Knowsley St
4 McIntock Wy
5 Nicholas St
6 Perseverance St
7 Pitt St West
8 Richard St
9 Richmond St
10 Springfield Pl
11 Stanhope St
12 Stanley St
13 Waterloo Rd
14 Well St
15 Westfield St

J7
1 Cranbrook St
2 Fife St
3 Havelock St
4 Helena St
5 Leopold St
6 Sandford Ct

J8
1 Dyson St
2 Ellington St
3 Kingstone St

K5
1 Aireton Rd
2 Churchfield
3 Church La
4 Church St
5 Eastgate
6 Lancaster Ga
7 Rosehill Ct
8 Sadler La
9 St Mary's Ga
10 St Mary's Pl
11 Victoria St
12 Westwood Ct

K6
1 Beaconsfield St
2 Fenton St
3 George Sq
4 Graham's Orch
5 Holden Ct
6 Lower Castlereagh St
7 Mark St
8 Nelson St
9 Peel Sq
10 Plumber St
11 Royal St
12 Wortley St
13 York St

Page 56

A5
1 Denton St
2 Hanson St
3 Harborough Hill Rd
4 Redfearn St
5 Vernon St North

A6
1 Burleigh St
2 Burlington Ar
3 Cheapside
4 Freemans Yd
5 Hayes Crt
6 Malthouse Rd
7 May Day Grn
8 Midland St
9 Pall Mall
10 Sherwood St
11 Wesley St

A7
1 Britannia Cl
2 Buckley Ct
3 Copper Cl
4 Denison St
5 Duke Crs
6 Duke St
7 Freeman St
8 Providence Ct
9 Quarry St
10 Rebecca St
11 Rosebery Ter
12 Taylor Rw
13 Upper New St
14 Wilkinson St

A8
1 California Crs
2 Chestnut Ct
3 Dickinson Pl
4 Dickinson Rd
5 Essex Rd
6 Frederic Pl
7 Hornby St
8 Howard St
9 Kelsey Ter
10 Kenworthy Rd
11 Stoneleigh Cft
12 Warren Pl

B1
1 Kingsley Cl

B2
1 Dunmere Cl
2 Edgecliffe Pl
3 Quarry St

B7
1 Clifton St
2 Gold Cft
3 Henshall St
4 Milnes St
5 Oakwell Ter
6 Osborne Ms
7 St Peter's Ter
8 Seth Ter
9 Sunderland Ter
10 Victoria Ter
11 Wilby La

B8
1 Crown Av
2 Crown St
3 Harriet Cl
4 Walton Ct

C4
1 Carbis Cl
2 Haworth Cl
3 Roche Cl
4 Sennen Cft
5 Sheridan Ct
6 Trewan Ct

C7
1 Applehurst Bank
2 Evelyn Ter
3 Lulworth Cl
4 Pindar Oaks Cottages
5 Pindar St

D4
1 Bude Ct
2 Chapter Wy
3 Cliffe La
4 Mylor Ct
5 St Lukes Wy

E1
1 Edenfield Cl
2 Formby Ct
3 Longridge Rd
4 Walney Fold

E4
1 Brookvale
2 Rectory Wy
3 Temple Wy

E8
1 Hunningley La
2 Neville Cl

Page 57

F7
1 Bridge St
2 New St
3 Oxford Pl
4 Pinfold Ct
5 Waterfield Pl

J7
1 Buttermere Wy
2 Crummock Wy
3 Ullswater Rd

Page 82

B2
1 Blackburn St
2 Brockfield Cl
3 Croft St
4 Henry St
5 John St
6 Kingwell Cft
7 Kingwell Ms
8 Mill Ct
9 Norman Cl
10 Osmond Pl
11 Osmond Wy
12 Parkside Ms
13 Sweyn Cft

B3
1 Ashover Cl
2 Charles St
3 George St
4 Hardwick Cl
5 Kendal Crs
6 New St
7 Robert St
8 Roundwood Ct
9 Thomas St

Page 90

B2
1 Farmhill Cl
2 Grampian Ct
3 Malvern Av
4 Mendip Cl
5 Ramsworth Cl
6 Roehampton Ri
7 Springfield Ct

C2
1 Charnock Dr
2 Farthing Gale Ms
3 Fernlea Cl
4 Rothesay Cl

C8
1 Gilberthorpe Rd
2 Hepworth Rd
3 Larchfield Rd
4 Milner Rd
5 Ranyard Rd
6 Ventnor Cl

D6
1 Beaconsfield Rd
2 Laneside Cl
3 Old Hexthorpe
4 Patrick Stirling Ct
5 Shirley Rd

D3
1 Cross St
2 Grange Av
3 Laurel Ter
4 Marshall Av
5 Mount Pleasant
6 Ronald Rd

Page 91

G3
1 Allerton St
2 Athron St
3 Copley Rd
4 Harrington St
5 High Fisher Ga
6 Market Rd
7 Milbanke St
8 Penistone St

E1
1 Barrie Rd
2 Browning Av
3 Burns Rd
4 Crookes Rd
5 Gray Cdns
6 Gurney Rd
7 Keats Rd
8 Lowell Av
9 Norfolk Rd
10 Suffolk Rd
11 Swinburne Av

Page 130

B2
1 Bents Cl
2 Berry Holme Cl
3 Berry Holme Ct
4 Nether Ley Ct
5 Nether Ley Cft
6 Nether Ley Gdns
7 Upper Ley Ct
8 Upper Ley Dell

Page 151

H1
1 Edge Well Pl
2 Edge Well Cl
3 Fox Hill Wy

H7
1 Brier St
2 Cannock St
3 Cheadle St
4 Hillsborough Pl
5 Hillsborough Rd
6 Holme Cl
7 Roselle St
8 Treswell Crs

J8
1 Bilston St
2 Blackburne St
3 Burnaby Gn
4 Cuthbert Rd
5 Langsett Crs
6 Normandale Rd
7 Walter St

Page 152

D7
1 Cawston Rd
2 Cayton Rd
3 Osgathorpe Crs

Page 155

G1
1 College St
2 The Crofts
3 Domine La
4 Down's Rw
5 Quarry Hl
6 Snail Hl
7 Stanley St
8 The Statutes
9 Unity Pl

G7
1 Blackbird Av
2 Buckingham Wy
3 Chaffinch Av
4 Chatsworth Ri
5 Cherry Tree Ct
6 Fairburn Gdns
7 Lyncroft Cl
8 Mendip Ri
9 Thorndale Ri
10 Thrush Av
11 Trentham Cl

H1
1 Catherine St
2 Chatham St
3 Doncaster Ga
4 Douglas St
5 Morpeth St
6 Percy St
7 Summerfield
8 Whybourne Gv

Page 169

H5
1 Burnt Stones Gv
2 Hallam Cha
3 Sandygate Cl
4 Stonewood Ct

K4
1 Coppice Vw
2 Melfort Gln

K7
1 Bramwith Rd
2 Carr Bank Dr
3 Hanging Water Cl
4 Pendeen Rd

Page 170

A1
1 Ivanhoe Rd
2 Middle La
3 Woodland View Rd

B3
1 Bosworth St
2 Chichester Rd
3 Colchester Rd
4 Flodden St
5 Newbury Rd
6 Suthard Cross Rd

C2
1 Bank House Rd
2 Eastfield Rd
3 Joseph Rd
4 Northfield Cl

C3
1 Ainsley Rd
2 Clementson Rd
3 Cobden Pl
4 Leamington St
5 Romsdal Rd
6 Spring House Rd
7 Spring View Rd
8 Warwick St
9 Warwick Ter

C4
1 Churchill Rd
2 Coombe Pl
3 Highnam Crescent Rd
4 Pisgah House Rd

C5
1 Ashdell
2 Ashdell La
3 Ashgate La
4 Caxton Rd
5 Chandos St
6 Hoole La
7 Nile St
8 Peel St
9 Taptonville Crs
10 Turners La
11 Watson Rd

D2
1 Alpine Rd
2 Birkendale Vw
3 Bransby St
4 Daniel Hill Ct
5 Upperthorpe Gln

D4
1 Claremont Crs
2 Damer St
3 Harcourt Crs
4 Palmerston Rd
5 Severn Ct
6 Severn Rd
7 Shearwood Rd
8 Tree Root Wk

D5
1 Broomgrove Crs
2 College St
3 Paxton La
4 St Mark's Dr

D7
1 Ashford Rd
2 Berresford Rd
3 Bruce Rd
4 Dyson Pl
5 Eastwood Rd
6 Gordon Rd
7 Harefield Rd
8 Hickmott Rd
9 Jarrow Rd
10 Lynton Rd
11 Rosedale Gdns
12 Rosedale Rd

D8
1 Cherry Tree Cl
2 Cherry Tree Dell
3 Cherry Tree Dr
4 Cherry Tree Rd
5 Meadow Bank Av
6 St Andrew's Cl

E1
1 Gilpin St
2 Primrose Hl

E2
1 Blake Grove Rd
2 Brandreth Rd
3 Brandreth Ct
4 Burlington Ct
5 Carnarvon St
6 Daniel Hill Ter
7 Gilpin La
8 Philadelphia Dr
9 Philadelphia Gv
10 Portland St
11 Shipton St
12 Straw La
13 Westmoreland St
14 Yeomans Rd

E4
1 Brightmore Dr
2 Conway St
3 Durham Rd
4 Favell Rd
5 Hounsfield La
6 Hounsfield Rd
7 Leavygreave Rd
8 Western Bank
9 Wilkinson La
10 Wilkinson St

E5
1 Broomspring Cl
2 Broomspring La
3 Exeter Wy
4 Gloucester Crs
5 Hanover St
6 Holberry Cl
7 Holberry Gdns
8 Mackenzie Crs
9 Monmouth St
10 Ruth Sq
11 Upper Hanover St

E6
1 Parliament St
2 Pembroke St
3 Sawdon Rd
4 Sunderland St

E7
1 Mackenzie St

E8
1 Kenbourne Gv
2 Kenwood Rd
3 Montgomery Dr

Page 171

F2
1 Bedford St
2 Dixon St
3 Downing La
4 Dun Flds
5 Dun La
6 Henry St
7 Infirmary Rd
8 Lancaster St
9 Lister La
10 Matthew St
11 Montgomery Terrace Rd
12 Percy St
13 St Philip's Rd
14 Sudbury St
15 Waterloo Wk

F3
1 Blue Boy St
2 Brocco St
3 Brownell St
4 Burnt Tree La
5 Craven St
6 Ellison St
7 Morpeth St
8 Netherthorpe St
9 Queen's Rw
10 Well Meadow Dr
11 Well Meadow St

F4
1 Abney St
2 Boden La
3 Broad Lane Ct
4 Canning St
5 Charlotte La
6 Chester St
7 Congress St
8 Convent Pl
9 Devonshire La
10 Devonshire St
11 Orange St
12 Pitt Cl
13 Pitt La
14 Portland La
15 Red Hl
16 Regent St
17 St George's Ter
18 St Thomas St
19 Siddall St
20 Westhill La
21 Wheeldon St

F7
1 Asher Rd
2 Bennett St
3 Crowther Pl
4 Croydon St
5 Grosvenor Sq
6 Mount Pleasant Rd
7 Penley St
8 Salmon St
9 Sitwell Pl
10 Smeaton St
11 Stemp St
12 Ventnor Pl
13 Ward Pl

F8
1 Ainsty Rd
2 Aizlewood Rd
3 Alcester Rd
4 Brookfield Rd
5 Cutts Ter
6 Dalton Ct
7 Farrar Rd
8 Herschell Rd
9 Marples Cl
10 Marples Dr
11 Miller Rd
12 Rampton Rd
13 Sellers St
14 South View Crs

G3
1 Bower Spring
2 Cupola
3 Lee Cft
4 North Church St
5 Paradise La
6 Paradise Sq
7 Paradise St
8 Plum La
9 St Peter's Cl
10 Silver Street Head
11 Water St
12 Workhouse La

C4
1 Barker's Pool
2 Bells Sq
3 Cambridge St
4 Chapel Wk
5 Charles La
6 Cross Burgess St
7 East Pde
8 Fargate
9 Holly La
10 Norfolk La
11 Orchard La
12 Orchard St
13 Penton St
14 Pool Sq
15 St James' St
16 Wellington St
17 West Street La

C5
1 Cambridge St
2 Clay La
3 Cumberland Wy
4 Duke La
5 Froggatt La
6 Hallam La
7 Jessop St
8 Matilda Wy
9 Moor Head
10 Newton La
11 Rockingham Cl
12 Rockingham Ga
13 Rockingham Wy
14 Union La
15 Union St

G7
1 Alderson Rd North
2 Atkin Pl
3 Batt St
4 Belgrave Sq
5 Harrington Rd
6 Holland Pl
7 St Barnabas La
8 Silver Mill Rd
9 Witney St

G8
1 Alderney Rd
2 Fieldhead Rd
3 Gifford Rd
4 Glover Rd
5 Guernsey Rd
6 Jersey Rd
7 Preston St
8 Sark Rd
9 Sheaf Bank
10 Staveley Rd

H2
1 Andrew La
2 Andrew St
3 Denholme Cl
4 Lopham Cl
5 Lopham St
6 Nursery La
7 Scholey St
8 Spitalfields
9 Stanley La
10 Stanley St
11 Stockton Cl

H3
1 Castle Gn
2 Harts Head
3 Haymarket
4 Johnson La
5 Joiner St
6 Lady's Br
7 Meetinghouse La
8 Shude Hl
9 Waingate
10 Wharf St
11 Willey St

H6
1 Cream St
2 Cromford St
3 Leadmill Rd
4 Lenton St
5 Manton St
6 Sheaf Gdns

J1
1 Bressingham Cl
2 Ditchingham St
3 Harleston St
4 South Grimesthorpe Rd

J3
1 Blast La
2 Cadman St
3 Effingham La
4 Malting La
5 New Street La
6 Stepney St

J4
1 Anson St
2 Blackwell Cl
3 Blackwell Ct
4 Crown Pl
5 High Street La
6 Manor Oaks Dr
7 Manor Oaks Gdns
8 Rhodes St
9 Talbot Rd
10 Weigh La

J5
1 Coates St
2 Glencoe Dr
3 Glencoe Pl
4 Robinson Rd
5 Samson St
6 Talbot Crs
7 Talbot Gdns
8 Talbot St

J7
1 Tower Cl

J8
1 Thornborough Cl
2 Thornborough Pl
3 Warburton Cl
4 Warburton Gdns

K1
1 Babur Rd
2 Norroy St
3 Windsor St

K2
1 Sutherland St

K4
1 Manor Oaks Ct

K5
1 Ingram Ct
2 Stafford La

K7
1 T Benedict Ct

K8
1 Kenning Hall Cl
2 Kenninghall Mt
3 Samuel Cl
4 Samuel Dr

Page 172

A5
1 Kestrel Gn
2 Magpie Gv
3 Maltravers Cl
4 Osprey Gdns
5 Partridge Vw
6 Plover Ct
7 Quail Rl
8 Starling Mead
9 Wren Bank

B1
1 Bodmin St
2 Chippingham St
3 Heppenstall La
4 Sleaford St
5 Slitting Mill La

C2
1 Bray St
2 Cattal St
3 Chinley St
4 Faranden Rd
5 Fearnehough St
6 Garth Cl
7 Harry Firth Cl
8 Ouseburn St
9 Spofforth Rd
10 Wilfred Cl

D2
1 Basford Pl
2 Bramham Ct
3 Bramham Rd
4 Flaxby Rd
5 Kashmir Gdns
6 Shirland Ct
7 Shirland Ms
8 Shirland Pl
9 Tockwith Rd

D6
1 Beaumont Ms
2 The Crossways
3 Dawlands Cl
4 Dawlands Dr
5 Noehill Pl
6 Normancroft Dr
7 Prince Of Wales Rd
8 Saxonlea Dr
9 Vikinglea Gld

D7
1 Castledale Cft
2 Castledale Pl
3 Princess Ct
4 Vikinglea Cl

E2
1 Basford Ms
2 Boden Pl
3 Craven Cl
4 Fulford Cl
5 Fulford Pl
6 Greenland Cl
7 Whitby Rd

E3
1 The Avenue
2 Catcliffe Rd
3 Jeffcock Rd
4 Main Rd
5 Ronald Rd
6 Station Rd
7 Studley Ct
8 Swale Gdns
9 Waverley Rd

E7
1 Angleton Cl
2 Angleton Gdns
3 Angleton Ms
4 Aughton Dr
5 Woodthorpe Crs

Page 186

E1
1 Archibald Rd
2 Gatefield Rd
3 Herbert Rd
4 Marden Rd
5 Violet Bank Rd

E2
1 Coniston Ter
2 Crummock Rd
3 Edgemount Rd
4 Grasmere Rd
5 Thirlmere Rd
6 Thorne Rd
7 Windermere Rd

Page 187

G2
1 Brooklyn Pl
2 Brooklyn Rd
3 Cross Park Rd
4 Cyprus Rd
5 Molloy St
6 Rushdale Mt
7 Rushdale Ter

H1
1 Farish Pl
2 Gerard Cl
3 Gleadless Ct
4 Jeffery St
5 Nicholson Pl
6 Richards Ct
7 Romney Gdns
8 Sturge Cft

J1
1 Abney Cl
2 Derby Pl
3 Hallyburton Cl
4 Hallyburton Dr
5 Hartopp Cl

J8
1 Hazlebarrow Gv
2 Jordanthorpe Vw

K5
1 Constable Wy
2 Landseer Cl
3 Mawfa Crs
4 Mawfa Rd

Page 188

C3
1 Crispin Cl
2 Crispin Rd
3 Hollinsend Rd
4 Kirkby Av

D1
1 Applegarth Cl
2 Bagshaw's Rd
3 Holbrook Dr
4 Penthorpe Cl
5 Pleasant Dr

Page 190

B5
1 Deane Field Vw
2 Purbeck Ct
3 Roydfield Cl
4 Thorpe Gn

B8
1 Church Ms
2 Kildale Gdns
3 Shipman Ct
4 Station Rd
5 Stonedale Cl

C7
1 Birchwood Cl
2 Birchwood Gdns
3 Birchwood Rl
4 Birchwood Wy
5 Challoner Gn
6 Garland Mt
7 Meadowcroft Gld
8 Meadowcroft Rl
9 Pedley Dr
10 Shortbrook Bank
11 Westland Gv

D4
1 Drake House La West
2 Primrose Crs
3 Sothall Ct
4 Sothall Ms

E5
1 Byron Rd
2 Charnwood Ct
3 Crizedale Ct
4 Hartland Av
5 Hartland Ct
6 Ringwood Rd
7 Rothbury Av
8 Rothbury Ct
9 Rufford Ct
10 Waltham Gdns
11 Wareham Ct
12 Willingham Gdns
13 Wychwood Cft
14 Wychwood Cln
15 Wychwood Rd

E6
1 Abbots Meadow
2 Bramshill Ct
3 Collingbourne Dr
4 Hursley Cl
5 Inglewood Av
6 Inglewood Ct
7 Inglewood Dell
8 Milburn Ct

Page 200

C6
1 Allestree Dr
2 Barley Ms
3 Belton Cl
4 Burnaston Cl
5 Chaddesden Cl
6 Hazelwood Cl
7 Ivan Brook Cl
8 Mapperley Rd
9 Newstead Cl
10 Ormesby Cl
11 Oxclose Dr
12 Repton Pl
13 Rockingham Cl
14 Snelston Cl
15 Stanford Rd
16 Thornton Pl

Page 201

H1
1 Dyche Cl
2 Dyche Pl
3 Hazlebarrow Rd
4 Lingfoot Cl
5 Whinacre Cl
6 White Thorns Cl

Page 204

C1
1 Ambleside Cl
2 Borrowdale Av
3 Borrowdale Cl
4 Ennerdale Av
5 Ennerdale Dr
6 Murrayfield Dr
7 Oakworth Cl
8 Ralston Cft
9 Twickenham Cl
10 Twickenham Ct
11 Twickenham Gld
12 Twickenham Gv
13 Wasdale Av

Notes